Praise for *Animal Factory*

"Immensely readable and should be required reading for anybody concerned with how CAFOs are changing the nature of livestock farming." —*Library Journal*

"*Animal Factory* is a beautifully written account of the danger industrial meat and dairy production represents to our health, environment, and democratic process. In a unique and captivating way, Kirby reveals the consequences of animal factories through the eyes of the citizen advocates who have fought the long and hard battle to civilize the barbaric and often criminal behavior of the meat barons. As the readers of Kirby's book will learn, nature's clock is ticking and much is at stake for the planet and all of its inhabitants." —Robert Kennedy, Jr.

"Nature did not intend for animals to live and die in a factory assembly line. In David Kirby's startling investigation *Animal Factory,* he gives a human face to the terrible cost our health and environment pays for this so-called 'cheap food.' This is a story that is seldom told and rarely with such force and eloquence." —Alice Waters

"*Animal Factory* documents the scandal of today's industrial food animal production system in the same compelling way Upton Sinclair alerted Americans to the abuses of the meatpacking industry in his 1906 *The Jungle.* The well-being of animals produced for human consumption, the fate of rural communities, the health of farm workers, and the protection of the environment are daily compromised for the sake of profit." —Robert S. Lawrence, M.D., director, Center for a Livable Future, Johns Hopkins Bloomberg School of Public Health

"Ol' MacDonald had a farm—until America's corporate animal factories plowed it under, packing living, breathing, sensate creatures into sewage plant conditions for your gustatory pleasure. Now, you're next. Bon appétit." —Deirdre Imus

"This book puts a human face on a well-hidden national scandal: the effects of large-scale raising of animals on the health and well-being of farm workers and their families, local communities, the animals themselves, and the environment we all share. By examining how CAFOs affect the lives of real people, Kirby makes clear why we must find healthier and more sustainable ways to produce meat in America." —Marion Nestle, professor of Nutrition, Food Studies, and Public Health at New York University

"*Animal Factory* tells how big agribusiness's industrial meat production is leaving our communities foul with unhealthy air, awash in untreated sewage, and increasingly buffeted by bacteria made resistant to the antibiotics. Anyone in search of why America's health care system is going bankrupt will find part of the answer in these pages." —David Wallinga, M.D., food and health director, Institute for Agriculture and Trade Policy

ALSO BY DAVID KIRBY

Evidence of Harm

DAVID KIRBY

ANIMAL FACTORY

THE LOOMING THREAT OF INDUSTRIAL
PIG, DAIRY, AND POULTRY FARMS
TO HUMANS AND THE ENVIRONMENT

ST. MARTIN'S GRIFFIN ❦ NEW YORK

www.stmartins.com

The Library of Congress has cataloged the hardcover edition as follows:

Kirby, David, 1960–
    Animal factory : the looming threat of industrial pig, dairy, and poul-
try farms to humans and the environment / David Kirby.—1st ed.
        p. cm.
    ISBN 978-0-312-38058-8
1. Factory farms—Environmental aspects. 2. Factory farms—Health
aspects. I. Title.
    TD195.A34K57 2010
    363.7—dc22

                                                        2009039692

ISBN 978-0-312-67174-7 (trade paperback)

First St. Martin's Griffin Edition: March 2011

10 9 8 7 6 5 4 3 2 1

To my only sister, Nancy Bue,

who taught me how to tie my shoes and helped me

to keep walking forward ever since

ACKNOWLEDGMENTS

Animal factories affect us all, one way or another. But the impact on some is far greater than it is on most. Among those brave and kind people who invited me into their homes and spent a good deal of time sharing their stories about factory farming—and its alternatives—were Karen and Rocky Hudson, Rick and Joanne Dove, Helen Reddout, Chris and Kristi Petersen, Terry and Linda Spence, Barbara Sha Cox and Dan Cox, Nina Baird, Charlie Tebbutt and Karen Murphy, Bill Niman and Nicole Hahn Niman, Diane and Donny Ward, Kim Ward and Dan Trent, Lynne and Doug Henning, Jordan West, and though I did not make it to her home, Carole Morison.

But those are just some of the people who spent time with me in person, on the phone, or in e-mail conversations. At the near-certain risk of omitting individuals who helped me (my apologies in advance), I want to extend deepest thanks to the following citizens.

In Washington State, there was Mary Lynne Bos, Doug and JoEtte Moore, Jim and Linda Dyjak, Jan Whitefoot, Linda and Kin Cornwall, Florence Howard, Jerald and Lorre Gefre, Larry Fendell, Wally Almagauer and Gene Martin. In North Carolina, Don Webb, Devon Hall and Dothula Baron-Hall and their friend and colleague Elsie, Gary Grant, Neuse Riverkeeper Larry Baldwin, Diane Baldwin, State Rep. Carolyn Justice, and the Raleigh staff of North Carolina Environmental Defense. In Illinois, Nancy Crosby and her family, Diana Smith and Angie Litterst.

In Indiana, Mike Platt, Dianne Richardson, Bonnie Hahn, Sharon Adcock, Allen Hutchison, Ron Chalfant, Tony Goldstein, Jerry Carter, Courtney Justice, Rick Hughes, Seth Slaybaugh, State Rep. Phillip Pflum, State Rep. Tom

Saunders, Phil Bir, Bill Grant, Bob and Barbara Hedges, Pat Pichon, Ira Johnson, Jean Witcomb, Gary and Julie Alexander, Bud Ashton, Mike Appleby, Kathryn Petry, Sandra Dalzell, Melinda Thomas, Nell Comer, Jetta Dungan, Barbara Pegg, Alan Hamilton, and Barbara Artinian. And special thanks to Andrew Miller, former director of the Indiana Department of Agriculture, and Thomas Easterly, commissioner of the Indiana Department of Environmental Management.

In Iowa, Lisa Whelan of Iowa Citizens for Community Improvement and the Simmons family of Kirkfield. In Michigan, Kathy Melmoth, John and Peggy Zachel, Lighthawk pilot Ed Steinman, local Sierra Club activist John Klein, and Floyd and Mary Lou McVay. In Arkansas, attorney Jason Hatfield and clients Beth and Mike Green, William and Virginia Vavakos, Whitney Green, Beverly and Tommy Johnson, Sue Mobley, Bob Smith, Carol Fidler, Wendy Wood-Wolber, Chris Rasco, and Lisa Stills. In Oklahoma, Ed Brocksmith, John Ellis, L. D. Stephens, and state attorney general Drew Edmundson. In Texas, Robert Bernays, Waco assistant city manager Wiley Stem, and former Waco mayor Linda Etheridge. In Ohio, Jane Phillips, Dave Weiss, and Dave Blessing, and in California, Bill Jennings, Tom France, and from the Center on Race, Poverty & the Environment, Brent Newel, Lupe Martinez, and Daniela Simunovic, who graciously drove me around the San Joaquin Valley.

From the august world of academy, I heartily thank people at the Center for a Livable Future and the Johns Hopkins Bloomberg School of Health, including Ellen Silbergeld; Shaw McKenzie and Ralph Loglisci, formerly of the Pew Commission on Industrial Animal Practices; JoAnn Burkholder of North Carolina State University at Raleigh; Steve Wing of the University of North Carolina, Chapel Hill; Larry Cahoon and Mike Malkin of UNC, Wilmington; Kendall Thu of Northern Illinois University; and Donald Boesch, of the University of Maryland Center for Environmental Science. At Purdue University, I wish to thank Rod Allrich, Paul Ebner, Donald Lay, Ed Pajor, Allen Schinckel, and others. Other very special thanks go to David Wallinga of the Institute for Agriculture and Trade Policy and John Ikerd of the University of Missouri. Finally, Robert Martin at the Pew Environment Group and former executive director of the Pew Commission on Industrial Animal Production, Fred Kirschenmann of the Leopold Center for Sustainable Agriculture at Iowa State University, and Robert Lawrence, of the Center for a Livable Future at Johns Hopkins donated time and attention to help with the manuscript in its final stages.

Many from the world of nonprofit environmental, farming, and public-health advocacy also helped out with this effort, including Natalie Roy of the

Clean Water Network, Dan Klotz of Keep Antibiotics Working, Margaret Mellon of the Union of Concerned Scientists, Michelle Merkel of the Waterkeeper Alliance, Diane Hatz of Sustainable Table, Ed Hopkins of the Sierra Club, Karla Raettig of the Environmental Integrity Project, Ken Cook of the Environmental Working Group, Martha Noble of the Sustainable Agriculture Coalition, and Mary Thomas of the Farm Foundation.

Among the producers, CAFO operators, and animal agriculture industry representatives, I truly appreciate the time and effort extended by Chuck Stokes, Don Lloyd, Malcolm DeKryger, Mike Beard, Randy Curless, Julia Wickard, Cecilia Vander Hoff-Conway, Art and Marion Venema, Richard Lobb of the National Chicken Council, and Don Parrish and Kelly Ludlum of the American Farm Bureau Foundation.

Several attorneys gave me their insights into filing nuisance and other lawsuits against CAFOs, including Ralph Epstein, Richard Middleton, and Fred Roth.

Very special thanks go to Robert F. Kennedy, Jr., who inspired me to write this book when he told me about the cancer situation among the residents of Prairie Grove, Arkansas; Bill Wieda of the Socially Responsible Agriculture Project; Deirdre Imus and Don Imus, who had me on his show to discuss the possible origins of swine flu; the Bono family of Durham; Arianna Huffington and the entire *Huffpost* crew; Sandy Goldstein; Marisela Taylor of the Western Environmental Law Center (WELC), for her wonderful assistance while I was working in Eugene; and Sue Haney, the former court reporter from the Yakima Valley who pulled out the e-transcripts of the *CARE v. Bosma* trial from her archives and gave them to WELC free of charge. I also want to recognize and appreciate the thousands of parents of children with autism who read my first book and have been terrifically supportive in anticipation of this one.

My family and friends have been of limitless value, including my parents, Barbara and Leo, my sister Nancy Bue and her great kids, Jennifer and Michael Bue, plus Matthew Singer, Gabriel Rotello, Rob Arnold, and Natalie Aaron in California, and on the East Coast, Doug, Art, and Judy Fredman; Lou Pansulla; David France; Shimon Attie; Laura Perry; Bob Lenartz and Patty Glynn-Lenartz; Johnny Ramos; Jane Berliner; Georges Piette; and Sasha Silverstein. Jay Blotcher provided extremely able and helpful editing prior to submission (contact me for his contact info), Nancy Hokkanen was my fearless and intrepid transcriber, and I will forever be indebted to my wonderful agent, Todd Shuster, and the world-class team at St. Martin's Press, including my editor George Witte, Rachel Ekstrom, Tara Cibelli, Terra Gerstner, Julie Gutin, and Sara Sarver. I also want to thank Carlos Jimeno, who helped me through the very toughest parts of writing a very tough book, and kept me sane and laughing in those moments when I wanted to abandon ship.

Finally, I think everyone should give a moment of thanks to the beautiful animals who populate our farms. Whether raised in industrial settings or pristine pastures, they help to sustain all of us (except the strictest of vegans) with their constant supply of meat, milk, and eggs.

farm \ färm\ 1. *n.*—a tract of land, usually with a house, barn, silo, etc., on which crops and often livestock are raised for livelihood

factory \ fak-t(ə-)rē \ 1. *n.*—a building or group of buildings with facilities to manufacture a uniform product, without concern for individuality

INTRODUCTION

MAY 27, 2009

Many Americans have no idea where their food comes from, and many have no desire to find out.

That is unfortunate.

Every bite we take has had some impact on the natural environment, somewhere in the world. As the planet grows more crowded, and more farmers turn to industrialized methods to feed millions of new mouths, that impact will only worsen.

The willful ignorance of our own food's provenance is curious, given our Discovery Channel–like fascination with the way in which everything else in our modern world is made. Some consumers will spend hours online reading up on cars, cosmetics, or clothes, searching out the most meticulously crafted or environmentally healthy products they can find, then run down to the supermarket and load their carts with bacon, butter, chicken, and eggs without thinking for a second where—or how—any of those goods were produced.

This is starting to change, of course. More Americans are coming to realize that the modern production of food—especially to provide for our affluent, protein-rich diet—has a direct and sometimes negative impact on the environment, the well-being of animals, rural communities, and human health itself. Some have joined in a contemporary consumer revolt of sorts that has put the corporate food industry on the defensive in recent years.

At the center of the storm are the large-scale, mechanized megafarms where hundreds of thousands of cows, pigs, chickens, and turkeys are fed and fattened for market, all within the confines of enclosed buildings or crowded outdoor lots.

Government and industry call these massive compounds "confined [or concentrated] animal feeding operations," or CAFOs (usually pronounced KAY-fohs), though most people know them simply as "factory farms." Chances are you have seen them from above, while flying in an airplane: long white buildings lined up in tightly packed rows of three, four, or many more.

CAFOs are where most of our animal protein—our milk, cheese, butter, yogurt, eggs, chicken, turkey, bacon, sausage, cold cuts, ribs, pork chops, and, increasingly, beef and fish—comes from these days. Old MacDonald's farm—with his big red barn and clucking chicks in the yard—is quickly fading away into a romanticized past. Today, MacDonald would most likely be working as a contract grower for some conglomerate, raising tens of thousands of animals inside giant enclosures according to strict instructions dictated by the company, which typically owns the livestock but is not responsible for the thousands of tons of waste left behind before the survivors are trucked off to slaughter.

Large companies with kitchen-table names like Perdue, Tyson, Smithfield, Cargill, ADM, and Land O'Lakes now control much of the poultry and livestock production in the United States. They own the animals, they control the all-important processing and packing plants, they often operate their own distribution networks, and they sell an array of brands to consumers in the supermarket.

This "vertical integration" model of production—some would call it an old-fashioned, illegal trust in need of a Teddy Roosevelt–style buster—leaves small and independent growers at such an obvious disadvantage that many of them give up animal agriculture altogether. Two percent of U.S. livestock facilities now raise 40 percent of all animals,[1] and the vast majority of pigs, chickens, and dairy cows are produced inside animal factories.[2]

Livestock and poultry are *very* big business in America. Like all industries, agribusiness has barons that wield extraordinary political and economic clout, with billions at their disposal to spend on K Street lobbying, local and national political campaigns, saturation advertising, feel-good PR (see: "California, happy cows"), and other means of creating a favorable business climate for themselves.

And like many big industries, factory farms are major contributors to air, water, and land pollution. Science and government have concluded without a doubt that CAFOs are responsible for discharging millions of tons of contaminants from animal manure into the environment every year—much of it illegally.

Unlike the steel, auto, or coal industries, livestock operations are not subject to the same stringent rules, regulations, laws, and controls on environmental discharges. After all, what could be more important than the guarantee of an abundant, safe, and affordable food supply? What could be more sacrosanct in American legend and law than the farms and farmers who make sure our food gets to the national dinner table night after night?

Besides, how could a farm be considered a factory? There are no smoke-stacks on a farm. There are no chemical plants or refineries, and very few ve-hicles. Where, then, is all that supposed pollution coming from, and how much of a problem could there actually be?

Consider this:

- Each year, the United States produces more than one ton of "dry matter" (the portion remaining after water is removed) animal waste for every resident,[3] and animal feeding operations yield one hundred times more waste than all U.S. human sewage treatment plants.[4]
- While human sewage is treated to kill pathogens, animal waste is not. Hog manure has ten to one hundred times more concentrated pathogens than human waste,[5] yet the law would never permit un-treated human waste to be kept in vast "lagoons," or sprayed onto fields, as is the case with manure.
- Manure can contain pathogens, antibiotics, drug-resistant bacteria, hormones, heavy metals, and other compounds that can seriously im-pact human health, aquatic life, and wildlife when introduced into the environment, according to the U.S. Environmental Protection Agency (EPA).
- The eastern shore of the Chesapeake Bay produces one million tons of manure a year, enough to fill a football stadium "to the top row, includ-ing all the concourses, locker rooms, and concession areas."[6]
- Agricultural waste is the number-one form of well-water contami-nants in the United States, where at least 4.5 million people are ex-posed to dangerously high nitrate levels in their drinking water.[7]
- A Centers for Disease Control (CDC) study of well water in nine Midwestern states showed that 13 percent of the supply had nitrate levels above the EPA standard of ten milligrams per liter.[8]
- Feedlot odors contain some 170 separate chemicals,[9] many of them known to cause respiratory ailments, diarrhea, depression, violent behavior, and other health problems.
- Rearing cattle produces more greenhouse gases than cars, a UN re-port warns.[10]

Animal-factory proponents say that CAFOs are the most cost-effective method in the world of producing meat, milk, and eggs. They credit modern American agriculture with yielding the cheapest food in human history—which is hard to refute—and also the safest, which is debatable.

Animal industrialists say that by confining poultry and livestock to CAFOs—as opposed to letting them roam free on ranges, pastures, and fields—they are providing warm and clean environments where farm animals can thrive, free from the threats of the elements, predators, or even attacks from other farm animals. The delivery of food, water, and veterinary care becomes more efficient, they contend, and animals can be moved more quickly to market, increasing profitability.

Besides, according to these industrialists, consumers demand cheap, lean, uniform cuts of meat, and using CAFOs is the only possible way to deliver that.

But animal-factory opponents, whose ranks are growing—they are not only consumers, but scientists, politicians, and farmers, as well—charge that the only way CAFO production can be profitable is by passing along, or "externalizing," certain costs associated with raising so many animals in such a small place.

In 2008, the Pew Commission on Industrial Farm Animal Production released a landmark report on CAFOs. It reached some very sobering conclusions about their impact on our health, the environment, rural communities, farm workers, food safety, animal welfare, and the looming threat of evolving microbes—including antibiotic-resistant *E. coli*, MRSA, and, of course, swine flu virus.

The Pew report reminds us that the price of protein, given the externalities of animal-factory production, often goes well beyond the price tag in your grocer's aisle.

"These 'externalities' may include anything from changes in property values near industrial farming operations, to health costs from polluted air, water, and soil, and spreading resistant infections or diseases of animal origin, to environmental degradation or cleanup costs—all of which are 'paid' by the public," the Pew Commission said, "even though they are not included in the cost of producing or buying the meat, poultry, eggs, and milk that modern industrial animal agriculture provides."[11]

Animal Factory is not strictly an anti-CAFO book, though many in the agricultural community will perceive it that way. I do not call for an end to industrial animal production, nor do I draw any personal conclusions myself. Informed consumers—whether of food or of information—are vital to a healthy democracy. I would never dream of telling people what to eat or, more important, what *not* to eat. But we all have a responsibility, even an ethical obligation, to know where our food comes from, and what impact its production has on the environment and public health, before we take it home and fry it up in a pan.

Wherever possible, I have tried to include voices from the animal-production industry and other CAFO supporters. Many farmers believe that industrial animal production is the only option open to them if they are to remain in farming, and they are grateful to the large companies for providing steady contracts and a stable economic environment for them to survive.

One powerful argument for agribusiness is that it offers a lower retail price of food to shoppers. For consumers, factory-farmed meat, milk, and eggs are usually considerably more affordable than their organic, free-range, or "sustainably produced" counterparts. Most working families do not have the luxury of buying high-end, "boutique" protein. Some opponents of CAFOs would counterargue that families should simply cut down on the animal products they buy.

I am not a vegetarian, and you will occasionally find me in line for fast food, so I have no business telling others how to eat. Food—like sex, politics, and religion—is an intensely personal, emotional, and complicated subject.

Moreover, farmers are not evil people. The farmers I got to know, including those who operate CAFOs, seemed to genuinely care about the environment, the animals, their communities, and the quality and safety of the food they produced.

On the other hand, I cannot dismiss or forget what I witnessed firsthand in my three years of reporting this story. I met with people living within smelling distance of animal factories in the chicken belts of Arkansas, Oklahoma, Maryland, Delaware, and Virginia, in the hog belt of North Carolina, in the upper Midwestern CAFO states of Illinois, Iowa, Missouri, Michigan, Indiana, and Ohio, and in the arid western dairy regions of Texas, central California, and the Yakima Valley of Washington.

Everywhere I went, the story was the same: CAFOs had fouled the air, spoiled the water, threatened property values, changed the face of local agriculture, and made life miserable for thousands of people, though certainly not everybody.

Sadly, I could only tell a fraction of the stories I heard. This book is not an encyclopedic history of all forms of animal production in the United States. Many people, for example, will notice and perhaps criticize the paucity of information about the raising of beef cattle and farmed fish in America. Though I am not trying to somehow "clear" beef of any responsibility, I do think that its production is the least problematic of all CAFO-related protein; most U.S. beef cattle are still owned and raised by independent producers—on open pasture, grassland, or through grazing permits on federal land—and spend only the last few months of their lives being fattened on grain in massive feedlots, which most certainly qualify as CAFOs, with all their attendant environmental issues. (Another reason I did not write about beef feedlots more is that, aside from residents of Yakima Valley, they were not an issue for any of the people I profiled.)

As for fish farms, they certainly present challenges that keep some environmentalists up at night, including farmed-salmon escapees that introduce harmful pests such as sea lice and viral diseases that infect wild fish populations. One could write an entire book on the environmental impact of fish farms alone. On the other hand, I have never heard anyone complain about foul odors or noxious gases coming from fish farms.

Animal factories of every stripe are currently under fire. So what does that mean for the future of CAFOs? Will they be reformed into universal acceptability? Will they be litigated into oblivion? Will they be driven out of the country? The truth is, none of those things is likely.

Only time will tell how this dramatic saga plays out. But humankind may not have the last word on whether CAFOs will be with us in twenty years.

That decision will belong to nature.

And nature did not intend for animals to live by the hundreds or thousands, crammed together inside buildings, raised with pharmaceutical products, with no access to grass, sunlight, or the clean, healthy scent of outdoor air.

PROLOGUE

The first time Rick Dove saw a hog factory, it was from a thousand feet up in the air. Finally, the carnage he had witnessed on the ground began to make some sense.

The fifty-three-year-old retired marine JAG and grizzled Vietnam vet was embarking on a new mission, perhaps the most important mission in his life. The flight he took that muggy afternoon over the coastal plains of North Carolina would change everything. Rick would finally understand what was killing the river. *His* river, a river called the Neuse.

Rick and his family had lived for years near the broad, muddy mouth of the river. Their home was built on the Neuse—the river was the family's backyard pool. The Neuse (pronounced "noose") sprouts from a reservoir below Durham and, 275 miles to the southeast, discharges its contents into the cloudy waters of Pamlico Sound.

With his steely gaze, silver hair, broad face, and sturdy frame, Rick looked every bit the retired Marine Corps prosecutor, out hunting down prey.

On this warm day in 1993, Rick had paid two hundred dollars for a bird's-eye view of the river, hoping it might reveal the secret of what was making the water so sick and killing fish by the millions. He had the mandate; the Riverkeeper Alliance had recently licensed Rick to serve as the "Riverkeeper" of the Neuse. He had since logged hundreds of hours plowing the brackish waters in his converted fishing boat, the *Lonesome Dove*, searching for illegal runoff from factories, sewers, and farms along the banks. He had found some violations, but nothing to explain the massacre of marine life ravishing this sleepy corner of North Carolina.

Something was lurking out there along the waterway. Rick was certain of it. Something had emerged in the last few years, something sinister and foul. Rick had vowed not to rest until he found out what it was—and put an end to it.

The most appalling fish kill had been in September of 1991. Typically, early fall marks the largest migration of the menhaden, a small, tender-fleshed silvery fish with a line of black dots along its flank. Menhaden lay their larvae in the open ocean, which are then washed into the Neuse Estuary, where the fish hatch. From there, young menhaden migrate up to the river basin's shady creeks and backwaters, where they spend the next several months feeding and growing. Most reassemble in September to swim back out to sea, where they live, spawn, and die. For small fry, they are unfathomably fertile: One mature female can produce over 350,000 offspring.

In 1991, the menhaden were running in numbers that Rick had never seen before. The water grew black with fish as they emerged from their bogs and creeks to gather in the middle of the wide estuary formed by the Neuse. From there, they were genetically wired to swim out to sea. But very few of them made it that year.

Rick first noticed a smattering of dead fish along the riverbanks in the weeks leading up to the run, but nothing too serious. Within the first two days after the fish began migrating, however, the kill was on in full force. Rick and his neighbors woke up one morning to the stench of hundreds of millions of dead menhaden lining the banks for miles. In the following days, bass, stripers, mullets, crabs, and shrimp also turned up dead. They were all pocked with round red sores, as though some specter had sucked the lifeblood from their flesh. Locals puzzled over how to deal with the carnage, but within days most of the rotting flesh had dissolved back into the water.

State inspectors rushed to the scene and ordered a battery of tests. They expected to find that oxygen levels in the river water had been depleted, which is usually caused by a large algal bloom—the usual explanation for fish kills and "dead zones." But oxygen levels were normal; something else had wiped out a billion fish at once. The largest fish kill ever recorded on an American river remained a mystery.

One evening soon after the kill, Rick went out to the Neuse with his teenage son, Todd. Together, they sat down on a riverbank, covering their noses against the stench. The river had meant the world to this family. It had given them years of fresh crab and fish. It had provided clean, healthy water for swimming and sailing. Rick sighed and put his arm on his son's shoulder. The hardened marine fought back a tear.

"Everything we loved about this place," Rick said, "it's all over." Inside, he was seething. This old marine had a killer to hunt down; he just wasn't sure where to look.

A few months later, the New Bern fish kill of '91 was little more than a bad memory for most people, the more quickly forgotten, the better. But not for Rick Dove. Over the next two years, he would work closely with local scientists, and, eventually, they would finger the killer: a microscopic organism with the bizarrely happy-sounding name of *Pfiesteria*. This deadly dinoflagellate, Rick was learning, had caused those appalling open sores on the fish.

But this explanation solved only half the murder mystery. Rick still wanted to know why what some called the "cell from hell" was appearing in numbers large enough to kill a billion fish. Why was it appearing now? And why was it in the Neuse?

The waters of the river would not relinquish the answer, so Rick decided to extend his investigation to the skies. On this first of several hundred sorties, Rick had asked the pilot to fly upstream all the way to Raleigh, the state capital. Outfitted with a high-tech camera and telephoto lens, Rick snapped images of factories, sewage plants, and housing tracts that lined the river. Rick had quickly become an amateur expert in environmental forensics, and he was looking for possible discharges of pollutants—especially nutrients like nitrogen and phosphorus, which can feed and sustain deadly outbreaks of parasites such as *Pfiesteria*. But nothing he had seen so far would explain dramatic changes in nutrient levels.

Frustrated but hardly willing to give up, Rick asked the pilot to head back downriver toward New Bern—a historically charming old fishing and timber town dating back to colonial times. One of the oldest settlements in North America, wonderfully preserved New Bern is perched on a sharp elbow of land where the Neuse and Trent rivers merge.

When they reached New Bern, Rick had the pilot head west, up the Trent River. Perhaps something had been built along it, he thought, that was dumping nutrient-laden matter into the water. They headed over neighboring Jones County.

Soon, several large dark ponds of water began to dot the misty green landscape below. They were of differing colors and various angular shapes. Some were black, some brown, and many a shocking shade of magenta, as though they had been filled with Pepto-Bismol. The ponds lay in random patterns across a vast swath of land, like massive swimming pools in a subdivision for giants.

"What are those?" Rick asked the pilot over the audio system. "Some sort of fishponds? Maybe catfish or tilapia farms?"

"No idea," the pilot crackled back through Rick's headphones.

The peculiar ponds were adjoined by long, narrow metallic buildings that stretched a hundred yards or so in rows of two to eight or more buildings. As they flew farther west, the weird-looking "farms" became more concentrated. Even through the haze, Rick could count one hundred or more ponds within his field of vision.

Then the smell hit them.

Noxious gases were infiltrating the aircraft, still potent after traveling upward through a thousand feet of sky. Rick gagged. Whatever was living—or dying—down there, it sure as hell wasn't fish.

They continued their northwesterly route, passing into Duplin and Sampson counties, among the poorest and most rural in the state. Now the strange longhouses and their ponds filled the landscape in unending succession. One after another after another. Rick continued to snap photos. The farms—or whatever they were—were packed so tightly together that many were wedged in between creeks, canals, and wetlands. Most of that water would find its way into the Neuse, Rick knew. He also noticed big spraying devices—giant sprinklers—on fields surrounding the farms. They were spewing reddish-brown liquid into the air and onto the soil. Some of the spray was caught by the wind and carried aloft as mist; much of it pooled into rivulets on the ground and ran off into nearby waterways. In some areas, sprinklers were spraying brownish water directly into streams.

The wetlands and waterways were choked with green, yellow, and even orange algae. Rick was sickened by the sight of it. "This is what hell must look like," he said to the pilot. "Let's heave back to New Bern. I've seen enough."

The next morning, Rick called his friend Al Hodge, who worked at the state's Division of Water Quality. Rick described what he'd seen from the plane. "So," he said flatly. "What am I looking at?"

"Pig farms," Al said. The ponds were actually waste "lagoons," he explained, and the sprinklers part of a "sprayfield" in which liquefied pig waste from the lagoon is distributed onto crops—usually Bermuda grass, hay, or corn—that absorb the nutrients.

"*Pig* farms?" Rick laughed. "If those are pig farms, then there are millions and millions of pigs living right there in Duplin and Sampson counties."

"There might be, Rick. We just don't know."

"But *millions*? What would that do to the environment? What about all that surrounding water?"

"We don't know, because we don't even know how many pig farms there *are*. We don't know *where* they are. We just have no control over any of it."

Rick was stunned. "Well, who the hell can tell me where these things are located, and what they're doing to the river?"

"The Department of Ag," Al said, "in Raleigh. But trust me, we've asked them for that information time and again. They won't share it with us. It's some kind of state secret. All they say is to stop breathing down their necks."

Now Rick was steaming mad. But at least the mystery of the Neuse was beginning to unfurl: Pig poop has nutrients; nutrients feed *Pfiesteria* outbreaks. *Pfiesteria* kills fish.

Rick smiled, just slightly. He had his suspect. It was time to start prosecuting his case.

YAKIMA VALLEY, WASHINGTON

"My God, what *is* that?" Helen Reddout shot upright in her bed, wrenched from the hazy dreams of a late-summer sleep. It was the summer of 1996. A stinging odor ricocheted through her nose and coated her mouth and throat. Her eyes were weepy. Helen cupped one hand over her face, fearing she might puke. It smelled as though someone had dumped an entire septic tank right onto the king-size bed. She turned to look at her husband, Don, who was still sleeping, oblivious to the stench invading the bedroom of their handsome two-story, 1920s white-wood farmhouse.

That man would sleep through a *tornado*, Helen thought, rolling her eyes and frowning. Then she remembered: Every window in the house was open, the better to attract the evening breezes that cool the sun-baked Yakima Valley, 150 miles southeast of Seattle.

There was only one place the stink could have slithered in from, Helen knew. It was those damn "milk factories"—massive open-lot dairies that had sprung up around the Lower Valley in recent years.

Helen plugged her nose and sprang out of bed to slam shut windows in every room. But it was too late. The stench was already entrapped in the house. She hurried to the bathroom and scanned the shelves, looking for anything to mask the odor. There it was: a dusty bottle of Tabu by Dana, left over from the Carter administration. As a grammar school teacher in her fifties, Helen didn't have much occasion for the syrupy parfum. But she admired its bottle and had kept it around. Helen plugged her nose and scampered back to the bedroom to begin spraying. *Pssshhht, pssshhht.* She lifted her hand slowly from her nose and sniffed. The treacly bouquet of Tabu had vanquished the stench. It no longer smelled as if a thousand Holsteins had crapped in her bed. It smelled like a French whorehouse.

But that was an improvement. "A whorehouse, I can sleep with," Helen said as she climbed into bed and pulled the sheets up to her head. "Cow poop? No way."

Minutes later, it was back. This time, her nightgown had absorbed the reek. She jumped up and flung the offending garment down the stairs before going to wash up in the bathroom. Helen selected a fresh gown from the dresser, slipped it on, and warily, so as not to trouble the midnight air, tiptoed back toward bed. But the odor lingered.

Frustrated and angry, Helen walked over to the window. She was freaking out. All she could think of was that scene in the movie *Network* when everyday folks, egged on by the crazed TV anchor Howard Beale, run to the window, throw up the sash, and bellow out, "I'm as mad as *hell*, and I'm not going to take this anymore!"

Helen seriously considered doing that. But she didn't dare open the window.

Instead, she peered out into the moonlight and down at her tidy rows of peppers and eggplants planted next to carrots, sweet corn, Brandywine tomatoes, and green patches of herbs. She gazed over the Yakima Valley, an irrigated patchwork of farms, orchards, vineyards, and dairies laid out across the scrubby high desert of south-central Washington. She saw the rich fields of corn, hops, alfalfa, and mint, bordered by wild bitterbrush and horse thistle, leading down toward the meandering Yakima River. Under the blue moonlight, she could see the looming outline of Snipes Mountain, which dominates the landscape from Granger in the west to Sunnyside in the east. On this low escarpment, the Reddouts had planted their seventy-five acres of cherry, pear, apple, and nectarine orchards.

Helen thought back on the years she had spent so happily in this small patch of paradise. But then the big dairies had moved in.

Many in the valley had watched with heavy hearts as family dairies with seventy-five or so cows went out of business, replaced by enormous, corporate-backed behemoths that could milk and feed five thousand or more cows within a single confinement. Over time, many more of these "milk factories" began appearing in the dry, wide-open valley.

There was no mistaking these newcomers. The old-fashioned dairies had pastured their cows on emerald fields of green, periodically moving the animals through well-timed rotations of meadows brimming with wild clover, alfalfa, downy ryegrass, and other ingredients of a natural bovine buffet. Helen was not exactly enamored of cows, but she had always delighted at watching mothers and their calves gamboling about the green pastures of their valley home. She figured they were doing whatever it is that cows *do*, at peace in their world. The pastured animals seemed healthy and robust, walking erect with straight spines and heads held high. To Helen, they seemed happy.

But the cows at the new milk factories were nothing like that. Instead, thousands of manure-smeared animals were jammed onto strictly confined tracts of land. Whatever grass had sprouted in these "feeding pens" was quickly shredded under constant hoof pounding, leaving behind open stretches of dirt, urine, and feces.

In the newfangled dairies, milking cows lined up in long metal buildings called freestyle barns. Outside in the open-air pens, or "dry lots," dairymen confined their "dry cows"—usually pregnant mothers within sixty days of giving birth—and "heifers," young females that had not yet calved for the first time.

During the arid summers, dry lots baked and crumbled under the blazing sun. Cows and heifers kicked up clouds of dust laden with ground-up feces and pathogens. Sometimes on windy days, the disgusting brown clouds grew so thick that drivers flipped on their headlights at noon. The winter was even worse. Rain and melting snow mixed with the crap-filled soil and left a thick coating of muck caked onto the cows' legs, bellies, and udders. Helen watched these creatures, penned in by the thousands, and felt they were the very picture of animal misery.

Without access to a single blade of grass, these "new" dairy cows depended entirely on trucks that delivered silage, a mixture of milled grains, ground soybean, and fermented cornstalk. Helen knew from her family's dairy days that grain was no substitute for grass, which ruminants can digest and transform into protein.

Then there were the pools of stinking crap. Each dairy cow produces 120 pounds of wet manure a day—the equivalent of what twenty to forty people would generate.[1] In a pasture-fed system, a farmer budgets up to 1.5 acres per cow. The land acts as a free-range toilet that can absorb the excrement. A confinement dairy does not have that option.

So what was becoming of all that crap? Dry-lot waste was left to cake in the sun and periodically scooped away with front loaders. Waste from the barns and the milking parlors was flushed into the lagoons. Before planting and after the fall harvest, farmers sprayed the liquefied waste onto their fields, spewing gases, pathogens, and particles into the semidesert air. The odor had been horrendous around the valley, though thankfully it had not reached the Reddout household—until now. And though Helen had joined with other neighbors to politely express concern over the smell, one dairyman had growled back at them. If they didn't like it, they could move, he said, adding: "My shit doesn't stink."

Tonight, sitting at the window, her eyes running, sick to her stomach, Helen made a silent vow to fight back. Until now, Helen admitted, she had only dabbled in the Yakima dairy battles. She'd been a halfhearted volunteer, a farmwife who cared. But on this putrid August night, Helen Reddout was emerging as a new person, a full-fledged warrior activist. I can and I will speak out, she thought. And maybe I might actually *change* something. Just like that man in *Network*. He first yelled out, and then someone else yelled, and someone else, until whole cities were filled with cries for change.

This would become her new job, Helen thought. This would be her *crusade*. She spritzed the room once again with Tabu and climbed back into bed next to her still-sleeping husband. "This war," she said as she closed her eyes, "is on."

ELMWOOD, ILLINOIS

Karen Hudson was worried about the rain. For days on end in February 2001, the weather in her little town of Elmwood had been wretched even by western Illinois standards. Periods of blinding snows and subfreezing temperatures were followed by warmer wet fronts carrying torrents of rain that fell around the clock. The result was an objectionable mess of icy mud and water, layered over a solid pack of frozen ground.

Karen knew that Inwood, the megadairy outside Elmwood, was about to have a major accident. Investigators had been out to the dairy to see how it was faring in the rough weather and found that its waste lagoon was just inches away from spilling over the rim and down into neighboring fields. A historic Civil War–era cemetery was threatened. Karen learned that dairy workers were frantically piling sandbags around the lagoon's rim to try to keep it from overflowing.

Local news accounts reported that before they left, investigators had ordered David Inskeep, the owner, to lower the lagoon by at least a million gallons, telling him to load the waste into rented tanker trucks and haul it away, six thousand gallons at a time. He refused.

Instead, after the government men were gone, Inskeep ordered his workers to lay hoses from the lagoon across nearly a mile of land to a long, narrow ravine, where the waste would be pumped and stored. It would end up being the worst livestock spill in Illinois history.

Karen and her husband, Rocky, watched the disaster unfold on the evening news. They saw that the lower end of the ravine was dammed with an earthen berm about ten feet high. Inskeep must have assumed it would be a fitting locale for some of the liquid from his waste lagoon, and he filled it with two million gallons of a foamy, brown-yellow stew.

But the berm didn't hold. Lagoon waste plunged through the breach and into the West Fork of Kickapoo Creek, which joins the Illinois River near the point where Peoria draws its drinking water. Dead fish were turning up, and the entire area was an environmental disaster zone.

"I knew this would happen!" Karen cried. "I knew they would mess up that cesspool. Everything we said would come true about this megadairy *is* coming true." It was neither a joyous nor a victorious emotion. Karen had tried to stop this from happening. She recalled that back in 1997, before the dairy was built, she had naively thought she could talk Dave Inskeep out of his plans. She had invited him over one day to talk "neighbor to neighbor" over coffee. "Don't do this, Dave," she pleaded. "Please don't put this god-awful animal factory here in Elmwood."

But Inskeep's mind was made up. "Karen," he said sincerely, "I'm not going to do anything to hurt this community. Please, trust me. Just keep quiet about this for now, and I promise you, I'm not going to do anything harmful." But Karen was unmoved. "Dave," she said, "we've known each other a long time. We got our dog from you. I taught school with your wife, and she taught my kids. I am asking you not to do this. It's going to be a disaster."

Inskeep looked hurt. "Why are you fighting me?" he asked.

"I'm not fighting you, Dave. What I'm trying to do, in a neighborly way, is to ask you not to do this to my family and my community, not to build the dairy."

"I'm going to do it, Karen. I've already decided. I've signed the papers."

"Well then, I'm going to do everything I can to oppose you."

"Do what you feel you need to do, but I am putting this in." Inskeep rose from the table and shook Karen's hand.

"God bless you, Dave," she said. "I guess we agree to disagree."

And out he walked, saying only, "We'll be in touch."

Now, four years later, Karen's jaw went limp as she pondered how her worst premonition was actually transpiring in Elmwood. "My God, how could someone do this?" she asked. "How could Inskeep be so stupid as to just go and pump millions of gallons of crap into a creek? Why didn't he seek help? That fool is paying the price for his own arrogance."

Karen thought about the twelve hundred acres that she and Rocky farmed just outside Elmwood, where they planted rows of corn and soybeans across gently rolling land that had been in the Hudson family since the 1890s. There, amid the oaks, willows, and wildflowers of the Illinois prairie, they raised food, raised a family, built a home, and built a life.

Elmwood is a pleasant, all-American farming town west of Peoria. People there—farmers, merchants, business types who commute to Peoria, and a few escapees from Chicago—cherish their lives in the Starbucks-free zone. Elmwood exudes a slightly upscale confidence not always found in the hardscrabble prairie towns of the area, where Ronald Reagan once shot high school hoops. Stately storefronts house a hardware store and an old-time drugstore on Elmwood's tiny Central Park. Under the park's classic white gazebo, bands draw large families on summer evenings filled with fireflies and the smell of fried chicken.

In 1996, Karen and her neighbors formed a little grassroots group called Families Against Rural Messes, or FARM, in order to fight Dave Inskeep's dairy—Illinois' largest. They had issued many dire warnings about the dairy's waste lagoon and "manure management" practices. The 1,250-head facility had already been cited for several violations involving land and water pollution, including an incident in late 1997 that had expelled a "turbid, gray-colored wastewater with a distinct manure odor" into Kickapoo Creek, Karen learned from state reports.

Yet despite all that, Inskeep had now let his lagoon level creep dangerously close to the rim during this season of extraordinary precipitation.

It was time for Karen to get to work. She summoned her FARM colleagues, who by this point had been fighting large-scale hog and dairy confinements for five years. Together they had filed lawsuits, staged protests, and testified at hearings. Those years were long on struggle and short on rewards. But maybe, at last, that would finally change. Maybe Karen could use this disaster to her advantage.

The Illinois media were used to calling Karen whenever a factory farm had an accident. Now her phone would not stop ringing. She spent much of the next few days on the line with reporters, and making trips out to the site for interviews. "What Inskeep should have done was call the state and have everyone work out a solution together," she told reporters. "But good old Dave, he didn't think he needed anyone's help and he refused to hire waste haulers—he thought he could do this on the sly, and on the cheap."

And, she noted, a new problem was besieging the dairy. The state had advised Inskeep to stop pumping any more waste into his lagoon. As a result, according to local media reports, a rising backwash of flush water was now spilling from the barns and milking parlor and pooling into a massive manure lake that engulfed the cattle confinements. The lake, growing by the hour, already held two million gallons of brown stinking water. Workers had to fence off much of the area after Holsteins were found wading around in fetid liquid up to their udders.

"Maybe this disaster will finally do something to strengthen the law; maybe this will be precedent setting," Karen told one journalist. "But even if that happens, isn't it sad that it takes a spill to give one hope?" She paused a moment, then said, "On the other hand, this terrible event has given us a very powerful weapon in the court of public opinion."

Another reporter asked Karen about Inskeep, her neighbor, the man who once gave her family a puppy. "We must never forget that Dave Inskeep dumped millions of gallons of waste into our waterways. This is the usual defiant arrogance of factory farmers," she replied without emotion. "These events verify exactly what we at FARM have been warning about: Factory farms are dangerous to the environment; they are ticking time bombs of manure just waiting to be spilled into public waters."

It was a tough time for FARM, but Karen's PR sense paid off handsomely. Aerial photographs and videos shot by group members and local reporters aired on local stations throughout western Illinois. The front page of the *Peoria Journal Star* was splashed with a four-color aerial photo of the dairy, taken by a FARM volunteer. Later, FARM's photos would be used by the Illinois attorney general's office to prosecute the case.

To Karen Hudson, Inwood Dairy was the poster child for what happens when too many animals are concentrated in one place at one time, and managed by someone evidently not up to the task. "The way our law is written, the bad actors are allowed to get by for quite a long time until there's a catastrophic event," she said at a FARM news conference a few days later. "All the things we warned about regarding this corporate dairy came to light."

At least she could take comfort from the sick humor spreading around town in response to the giant dairy, which was using Monsanto's artificial bovine growth hormone, Posilac, to boost milk production by up to 30 percent. Some people were now sporting T-shirts that said, WELCOME TO ELMWOOD. THERE'S NOTHING WRONG WITH OUR WATER.

Below that was an illustration of two children growing udders.

PART I

RAISING A STINK

Rick Dove loves the Neuse. The cloudy river, two million years old, seems to possess a spiritual quality that he finds irresistible. The Neuse was named after the Neusiok Indians, who thrived along its southern banks before the English began exploring Pamlico Sound in 1585. By the mid-1700s, the Neusiok were nearly gone.

The Neuse is born outside Durham and runs in a southeasterly direction until it reaches New Bern, two hundred miles away, at the juncture of the Trent River. There the water goes brackish, then spreads out for several miles wide before crawling through a forty-mile tidal estuary that empties into Pamlico Sound. At roughly ten miles across, it ranks among the widest river mouths in the continental United States.

Rick always loved rivers. He grew up next to a little tributary of Bear Creek near Dundalk, Maryland—just five miles southeast of Baltimore. As kids, Rick and his buddies would splash around in the creek during the sweaty months of summer. But one afternoon in the 1940s, that dreamy world came to an end. Rick's mother took her six-year-old by the hand and led him down to the water's edge. She pointed to a new housing development built upstream. When those people flushed their toilets, she said, it went right into the creek.

"You can't swim here anymore, Rick," she sighed, kissing his forehead.

The six-year-old frowned at the prospect of swimless summers to come. Then his face lit up. "Don't worry, Mom! It's okay," Rick said. "We'll just go over there and tell them to stop!" Many years later, he would remember that day as his start as an environmentalist.

As Rick grew older, his maritime vistas expanded beyond polluted Bear

Creek to Chesapeake Bay and the Eastern Shore. His dad built warplanes for the Glen L. Martin Company (now Martin Marietta) and his mom ran a dry cleaning business. Rick and his dad were able to embark on many fishing trips to remote inlets of the sprawling bay.

Rick earned his law degree at age twenty-three from the University of Baltimore in 1963. But the Vietnam War was rumbling, half a world away. Rather than risk being drafted, Rick applied for the marines' four-year officer program in Quantico, Virginia. He wanted to "take orders, and learn how to give a few," he likes to say. Officer boot camp was sixteen weeks long and nearly half his class dropped out—but Rick held on and graduated as a second lieutenant.

In 1964, Rick married his childhood sweetheart, Joanne Rose Tezak, and, after he passed the Maryland bar, Rick and his bride were stationed at the Marine Corp Recruit Depot in Parris Island, South Carolina, where he worked as a judge advocate in a law office. Soon after that, Rick signed up as a career officer in the marines. He was then sent to a big naval base at Yokosuka, Japan, where he and his platoon guarded against demonstrators protesting U.S. nuclear ships docking in the harbor. Rick was grudgingly impressed by the passionate activists.

Rick did two tours of duty in the Vietnam War and took incoming missiles on his first night in-country. Eventually, he ended up working as a defense counsel in a supply depot called Red Beach, not too far from Denang. There he defended marines who had been court-martialed for murder, fragging, and rape.

By 1972, Rick was stateside again, working as a marine liaison to Congress during the final years of the war. He and Joanne lived in Washington, D.C., and adopted two children, Todd and Holly. In 1975, Rick transferred to the Marine Corps Air Station at Cherry Point, North Carolina, fifteen miles southeast of New Bern, on a wide bend in the Neuse River.

The fishing, Rick quickly learned, was incredible. The Neuse feeds river water and nutrients into the Albemarle and Pamlico sounds estuarine system, a vast nursery for 90 percent of all commercial species caught in North Carolina. Its feeder streams and shady backwater creeks provide spawning areas for herring, shad, and striped bass. Much like salmon, these fish live as adults in the open sea but swim upriver when it comes time to spawn.

Rick became the staff judge advocate for the 2nd Marine Aircraft Wing at Cherry Point, and in 1983 the family settled into a Mediterranean-style home right on the Neuse, in the prosperous subdivision of Carolina Pines. Rick built a wooden deck and a good-size pier out on the water, and purchased his dreamboat: a twenty-three-foot riverboat with a 200 horsepower engine manufactured by Hydro-Step Corporation. Designed to carry extra weight, she was perfect for crabbing, when a full cargo could reach two thousand pounds or more.

Life could not have been sweeter. America was at peace, and the river was swollen with bass, flounder, crab, and shrimp. They were so bountiful, Rick couldn't give them away to his neighbors. Now a colonel in the marines, he told Joanne that one day he would retire from the Corps and launch a fishing business right from his backyard. Rick loved the Neuse so much that when he was transferred to serve as a military judge at Camp Lejeune, fifty-five miles to the south, he chose the two-hour daily commute over moving off the river.

Nothing could keep Rick from the Neuse, not even when he began forgetting things after spending his days on the river in the fall of 1986. It wasn't simple memory loss, like forgetting where you put your car keys. He couldn't remember which courtroom he worked in, or find his way back to chambers from the law library. Rick was convinced he had a brain tumor. But doctors found nothing wrong with him. He took some time off to recuperate, and within three weeks, the problems abated and he returned to the bench.

At the same time, Rick began noticing that some of the menhaden in the Neuse were turning up dead, with open, bleeding lesions on their silvery flanks. It would be years before he understood the connection between his memory loss and the ghoulish fish kills.

In June 1987, Colonel Richard Dove turned in his retirement papers and walked out of Camp Lejeune's main gate, leaving the Marine Corps behind. Rick could have waited five years for full retirement benefits. But all he wanted was to grab his son, Todd, jump in his boat, and go be a fisherman on the Neuse.

Rick and Todd rigged up the boat into an operable commercial fishing vessel. They bought a seventeen-foot fishing skiff that was ideal for crabbing and christened it the *Little Dipper*. Rick rented a store in nearby Havelock and opened a fish market, Todd's Seafood. The catch was consistently generous and the customers voracious. Business boomed.

For two years, Rick lived in bliss. But in the autumn of 1989, he again noticed dying fish turning up in his own seafood catches. The lesions began appearing on menhaden, but quickly spread to other species.

Then the sores started to appear on people.

One day Todd pointed out to his dad a couple of puzzling red spots on his hands and lower leg. Rick didn't think too much of it—until he found similar spots on his own forearm the next day. Within days, their wounds had grown into weepy open sores, and no antibiotic seemed to make them go away. Rick and Todd realized that anywhere they got wet, they got lesions. Whatever was killing the fish was now stalking them.

Then, in 1990, more than two million fish perished in the Neuse River from August through October. These are the months that the menhaden gather for their annual exodus to the Atlantic. Rick knew that the massive fish migration is nature's way of exporting excess nutrients out of the Neuse River Basin. Throughout the year, young menhaden gorge themselves on tons of plant material that end up in creeks and streams feeding the river and estuary. In the late summer or early fall, a billion or more menhaden converge to swim en masse out to the ocean. Once there, they breed and then die, releasing stored-up nitrogen and phosphorus into the open waters. But when millions of fish instead die prematurely in the Neuse, those excess nutrients remain where they are.

Rick began to hear other fishermen around New Bern speaking of odd experiences on the water. Their problems went beyond skin sores. Some suffered from memory loss and worse. Some guys were passing out in their boats, then drifting for miles unanchored and unconscious. When they finally came to, they did not recognize their surroundings and could not remember where they had launched their boats. Once ashore, they had no idea where they'd parked their vehicles. The hapless fishermen would wander aimlessly around, trying to sort through a cloud of confusion to find their way home.

Rick realized that his own memory troubles had returned. He was missing business appointments. It was out of character for a disciplined marine.

What, then, was happening to the Neuse? Rick began reading every book he could find on the history of the Neuse River, Pamlico Sound, and fishing along the Carolina coast. He learned that fish kills had occurred for centuries. When colder seawater creeps in under warmer river water, it can create a condition called a salt wedge, which can turn water into a hypoxic (low oxygen) or anoxic (zero oxygen) death trap for fish.

Salt wedges can kill a few thousand fish at a time. But not millions. And the history books said nothing about fish with gaping sores in their sides. Rick sailed his boat up and down the river, visiting with old-timers—some whose families had settled here in the 1700s—to probe their recollections. No one had ever heard of anything like these fills kills.

By 1990, Rick and his family closed Todd's Seafood and reluctantly gave up eating local fish. In 1991, he began downsizing the fishing operation, save for some six hundred crabbing pots he kept going. It wasn't much, but it brought in some income. Eventually, Rick stopped doing that, too. "If I won't eat it myself, how the hell can I sell it wholesale?" Rick told friends. "My conscience won't let me do this anymore." The *Little Dipper* and other small craft were sold off.

Todd was relieved to be off the water. By now, red sores—large, pus filled, and painful—covered parts of his body. The sores even started appearing on his face. Rick realized he was trying to hold on to a boyhood dream of being a fisherman, but that dream was becoming nightmarish. It was time to stop. "It's just no fun anymore," he told Joanne one night at dinner. "It's not like it was a few years ago. When the fish are sick, and you and your son are getting sick, well, it's just too damn depressing."

In the summer of 1991, Rick quit his life on the river and returned to law, opening a small firm specializing in criminal defense for military personnel charged with everything from rape to murder to desertion. Now off the boat and in a suit, Rick was back in the same military courtroom at Camp Lejeune where he himself had been a judge. It was depressing to be there, arguing cases before former colleagues, but pining for the river—the river as it was *before* the fish started dying.

With more time spent on dry land, though, Rick could also linger in the law library, searching for the answer to what was killing the river. In the summer of 1992, he was reviewing the latest issue of the journal *Nature* when he came across a published letter from researchers at North Carolina State University, Raleigh. It was titled "New 'Phantom' Dinoflagellate Is the Causative Agent of Major Estuarine Fish Kills."

Rick wondered if this phantom protozoan might be connected to the massacre on the Neuse. He read on: "A worldwide increase in toxic phytoplankton blooms over the past twenty years has coincided with increasing reports of fish diseases and deaths of unknown cause. Among estuaries that have been repeatedly associated with unexplained fish kills on the western Atlantic Coast are the Pamlico and Neuse Estuaries."

Suspect identified, Rick thought.

The term "dinoflagellates" describes a large group of common plankton with plantlike features, including the ability to photosynthesize. But they can also take on animal-like characteristics, including the ability to move around at will. The protozoa have flagella, or whiplike tails, for locomotion and steering, and typically move around in a distinctive whirling fashion (*dinos* is Greek for "whirling").

The authors went on to describe a certain type of toxic one-cell organism with "phantomlike" behaviors that kill huge numbers of fish in the estuaries. The creature can lie dormant in a cystlike state for extended periods on river bottoms, until it detects the presence of live fish. That triggers the alga to break free from its cyst form and move toward its prey, releasing an extremely potent toxin that stuns them. In laboratories at North Carolina State, the removal of live fish from tanks was followed by "rapid algal encystment and dormancy," the letter said. When new fish were put back in, the cycle of death started anew.

"This dinoflagellate was abundant in the water during major fish kills in local estuaries, but only while fish were dying; within several hours of death where carcasses were still present, the flagellated vegetative algal population had encysted and settled back to the sediments," the authors wrote. The toxin produced by the phantom plankton was "highly lethal" to finfish and shellfish in the laboratory. But this vampire alga was interested only in live fish.

The Neuse River Estuary—its salty, murky water overloaded with phosphorus and nitrogen—was the ideal habitat for these particular dinoflagellates. The farms, factories, and cities upstream, Rick realized, were feeding a frenzy of fish kills down toward the river's mouth. "Given its broad temperature and salinity tolerance, and its stimulation by phosphate enrichment, this toxic phytoplankter may be a widespread but undetected source of fish mortality in nutrient-enriched estuaries," the authors concluded.[1]

Soon, news of the dinoflagellate went mainstream. Local papers reported that the creature in question had been given two different names—one scientific and one colloquial. Science's name was *Pfiesteria* (fist-AIR-ee-ah) *piscicida* (pis-ki-SEED-ah). The genus name came from a late friend of the researchers, Dr. Lois Pfiester, who pioneered studies into the sexual habits and life cycles of dinoflagellates. *Piscicida* is Latin for "fish killer."

The vernacular term was much easier to remember. The press called it "the cell from hell."

Happily for Rick Dove, his days as a private attorney defending GIs were short-lived. One chilly afternoon in December 1992, he drove home from work, opened a beer, and picked up the paper. What he saw on the front page would change his life forever.

A local conservation group, the Neuse River Foundation, had received a small grant to hire a "Riverkeeper" for the Neuse. It was part of the fledgling Riverkeeper movement started in the 1980s on New York's Hudson River. The term was coined in medieval England to describe men who policed common fishing grounds against poaching. The foundation was seeking an individual to patrol the waterways of the Neuse River Basin, searching for illegal discharges from farms, factories, and towns.

"Man, this is the job I want," Rick said to Joanne. He smiled, kissed her forehead, handed her the paper, and went off to his office to bang out a letter of application. He knew there would be stiff competition, but he felt that he'd been born to do this work. In March, the call came in and, on April 1, Rick started his dream job. He still needed to wrap up a few legal cases, but for now, he was back on the water.

Former law colleagues were dismissive. What can one individual do on the water by himself? They called him Don Quixote of the River. Rick put up with the ribbing. And he took comfort in knowing that while these guys were getting rich defending polluters, he would be making their clients' lives hell.

"I'm going to find out who did this to our river," Rick vowed to his family at dinner, the night before his first day as Riverkeeper. "I'm going to get even. I'm going to make the people who are responsible pay for what they did to the water and to us."

It didn't take long for Rick to rig his vessel into an efficient eco-patrol boat. An old friend who worked at the North Carolina Division of Environmental Management lent him a kit to facilitate onboard water testing (for turbidity, salinity, dissolved oxygen, etc.). Rick added casting nets and crab pots for collecting marine samples, and bought a video camera. He also fixed lights to the boat to illuminate it "like a Christmas tree" during night missions.

Rick designed his own "uniform," too—a khaki short-sleeved shirt made of thick cotton, with epaulets on the shoulders. He had the words NEUSE RIVER-KEEPER stitched in red on the pocket, and his name stitched on the sleeve. He also wore brown field boots, an orange life vest, and a navy blue cap with the words NEUSE RIVERKEEPER printed in white. "I've got to have people recognize me for who I am and what I am doing," he explained to Joanne. "When I go to hearings and other events, the media will know who I am, because of my clothes. This outfit tells a story." Soon enough, Rick would become well known around New Bern for his Riverkeeper uniform.

The words NEUSE RIVERKEEPER were also painted in dark blue on each side of his boat's bow. His wife suggested the boat's name—*Lonesome Dove*—as a gentle dig at his long, obsessive solo river patrols that left her home alone. But Rick prefers to call his boat the *Lonesome D*.

The entire operation had an annual budget of just twenty-five thousand dollars—and that had to cover fuel, maintenance, lab testing, equipment, photography, and Rick's salary. By the time expenses were paid, there was no salary left. So he dipped into his own pockets—a military pension that kept him comfortable—to keep the project afloat.

Rick was overjoyed to be back on the Neuse. He spent the first weeks inspecting known "point sources" of pollution, such as municipal waste treatment plants and certain factories. He even lectured his own neighbors about their manicured suburban lawns. The nutrients they used to keep them so lush and green mostly ended up running into the water, causing serious algal blooms—some so severe that boats belonging to the affluent were being locked into their slips by the thick green mass.

About a week after starting his new job, Rick called a young college professor from North Carolina State University in Raleigh: JoAnn Burkholder, a professor of environmental science. He had heard that she was doing research on the fish kills, and asked if she would meet with him. Burkholder holds a doctorate in botanical limnology, the study of inland water ecosystems. More important, she had coauthored the letter Rick saw in *Nature*, and she was a codiscoverer of *Pfiesteria piscicida*, the "cell from hell."

JoAnn had read about Rick's appointment as Riverkeeper in the New Bern *Sun Journal*. He asked her if she would tell him more about the fish kills. She wanted to test water conditions, especially for nutrients, and collect samples to test for toxic *Pfiesteria*. The two arranged to meet at the restaurant in the Havelock Holiday Inn, and they ended up glued to their corner table for three hours and two pots of watery coffee. Rick was spellbound by JoAnn's intelligence and analytical drive.

JoAnn is the type of no-nonsense scientist who strikes fear in polluters who come within view of her academic crosshairs. Tall and sturdy with shoulder-length, wavy dark hair and pale blue eyes, JoAnn was raised in northern Illinois, with the modesty and understatement that attend a Midwestern upbringing. In short, the young aquatic botanist is both likable and seriously credible.

"We first discovered it in the Pamlico River during a major kill of juvenile menhaden, and have also tracked it to the Neuse River during some fish kills there," she said of *Pfiesteria*. "This is a very unusual microbe. I've never seen anything like it. It changes into several very distinct forms across its life. It might be dormant as an inert cyst. Or it might assume various active forms. It usually eats other organisms, from microalgae to fish, but sometimes it can use photosynthesis for nutrition, like a plant. And it can reproduce rapidly, but its toxin allows it to kill fish in fairly small cell numbers, only a few hundred to several thousand cells per milliliter."

While she studied *Pfiesteria*, JoAnn discovered that using bleach to clean lab tanks where the dinoflagellate had killed fish was not enough to kill *Pfiesteria*, which formed protective coverings and lay dormant in cyst form. When JoAnn refilled the tanks with live fish, they would begin their sickening dance of death, sometimes within a few minutes. In other tanks, with smaller numbers of the dinoflagellates and therefore less toxin, the fish died more slowly, though they sometimes became covered with hideous red sores.

"I know that sign all too well," Rick said.

JoAnn explained, "The toxin or toxins can destroy the fish skin, and also apparently can affect the immune system and nervous system." Rick scribbled notes furiously as she went on to explain how the organism moves in to eat blood and flesh from the doomed fish's cells.

"Yep," Rick said, "And I know what comes next. Millions of dead fish washing up on shorelines and rich people's beaches, so many rotten fish you can't bulldoze them away."

"But here is where it gets even stranger," JoAnn said. "By the time all the fish are washing up dead, often with sores, nearly all traces of the cellular organisms that killed them have disappeared." After their feeding frenzy, the cells almost instantly leave the water by attaching to fish tissue or settling back into the riverbed, leaving little trace behind and making them exceedingly difficult to track.

Rick thought about this diabolical life cycle. Then he thought about the scores of people boating, fishing, and swimming in the Neuse at that very moment. "So, if it does that to fish, what does it do to people?" he asked. "Is this stuff dangerous to humans?"

"We think so, but we need more research. We do believe it may cause sores on humans as it does on fish," JoAnn said.

Rick got the shivers thinking about the "cell from hell" and its implications— for fish, for people, for the river. Not to mention for tourism and sportfishing. And there were YMCA camps and other summer retreats for kids all along the estuary. Would that all come to a halt? It was a chamber of commerce nightmare. How to convince people to visit, when the Neuse was infested with a one-cell vampire?

"My God," Rick said, "it's one thing to have people swimming in polluted waters and getting sick. But exposing them to a thing that's after their blood? It's worse than *Jaws*. A shark is big and real. A shark you can see." Rick stirred his coffee for a moment in silence. "I've lived here since the seventies and never seen anything like it. What's changed?"

"We are looking at nutrient pollution, like the excessive nutrients that come from sewage treatment plants and hog farms. But we're not sure yet. We need to study it further," JoAnn said.

A few days later, Rick made the three-hour drive to Raleigh. JoAnn showed him the protocols on testing river water for *Pfiesteria*—how to take the algal samples, how to package and document them, where to ship them.

Rick also met JoAnn's trusted colleague Howard Glasgow, who worked at the same North Carolina State University lab. Howard explained how the stretch of river where Rick lived lay right in the heart of the "kill zone"— where water was still and murky, so algal blooms were more likely.

Howard helped Rick borrow an instrument called a Hydrolab—an expensive piece of scientific machinery—for the *Lonesome Dove*. Its electronic probe was dropped in the water and programmed to test for salinity, temperature, oxygen, pH, and conductivity. Testing for oxygen levels was crucial—they were an omen of murderous things to come. High readings during the daytime, followed by very low levels at night, usually meant the presence or imminence of a large algal bloom. This would at least allow Rick time to prepare for a new emergency round of studying and testing.

As algal blooms grow during the day, they convert carbon dioxide into oxygen through photosynthesis. But when the sun sets, they begin their nightly process of respiration, taking pure oxygen from the water and replacing it with carbon dioxide within hours. The fish die at night in droves.

Rick knew what came next. He had witnessed it dozens of times before: the horrific "fish jubilee," when millions of menhaden, eels, flounder, crab, and shrimp—species that never comingle—scrambled en masse toward the shoreline, flopping and struggling in one inch of water, trying to extract oxygen from liquid as it passed through their gills. Locals with metal spears would turn out for a jubilee, harpooning flounder by the dozens to take home for a free meal. By morning, most fish were dead.

Rick could soon predict when the fish would begin dying from low or no oxygen. Likewise, when fish began to die during normal oxygen conditions, he knew the *Pfiesteria* might be amassing, attracted by the dying fish. During these tense periods, Rick would call JoAnn for information and support. Often she or members of her lab would travel to New Bern on steamy summer nights and join Rick to take readings and net fish up and down the river. To protect his skin, Rick would don elbow-length rubber gloves before collecting water samples during algal blooms or fish kills. After a long day on the Neuse, he would often work in his office until midnight, completing the paperwork on the day's haul.

But Rick still could not discern any direct point of pollution that might explain the *Pfiesteria* outbreaks and fish kills. Perhaps the answer wouldn't be found by boat, he realized. And so he dipped into his own pocket and paid two hundred dollars for a pilot and plane to take him up high over the Neuse to see what he could see.

Large-scale hog farming had come to North Carolina in the late 1980s—right around the time that Rick Dove began to notice an unsettling decline in the river's health. During the summer of 1993, he opened his own little investigation into the strange-looking pig farms he had seen from the air. He discovered, for example, that most farmers were little more than hired animal caretakers contracted to feed the pigs, which were owned by huge livestock conglomerates such as Carroll's Foods and Prestage Farms. The biggest and richest of them all, Murphy Family Farms, was founded in 1962 by Wendell H. Murphy. Murphy, a former state senator and down-country power broker, had supported a raft of pro-pig legislation through the statehouse even as he built his own lucrative empire of swine.[2] This apparent conflict of interest did not violate any North Carolina ethics laws.

Under the efficiency-loving contract system, pig production is usually divided into three succinct stages, much like an assembly line, only each stage is often completed at a different farm. It starts at the breeding facility, or farrowing operation, where baby pigs are delivered from (usually) artificially inseminated sows that live much of their cramped lives in small "gestation crates" that afford them no room to stand up or turn around. For many animal activists, farrowing operations are barbaric and inhumane—concentration camps for sows. Banned in Europe, they are now gradually being phased out in at least some parts of the United States.

After the piglets are weaned, some gilts (young females) are set aside to be raised as replacement sows. The other gilts and boars are trucked away to nearby nursing operations, where they are kept in pens inside long barns. After castration, the young boars are called barrows. These animals will never go outside, breathe fresh air, or feel natural sunlight. They will not get a chance to grub in dirt or wallow in mud, as pigs are meant to do. They will never chase siblings through a field or have sex with a mate.

Modern hog nurseries can contain well over twenty-five hundred piglets. The farmers at these nurseries are responsible for fattening young pigs for several weeks, until they weigh about 50–60 pounds. Then they are transferred to "finishing facilities," where they are housed and fed on high-calorie grains until they reach market weight, about 250 pounds, at about six months of age. Some large "farrow-to-finishing" operations complete all three stages at one location.

By the time the animals near market size, they are so large that they have to be packed into their small indoor pens. There is little room for them to move around. This often results in higher incidences of infectious diseases, bloody fights, and highly stressed animals with weakened immune systems. At about five months of age, the hogs are dispatched to the slaughterhouse.

Under the contracting system, farmers are responsible for financing and constructing all barns, buildings, and waste lagoons. They often incur debts well over a million dollars just to get started. Contract farmers are also responsible for feeding the pigs and maintaining the health of the herd. Some describe it as raising animals according to a recipe: Farmers feed company-supplied rations to company-owned animals. They administer company-prescribed antibiotics whenever the company instructs them to in order to promote growth, stave off infections, and treat outbreaks. The farmers even maintain barn temperatures within a precise range determined by the company. Often they must erect their barns using company-approved designs, dimensions, and materials.

Farmers commit to delivering the animals to the next stage of the production line, or the slaughterhouse, at a predetermined time. The idea is to send uniformly sized hogs to the processing plant on a steady schedule that can keep the place working twenty-four hours a day with three shifts of labor. The farmer, of course, is also responsible for disposing of the thousands of tons of manure and urine left behind daily by the pigs, and for disposal through composting of the pigs that die. Mortality rates up to 5 percent are not uncommon. The contract farmers are liable for any environmental infractions that occur.

The company, meanwhile, provides young sows and semen stock to the farmers. It sells to farmers (and makes a profit on) the animals' feed, medications, and other additives, provides staff veterinarians, and sends company trucks on specified days to collect pigs and haul them to their next or final stop. What the large companies don't do, however, is assume any liability for manure spills. And they don't tie up large sums of their own capital building expensive animal confinements and other structures.

In North Carolina, the new-style hog farms—folks had started calling them hog factories—began sprouting up from Interstate 95 eastward to the tidewater. People who lived near them—rural, usually poor, and often African American—soon began complaining about wretched odors, noxious gases, breathing difficulties, general health problems, and even mood swings. Their troubles largely went ignored.

But by 1993, that was slowly changing. The media were starting to take note of the state's hog "situation." On July 18, Rick woke up to read an article in the Raleigh *News & Observer* called "Raising a Stink"—the first in a long and prizewinning history of coverage.

The hog industry was moving in with "warp speed," reporter Jim Barnett wrote.[3] In just two years, the hog population had exploded by more than 60 percent in the state—from 2.8 million to 4.6 million, making it the fourth-largest U.S. producer. By 1996, the article stated, North Carolina might have more pigs than people, or some seven million animals. Only Iowa had more.

And with all those hogs had come the lagoons. They were often twenty feet or more deep. Newer models were lined with clay as a sealant. Manure and urine were collected in pits under the animal barns and periodically flushed through gutters into the lagoon, where bacteria broke down the waste and helped reduce the smell.

To prevent lagoons from overflowing, growers pumped wastewater onto surrounding land, where it was mechanically sprayed onto fields and crops.

Most lagoons were designed to maintain an extra margin of safety, or free-board, of at least two feet. But critics said many farmers ignored that rule and let their lagoons overflow. Others sprayed wastewater onto obviously oversaturated fields that could not absorb more nutrients. "Either way, hog waste can work its way into the water supply," Barnett wrote. "And with the rapid growth of the state's hog population, activists fear that wastes could begin fouling drinking water."

Not too long before this, farmers could only raise a few hundred pigs at one location. But under the new system, they could house thousands of animals on just a few acres of land. One Duplin County grower, Ronnie Jarmon, said he'd be out of farming altogether if not for the hog-contract system. Jarmon had gotten by on corn and soybeans, but those crops could no longer support him on the land he owned.

But the hogs—there was money in the hogs. That income could keep him on his land and out of a dreary day job somewhere in town.

Jarmon built his first finishing barn in 1990, and later installed two more with a total capacity of thirty-six hundred pigs. For every animal he successfully raised and sent to the slaughterhouse, he earned on average $9.17. Every eighteen weeks, when all the animals in his barns were turned over, he could make about $33,000, enough to keep him on the farm, albeit with some considerable payments to deduct for his construction loans, feed costs, electricity, labor, and affiliated expenses.

Still, many growers said they were making money, though some had to supplement their income off the farm. Phyllis and Eugene Parker raised twenty-six hundred hogs in Duplin County for Murphy Family Farms. Eugene worked a regular job in town while Phyllis spent two or three hours each day feeding the pigs and cleaning the barn. In their first year, they netted $20,000. They would be able to pay off their ten-year, $143,000 bank loan in just six or seven years.

But the boom had not been good for everyone. The rapid growth was already affecting the staid and traditional character of eastern North Carolina. Many people said the stench was overpowering, and the threat to property values was real. Worse, there was virtually no regulation. "They can build and operate huge barns virtually without oversight," the article said, "as long as they don't dump their wastes directly into streams." Rick had to laugh at that one. He had personally caught dozens of farmers spraying wastewater directly into waterways, often unaware they were being photographed from the air.

Then there was the maximization of earnings through "vertical integration" of the corporate food chain. Under this model, companies control every stage. Many big hog producers were also hog processors. Take Smithfield Foods, Inc., one of the largest. It built a multimillion-dollar slaughterhouse in Bladen County in the early 1990s, and now processed hogs from Murphy Family Farms. But Smithfield also raised its own pigs in partnership with Carroll's Foods. This deal gave Smithfield control of its meat from insemination day to shopping day at the supermarket, much like oil companies controlling their own wells, refinery, and gas stations.

Verticalization of the industry was prohibited in most big hog states, including Iowa and its upper Midwest neighbors, where companies that owned hogs could not slaughter them. The laws were enacted to protect the viability of small and independent producers. Without access to an abattoir, these small producers would quickly be driven from business. The slaughtering plant is a hog farmer's sole gateway to the global meat marketplace. If a plant is owned by a single hog company, that firm can deny access to other farmers in the area.

Rick was disgusted. He had to put down the paper and go walk off some steam. He headed out the back door and down to the dock, peering out over the rippling waters and across to the distant north shore. Pig farms were not just hurting the river, they were hurting and killing small towns and family farms as well.

Joanne walked out to join her husband in the warm, soupy air. She put her arm around him. "It's not fair and it's not right," Rick said. "These damn pig factories, they're everywhere. And they'll keep growing, and keep polluting, and keep killing our fish, because it's a sweet deal for the companies. But it's not always so sweet for these poor farmers."

Joanne shook her head. "Then why would the farmers agree to it?"

"They have no choice," Rick said. "If they want to raise hogs, they gotta do it with the big boys. These contracts—they are signing away their lives, their independence. They agree to be mere servants. They don't make any decisions that a normal farmer makes. They're employees, sharecroppers. They don't even own the pigs! But they do own whatever comes out the other end."

"Rick," Joanne said, laughing. "You're a Republican. You sound like a socialist."

Rick laughed, too. "But really, Joanne, this whole business sucks," he said. "The farmers get screwed by the companies, and the neighbors get screwed by so many pigs confined in one place. Those poor people are drowning in fumes."

Rick was convinced that the pig boom was hurting the Neuse. And things would only get worse, he feared. Most lagoons were fairly new. Damage from spills and leaks might take years or even decades to become apparent. By then, an entire swath of the state would be pocked with these damn things, he thought.

Rick was hardly comforted by the soothing reassurances echoing from industry spokesmen, who uniformly extolled the safety of hog lagoon technology. One Murphy executive said it was all state of the art. It was simply not possible for a lagoon to leak. "I don't have the evidence," he told the reporter, "but I don't think there's any evidence to the contrary."

One day in the late summer of 1993, Rick got a call from Bob Roth, a founding member of the Neuse River Foundation. "There's someone you should meet," he said. "He's a lot like you, trying to bring the hog farms under control. He left the business because he just couldn't take the guilt," Roth explained. "He couldn't stand knowing he was making his neighbors sick. I think you'll like him. He's what they call a very colorful character."

Don Webb was a retired hog farmer up in Wilson County, about halfway between New Bern and Raleigh, near the epicenter of swine operations. Rick and Don spoke on the phone the next day. Don's voice boomed, but it also drawled in that classic backcountry Carolina way, where an unhurried accent can sometimes stretch three letters into three syllables, and the word "pen" might come out more like "*pay*-yen-nuh."

Don spoke like a good old Southern boy, but his angry words against corporate farms made him sound more like a radical. He lashed out at what he called the godless theft of America's promise, stolen from anyone unlucky enough to live near a hog factory. "We're warning people 'round here about the damn corporate greed that's turning our state into a big stinkin' pigpen," Don said. "It'll just get worse if we let these company-owned piggies run all over us. These factories wreak havoc on our health and happiness. People are being robbed blind of the American dream, forced to smell urine and feces all day and all night."

Don had grown up dirt poor in Stantonsburg, North Carolina, having been born by an old graveyard along the train tracks; the house where he had lived had no water or electricity. After graduating from East Carolina College with a degree in physical education, Don became a high school coach. He ultimately traded that for a desk job, but his heart wasn't in it. "Being an old country boy, and all," Don explained, "I thought I just might go and raise me some hogs. And so I did." He and a friend bought and managed several hog barns with some four thousand pigs, which they finished and sold to Smithfield (though they owned their own animals).

"We kept it all in lagoons, but we didn't have no sprayfields," Don drawled. "All you had to do was drag it out and throw it on the ground. Back then we didn't have modernization, and frankly, we polluted like hell. The government knew it, too. They told us it was no problem at all. Did I pollute? Yes. Did I stink up people's homes? That's why I got out."

"What about your own home?" Rick asked. "Didn't that stink up too?"

Don laughed. "Hell, no! I didn't live anywhere *near* those barns. Few big producers do. I lived in a nice subdivision in Murfreesboro. Polluting didn't bother me none because I didn't know I was polluting. Then one day, a man who lived by my barns come up to me and said, 'Mr. Webb, I don't want to upset you, but you know some nights we can't even sleep, especially on warm nights when we got windows open. And we've got a sick little girl at home, and she's up crying all night because of it. *Please* do something.'

"So I go down to the County, and they say, 'All you do is get yourself some yeast, get in a boat, throw that yeast out there and stir it up.' So I got a pile of it and I got in a little motorboat and I went out and spread that yeast around. Then I stirred her up, *rrrrrrrr!!!* Three days later I see the same guy. 'Don!' he cries. 'I appreciate you trying to stop that odor. But whatever the hell you're doing back there, please stop! Don't do it no more because we can't stand it. It's ten times worse!'

"Well, I couldn't do anything more. And I was thinking about my mama and my daddy, and how they raised me. So I went to those neighbors and said, 'I'm gonna sell the hogs.' My business partner, he didn't want to. But we finally sold the herd and made some money. And I got out of the business. I'd have to be a no-good human being to keep on like that."

In 1989, Don bought an old farm, with twin lakes and lazy Contentnea Creek winding its way through the property. Months after moving in, Don noticed that several mega–hog farms were being built within a mile or two of his home. That's when he really rolled up his sleeves and fought back. He invited small hog farmers and others to stand up against the hog factories, and the Association for a Responsible Swine Industry (ARSI) was born.

Rick was impressed by Don's initiative, and he recognized a major potential ally. He told Don about the Neuse River fish kills, the *Pfiesteria* problem, and his work with JoAnn Burkholder. And he described his eye-opening plane ride over the mega–hog farms.

"I'm really getting pissed off," Rick said.

"Join the club!" Don crowed. "We don't want more of these hog factories in North Carolina. That's why we formed ARSI. In fact, we're having a community briefing this Sunday in Black Creek, near Wilson. Why don't you come and tell us what you've seen on the river, and from that plane?"

That weekend, Rick drove up to Black Creek, a timeworn town with a sad strip of stone buildings for a Main Street. One modest storefront housed the city meeting hall. It was packed with fifty or sixty people, about half of them white and half African-American. They looked like poor, worried farmers, Rick thought.

Don Webb went up front and introduced himself with a wave of his big paw and a hearty smile. He was six foot four inches and well over two hundred pounds, and the minute he opened his mouth he showed why Southerners so easily dominate the American art of florid oratory.

"Afternoon, my friends!" he began. "I am Don Webb from right here in Wilson County, home of feces and urine, the cell from hell, heaven for hogs and hell for humans. Over the past few years, the eastern region of North Carolina has been inundated with large intensive corporate hog operations. They have invaded our neighborhoods and communities, forcing our people into the bondage of feces and urine.

"Thousands of North Carolinians have begged for relief from the stench of these factories, but there has been no relief from the devastating odors, permeating from open earthen cesspools. They aren't lagoons. A lagoon is something a beautiful girl in a South Seas island swims in. A cesspool is something you put feces and urine in. There's so much that fields can't absorb it all. It's poisoning groundwater and our drinking wells."

Don said a new study by Duke University professor Susan Schiffman, who had researched odors, showed that people living close to commercial swine farms were less energetic, and more depressed and fatigued.[4] "Odors from these operations are harmful to humans, it's obvious," Don continued. "These factories force neighbors to leave their homes, or endure the impacts of this industry. Some have made the painful decision to sell homes at a loss, in order to regain a decent quality of life. Why should people have to leave their homes in order for a few people to make money?" he growled.

Don pointed out that many hog farms were actually owned by lawyers, sheriffs, county commissioners, and state elected officials. "These are not family farms," he said. "These are industrial endeavors by investors, who are making money while at the same time making sharecroppers of our true American farmers!" The crowd leaped to their feet and cheered. Rick joined them. Don Webb could tell one hell of a good story.

"Now, I know what it's like to stink up people's lives," Don confessed. "But if you knowingly go and stink up someone's home, and continue to do so, you're not a good American; you're not a good Christian. That's common sense. If you're this great Christian, this Paul Revere American, then you're going to stop hurting your neighbors. You don't have to get Billy Graham to come down here to tell you it's wrong. You know it's wrong."

Don welcomed others to share their stories of living within the "stink zone." Rick listened to a litany of misery as people rose to describe how their lives were disrupted when the "pig factories" moved in to Wilson County. People spoke of stench clouds and gaseous odors so foul they made small children vomit and old ladies faint. They spoke of burning throats, watering eyes, throbbing heads. When the wind shifted, women grabbed laundry from the line and ran for their houses, slamming windows to keep the stink from slithering in.

Odor was just part of the problem. Waste lagoons would often overflow, sending hundreds or thousands of gallons of stinking brown water onto neighboring farms. Manure spraying was so routine that people often found their homes engulfed in a sticky brownish mist.

Everyone who spoke had called state authorities for help. But their complaints went unheeded, they said. One African-American man came from a family who'd farmed beans and tobacco on their land for over a century. When his next-door neighbor wanted to build a thirty-two-hundred-hog facility, he begged the man not to. "I told him, 'We're all farmers around here; farmers are supposed to support farmers,'" he recounted sadly. "But he didn't care. Now he's got his swine contract, and we're getting sick."

When Rick's turn came to speak, he felt almost guilty for living down near New Bern, where hog odors were not a problem. He displayed photos and video footage he had taken from the air, and explained the images' connection to the *Pfiesteria* outbreak.

"Before I came here today," Rick said, "I saw this issue purely from the viewpoint of the river and the fish. But now, after listening to all of you, I realize the much wider and more serious nature of this problem. These new hog farms are polluting communities, polluting people, and polluting the river. I want to help stop it from happening more."

CAFO. The first time Rick heard a friend utter the term, he thought it must be some kind of new espresso place. But it's an official designation used by the U.S. government to describe any poultry or livestock operation with concentrated numbers of animals confined for at least forty-five days a year within a building or outdoor pen, without access to grass or other foraging vegetation within the confinement area.[5]

Any feeding operation with more than one thousand "animal units" (one beef cattle equals one animal unit) is automatically designated as a CAFO. The equivalents for one hundred animal units are: beef, 100 head; dairy, 70 head; swine, 250 pigs more than 55 pounds; poultry, 12,500 broilers or 8,200 layers.[6] Within a CAFO's rows of climate-controlled buildings, thousands of creatures could be fed and watered by a network of whirring, computer-driven machines.

CAFOs are more commonly called factory farms—a term generally loathed by the animal farming industry. They are distinguished from traditional farms because most of their land is dedicated to the housing, feeding, and (at dairies) milking of animals, and waste for disposal is stored somewhere else. A typical family farm usually has sufficient acreage to dispose of its own animal manure in a healthy, agronomic fashion. But a CAFO, by definition, has far too many animals per acre to absorb the waste. Urine and feces are distributed off-site from the confinement—at least in theory. But too often, critics say, the dissemination is poorly executed, resulting in an overloading of nutrients such as nitrogen and phosphorus, or heavy metals and antibiotic-resistant bacteria into the soil. When overapplication becomes acute, arable land can be ruined for generations.

Most factory farms—with the exception of dairy and beef lots in western states—confine animals within an enclosed building for most, if not all of their lives. Structures that house poultry and livestock are sometimes called parlors or barns—though they bear no resemblance to the quaint red structures with haylofts that are so iconic to American country life. CAFO houses are usually massive, hangarlike structures made of concrete and aluminum or heavy canvas. In some megadairies, they are a quarter-mile long.

Cages, crates, pens, and "veal hutches" restrict animal movement. Breeding animals, such as sows, are usually artificially inseminated. Mother pigs spend most of their lives locked into abusively small crates during pregnancy, farrowing, and nursing (though this practice is slowly being phased out in the United States). They barely have room to stand up, and they can't turn around.

A typical hog "finishing" operation might have around eight barns, or 5,000 animals in total, on just an acre or two of land.[7] Each tightly packed barn holds twenty-five pens, crammed with twenty-five hogs apiece, for a total of 625 animals per barn. As the animals eat more and near market size, they barely have room to fit. Fights are not uncommon. The amount of waste generated daily is equivalent to the raw sewage of twenty thousand people.[8]

Big Ag preferred this method because it was designed to maximize profit. The goal of factory farms is to produce as much beef, chicken, turkey, milk, or eggs at the lowest possible cost per unit. Economies of scale are achieved by buying feed, drugs, equipment, additives, and vet care at negotiated bulk rates that smaller producers could never obtain.

Animal welfare activists charge that meat-industry wealth is amassed at the cost of animal misery. But producers insist that farm animals are better off confined than set loose on pastureland, where they fall prey to the elements, predators, and disease.

Rick was stunned to learn all this. Most shocking, perhaps, was how quickly the pigs were being "finished" to market size. "They go from little piglets the size of your fist to 250-pound beasts in under six months," he told Joanne one evening, after researching the topic for hours online. "If the piggies aren't eating all the time and getting to market weight, they are losing money for the producer. It's an animal factory, plain and simple."

If Rick Dove was not out patrolling on the *Lonesome D*, marching through swamps, or sometimes sinking into the soft ground up to his waist, he was collecting water samples for JoAnn Burkholder. He also began traveling around the state, delivering community talks about how factory hog farms were killing the Neuse River.

It was not a popular message to be broadcasting in eastern North Carolina in the early 1990s. Everywhere he went, hog farmers and industry types materialized, sitting in the back, arms folded, glaring. Inevitably, one would rise and shake a fist at Rick. "You don't know what the hell you're talking about, you dang fool!" Rick had fought in Vietnam; he reckoned he could handle these gentlemen. And he began noticing that his detractors rarely came up with legitimate responses to the concerns he raised.

Sometimes Rick brought the issue literally to a farmer's own turf. He'd drive out to farms known to be polluting and park his big red truck where it could easily be seen, and then begin taking waste samples and pictures. Once in a while, the pig workers would invite him onto the farm to have a look, maybe even meet the boss. Usually, though, he was met with anger.

The aerial surveillance program also picked up at this point. Rick recruited his old friend Phil Bowie—a writer and a small-craft pilot—to help document the number and position of CAFOs in the region. In his late forties, with rabbit-white hair, a matching beard, and wire-frame glasses, Phil resembled a scruffy version of CNN news anchor Wolf Blitzer. He would help Rick compile a photographic encyclopedia of spills, leaks, runoff, and other violations.

Rick and Phil were shocked to discover that the state government of North Carolina did not keep a central registry of CAFO locations. The Department of Agriculture knew, but would not share the data—not even with fellow agencies. And so Rick and Phil, often corralling volunteers with small planes, began mapping hog farms from the sky. The Neuse River Air Force was born.

Rick was steadily making a name for himself in the small but growing world of North Carolina environmental activism. By the late summer of 1993, his reputation as a tenacious maritime investigator was confirmed by the Raleigh *News & Observer*, which ran a glowing front-page profile of him, simply titled "The Riverkeeper."

The article portrayed the Neuse Riverkeeper as a roving crusader against human complacency, the river's mortal enemy:

> His ultimate goal is daunting. He wants to change the way the million people who live in the river's basin think. He wants city officials, factory owners, hog farmers, tobacco and corn growers, foresters, and

gardeners to see what they're doing to the river. His main weapons are video, a spotlight, and plastic tubs for water samples. With those, he documents the offenses and the offended, dead and dying fish.[9]

The reporter, Julie Powers, made several trips to New Bern for her research, and Rick took her out on the *Lonesome D*. He showed her the various sewage treatment plants. He drew nets and looked for fish with sores. He took her out on night patrol, searching for illegal discharges into the river.

"You know, Julie, when I was a kid, I watched the Chesapeake Bay die," he said one muggy afternoon, when the sky was heavy with thunderclouds. "And then years after I moved here, I saw the Neuse River heading on the same trajectory." He paused for a moment, staring out at a soaring flight of wood ducks. "The positive thing about the Neuse, though, is she's not dead. She can be fixed. That's the reason I went for this job."

Julie asked how the fish kills had affected people along the river. Rick thought for a moment. He would have loved to say the kills had mobilized the population and shaken folks from their complacency. But he couldn't. Sadly, the disasters seemed to engender resignation among the public. "People accept the kills," Rick sighed. "It's something that's not alarming anymore."

On a windy morning in February 1994, Rick Dove awoke to make coffee and check his overnight e-mail. He slid open the glass doors onto the back lawn and walked down the slope to the water. Normally on windy days, he would expect to see whitecaps skipping across the watery expanse. But today, Rick had to rub his eyes to make sure he was seeing correctly. He was looking out at carrot-orange caps; a frothy sea of Tropicana juice.

"Joanne! Honey, get out here!" he called. "There's something you gotta see." Joanne joined him by the waterside. "My God," she said, "it looks like the end of the world."

They had observed just about every other color spreading across the Neuse—the river had turned red and yellow and green and even black in the past. But this was the first time it had gone orange. Rick presumed the orange murk was the result of yet another bizarre bloom of algae, heretofore unseen in these parts.

The phone rang. A staff member from the Neuse River Foundation had already received twenty calls. Six people had come by the office to drop off water samples. Rick jumped in his boat and went out to take his own samples. As he sped away, the *Lonesome D* began spewing a giant plume of fizzy Orange Crush.

Scientists tested the water and confirmed that another algal bloom, caused by an excess of nutrients, was responsible for the discoloration. There was no evidence that the organisms were toxic, nor were any fish kills considered imminent.

It took three different types of algae to bloom at once to create this particular shade of water, scientists said. Those species had appeared before at this time of year, but never in such massive numbers: The great orange bloom of 1994 stretched for more than ten miles. Scientists warned that algal blooms of many types, colors, and toxicities were growing larger, more severe, and more frequent. There was little they could do. As one UNC researcher put it, "All we can hope for is that Mother Nature is going to be kind to us."

The Division of Environmental Management (DEM) did not have a clue about the number, size, or location of mega–hog farms that had moved into the state in recent years. So the Neuse River Air Force was doing the surveillance job for them.

The Neuse River Air Force assembled a crew of twenty observers to collect data. These eyewitnesses accompanied volunteer pilots to shoot film and video, or fanned out on the ground to locate the facilities and mark them on a road map. Very often, it was odor complaints by neighbors that brought a CAFO's location to the attention of the Neuse River Air Force. Since it was difficult to follow a county road map from the air, the solution was for ground crews to stake down giant orange sheets wherever they spotted a CAFO. They would then stand by the sheet and radio in their general location, until the pilot found them.

The air observer would photograph and videotape the facility, including its lagoons and sprayfield operations. When they returned from their missions, they delivered their reconnaissance films to Rick, who was plotting the CAFOs on a master map of the state. Rick felt as though he was back in the military.

By late 1994, the Neuse River Air Force had compiled a tall stack of documentary evidence on hog-farm violations across several counties. Everything they gathered, they took to DEM, demanding that agency investigators stop the spillage, overspraying, and runoff. "Look," Rick told the officials one afternoon, "we can forgive you for not going after these animal factories in the past; you didn't know where they were. But now you have that information; you've got no more excuses." If they chose not to act on the information, Rick vowed, he would go over their heads—and to the media.

He made good on his promise. Packets of photos and videos confirming the unchecked polluting were dispatched to the governor and key lawmakers in Raleigh.

Rick also phoned his contact at *The News & Observer*, Julie Powers. She had been interviewing Don Webb in recent days, and said the newspaper was considering a major exposé of the swine industry. One weekend, Don and Rick arranged to meet Julie in Greene County and bring her to see the hog farms that neighbors were complaining about. They stopped for lunch at a barbecue place off the highway. Don surveyed the room, looking for acquaintances. He raised his eyebrows, suppressed a howl, and nudged Rick with his elbow.

"Hey! Look over there," Don said, nodding at a half-dozen people, some in suits, eating North Carolina–style shredded pork barbecue around a table. TV news equipment was piled next to them. "You see them folks? Now, that guy there in the cap is a contract grower, one of the bigger ones in Greene County. He raises pigs for Murphy. Those other folks, they're Murphy executives. And those ladies are PR people. They got a TV crew with 'em, looks like the FOX channel up in Raleigh."

Don explained that the grower maintained a "model" hog farm—with barns that were new and clean, aerated and disinfected—to show off to lawmakers, reporters, and the curious public. "They're going to take that film crew over there to *ooh* and *ahh* at the cute little piggies, and show everyone what modern wonders these hog factories are. You watch." Don got up to leave. "Those folks, they won't want to talk to me. But you two should go introduce yourselves. You might get an interesting afternoon from it."

Rick and Julie wandered over. Julie said she was doing an article on the health of the state's rivers. Rick was helping her out. They were invited to come along on a hog-farm tour. The party piled into a small caravan and drove fifteen minutes past streams and pine forests until they arrived at the "model" swine farm. The grounds were groomed and manicured; the white barns sparkled in the sun. The waste lagoons were kept well below their rims; and the sprayfields, where hay was grown, were a safe distance from any water sources.

Rick was impressed. But he knew this tightly run operation was not a typical example of pig CAFOs. He had seen the evidence himself. In fact, he knew there was a heavily polluting hog farm just about a mile down the road.

When it came time to tour a barn, everyone was required to shower and don special synthetic bodysuits with zip-on booties before going in the confinement. Rick couldn't get over the irony: People on the outside were worried about getting sick from the pigs on the inside. And yet, the hog growers were worried about the opposite problem. One bad virus tracked in by a visitor could potentially wipe out an entire pig parlor. The humans had to be disinfected to go before swine. What a world, Rick thought.

The confinement building was swept clean, and its walls had obviously just been washed down and disinfected. There was an unmistakably sharp odor in the barn, but nothing that Rick would consider overpowering. The pigs were relatively young, pinkish, and cute. They ran around and played with one another.

Rick wondered if the guests knew these pigs had never—would never—see the sun, breathe fresh air, or dig for grubs. They would live their days and nights under artificial lights, in reasonably sized pens, on top of freshly washed concrete floors with slats between them. The floors covered an underground waste pit into which the animals' feces and urine fell.

"This must be the best-run hog factory in North Carolina," Rick whispered to Julie at one point. "This is their pig-and-pony show. They're not going to take us to a *bad* factory."

After the tour, the PR people asked Rick if he wanted to go on camera to describe what he'd seen. He agreed. Rick described the pleasant conditions of the building while the Murphy Family Farms people smiled and nodded. "But you know something?" Rick frowned. "I think you should take me to some other swine facilities around here—to compare. We passed one, a Murphy contractor, not too far back. Why not go have a look at *that* one?" Rick noticed that the pork people had stopped smiling and begun to glare. He pressed on. "It's just back down the road about a mile. Take me to see what *those* animals live like."

Oblivious to the beet-red-faced Murphy folks, the FOX reporter echoed Rick's suggestion. Julie also asked to see the other farm. They drove down to it. Don had told Rick the place had fields oversaturated with pig waste, and effluent running into a nearby creek. When the caravan arrived, the gate was closed. "Well now, that *is* a pity," a Murphy staffer said with feigned sympathy. "It looks like the owner isn't around. We can't enter without permission." Rick smiled. "Follow me," he said.

Rick grabbed his camera, tugged on some hip boots, and hopped over the chain gate. "Wait! Mr. Dove!" a Murphy man shouted after him. "You can't go down there!" But Rick was marching briskly toward the field where Don said the hog water was pooling up and had been running into a ditch that ran to the creek. Everyone tore after him—Julie, the FOX crew, the Murphy executives in their tailored suits, the PR women in their Gucci shoes.

As Rick tells it, he continued his stomp across the soggy field. Soon, everyone else was wading after him through reeking pig effluence. Women gagged. Men wiped at their teary eyes. Rick kept going, searching out the wettest, muckiest spots to walk through, knowing everyone would follow. The Murphy bigwigs kept up—*squish-squash-squish*—the brown liquid now oozing over the rims of their very pricey shoes. Rick grinned as he traipsed on in his dry and cozy hip boots. He kept going until he got to the end of the field, where it was obvious that runoff had reached the creek.

"Look!" he shouted, pointing at the ground. "Over here! You can see where the pig waste was running right into the water." They all came slogging over.

Rick heard some of the Murphy men swearing under their breath. "Mr. Dove!" one shouted. "You don't know for a *fact* that this is hog poo! You don't know *what* was running into that river! You need to be careful. Our lawyers will be reviewing this footage." Rick smiled triumphantly as he explained what a Clean Water Act violation looked like. "You see? Hog poo does not mix with streams," he said. "And it doesn't go with Gucci shoes too good, either." As he trudged back to his truck, Rick murmured to himself, "Oh man, I can't wait to watch TV tonight."

2

Helen Ann Brower was born during the Great Depression into a fourteenth-generation farming family (going back to England) in the southwestern corner of dust-bowl era Missouri. She was reared in a world where luxury never came knocking at the farmhouse door. But Helen was comforted by two loving parents, good home cooking, and three rowdy brothers. As the only girl, Helen soon learned to assert her will in the rough-and-tumble world of boys.

Soon after World War II the family moved to California, where her parents worked in a defense plant. When Helen was thirteen, the family bought a small dairy back in Missouri. Leaving Southern California to live in the Ozarks was a culture shock; Helen changed from a California girl to a milkmaid. She was handed a milk pail and marched toward the barn, where she was shown how to milk a cow. Other chores included hand-pumping the well and feeding the chickens and pigs.

Helen hated every second of it. Milking was the most loathsome of all. Twice a day, she and her brother trudged out to squat in the barn until all twenty-seven udders were emptied. One cow really had it in for Helen, she could swear. The Guernsey would whack her face hard with a raspy tail, or wait until her milk bucket was nearly filled, and then knock it over with a petulant hind kick.

Helen was a tall teenager, with soft gray eyes and a mane of wild, wavy brown hair. She was smart, too, so school was easy. She was accepted to several big colleges, and even offered some scholarships, but it was still not enough to cover the costs for the struggling family. Then, in the summer of 1952, a girlfriend told Helen about a job out in Washington State in an exotic-sounding place called Yakima Valley, home to a massive Libby fruit cannery and packing house. Young Helen jumped at the chance to break free of the Midwest, and her family. But her parents had other plans.

"We're going to spend the summer there with you!" they announced with smiles that Helen found slightly malicious. As it turned out, her parents had friends in the Yakima area who owned several orchards and needed help harvesting cherries, apples, and pears. "We are all going to pick fruit together!" her mom said, a little too gaily for Helen's taste. Helen pouted and pleaded. But when she heard about the wages paid to fruit harvesters, she relented. "For three bucks an hour," she told her girlfriend, "I can tolerate anything."

It took several days to drive to the wide and shallow Lower Yakima Valley, or Lower Valley for short. The word "Yakima" derives from one of two Yakima Indian legends. In the most popular version, "Yakima" means "runaway," and refers to an Indian chief's daughter who did just that. Others believe the word means "bountiful," "beginning of life," or "big bellied," leading some to wonder if pregnancy was the reason why the Indian girl had to run away in the first place.

As Helen entered the valley, she saw the scrubby low Rattlesnake Hills—bleached a golden tan color from the unforgiving western sun—and the towering green Cascade Mountains off to the west. The snow-topped range blocks most of the Pacific marine drizzle that infamously dominates Seattle and keeps everything west of the mountains emerald green, but creates a dry desert area to the east.

Making its way through the five-mile-wide valley was the Yakima River, whose waters tumble down the eastern slopes and zigzag through Yakima Valley to the Columbia River.

The family arrived at the orchards to find attractive acres of Bing cherry trees climbing over low hills and down into shallow dells. Helen was uplifted by the beauty of the place, until she saw their accommodations: dingy migrant-worker shacks that she was sure were infested with cooties. To make things worse, Helen looked across the road at workers camped out on the ground. "It looks like *The Grapes of Wrath*," she said to her mother. Helen attempted a prima donna act of refusal, but eventually resigned herself to the conditions.

Everyone rose early for their first day in the orchards. Brushing her teeth at the outside sink, Helen caught a glimpse in the chipped mirror of a lad hauling buckets of cherries across the grove. A handsome young man, he had a dark blond crew cut and rounded muscles under suntanned skin.

Hmm, Helen thought, maybe picking fruit from trees all summer won't be a total loss after all. She ran back inside and put on her favorite chartreuse short shorts, grabbed a ladder and bucket, and merrily set off for work toward a row of trees, keeping one eye on the good-looking tractor driver.

Minutes later, she saw him driving a tractor down the rows, retrieving buckets filled by pickers. Helen spent most of that day trying to position her ladder where their paths might cross. It happened late in the afternoon. His name was Don Reddout. To Helen, he was a dreamy John Wayne type. On their third date, Don told Helen he was going to marry her. She laughed. But that November, when she was just eighteen and he was seventeen, Don kept his promise.

One year later their first daughter, Terri, was born in November 1955. Lisa arrived two years later, in November 1957, and Linda in December 1959. Their first son, Donny, was born in August 1962. The following year Don and Helen bought their first orchard—ten acres of Bing cherries on Snipes Mountain, which most folks call Cherry Hill. Their second son, David, was born in May 1966. Helen raised what she called a working family, in which everybody had responsibilities.

The young family was exceedingly happy for years, and though money was hardly flowing, the couple saved enough to purchase seven more acres of prime orchards on Cherry Hill. In 1969, Helen decided it was finally time to go to college. Every day, she made the three-hour round-trip trek to Central Washington University in Ellensburg, managing to wrangle her four-year education degree in just three years of very hard work. She graduated cum laude as her children and husband watched proudly from the gym seats.

In 1972, Helen started teaching English at Granger Junior High School. That same year, the Reddouts moved to a white wooden house in the valley town of Outlook, just east of Granger, on an acre of shady, elevated land with views out over the valley.

Between 1981 and 1982, four kids were wed within an exhausting eighteen-month whirlwind of cakes and flowers. At the end of this joyous but chaotic time, Helen and Don found themselves rattling around alone in their big old house. By the late 1980s, the Reddouts completed their orchard holdings. They owned six different parcels covering sixty-five acres of Bing cherries, plus apples, pears, apricots, and nectarines.

It was during this time that Helen began to hear from neighbors about large, strange-looking dairies setting up shop around the Lower Yakima Valley. One by one—slowly at first, and then at an accelerated clip—the area's small, pasture-based dairies of seventy-five or eighty head began going out of business. Meanwhile, outsiders, reportedly from California, were snatching up the defunct properties for very little money. These new dairymen were also buying up large tracts of cropland around the old dairies.

But these new dairies were nothing like the old ones. Their barns housed hundreds of milking cows who lined up to rest on sand bedding, or wandered over to stick their heads between steel bars to munch on feed that was periodically dumped before them. They looked like a long row of fat black-and-white bicycles parked at an enormously long metal rack.

To Helen, the cattle looked demoralized, sick, broken. They were walking around in deep puddles of their own urine, crap, and filth. And my God, she thought, they smell awful. The stench was unlike anything Helen had experienced in her life.

Helen had been around cows when she was younger. "I know perfectly well what cows are supposed to smell like," she told Don one day. "The cows we had would manure all over the field. They'd wander around a pasture, and the waste would never build up. It was used up by the growing grass. It smelled like manure, not fermented sewage. The cows fertilized the grass that fed them—recycling nutrients over and over. It was a nearly perfect, sustainable system."

But in these new megadairies, five thousand cows were often jammed into a corral no larger than a few acres. "Those poor creatures are living right on top of one another, without so much as a blade of pasture to absorb anything," Helen lamented. "And the smell is like fermented sewage. It burns your eyes and coats your throat."

Most of the new dairymen were Dutch immigrants who relocated to Washington after California environmental regulations grew more stringent. In the 1980s, the dairy industry had suffered through a period of upheaval, rocked by spiking overproduction and plummeting milk prices. The Reagan administration was compelled to offer a massive federal "cow buyout" to avert catastrophe. Farmers were literally paid to kill off their livestock and thin the national herd, in order to stabilize milk prices.

At the time, the hot, smoggy Chino Basin east of Los Angeles was one of the nation's leading milk producers. There, amid the dusty back roads and sandy-colored sagebrush, several massive dairies—many run by Dutch immigrant families—were operating virtually unnoticed by the rest of the state. But California's voracious real estate sector was constantly demanding ever more rangeland and semidesert to devour for tract housing and in-ground pools. By the end of the 1980s, California's skyrocketing land prices and ever-stricter environmental laws lured many dairy farmers to search for "greener" pastures.

The Dutch dairymen had specific needs: affordable property, fair and dry weather, plenty of cropland to grow feed and absorb lagoon water, cheap unorganized labor, and a pro-growth economic climate. And they wanted a state where environmental intrusions could be kept to a minimum through the proper care and feeding of political figures who would be counted on to keep their regulatory hands off the dairy cattle.

Yakima Valley, Washington, clearly fit the bill.

On Sunday afternoons in the late 1980s, Helen and Don Reddout would often drive their pickup into Sunnyside to shop at Safeway and enjoy a late lunch out. Their route took them right past one of the valley's first industrial-style dairies, run by the DeRuyter family, recent arrivals from Chino. A mile before reaching the place, Helen would insist that Don shut the windows and turn off the air conditioner. But they'd still be assaulted by head-spinning mixtures of ammonia, methane, and hydrogen sulfide. Helen, often coming close to vomiting, would pull her coat over her face.

"How can they do this, Don?" her muffled voice inquired on one such occasion.

"It's not good," Don said. "Not good at all."

"Hell must smell like this, Don. It's putrid. These new dairymen are going to wreck our valley. Mark my words."

"Oh, Helen," Don replied—an oft-repeated comeback to her deep concern. "C'mon, what're you going to do? They're our neighbors now."

"Well then, why don't they *act* like it? We've got to do something about these folks."

Don flashed his signature white-toothed grin. "Oh, Helen," he said soothingly. "They aren't *putrid*; they're from California. They just don't know how we farm up here."

"Then somebody needs to teach them," she said.

Each time they drove into Sunnyside, Helen's ire grew stronger. "That's just not how it is supposed to *be*!" she would say. Don would gently roll his eyes and adjust the radio.

In the summer of 1989, another megadairy started to move in across the road from two friends of Helen's—John and Florence Howard. The dairyman, John Bosma, a Dutch immigrant and transplant from the Southern California dairy wars, began to dig his manure lagoon just fifty yards across the road from the Howards' kitchen door.

As Helen recalled, one Saturday when she was correcting English papers at home, John Howard knocked on her door, looking glum.[1] "It's bad, Helen," he said. "This guy Bosma dug up earth and moved it all over the place; he's building right in the middle of a natural wetland. The cattle have torn up all the hillside, and now there's nothing left over there but dirt and cow pies."

"So what now?" Helen asked.

"He's got his lagoon in place. We look right out our living room window at a cesspool. The stench is like something you can't even imagine. It's ungodly. It's going to kill us."

"I don't see how this can happen," Helen said. "There was no public notice, no announcement in the paper, right? You mean to tell me he can come in here and dig a hole and fill it with sewage right near your front door. And he doesn't even have to give anyone notice?"

"Apparently not," John said. "Oh, and now we discover that Bosma's lagoon is actually leaking. We can tell because there's crap water running through a culvert under the road—that culvert is always dry at this time of year."

Helen asked John what he had tried to do. "I'm nearly at wit's end but no one will do anything," he said. "I do have one more trick up my sleeve. Water samples from the culvert. Next week I'm driving up to the Departments of Health and Ecology, and getting this settled. I believe in the system, Helen. This is America."

A week or so later, John returned to Helen's door, practically in tears. "I tried everything, everyone," he fretted. "The Department of Health, Department of Ecology, the valley clean air officials, the county commissioners in Yakima."

"And?"

"And I am in shock, Helen. I had the culvert water tested and it was totally beyond the limits for *E. coli*, nutrients, and other contaminants. I took those results up to the state officials in Yakima and told them what was happening down here in the Lower Valley. I showed them the water reports."

"What did they say?" Helen felt blood rushing into her forehead. She knew the answer.

"They told me that Bosma could do whatever he wants. He could build his filthy, stinking open sewer right under our window and we can't do a damn thing about it."

"My God," Helen sighed. "What is going on around here? This is crazy. It will destroy our valley."

"Helen," John said, "do you think you could come over and have a look?"

On Helen's tour, she saw that John Bosma was digging two more lagoons to supplement the one already filled with waste. John Howard was right: All three were situated in natural wetlands. The stench was overwhelming.

John led Helen down to the culvert that went under the road. He pointed to a foot of fetid, fly-covered water collecting into a ditch. "That lagoon is leaking so badly that I can't even walk across this drainage ditch, and it hasn't rained in months. It's that lagoon of his. It doesn't even have a liner."

"Well," Helen said calmly, taking a deep breath, "what do you plan to do now?" John drew himself up to full height. "Maybe I should just go talk to Mr. Bosma. The government won't listen, but maybe he will. I'm sure he will understand once we explain how we do things here in Washington—how we farm up here without upsetting one's neighbors or the environment. 'This isn't California,' we'll tell him. 'We farm differently up here,'" John mumbled as he walked back to the truck.

The following Monday, a small klatch of neighbors came together to confront Bosma, in a respectful and neighborly way. Recruited to the effort were two rather prim farmwives, dressed in floral dresses and sensible shoes. Helen thought they looked like Sunday-school teachers.

That morning, when the valley air was redolent with ripening hops and fermenting poop, John Howard walked across the road to visit John Bosma. He was followed by Helen, the two proper farmwives, and a neighborhood man.

John Bosma, a tall, good-looking middle-aged man was waiting for them outside his milk barn, arms folded across his chest. His eyes intensely watched the troupe parading up toward his door, a "slick," almost too-friendly smile on his face, Helen thought.

"Good morning, Mr. Bosma!" John Howard said. "We thought we might have a word with you." Bosma stared at them in silence for an uncomfortable amount of time.

"A word about what? Why are so many people on my property?"

"Well, we are concerned about the lagoon," John began. "And the smell. And the flies."

"*And?*" Bosma said.

"And the wetlands. You're destroying wetlands. I'm not even sure if that's legal."

"What makes you think I care about wetlands?" Bosma said. "Who are you with? The friggin' Sierra Club?"

As John recounted the story that evening, Helen suppressed a laugh. Sierra Club! This was the most nonactivist bunch of farmers you could ever find. They were Republicans. But she kept silent as John told his story.

"No, sir," John Howard said. "We're your neighbors. We aren't environmentalists. I mean, sure, we care about the earth. But good farmers have always cared about the earth."

"So what? I'm a good farmer, too," Bosma growled, growing agitated. "Look, my shit doesn't stink. If you don't like what I'm doing, go move somewhere else. This meeting is over."

That night, as Helen told Don about the failed encounter, they both shuddered at Bosma's attitude. "He couldn't be much of a farmer if he does that to a wetlands area," Don said.

Helen agreed. "And allowing your animals to live in that filth—I don't think a real farmer would do that, either. I've got to do something. This makes me mad."

"You've been mad as hell for a while, Helen."

"No, I've been *concerned*. There's a difference. But now I am just in shock. You don't treat people like this. You don't just tell your neighbors, 'Move somewhere else.'"

"Helen," Don said, "you know I love you. But either *do* something about this—or shut up. Because I can't stand another day listening to you complain about these dairies."

Don was right. Helen went silent.

But not for long. A few days later, Helen got out her phone book and started dialing state agencies in the city of Yakima. The days turned to months and yet she kept calling, trying to get someone to listen and not make excuses. She finally found a friendly guy at the Washington State Department of Ecology. "Please," Helen begged him, "tell me where to go, tell me what to do. We're choking out here in the Lower Valley, and the dairymen won't even talk to us! The agencies here ignore us. Tell me what agency to go to, tell me who to contact. We will do whatever we need to do," she continued. "We'll travel to Olympia or Seattle. We'll do it at our own expense. Just help us!"

The official was silent for a while. "I hate to tell you this, Mrs. Reddout," he finally said, "but nobody's going to help you. Not in Seattle, not in Olympia."

Helen felt like she was in a bad Lifetime movie. "Well then, sir, what on God's green earth *can* we do?"

In hushed tones, the man suggested that Helen attract media to the story, like a newspaper. Or better yet, TV news shows like *60 Minutes* or *20/20*. Helen shut her eyes and shook her head. How was she—a little cherry farmer—going to get *60 Minutes* to come out to the Yakima Valley?

Maybe more people will help, she thought. Within days, Helen formed her own lobbying group, including the church ladies from the John Bosma visit. They scheduled meetings with bureaucrats up in Yakima, a tidy and prosperous little city near the Cascade foothills, forty minutes to the northwest.

Once downtown, the women would meet with any number of agents from health and environmental bureaus and divisions. They made sure to adopt sweet, almost girlie voices, uttering things like: "You know, sir, we think they are doing some *bad* things down there. Can you please come and see what's going on? Look, we even have *pictures*!" They then produced photos of the big dairies and politely explained how so much urine and manure was being created that it was spilling off property lines onto local roads, into drainage ditches, and eventually into streams that feed the Yakima River.

In other places, the women discovered dairymen deliberately pumping over-flow wastewater from their lagoons directly into irrigation and drainage ditches. Elsewhere, dairies that grew their own feed, or crop farmers who were contracted to spray lagoon water on their fields, were applying the stuff far in excess of the ground's ability to absorb it all. The women had photos of waste running into wetlands, streams, and canals.

"We can't accept that as evidence," one typically blank-faced official said.

"Why not?" Helen smiled. "It's not like we *faked* them."

"It wasn't taken by one of our agents."

"Well then, how can we *get* one of your agents out there to take pictures for themselves?"

Helen knew they were getting the runaround. What she didn't know, however, was that *years* would pass before a single state inspector would take action against factory dairies in the Lower Valley.

"You know something, Don?" she said that night as they were climbing into bed. "I used to think our government was here to serve us. And I walk into these plush buildings, all air-conditioned and carpeted, and I think, I'm paying for this? Why aren't they protecting me? Why aren't they doing their job?"

"Did you ask them, Helen?"

"Of course I did! You know what they told me? 'We're understaffed and overworked.' And I said, 'Well, what's it going to take for you to come down and look, then?'"

"And what did they say?"

"They said, 'We'll call you.'"

Helen Reddout had hit a bureaucratic wall, but she decided to go around it. In the early 1990s, she found a powerful new ally—the Internet. Surfing one night late in her small home office, Helen came across a rare 1982 study by county agents on dairies and the Yakima Valley. Even back then, officials were worried that cow manure was contaminating rivers and lakes, as well as groundwater sources like wells and springs.

"They knew!" she said to Don that night at dinner. "They had the scientific proof that this was happening. So why in God's name aren't they monitoring these new milk factories?" She decided to take the advice of that one state agent and contact the media. Helen called the agriculture reporter from the *Seattle Post-Intelligencer*, Rob Taylor.

Taylor listened patiently for several minutes to Helen's pitch. When she finally stopped, he responded. "Well, Mrs. Reddout, thank you very much for alerting me to this. It sounds like you have really done your homework."

Helen considered this the verbal equivalent of a patronizing pat on the head. He must think I'm imagining things, she joked to herself. Or menopausal. But Helen was in no mood for condescension. "Mr. Taylor, *please*. Come to Yakima. I will show you things you've never imagined." There was a long silence on the other end. Helen pushed ahead.

"If you were *truly* interested in factory farms, you'd have been here by now. You folks on the coast have no idea what's happening out here. You *should*." Helen knew she was getting nowhere. "This is a prizewinning story if you took the time. I'm not going to bother you again," she said. "But remember, if you have a slow news day, there is a story here. I'll make sure you get it."

Then, one day, the agencies began to realize that Helen was not going away. To appease her they assigned an inspector at the Department of Ecology named Ray Latham. Ray was a well-meaning man but, in Helen's view, not prone to getting results. He responded to their calls by coming to the area in person once in a while, but it took a few days for him to get there.

One morning Helen noticed a large amount of liquefied cow manure spilling from a dairy near the old Yakima Valley Highway. She called Latham to report it. "It's pretty bad," she said. "You should get out here. The spill is in on the northwest corner." But it took four days before he drove down to inspect the site. He called Helen. "Well, I was there today, on the southeast corner, and I didn't see anything," he said.

"Ray," Helen sighed, "it was the *northwest* corner, and it happened four days ago."

Even though Ray lacked directional ability, at least he tried. So when Helen received a call for help from her neighbor Linda Trevino, the best she could offer was Ray. The Trevinos lived directly across Independence Road from the S&S DeRuyter megadairy. Helen learned from Linda Trevino that she had called Ray to tell him Steve DeRuyter was spraying sewage water into his fields, but it was running off across the county road into her yard and on her house. Linda's patience had reached its limit. She was undergoing cancer treatment and she needed her rest. In desperation, she had called DeRuyter and asked him to stop spraying. He did stop for an hour, and then turned up the intensity even more. The Trevinos' quiet little bungalow should have been a perfect place to rest, but the dairy was turning it into a torture chamber, she said.

Robert Trevino had worked as an organizer for César Chávez in California during the seventies, but he was at a loss. "I don't know what to do with them. They don't listen, they don't care," he had said to Helen during one of her visits. "Linda needs her rest. I hope this Ray guy will be able to do something."

When Ray arrived, Steve DeRuyter was out on his land spraying lagoon water onto fields that stretched right up to the road. A stiff breeze was blowing the stinky, mocha-colored mist onto the Trevinos' property.

"Linda just got out of the hospital, Ray," Robert said, pointing at the house. "She is being treated for cancer. And she has to come home to *this*. Linda couldn't even sleep because of the stench." Robert showed Ray how overflow from DeRuyter's lagoon had run through a culvert under the road and spilled onto the other side, smothering huge swaths of the Trevinos' property. Much of it had gathered in their vineyards, leaving a fermenting, stinking, fly-covered mess.

Linda Trevino, pale from chemotherapy, came out to speak with Ray. "Mr. Latham, please, you have *got* to help us," she pleaded. "Look at our place. It's in ruins. There's crud all over the property, dried manure in big chunks on our lawn and our vineyards. We can't even go out in the yard!"

Latham looked truly concerned and scribbled a few notes in a little book. "Now he gets it," Linda whispered to her husband. Ray drove over to the De-Ruyter barn area. He was there a good twenty minutes before he finally came walking back across the road. "I think we've got the problem solved," he said.

"Well, thank God for that," Linda sighed. "So? What's the plan?"

"Mr. DeRuyter is going to run a flag up his flagpole, a red flag, I suggested, whenever he's getting ready to spray. That'll give you time to get in the car and leave your property, Mrs. Trevino."

"That's right, Linda!" Robert said sarcastically. "Gather your cancer meds and your pain pills and put on some clothes, tell the kids to get in the car and evacuate your home. Just go someplace else so Mr. DeRuyter can do his thing. Then come back in a few days. *That's* reasonable. Isn't it?"

Ray shuffled his feet and looked at the ground.

"Is *this* the kind of brilliance we can expect from the department, Ray?" Robert demanded.

"It's the best I can do. Mr. DeRuyter has a right to make a living, and that includes fertilizing his fields."

A few days later, Helen got a phone call from Linda Trevino. The couple was trying to sell off some of their vineyards, lot by lot. But no one wanted them. Who could blame them? When prospective buyers pulled up to their property, it smelled. Adding to the injury, Steve DeRuyter had put up a sign on his property across the street. Potential buyers were now greeted with this four-by-eight-foot plywood announcement: "ATTENTION: THIS FIELD IS LOCATED IN AN AGRICULTURAL AREA. IT IS SUBJECT TO NOISE, DUST AND ODOR. THIS FIELD IS A DAIRY SPRAY FIELD AND POSSIBLE LAGOON SITE. PUNGENT ODORS ARE TO BE EXPECTED."

By the early 1990s, dairy was king in the Lower Yakima Valley. Fueling the boom was an ultra high-tech, $22 million powdered-milk plant built in Sunnyside by Darigold, Inc., a hugely successful Seattle-based corporation. Darigold was wholly owned by members of the Northwest Dairy Association, a co-op of hundreds of producers in Washington, Oregon, Idaho, and northern California. The corporation produced millions of pounds of milk, powdered milk, butter, cheese, yogurt, cream, and ice cream, with wordwide sales approaching the $1 billion mark. Darigold was counting on a steady supply coming in from Yakima County dairies to keep its new Sunnyside plant purring at full capacity.[2]

The valley was alluring to megadairy families—especially Dutch ones—for several reasons. Aside from a dry climate, the main attractions were, essentially, God, grains, and Mexicans. Sunnyside Christian schools were a big draw for Christian Reformed and Netherlands Reformed families. Meanwhile, grain and other feedstuffs were cheap, plentiful, and close by, with crops surrounding most towns in the valley.

Perhaps most important, thousands of low-wage workers, mostly from Mexico and Central America, had joined the large Latino community already living in the valley. They were an ideal workforce. More than 90 percent of county dairy workers were Latino, though they comprised just 35 percent of the population. As one newspaper wrote, "Hispanic milkers are thought of as hardworking and loyal, and their labor is relatively cheap."[3]

One evening in 1995, Helen and Don Reddout were watching TV after dinner when the local anchorman promised a story about a Sunnyside family whose life was turned upside down by a megadairy next door. The news that night really got under Helen's skin.

The Bos family lived next door to a rapidly growing CAFO called Sunnyveld Dairy, owned by Herman and Sharon teVelde, members of a Dutch dairy family from California's Central Valley. In 1951, when Fred and Mary Lynne Bos moved into their tidy white-brick ranch-style house, the news report said, there was a small beef feedlot next door, with maybe fifty head of cattle. But when the teVeldes moved in, Herman teVelde had asked his new neighbors if they objected to him putting a "small dairy" on his property. The Boses were farmers, too; they grew squash and asparagus. They had no problem with it.

But the small next-door dairy soon expanded from small to big to enormous. Dust, odor, and flies began blowing into the Boses' home, garden, and even their new pool, the pride and joy of the family. Before long, swimming became unthinkable. By 1995 Mary Lynne and Fred decided to fill in the pool.

"We're destroying our swimming pool," Mary Lynne, a woman of short stature but kind face and gentle demeanor, told the news reporter. Behind her, a granddaughter sat on the back steps, head buried in her lap. "It's all due to the stench from this dairy, and the manure dust that's coming in. We can't keep the pool clean. It's unhealthy for our kids and grandkids. And the Department of Ecology won't do anything about it. It makes us very sad, but we're going to have to close it up." The bulldozer pushed the first scoop of dirt into the pool.

"*What?*" Helen said, shaking her head. "If I had a swimming pool like that, I would fight like *crazy*! This just rips my heart out. Why is she giving up?"

"Helen," Don said. "We don't even know these people. Calm *down*."

"She should fight back! Somebody needs to show some backbone."

Animal-factory emissions are unpredictable things; the olfactory insults they inflict can change in minutes. Distance helps, of course. But wind, temperature, humidity, time of day, and geography can confound factors. One moment the air lifts you up with country honeysuckle; the next, it slams you down with a mist of piss, shit, and ammonia. *Not* knowing when an onslaught might come is what drives many rural residents to despair.

Helen and Don had never suffered the assault of that stench in their own home. That is, until that terrible August night in 1996, when Helen had awoken to a bed smelling of septic tank and ran around like a madwoman, slamming shut windows.

"This war is officially engaged," she announced to Don that next morning. "We've been here forty years, long before these dairymen even *thought* about our valley. My new job is to stop them."

As a "job," fighting megadairies and the Washington milk establishment was surely a thankless one: long hours, no pay, little recognition. Fringe benefits included head-banging against a wall of bureaucratic indifference. But one rainy November day, while teaching a class of fidgety preteens, Helen was told she had a call at the office. It was important, the messenger said.

On the line was Rob Taylor, the agriculture reporter from the *Seattle Post-Intelligencer* who had seemed to brush her off a year or so before. Helen's heart raced. "I'm going to be in the area on Thursday," Rob said. "Okay if I stop by?"

"Why, sure it's okay!" Helen cried. "When? Where? I'll be there!"

That Thursday, Helen drove out to meet Rob Taylor at the Granger exit on Interstate 82, joined by Gary Ostby, a friend and science teacher at Granger Junior High School, and Curt Porter, the shop teacher from school. First, they took the reporter to see and smell the dairy belonging to John Bosma, across from John and Florence Howard, and another two, Bosma Dairy and Liberty Dairy, owned by Bosma's brother, Henry.

The Cow Palace was next, then on to the Sunnyveld Dairy, next to the Boses' now filled-in swimming pool. Along the route, Helen pointed to rivulets of liquid manure running beside the roads, running into ditches, or pouring through culverts into marshes and streams. Each time they passed a sprawling, muddy CAFO, Helen lowered her window to let a rush of foul air fill the car.

"Oh man!" Rob shouted, holding his nose. "That's terrible! Roll up the window!"

Helen would roll up the window and suppress a devilish smile.

She knew that, whatever Rob wrote, it would not be favorable to the dairymen.

On November 20, 1996, Helen woke up early. Rob Taylor's story was due out today. She drove to Safeway in Sunnyside and grabbed copies of the *Post-Intelligencer*. The story was teased across the front page under the headline AS DAIRY FARMS GROW LARGER, SO DO SOME COMPLAINTS ABOUT THEM.[4] Beneath that it said, "Washington's dairy farms are polluting streams and groundwater 20 years after federal laws were passed to control livestock runoff." According to the paper, existing rules were nothing but industry loopholes, the "laughingstock" of dairymen. The paper promised to examine "the economics and politics that have left some farms, streams and rivers literally awash in manure."

When Helen got home, she and Don sat down to read the coverage. There were five articles, four by Rob, including the lead story. Helen almost screamed with joy over the first sentence: "Yakima Valley dairies are becoming milk factories." She felt vindicated.

Helen wondered what the dairymen thought as they read their papers that morning. Indigestion, she imagined; maybe a little nausea. "Dozens of industrial-strength dairies are visible along the roads between here and Yakima," Taylor wrote. "Driving by, a visitor sees thousands of cattle standing in a series of muddy lots stretching for a quarter-mile or more in a single dairy. Trucks rumble in with feed, others haul out mountains of manure and oceans of milk."

The industry's consolidation had increased tensions in the valley, and led to growing demands for tighter regulation in Yakima County, where the dairy herd doubled from twenty-eight thousand to fifty-six thousand in just six years. The big operators were causing most of the problems and complaints, according to then state senator Marilyn Rasmussen, a Democrat and former dairy owner. Smaller farms rarely pollute, she said, but they were being driven out by big dairies that "milk too many cows on too little acres with no manure management plan."

Most complaints were about odor. But the Department of Ecology and farm agencies had little sympathy about it. Usually, the protests centered around lagoons that the agencies themselves had recommended to keep Yakima Valley's waterways clean. The Yakima Conservation District's director, Walter George, scorned anyone who complained about odors. "They want to live in the country, but they don't want dust, noise or smell," he told the paper. "They'd shut down farming."

The next article, "Dairies Spread Danger," centered on water pollution. "From contaminated drinking water to closed shellfish beds and increasingly frequent outbreaks of E. coli infections, dairy farms are blamed for much of the state's water pollution," the article began. "Yet they remain virtually unregulated."[5]

The phrase "virtually unregulated" was an understatement. One official said the threat of inspections was something that dairymen "laugh about over coffee." They weren't worried about compliance because there simply was no enforcement. And the few dairies that were actually confronted were routinely given years to clean things up. Meanwhile, manure and wastewater from the state's 263,000 dairy cows left behind two billion gallons of slurry a year— enough to fill thirty Exxon Valdez tankers.

A third article, by Tom Paulson, looked at what was contained in that "slurry," and where it all ended up.[6] "Cow manure in pasture run-off may contribute to the spread of the dangerous strain of E. coli bacteria, like that in a recent outbreak linked to Odwalla fruit juice," he wrote. Irrigation water contaminated with the bacteria was a possible cause of a recent outbreak that killed a two-year-old girl and sickened at least sixty other people in Washington, California, Colorado, and Canada.

Manure in irrigation water might also explain why the most deadly form of E. coli, O157:H7, was increasingly found on fruits and vegetables. Contamination of lettuce from Montana, for instance, had been traced to cattle effluent. As Dr. Robert Mead, chief veterinarian at the state Department of Agriculture, put it, "If you're irrigating with water from dairy barns, there's a potential for it to get on anything."

Helen felt certain that this extraordinary news series would mark a turnaround in the sad saga of Yakima Valley. But days went by, and then weeks. Christmas gave way to New Year's, and absolutely nothing happened. The public response, if any, was undetectable. "Why is no one speaking out?" she asked her husband. "There should be an outcry against what's happening. But there's *nothing*."

The *Seattle Post-Intelligencer* series had sparked a reaction, but not where Helen had expected. Powerful people from Olympia to Washington, D.C., were paying close attention to the dairy situation in the state. On January 31, 1997, the agricultural trade paper *Capital Press* warned that Washington's dairy industry was falling "under scope" and on the radar screen at Bill Clinton's Environmental Protection Agency (EPA), which was lining up suspected polluters in its sights.[7] The article said that dairies should brace themselves for "teams of inspectors, armed with the power to levy heavy fines, poised to begin unannounced visits." Failure to comply with the EPA orders could bring fines up to twenty-five thousand dollars a day. The wagons were circling.

It was highly unwelcome news for Yakima Valley dairymen, who complained that an EPA crackdown would bring new rules and higher operating costs that would drive dairies out of business. On the other hand, EPA oversight wasn't entirely undesirable. Debbie Becker, then executive director of the powerful Washington State Dairy Federation, said current inspections were not taken seriously by state officials, who had refused an EPA offer of help in 1995. Some operators actually welcomed EPA involvement, she said, prompting one newspaper editorial to quip: "When a farmer speaks highly of an EPA inspection, you wonder about problems with state government."[8]

The EPA had reason to intervene. Its inspectors had found "brown streams of manure running directly into ditches and creeks," according to one EPA manager. "Everywhere we go out into the field and look at dairy operations, there's a direct relationship with water-quality problems."

State officials had little defense. "Our dairy waste-management program is broken and is in need of repair," confessed one Department of Ecology official. He blamed weak laws and a skeleton staff of just four part-time inspectors to cover the state's 935 dairies. Meanwhile, the EPA said farming operations of all types had contaminated some fifteen hundred miles of state rivers, more than twice the amount polluted by manufacturing and city sewage plants *combined*.[9]

In the summer of 1997, Helen ended her twenty-five years of teaching. Given her work against the dairies, she was not only retired, she was also just plain tired. "You know," she said to Don one night, "I feel so desperate. There were days when I'd get up, and feel so determined to defeat these factories. I thought this would be over by now. I was so wrong. I'm tired, so tired." She stared out the window at her tidy vegetable garden. A few moments passed.

"Helen, it's taking a toll," Don said at last. "I've seen it. When I leave the house in the morning, you're at the computer. When I get home—you're still in your nightgown, roving the Internet, looking for research. Sometimes I think, 'My God, are you possessed or something?' "

The words shook Helen. Don was right. The next morning, she gathered every last file of papers, letters, photos, and articles on animal factories. She carried them into the yard, dumped them in a metal bin, and set them ablaze. "There," she said. "If nobody else cares, why should I? I'm done."

But fate was not done with Helen Reddout.

One blazing August afternoon in 1997, Helen and Don were on their Safeway sojourn when she asked him to take the old Yakima Valley Highway, for a change of pace. They passed a squat but stately white farmhouse that Helen had long admired. She had an inexplicable fascination for old staircases, and this early-twentieth-century gem looked like a good prospect.

As luck would have it, a yard sale was in progress and people were picking over the standard clothes, toys, and pottery of another family's life. "Can we stop, please?" Helen asked. "I want to go inside and see the staircase!"

Behind the house, Don noticed an old shed filled with yard and garden equipment for sale. An attractive Latina woman in her midthirties introduced herself as the owner, Marcella Garza. Don said he was itching to see the tools in the shed. As Marcella walked him over, Helen went inside the house to see what was for sale and take a peek at its staircase. Marcella gestured for Don to look at the green pasture beyond her property line. "They're going to build a calf operation, right there," she said. "Just 150 feet from our well. It scares the hell out of us."

Don stared at the future CAFO site, which would be dedicated to impregnating dairy heifers and birthing their calves. The female calves would be sent to dairy farms for lives of production. But male calves are not needed on a dairy. All they do is consume food. These infant bulls would be destined for the veal market. They would live for a few months in veal hutches that would prevent them from moving around and developing muscle tissue. Then they would be slaughtered.

"I wish there was someone who knew how to fight these things," Marcella said. Don hesitated. He knew Helen was burned out, and had just incinerated all her research. Incredibly, he still found himself telling Marcella, "You might want to talk to my wife about this."

Marcella was thrilled. She grabbed Helen as she emerged from the house. "Your husband said I should find you!" she said. "I hear you fought the CAFOs around here. Can you tell me what you did?"

Helen felt a wave of dread wash over. "Well, I wrote some letters, took some pictures," she said noncommittally. "But it never really went anywhere. I kind of lost my drive."

"But can't you help me?"

Helen wanted out, but found herself saying, "I'll help." She invited Marcella to come over later that evening.

After dinner, there was a knock at the door. It was Marcella.

"Helen," she said, "I cannot wait to get started fighting."

"Come in," Helen said, unsure where all of this was going to lead.

Marcella Garza proved to be a natural-born activist. She peppered Helen with questions about dairies, manure, disposal plans, soil absorption, and well contamination. Marcella and her husband, Ed, had already met with some of the neighbors to figure out what to do about the new dairies.

At Helen's first meeting at the Garza home, she met sixteen other valley residents who were wound up and ready to fight. Helen shared what she had learned with her neighbors, but went no further. She couldn't help but feel a certain excitement from the energy and drive of these folks. As the meeting progressed, a woman who had arrived late stood up to share an idea. It's the woman who filled in her pool on TV, Helen thought. What's she doing here?

Mary Lynne Bos clutched a petition she and her daughter Debb had circulated earlier. The letter was passed around. Helen read, "We the residents of the once beautiful Yakima Valley would like to have some updated regulations, and closer scrutiny of the dairies in our county." In a week, more than one hundred other concerned citizens had signed the petition.

Marcella thought the petition was a good idea. The group's first objective would be to canvas the valley to solicit signatures on a similar entreaty. Since two-fifths of county residents were Latino, Marcella translated the words into Spanish.

Helen very reluctantly agreed to join the group, but only in an advisory capacity. There was no way, she told Don, that anyone was dragging her back into that crap, "and I mean that literally." Still, no harm could come from sharing information and listening. Over the next several weeks, Helen attended more meetings, but just enough, she assured herself, to provide information so the group could move forward without her.

But then Helen got a call that would change everything.

"Hello, Mrs. Reddout?" It was a male voice, middle aged and nonthreatening. "My name is Bill Bean. I'm an organizer for the Columbia Basin Institute and I want to talk to you about your work on dairy issues in the Yakima Valley."

A million alarm bells went off. Who was this guy? Someone's ratted to the dairymen, Helen thought. Columbia Basin Institute, sure! And that name? Bill *Bean*? It all sounded so improbable. Helen had reason for caution. One of the "concerned citizens" had recently broken ranks with the group, and was suspected of feeding everything they knew to the dairymen. Maybe this was one of them, Helen thought.

Bean explained that the Columbia Basin Institute (CBI) organized poor and Latino groups in the river basin for political and legal campaigns on environmental justice. "Right now, we are ready to take on the dairy pollution in your area. It's threatening the Yakima River, which feeds into the Columbia," he said.

"How did you get my number?"

"Rob Taylor at the *Seattle P-I*. We met at a party a while ago. He told me about his reporting in Yakima, about the livestock pollution, about you."

"About *me*?"

"I was commenting on how strange it was that all these dairies are coming into the valley, yet there's no protest, no one who's screaming bloody murder. And Rob said, 'Oh yes there is. Believe me.' And he gave me your number."

Bill wanted to help people in the valley obtain top-flight, and maybe pro bono, legal counsel. In exchange, CBI would ask for a portion of the money raised from charitable foundations for the legal campaign. "It's the only way we can finance our operations, and yours," he explained.

Helen wasn't biting. Mostly, she wanted out of the activism business. Several members of Marcella's new group had been subject to veiled threats, under-the-breath nasty comments, and drive-by obscenities while going about their business. No one felt physically in danger—not yet, anyway—but it sure was creepy, and it wasn't much fun.

If you think I'm going to spill my guts about what Marcella's people are doing, you're crazier than a bedbug, Helen said to herself. And what the hell is this "Columbia Basin Institute"? I could call myself Alexander's Ragtime Band, but it doesn't mean I can *play*.

Helen kept up her guard. "I'll tell you what, Mr. Bean," she said. "Send me your pamphlets and such. And after I've read everything, perhaps I'll get back to you." She hung up, still believing Bean was a corporate dairy spy. Ha! she laughed to herself. I've got you now, Mr. Dairyman. So let's see your, um, *brochures*.

But a few days later, a fat packet of materials arrived from a B. Bean of the Columbia Basin Institute, in Portland. When a friend from Portland confirmed Bean's reputation, Helen called him. "Okay. You got a deal," she said. "But you've got a bunch of green, nonactivist people who just want to *do* something. We're flying by the seat of our pants."

A week later, Helen was back at her post, driving Bill Bean around on a "farm stench" tour. Bill came from an organizing background, having passed through the Saul Alinsky (creator of the phrase "Think globally, act locally") school in Chicago, with union roots from Boston. He took pictures and notes. The pair really hit it off.

Bill told her about a flyover that his colleague Mike Tedin had done a few months earlier, along with Charlie Tebbutt, staff attorney for the Western Environmental Law Center (WELC), a public-interest firm out of Eugene, Oregon. WELC was a well-known foe of industrial agriculture from California to Idaho.

During Bill's next call to Helen, he said he was reasonably sure that the WELC would take the case pro bono. Helen explained the situation to the group. "This is an answer to our prayers," someone said. They agreed to invite Bill to come make his case. At the Garzas', Bill repeated what he had told Helen: The lawyers would get their fees paid by the defendants, assuming they won the case. If not, the firm would eat the costs.

The group agreed to meet with the lawyer from Eugene, Charlie Tebbutt. Bill handed Marcella a list of things that needed to be done before the next meeting. "Tonight you need to think of a name for the group. Something that says what you stand for," Bill said as he walked to the back door. Helen agreed. "We should come up with a name that means something. Like at the school, we have the D.A.R.E. program—Drug Abuse Resistance Education. Maybe something along those lines."

"Why don't we also call ourselves D.A.R.E.?" someone shouted from the kitchen. "It will stand for 'Dutchmen Are Really Evil.'" Nervous chuckling spread around the room, but Helen put the kibosh on it. "We're here to be *neighborly*. Other suggestions?" Her schoolmarm side was kicking in.

Eventually, they settled on CARE, for Community Association for Restoration of the Environment. Their mission statement was simple and straightforward: "CARE is a nonprofit, volunteer organization that works to protect and improve the environment in the Pacific Northwest. The organization supports family farms that operate in a sustainable manner, promoting public health, economic vitality, stewardship of the land, and protection of air and water resources. CARE opposes any agricultural operation that pollutes and degrades rural communities."

Marcella would be the group's president. Her vice president was Helen Reddout, who was now officially back in the game.

3

Elmwood, Illinois, is a tiny speck of a place just west of Peoria, built along the razor-straight line that separates Knox County from Peoria County. It lies about three hours southwest of Chicago, near Kickapoo Creek and the fabled Spoon River, made famous by Edgar Lee Masters's *Spoon River Anthology*.

A pleasant, manicured, all-American farming town, Elmwood—all 1.5 square miles of it—is home to just two thousand residents, 98 percent of them white. Elmwood is surrounded by unyielding stretches of corn and soybeans that, in growing season, climb up and over the undulating green hillocks like something on the outskirts of Oz. White farmhouses, old red barns, and gleaming silver grain silos dot the *American Gothic*–like landscape.

Elmwood is in the epicenter of the Great American Corn Belt. Loamy soil and good drainage combine with warm, humid summers and usually enough rainfall to raise cornstalks higher than an elephant's eye. In the age of ethanol, corn is king. The stuff is ubiquitous; it sprawls out in every direction toward the unbroken horizon. Around Elmwood, corn rises from behind gas stations and borders parking lots. It is sowed between suburban-style ranch houses, around golf courses and even in place of front lawns. Out in the fields, the vast blanket of green stalks is rotated with acres of low-growing soybeans, planted to restore nitrogen sucked from the soil by all that maize.

The corn crops are lush, but none of the produce will be consumed fresh by humans. Much will wind up as feed for billions of chickens, turkeys, pigs, and cows within a half-day's drive from here. Even grain destined for ethanol refineries, postprocessing, finds its way into the bellies of livestock. Some corn not consumed by Midwestern animals will be delivered in trainloads to swine in faraway places like North Carolina.

These lonely cornfields of western Illinois are perhaps the last place on earth where Karen Hudson imagined she would end up. But it's been her home for thirty years now.

Karen Santoro was born in Chicago and recalls growing up in the leafy suburbs west of the city, saying good-bye to her father every morning as he left for his job as a commercial graphic artist downtown, working for clients like Marshall Field's and Walgreens. As a child, Karen didn't particularly like the country. At six, she developed an inexplicable fear of tractors. Her fantasy was to flee the Midwest altogether for the high peaks of Colorado, where a life of skiing and hiking awaited.

But then she met Howard Rockwell "Rocky" Hudson. Karen was on a date at the time—with another guy. But the rugged farm boy caught her eye. The two were both wild about swimming, diving, and classic rock bands of the sixties and seventies. Their first date was at a Beach Boys concert—Rocky was a box office manager and he bribed her with center-front tickets. Soon, he won her heart.

Rocky came from solid German immigrant stock and his family had farmed in Peoria County for three generations. Karen, who thought eggs came from the grocery store, had never heard of Elmwood.

During the Christmas break of 1976, when they were juniors in college, Rocky brought Karen out to stay in Elmwood and meet his family, who managed the working farm. City-girl Karen had outgrown her tractor phobia, but was even more unsettled about meeting her potential in-laws. When Rocky and his mom led Karen upstairs to her guest room, Karen asked how to lower the bedroom shades.

"There are no shades," Rocky said.

"But what about the neighbors? They'll see me getting dressed."

"There are no neighbors," Rocky said.

Karen was dumbstruck. Everyone had neighbors. But the next morning, as the low winter sun rose over the heartland, Karen saw nothing but brown stubbly fields stretching to the distance. Not another house in sight.

On her second visit, Karen arrived in time for "chicken day." The Hudson family kept a sizeable coop in their backyard. Until this point, Karen had only ever gotten her chicken from the grocery store, cleaned and antiseptic in its Styrofoam tray and shrink-wrap.

First thing after daybreak, live chickens were trucked off to meet their demise and, by late morning, dozens of dead and cleaned birds were returned to the farm from the plucking house. Next came four hours of cutting, wrapping, and freezing, requiring the efforts of the entire Hudson clan. The Hudsons' chickens had been returned in tubs of ice. Karen found herself separating icy chicken pieces at the joint with cleavers and scissors. But she got through the day, proudly filling dozens of two-gallon ziplock bags with bird parts.

For "dinner" (served at midday, much to Karen's bewilderment) the Hudsons sat down to mashed potatoes and gravy with heaping platters of country fried chicken, fresh from the backyard. Karen realized it was the first time she had eaten a hen that was alive only a few hours earlier. Her taste buds had grown so used to mass-produced birds that this chewier, gamier meat tasted downright odd, but truly better.

After graduation, Karen followed Rocky back to Elmwood, where he had returned to farm. The two were married in August 1978 at the Elmwood Presbyterian Church, and Karen became a substitute teacher in the Elmwood public schools. All the kids in town already knew her, so showing up as a sub was no big deal. Karen stayed there for nine happy years, working part-time while Rocky tended to the corn and soybeans. Rocky practiced "no-till" farming, where the detritus of the old crop is left behind to cover the surface over the winter, preventing erosion while amending the soil with a rich humus.

In 1980, Rocky phased out his cattle, followed by the chickens in 1983. The pigs had been phased out in the early 1970s by Rocky's father, Lester.

The 1980s were comfortable times for Karen and Rocky; a steady farm income allowed them to start a family. Daughter Alisha was followed by a son, Sam. In 1985, Karen took a job at the Central Illinois Light Company as a troubleshooter who helped unhappy customers. When a meter reading was indeed wrong, Karen went to bat for her customers. Helping them gave her a feeling of accomplishment, a sense of justice done. Later, she became a drafting and engineering troubleshooter.

Life felt good. But disturbing rumors were beginning to circulate around town; something to do with hog farms and confinement barns. No one really knew what it all meant, but some people had bad feelings in their stomachs about it. Karen was one of them.

In late August 1996, Karen Hudson returned from a weekend at a farm conference in Chicago. Rocky passed her a copy of the *Peoria Journal Star*. "Welcome home. Take a look," he said.

Karen read the headline. A livestock facility, raising either dairy or swine, had been proposed outside of Elmwood. "So? Why that look on your face?" Karen looked at Rocky, puzzled. "It's just a pig farm."

"They want to put seven thousand hogs just south of town here," Rocky said.

Rocky must have misread, Karen thought. Or maybe it was a typo. Maybe there were seven hundred animals planned. But seven thousand? How could that be? "Are you sure?" she asked.

"Says so right here," Rocky said. "It's Dave Inskeep who wants to do it."

Karen knew the name well. Dave was an elder in the local Catholic church, a Caterpillar executive and hobby farmer. This being a tiny town, there were connections: Inskeep's wife was the principal at the school where Karen had substituted. Rocky's brother and sister-in-law were two of Dave Inskeep's best friends. Karen and Rocky had even adopted a puppy from the Inskeeps, which they named Butler for his shiny black coat.

Karen couldn't imagine that many pigs crowded together on one farm. It didn't make sense. When Rocky raised pigs, they lived out on pasture, with little A-frame houses for farrowing the sows. The pigs would spend their days outside, grubbing for food or eating table scraps. Many farmers kept a hundred head or so. But seven *thousand*?

Karen read the article more closely. Inskeep wanted to develop eight hundred acres of land out on Route 78, about two miles south of Elmwood. Previously a strip mine, the tract was still owned by a coal and energy company. Karen looked up from the paper at Rocky. "Are they *nuts*?" she said. "Can you imagine what this is going to smell like?"

"We're screwed," Rocky said with a frown.

Karen read aloud. "'The Illinois Pollution Control Board will approve rules involving potential environmental pollutants, but the rules have yet to be developed and final adoption may be a year away.'[1] Oh, swell, by the time they're adopted, Rocky, we'll be swimming in crap. My gut tells me we're going to have one giant, open sewer move right into town. But not if I can stop it!"

From the first day that Karen read about the proposed seven-thousand-head pig farm in the *Peoria Journal Star*, she found it hard to sleep. Inskeep was now telling the media he had settled on a farrowing operation, where he would breed piglets. He had signed a ten-year contract with a company out of North Carolina called Murphy Family Farms. This would be the first Murphy venture into Illinois. Inskeep told the media that he would grow his own feed, and hire about fifteen people to work at the facility where he would, under contract, breed seventy-two thousand piglets annually from a herd of thirty-six hundred sows. The animals would belong to Murphy, and Inskeep would be paid a per-pig "fee" for managing the operation. He would also need to finance and build five barns and a waste lagoon on the eight-hundred-acre property. The lagoon, designed by a Missouri engineering firm and sealed at the bottom with a one-foot-thick clay liner, would be built to "minimize odors," Inskeep said.

Karen knew nothing about mega–hog farms, North Carolina, or waste lagoons. But she sensed enough to grow alarmed. "What the hell is a waste lagoon?" Karen asked Rocky. "I am pretty damn sure that isn't any tropical paradise."

Meanwhile, at the farm, piglets would be weaned at three weeks and shipped off to a nursery farm, to be located "somewhere" in western Illinois. From there, after seven weeks, they would be transferred to so-called finishing farms in Iowa.

Karen did not understand what Elmwood would get from the deal, apart from stinky air. "This town is doing well, so it's not like we desperately need those fifteen jobs," she said. "Besides, his lagoon is being built by a company in Missouri. And Dave is going to grow his own feed, not buy it from others. So who exactly will benefit in the local economy?"

Karen was not alone in her doubts over the "hog factory." There was a rising chorus of trepidation coming from other people in Elmwood, including its representative on the Peoria County Board, Eldon Polhemus. Polhemus vowed to enforce every law on the books to protect local residents from drifting odors. "Being an old farm boy," he said, "means knowing that two miles away won't stop the smell."

Elmwood mayor Joe Almasi also opposed the project. "With this stuff, you never know what can happen," he said. Almasi and other town leaders had visited a Murphy Family Farms site in Missouri, where neighbors spoke out against the animal factory, citing a big drop in land values and a terrible stench in the air, especially when the lagoon water was sprayed on fields.

Opposition to Inskeep's pig farm was beginning to gel, Karen realized. More people were speaking out. Even the library got involved, saying the hogs would threaten a nearby nature trail and possibly pollute an artesian well located on library property.

"The smell is going to permeate clear down through Peoria," one local official predicted. He also pointed out that the site was just one mile from Kickapoo Creek. "What happens if there is an accident?" he said. "What will happen to the fish in that creek?"

No one could know just how prophetic that question was.

In many small Illinois towns, one unofficial social center is the grain elevator, where tons of corn, wheat, and other grains are stored before being sent off to market. The Elmwood elevator was no exception. Rocky, like many farmers around town, loved hanging out there, sipping coffee, shooting the breeze,

checking commodity prices, and catching up on local births, deaths, wed-
dings, and divorces.

One humid morning in early September, Rocky heard talk of a community
meeting on the proposed livestock facility. He rushed home to tell Karen. "We
gotta do something, Rock," Karen said when she heard. "This situation is bad
for everyone, but it's worse for us farmers, you know? We can't just pick up
and leave. We can't just flee from all this."

Karen continued. "I've been reading up on this Murphy Family Farms in
one of your trade magazines. There's nothing 'family' about them. They are
big, disgusting pig factories. Murphy claims to have a zero-tolerance policy for
environmental problems, but that doesn't seem to match their actual record."
Karen paused to sip some wine. "If Dave Inskeep's pig farm is half as bad as
some of these Murphy sites, then we are in deep shit."

"But why here, I wonder?" Rocky said. "Why this area? Why Elmwood?
Why us? There's got to be a reason why they are coming to Illinois." It wouldn't
take long for Rocky and Karen to learn the answers.

The evening of September 6, 1996, was an uncomfortably warm one in
Elmwood. The darkening sky tumbled into a hazy orange horizon. Karen
and Rocky Hudson arrived at Elmwood High School a bit early, but watched
as the two-hundred-seat auditorium quickly filled up. People greeted one another with grim but neighborly "we're in this together" looks. Townspeople
whom Karen had not seen in months turned out. One was Bill Knight, a professor at Western Illinois University in Moline, and co-organizer of the meeting.
Bill, in his forties, with thinning brown hair and a trim mustache, was casually
dressed, yet spoke in a clipped, get-to-the-point manner. Karen found his demeanor refreshing.

Mayor Almasi stood up to report on his fact-finding mission in Missouri.
Karen had always liked the middle-aged Greek-American, with his smiling,
chiseled face, longish gray hair, and cuddly disposition. But Almasi was serious
tonight. Missourians who lived near the Murphy site were not happy people.
"They have to deal with foul odors all the time. And that smell that they deal
with? That smell will come here to Elmwood soon."[2]

Murmurs of indignant agreement echoed through the auditorium. The mood
was hardly lifted by State Representative Mike Smith, a Democrat from nearby
Canton. "I am sorry to have to say this, but there is absolutely nothing that
you—or I—can do to stop this facility from entering your community," he said.

The room erupted in protest and disbelief. Karen had never seen anything
like it: Traditionally mild-mannered farm people were ready to explode.

"This is outrageous; unbelievable!" one man stood up and shouted. "How can that be?" a woman cried. "Don't we have *rights*?" Smith merely shook his head. "Maybe one day we can seek a moratorium. But right now there's nothing we can do. The county simply has no control over where these things are put. This is agriculture—and this is Illinois."

Smith had voted for a big livestock law the previous May, he noted, designed to regulate large facilities and reduce pollution. It was a first step. Clearly, it didn't go far enough.

"That's because this bill is garbage!" said a large, husky man who rose to speak. He was Bill Emmitt, an ex-cop who raised buffalo in nearby Greene County. Emmitt said the committee that drafted the bill was headed by Becky Doyle, the state agriculture chief. Doyle was sister to one of the biggest hog growers in Illinois—and was married to a hog farmer herself. The new law exempted any facilities with fewer than seven thousand animal units, but very few farms had that many, he said. "That law was designed to bring megapork to Illinois, and it will put smaller farmers out of business. We need people in Springfield who have guts enough to stand up and say what's right," Bill said to raucous cheering. "These hog factories are industries, not farms. They should be regulated accordingly!"

So what was Murphy promising to local farmers in exchange for raising contract pigs? A fair question that no one could answer, since neither Dave Inskeep nor anyone from Murphy Family Farms showed up to the meeting.

But Elmwood farmer Wayne Davis had been at a Murphy recruiting meeting back in June, and told of his experience. He said Murphy officials had tried to entice him with slick brochures and guaranteed profit streams. But Davis didn't bite. "They said they were looking for contracts with twenty farms or so in a sixty-mile radius of here," he said. "They plan to breed upwards of seventy thousand sows, which will produce about 1.4 million piglets a year."

Nearly a million and a half piglets in a county with fifty-five thousand people? This was farming on a scale unlike anything seen in this area before.

Just one sow factory, with thirty-six hundred sow animals, required an initial farmer investment of $2.2 million, Davis continued. "They said you could make a decent living and pay it off in fifteen years, but it just didn't make sense, not to me, anyway."

A representative from the Illinois EPA, Lyle Ray, stood up to reassure people. "Murphy Farms have been warned of their obligations," he said. "They know they can be prosecuted if odor or water pollution problems occur."

Karen turned to Rocky. "That's supposed to make us feel better?" she whispered.

Toward the end of the long night, a tall, slender, middle-aged man in a topcoat stood to speak. To Karen, he seemed rather well groomed for a farmer. Phil St. John explained how he had fought against a pig farm in Stark County. There he met a young public-health professor from the University of Iowa who was quickly becoming an expert on Midwest factory farming. He had invited the professor, Kendall Thu, to address the crowd from his office in Iowa City. He now pressed a button on a machine that connected the telephone to the school PA system, and a disembodied voice crackled over the speakers.

"These are factories, they are not farms," Thu's voice shot through the crowd, which burst into applause. "And they are no good for rural communities, no matter what their promoters and sponsors tell you." Thu described the "industrialization of livestock" and the many social, environmental, economic, and public health problems that factory farms had created in towns that initially welcomed them.

Karen listened with trepidation to the voice on the speakerphone. It was surreal to hear this dispassionate, disembodied person of science calmly detail the dreadful things to come. Looks of disbelief pervaded the room.

"Big Ag has set its sights on Peoria County," Karen said to Rocky, "and we have nothing to say about it. But you know what? This community is worth fighting for." When Thu mentioned his most recent paper, on the impacts of large-scale swine production, she made a note to order a copy.

By the time the evening ended, several people had been transformed into activists. About a dozen of them gathered afterward to discuss their next steps. Karen joined them. Bill Knight had drafted a petition against the proposed hog farm, and everyone signed it. Phil St. John suggested a meeting for the following night at Elmwood Town Hall.

Karen approached Mayor Almasi and Bill Knight. "I can't help but notice that Dave Inskeep isn't here," she said. "It's like a salesman trying to sell you shoes without being in the store." They all laughed. "Instead, we had two hundred people here, and not one of them spoke out in favor of this thing. If this project is so great, then where's Inskeep?"

On the drive home, Karen felt an odd mixture of hope and dread. "We're going to stop this thing, Rocky," she said. "We're going to get folks together, and pass ordinances, and win this! Democracy at its best: local people pushing for local control."

But Karen did not realize how factory farms can vex even basic, localized democracy.

Bill Knight, who helped organize the Elmwood meeting, was a former reporter at the *Peoria Journal Star*. His wife, Terry Bibo, had a lively column in the same paper. Taking a cue from her husband's work, she wrote about a cattle feedlot near her parents' home in Lamar, Colorado. It was "nearly impossible" for anyone to leave their homes when the wind blew the wrong way, she said. Her father called it "the smell of money." In Illinois, the situation would become even worse, she said, given that state environmental laws were "about as tough as Kleenex":

> Trust me, once Murphy gets its snout in the Illinois trough, our own independent farmers are doomed. You think I'm kidding? Check out the hog factory record. Murphy is headquartered in Rose Hill, N.C. Owner Wendell Murphy was a state senator there during the 10 years he became a corporate hog-boss. The results? Since 1983, almost two-thirds of the hog farmers in North Carolina, 16,000 of the 23,400 producers, have left the business.[3]

"To put it bluntly," Bibo warned, "the village of Elmwood, or even the county of Peoria, is no match for the Big Pig." And despite corporate sweet talk of new jobs, "nothing I've seen indicates that a handful of $6–$7-an-hour jobs is worth it. Unless these porkers can guarantee not to have a bad impact on groundwater or air, and my information indicates they can't, they stink bad."

Karen pulled up to Elmwood Town Hall, a redbrick Victorian building with a black slate mansard roof. It was the first meeting of the anti–Murphy Family Farms brigade. Most of her new colleagues were already there: Bill Knight, Mayor Almasi, County Commissioner Eldon Polhemus, Phil St. John, a sweet elderly couple named Joe and Jane Kuck, and about fifteen others.

Virtually everyone came with news clippings: articles about the impact of factory farms on local communities, mostly in North Carolina. These were assembled, collated, and copied on the Xerox machine in the town hall office. Phil St. John had photos of a CAFO in Cass County where a lagoon was being dug in sandy soil with a shallow water table. The hole had filled with aquifer water.

One of the first orders of business was to create a name for the little cabal. Bill suggested FARM—for Families Against Rural Messes. Everyone loved it. People vowed to gather research on the megafarms and their impact on the health and environment of rural communities. Jane Kuck even invited Karen over to explore the "search engines" on her home computer, with its dial-up modem.

Karen had never been on a computer before, let alone one that connected to the World Wide Web, whatever the hell *that* was. Jane, a librarian, offered to conduct the searches for her. Within days, she was printing out neat piles of agribusiness information for Karen to come and collect.

When Karen arrived home that night after the FARM meeting, she was unable to sleep. The idea of saving Elmwood had entered her blood and stayed there. I need to learn everything I can about these factory farms, her racing mind told her as she tossed in bed. Research. I need more research.

The next morning, Karen woke up, called the University of Iowa, and ordered Professor Kendall Thu's paper, "Understanding the Impacts of Large-Scale Swine Production," express delivery.

Karen was ready to take on Dave Inskeep, his Murphy Family Farms backers, and the State of Illinois, if need be, to protect Elmwood. But not everyone felt warm and cozy about her newfound political activism. Friends, neighbors, and in-laws questioned her opposition. After all, the pig facilities would be state of the art. And they'd be located miles away from the Hudson home; Karen would never be bothered by foul smells.

"I know we're four miles away, but that doesn't matter," Karen told them. "Elmwood's town square is much closer. And look what happened in North Carolina—lagoon breaches, fish kills, people getting sick. This hurts everyone. I'm not doing this for me." To Karen, this was a moral issue. "It isn't right when you have to make someone else sick to make a living for yourself. It isn't right to degrade property, and degrade the earth, and abuse the animals, just to extract every last cent you can.

"Besides," she said, "waste lagoons are anything but *high-tech*. It's simply digging a hole and putting crap in it. That's not state of the art. That's caveman mentality."

Kendall Thu's speakerphone speech had left Karen with a queasy feeling. A few days later, his report arrived in the mail. After supper, Karen grabbed a highlighter pen and a glass of Chianti and cracked open Thu's big pig paper. She read through most of the night, taking furious notes.

The 207-page report had resulted from a workshop held in June 1995 in Des Moines, organized by Thu and Kelley Donham, professor of agricultural safety at the University of Iowa, and others. Its introduction read like a war history:

Large-scale swine production has resulted in factions that pit farmer against farmer, rural residents against farmers, citizens against the government and academic institutions, the agricultural community against different segments of the academic community, different farm groups against one another, and smaller independent family-oriented pork producers against large-scale corporate-style producers.[4]

The academic community, the authors said, had been besieged with requests from both sides—the anti-CAFO and pro–factory farm people—to provide evidence that one group was correct. Most pressure had come from industry, but the tug-of-war split academia. "Academic freedom is being challenged from various forces connected to swine industry change," Thu and Donham wrote. Their findings on the impacts of hog CAFOs included the following:

Water Usage: There were no studies on water consumption at large sites, so researchers could only offer "a theoretical range of possibilities." Finishing hogs consume 3–5 gallons per day, while sows and their litters drink up to 8 gallons. But the real usage comes in flushing of barns: 15 gallons per finishing hog and 35 per sow and litter. So, a five-thousand-sow farrowing operation would consume 215,000 gallons each day. The average U.S. household uses about 69 gallons of water a day.

Waste Treatment: Human waste, unlike manure, is treated before being discharged into waterways. Through aerobic composting, human-waste pathogens are killed and biochemical oxygen demand (BOD) is vastly reduced, while remaining solids are settled out as sludge (which is sold as commercial potting soil). But hog waste is stored in anaerobic lagoons that are much less effective at eliminating pathogens, BOD, or heavy metals.

Water Quality: "There is some potential for microbial contamination of ground- or surface water," Karen read. GI diseases from contaminated water threatened human health, especially in rural areas, which often lack adequate testing.

Pathogens: About 85–90 percent of viruses and 45–50 percent of bacteria are killed in lagoons. (Oh great, Karen thought, that means 15 percent of viruses and 55 percent of bacteria survive.) "*Helicobacter pylori*, a human pathogen associated with gastric ulcers and possibly stomach cancer, has been found in swine lagoons," the paper said. Other pathogens included salmonella, listeria, viruses, protozoa, and worms. Meanwhile, CAFO hogs are routinely fed antibiotics, creating bacterial resistance. Resistant genes are passed between bacteria, even other genera, and confer resistance to antibiotics that humans need.

Excessive Rainfall: All lagoons must be designed to withstand a "twenty-five-year, twenty-four-hour precipitation event," but more precipitation than that will cause spillovers and breaches. "Several days or weeks of persistent rainfall coupled with failure to distribute excess lagoon volume (for instance, if it is impossible to get into the field with spray equipment) could also cause the dikes to overflow or fail," the report said.

Manure Application: Even if lagoons were 100 percent effective, they are only temporary holding ponds. Eventually, millions of gallons of waste will have to go *somewhere*—usually onto nearby croplands. And there was "ample documentation" of water pollution from runoff of animal waste used as fertilizer. More than half of all U.S. fish kills have been attributed to livestock runoff.

Barriers to Absorption: The soil must absorb whatever liquid waste is applied to it to prevent runoff. But rates of soil "infiltration" can vary wildly, and depend on things such as frozen or snow-covered ground, soil texture and structure, surface slope, and cover conditions. Flat cropland with deep sands and good cover will absorb sprinkler applications at 32 millimeters per hour, which is sixteen times greater than bare clay soil on a 10 percent slope, which will only absorb 2 millimeters an hour. Everything else will run off. At any CAFO where there is more wastewater than the surrounding land can absorb, "water contamination from overapplication is almost guaranteed."

Manure vs. Chemical Fertilizer: This was a topic of great interest to Karen. After all, Rocky used chemical fertilizer on his row crops. Was that contributing to nitrogen runoff? Probably so, the report said, but not in the same proportions, though it was a difficult comparison to make. For one, the exact nutrient content in manure is often untested, while inorganic fertilizers are pretested and precise. Commercial fertilizers can be applied more evenly to soil than animal waste on a field, and it can be purchased and applied whenever appropriate. Animal waste, however, must be removed when a lagoon is nearing capacity. "This schedule may not coincide with appropriate field conditions for application, e.g., frozen or saturated soil, or for the crop's needs," the report said. Karen also knew that commercial fertilizer wasn't cheap; farmers tended to use it sparingly.

N-P-K Ratio: The ratio of nitrogen to phosphorus and potassium (or N-P-K, as any good gardener knows) in manure does not always meet the demands of the crop being grown. Swine waste is particularly rich in phosphorus—usually in excess of most crop needs. Corn, for example, needs about 1 part phosphorus to 6 parts nitrogen; but hog manure delivers that same 1 part phosphorus to only 1.5 parts nitrogen. In other words, from hog waste, the corn gets four times more phosphorus than it needs to bring nitrogen amounts to beneficial levels. In Holland, hog waste had caused phosphorus oversaturation in more than a million hectares of precious farmland the small country could hardly spare.

Heavy Metals: Phosphorus, sodium, potassium, copper, and zinc can build up in soils where swine manure is applied. Copper and zinc are added to pig feed to promote growth. Crops require very small amounts of these metals, which accumulate in soil "nearly as fast as they are spread." Too much can ruin cropland for decades or more.

"Nitrogen Rain": Atmospheric nitrogen from hog confinements may fall in the form of rain, and could be viewed favorably by nearby crop farmers as "free fertilizer." But that nitrogen is also falling onto "roads, parking lots, fallow fields, fence row weeds, lakes, streams, ponds, forests, wetlands and prairies," the report noted. Nitrates can leach or run off the soil surface. Atmospheric nitrogen also damages wildlife habitats.

Air Quality: With hog CAFOs, "odors, gases, and airborne particles are carried from the buildings by ventilated air." The stench is from decomposing "protein waste material": feces, urine, skin cells, hair, feed, even bedding. Principal gases include ammonia, carbon dioxide, hydrogen sulfide, and methane. Also, particulate matter may contain "endotoxins, possible steroids, and gases generated from feed, the pigs, feces, and building materials."

Karen was about to be sick, but she read on. At least half of all dust particles from hog confinements were tiny enough to be inhaled by the lungs. Meanwhile, dead animals and rotting wet feed added to gases, too. Odor was also coming from a compound called skatole. "*Skatole?*" Karen laughed. "Is that the scientific name for the smell of shit?"

Health Effects of Gases and Odor: "Odors may elicit nausea, vomiting and headache; cause shallow breathing and coughing; upset sleep, stomach and appetite; irritate eyes, nose and throat; and disturb, annoy and cause depression," the report said. Sometimes the gases can even alter behavior. "People living near intensive swine operations in North Carolina report significantly more anger, confusion, tension, depression, fatigue and less vigor" than those who don't. Inside a hog barn, the air is heavy with pig protein (urine, dander, serum), feces, mold, pollen, grain mites, insect parts, and mineral ash. Any workers allergic to

one of these contaminants face permanent lung damage. "Subsequent exposures trigger the immune system to work against inhaled foreign material, but
permanent scar tissue may form within the lungs and increases with each exposure," the paper said. "The lungs' internal defense system may remove much of
the dust before tissue damage can occur. However, the inflammatory and irritant nature of this dust can result in bronchitis and occupational asthma." Another condition, organic dust toxic syndrome (ODTS), is caused by exposure to
high amounts of organic dust. Symptoms include fever, malaise, muscle aches
and pains, headaches, cough, and tightness of chest.

Greenhouse Gases: Manure-based emissions of methane and other CO_2 containing gases contribute 7.4 percent (two million tons) annually to total greenhouse gas emissions in the United States, which was among the five worst
offenders in the world. High concentrations of animals create greater environmental risks for the atmosphere than if those same animals were spread out in
smaller herds over more land. Why? The lagoons. They become "greater sources
of emissions than if the same number of animals were being managed in a less
intensive manner," the report said.

Ammonia, Acid Rain, and "Acid Mist": Ammonia is not a major greenhouse
gas, but it does contribute to acid rain. As it spreads upward into the air, it binds
with hydrochloric acid, nitrous acid, and sulfuric acid to form a highly toxic,
aerosolized form of ammonia that is carried over great distances, "making it a
pollutant on a large scale." It can even change cloud chemistry. In Europe, highly
acidic clouds were producing "acid mists" that covered hilly woodlands and
caused significant damage to foliage. And it was coming from agriculture. In the
Netherlands, 94 percent of all ammonia was due to farming, mostly from manure applications, animal confinements and waste lagoons. Again, it was animal
concentration, as much as sheer numbers, that caused the ammonia "acid mist"
of western Europe.

Odor and Quality of Life: Here, Karen read about a landmark 1994 study by
Thu and Durrenberger of one hundred North Carolina residents. They found
that swine odors had altered outdoor family activities such as barbecues and
child play and visiting of friends. An Iowa Farm and Rural Life Poll found that
only 2 percent of respondents said a neighboring farm detracted from their
quality of life "a great deal," and 21 percent said it detracted "some." Among
the 23 percent impacted, nearly all of them said odor was the main concern,
followed by flies (reported by 41 percent), manure runoff (27 percent), noise
(14 percent), and dust (10 percent).

Political Influence: "Some evidence exists to support the claim that local residents are disadvantaged when they seek to redress problems emanating from the operation of large-scale swine facilities in their communities," Karen read. "This evidence typically comes from individual case studies, industry exposés and investigative newspaper reports."

Men like Wendell Murphy and his company were prime examples, Karen was distraught to see. This man had influence, the likes of which she and the little FARM group, with their photocopies and worried faces, could never imagine. "Agribusiness leaders have political contacts and access to government uncharacteristic of the average citizen," the authors wrote. Activists like Karen and groups like FARM that tried to take on agribusiness were not taken seriously by state officials. "When individual concerns and complaints are taken to the state level," the report said, "they are regarded as being scientifically unfounded and emotional in nature."

Emotional! Karen thought as she read that. You're damn right it's emotional. These are people's homes we're talking about. Besides, it was hard data—not "scientifically unfounded" rumors—that made this issue so emotional in the first place. "Private citizens find that unless they make 'nuisances' of themselves, e.g., dozens of phone calls, their concerns receive little official attention," the report said. "Government protects the prevailing system, the status quo. The burden of proof falls to a private citizen with little experience collecting and interpreting sophisticated scientific evidence."

Social and Ethnic Issues: Many livestock industries actively recruit foreign immigrant workers, especially Mexicans and other Hispanics. "These new community members have imposed considerable costs in education, health care, and law enforcement on the community," the report said. There was often an "explosion" of non-English-speaking students, taxing school districts trying to provide English-as-a-Second-Language (ESL) instruction. Meanwhile, immigrant influx had been responsible for increased emergency-room visits, rising crime rates, and additional police costs.

Stifling Competition: Concentrated hog production can make it extremely hard for smaller, independent growers to compete and stay in business. CAFOs increase demand on feed, labor, and other "inputs," increasing costs. But the real harm was being done at the abattoirs. "Large hog operations bring new processing facilities to rural communities, but over time, as processing firms supply more and more of their own needs from either owned or contracted production, 'outside' hogs may become discounted or not accepted by the processor." Without access to a processing plant, a farmer's pigs are worthless.

Citizen "Resistance": "Resistance organizations" against hog CAFOs had emerged in Iowa, North Carolina, Missouri, Kansas, Illinois, Michigan, Minnesota, Nebraska, Utah, Colorado, and Ohio, Karen was thrilled to read. They all charged that their "rights to enjoy their property and family have been violated," the report said. People such as Karen join the resistance "as both a political strategy and as a support mechanism." Meanwhile, odor was not the only motive for citizen resistance. In fact, even if odor was removed from the equation, the authors said, "it would not make opposition groups go away." That's because there was no *single* issue fueling the conflict: not odor, property values, health risks, or water pollution. "More fundamental," the report said, "is a sense of frustration at the lack of official respect for their problems, and the resulting skepticism that their situation will be remedied through political and/or legal channels."

For Karen, it got more depressing from there: "There is a growing conviction that government selectively serves the interests of money and power and that no amount of citizen protest will affect meaningful change," the paper said. "A 'we vs. them' mentality produces additional paranoia and distrust both within and beyond the community. The conflict polarizes community residents and tears at the fabric of community life, transforming neighbors into enemies, severely straining friendships and families."

And there was one final word of caution for anyone thinking of joining the resistance. "Local activism depends on the mobilization of volunteered efforts and resources, it demands an obsessive identification with 'the cause,'" the authors wrote. "This contrasts with the purchased manpower and expertise available to large-scale swine enterprises. Not only does this obsession continue to rigidly define 'sides' within a small population, it can also result in the physical and mental exhaustion of heavily committed residents." It was a warning that Karen would have done well to heed.

This was the first of many late nights to come for her, researching, reading, collecting facts, and making presentations on animal factories. It was a stretch of time that put great strain on her family, with late dinners and the exhaustion that came from being a wife, mother, and activist. Her weight plummeted as she worried about the outcome of the fight. Nothing tasted good, and she felt too busy to eat, anyway.

On September 10, 1996, Murphy Family Farms announced it was pulling out of its swine deal with Dave Inskeep. Engineers discovered that the eight hundred acres designated for the CAFO rested over an old coal strip mine. It was pierced with sinkholes and mineshafts that would prevent the safe operation of a waste lagoon.[5]

Karen and her FARM comrades were elated. But they were not off the hook yet; Murphy was still scouting around for other sites between the Illinois and Mississippi rivers. Its minimum requirement for farm size was two hundred acres. To Karen's disbelief, a local politician from a neighboring county was considering a Murphy contract.

Jim Baird, then chairman of the Knox County Board, owned land about twenty minutes northwest of Elmwood, near the village of Williamsfield. Baird was awaiting test results on his property, according to the *Journal Star*. "Agriculture is changing so fast that the changes are coming whether we like them or not," he told the paper.[6] Karen was appalled and saw through his cynical quote: If CAFOs were the next wave of farming, then Baird wanted to cash in early. The Illinois animal-factory wars were just getting started.

By the autumn of 1996, Karen Hudson and Families Against Rural Messes were taking their first baby steps through the corridors of power. They began in their own backyard. On September 12, FARM members attended a meeting of the Peoria County Board, which was to take up the hog issue for the first time. Karen drove to the meeting with a sense of urgency.

Eldon Polhemus rose to call on Governor Jim Edgar and the state legislature to impose a one-year moratorium on new CAFO construction. A suspension would allow time to study the situation. Only then could "proper rules be put in place to protect people," he said, warning that the Inskeep deal's termination did not mean Murphy had withdrawn. "They intend to have operations somewhere, and it could be devastating," he said. "Don't think they've backed off."[7]

Bill Knight got up to support the CAFO moratorium, citing air and water pollution from similar farms. "If we don't do the same thing here and fight back, if we don't make a stink, I think we're going to smell one," he said. Knight noted the waste potential for the original Murphy CAFO would have been equivalent to a town of twenty thousand people. Any resulting damage, though caused by the corporation, would ultimately be cleaned up at taxpayer expense.

The board voted to back the moratorium. They also agreed to explore laws in other places that regulated CAFOs, and considered the idea of an outright ban in their county.

Karen was feeling some power, and FARM was on a roll. Local media supported the ragtag group with surprising gusto. "It's time to declare a moratorium on huge pig farms in Illinois," a *Journal Star* editorial blared.[8] Karen was amazed.

Warning that the fight was not over, the paper urged the public to band together against corporate giants. "Individuals still are in charge here. Individuals can say no. And individuals who get together can be potent," it said, noting that, among the two hundred people who showed up at Elmwood High, "No one, absolutely no one, spoke in favor of an operation designed to produce 72,000 piglets a year." Tipping its hat to the scrappy members of FARM, the *Journal Star* warned politicians, "State legislators need to know that pigs aren't the only central Illinoisans who can raise a stink."

Karen had developed a ritual of visiting Jane Kuck to hunt down factual treasures from the mysterious World Wide Web. One search turned up a Minnesota woman with a jaw-dropping tale. Julie Jansen, a wife and mother of six, lived in Olivia, about sixty miles west of Minneapolis, where she ran a day-care center.

Within a two-mile radius of the Jansen home, two hog megafarms had been built. Since then, the entire family—and most of the day-care children—had suffered from a plague of maladies: headaches, nausea, fatigue, dizziness, vomiting, lung congestion, even blackouts. Jansen documented the suffering and sent a copy to Jane.

"Doors and windows shut, and air-conditioning running and still the sewer gas smell was unbearable," Julie wrote. "Everyone in my home was ill once again." Julie called the Minnesota Poison Control System to ask about two common gases from animal waste: methane and hydrogen sulfide (H_2S). She described the symptoms her family was experiencing. They were consistent with exposure to H_2S. "I asked what else H_2S could do," Julie's letter continued. "I was told the only symptoms we were *not* experiencing were seizures, convulsions—and death." Subsequent calls to health departments and pollution agencies resulted in no action. Julie realized she would have to undertake the "search for the truth myself," she wrote.[9]

Karen wholly identified with Julie's plight. She felt as though this were a letter written from the future—*her* future. "I am so inspired by this," Karen told Jane. "Here is a mother, compelled to speak out because she couldn't protect her kids and home from a chemical invasion. We are in the same position in Illinois. We all need to become Julie Jansens."

Elmwood, Illinois, may have dodged Murphy's pig bullet for the time being, but that hardly meant the CAFO fight was over: Rumor had it that Murphy was negotiating with Knox County Commissioner Jim Baird on a farrowing operation. Folks said that Baird was close to signing a contract similar to what Inskeep had sought. The proposed thirty-six-hundred-sow facility would go up on Baird family property and produce some seventy-two thousand piglets annually. Jim Baird said no decisions had been reached, and denied there were any done deals.

Fresh off their victory at the meeting with the Peoria County Board, FARM now had another mission. The Knox County Board would discuss the Baird CAFO deal at its September 18 meeting. That day, Karen and her fellow activists drove up to Galesburg and the Knox County Courthouse, an imposing 1886 Romanesque Revival building. The public would be allowed to speak at the meeting, which would be run by Jim Baird.

The hearing began at 6 P.M. sharp, in front of more than a hundred people who had crammed into an old-fashioned courtroom on the third floor. The members of FARM weren't the only people spoiling for a fight this evening. An unexpected ally was none other than Baird's sister-in-law, Nina (pronounced *nye*-nah). Nina and her husband, Bill Baird, lived down the road from Jim's proposed site. This was shaping up to be a family feud unlike any other in Knox County, the second-largest pork-producing county in Illinois.

When the hog-confinement issue came up, Chairman Jim Baird recused himself and passed the gavel to his vice chair. Newspaper accounts said the standing-room-only crowd was evenly divided between the pro- and anti-megafarm camps. The board would now consider support for a statewide moratorium on CAFOs, until Illinois' new livestock law could be amended and tightened.

Opponents got up to argue passionately about air and water quality, migrant workers, and the economic benefits, if any, that CAFOs would bring to Knox County. "There should be some type of control over these things," said Mayor Almasi of Elmwood. "How is it possible that someone building a house is subject to more restrictions than someone raising thousands of pigs?"[10] Half the crowd went wild. Most of the board appeared supportive, Karen thought. Chairman Baird looked as if he had indigestion.

Speaking on the pro-pork side were people like hog grower Jerry King of Victoria, about ten miles from Williamsfield. The controversy had grown too "emotional" he said, but residents had nothing to fear from hog confinements. "A moratorium could be devastating to the industry that exists in Illinois," he said, echoing the "grow or die" mentality common at the time among hog farmers in the area.

After two hours of debate, the vice chair called the vote. Karen held her breath. Baird was a powerful man; would fellow commissioners oppose him and risk losing his favor? Karen soon had her answer. With Baird abstaining, the vote was a bruising twenty-three to one to support a statewide moratorium on new large-scale hog confinements, pending "better regulations to control and monitor them."

The lone dissenter was Randy DeSutter, a prominent member of the Knox County Farm Bureau. He argued that a moratorium was against the county's economic interests, without distinction made between small-time farmers and animal factories. "This is a strong agricultural county. It's full of hog farmers already raising large numbers of pigs," he said. "We should support these farmers, and the industries that support them."

Karen was thrilled, but the board wasn't finished just yet. Before adjourning, it voted fifteen to nine to urge the state to accelerate new laws to give more teeth to livestock enforcement. As Karen and her FARM allies celebrated the dual victory, she saw Jim Baird quietly slip through a side door and out of the courtroom. "Look at him, skulking away," she said to Rocky. "I almost feel sorry for him."

FARM was on a roll, and its members knew it. First Peoria, now Knox County. The jubilant members of the "resistance" movement spilled from the courthouse and over to a local brewpub for burgers and back-slapping. They crowded around a long communal table and toasted their flexing political muscle with chilled drafts.

But not everyone there was savoring their victory. People from the "other side" had arrived. Members of FARM and their opponents eyed one another warily. The door opened again. In walked a tall, slender, and well-dressed woman, out of place in this farm town, Karen thought. Joined by friends, she sat at the FARM table.

"Mrs. Baird," someone whispered to Karen. But which Mrs. Baird? Commissioner Jim Baird's wife, Nancy? Or his brother Bill's wife, Nina? "Is she the good Mrs. Baird, or the bad Mrs. Baird?" Karen whispered. Everyone laughed, but nobody knew the answer.

"I'm going to feel her out," Karen said, and she walked over to join the newcomers at the table's end. "Hi, I'm Karen Hudson, from Elmwood, Mrs. Baird," Karen said cautiously. "Um, do you mind if I ask you a question?"

"Not at all."

"Are you opposed to the pig factory?"

"Yes." Nina smiled. "Very much so."

"What a relief!" Karen confessed. "We didn't know if we were dining with the enemy."

Not only was this the "good" Mrs. Baird, but she had been so concerned about the Dave Inskeep situation down in Elmwood that she had attended the meeting at the high school. It turned out that Nina was very friendly with Jane Kuck, who kept her informed about the project from their encounters at the local library. Jane had told her about Murphy's plans to build a hog factory near Elmwood, and Nina had been horrified by the idea.

"It was such terrible news," Nina told the FARM people at the table. "Your town is so nice. I just couldn't let that happen." But after Inskeep pulled out, Jane still warned Nina: "That Murphy company is coming to your town next." Nina had gone from "concerned citizen to potential victim overnight," she said.

That night, Karen convinced Nina to join forces with FARM. Instead of dining with the enemy, Karen was dining with a new, lifelong friend.

Nina Baird's husband, Bill, was once the largest beef cattle farmer in all Knox County, with some one thousand head grazing on his land. A well-known fixture in state livestock circles, he was also a former chairman of the Illinois Cattlemen's Association, and still sat on state livestock and meat boards. Bill and his brothers, Jim and Dick, were fifth-generation farmers with deep Midwestern roots. Bill had met Nina when they were both at the University of Illinois at Urbana-Champaign. Nina had grown up on a farm, raising Angus cattle for 4-H. At college, she majored in animal science with the goal of one day landing a plum job as a spokesperson for the National Livestock and Meat Board.

The newlyweds built a house across from the old Baird homestead that Bill's grandfather built a century before, a few miles south of Williamsfield. They raised three daughters; untold tons of soybeans, corn, and oats; and, until the 1980s, cattle for the Chicago and, later, Joliet markets.

The Bairds also raised hogs for a number of years—but nothing on the scale that Murphy Family Farms wanted to build. The Baird pens were large and clean. Small A-framed farrowing houses dotted the grounds. Manure was scraped up with tractors and spread over hundreds of acres and plowed under; it was never liquefied or sprayed, and it was never allowed to smell like fermenting sewage. "Back then, when you began to notice odor, it just meant that it was time to clean the pens," Nina told Karen.

Eventually, Nina began teaching school, and got a master's degree in counseling from Bradley University in Peoria. By 1986, the couple began to sour on livestock farming, fretting that it had become far too dominated by corporate interests. Bill ran a seed-farm partnership with his brothers, Jim and Dick, for several years, but later decided to take over the family insurance agency.

Bill's brother Jim and his wife, Nancy, had five kids—all very close to Nina and Bill's children. The Baird clan lived a happy existence for many years. Nina and Bill dreamed they would live out their lives in their cherished farmhouse, with its shady oaks, tidy vegetable garden, and exuberant flowerbeds. But then rumors began circulating that Jim Baird was quietly meeting with men from North Carolina—Murphy men. Soon, more local people learned of the conglomerate's plans. A cloud of tension began to form over the various Baird family members, and over the peaceful hamlet of Williamsfield itself.

Jim Baird denied he was making a deal with Murphy Family Farms. But one morning, after Jim had walked over to Bill and Nina's for coffee, Bill confronted his brother about Murphy's intentions, and an anonymous letter that had been circulating around the community alleging that a deal was being brokered.

"What the hell? Nobody was supposed to know about this until it was done!" Nina remembers Jim saying, as he tossed the letter onto the kitchen table.[11]

"Then it's *you*?" Bill was floored.

Jim looked uneasy. "Nope," he said after a pause. "It's not me."

Nina forgot about the matter for a while. But one day Bill came home and reported that, indeed, Jim and his son Doug were negotiating with Murphy. That day, Bill and the third Baird brother, Jack, went over to confront Jim and his son.

"Look, we've been searching for ways to save this farm for three years," Doug Baird explained. "It wasn't until we started running the numbers that I figured out the solution. It was livestock manure."

"Come again, Doug?" Bill said.

"We found that manure's been undervalued for years," Doug said. "Plus, the hogs will bring in enough income to save the farm." Silence engulfed the room. Doug broke it: "It just doesn't pay anymore to put in twelve hundred acres of corn and beans when we've got taxes, equipment costs, rising rents, and two children in college," Doug said. "We either get into big livestock, or we get out of farming altogether. It's that simple. Me, I plan to survive."

Doug and his father, Jim, had been speaking to hog companies for three years about various CAFO configurations. Bill was growing angry. Why hadn't they been told about this? "We spent time with the Murphy people, visiting farms outside Kansas City," Doug said. "And I was impressed. I was absolutely impressed. It's not like hog farming when we grew up." Then he added, "Plus, they really want us to be their first operation in Illinois."

Bill and Jack stared in silence at their nephew. "Now, I know they say hog confinements stink," Doug pressed on. "But there's been so much research and effort to control odors."

Bill had heard enough. "Doug, Jim, this is not going to work," he said. "This is not good stewardship of the land. This isn't the way we've farmed here all these generations. You know that. With so many sows in one place, with all that hog waste, whatever land you site this on, you'll be condemning it. You won't be able to farm that land anymore."

Jim disagreed, insisting the Murphy engineers would make sure the place was environmentally sound and "state of the art."

Back home, Bill went over the tense family meeting with Nina. It didn't look good. "I think what we have coming in here," he said, "is a hog factory."

Nina, once only vaguely aware of CAFOs, started her own research. "They're going to have problems keeping those pigs and their babies warm and lit," she told Bill. "And they're going to have labor problems, too, because from what I read, it's hard to keep a steady workforce in that sort of environment. The work is so wretched, people just walk away. You can't pay them enough for what they must endure in those pig parlors."

Then there were the disturbing studies from North Carolina, Iowa, and elsewhere. "What about the foul air and polluted groundwater?" Nina said. "What about pathogens in the air? What about the sick neighbors?" she fretted. "Will we become 'sick neighbors,' too?"

B y early 1995, the situation in the Neuse River Basin was reaching crisis proportions. In some creeks and tributaries, green gossamer algae covered the water from shore to shore. Even the most affluent residents no longer enjoyed unfettered boating access. Boat engines could not break through the slimy mass. Meanwhile, fish were still dying each fall, and people were still getting sick after being on the water during fish kills.

Rick embarked on a marathon letter-writing campaign to officials in Raleigh, describing the desperate plight of the Neuse. He targeted two men in particular: Dr. Ron Levine, then director of the State Department of Health (now the Department of Health and Human Services), and Dr. Levine's boss, Jonathan Howes, then secretary of the North Carolina Department of Environment and Natural Resources. Howes was a close ally of the current governor, James P. Hunt, who in turn was an old college chum of Wendell Murphy—the former state senator and Democratic Party powerhouse, and head of the Murphy Family Farms pork empire.

Rick sent several letters and e-mails to Dr. Levine, begging him to send agents down to New Bern to investigate the mysterious ailments afflicting fishermen and others on the river. When Rick got no response, he picked up the phone. One time he actually got past the staff and right to the health chief. "You've got to get some doctors down here now to have a look at these poor folks, Dr. Levine," Rick demanded. Levine claimed he would look into the matter, but Rick still felt he was getting the Raleigh bureaucratic brush-off.

Dr. JoAnn Burkholder, the *Pfiesteria* expert at North Carolina State, told Rick about similar treatment she had received from Dr. Levine. One of his underlings had told her that health officials had no intention of looking into *Pfiesteria*, because to do so would threaten tourism and the coastal economy. JoAnn was fed up. Rick was, too. "What they're really saying with their silence is, 'We just don't believe you,'" Rick complained. "Those big boys up in Raleigh, they just want us all to go away. They don't want to hear about hogs. They don't want to hear about any cell from hell. North Carolina is counting on pork and tourism to bring in money. They won't let anything upset that plan."

Meanwhile, there was a new wrinkle. Rick had learned that the nutrient surplus in the rivers, of nitrogen especially, was not just coming from liquid runoff and discharges. Some of it was coming from the sky.

Rick first heard about this phenomenon from Doug Phelps, a retired IBM specialist and sailor who shared a love for the Neuse. Doug had read a European scientific paper that explained how ammonia emissions rise into the air from animal confinements, waste lagoons, and sprayfields. Once into the "airshed," the nitrogen-laden gas can be carried for miles before it settles back down to earth and onto waterways and river basins. Once in the water, it can incite algae to bloom.

"My God," Rick said to Doug, "even the best-run CAFO, with zero seepage, spills, or runoff—if there was such a thing—is poisoning the river. I had no idea."

Working with UNC researcher Vinnie Aneja and others on the airborne ammonia issue, Doug learned that, depending on the wind, ammonia emissions from a CAFO can deposit nitrogen from sixty to three hundred miles away.[1] In North Carolina, ammonia was known to be coming from sewage plants and pulp mills, but also from nonpoint sources such as agriculture, especially livestock. It was hard to believe, but as much as 80–90 percent of the nitrogen in a hog lagoon is released into the atmosphere as ammonia.[2]

Some researchers estimated that 80 percent of this highly potent form of nitrogen in the river had originated as ammonia emitted into the Neuse River airshed.[3]

Rick and his colleagues presented their findings to astounded DEM agents in Raleigh. He still says it was the big breakthrough that helped set the North Carolina hog wars afire.

Rick knew it would be big, but not this big. The Raleigh *News & Observer*'s series on the North Carolina hog industry ran for five consecutive days. The coverage shook the North Carolina political establishment and, in many ways, carried reverberations that are still felt today. People in New Bern were exultant.

The five-part investigative series "Boss Hog: The Power of Pork" was coau-

thored by reporters Pat Stith, Joby Warrick, and Melanie Sill.[4] After seven
months of research, they dissected North Carolina's "pork revolution" as no
one had ever done before. The series arrived at a propitious time: North Carolina had just taken over the number-two slot for pork production (after Iowa).
In 1994, hogs earned some $1 billion in revenue, more than tobacco. By 1995,
they were poised to top broiler chickens as the number-one farm commodity in
the state.

North Carolina now had its own "hog belt," a long stretch of CAFOs that
had popped up in the past ten years in two dozen coastal and piedmont counties. The top four counties—Sampson, Duplin, Wayne, and Bladen—were home
to some 2.8 million pigs—far greater in number than all the other counties in the
state combined. Sampson and Duplin each saw their hog populations soar by
about 350 percent between 1983 and 1993, the most staggering rises of all. By
this point, they were the top hog-producing counties in the nation.

The reporters had select criticism for state agencies. While these agencies
eagerly helped the swine population expand, they were less attentive to the
mounting array of problems caused by the population's rapid and unchecked
growth. Odor and pollution problems were now of primary concern to "a
growing chorus of residents, local leaders and environmental groups, pressing
the state to address worries about hog farming," wrote the editors, who promised to reveal "who wins, and who loses, when a major industry is given special treatment."

This expert display of hard-hitting reporting and good old-fashioned muck-
raking earned the "Boss Hog" team the 1996 Pulitzer Prize for meritorious
public service reporting.

DAY ONE: LEAKING LAGOONS, DIRTY WATER

Warrick and Stith opened the series by addressing the subject of filthy water. To
help readers understand the enormous problem of factory farms, they suggested
imagining a city twice the size of New York. "Now imagine that this city has no
sewage treatment plants," they wrote. "All the wastes from fifteen million inhabitants are simply flushed into open pits and sprayed onto fields. Turn those
humans into hogs, and you don't have to imagine at all. It's already here."

It was going to be a long week for the pork people, Rick thought with a
grin as he settled into his Sunday paper that morning.

Hog industry leaders insisted the lagoon-and-sprayfield system was proven
to keep chemicals and pathogens away from water supplies and claimed that
lagoons were nearly leak-proof. Heavy solids in animal waste sink to the bottom

and form a "seal" to prevent seepage into the soil, they said. DEM officials confirmed that the "self-sealing" process usually happened within months and could even plug up sandy soils.

Wendell Murphy himself made the same claim. "There's not one shred, not one piece of evidence anywhere in this nation that any groundwater is being contaminated by a hog lagoon," he said. If there was any evidence, he added, "I am totally oblivious to that."

Murphy may have been oblivious, but he was also wrong. New data showed plenty of leaching into groundwater. One report said half of all lagoons leaked badly enough to pollute wells, springs, and aquifers. Huge numbers of families in eastern North Carolina depended on wells for drinking water. Excess nitrates in water can cause the potentially fatal "blue-baby syndrome" (methemoglobinemia) in infants, among other health hazards.

Lagoons did more than just leak. Marvin Angel, a former manager for Carroll's, said it was routine for them to overflow. "There are so many ways to have a spill that it's impossible NOT to have one," he conceded to the newspaper. "Pipes fill up with leaves. Drains get stopped up." Barely a week went by, he added, without some kind of leak or overflow accident. When that happened, workers tried to fix the mess. But mostly, he said, their motto was "pray and keep your mouth shut."

Meanwhile, North Carolina pig producers were running out of places to spray all their effluent. In the big swine counties, growers were producing far more nitrogen and phosphorus than the land could absorb.

The hog industry was aware of the problems, and sponsored studies to address waste and odor control. "They say no one works harder than they do to prevent the contamination of water supplies," the article said, but "nowhere else has this waste-intensive industry grown so much so fast, with so little known about long-term consequences."

Even industry-sponsored tests revealed problems. Carroll's Foods drilled test wells next to lagoons at three pig facilities in Northampton County. In 1994, ammonia nitrogen levels were almost ten times more than the normal level of 2 parts per million. Months later it bumped up to 27 parts per million, and then 57 parts per million. By the fall of 1994, it was out of control, at 178 parts per million. Carroll's dismissed its own findings as "nonmaterial variation."

DAY TWO: CORPORATE TAKEOVER

Nearly all the explosive growth in North Carolina's hog population had occurred at contract farms for corporate clients. State policy blessed the system as sound and desirable. It was a sweet deal for corporations. They could saddle hundreds of farmers with debt in exchange for the care and feeding of their pigs. "Why own the farm when you can own the farmer?" one former executive explained.

Still, there was a twelve-month waiting list to land a contract. Wendell Murphy called it his greatest contribution to hog production. "These contracts are very good for the growers, and they work good for the integrators," he told *The News & Observer*.

But some ex-growers disputed the hog boss. "The contract looks a whole hell of a lot better when they're presenting it than the actual value is," said Jack Sauls, a former contract farmer. "It's a good deal for a man who doesn't have any money and can't borrow the money. You give him a string to hold on to, and he thinks it's great. And it turns out to be . . . for the company."

Contract farmers were borrowing $200,000 to $1 million to finance construction, often putting up their houses and land in collateral. But even as they carried that debt for seven to ten years, the hog company could cancel the deal with just thirty days' notice. Most hog contracts lasted one year; if they were not renewed, farmers scrambled to find a replacement.

Some farmers had already gone bust. John Cooper said he was "lured" into a contract with happy talk of $100,000 profits a year. But he had to expend $56,000 annually on his $750,000 loan. His first year, he finished $8,000 in the red. "I would tell people that each and every contract should be looked at carefully, and nothing should be taken for granted," he warned.

"People generally don't ask you to go borrow $150,000 to get an $8-an-hour job," one law professor explained. "These relationships shift an awful lot of risk to the producer—the risk of owning the building, the risk of environmental damage, the risk that the contract won't be renewed." No wonder some farmers were calling themselves glorified sharecroppers.

On the other hand, many hog growers praised their contracting companies. George Garner, who raised pigs for Carroll's Farms, said the firm had been "nothing but good to me." It was good for companies, too. Smithfield earned $7.8 million in the second quarter of the 1995 fiscal year, 8.5 times more than it made in the second quarter of the 1994 fiscal year.

DAY THREE: MURPHY'S LAW

"God gave eastern North Carolina a fine, sandy soil that grows the world's best tobacco. It took a man named Wendell Holmes Murphy to make it sprout pigs," the reporters said in profiling the real Boss Hog. "Murphy took an old idea, adapted it to swine and literally changed the way pigs are raised. Twenty-five years later, Murphy is America's undisputed King of Hogs."

Murphy Family Farms had become the "General Motors of a hog industry empire" reaching from North Carolina to Utah. In 1995, it would raise some 3 million hogs in North Carolina alone, 8,200 every day, 365 days a year. The company's founder was a former schoolteacher, self-proclaimed "country boy done good," and lifelong Democrat. During his ten-year tenure in the North Carolina General Assembly, he became the largest hog producer in America.

Murphy's influence in Raleigh is the stuff of legend; he is known as "a back-room wheeler-dealer, a man who knew how to get things done," the paper said. The Duplin County pig tycoon helped pass numerous laws benefiting his company and the hog industry, often without public notice or a single vote of opposition. Ethics laws were hardly a concern—general assembly rules allowed members to earn money from the results of their own bills and votes, provided they declared that their financial interests had not influenced them. Murphy said he was acting in the interest of hog growers in his district. The fact that he was also a hog grower was immaterial.

In 1992, Wendell Murphy left lawmaking to oversee his expansive pig empire, which by that point reached the Midwest and beyond. But he remained a deep-pocketed donor to other power brokers at home. County officials, state legislators, members of Congress, and his buddy Governor Hunt were all regular beneficiaries of Murphy's political largesse. Murphy Family Farms had practically become a branch of state government, the article went on. From 1992 to 1994, records show, Murphy family and company executives logged an average of fifty phone calls per week from state officials, including people in Hunt's office.

Employing his famous "aw shucks" demeanor, Murphy downplayed his legendary influence in an interview with the paper. "I'm just a country boy who grew up on a small farm with tobacco and a few pigs in the backyard," he said. "Frankly, I don't know much about raising hogs. But fortunately, we have some people that do.

"Our trademark, our hallmark if you will, has been our willingness to recognize that change is inevitable; we cannot continue to do in the future exactly what we've done in the past. People who resist change are just going to get left behind."

DAY FOUR: THE SMELL OF MONEY

Huge sums of revenue were being generated from the sprawling hog farms, but the boom had its downside, especially among neighbors living downwind from a CAFO. For hog growers, the odor at their facilities was the "smell of money." But for those gagging and choking nearby, it just smelled like shit.

In Duplin County, people were choosing cleaner air over the economic bliss of industrial swine. Residents in the village of Faison (population seven hundred) had jammed the local firehouse to speak against a proposed hog-processing plant, even though it would bring fifteen hundred new jobs to the area. "They jeered and hissed every time the county's industrial recruiter mentioned pigs or the plant," the story said. "'I want to know two things,' thundered one burly speaker, thrusting a finger at Duplin County development director, Woody Brinson. 'How can we stop this thing, and how can we get you fired?'" In the end, the town council voted three to zero against the slaughterhouse, though it was powerless to stop it.

Then there were the jobs lost when labor-intensive independent farms converted to capital-intensive factory farms. One farrowing operation in Sampson County needed just eight workers and a manager to oversee two thousand sows and their piglets. At finishing farms, even fewer were needed: Some had no full-time staff at all. Meanwhile, many of those jobs went to people from outside the community, such as Latino migrants and prison inmates.

Mostly, neighbors expressed sadness, fury, and resignation. One Greene County woman complained of being engulfed in a sticky cloud of foul odor each morning at 5 A.M. when she departed for her factory job. The stink would stay with her all day. It fused to her car's interior. It stuck in her hair and settled into her clothes. She would track it into work in the morning, and it would be there to greet her when she got home. "The owner lives miles away from here, and he can go home and smell apples and cinnamon if he wants to," she said. "But we have no choice."

Thomas "Pick" Robbins, a retired tobacco farmer, had no choice when a forty-eight-hundred-hog facility went in upwind from his farm. Now diagnosed with bone cancer, he would likely be breathing hog odors until the day he died. "People don't know what we go through," he said. "Some days I can't even walk out to my barn without feeling like I want to vomit. It ain't fit for a dog to live like this."

Life had also become hell for many in the hamlet of Brown Town, a struggling community of low-income African-Americans and mixed-race residents that dated back to the Civil War era. Hog barns had popped up only a hundred yards or so away from the center of town. The smell was often hellish:

Virtually everyone has their own "stink story" to tell. Lisa Hines' starts before dawn with a raspy call for help from her 10-year-old son, Jazz. Jazz has suffered from asthma since age 4. Two years ago, when a large hog farm opened directly across the road from the family's home, his condition grew dramatically worse. "There have been times when I've had to take him to the emergency room two or three times in a week," said Hines, 34. "I'll hear him call out, "Help me, Help me!' in a whispery voice, because he can't get his breath. He'll be on his knees beside the bed with his eyes rolled back in his head."

If Murphy harbored any compassion for these suffering neighbors, he did an admirable job of concealing it. "Should we expect odor to never drift off the site to the neighbor's house?" he asked. "We all have to have inconvenience once in a while for the benefits that come with it."

The odors were clearly taking their toll, emotionally, physically, and medically. No one in the state had studied the effects of swine stench on humans more extensively than Dr. Susan Schiffman, the odor researcher at Duke University. According to her studies, the swine odors were intermittent and somewhat unpredictable, making them even more unnerving to most residents than a single, predictable scent. During the day, when breezes are more common, the stench was lighter, even imperceptible. "Other times you go there and it's just horrible," she said. "And that seems to bother people more than a constant odor."

But even when CAFOs were not stinking, the hog smell persists. It can literally adhere to homes. Shingles, siding, and other materials absorb and trap odors during the night, off-gassing them in the sunlight of day. In people, fatty tissues act in much the same way. "That's why some people say they can smell the odor on their breath long after they left the farm," Schiffman said. People living nearest to hog CAFOs showed "more tension, more depression, more anger, less vigor, more fatigue and more confusion" than others.

FINAL DAY: POLITICAL PORK

Pork and politics have always gone hand-in-hand, but perhaps not quite so literally as in North Carolina. By the mid-1990s, pig profits permeated the political power structure. U.S. Senator Lauch Faircloth, a wealthy Republican who chaired an environmental subcommittee, made a fortune from hogs. The chairman of the general assembly's environment committee, John M. Nichols, a Republican of New Bern, was constructing his own hog CAFO in Craven County, in order to raise pigs for Murphy. In the Senate, Democrat Charles W. Albertson of Duplin County, chair of the Committee on Environment and Agriculture, was not only a Murphy confidante, but also the number-one beneficiary of donations from the entire pork industry.

In Duplin County, residents fighting the planned abattoir accused state and
local politicos of belonging to a powerful cabal led by the hog industry and
allied interests. "We have a political process in which everything is done under
controlled conditions," said Derl Walker, the Republican county commissioner.
"You can't find out what is happening because everybody else is working to
keep control in the hands of a few people."

To Rick, that pretty much summed up North Carolina pork.

For weeks after the series appeared, nobody in New Bern was speaking of
much else. Rick had never known the power of the press to advance an issue
this quickly. Before the series, the industry had kept a tight lid on its dirty little
secrets. Negative hog stories in the media were sporadic and ineffective. "But
this is a whole new ball game," Rick told colleagues. "There's no way the hog
industry can hide anymore. It's all out there for everyone to see: the pollution,
health problems, corporate control, corruption. The public just got a good
whiff of all the many ways this industry stinks."

From now on, Rick predicted, their complaints would not fall on deaf ears.
Letters to the editor of *The News & Observer* reflected public approval of the
series and its prevailing message that the hog industry needed tighter controls.

Some responses, however, remained firmly within the Murphy camp. "The
writers make Murphy sound like some kind of monster out to destroy the industry and wipe out the family farm for his own gain. Nothing could be further from the truth," wrote Susan Bowman of Henderson. "If he is guilty of
something, it is using his sharp mind and intuition to create a better, more efficient industry for the benefit of his company and pork producers worldwide."

The town council of Wallace, in Duplin County, said Murphy had saved
many towns and farmers from going broke. "The reduction or loss of this revenue would lead to serious financial distress for many of our local businesses,"
Wallace's mayor wrote.

Rick thought the series would have an impact. But looking back now, he
feels a tinge of embarrassment for his naive enthusiasm, quipping that, "A few
of the rules have changed, but it's the same field in the same ballpark."

In June 1995, Rick got a call from Tom Madison, Riverkeeper on the New
River, which flows past Jacksonville into a large estuary that cuts through
Camp Lejeune before emptying into the Atlantic.

"Rick, we need you down here right away," he said. "There's been a massive lagoon spill on the New River, fifteen miles upstream. The sludge is now moving toward Jacksonville. They say a whole slew of fish are dying upriver already. When can you get here?"

Rick went outside, cranked the *Lonesome D* onto its trailer, loaded in his monitoring machines, and drove the eighty miles down to Onslow County. The spill was three days old by this point and DEM had said nothing, hoping the crisis would just go away, Rick reckoned.

He met Tom in Jacksonville, a town of twenty thousand people next to Camp Lejeune. They dropped the *Lonesome D* in the water and steered her upriver. As they cruised along, Tom explained the genesis of the spill. It had happened near the town of Richland, at a huge operation called Oceanview Farm. The Purina-run site had eleven barns housing one thousand animals apiece. One of the earthen berms of the eight-acre lagoon had given way, leaving a twenty-five-foot gash in the side. Within several chaotic minutes, twenty-five million gallons surged across roads, driveways, crops, wetlands, and woods, before draining into a New River tributary.

For more than a mile around the lagoon, surrounding property became a nightmarish moonscape of tobacco and soybeans painted black in a sticky, malodorous coating. On State Road 1235, motorists were forging a foot-deep river of brown water. Cleaning the shit from their undercarriages would be a nasty job. All around the accident, black, brackish pools of sludge had formed into mini–waste lagoons, each emitting a vomit-inducing stench. Much of the neighborhood was choking in a dank, heavy cloud of gases. Downstream, dead fish dangled from mucky bushes like devilish ornaments.

Nearby stood a sign: WELCOME TO RICHLAND—TOWN OF PERFECT WATER.

"They're calling it the worst manure spill in North Carolina history," Tom said.

Ironically, the state's biggest spill had happened at its first hog farm to meet new requirements for protecting waterways. "Way to go, boys," Rick said sarcastically.

Two miles north of Jacksonville, Rick took his first reading with the water probe. The oxygen level was at zero. "Damn," he muttered. "We're going to have a very long day here." Another mile upriver, the men began noticing streaks of discoloration flowing downstream—wide bands of foamy grayish-yellow, with flecks of maroon around the edges. By now, Rick knew what hog odor smelled like; this was hog odor. A few miles later, oxygen readings rebounded somewhat, suggesting the worst of it was behind them.

"This big old blob of crap is going to reach Jacksonville in a couple of hours," Rick said. "We need to alert the officials there." They spun around, throttled the *Lonesome D* to her max speed of 50 miles per hour, and headed south through the foamy water. Back in Jacksonville, on a warm Sunday afternoon, the riverfront was teeming with vacationers and U.S. Marine Corps families unaware of the incident. People were boating, waterskiing, and frolicking on Jet Skis in wide lazy circles. Rick could not believe his eyes. "It's been three days," he said, "why have no warnings been posted? Where the hell is our government?"

Rick reached for his cell phone and dialed the Onslow County health director. Nobody was there on a Sunday, so he left a message. He called Ron Levine, the state health director—same story. He even tried the local hospital, but they had no idea what to do. Ticked off, Rick asked Tom to help him hand-letter warning signs alerting people to the animal waste and dangerous pathogens in the water. They posted them on docks and bridges. They also opted for a more direct approach.

"Hog crap!" they cried to anyone in sight. "There's hog crap coming downstream! Bacteria! Viruses!" As it dawned on vacationers that something dreadful was heading their way, they quickly abandoned the water. Within an hour, the riverfront was deserted. Still disgusted by the nonaction of the "authorities," Rick pulled the boat onto its trailer and drove home.

The next day, he gave Ron Levine hell. "What is wrong with you folks?" he yelled. "I've been after your butts for months, begging you to come down and have a look at our rivers, our dead fish, and our sick people. But you did nothing, Dr. Levine. And now there are millions of gallons of hog crap floating past Jacksonville, and you do nothing to warn folks. You *are* the health director, *right*?"

To Rick's surprise, Levine apologized. He said he would get people on the matter right away. By noon that day, he promised, warning signs would be posted up and down the river. But by this time, the worst of the muck had moved past Jacksonville and toward the sea.

The same day, members of JoAnn Burkholder's lab arrived at the New River to begin testing water conditions for oxygen levels and high concentrations of nutrients like ammonia and phosphorus. They also tested for various harmful algal species, including the dreaded *Pfiesteria piscicida*. They were joined by a team from UNC Wilmington, headed by Michael Mallin, an associate professor in marine and estuarine ecology. Mike and JoAnn had collaborated on similar projects in the past. DEM also sent its agents to the site for water sampling. Meanwhile, state wildlife officials picked up dead fish by the bucketful.

JoAnn and Mike found extremely high levels of turbidity, ammonia, and phosphorus in the New River, and very low levels of oxygen. They tracked the swine wastes and associated fish kills for some twenty miles downstream from Oceanview. As the "nutrient plume" reached Jacksonville Harbor (where the current slows down considerably) the phytoplankton bloom reached concentrations of at least three hundred micrograms of chlorophyll per liter. Concentrations over forty micrograms indicate a "nuisance algal bloom."[5]

Downstream from Jacksonville, in the estuary, they found another algal bloom. This one contained *Phaeocystis globosa*, a harmful organism never before seen in these waters. The bloom also contained potentially toxic levels of *Pfiesteria*, which they estimated had killed ten thousand menhaden.

As for the spill itself, Oceanview officials blamed the foot of rain that had deluged the area. It had prevented operation of the sprayfields, and subsequently prohibited the draining of lagoon levels. But state officials had another explanation. Oceanview had installed a new drain pipe right through the berm, which may have weakened the structure.

Charles Carter, a partner in the firm that built the lagoon, told reporters: "Didn't nobody mean for it to happen. It just happened." Even so, an investigation was under way.[6]

The environmental mishap had lasting effects, ruining the Fourth of July weekend for Jacksonville, usually packed with revelers over the holiday. Media coverage only made things worse. "Right now people are at home reading about this spill," Mark Ivey of the Marina Café told *The News & Observer*.[7] "They're not coming down here to sit by a cesspool." In fact, the only real activity in town was from news teams—some from Europe and Asia—who descended on Jacksonville to cover North Carolina's largest hog spill. As Ivey spoke, a "stream of chocolate brown water" continued to flow down the river.

Upriver, things were no better. Researchers from North Carolina State, including JoAnn Burkholder, had sampled water several miles above Jacksonville and found ammonia levels twenty times over the lethal limit for most fish. In some places, fecal coliform bacteria were more than ten thousand times above the state standard for safe swimming. JoAnn told reporters that it might take years for the affected areas of the river to recover their populations of fish, clams, eels, crabs, and healthy riverbed animals. And every time it rained, pollution and pathogens such as *Giardia* and *Streptococcus* that had settled to the bottom could be churned up anew.

The Oceanview spill in the "Town of Perfect Waters" was not an isolated incident; it was in fact the first of several CAFO accidents in North Carolina that summer. A second lagoon breach—smaller and barely reported—occurred on a New River tributary in Sampson County on the same day as the Oceanview spill. Shortly after that, a third lagoon ruptured at a huge egg-laying operation in Duplin County, spilling nearly nine million gallons of chicken waste into Limestone Creek, a tributary of the Northeast Cape Fear River. State engineers from Wilmington said a ruptured storm-water pipe on one side of the lagoon may have allowed water to erode the earthen berm.

Two days later, most of the chicken waste flowed from the creek and into the river. Once again, Rick got a call about the spill and drove to Beulaville, about twenty miles northwest of Jacksonville. There he met up with JoAnn, Mike Mallin, and their teams. The river was too shallow and narrow to accommodate the boat, so they did their inspections from the banks. They found extremely low levels of dissolved oxygen—less than one-tenth the levels upstream from the spill—and a large fish kill in the creek and the river it fed.

Later that day, Rick happened upon a small recreational spot where a young family had stopped for a picnic. He saw the father and his young daughter splashing around just yards from a passing yellowish plume of foam. Rick shouted at them to get out immediately. The father looked terrified as he hustled his daughter to shore.

When Rick got home, he again called Dr. Levine and chastised him over the absence of any response from his health agency. "You did it again! How could you let this happen again?" Rick shouted. "You *know* there's been another animal-waste spill on the Northeast Cape Fear, and again you've done nothing. There are no signs posted anywhere down there. And now you got people swimming around in chicken poop."

North Carolina governor Jim Hunt may have been college buddies with Wendell Murphy, and a friend of the hog industry, but in the end, he was first and foremost a politician. Hunt knew that one lagoon spill could be written off as a tragic accident, and two could be considered a bizarre coincidence. But when the chicken lagoon blew, he knew he needed to speak out. "Three lagoons bursting in two weeks is three too many," Hunt said in a statement, even as poultry poop was oozing down the Northeast Cape Fear toward the city of Wilmington. "Our goal is to find and fix the next lagoon before it becomes an environmental problem. We can't wait for another multimillion-gallon spill."[8]

Hunt vowed to ramp up oversight of the hog and poultry industries, and ordered the DEM to transfer twenty inspectors to eastern North Carolina to collaborate with local officials and determine which lagoons were at the greatest risk for problems. Borrowing a page from the Neuse River Air Force, Hunt said regulators would take to the skies in small aircraft for aerial surveillance of the CAFOs and waterways.

"Environmentalists applauded the measures but questioned why it took three accidents and several weeks of steady rain for state officials to intensify their oversight of North Carolina's 4,000 livestock farms," *The News & Observer* reported. Bill Holman, a lobbyist for the Sierra Club, Conservation Council, and others, demanded a more powerful state response. "The solution has to be that large hog operations pay permit fees and face inspections just like every other industry," he said.[9]

Stung, Hunt wrote to key lawmakers urging an appropriation of $1.5 million for a permanent, statewide practice of inspecting and certifying manure management systems. "State environmental engineers tell me that at least one of the recent spills was the result of poor management and operation. It is vital to ensure that animal waste systems are operated as professionally as other wastewater systems," he wrote.

A few weeks later, the governor's office released initial data from the lagoon inspections. Agents found that nearly one-fourth of lagoons inspected so far were "dangerously full," and many had seepage at their base, a sign that some walls were weakening. Reports from 1,103 inspections had been returned. Of these, 393 lagoons exceeded their normal storage capacity. In some cases, record rainfall was to blame. But in many others, inspectors cited sloppy management practices.[10]

Meanwhile, the USDA's Natural Resources Conservation Service released another report, this one on the Oceanview spill. Though rainfall contributed to the disaster, incompetence and negligence by farm operators ultimately was to blame. Oceanview was supposed to have leveled 102 acres of timberland around the CAFO to plant enough crops to absorb the nutrients generated from ten thousand hogs. But they cleared only half that amount, creating a dangerous buildup of waste. "The failure would not have occurred if the lagoon had been maintained at proper levels," the federal report charged.[11]

This accident was only a foul omen of more to come. After reading the federal report, one state official commented glumly: "Oceanview isn't the only farm with these problems."

The summer of 1995 was not a good one for the Neuse River and the people who depended on it for a living. By mid-July, monumental fish kills had returned. Algal blooms, plus a streak of warm, wet, windless weather, had created another dead zone in the river. UNC scientists dubbed the Neuse "an absolute disaster" and described its bottom as a graveyard of dead fish, shrimp, and worms. Everything had suffocated.

Rick estimated that by the end of the month, half a million fish had come down with open bleeding lesions and died. *Pfiesteria* was back, so Rick called

JoAnn and asked her to investigate. She and several lab members, incidentally, had gotten severely ill a few years before while working with toxic cultures of *Pfiesteria*. The lab had been shut down and redesigned as a biohazard 3 containment system to protect the researchers from toxic aerosols emitted by the cultures, so that they could resume their work.

Over the summer, Rick received more reports of illnesses afflicting fishermen and other Neuse River people. More men were passing out in their boats and waking up lost and disoriented. Rick was appalled. Again he begged health department agents to come investigate.

This time, he got a call back from one of Ron Levine's deputies, Dr. Peter Morris. "Rick, we want to help," Morris said. "What I'd like is for you to give me the names of all the people on the river who you think might be affected."

Rick laughed. "Hell, Doc, I might as well send you the New Bern phone book!" he sarcastically joked. "But if you won't come see for yourself, I will send you the names starting with fishermen, marine construction workers, boaters, and water-skiers, as well as those reporters I am taking out on the water to see what you refuse to look at." Rick knew the cases well. There was Joseph Lopes, for example, a marine construction worker who, after working in the water, climbed out from the river in a daze to find open bleeding sores on his body. He was short of breath and then blacked out, before being rushed to the ER.

But Dr. Morris did not send anyone to investigate. "I think the health people are under orders to stay out of it," Rick told JoAnn. "Hunt's people don't want to admit that North Carolina has a health problem. They don't want to upset the hog industry, and they don't dare disrupt tourism. If people found out how sick this river is, they'd never come here."

Rick's own health was troubling. His memory was slipping, he felt fatigued but couldn't sleep, and he began developing migraines. They were the same symptoms that JoAnn and her team members had had when they'd been exposed in the lab. Eventually, Rick consulted his physician, who could offer little in terms of treatment.

In August, the seagulls arrived—by the hundreds of thousands, drawn by the presence of countless dead and dying fish in the Neuse. Rick had never seen so many birds in his life—"There were so many you dared not look up," he said—but even they were not enough to clean up the mess. Millions of fish had again piled up on shore. Normally the state would send inspectors to tally the kill, but the inspectors were too busy inspecting failing sewage plants and hog lagoons. The DEM asked the Neuse River Foundation if they could do the count. Rick agreed to carry out the grim task. On his first day out, he counted two hundred thousand dead fish in just one small area surveyed.

The pork industry in North Carolina was acutely aware of the potential backlash it faced among the public, the media, and even its powerful friends in the capital. It was time for some image burnishing. But those damn lagoons kept getting in the way.

"A week-old campaign to improve the swine industry's image hit a snag Friday when North Carolina investigators found evidence of violations in the worst possible place: a farm owned by the president of a national pork producers' group," *The News & Observer* reported in August. "It was a fresh tide of bad news for an industry that is still trying to recover from a string of lagoon breaks in June and July."[12]

The violations—illegal discharges into state waters—occurred at a facility in Edgecombe County owned by R. H. Mohesky, president of the National Pork Producers Council, which represented one hundred thousand growers nationwide. Investigators found that a pipe was draining waste directly from the lagoon into a nearby ditch that ran into a creek. Mohesky said the pipe was hidden by brush, and he had had no idea it was there. He vowed to have a contractor remove the pipe immediately. "There's nothing else I can do," he told reporters. "Obviously I have to be embarrassed that we're not doing the job we're supposed to do."

Rick laughed bitterly. You should be more than embarrassed, buddy, he thought; you should be in *jail*.

The spills just kept on coming. During August, DEM officials announced a "partial" lagoon collapse that spilled into a small creek in Duplin County. It occurred at Herschel Jenkins's Cypress Creek Farm, a Carroll's Foods, Inc., contractor with about one thousand hogs. The DEM said nearly one million gallons of waste had discharged into Back Swamp Creek, a tributary of the Northeast Cape Fear River.[13]

Then, at the end of August 1995, Rick heard from a Riverkeeper volunteer who had stumbled on a major disaster in Greene County, at a huge facility with twelve hog barns and three lagoons, all backing up to a large swamp. The volunteer noticed that the swamp was covered with red and yellow algae. When Rick arrived, he almost got sick, not just from the stench but from the devastation. Dead trees studded the swamp. Flies swarmed around in black squalls. Even worse, fetid water was draining into Middle Creek, whose banks were lined with dead trees. A tributary of Contentnea Creek, Middle Creek winds up in the Neuse.

This was not a one-time accident. It was deliberate pollution of the worst sort. But in the end, the farm received a DEM fine of just five thousand dollars.

Environmentalists were enraged by the relatively lenient penalty, given the chronic pollution discharged from the site.

Some of that anger was tempered soon after, when officials said they were slapping a considerably more stringent penalty on Oceanview Farms for its twenty-five-million-gallon lagoon spill into the New River in June. They fined Oceanview $110,000, including $6,200 for the fish kill, $92,000 in civil penalties, and $11,800 in enforcement costs. Eventually, the CAFO settled with the state and paid just $61,800 over five years. It was by far the biggest fine ever imposed on a North Carolina hog farm. The previous record was $10,000.[14]

"It is meant to put others on notice that if you do something like this, here's what you'll be up against," a DEM spokesperson said. Perhaps Raleigh was getting serious about cracking down on hog factories after all, Rick thought. There had now been at least seven significant CAFO violations in the past three months—six of them at hog factories. Rick and others could sense the tide turning. Sentiment against the porcine invasion, they thought, was finally reaching the highest halls of power.

Even Governor Hunt's administration was "daring to suggest that large hog farms aren't really farms, but industrial operations that should be regulated as such," *The News & Observer* reported. "A race is on to find alternatives to open-air lagoons for storing waste."[15] Rick was amazed. To think it all started back in June, when the manure siege of Jacksonville had become an "environmental Alamo."

North Carolina politicians knew they had a big problem; unhealthy locals are one matter, but allowing tourism dollars to dry up was electoral suicide. In early October, New Bern mayor Tom Bayliss organized a town hall meeting on what was ailing the Neuse.

It took place on a warm Tuesday evening in downtown New Bern, where four hundred people packed the high school auditorium. Mayor Bayliss, a plain-looking man in his forties with thinning dark-blond hair and a strong Southern lilt, opened the evening with a plea for civility among attendees, no matter how pissed off they were.

He would not get his wish.

Both Rick and JoAnn Burkholder sat on the panel, joined by Jonathan Howes, secretary of the North Carolina Department of Environment, Health, and Natural Resources (DEHNR, now known as DENR); Pete Petersen from the University of North Carolina at Chapel Hill's Institute of Marine Sciences; Dr. Greg Smith, a public health physician with DEHNR; and several fish and wildlife experts from the government. In the audience were then Democratic state senator Beverly Perdue, Republican state representative John Nichols, and then Craven County Commissioner Gary Bleau, who owned a hog operation with Nichols.

Mayor Bayliss invited Rick to kick off the discussion. "Over the past three years in my job on the river, there've been increasing signs that something's wrong in our waters," he began solemnly. "One is the vegetation, including algae. All different kinds are clogging up creeks. Meanwhile, we're seeing dead fish in ever-increasing numbers."[16]

"There is no doubt in my mind that our river is broken, and it's been broken for some time," Rick continued. Then, breaking the mayor's request for comity, he added, "There are people sitting up here at this table who are going to be speaking to you tonight who, in my opinion, are responsible for that river being broken. It's ours, and we need to get on with the job." The room erupted in applause.

But not everyone was clapping. Among the unsmiling bureaucrats on stage who visibly grimaced at Rick's aggressive populism was Dr. Greg Smith, the public health physician from DEHNR. Smith would later clash with JoAnn over her *Pfiesteria* findings and her conclusions about the potential for the microorganism to threaten human health.

"*Pfiesteria* is not the same in the river as it is in Dr. Burkholder's lab," Smith sniffed, without offering evidence to support his claim. "And besides, if we were to post health advisories on the Neuse because of algae, we would need to put warnings up on every creek in the state, because they also have algae, which sometimes cause health problems. We have to look at the other consequences. Economic costs. A man who wants to take folks on his boat, that's *income*. We must remember that before we go posting warnings."

The mayor asked the panel which of them believed nutrients were contributing to fish kills and excess vegetation. Everyone raised a hand. He then wanted to know the source of the nutrients: what percentage from municipal sewage, from farms, from lawn fertilizers.

No one could answer, though Rick offered an observation. "We've just lost four and a half million fish, and we now got grass growing out our ears," he said as the audience offered murmurs of support. "Wherever the nutrients are coming from, we already have too much!"

Mayor Bayliss attempted a comeback but fumbled nervously. He never fully recovered throughout the two-and-a-half-hour meeting. He said he wasn't sure that an increase in nutrients was to blame. The room filled with boos. "We think it *does*!" someone cried out. Louder boos, more derisive laughter. The mayor looked hurt.

"Well, folks," he said, trying to force a grin, "maybe there're more scientists here than I thought. Let me explain what I'm sayin'. Everybody here knows, and I believe, and we all believe, that it will have an effect, and it will have an effect that we don't like. But, but . . . do you understand what I'm saying?"

"No! No we don't!" came the cries. His Honor was beginning to cut a rather sad and hapless figure. This particular gathering was not going as he had hoped. "What we are trying to do," he stumbled on, "or, what I think should be done, is to figure out what the problem is, and do something about it!"

"We know what the problem is!" one man shouted. "What we came here tonight looking for are solutions!"

"Well, yes, we are looking for solutions," Bayliss pleaded. "And that is my point. We can't just throw our hands in the air, or dump money in the river."

The crowd grew silent after that rather incongruous statement, but Rick spoke up. "The mayor is right about *one* thing," he said, emphasizing the word "one" to great effect. "For us to fix the river, we've got to get the nitrogen levels in the waters down. But you are right, Mr. Mayor, it's not just the wastewater treatment plants. It's a cumulative thing. We get it from the hog farms, and from everywhere."

An elderly man in a tailored blue suit and striped tie rose to speak. He was Harold Hart, a retired navy captain, pilot, and member of the Neuse River Foundation and "Air Force." Hart lived on the river with his nine-year-old granddaughter. During the summer months, her swimming resulted in an outbreak of hives on her face, arms, and legs. "She looked like a hundred-year-old woman in just a couple of minutes in the river.

"Mr. Secretary, all parties seem to agree there is something going on in the waters of the Neuse River that may affect public safety," he said. "As a citizen, I feel as if I'm involved in a Kafkaesque tragedy. What I'm trying to obtain is a straight answer to a simple question: Can I safely swim, boat, fish, clam, and crab in front of my house on the river? All I want is a simple yes or no."

"No! *No!*" came shouts from the audience.

Bayliss hushed them and snapped at Hart. "Excuse me a second," he said. "Do you fertilize your lawn? I'm just tryin' to run a little survey in my mind, see where it's all comin' from." His query was met with silence. "Okay. Next one," His Honor commanded.

George Beckwith, a young fishing captain with a mop of auburn hair and boyish good looks, went next. He had obtained a degree in marine biology and earned his commercial captain license. "But right now, I am scared to death," he said. "And there are questions that I need answered, to know if I can continue to work. Because my conscience will not allow me to take people out on the water and take them fishing, when I am afraid to handle the fish, or eat the fish, or even be on the water. So answer my question: Is it safe for me to take people out this weekend and to catch fish and eat those fish? Answer that question!"

The mayor looked ashen. "Well, that's several questions, that . . . I don't . . . I don't have . . . ," he stuttered. "I don't know what the answer will be. It may be *stormin'*, it may be *rainin'*, there may be no *fish* in the river. Though my son caught a bass just the other day!"

A rash of boos broke out in the hall again. "Answer the question!" one man yelled. "It's the same question that you did not answer before. Can we go out and catch fish, or not?"

The mayor was marooned, clinging to his podium. He looked plaintively at the panel members. "Does somebody want to answer that question and then we will move on?" he asked. "I promise."

Dr. Smith tried to offer a statement, though it fell short of an actual answer. "We need to make sure that we don't turn *Pfiesteria* into hysteria," he said, to audible groans. "And I think that is where this discussion is going. Now, in 1989 I came down to this region because there were many fish kills along the coast. At that time, there was a condition on the fish termed ulcerative mycosis— a fungal disease, and it caused sores on the fish. And there were many of the same questions from the public along these lines, the same types that came forth with the recent hog waste spill in Onslow County on the New River.

"Nobody has all the answers to all these questions and I don't pretend to have all the answers," Smith added in a sudden outburst of candor. "Use common sense. If you see dead fish on the water, don't swim, don't wade, and I don't think you should fish in that water, personally. Should you eat fish with sores on them or caught in the area with dying fish? My recommendation to that is no."

JoAnn Burkholder shot right back at Smith. "The current kill is from *Pfiesteria*, not low-oxygen," she calmly stated. "And the sores on these fish were not caused by fungus. I don't think we should be expressing anything close to hysteria about *Pfiesteria*. But for about three years now, folks in this county have expressed concern, not alarm but concern. And those concerns need to start being addressed in a very sound and rigorous manner."

Then Rick jumped in. "The problem is, none of these folks from the health department had come down here," he said, directing a question at Dr. Smith. "May I ask you, sir, have you been here over the last three weeks while 4.5 million fish died, while people have been on the piers fishing and catching fish and taking them home? Have you spoken to any doctors in New Bern?"

"No," Smith replied, somewhat defensively. "I haven't been here. We only have two physicians in my area of expertise for the whole state. This fish kill is important, but we have a priority list."

The next questioner was Bill Harper, from Onslow County. Harper had clearly practiced the art of political theatrics. He strutted around in front of the stage like a preacher, growling in a deep Southern voice as he lectured the panelists. "Folks, everybody knows that a hog produces more good stuff than seven, eight, nine times a human," he began softly. "Now, me and my honey-pooh can't get a permit to put a septic tank down by our trailer. But our government will let you build a hog farm right on the edge of the riverbank." He allowed a long pause for effect. "*Why* can they do that, but I can't put a tank down?"

Dr. Smith took the question, but may have regretted his words even as they passed over his lips. "One reason," he suggested, "is because hog waste doesn't contain HIV, and it doesn't contain the hepatitis virus."

Smith did not mean to imply that Bill Harper was a vector of infectious disease, but that's how the crowd took it. They erupted in protest. Harper ignored the gaffe and pressed on. "All of our elected officials, almost, are in the hog business, chicken business, turkey business. Hell, even old Hunt is in the beef business. And they're not gonna let environmentalists speak up." Harper's voice started to rise. "It wasn't until people started speakin' and hollerin' and screamin' that we only had one part-time hog inspector for four thousand hog farms that the state did anything at all." The room fell silent. Harper was good.

"It's my government's fault," he finally announced with a bellow, prompting fits of applause again. "It comes from the commissioners who are in the hog business, from our state legislators who are in the hog business. Why, it even comes from my senator, Mr. Faircloth, who's in the hog business," he roared. Some shouted, "Amen!"

The night was dragging on and many were unhappy. Mary Ann Harrison, president and a director of the Neuse River Foundation, rose to voice the general unhappiness in the room. "I think we're entitled to some specifics," she declared. "I talked to several people who left because they were, quote, 'disgusted' because there was nothing specific being proposed tonight, just a lot of talk. So I'm asking you for some specifics, and some action. You all have been skirting the issue of health, and I know lots of people who've gone into that river and come out sick as dogs, with sores over their body, like the fish. Are you all going to wait until people get sicker and drop dead of this before the health issue is raised to where it should be? What do we tell people who are afraid to let their kids swim in the river?"

Mary Ann Harrison was right—the night was long on chatter and short on deeds. It was time to leave, Rick thought. No one was getting anywhere.

On the drive home, Rick tried to imagine what the mayor had expected from this meeting. Had he wanted to quell the issue—or just quell the conflict?

Bayliss had not impressed many that evening. Nicole Brodeur, of *The News & Observer*, reserved particular disdain for his inability to grasp the severity of the river pollution problem. "The whole thing reminds me of the movie *Jaws*," she wrote. "The good tourists of Amity were getting munched left and right by a great white shark. But Amity's cheesy chump of a mayor refused to close the beaches or warn people of the danger they faced. He just couldn't lose sight of the almighty dollar. Citizens' health remains at risk while officials hem and haw."[17]

Weeks later, Rick was thrilled when Bayliss became a leading voice for environmental reform, and heartily supported Rick and JoAnn's work. Looking back, Rick realizes the meeting opened the mayor's eyes. If the meeting had done nothing else, it had accomplished that first huge step.

On the day after the heated showdown in New Bern, Rick took Secretary Jonathan Howes out for a tour of the Neuse.

It was a rainy morning, and an eerie fog covered the river. Howes arrived with his staffers at the New Bern dock where the foundation's boat, *Saint Mariana*, was moored and ready for launch.

As Rick extended his hand to greet the secretary, Howes asked, "Rick, what's that smell?"

"You'll see, just follow me," Rick answered. As they boarded the boat, rotting dead fish clustered along its hull. The dead fish were everywhere along the shoreline as well. There was no need to say anything. Howes's watery eyes and stinging nose answered his own question. Rick could tell by his expression that it sickened him.[18]

About time, Rick thought. As he skippered the boat out into the river, they quickly disappeared into the fog. Rick only needed to run the boat a short distance to get to the middle of the river. But he would have to rely on his compass. Soon he cut the engines and a deadly silence settled in. The boat drifted for what seemed like hours. It shortly came to a spot where the fog lifted enough to allow everyone to see the water. Fish were dead and dying in every direction. They could see them by the thousands. Many of the fish were spinning out of control in a death spiral well known to Rick—a result of *Pfiesteria* attacks. They were covered with bleeding lesions, some with holes right through their bodies.

Howes had seen enough. "Take me to shore. Take me to your office," he insisted between gasps. Back at the foundation office, Howes made several calls: One was to the governor. "The river is broken and it has to be fixed," he said. To Rick, it was a most profound statement—and it changed the state's mission from river protection to river restoration. Rick smiled. The river had finally gotten to speak for itself. It had been a hell of a good couple of days.

Rick was thrilled; he had actually gotten two high-ranking officials, the mayor and the secretary, to back his cause. Help was on its way. "It's a new day in North Carolina," he said to colleagues. And unlike the wishful thinking engendered by the newspaper series, this incident achieved results. Rick remembers it as the morning that changed everything.

Two days later, officials issued "unprecedented" state health warnings for the lower river.[19] People were advised against swimming, fishing, or coming into contact with any waters where *Pfiesteria* had been attacking fish over the past three weeks. Levine said scientists were still uncertain about health effects associated with *Pfiesteria*, but he issued a written statement saying "we want to err on the conservative side." Among the precautions (quoted verbatim) were:

- Do not consume any part of a fish with sores or other indication of disease. Do not collect dead or dying fish.
- Do not swim in water proximate to a fish kill. This applies to recreational activities that would involve skin contact with the water.
- People whose work requires water contact should postpone such work in the event of an ongoing fish kill. If contact cannot be postponed, protective gear should be used to reduce water contact.
- Items that have been immersed in the waters of a fish kill should be handled with gloves or other protective gear.
- A person who falls into the water at a fish kill site should wash the exposed areas with soap and clean water.

Some environmentalists were pleased with the action, but it left Rick short of impressed. "It's not like the state was hit blind with these fish kills; they could have responded a lot more quickly than they did," he told reporters. Ironically, the very people meant to be protected by the move—fishermen—were complaining bitterly. They were just starting to set gill nets for flounder and other market fish when the new rules were established. The state had overreacted, they said. It would damage their livelihood.

But their protests went unheard. Within a week, the North Carolina Marine Fisheries Commission decided to completely close down a ten-mile stretch of the river to all commercial and recreational fishing. Rick saw state patrol boats on the river, enforcing the ban and warning people away. There were even signs posted: IF YOU SEE DEAD OR DYING FISH, STAY OUT OF WATER.

The ban would not be lifted until late November, after the local fishing industry had suffered hundreds of thousands of dollars in lost revenue.[20] But the state was finally paying attention. Government dollars would soon pour into river research. Scientists across the globe would find their way to North Carolina, and so would the national media.

They all wanted to interview the Neuse Riverkeeper. Finally, the word was getting out.

During the fall of 1997, Bill Bean helped the Community Association for Restoration of the Environment craft a mission statement, form a board of directors, and establish itself as a nonprofit group. But the next step was more difficult: to raise funds to help start a Clean Water Act citizens' lawsuit against the most polluting dairies in the valley. Bill scheduled meetings with funders in Seattle, and briefed Helen Reddout, Mary Lynne Bos, and Shari Conant—a new member whose role in CARE was growing—on talking points.

At the Seattle meetings, Bill would make the opening pitch on ecological havoc in the valley. This part always amused Helen. "It's like we're part of the Christian Orphan Foundation, or something," she chuckled. Next, Helen would give her own presentation using an overhead projector, just like any good junior high teacher. She showed transparencies of cows wading through waste, of liquid manure running into ditches, of sprayfields where wastewater pooled on the ground and ran into streams.

Despite their best efforts, only one charity donated five thousand dollars in seed money. CARE would split it with Bill's group.

But nobody was giving up their fight yet. The group voted to divide the valley into "surveillance units," and appoint one member to each. Their mission: to observe, detect, and document any environmental infractions they saw. They agreed on the official-sounding name of Yakima Valley Dairy Watch.

The new group soon had its opponents. One day Helen was out and about, alone, taking pictures near a dairy, when she noticed a farmwife approaching quickly—and carrying a baseball bat. "Crap!" Helen cried before jumping into her white pickup.

At the next meeting, it was decided that Dairy Watch members would always go out in pairs.

"This is scary," Helen said. "You know, Bill Bean and Mike Tedin can come and go from this valley whenever they like. But not us. We don't have that option. This is our valley, and the dairymen are trying to destroy it."

A week later, the environmental lawyer Charlie Tebbutt arrived at a specially arranged meeting in Outlook, joined by Bill Bean. It was a hot September night, and Charlie's first meeting with the CARE group marked a rocky beginning. He walked into the room in a pair of faded blue jeans, a well-worn button-down shirt, and an Australian outback hat. A bushy red beard hid much of his face.

He looked like Yosemite Sam, come to save the day.

The farmers, dressed in their Carhartt shirts and Timberland boots, exchanged looks but remained silent. Charlie removed his sandals and stood barefoot. With one final flourish, he removed his hat, and the mane of long reddish-brown hair tumbled down to his shoulders.

"Oh brother, get a load of *this* one," Helen whispered to Mary Lynne. "I was expecting a lawyer in pinstripes. And what do we get? A hippie."

"He's scary," Mary Lynne said.

Charlie either didn't notice their conversation or pretended not to. He began his usual spiel for prospective clients. That included the occasionally awkward part about legal fees. "The Western Environmental Law Center is a not-for-profit operation, and we generally don't have funds to finance lawsuits. Of course, we will work in partnership with you, to try to raise some of the costs," he said.

A roomful of farmers' jaws dropped. Bill had neglected to tell Charlie that the CARE people were expecting his law firm to cover the costs.

"And just how much would those *costs* be?" Helen spoke up.

"About ten thousand dollars to get started," Charlie said without blinking.

"*No*, this was not what we were told," Helen said. This is nothing but a bait-and-switch shell game, she thought, embarrassed that she had misled the group. She stood up. "Now just stop right there! Ten thousand dollars? We don't have that kind of money, Mr. Tebbutt."

Charlie shuffled his bare feet uncomfortably as Helen pressed on. "I just retired, and I have no intention of spending my golden years having bake sales to raise ten thousand dollars."

Charlie looked perplexed but attempted to make peace. "Maybe we can work something out?" he offered. "I was under the impression you were willing to cover the legal fees."

"Well," Helen fumed, "until this gets straightened out, we're done here. And if it *does* get settled, then whatever agreement we reach, I want it documented because we can't afford anything close to ten thousand dollars. We're farmers. We can't tie up our revenue to file a lawsuit. Especially when these agencies should be taking care of this mess themselves!"

The room burst into applause. Helen had inadvertently become CARE's de facto leader. Later, her colleagues designated her "legal liaison" to the unusual Mr. Tebbutt. "Do I really have to do this?" she asked at the time. "I've got enough troubles in my life and I don't need to have that little banty rooster running around causing me problems."

Charlie felt pretty much the same. He left Outlook a tad shell-shocked—an uncommon emotion for him. It was a long drive back to Seattle-Tacoma Airport. Charlie wondered about dealing with the irascible Helen Reddout.

"That woman, the cherry farmer," Charlie said. "She's trouble."

A few weeks later, Charlie mapped out the financial plan: The Western Environmental Law Center would cover all expenses for the litigation, which they would recoup after they won. CARE would be responsible solely for filing fees, costing perhaps a few hundred dollars.

Helen reviewed the contract and called Charlie. "It looks good," she said. "We'll do it."

CARE had to decide who they were going to sue, and for *what*. "What goals can we establish that are achievable and realistic?" Charlie asked during another journey up to the Yakima Valley to meet with the group.

"We want this place cleaned up, we want the pollution to stop," Helen said.

"I want the smell to stop," Marcella added. "And I don't want our well water getting contaminated."

"And the *roads*, they're a mess," Mary Lynne said. Trucks delivering grain and hauling out milk were tearing up roads, and the county was not fixing them. And liquid manure spilled on the highways was a driving hazard. A few months earlier, several children were injured when their school bus skidded on a patch of goo.

Charlie listened and then explained that the best chance for victory was through the federal Clean Water Act (CWA). "It's the least complicated and least challenging way," he explained. The act, passed by Congress in 1972, prohibits industries from discharging pollutants into surface water without obtaining a permit. Most industries treat waste before discharging it—CAFOs do not. Under the CWA, CAFOs must comply with a standard of zero discharge; anything else is a violation, carrying civil or criminal penalties and possible jail time.

Following a review of the DOE records, several prospective defendants emerged among the valley's most problematic dairymen. CARE eventually selected ten dairies they considered the worst offenders: Cow Palace, Viewpoint, Liberty, Henry Bosma, DeRuyter Brothers, John Bosma, S&S DeRuyter, George DeRuyter and Sons, Sid Koopmans, and Sunnyveld.

The next step was to start the proceedings for a "citizens' suit" against them. The CWA requires that letters of intent be sent at least sixty days before filing suit, and CARE mailed theirs on October 31, 1997.

News of the potential suits swept across the valley like an autumn wind, appearing in many local papers, and even online at Environmental News Network (ENN). "Yakima Valley residents, frustrated after years of being ignored in attempts to clean up their water, sent notices to bring civil complaints against 10 factory dairies," ENN reported.[1]

"We've been trying to get the state and the county to do something about these milk factories that have invaded our community," Marcella told ENN. "They've driven people from their homes, polluted air and water. We're ready to do whatever we can to stop it." Yakima Valley's cow population was nearing one hundred thousand, she added, creating as much waste as a city of 2.5 million people

Meanwhile, the Sunnyside *Daily Sun News* profiled Marcella and CARE in a story headlined IS THE WATER SAFE? Marcella had tested her well water and found it was contaminated with nitrates. A large front-page photo showed her standing in front of cattle pens and holding aloft a tainted glass of H_2O.[2]

Local officials took at least some of the blame for the problems. "We admit our dairy waste management program is lacking. It's in need of repair and improvement," said one Department of Ecology employee. Understaffing was a huge problem; his office employed just three part-time dairy waste inspectors to cover all of central Washington.

The dairymen were less deferential. "I don't really know what the Clean Water Act is and I'd rather not talk about it," Jake DeRuyter told reporters. "This came as a surprise."[3]

Then the pushback started getting personal. Mary Lynne Bos received a letter from "a fellow farmwife" written in neatly formed cursive on unlined paper. She warned Mary Lynne that CARE's alliance with the Columbia Basin Institute was an attack on "our fellow farmers, the dairymen. You, a farmwife yourself, should know how hard they work, as your husband does." She said the suit was motivated by CBI greed and accused Mary Lynne of "being used as a pawn to get in the dairymen's pockets." She beseeched her to "stop this farce now!" and signed the letter, "A concerned farm wife!!"

Meanwhile, CARE's newest member, Shari Conant, and her husband, Ty

Kamphuis, operated several orchards along the Roza Canal near Grandview. Shari was thirtysomething with brunette hair and a winning smile. A private detective and bookkeeper in previous careers, she would be a great asset to the group.

Shari was inadvertently drawn to the cause by some of the local dairymen themselves. One evening she and Ty were eating at Snipes Mountain Brewery and Restaurant, a local pub popular among dairy operators. A ball game was on the bar TV, and the men were talking loudly over it. Shari subtly took notice of the conversation.

"People were running around whispering and excited about something," she later told Marcella. A man at the next table said he'd received one of the letters of intent from CARE. He dismissed the tactic, saying, "As long as you clean things up within the next sixty days, then you won't have any problem." The next day, Shari saw the newspaper story of Marcella and her glass of water, "and it really made me angry," she said, "especially after hearing their cavalier attitude about it. It was like they felt they were above the law."[4]

Yakima Valley was rumbling over the impending dairy wars, and CARE members were beginning to feel the heat from neighbors who blamed them for threatening their livelihood. Stray comments at Safeway told the story; people were accusing CARE of seeking to line their pockets with lawsuit dollars, at the expense of the economic health of the valley. It was the same argument used in the anonymous housewife letter.

But CARE members had no intention of pocketing any court award they might get. Award money would eventually be directed to well-water testing in the valley. "I'd be glad if we didn't have to sue at all," Helen told Don. "I'd be glad if they just cleaned up and we could all move on."

Hostility toward CARE members and their intent to sue was growing, and Bill Bean felt it was time to address it. He suggested a town hall meeting to separate rumor from fact—and from hurt feelings. Perhaps an agreement between CARE and the dairies could be reached, he said, thus avoiding court. Helen agreed. "We're all farmers; we can fix this together," she said.

Everyone supported the meeting—except for Charlie Tebbutt. He worried that CARE would be overwhelmed by pissed-off dairymen backed by the powerful Washington State Dairy Federation. He forsaw intimidation and threats: legal, social, even physical.

But CARE wanted the meeting. Marcella reserved the Outlook Grange Hall, which had been a local center for farm meetings and policy debates since 1908. Debbie Becker of the Washington State Dairy Federation called Bill Bean and asked to be invited. "Why, that's just wonderful!" Helen said to Bill. "She wants to be part of the solution as well!"

On November 16, Helen and Mary Lynne arrived an hour early at Grange Hall, planning to set up the room. But the place was already crawling with people—virtually all of them dairy industry supporters. It was an ambush: The Dairy Federation had taken CARE's invitation to heart, and brought in scores of dairy families. The well-rehearsed crowd recognized the CARE women and shouted, "Save the small farm! Save the small farm!"

"Tell me again," Mary Lynne said sheepishly, "why I thought this was a good idea?"

"A *darned* good idea," Helen replied in a dry whisper. "You said it was darned good."

TV crews from three stations buzzed around, gathering images. Rob Taylor from the *Post-Intelligencer* had come in from Seattle. Dairy Federation men and women dominated the room, wearing big yellow buttons that read DAIRY DOLLARS SUPPORT THE COMMUNITY, or carrying placards claiming ENVIRON-MENTALISTS ARE DESTROYING THE SMALL FARM.

Only five CARE supporters were able to make their way in before the crowd limit was reached. Marcella, dressed in a red wool suit and bookish glasses, arrived just in time. She braved the unfriendly crowd and made her way up to the little stage, where she gamely tried to welcome the scowling dairy farmers to the meeting.

Many booed as she walked to the stage. Others called out "AY-AY-AY!" to mock her Latina heritage. Mary Lynne sat in the audience, shell-shocked and shivering, desperately wanting to crawl under a chair. Helen, by this time, had slipped quietly to the back. She was sickened to hear what some of the men were shouting.

"Hey, lady, go back to where you belong! Go back to May-HEE-co!" said one.

"You know what? We oughta bring our manure guns down here and turn 'em loose on *her*!" another shouted.

Marcella pushed ahead, undaunted. "We deserve the right to have the use and enjoyment of our own properties," she began. "We have a right *not* to get sick from the smell of your animals, and we have the right *not* to see our wells poisoned by feces."[5]

Boos and hisses spread through the room. A sturdy middle-aged woman rose to her feet shouting, "Well, *we* have a right to survive!" Supporters cheered her. "These days, our farms need to get bigger just to survive. Do you have any idea what falling milk prices are doing to us?"

Marcella, caught unaware, shook her head no.

"Do you even *care*?" the woman cried. "Don't you realize that you need more cows, or else you go out of business? Is that what you want to happen to us?"

Another man two rows behind jumped up. "You want us to control our manure, but those pollution measures are very expensive," he pleaded. "There's just no way we can pay for them. We're going broke as it is, just like the lady said."

"That's right!" another woman said. "Dairy size is a free choice! There's no right or wrong to it." Mary Lynne gestured to catch Helen's attention, as if to say, "How soon can we get out of here?"

Marcella took a deep breath, tried to smile, and continued. "Look," she said softly. "If you don't stop polluting, you'll force yourselves out of business. It's against federal law. This is very serious." She went on to describe how state agencies had spent years ignoring complaints about odors, flies, polluted water, and roadways covered in animal waste. "We would never have taken this issue so far if the dairy families had been willing to discuss our concerns, and work out a compromise. But when that failed, what other option did we have?"

One of the women spoke up again: "Well then, Mrs. Garza, why can't we just settle our gripes *without* resorting to litigation? Drop the lawyers and we'll talk."

"We want to work with you. This problem *can* be solved," Marcella answered. "So yes, maybe we can settle this . . . um, without litigation."

Mary Lynne looked at Helen with a look that said, "What the hell is she talking about?"

Helen shot back a look that said, "Over my dead body will we drop the lawyers."

When Bill Bean's turn came, the animosity made Marcella's reception seem downright cordial. "These are not farms, these are huge factory operations, and they are polluting the water," he began.

A man raised his hand. Bill nodded at him. "Sir, we feel you are just a bunch of legal extortionists," the man said. "You just want to drive us dairymen out of business."

"That's right!" another woman chimed in. "We don't need lawyers from Portland telling us how to run our farms!"

Bill continued, explaining how the valley's dairy herd had grown to more than seventy thousand in the past decade. The result was "measurable increases in water pollution" including nitrates and fecal coliform, he said. Since 1988, coliform levels had tripled at the mouth of the Granger Drain. Bill said more large dairies would worsen the situation, but insisted he fully supported smaller farmers. "Big agribusiness is driving out the small-family dairy," he declared over booing. "And this country has done nothing to protect small farmers from market forces."

When Debbie Becker, director of the Dairy Federation, rose to speak, she was bathed in warm applause. She discussed the plight of small farmers amid falling milk prices. Then she addressed the CARE campaign. She spoke with heartfelt sympathy about "tough times" facing many dairies. Conflict wasn't going to help anyone. "This has turned your area upside down," she said. "It has pitted neighbor against neighbor and cast a blanket of fear across this valley. As a community, it would be far more productive to resolve this issue without listening to these out-of-towners promoting their own agenda." Supporters whooped themselves hoarse.

The Grange meeting ended with a whimper, not a bang. Helen felt beaten and frightened. When it was over, Helen ran to her car, locked the door, and got the hell out of there, taking a circuitous route to elude any hotheaded farmers. She did not relax until she was in Don's arms. "If this case goes to trial," she told him, "and we're not beaten to death on some lonely highway, then we're going to win."

The meeting was widely reported in the media. Rob Taylor wrote: "Fear and anger were palpable Thursday night, when hundreds of farmers and their supporters packed the Outlook Grange." Inside, "The crowd bristled with hostility for the outsider they blamed for this conflict: Bill Bean—who had set up the meeting to explain the litigation threat and recruit more dairy critics."

Dairymen refused to speak to the press "for fear of being singled out for litigation," Taylor wrote. "They're scared to death," Debbie Becker told the paper. "People are wondering, 'Am I next? Is my neighbor going to do this to me?'" She added that three-quarters of valley dairies had "best-practice" manure plans in place or in development.

"The attack over environmental concerns is the most aggressive yet against the Washington dairy industry," Taylor wrote, "and it signals the increasing scrutiny operators could face as dairy farms become larger and larger in order to compete."

If successful, the lawsuits could cost the dairies upwards of $1.6 million.

Marcella Garza had hoped to meet with the dairymen and discuss an out-of-court settlement, but she was at odds with her comrades: Most of CARE had already decided on legal action as the best route, and they were ready to file suit on December 4. Charlie Tebbutt caught a flight from Eugene and arrived at the Conants' forty-acre farm in the early evening. When he arrived, Marcella, Helen, Shari, and Mary Lynne were sitting around the kitchen table, enjoying cookies and homemade cider.

For Charlie, here was a perfect chance to sit down and work out any re-sidual mistrust with the group's core members "Tell me," he said, "what are you demanding? What exactly is it that you *want*?"

The women collaborated on a list. It included a strict policy of no dis-charge for all CAFOs; a requirement to obtain all proper permits; the inclusion of setbacks from canals, roads, ditches, and neighbors' homes; a ban on spray-ing near waterways; safe road conditions; monitoring of surface water up-stream and downstream of dairies; tree buffers around pens and lagoons to block odor; best-management practices to stop pollution; fly control; air-quality control; and odor control.

Now that the group had its demands, who would be first to receive them? Charlie became convinced that the first defendant should be Hank Bosma, who owned Henry Bosma Dairy and Liberty Dairy, both in the Lower Valley. It was a shrewd choice: Bosma had a well-documented history of violations in Washington State, Charlie explained, with an ecological rap sheet that dated back to the 1970s. All Department of Ecology communiqués with Bosma, most citing overapplication of manure and runoff into waterways, had been flatly ignored.

Born in Holland, Hank Bosma moved with his family to America in the 1950s. His father bought a dairy in Southern California, while Hank opted for an accounting career. But after seeing colleagues develop ulcers at work, he decided to return to the family business. In 1972, Hank moved to the Yakima Valley and started a dairy with twenty-three cows. About a year later, he pur-chased his current land at a discount from a bank that was anxious to unload it. Gradually, his herd increased, from about 120 when he moved to the new site, to the adjoining 5,000-head operation he was running by 1997.

Charlie cautioned the women of CARE about their quarry—and his allies. "I've worked with citizens taking on big industry before, and the MO of the other side is always the same: Divide and conquer," he cautioned. "We've seen that the Dairy Federation is already mobilizing against us." He looked at Mar-cella as he said this.

On the bright side, CARE had already made an impact. Charlie learned that many local dairies, not just defendants, were already building up berms to protect streams and constructing better lagoons. A DOE agent affirmed that valley dairies had achieved more cleanup in the month after CARE threatened lawsuits than in the previous ten years.

Meanwhile, the Washington State Dairy Federation called for a meeting with the DOE; they were begging the state to intervene, and fine them.

"Our letters have stirred up quite a hornet's nest," Charlie reported. "Within a week of their delivery, the Dairy Federation wanted to discuss ways to preempt our enforcement actions with DOE." This was something the group had worried about: The CWA prohibits any legal action for sixty days after notice, in order to give authorities time to intervene. In past cases, officials would hit the offender with relatively modest fines, thus freeing the farmers from costly and distracting litigation in federal court.

But DOE agent Bob Barwin, who accepted a lunch invitation to hear the Dairy Federation's plea, had a speedy reply. "Sorry, not going to do it," Barwin told them. "We at DOE made a choice, going back to 1994 or 1995, to allocate our enforcement resources according to our priorities, and not to intervene in citizen suits."[6]

Charlie had a good chuckle over that one. "In this case, government inaction was a beautiful thing." He smiled. "They chose *not* to enforce the law—especially since they never did anything in the first place—so that we could exercise our rights without hindrance. Thank you, State of Washington."

A few days later the Washington State Dairy Federation offered its backing for a new bill in Olympia calling for increased scrutiny of its own industry. If it passed, every dairy would have to implement a formal manure management plan that would be enforced by regular state inspections. (At the time, 58 percent of the dairies had no waste plan at all, and just 13 percent had carried out the requirements of their plan.)[7]

Debbie Becker said she vowed to give the legislation "everything we've got," as she told *The Seattle Times*. "We as an industry don't want a repeat of what's happening in the Yakima Valley."[8]

Helen smiled when she read that. Clearly, CARE's saber rattling about a lawsuit had suddenly made dairy reform a very high-profile issue.

Marcella Garza still had not abandoned her desire to settle with the dairies. An arbitration session was held in December 1997 in which she convinced her CARE comrades, against Tebbutt's strong recommendations, to meet with the ten dairymen. But mediation went nowhere.

Henry Bosma appeared at Marcella's house with a message: Drop the litigation or face legal retaliation. He was going to sue them for suing him. Soon after, Marcella Garza resigned from CARE and removed her name from the lawsuit.

Bosma continued his litigation threats. On December 20, a chilly afternoon, he showed up at the door of the Conant home. Shari and Ty were enjoying a cozy holiday fire, but this was no friendly Yuletide visit. After he left, Shari faxed a note to Charlie.

"Hank Bosma arrived at my home unannounced or uninvited," she wrote. She said that Bosma had just come from a meeting with Marcella, who sent him to see Shari about trying to reach an agreement to head off a lawsuit. "He said he had done $150,000 worth of property improvements and invited me and my husband, Ty, to tour his facility. I declined," Shari said. "I explained I was in no position to negotiate on behalf of CARE and invited him to contact you. He said you would not talk to him and he hoped I would be the 'voice of reason' and settle this thing between the two of us."

Shari wrote that Bosma had claimed that the CBI and Charlie's law firm were just "using" Shari and had no interest in stopping pollution. "When his angry rantings provoked no response from me, he said, 'You are aware that we will be starting an investigation on you personally and that we will be filing a lawsuit against you in response to your activity with CARE,'" she said. Shari told Bosma he was free to do as he pleased and, after that, "he left in anger."[9]

By this point, the dairymen's harassment and threats of a countersuit had persuaded four of the nine board members to resign. Shari confessed to Charlie that a countersuit would force her resignation as well.

And then things started getting creepy.

The day after Bosma's visit, an envelope appeared in the Conants' mailbox, postmarked from eastern Washington. It wasn't a letter, but rather a piece of paper with cut-and-pasted words and definitions taken from a dictionary. Its random pattern suggested a ransom note. Among the unsettling words pasted onto the paper were: "stalk," "fraud," "frivolous," "orchard," "investigation," "charge," and "stop." A few days later, Mary Lynne received a similar mailing.[10]

Helen and the Reddout family were away for the Christmas holidays at their seashore retreat on Copalis Beach. Helen was happily out of the loop. But her time was coming.

When Helen returned from vacation in January, she received a worried call from Shari about Bosma's harassment. After the Conants, he visited the Bos home, Shari said. "He told Mary Lynne she could, you know, 'get into a situation,' and they could lose their farm. But she kind of blew him off. He's trying to get all of us to ditch the lawyers and drop the suit. But I said, 'Hank, why would we want to do that?' He didn't have an answer. He just walked away in a huff," Shari said.

"Well, he hasn't been over to my house."

"Don't worry, Helen. He will be. He said so."

Helen hung up and quickly developed an acute case of the willies. She was alone in the house; Don was over in the orchards. Suddenly, she remembered a pamphlet she had picked up during a visit to Seattle. It was called *When Activists Are Harassed.*

When expecting "unpleasant or threatening company," the brochure said, the most important thing was to set up a hidden video camera and make a tape of the occurrence. Well, that's not going to work, Helen thought. That's a little too James Bond-y for me. However, the brochure explained that an audiotape would suffice. Don owned a small tape recorder that he kept at the office. Helen called Don, explained the situation, and asked him to bring the tape recorder home with him.

But then Helen considered a way to deter Bosma. She really didn't want to do a face-to-face with him. She went to her computer and typed up a sign in bold letters: THE PEOPLE IN THIS HOUSEHOLD RESERVE THE RIGHT TO TAPE ANY CONVERSATION. She signed her name and popped the sign into a simple wooden frame and hung it on the door. That should cool him down a bit, she thought as she sat and waited.

Eventually, a man appeared at the picture windows of the glassed-in porch. Helen took a deep breath, switched on the recorder, and went outside to greet her visitor. Henry Bosma was unsmiling but introduced himself politely and asked Helen if he could come in.

"Of course," Helen replied cordially. She smiled as he removed his boots before entering. Don doesn't even do that! she thought. Maybe Bosma's not so bad after all.

Bosma followed her into the family room. As he sat on the sofa, Helen's heart was racing. Had he seen the sign outside? Would he notice the tape recorder? It didn't seem like it. Bosma launched into a prepared speech:

"If my lawyer knew I was here talking with you I would get into a lot of trouble," he began. "But I thought that we neighbors should be able to talk, and settle their problems."[11]

Helen merely sat with a gentle smile on her face, which seemed to unnerve Bosma.

He continued. "I understand you guys want to sue us, and I really don't know why," Hank said. He admitted having violations in the past—a confession that was immediately committed to Helen's tape recorder. But he was committed to complying with the DOE. In fact, Bosma had spent a hundred grand in improvements—even before talk of a CARE lawsuit. He produced a large manila envelope. The documents inside listed the specifics of his advanced waste-management plan.

"Now, I don't feel that I need to do this, but I want you to have information before you get into whatever you're trying to get into," Hank said. And he challenged the information CARE had collected on his dairy. Then he looked her in the eyes and asked, "Why do you really want to do this, Helen? What do you hope to accomplish?"

Helen didn't pause for a second. "I hope to get the water cleaned up," she told him flatly. "I hope to get the smell cleaned up. I've lived in this house for twenty-two years and we've always had dairies around us. And I was raised on a dairy farm, so I'm not an antidairy person. But I am an antifilth person. And what we are dealing with here are factories. These factories are abusing the regulations—"

Hank scowled. "Well, you know, I don't know about regulations," he said.

Aha! Helen thought with delight. Another incriminating remark caught on tape.

Hank insisted that most Washington dairies try to comply with state and federal laws. Helen looked at her guest askance. Was he kidding? Instances of runoff, he continued, were inevitable in such hilly country.

"We're talking about sewage running down the road," Helen replied. "We're talking about the fact that the Conservation Service says you are not supposed to be spraying this fermented manure in those big guns on the frozen fields. Yet all around me, anyplace I want to go in any direction, I find farmers doing just that."

When Helen asked why Bosma couldn't follow the model of organic farms, which were cleaner than factory farms, he scoffed. "Those types of dairies, with forty or fifty cows, are going out of business! They can't make it! That's an era that has come and gone."

Helen was losing patience. "You know, Hank, if you want to run your five-thousand-cow dairy, fine," she said. "But let those poor cows out on pasture and eat grass, so they're not—"

Bosma cut her off. "Helen, you can't *do* that. You can't buy enough land to put the cows out to pasture. You know, they do that in Wisconsin, but they don't do that here anymore. And they don't do it in California, they don't do it in Arizona, or even in Mexico."

Helen reminded Bosma that the spike in nitrate levels in the area came from megadairy manure runoff. He insisted the culprit was chemical fertilizer, and Helen countered him: "There's a clear correlation between increasing dairy cattle and levels of nitrate pollution in the valley," she said coolly. "I've been told that by researchers working on this."

Hank reminded Helen that all dairies were required to have a manure-management plan, something that wasn't required for applying commercial fertilizer. "That's just a paper trail!" Helen laughed. "No one actually has to follow the plan they file, you know that, Hank. I mean, I can say, 'Okay, ten years from now I am going to lose weight, have curly hair, and look like Farrah Fawcett.' Then ten years go by and I still look like me."

Bosma admitted that the record weather of the past winter—excessive rain and snow—had wreaked havoc on farm waste management. It taught dairy farmers that new strategies had to be adopted regarding waste storage.

Helen was unimpressed. "But this is not just a 'this year' or 'last year' problem," she cut him off. "I have videotapes and photos going back seven years. There have *always* been violations." She cited the DeRuyter Brothers Dairy and CARE's allegations that Jake was running sewage directly from his lagoon into a drainage ditch flowing past Marcella's property.

"Jake is not a good neighbor," Hank said. Helen perked up; was Henry Bosma really going to trash a fellow dairyman, right there in her family room, on tape? Bosma took a deep breath. "I'm going to tell you, Helen, I never had any inkling about this at all. But you know, I have fought the elements, and I worked hard on my property. But I've never seen Jake put in that kind of labor on his place, like I was doing, or Cow Palace was doing. So I think that, on some of it, you're probably right. I think Jake had a way of dumping his waste down the drainage ditch. I've heard this, but never seen it.

"I think, Jake, for one—and I don't know about Herman teVelde—but I think Jake for one has been a real asshole to people that complain," Bosma said. "He treats some of them like shit. And that's where the problem basically started."

If this tape ever makes it to trial, Helen thought, these guys are *doomed*. She discreetly glanced toward the recorder on the end table. The red Record light still glowed. She prayed there was a ninety-minute cassette in that machine.

Amazingly, Hank continued to trash DeRuyter. "Whenever we were trying to handle our own waste overload with spray guns in the fields, during different times of the year, there seemed to be nothing going on over at Jake's place," he said. "His lagoons would be half empty and ours were full. And I could never figure that out. Now I am told that Jake has done a lot of work out there at his place. But even so, Marcella has a legitimate gripe. And so does Mary Lynne."

Helen arched an eyebrow, fighting the urge to look at the recorder. This was good stuff.

Then Hank suggested that other sources of pollution, including her own orchards, were just as culpable as any dairy in the valley. "You know, Helen, when you have frost protection, you have a tremendous amount of water that is being used in these trees. I would say that is probably as illegal as anybody else's. It goes down the drain. It's full of stuff. It's full of pesticides and whatever else is in the orchard."

Helen looked at her watch. More than fifty minutes had gone by. What if that was only a sixty-minute cassette in the recorder? What if the machine made a loud click—or worse, a beep—as it switched off? Helen began to fret. "Hank," she said, "I'm going to have to cut this short. I have an appointment in Sunnyside at one fifteen. I'm sorry."

"No, no, that's okay," he said politely. "I just wanted to have this opportunity and, and . . ." Hank stopped in midsentence. The politeness seemed to disappear. Helen thought she detected a dark look crossing Bosma's face, and she braced herself with a deep breath. "There's one other thing I wanted to say, Helen."

Oh boy, she thought. Here we go.

"I've told Mary Lynne this, too." Hank frowned. "I said, when you file a suit against me, then I am going to have to file a countersuit against you." Helen stood up but remained motionless, looking him in the eye as he spoke. "And what will happen in cases where there is farmland, they will probably be monitoring whatever runoff comes down the pike."

Don't threaten me, Helen thought. You can monitor my runoff all you want.

"And what you've done," Hank said, "if you decide to file these suits, you've made every farmer and every orchardist and every irrigation district vulnerable to the same type of thing. And that is why I was hoping you would read those materials I brought you. You will not accomplish what you set out to do. So you'll consider reading them?"

"I'd be glad to," Helen said. "But what I see is just tons of manure being put on this land. I went to a meeting and heard the government guy tell the dairy people, 'If you guys don't start fixing this problem, you're going to be in trouble. This is a violation.' And everybody kind of joked around about it. Ha-ha, ho-ho. It's an attitude you all have!"

"Well, no Helen. No—"

"And it has to be corrected."

"A lawsuit is not the way, Helen. I spent over $125,000 on that, this year alone . . ."

Helen had heard enough about Hank's expenditures. And she was still nervous about the tape making a noise if it clicked off. She showed Bosma to his boots and the door. "Well," she said, without smiling, "thank you for stopping by." Bosma stepped out into the sunshine on the porch, put his boots on, and again asked Helen to read the papers he had brought.

As soon as Hank Bosma left, Helen ran to the tape recorder and threw it into rewind. "Oh please, please let it work," she prayed aloud. It did. She ran to the phone and dialed Charlie down in Eugene.

"Charlie? Hank Bosma was just here!" Helen could barely hold the phone steady. "Not only did he admit that he knew what the Clean Water Act was, he admitted that he and the others had violations!"

Charlie was excited, too, but cautious. "You taped the conversation? You haven't let anyone else hear that tape, have you?"

"No, I'm here by myself, Charlie. Why?"

"Just overnight it to me right away. And don't tell anyone you taped him, okay?"

Helen drove to FedEx and got the tape off to Charlie. Later, over dinner, she recounted the tale to Don. "And there he was, just sitting there, not only admitting he understood about Clean Water violations, but totally lambasting these other dairymen and saying that they were also in violation!" Helen kept smiling. "I mean, when you think about it, Bosma has essentially just become a witness for our side."

Don smiled at his wife's sleuthing, but wondered just how deep Helen was getting into this battle.

Helen's merriment was short-lived, however. A few days later, a cut-and-paste letter showed up in Helen's mailbox. IT PAYS TO ENRICH YOUR WORD POWER, the heading said. Pasted around the page were thirty-eight words, and their definitions, again clipped from a dictionary. The words chosen revealed a scattered line of thinking.[12]

Some words seemed to pertain to Helen: "farmland," "orchard," "profession." Others referred to the lawsuit: "target," "falsify," "frivolous," "extortion," "liability," "aspersion," "fraud," "insidious." Some were obtuse: "proton," "orb," "history," "Friday," "imposter." And others were downright sinister: "haunt," "reprisal," "countermeasure," "vulnerable," "victim," "vicinity," "stalk," "fret," "exposure," "expire."

Helen immediately called Charlie. Again, he instructed her to put the envelope in a plastic bag, not to handle it, and to mail him the evidence immediately. On January 7, Charlie fired off a letter to Jerry Neal, attorney for Henry Bosma and other dairymen.

"I am writing to insist that Mr. Bosma, and any employees or agents of Mr. Bosma, have no further personal contact with any member of CARE concerning impending litigation," he began. "Mr. Bosma has made unannounced and uninvited personal visits to the homes of a number of CARE's board members," he continued, citing the farmer's additional threats of investigations and countersuits. "This blatant attempt at intimidation of my clients is without basis in law or fact and, along with other recent occurrences which will be discussed herein, has prompted me to send this letter." Charlie also recounted the cut-and-paste letters sent to CARE members, which he cited as "an attempt to intimidate."

"It is because of this pattern of behavior that a copy of this letter is also being forwarded to appropriate government agencies," he said. Among those carbon copied were Annette Sandberg, then chief of the Washington State Police; Doug Blair, the Yakima County sheriff; U.S. EPA administrator Carol Browner; and then attorney general, Janet Reno.

Yakima Valley's dairy war had just accelerated.

6

Dave Inskeep had not abandoned his plans for an animal factory in Elmwood. Though pigs were out of the picture, he was considering other animals. Most people assumed it would be dairy cows, but Inskeep was keeping mum on specifics.

"Everybody that needs to know knows, and those that don't, don't," he coyly told the *Peoria Journal Star*.[1]

Karen decided it was time for a town hall meeting. Since few Elmwood people had Internet access in 1996, old-fashioned gatherings were still the best way to alert people to community developments. FARM called the meeting for the evening of November 2, at Elmwood High School.

They also hoped to secure a face-to-face discussion with Illinois' governor, Jim Edgar, in order to demand more government action on CAFOs. What they got instead was a meeting with gubernatorial aide Allen Grosboll, just one day before the high school gathering. Karen, Nina Baird, Eldon Polhemus, and a local family physician, Lee Hammond, drove down to Springfield to plead their case for local control and better oversight of CAFOs. Grosboll sat and listened to them for two hours, arms folded.

"I'm sorry, but there's nothing we can do," he finally said. FARM members were stunned. "The legislature needs to address these issues through state law; the governor has no say over local control, or the regulation of livestock."

Karen was disgusted. If the governor was not going to help them, Grosboll should have said so up front. "He wasted two hours just sitting there only to tell us to go away?" she grumbled on the drive home from Springfield. "He could've saved all of us the trouble."

The next day, Karen recounted the frustrating meeting to more than a hundred people at the high school. To drive home her point about CAFO dangers, Karen held up a photo that she said was an aerial shot of a newly dug hog lagoon in nearby Cass County, built by Land O'Lakes. The lagoon was nearly full of liquid. But it wasn't hog waste; it was fresh water. Its construction had pierced an aquifer. A grunt of concern rippled through the crowd.

Karen watched as heads shook in sad silence. "This is why we are fighting," she said. "If the aquifer can get into the lagoon, the lagoon can get into the aquifer." Illinois drinking water was not safe from factory farming, she contended.

To bolster her anti-CAFO case even further, Karen read from the letter from the Minnesota mom Julie Jansen, who had been fighting hydrogen sulfide pollution in her home. She had some solid suggestions for Elmwood:

> Because of the odor and health effects, we have banned lagoons and earthen basins in Renville County. We have also limited the animal units to no more than two thousand animal units. If the producers cannot fix the problems by this legislative session I am sure we will get lagoons and earthen basins banned throughout the state. There is not a reasonable setback for these lagoons. At least four to seven miles would be required to protect the health of all citizens. My children cry in their sleep, hold their heads and tummies. My children tell me, "Mommy I never feel better anymore." You have a duty to protect your citizens' health.

When the meeting adjourned, most people seemed determined to fight. Karen was thrilled with the response. But she knew this was just the start of a long journey to raise awareness and to convince people they could make a difference.

A few days before Thanksgiving 1996, Jim and Doug dropped by Nina and Bill Baird's house to chat about their hog farm idea. Again, the mood was tense. Bill and Nina wanted answers: Where was the initial investment coming from, and how much debt would they have to assume to build the damn thing? The answer shocked them: probably $2.25 million. Jim would borrow it from Farm Credit Services.[2]

The confinement would be placed on land upwind from Bill and Nina's property. "Why aren't you building it over on your own property, Jim?" Nina asked. "You're south of us, so we wouldn't catch the wind so much."

"Well, I don't want to smell the damn thing," Jim replied.

Nina blew up. "Neither do *we*!"

Jim smiled. "Relax; based on the info I have from Murphy, this thing will be virtually odorless, high-tech, sanitary. I assure you it won't be a nuisance to any neighbors."

Nina glared at her brother-in-law. "If it's so harmless," she asked, "then why don't you want it by your own house, Jim?"

Jim and Doug went to the Knox County Board of Zoning Appeals and filed for a building permit, calling their operation the Highlands LLC. Two days later, the first construction trucks began rumbling toward the Baird property, traveling a country lane that locals would soon label "Pig Factory Road."

The next time the Baird brothers would communicate was through private attorneys in court. Despite their anger, Bill and Nina were genuinely worried about Jim and Doug's new venture. "I think they are being used by Murphy," Nina said. "They are going to lose every penny. Murphy will get the money, and they'll be left with the hog waste."

On December 4, 1996, the guessing game was over: *Peoria Journal Star* reported that Dave Inskeep had planned a massive dairy for Elmwood. Spurned by Murphy, Inskeep had turned his sights from sows to cows.[3]

Inskeep planned a "private, invitation-only meeting" for state officials for that night, at Elmwood's Saint Patrick's Catholic Church, the *Journal Star* reported. "No invitation has been extended to the *Journal Star* and our guest list is now full," Inskeep told the paper.

It wasn't clear to Karen why the strip-mined land, deemed inappropriate for a swine operation, was considered ideal for a megadairy. Inskeep claimed cow manure would "improve" the hole-riddled tract. What he didn't explain, Karen noticed, was how he would keep the manure from leaching down and contaminating the aquifer below.

Private meetings aside, Inskeep realized the time was nigh to explain things to his neighbors. He set a public meeting on February 17 at Elmwood High. More than one hundred people showed up, including Karen and most of FARM.

The project, Inwood Dairy LLC, would house twelve hundred Holsteins, making it the largest milking operation in Illinois. Inskeep said he would begin construction by May. His show-and-tell included images of a dairy CAFO in California. It looked like a country club, bordered by manicured strips of grass and dotted with bushy trees and blooming roses. The cows, barns, dry lots, and milking parlors were out of view.

Karen was not sold. "I don't think this is what we're getting," she whispered to Rocky.

Karen had good company in her skepticism. Aggressive questions were lobbed at Inskeep all evening. "All a' sudden, you're going from hog factory to megadairy, with no prior experience in animal husbandry?" a woman asked. "That alone seems very unusual."[4]

"She's right!" another man said. "You're a Caterpillar executive, Dave. A hobby farmer. If you start raising thousands of animals on your property, you're taking on a lot of liability—for you and your family. This thing could really land you in a heap of trouble."

"It's true, I have no experience as a dairy farmer," Inskeep said. "But I promise to hire very experienced management. They will know what they're doing."

"But what about the smell?" one farmer demanded.

Inskeep flashed a cool smile. "It ain't going to smell," he said. "It's going to be state of the art. I'm going to cover my lagoon, capture the methane, and burn it off."

Others voiced concerns about the shallow water table and possible contamination of the aquifer. "It's not going to happen," Inskeep said again flatly. How could he guarantee that? "I can't," he said. "But I *know* it's not going to happen."

Karen rose to ask about the instability of the strip-mined soil. "Murphy pulled its pig farm out because of the soil situation there," she said. "So why is this any different?"

"It's different because it will be built on virgin soil, and not on the strip-mined area," he replied. The project would include a two-stage sewage system. Treated wastewater would be used to clean barns, while liquid and solid waste would be spread on the cropland.

He added that his lagoon would be three to five acres, with a clay lining. For his water supply, Inskeep was digging two wells, one thousand feet deep. He would tap the same aquifer as the town of Elmwood, and expected to use one hundred thousand gallons a day. As for feed, he would grow some, and also buy grain from local farmers or the Elmwood elevator. The dairy would bring twenty new jobs to town, with a half-million-dollar payroll.

Then someone asked Inskeep about bovine growth hormone—a new drug from Monsanto called Posilac that could increase milk production by 30 percent over the life of a cow.

"I want to use it in my feed," he said to groans, "if my wife agrees. But I believe in it."

Dave Inskeep went on to say that, essentially, the dairy was coming to town whether people liked it or not. To Karen, his attitude seemed dismissive, above it all. She saw that the meeting had grown contentious very quickly. Inskeep did, too, and he grew more defensive. "There's been a whole bunch of misinformation spread around this town. And the result has been for the activists to be spreading fear all over the place," he said, glaring at the FARM people. "But you folks are just plain misinformed."

It did not go over very well. He also said he would ask the town to honor his request for some $500,000 to improve the road leading up to his site. But few in the auditorium were feeling very generous that night. "I'm living on a gravel road," one man said. "When will they blacktop my road?" Others demanded to know why Inskeep hadn't identified his investors. He smiled ruefully.

"Everybody is picking on Dave Inskeep," he said. "These guys, my investors, they're smarter than that. *They* don't want to stand here and get picked on."

By March 1997, factory farm opponents in Knox and Peoria counties were busy, working to block the pig operation near Williamsfield and the megadairy outside Elmwood. They knew their opponents had power and money. But they also knew the stakes were too high to walk away. They vowed not to give up.

Nina and Bill decided on two approaches to the crisis: espionage and psych-ops. That is, they would identify opportunities to catch Jim and Doug Baird in public deceptions, and then discredit them in the eyes of the community. It gave Nina and Bill no joy to carry out their tactics on their family. But what other weapons did they have in the face of so much impending pork?

Jim and Doug Baird had been insisting that their mega–hog farm would bring ample jobs to sleepy little Williamsfield; contractors, lumber dealers, metalworkers, and other local tradespeople would benefit. But then the trucks started arriving, hauling in supplies from other areas. Nina watched it all through a pair of binoculars. Murphy had recruited a building crew from out of state.

Jim and Doug had also extolled the virtues of all that natural hog fertilizer— it was great manure for their neighbors, they said. "Great manure, my football suit," Nina fumed. "That crap is loaded with heavy metals, resistant pathogens, and goodness knows what else that'll kill you. I wouldn't put it anywhere near my land."

And so the Manure Covenant of 1997 was born. (Nina purposely used the biblical term "covenant" to give the plan a sacred and inescapable feel.) A friend with some legal experience drafted an agreement that no one within a ten-mile radius of Jim Baird would agree to accept any of his pig waste. Nina and supporters canvassed the entire area around Jim Baird's farm and collected dozens of signatures. The extra cost of hauling the heavy crap away, one tanker at a time, would be discouraging, maybe even prohibitive.

When Jim and Doug found out, they were enraged. But Nina did not stop.

The animosity between Baird family members was reaching a breaking point. The entire clan still attended the same church, but now they worshipped on opposite sides of the aisle. Some refused to acknowledge one another, even on the Lord's day.

Before long, the hog-factory dispute began cleaving the town itself. "It's strange. Some folks are violently opposed to this thing, and some don't see anything wrong with it," Nina told Karen one day. "And these days it's getting to where the two sides won't even *speak*. Some folks who see me in town? They turn right around and walk the other way."

Karen would soon discover how tense things had become. In fact, they were about to turn nearly violent.

As part of their effort to stop the project, Nina, Bill, and others, with the help of then Knox County state's attorney Paul Mangieri, had sought and won a temporary injunction against building on the site, pending court review. But Nina complained that construction had continued anyway and said she had the photos to prove it.

The members of FARM were livid about what they considered to be illegal construction. To them, Jim Baird's flouting of the law was a slap in the face to family, neighbors, and the community. They decided to go directly to the media.

One spring afternoon, Karen and her son Sam, age twelve, drove out to the lonely country road that runs past the Highlands, where they would set up for a FARM press conference. Sam helped get everything out of the van as they put an impromptu podium in the prairie grass lining the road. Karen took pains to ensure they remained well within the public right-of-way. There would be no illegal trespassing on Highlands property.

Every good press conference needs a visual prop, and Karen had brought one along. It was a doghouse—to symbolize the Bairds' spotty relationship with the law. "We want the media to see how Jim Baird thumbs his nose at the state, Karen would tell reporters. "It's got him in the doghouse."

Suddenly, she heard the screeching of tires. Karen saw a big pickup barreling down the blacktop at nearly 70 miles per hour. It careened toward them, on the wrong side of the road. For an instant, Karen thought it must be some drunken teenager, out for a joyride. But then she recognized the snarling face behind the wheel. It was a local man who worked at the Highlands. His truck was heading right for them.

Karen screamed, grabbed Sam, and dove into a ditch. The pickup slammed on its brakes just a foot or two from where they cowered. The man jumped out. Karen cautiously rose up and dusted herself off. "What the hell is *wrong* with you?" she demanded.

"You gotta pick that crap up, put it back in your van, and get the hell out of here, lady," the man shouted. "*Now!*"

Karen was shaking, but her anger overcame her fear. Nina had warned her about this guy. He was well known around Williamsfield for being a hard-drinking tough guy. For all Karen knew, he had a gun.

"Please don't talk to us that way," she said, trying to remain calm. "We're on public property here. We're not doing anything wrong." The man jeered but said nothing. They stood there for a moment in the sun. Karen could hear a distant cow calling for her calf. She pulled Sam close.

"Listen, lady, I know who you are," the guy broke the silence. "You're that Karen Hudson bitch who causes so much fuckin' trouble down there in Elmwood. Well, let me tell you—you're going to be sorry about this. Very, very sorry. You all better *watch* yourselves."

Karen quietly pulled out her cell phone and punched in three digits: 9-1-1. Before she could press Send, the man climbed into his truck and sped away.

Karen fought back tears as she explained to the dispatcher that she had been threatened on some lonely backcountry road in the vast green cornfields of Knox County. When the police arrived, they told her the man had committed verbal assault. Karen was still shaking as she signed the official complaint.

But Karen had a press conference to conduct. She was comforted to see Nina and the other FARM members show up, followed by reporters, photographers, and TV crews. The factory farm battles were now standard news fare from Peoria to the Quad Cities.

The visuals could not have been better. Even as Karen spoke about Baird ignoring a stop-work order, bulldozers rumbled around the work site behind her. "A hundred pigs out in pasture is agriculture. The thirty-six hundred sows that Jim wants is heavy industry," she said.

Just then, one activist in attendance, practically in tears, ran to lie down across the Highlands' driveway, blocking a truck trying to enter the property. It was a stunning act of civil disobedience, but Karen disapproved. She approached the man and nudged him out of the roadway. "You can see how desperate some folks have become," she explained to the reporters. "I'd heard of things like this in other states, but I never thought we'd get to that point here. We're a law-abiding group."

The press conference helped publicize the Bairds' disregard for court orders. So did Karen's criminal complaint about the menacing employee, which appeared in the police blotter. The incidents ramped up the heat in the already-simmering hamlet of Williamsfield. In the end, Karen decided not to pursue verbal assault charges, concerned it could bring greater harm to her family.

But the escalating stress was getting to everyone. A day after the press conference, Bill Baird awoke to chest-thumping pain. Nina rushed him to the hospital, but the doctors there could find nothing wrong. "Physically, he's all right," Nina told the *Journal Star*. "But a broken heart doesn't show up on an X-ray."[5]

The feud that made Bill so sick was about to grow even more anguishing.

K aren, you won't believe this." It was Nina on the phone.

"What's up, Nina?"

"They're suing us."

"What? Who is?"

"The Highlands LLC. Otherwise known as Jim and Doug. They're trying to get us to stop harassing them."

"But they can't sue us! We didn't do anything."

"I'll bet this is all Murphy's doing. They had to make an example of us," Nina speculated, "because they intend to invade Illinois, and they're not going to have any local folks causing trouble and running off to zoning boards. So they got Jim and Doug to sue everybody that showed up at that hearing back in Galesburg. It's their way of sending us a message."

When Karen finally saw a copy of the lawsuit, she was stunned. She had no idea you could be sued just for attending a public hearing. Mild panic began to spread that Murphy or its contractors were going to take folks for all they had: homes, farms, savings.

"It's called a SLAPP suit," Nina told Karen a few days later, "a strategic lawsuit against public participation. Corporations and large developers sometimes use SLAPP suits against citizens' groups who try to get in their way. It's illegal in some states. But not in Illinois. It's meant to scare people."

"It's working," Karen answered.

"I guess the bottom line is, no one messes with those guys," Nina laughed bitterly, "or you get squashed like a bug. Do you know any lawyers?"

W hy was there such a gold-rush feel to the pig business in Illinois in the late 1990s? Pork was a hot global commodity. It was a great time to grow hogs, and 1997 was shaping up to be one of the most profitable pig years in history, experts said. Demand from processing plants was keeping three-shift-a-day operations humming around the clock, turning animals into canned hams and frozen sausages at a frighteningly efficient rate. An epidemic of hoof-and-mouth disease that decimated swine herds in Taiwan had created new export opportunities for the United States in the lucrative and insatiable Japanese market.

"If you're the hog farmer, you're doing great because prices are high," Bonnie Wittenburg, a Minneapolis investment analyst, told the media. "There is excess slaughter capacity chasing too few pigs, driving up the price of pigs." And those prices were golden. The cost of thirty-to-forty-pound "feeder pigs" was forty-eight dollars per hundred pounds at auction in Iowa City, up from eighteen dollars the year before.[6]

Even the *Chicago Tribune* was taking note. In an article titled "Going Hog Wild Down on the Farm," the newspaper heralded the imminent arrival of the new Baird facility. Doug Baird assured the paper the new facility would be eco-friendly, citing a "tremendous amount of improvement in the technology . . . Murphy's has looked at this from an environmental standpoint, at the safety of the water supply and the proximity to neighbors," he said.[7]

Amid this boom of activity, Karen Hudson got a call from State Representative Mike Smith—the politician who had declared at the original Elmwood meeting that there was no way to stop the megafarms from moving in. The legislature was putting together a special livestock panel, and Smith wanted Karen on it. "You'd be a community representative on the committee," he said. "You would review the current livestock law and make recommendations on how to strengthen it." Karen was the most visible and vociferous citizen activist on the issue that he could think of, he said. She was honored to sign on.

"It's very encouraging, a good sign," she told Rocky that evening over lasagna. "It's exciting that an actual citizen has been chosen to sit on such an important committee—one that can make real change!" Only later would Karen have reason to laugh at her own naive optimism. Of the twelve members appointed to the House Senate Joint Livestock Advisory Committee, most came from government or industry. Only two people were environmentalists: Karen and committee cochair Lynne Padovan, executive director of the state-funded and mainstream Illinois Environmental Council.

The question at hand was fairly straightforward: Did the state's new Livestock Facilities Management Act need revision? The committee was scheduled to meet several times in Springfield over the next few months to hear testimony before making any recommendations on this contentious issue.

Over that summer, Karen tried to educate the other panel members on all the information she had compiled—from the reliability (or lack thereof) of clay-lined waste lagoons to the fish kills and protozoan outbreaks of coastal North Carolina. She collated the information into one large master set and brought it down for the next meeting. But the committee cochairs claimed there was no money in the budget for photocopying.

On hearing days, members of the public would line up for hours waiting to testify. Karen felt like an elected official, listening to the concerns of her constituents. One by one, people who supported or opposed megafarming presented research and opinions.

At a September meeting, Karen moved to present her own recommendations. Among them:

- The public should be notified immediately whenever a lagoon spill occurs.
- Any facility with more than five hundred "animal units" should be inspected before, during, and after barn construction.
- Large farms should be required to file plans for disposing of dead livestock.
- The minimum distance between homes and CAFOs should be increased beyond the current requirement of three-eighths of a mile.

Over the summer, Karen had received a call for help from some FARM-affiliated residents in Eldred, a small town in Greene County, about a half hour west of Springfield. There, Bill and Judy Hobson owned a small bed-and-breakfast at the foot of a large bluff. The escarpment was formed from karst—extremely porous limestone. Directly above them, atop the bluff, the largest hog confinement in Illinois was being completed. It would house some eighty thousand hogs.

Once again, FARM launched into action. They got a volunteer pilot to take them up in a small plane, to snap aerial photos of lagoons already being filled with hog waste. As the day wore on and the sun warmed the air, gases began to rise. Even fifteen hundred feet aloft in an airplane, they could not elude the overpowering stench. Everyone on board developed such severe headaches, they had to put down to get some Tylenol.

The Hobsons knew that the state livestock committee was already scheduled to visit Greene County, so they invited all twelve members to stop by for a lunch meeting at their place in Eldred. They offered to brief the committee about the impact of the megafarm industry on their place of business. Karen told cochair Lynne Padovan it would be helpful to tour a business affected by factory farms.

But not everyone agreed. That weekend Karen got a call from another committee member who warned her, "You're being too aggressive. You have to back off."

"Back off? Oh *really*?" Karen said defiantly. "Well, let me tell *you* something. Your little phone call is giving me all the more reason for me to move forward." She grew angrier, telling the man, "This committee we sit on, the majority of the members have very close ties to industry. I really don't think that people like you want anything done. *Do* you?" The man hung up.

At the next livestock meeting, Karen announced the invitation by the Hobsons and recommended that the committee accept. Karen expected Lynne Padovan to second the motion. Instead, the cochair turned to Karen and said brusquely, "*That* is not going to happen." Karen was mortified. What could have transpired between Saturday and Tuesday to cause this change of sentiment? Or rather, who got to Lynne?

"It would not be appropriate to accept a lunch invitation at someone's place of business," Padovan rationalized. "There could be the appearance of a conflict of interest." Karen thought that was preposterous. When she left the chamber later, Karen was swarmed by reporters who also noticed how Padovan had turned on her putative ally.

Karen felt betrayed. Later, Nina told her, "You needed a towel to wipe the blood off of your back." Yet it wasn't the only surprising event of the day.

That afternoon, Karen was called out into the hall to take a panicked call from a FARM volunteer. A hog CAFO in Hancock County had just reported a huge lagoon spill after several days of rain. This wasn't just any pig farmer, either. The operation was owned by Dan Carlyle, brother of the state agriculture director, Becky Doyle. More than eight hundred thousand gallons of liquid manure had spilled into Bear Creek, a tributary of the Mississippi River.

"They had a very full lagoon to deal with," the caller said. "So they just opened a breach in the earthen dam and let it all flow out." Nobody—neither the operators nor the Illinois EPA—had notified the public. Finally, days later, Hancock County health officials were warning the people not to drink water from shallow wells near the creek, and to avoid contact with the creek itself.

Karen returned to the committee meeting to announce the spill. As she relayed the news, she scanned her colleagues' faces. Nobody seemed too troubled by the massive Bear Creek spill. Their passivity only confirmed her suspicions.

"This committee is a dog-and-pony show," she told Nina. "It's a farce."

In August 1997, Dave Inskeep won approval from the Illinois Department of Agriculture to build a waste lagoon for his planned twelve-hundred-head dairy south of Elmwood. The 8.3-acre lagoon (at the town meeting he had said it would only be two to five acres) would hold five million cubic feet of waste. Inskeep got the green light to position the lagoon a mere forty feet from a small stream that flows into Kickapoo Creek. Though Illinois required a hundred-foot "setback" between lagoons and wells, no such restrictions were placed on surface water. It's just another loophole in the law, Karen thought, one that must be easy to fix.

She was wrong. An agriculture department spokesperson said that setbacks were unfeasible. "If you start having setbacks from waterways, you would not be able to have the livestock industry in the state. There are waterways all over the place," he said. Setbacks would "doom" large operations. "Obviously, accidents happen. But the law tries to balance food production and the environment," he said. "The goal is to keep the waste in the lagoons."[8]

"That's the *goal*?" Karen asked Rocky. It was like saying the "goal" of an airline is to get you to your destination without crashing. The lagoon engineer hired by Inskeep said it was "unlikely" the lagoon would fail, "unless ten years down the road they let it fill up and water goes over the top." But, Karen wondered, might that scenario equally occur within two years, or six months—or during the next heavy rainfall?

Karen's speculation would ultimately become dead reckoning.

On September 24, the Illinois House Senate Joint Livestock Advisory Committee was abruptly disbanded.

"We feel that the committee's work is finished," cochairs Lynne Padovan and Michael Plumer said in a brief statement. The committee had developed a "list of proposals" and forwarded them to members of the legislature, they said.[9] There was nothing more to do. The decision came just one day before the panel was supposed to debate and vote on recommendations for its report to Springfield.

Karen learned of the disbanding only when the *Journal Star* called to get her reaction. She was furious, but soft-pedaled her reaction, reluctant to come across as a crazy radical.

"We view this situation with cautious optimism," she told the newspaper. Right after hanging up, Karen thought her comment was a stupid thing to say. The committee hadn't even gotten into the real meat of its appointed task yet. There were reams of testimony against these hog factories, she thought, and yet these guys have no recommendations other than "Just let it lie."

The animal wars of western Illinois were starting to take their toll on Karen, who worried that the fight had become an obsession. Many nights she would realize at 11 P.M. that she'd been at her computer the entire evening, away from her family. Laundry would pile up; help with homework was postponed. Karen reassured herself that she was offering her kids an example of self-sacrifice and standing up for what is right. But deep down, Karen worried more about what the consequences would be if she were to exit the battlefield.

Even in her downtime, the phone would ring seeking FARM's help, and she would find herself aiding other families at the expense of her own.

The situation at the Hudson homestead was nothing compared to the rift in the Baird family. Jim's son Doug told the *Journal Star* that contracting with Murphy had hurt his own family's relations, but insisted that it was a private matter. "We didn't think it would get as bad as it actually did," he said. "We're just not like that. It's been very frustrating." But he added: 'If I knew what I know today, would I still do it? Yes. If I wanted to continue farming, I didn't have a choice. I'm doing what I always wanted to do, and that is to farm, and farm with my dad."[10]

Recent research had revealed that strained family relations were not uncommon when "factory-size livestock operations" moved into rural areas, the *Journal Star* said. "It's just one violation of core values that rural residents may experience as more and more mega–livestock facilities establish throughout the Illinois countryside."

Nina Baird was interviewed, and she held out an olive branch. "All we want is Murphy to be accountable," she said. "The person who owns the hogs should be responsible for what happens, not just Jim and Doug, who own the buildings and lagoons. I still love them."

Anti–hog factory signs were sprouting up everywhere around Williamsfield, Elmwood, and other parts of west-central Illinois. They could be seen on front lawns, in bean fields and cornfields along county highways, and even out on Interstate 74 heading north to the Quad Cities. On the road to Williamsfield, motorists were treated to a colorful mural covering the entire side of a barn, depicting a cartoon pig sitting on a toilet. The slogan above: MURPHY, YOU STINK!

But by the fall of 1997, many of the hand-lettered signs—MURPHY GO HOME! and FARMS NOT FACTORIES were falling victim to vandalism. One weekend, vandals began chopping up signs with chain saws, destroying them under cover of night.

Each time signs were destroyed, FARM would call the police and call the press. One night, during the height of the sign topplings, someone approached the Hudson home and dumped a bucket of raw manure on their front porch, leaving it there to greet them along with their Sunday paper. TV stations came over to cover the bizarre story. It was the bucket of poop heard 'round western Illinois.

In October 1997, Bill and Nina Baird did the unthinkable: They put their home on the market.

They knew their location—just three-quarters of a mile from the future home of thirty-six hundred sows, their piglets, and their stinking effluent—would make this a hard sale. The couple ended up consulting with four different appraisers before one would even consider their demand for a fair-market value. "They were afraid they'd land in court with the buyers," Nina explained to Karen. They finally got an appraisal of $149,000.

Over the next several weeks, only two prospects came to see the house, located in a particularly bucolic stretch of Illinois farmland. Neither made an offer. "I hope we get a buyer," Nina told Karen. "Because, for the sake of our mental health, we're better off relocating somewhere like Peoria. But don't worry, we'll continue to fight these darn factories from there, I promise you. They are raping the countryside, Karen. And it's heartbreaking to see something destroyed that you held so sacred—like your own home."

With positively zero buyers coming forward to make an offer, Jim Baird finally told his brother and sister-in-law he would take the house off their hands—for $132,000. Jim planned to house farm workers there. "The only reason he offered to buy us out was to take away any legal claim from us," Nina told Karen. "And now he's stuck with this useless piece of property for the hired help."

Nina was ready to fold. "Listen," she said to Bill, "we can stay here and be miserable and watch this go on the rest of our lives, or we can move. Let's take the money and run." And so they moved away from Williamsfield, right before Thanksgiving Day, to a nice house in a leafy subdivision of Peoria, "where they have zoning," as Nina put it.

On moving day, Phil St. John, Karen, and Rocky showed up with a cattle trailer in tow. There was no way Nina's friends were going to let them move on their own. Three television crews also appeared on the front lawn, wanting to ask Nina how it "felt" to have to move.

"You folks are real sensitive with your questions," she said off camera, trying her best to be polite. Then she mustered the will to speak on camera. "I think it's a very sad commentary to what's happening in rural America today," she said, fighting back tears. "It's being replayed throughout America. It's very sad that greed is taking the place of values. We were told in the very beginning that we were up against a powerful force. I guess we're just starting to recognize how powerful that force truly is."

Jim Baird never came to say good-bye. The check for the house, however, arrived right on time.

And then off Nina and Bill went, making their way from the corn stubble of Williamsfield over to Peoria. When their odd little caravan—a loaded sedan, pickup trucks, and a cattle trailer filled with beds and sofas—pulled into the suburb that would be their new home, Nina said to Bill: "Everyone must be thinking: 'Oh my, there goes the neighborhood. The Clampetts are coming to town.'"

On December 7, 1997, bulldozers began roaring down the road heading for the new Baird hog farm to finish the lagoons. Within weeks, trucks carrying thousands of gilts (young female pigs that have not yet bred) would arrive. The "virgin sows" would be six months old on arrival. They would be given three weeks to settle in to their "gestation crates" (the cramped steel pens) before insemination began.

Jim and Doug Baird announced an "open house" for the following Saturday, December 13, for those eager to tour the new facility. "After months of debate and litigation among friends, neighbors and people from across Illinois, Jim Baird and his son, Doug, are now ready to show the public what all the fighting was about," the Galesburg *Register-Mail* reported. "It's a chance for us to dispel some of the rumors," Doug Baird told the paper.[11]

FARM voted to send members on the tour, though they vowed not to disrupt the day. "We are not going to cause a problem for them; we don't want to look like unreasonable people," Karen told reporters. "We don't want to look radical. We want to look like level-headed people who are concerned about the community." Karen also announced that FARM would hold a press conference that day, and a spaghetti-supper fundraiser to support its legal defense fund in the SLAPP suit against its members. Everyone had a lot of pasta to boil.

Saturday the thirteenth was freezing. The weak sun lay low in the cobalt sky as a northwest wind tore across the corn-stubble plains. By 10:00 A.M., cars and trucks were lining up in downtown Williamsfield as people ran into the warmth of the Legion Hall for the press conference and spaghetti-supper fundraiser.

The cozy room was festooned with a tree, garlands, and lights for Christmas—as well as signs that said REGULATE HOG FACTORIES, and WE LIVE NEXT TO THE MUCK, YOU RAKE IN THE BIG BUCK. Nina greeted neighbors with a warm smile. The event combined holiday cheer with the crackling energy of political protest. On the table, a booklet titled *Rural Rights Now!* lay next to some home-baked cookies. The *Register-Mail* called the place "a cross between a Christmas party and a pep rally."[12]

Karen spoke briefly to reporters, including all three network affiliates, and some two hundred people who filled the hall. She discussed FARM's concerns over the encroaching mega–hog industry in the area. "We do not welcome Murphy Farms into our community today," she declared, and the crowd chanted back: "Murphy go home!"

"Are we to trust these new neighbors moving into this community?" Karen continued. "I say no. Assurances made by the Bairds and Murphy are just empty promises, and the threat to our water, air, and land still exists. Wendell Murphy's promises last as long as footprints in the snow!" The crowd went wild.

Karen held up a letter that FARM had received from a Mr. Gene Andersen of Sheridan, Missouri. Andersen described what it had been like when Murphy Family Farms came to his own corner of the heartland. "'We were totally unprepared for the entrance of Murphy's into our area,'" Karen read. "While suspicious of their approach, we really had no grounds to dispute them. We learned that, while Murphy's was a very promising company, they were all promises." The promises, from vows to reduce odors to insistence that hog confinements would not impact groundwater or drinking wells, were not kept.

Karen then read a list of FARM demands that she would deliver personally to Jim and Doug at the open house:

1. Inject or incorporate all manure onto the surrounding land, rather than use liquid spray.
2. Post bonds for cleanup in the case of a lagoon spill.
3. Guarantee replacement of water supplies if they are depleted.
4. Notify the Knox County Health Department immediately of any spill.
5. Pay for road damage from trucks bringing feed and supplies, or hauling out piglets.
6. Stop construction until all proper county permits are secured.

After the press conference and the spaghetti dinner, everyone drove out to the Baird place.

Some were curious and some were furious—they came by the carload and kept on coming," the *Register-Mail* described the scene on open-house day at the new Baird farm.[13] The turnout was incredible: More than twenty-five hundred people—from all over western Illinois—lined up on the frozen ground and patiently waited an hour in thirty-degree air. People outside the offices of the Baird Seed Company boarded chartered buses that took them over to the hog facility.

Among the throngs were reporters from five area newspapers and all six TV news stations from Peoria and the Quad Cities. They were chaperoned by Murphy employees brought in from Oklahoma and Missouri for the day. Dressed in blue denim shirts and handing out barbecued pork sandwiches and souvenir refrigerator magnets, they put a wholesome, friendly, family-oriented spin on the nation's largest swine-producing corporation.

The tour took folks over the concrete slatted floors of the confinement area with its metallic blue boar pens, still empty. Visitors marveled at the gleaming railings, corrugated aluminum ceilings, and swept floors, all unsullied by swine waste. Water and feed distributors hung from the ceiling like oxygen masks on a troubled jetliner. The two-foot-by-six-foot farrowing crates, where sows would remain immobile while nursing, were lined up in endless rows.

At one table, employees handed out slick brochures explaining Murphy's commitment to environmental excellence. Nearby were samples of inoffensive composted manure for folks to touch and smell.

"I'm tickled to death about it," Duane Gibbs of Gilson, three miles to the west, told reporters. "I've worked the land for fifty years, and I now have a farrow-to-finish operation that has more than thirty-three hundred hogs at any given time. And they don't bother me any." Regarding the Bairds, Gibbs displayed the same bedrock philosophy common to many conservative Midwestern farmers: "It makes no difference to me what they do. I think anybody who owns land should be able to do what they want with it."[14]

Later in the afternoon, Karen, Nina, and the FARM brigade boarded a bus for the short trip over to the CAFO. Protestors began handing out flyers to people waiting in line. "We are Families Against Rural Messes," the flyers said. "We advocate for balance between individual and community economic development, and industrial and ecological interests." Their buttons read: STOP FACTORY FARMS.

Out on the road, dozens of FARM members began a "rural drive-by protest" by picketing with their vehicles, crawling slowly up and down the stretch in gloomy silence, their flashers and headlamps turned on high beam.

The Knox County sheriff and two deputies met Karen and her comrades at the gate. Karen told them she had a list of demands she wished to hand personally to Jim Baird. A Murphy rep told her to send them in via registered mail.

"I'm going in," Karen finally announced, like a soldier heading for battle.

Karen found the unoccupied pig house to be factory-fresh and squeaky clean. No awful smells, no emissions, no flies, no fecal particulate, no dust, no endotoxins, no antibiotics, or resistant bacteria wafting through the air. Not yet. But Karen knew what was coming. She looked at row after row of newly installed farrowing stalls. Soon enough, she thought, they would be crammed with animals squealing or biting at their tails or on the bars, trying in vain to find a way to escape their tiny confinements.

And there was no need today for the gigantic fans that lined the end of the CAFO, the ones that must endlessly push what is inside to the outside just to keep the animals from being killed by the gases in their own waste. This is a perfect Murphy's moment, Karen thought. It's their one and only time to present a pristine Pork Palace to the people.

A reporter from the Galesburg *Zephyr*, a populist weekly, asked Karen what she thought. "I think I don't trust Doug Baird when he says he'll keep odors to a minimum," she said. "There are hundreds of mega–hog operations across this country and this industry has demonstrated very little interest in being a good neighbor."[15]

Later that afternoon, Doug Baird countered Karen's claim, telling reporters he would keep emissions and other problems to a minimum. "From day one, I've been concerned about the odor issue," he said. Doug introduced Steve Pagano, an engineer from Bion Environmental Technologies of Smithfield, North Carolina (now Crestone, Colorado), which developed the Highlands' waste lagoons. Pagano echoed Baird, saying the lagoons would offer a continuous mixing and oxygenation of manure, prompting faster waste decomposition and an 80–90 percent reduction in odors.[16]

But not everyone was buying the happy talk. Edith Galloway, a grain and cattle farmer—and FARM member—from Hancock County, knew firsthand about living near a brand-new giant hog farm. "It reeks a mile away," she told the reporters, "and they haven't begun to fill the lagoon yet. That is just from the pigs! Already, I've had swollen glands, sore throats, and awful tastes in my mouth. I don't care what they do to those lagoons; it will do nothing to stop the barn gases."[17]

7

North Carolina's government was finally getting serious about fighting the deteriorating state of the Neuse River Basin. But the fish kills and hog spills just kept on coming.

In mid-October 1995, state inspectors were trying to locate the cause of a kill in Stantonsburg, on Contentnea Creek, a popular canoeing river that runs right through Don Webb's wooded property before emptying into the Neuse River near Grifton. Don and other neighbors reported that hundreds of fish—bass, bream, and crappie—were beginning to turn up dead along fifteen miles of the Contentnea from State Road 1628 on down to the bridge near Stantonsburg.[1] Flies swarmed around the rotted fish. Don Webb and his neighbors were furious. One old friend, Roy Davis, used to swim and fish in the creek as a boy, but in the last four or five years, the creek's health had deteriorated. "The water is a lot darker." He frowned. "I don't care to fish here anymore."

Officials tried to pinpoint the cause. Oxygen levels were normal, so it wasn't hypoxia, and they also doubted that *Pfiesteria* was to blame. So far, the vicious critter had only appeared in the brackish waters of coastal rivers and estuaries, not in freshwater streams. Don Webb told friends the problem was caused by hog feces in the water.

Just days later, officials announced that a swine CAFO in Robeson County had contaminated drinking-water wells at three nearby homes. Testing showed very high levels of nitrates in water near the Oxendine Pork Farm, a twelve-hundred-head facility in the hamlet of Shannon.[2] It was the first known case of a hog farm polluting wells in the state. No one had fallen ill, but Governor Hunt's administration made the unprecedented offer of free well testing to anyone living near a hog farm.

Nitrates in drinking water are a potentially deadly problem. Measurements above ten parts per million can cause methemoglobinemia, or blue-baby syndrome, which can kill infants by blocking the blood's ability to absorb oxygen. In Robeson County, four out of ten wells tested had nitrate levels up to a hundred parts per million, or ten times over the limit. "The contaminants appear to be from the hog farm owned by Curtis Oxendine," a DEHNR spokesperson said. The two lagoons, built in the 1980s, were unlined. In his defense, Oxendine, a local minister, said, "I was always told that lagoons seal themselves. I never wanted to do anything that would cause problems for my neighbors."[3]

The department ordered Oxendine to stop any further pollution, but admitted little could be done about the pollution that had already occurred. "It will take a long, long time before this is cleared up," one official lamented.

The two unlined lagoons on the Oxendine farm were built within 150 feet of the nearest home. All the affected wells were less than 50 feet deep, which was shallow but typical for the area. Counties with the largest hog counts were also among the poorest, and more apt to use private wells rather than town water. In Duplin County, 56 percent of all households relied on them, and in Sampson, it was 70 percent.

But some experts wondered whether leaky lagoons were entirely to blame. Sprayfields, they said, should also be considered as potential sources of contamination. In Duplin and Sampson counties, citizens' complaints were piling up against farmers spraying animal waste in abusive ways. Some farmers were spraying manure directly onto neighboring property, cars, and homes. While lagoons are typically located several hundred feet or more from neighboring homes, sprayfields bring contaminants much closer to the door, or well. Seepage of nutrients into sandy soil could easily reach a well fifty feet deep.

Oxendine's nearest neighbor, Othella Locklear, described her ordeals with airborne hog crap to *The News & Observer*. Whenever spraying occurred in the cornfield next to her mother's property, she said, a "foul black mist" would drift into the yard. It would deposit a greasy film on vehicles and buildings and coat the lawn. "If you were crazy enough to stand out there, you'd be soaked within a few minutes," Locklear said. On some days, the neighbor's dogs would drag dead pigs onto the property, leaving them to rot in the sun. "It just makes me so mad," she said. "I don't see how you can put people through things like this and still call yourself a good neighbor."

B y late 1995, it was quite clear that the hog factories of eastern North Carolina were a growing environmental threat. That view was reinforced by a report presented in November to the state's Blue Ribbon Commission on Animal Waste, following the inspection of nearly all the state's large-scale hog farms. In dozens of cases, pork producers had allowed discharges into public waters.[4] Of the 3,554 farms inspected:

- 15 percent (533 farms) failed to keep a proper safety margin, or free-board, in their lagoons.
- 13 percent showed "serious erosion problems" that could cause leaks and dike failures.
- 3 percent had lagoons that were visibly seeping waste.
- 3 percent lacked enough land to absorb the waste being produced, and 6 percent were found to be operating sprayfields where no crops had been planted to absorb the waste.
- 26 percent failed to keep adequate records on their waste-management practices.
- More than one in four farms were cited for some type of gross negligence, criminal violation, or management lapses.
- 4 percent (142 farms) were charged with deliberately discharging their waste.

There were other small victories. In December, then state attorney general Mike Easley announced that two CAFOs would be permanently shut down. "These animal operations polluted our rivers and streams and put people's health and safety in jeopardy," Easley said in a statement.[5] It was a stunning development, and Rick Dove was impressed.

The first farm to be closed was J & H Milling Company, a twelve-thousand-head swine facility in Greene County, charged with dumping lagoon waste directly into a swamp for several years. The operation had never even bothered to buy spraying equipment or to clear land, knowing it could just pump its waste into the swamp, *The News & Observer* reported.

The other facility was Sexton Dairy Farm, of Henderson County, which had illegally dumped waste over a seven-year period into nearby Mud Creek—despite several previous warnings. "I have lost my patience with polluters who put profits ahead of the public's well-being," Easley said. "If state inspectors continue to find animal operators who break the law, we will continue to shut them down."

Rick was hopeful that 1996 would be a much better year than 1995. It couldn't be any worse, he thought.

T he New Year was about to bring unspeakable personal pain. And despite some significant progress up in Raleigh, before the wretched twelve months came to a close, two massive hurricanes would heap devastation over the hog-rich lowlands of North Carolina.

But no month was as black as January.

During the early morning hours of January 8, Rick and Joanne were awakened by the sound of the doorbell. It was freezing outside, and icy rain slammed against the big picture windows that looked out onto the dark and angry Neuse River. He opened the door: Two wet and sad-faced Craven County Sheriff's deputies stared Rick in the face.

"Mr. Dove? I'm afraid I have some disturbing news for you. It's about your son, Todd. We believe he's been the victim of a homicide. We need to ask you to come down to the morgue right away, sir."

The words made no sense. Rick wondered if he'd heard correctly. Maybe it was a *Pfiesteria*-induced hallucination? Maybe he was still dreaming, and would wake up cozy in bed? No, the morning was too cold, and the rain on the window too loud to be a dream—and those two deputies were very real.

Rick drove with the deputies through the early-morning dimness to the county morgue. As the sheet was pulled back, Rick closed his eyes and prayed that it would be someone else—somebody else's son, not his. The face and body were horribly bruised and lacerated. It was difficult to determine at first if this really was Todd. Rick's heart pounded as he gazed closely at the gruesome visage. The instant of recognition was the most painful and difficult moment of the marine's life.

Todd had been stabbed more than forty times and shot in the head. After that, his body had been hurled into a filthy, watery ditch, where it remained for nearly a day before it was discovered.

Todd's death was profoundly wounding for Rick and his wife. God had blessed them with two wonderful children, he thought, and then took one of them away—without cause or reason. "Todd was my fishing buddy," Rick said through quiet tears as he filled out the paperwork required to have his boy's corpse released.

The homicide's details read like something from pulp fiction. Todd had married the wrong girl back in 1992. The marriage was fraught with battles and tension, and the couple divorced a year later. Todd's ex-wife ended up hating him. He tried to avoid her after the divorce, but that proved to be impossible.

Often, Rick was certain, she deliberately crossed Todd's path just to upset and harass him. After they split up, she moved in with "Tattoo John," the chieftain of a local chapter of the Pagans, a national motorcycle gang. In the same house lived a wannabe gang member, Michael Patrick Ryan. By some accounts, Ryan was told to kill Todd to gain favor with the motorcycle gang.

According to these accounts, Todd was lured to a local bar on a cold rainy night with the promise of meeting a girl, and then he was separated from his friends. He was hustled outside and ended up in Tattoo John's truck. He was then driven out to a road less than half a mile from the gang's house. Somehow, perhaps through Todd's actions, the truck went off the muddy road and became hopelessly stuck in a deep ditch. There Ryan, and possibly other gang members, stabbed and shot Todd. Their plan, as related by a number of sources, was to dump the body into Cahooque Creek and let the alligators have at it. That creek also happened to be one of Todd and Rick's favorite fishing spots.

Although gang members tried desperately to get Tattoo Jack's truck back on the road, it could not be pulled from the ditch. They panicked. Todd's body was unceremoniously dumped and the gang fled. Had the gang members freed their truck, the Doves might never have known what happened to their only son.

It took two years before a full accounting of the events was unveiled. Todd's ex-wife failed to pass multiple polygraph tests, according to Rick, and also made admissions to friends that implicated her. But the district attorney felt the evidence against her was not sufficient and she was never prosecuted. As for the other gang members, they all clammed up. Many left town. The Doves hired their own private investigators to help the sheriff and district attorney track down witnesses and obtain the evidence needed for a conviction. In the end, they were only able to secure one murder rap, in the case of the gang pledge Michael Patrick Ryan, who was convicted of first-degree murder and given a life sentence without chance of parole. No one else has been charged.

To this day, Rick regrets there wasn't enough evidence to prosecute the others. And though all of them have now scattered to the wind, as far as the Doves are concerned, the case against them remains open. Todd's murder became a motivational force for Rick's crusade to rescue their beloved waterway. "I have lots of reasons for fighting for the Neuse. One is the memory of the joy this river once brought to my son and me when it was a safe and healthy place to fish and play," Rick says today. "Another is Todd's little sister, Hollyanne, her husband, Joe, and my four grandchildren. Hollyanne is my lightbulb. No matter how down and out I get, she always finds a way to brighten my life. That sure came in handy in the year following Todd's murder, and it still does.

"My daughter and grandkids want the river back the way it was," Rick says. "They don't want stories of what *used* to be—they want what is legally theirs, a healthy river full of healthy fish, fit to catch and eat, not a river plagued by hog lagoons, sprayfields, and toxic swine waste. There's no quitting until all the cesspools are gone—after that, maybe there will be some peace for me about Todd and the river we once shared."

In February 1996, two highly anticipated reports related to pigs and rivers were released in North Carolina. One dealt with curbing the rising tide of hog waste; the other focused on reducing nutrients in the threatened Neuse River. Insiders recognized the causal relationship of these environmental problems.

In the Neuse River report, the state Department of Environment and Natural Resources (formerly DEHNR) set a precedent by proposing certain notable regulations.[6] These required first-time permits for CAFOs in the Neuse basin, mandated that there be fifty-foot "forest buffers" along streams to filter out nutrients in runoff, reduced the amount of nitrogen that sewage plants could discharge into the river, and banned so-called package plants—small, local waste facilities favored by developers.

Some parts of the plan read like a page from the Neuse River Foundation playbook. It called for cities, industries, and farms to reduce nitrogen discharges into the Neuse by 30 percent by 2020 and called for a ban on the spraying of animal waste within twenty-five feet of drainage ditches, among other conservation tactics.

Rick hailed the report's proposals. He told himself, proudly, that the ball really got rolling after he took Secretary Howes for that eye-opening ride on the Neuse.

Still, there were challenges to these proposals, especially from factories and hog farms. One hog grower, Dennis Loflin, accused the state of treating all farmers as criminal polluters. Furthermore, he said, if the measures were adopted, the hog industry would be forced to spend millions of dollars in upgrades in order to come into compliance.

The next day, the governor's Blue Ribbon Commission on Agricultural Waste issued its recommendations for state manure management.[7] Critics had noted earlier that the commission was richly stocked with livestock and poultry representatives, and predicted that the panel would be incapable of serving up anything harsher than a gentle slap on Big Ag's wrist.

But the commission surprised everybody. Under the Blue Ribbon plan, CAFOs would need general permits to operate (currently, they were simply "deemed" to be permitted and allowed to handle waste providing they incurred no violations), pay state fees, submit to annual inspections, conduct soil tests, and keep detailed records of soil application of nutrients. The cap on fines, currently at five thousand dollars per day, would be doubled to match other industries. Like the Neuse River plan, this Blue Ribbon report called for buffer zones along rivers and streams.

Joby Warrick, in *The News & Observer*, called it the state's "second pork revolution: a new system of rules and standards that would change the way large hog farms are managed and regulated." It would finally "turn up regulatory pressure on animal feedlots, subjecting them to many of the same rules as other waste-producing enterprises."[8]

Rick could not believe the results. "Well, it's about damn time," he said.

Perhaps most radically, CAFOs would be forced to devise their own legally binding odor-reduction schemes, the costs of which the state would help to offset. Present rules covering livestock farms would be extended to large poultry operations, since chicken CAFOs were moving into the state in record numbers, largely under the radar.

Finally, the panel called for "aggressive pursuit" of new technologies to replace the dirty, dangerous, and outdated lagoon-and-sprayfield system. "Lagoon technology served the industry well in the past," said Dr. J. C. Barker, a professor at North Carolina State and a commission member. "But it's not the technology that will take the industry into the next century."

If North Carolina adopted these rules, *The News & Observer* reported, it would follow big Midwestern livestock states and shed its "laissez-faire image that helped foster the explosive growth in high-volume swine factories in the past decade."

"Oh man, this is good, this is *real* good!" Rick chirped to Joanne over coffee. "You know why all this is happening? These hog factories, they don't like being singled out. Well, that's just too damn bad. They are unregulated; they've done nada to stop their own pollution."

If Rick was happy about the new proposals, farmers in the Neuse River Basin were despondent. They said a fifty-foot buffer requirement would hurt farmers whose land was crisscrossed with streams. Some complained that 10 percent of their cropland would be lost to conservation.

In the flat tidewater counties of eastern North Carolina, much of the lowlands were etched in a latticework of drainage canals, built by previous generations of farmers to empty the swampy landscape. Many farms were tucked between such waterways, with little crop area to spare. "A fifty-foot concession to the river is a sacrifice they literally can't afford to make," Warrick reported. As one farmer put it, if you have canals that run every two hundred feet, and you put a buffer on each side, "that's half your land."

But officials countered that a fifty-foot buffer would take only 2.3 acres of land out of use for every one thousand feet of stream, or twelve acres per mile. They estimated the value of that land—based on the market rent for one acre of prime "bottomland" with the richest soil—at about forty dollars per year, and asked that the state help offset some of those losses. Even Rick agreed with that. Whatever it took to clean up the river, he was in favor of it. "Let's put the buffers in, but in a way that farmers don't have to bear all the cost," he told Warrick.

But riled farmers could not be placated, even with offers of financial help. A series of state workshops on the plan drew hordes of balking men and women to town hall meetings around the basin, demanding to know why they were being picked on. "Why should farmers bear the brunt of cleaning up a river that everyone else helped to pollute?" one incensed swine farmer shouted at a workshop in Smithfield, about thirty miles south of Raleigh. Howard Hobson, a hog farmer who raised pigs for Carroll's Foods, told *The News & Observer*, "It just bothers me that we're being singled out."

Farm groups disputed state figures showing that up to 60 percent of the nitrogen levels in the Neuse came from agriculture, and most of that from pigs. Hog farmers decided to fight back. The North Carolina Pork Producers Association (NCPPA), claiming its members had been unfairly maligned, declared war on their enemies—the press and environmentalists—at a national Pork Industry Forum in Charlotte. "We are greatly concerned that misinformation and emotion have often replaced intelligent discussion in much of the debate during the past year with regard to future pork production in our state," said the NCPPA president, Nash Johnson, a hog producer from Sampson County.[9]

Johnson released a statewide survey showing that 75 percent of North Carolina residents felt positive about its $1 billion-per-year hog industry. The poll was conducted by professors at North Carolina State—but was commissioned by Epley Associates, a Raleigh PR firm with swine-industry clients. (The survey questions were not released.) "Many people mistakenly believe that producers violate environmental regulations. In fact, nothing could be further than the truth," Johnson said, adding that his group had funded a $350,000 study on the effects of odors from pig farms.

But Rick wanted to know something: If 75 percent of residents held a positive view of hog farms, then why were the pork people gearing up for a huge PR campaign, including a much-ballyhooed $500,000 "media blitz" to improve the image of pig CAFOs? In one ad, the announcer said that 97.2 percent of hog farms in the state had zero water-quality problems, a claim that critics disputed. The ads were written by Epley Associates.

In early July 1996, meteorologists announced that a tropical depression was forming far out in the Atlantic, off the coast of Africa. It would eventually hit the United States as Hurricane Bertha. Rick shuddered to think what a major hurricane might do to the waste lagoons in the area. They were, after all, simply open toilets brimming with piss and shit.

After chewing through the U.S. Virgin Islands and Puerto Rico with 90 mile-per-hour winds, Bertha ramped up to a category 3 storm and set its sights on the Carolinas. The Doves moved all outdoor furniture indoors and boarded up their windows. Rick pulled the *Lonesome Dove* onto her trailer and stowed her out of harm's way.

Bertha made landfall on July 12, about seventy miles southwest of New Bern. It rampaged up the tidewater region with 80 mile-per-hour winds, ripping down trees and power lines, washing out bridges and piers, tearing roofs from homes and flooding a number of towns.

Doppler radar showed that more than ten inches of rain deluged New Bern and the rest of Craven County, where a Mr. Cecil Rhodes owned a twenty-four-hundred-head hog-finishing facility. After several hours of unrelenting rain, Rhodes's 4-million-gallon lagoon burst its berm and sent 1.8 million gallons of pig waste into a tributary of Swift Creek, which flows into the Neuse. Bertha had turned his three-acre lagoon into a churning wave maker that eroded a three-foot hole in the wall. Rhodes insisted he had done nothing wrong, and blamed the accident on an unpreventable act of nature.[10]

Secretary Howes rushed to Craven County the next day to survey the damage by land and air. He claimed that initial testing showed no water contamination in the Neuse. But Rick knew that was untrue. He had been up in the air and seen for himself that a ribbon of milk-chocolate waste was flowing from Swift Creek into the Neuse. Rick took out his cell phone and called Erick Gill, a reporter at the New Bern *Sun Journal*. "Howes doesn't have his damn facts straight!" Rick yelled over the roar of the propellers. "We are over the Neuse right now, and you can see the waste from up here. The river looks just terrible; it's all sorts of colors. It's not a pretty sight. You should come up and see for yourself."

It was not clear if Rhodes would be fined for the spill, though penalties could go as high as ten thousand dollars per day. But state law exempted spills where it could be proven that the twenty-four-hour period of rainfall had exceeded the previous record for the past twenty-five years, and that had not yet been determined.

Even so, Rhodes had been warned twice about poor waste management just one year before the storm. In July 1995, DEM inspectors found zero freeboard in his lagoon; its contents were spilling over the rim into a ditch. On a return inspection, the officials noted the lagoon was still 100 percent full. Even in dry weather, Rhodes had failed to run his sprayfields efficiently to lower the level. To be fair, the hog farmer wasn't alone; agents had inspected ten lagoons in Duplin and Pender counties in the months prior to Bertha, and found that most would not withstand ordinary storms, let alone a big hurricane.[11]

Rhodes's troubles were not over yet. Cargill, Inc., his contracting company, came and hauled the twenty-four hundred pigs on his site to another farm in Lenoir County, where they would stay until Rhodes brought his lagoon up to spec. The media had little sympathy for him; a July 17 editorial in *The News & Observer* scoffed at his claim that the accident was an "act of nature":[12]

> Nature did not plunk down 2,400 hogs on his land, just as nature did not create the hundreds of waste lagoons across the coastal plain. This is a manmade problem. Besides, these waste pits are supposed to be built to withstand heavy rains, and operators know full well they need to keep them pumped down to prevent spills.

The paper also ridiculed the industry's recent efforts to polish its image:

> The pork industry, a North Carolina powerhouse, has taken out ads to try and sell itself as an environmental paragon, but ongoing problems suggest otherwise. Despite much publicity about the pollution threat from large-scale swine operations and heightened state attention, some operators have been as careless as ever, undercutting the image the "Pork Proud" industry is putting out big bucks to create.

Within a week after the Rhodes spill, the fish kills resumed. At least five separate incidents were reported in Onslow, Brunswick, and Duplin counties. In Pender County, a five-acre lagoon at the Jennings Humphrey swine CAFO began to overflow with heavy rains in Bertha's wake.[13] Meanwhile, dozens of dead fish and crabs were turning up in the New River near Jacksonville. The cause was low oxygen levels: Bertha had swept organic matter into Neuse River Basin streams. Bacteria that broke down the extra matter consumed oxygen in the process.

A few weeks later, another hog lagoon spilled its contents at a Browns of Carolina site in Jones County. Again, the cause was human neglect. This lagoon had been built over an aging "tile drain" (typically made of terra-cotta pipe) installed decades before to remove rainwater from the soil. The tile had been clogged for years but suddenly cleared, draining pig waste into a nearby stream.

A million gallons poured into a tributary of the Trent River. No fish kills were reported, though near-zero oxygen levels were found a half-mile downstream.[14] It was the second time in recent memory that a tile drain at a Browns facility was implicated in a spill. In August 1995, two million gallons escaped through a tile drain at a Browns lagoon in New Hanover County, entering the Cape Fear River.[15]

Much of North Carolina was still wringing out from Bertha when news came of another storm in the Atlantic. This tempest was named Fran, and it, too, was heading for North Carolina.

Farmers braced for another round of pounding. In Sampson and Duplin counties, hog growers were out spraying their fields at full tilt, desperately trying to lower their lagoons before the deluge.

Fran made landfall near Cape Fear, with 115 mile-per-hour winds, on September 5. It tore northward and inland, dumping a foot or more of water across the hog belt. It was a ruinous event—the strongest hurricane in half a century—and flood damage was extensive. In Kinston, the wastewater plant was forced to discharge four million gallons of raw sewage every twenty-four hours into the Neuse, compounding the existing pollution.

When the rain and wind stopped, the toll was formidable: twenty-six deaths and more than three billion dollars in damage—much of it in North Carolina. But remarkably, the hog lagoons were spared. The emergency lowering of waste levels before Fran hit seemed to have worked.

The animals did not fare as well. Thousands drowned as their livestock and poultry houses were flooded. In other places, terrified turkeys and chickens smothered one another as they ran about their confinements in a panic. Incredibly, the suffering was about to intensify. After Fran, torrential rains moved in and dumped even more water on the flooded ground. Without power, hog farmers could not pump their wells. Downed trees prevented feed-truck deliveries. In Sampson and Johnston counties alone, more than five thousand pigs and one hundred thousand birds perished from hunger and thirst.[16]

And still the rain fell. Hog farmers and state officials watched helplessly as lagoons rose and freeboard safety margins shrank. Then the lagoons began to overflow.

The first to go was a Pender County lagoon that overtopped into a feeder creek of the Northeast Cape Fear River. Another hog CAFO in the county, situated in the flood plain, was contaminating the river, officials said. It was called the Ham Hog Farm. When the nearby Neuse flooded, it devoured much of the property, stranding thousands of pigs and rising to just inches from the rim of the fifteen-million-gallon lagoon. It had been an accident waiting to happen, as *The News & Observer* reported:

> The Ham farm was built in the Neuse River's floodway, an area so vulnerable to flooding that federal guidelines caution against development of any kind. Goldsboro city officials approved the farm's building permit after owners—one brother who serves on the county planning board and another who was on the state's Blue Ribbon panel on livestock waste—commissioned an expensive study showing that their farm would pose no risk to neighbors in a flood.[17]

Officials confirmed that a "significant portion" of the state's CAFOs were built in floodways or floodplains. That's why, in Pender and Onslow counties, at least sixteen lagoons were close to calamity. In the end, more than ten were partially or completely covered by rising floodwaters, which flushed their contents out like open cisterns. One official described a particular riverside farm as "an island of pigs in a sea of murky brown water." Roofs were blown off the barns, and miserable pigs could be seen running around inside. Meanwhile, farmers were pumping tons of hog waste onto flooded fields to avoid the alternative: catastrophic failure of their lagoons. The result however, was similar: Most waste ran into nearby streams and wetlands.

Rick Dove and Phil Bowie took to the air and documented a dark plume in the river and dozens of "compromised" lagoons. Back on the ground, they saw fish dying off, beginning in obscure streams and spreading down the waterways where it quickly blossomed into a massive river kill as the wave of filth swept down the Neuse. Oxygen levels fell to one part per million—low enough to wipe out most fish. Boat captain George Beckwith told reporters that "every kind of fish that can't get out of the way is dead. Menhaden, puppy drum, flounder. Even the crabbers say that everything in their pots is dead."[18]

Environmental officials were quick to state that the hypoxic conditions were caused by natural organic material flushed in from swamps, and not sewage or hog spills. Swamps smell, said Secretary Howes. "That organic matter carries the same unpleasant odor that some people attribute to swine or municipal waste operations," he told *The News & Observer*.[19] But Rick disagreed. "It's not hard to see swine waste running into and down the river. I have seen this many times before," Rick insisted to the media. "I can definitely smell the feces in this river. I know the difference between rotting leaves and swine waste. The river is an absolute mess, and it's not just from one source. It takes all these things together, and anyone who says anything else doesn't know what they're talking about."

Don Webb also scoffed at the "natural" explanation for the disasters. He estimated a kill of two hundred thousand fish up at his Wilson County place. "It's the hog factories that are to blame," Don growled. "There have been floods here for longer than we've been alive; there's never been anything like this."

For all their destruction, Bertha and Fran left some good news in their formidable wakes. They swept the Neuse River Basin—its creeks, streams, and riverbanks—clean of thousands of tons of natural and man-made nutrients, and washed it out to sea. After the storms, oxygen levels improved, fish stocks rose, and *Pfiesteria* blooms returned with much less deadly force. The giant toilet, as Rick liked to say, had been flushed. The next few years would be better ones on the Neuse.

That is, until 1999, when an even mightier hurricane came killing in North Carolina. Its name was Floyd.

In late 1996, Rick received a call from Gary Grant, a resident of tiny, isolated Tillery, a community eighty miles northeast of Raleigh. Tillery is a poor town in a poor county. Established in 1939 as a New Deal resettlement, it was home to just twelve hundred people, 98 percent of them African-American and 85 percent of them over the age of sixty. Most were women—single mothers and grandmothers. Tillery's county, Halifax, near the Virginia border, was the fourth poorest in the state, with the highest ratio (nearly one in five) of households with substandard or no indoor plumbing.[20]

Gary was the director of Concerned Citizens of Tillery (CCT), a group formed in 1978 to "build on the legacy of those who toiled before us for civil rights and social justice for African Americans in the county and beyond," he told Rick. "We fight for the well-being of our citizens through self-development: From adult education to voter registration to land ownership and debt control to African-American culture and heritage."

For the last few years, CCT had been taking on the hog industry. Four large swine confinements were operating in Halifax County by this point. "The state ranks us as tied for third place among counties with the worst lagoon problems; we got four lagoons in danger of blowing right now," he said. Ironically, Halifax also had the state's toughest county health rules for lagoons and water monitoring, due to CCT's efforts. But it was not enough.

"When I first started organizing folks against the pig factories, I really caught hell from the powers that be," said Gary, a firebrand rural community organizer in his early fifties, who never fears to speak his mind. "I'd come home evenings to threats on my answering machine: 'Mind your own business, nigger,' and, 'Nigger, you're going to get killed.' That sort of crap."

Gary had been working closely with a young researcher at University of

North Carolina at Chapel Hill, Steve Wing, to study the impact of hog CAFOs on counties like Halifax. "We've got documentation on how the hog explosion happened mainly in poor African-American communities," he said. Twelve of the top fifteen hog-producing counties had black populations over 30 percent, while statewide it was 22 percent. Income in all but one was below the fiftieth percentile.

But the federal government was stepping in to help. "In 1994, President Clinton ordered federal agencies to begin addressing environmental injustice, including environmental racism," he explained. "The National Institute for Environmental Health Sciences offered money for partnerships among community groups, university-based environmental scientists, and community health experts. And in September, we got our grant—to fight environmental racism in Halifax County."

The project, conducted with the Halifax County Health Department and faculty at the UNC School of Public Health, was called South-East Halifax Environmental Reawakening. The reawakening in the title referred to regaining "fundamental environmental values that people forgot as they lost close contact with the land," Gary said.

The result of Gary's work with Steve Wing and others was a paper published in *Environment and Urbanization*, which stated: "Industries considered to be undesirable neighbors because of their pollution and poor working conditions have been attracted to rural areas with large African American populations," they wrote, "because land and labor are cheap, workers are not unionized and communities lack political power to oppose them."[21]

Swine CAFOs were remanded to poor black communities that were "disenfranchised in a system that began during slavery and continues today in the form of racially segregated schools, housing and job opportunities," the authors said. "Industry chooses these locations because of the lack of local political power and acceptability in the dominant society of sacrificing poor blacks, their communities and the value of their property." Rick was not surprised by what Gary told him. It sounded a lot like the stories he had heard at that 1993 meeting in Black Creek, when he first met Don Webb.

Gary saw an opportunity for partnering with the Neuse Foundation. "Listen, Rick," Gary said, "we're forming a little group called the Hog Roundtable, a coalition of grassroots, legal, and environmental people." He invited Rick to the first meeting in Goldsboro on December 14.

Rick was honored. On December 14, a Saturday, he and the New River Riverkeeper, Tom Mattison, took the hour drive up to Goldsboro, where they walked into a who's who collection of environmental activists in the state, gathered together for the first time.

Rick and Tom arrived early so Rick could meet his host. Gary Grant was a stout and sturdy man, balding with a swath of silver on either side, a warm smile, and an easy country charm that tempers a burning rage within. There were several African Americans at the Hog Roundtable, including people from Duplin County who were literally being sprayed with hog waste on their own property. Others from the more mainstream—and predominantly white— environmental groups included Joe Rudek and staff from the North Carolina Environmental Defense Fund; Bill Holman, a lobbyist for the Sierra Club; Don Webb and his ARSI members; the North Carolina Coastal Federation and North Carolina Wildlife Federation; and representatives from sixteen other groups.

Rick was impressed by Gary's ability to whip up an audience and speak truth to power. To hell with it if some people got uncomfortable, even the most well-intentioned people. Gary started the Roundtable calmly and straightfor- wardly, declaring that industrialized hog farms were the reason for numerous community problems, and that the main victims were black. "People who've been denied access to education, to voting, are now threatened when they raise questions about their wells being polluted, the air they breathe, and even their children who can't go outside because it smells like hog shit.

"People live like this every day," he continued, "where you can't raise your windows, where you run from your car into your house, when you sit in church and find something stinking and realize that it's you, because you didn't get into your car fast enough from your house." Many nodded in recognition. "There's *no* reason for an industry to continue to dump this kind of waste on our citizens, on our land, and in our water." Gary's pitch was rising. "We will *not* allow them to come in to pollute and kill off our people, nor to come in under the disguise of economic development but bringing destruction to us. We will *not* allow it." Applause broke out around the table.

As he focused more on the racism inherent in this trend, the white environ- mentalists began to shift uncomfortably in their seats. "We are disillusioned by the refusal of the environmental community to recognize environmental racism and injustice," he said. "Where is the adequate representation of communities of color? Where are the mentions of justice issues in your mission statements? Why neglect issues other than your specific environmental concerns?

"I ask you to think about this as we move forward, because we will not allow people of color to be taken for granted, patronized, excluded, or used by traditional environmental groups who refuse to expand their agendas. Fighting environmental injustice is important," he concluded, "but it's just one symp- tom of the sickness that plagues all of white America: racism."

The remainder of the afternoon was spent planning ways to protect rural communities (of any and all colors) from further degradation. The Roundtable members and their allies agreed to lobby together for county zoning control, for stricter rules on lagoons and sprayfields, and for new technologies to eliminate anaerobic (liquid-based) manure systems altogether. They hoped to persuade then USDA secretary Dan Glickman to come visit the area.

The environmentalists had their detractors. One of them spoke to an Associated Press reporter whom Gary had invited to the meeting. Nick Weaver, president of a new and well-funded hog industry group called Farmers for Fairness, told the reporter that the environmentalists' complaints were "ridiculous."[22]

Weaver insisted that factory farms are held to stringent standards for everyday operations, and said the biggest hog farms "probably have to meet more regulations and a higher standard than most." It was an argument that Rick and the others had heard repeatedly, and disputed. Weaver added, "If you went to one of our farms, you'd find a situation where we're meeting every single requirement. The bottom line is, if we do something to screw up our environment, we pay for it."

By early spring 1997, swine-belt skirmishes were escalating. But nowhere did they grow quite as tense, dangerous, or well-publicized as at one standoff on Gray Road near the hamlet of Vanceboro, about ten miles north of New Bern.

Several heavily armed and burly men used trucks and SUVs to blockade the Craven County road. They were farmers, mostly, and they had been fighting to stop CAFOs in their territory for more than a year. They wore farmer's caps and holstered sidearms. Some sipped coffee while cradling semiautomatics.

Their mission was to prevent heavy construction machinery from reaching two proposed hog sites—a nine-thousand-head operation called Forest Edge Farms, and a twenty-seven-thousand-head project on land being offered by Vanceboro's mayor. The protestors also demanded that Craven County commissioners deny building permits for the sites, citing the county's adoption of a one-year moratorium on new hog confinements. But that moratorium didn't apply to CAFOs already under construction—hence the urgency to block traffic.

The protestors' tactics had been increasing in vigor. At public meetings in New Bern, some would soak their clothes in swine waste to be as offensively malodorous as possible. Others shouted out at hearings and badgered politicians such as County Commissioner Gary Bleau and State Representative John Nichols, both of whom owned swine farms. These were not always tactics of which Rick approved, but they did earn his respect.

Not that he supported an armed standoff. He had advised his friend Bill

Harper, a member of the group (who had spoken out at the New Bern town hall), not to go the demonstration, saying that "violence begets violence."

Print reporters and TV crews swarmed to the standoff. So did county sheriff deputies, who surrounded the scene and ordered demonstrators to disperse, but were refused. In the end, the officers took no action, and just warned the protestors to "stay out of trouble."

Joe Laughinghouse, who lived next to one of the sites, positioned his .308 caliber rifle on the hood of a pickup and yelled out to reporters, "If they come down this road to try to build, there's going to be bloodshed." His buddies whistled and cheered. "These men who want to build the hog factories, they've chosen money and greed over the citizens. But I'd rather die with a bullet between my *eyes*, than be diseased all my life smelling hog feces and urine."[23]

But Glenn Buck, president of Stop the Hogs in Craven County, appealed to his members to shun any talk of gunplay, at least while outsiders were within earshot. Buck was a full-time tobacco farmer and part-time minister who preached at various local churches. On this day, he brandished a gun in one hand and a Bible in the other.

"Don't tell 'em we're gonna kill nobody!" Buck warned his posse. "If you open your mouth, the other side's gonna put us behind the eight ball." He handed reporters a statement declaring that "the people of Gray Road just wanted to be left alone." It called the agenda of the county livestock association's president "equal to that of a warmonger."

By day's end, the construction trucks hadn't arrived and folks dispersed, including the media, who rushed back to New Bern and Raleigh to file rather dramatic accounts. Ultimately, the protestors got their way, and the CAFO permits were denied.

For better or worse, the greater New Bern area was becoming famous—or infamous—for its farm and river battles. Media scrutiny was so intense that the Neuse River practically needed a press agent. Rick Dove could have used some help, too, as he welcomed and worked with reporters and crews from Los Angeles to London.

In March 1997, it was *Dateline NBC*'s turn.

NBC correspondent Dennis Murphy was dispatched to New Bern. Rick chaperoned him and his crew out on the water and up in the air to identify the CAFO pollution and fish kills. Much of Murphy's stand-up narration was delivered from Rick's dock.

"You're the Riverkeeper," he said. "How sick is your river?"

Rick looked somber as he pondered the question. "She is really on the brink," he said. "We have enough information to know that we have a true monster on our hands. This *Pfiesteria* puts a neurotoxin in the water, and when you're out there you can see fish attempting to escape the water, literally jump out of the water, or beach themselves—like something is after them."

"Would you advise someone to come down and get in the river?" Murphy asked.

"No. I don't use the river. I don't put my hand in it. I don't eat the fish, because I do not trust it."

Later, as Murphy and his crew filmed Rick on the *Lonesome D*, the reporter said to him, "You don't strike me as a tree hugger." Rick jumped at the chance to explain himself. "No, I am not." He grinned. "I am a Republican. And I am a capitalist. I believe that industry is good and development is good. But it's got to be right, or we're shooting ourselves in the foot."

"But you know what the guys in Raleigh are going to say," Murphy countered. "Rick Dove: You are *killing* us. You are going to murder our fishing business. The tourists are going to go right past the state with their boats on the trailer."

Rick looked at the NBC reporter, but his challenge was meant for the officials in Raleigh: "Then fix my river."

The grotesque signs of *Pfiesteria* were arriving earlier in the season. It was June 1997, and rotting fish with telltale lesions were crowding the Pamlico and Neuse rivers and tributaries. Rick, Howard Glasgow, and others from North Carolina State and University of North Carolina Wilmington raced out onto the waters to pick up dead menhaden for research.

The state also sent its newly formed Neuse Rapid Response Team, who reported low levels of *Pfiesteria*-like dinoflagellates in Vandemere Creek, a condition that may have stressed the fish, but not killed them. Back in Raleigh at JoAnn Burkholder's lab, technicians found concentrations of eighty to one hundred *Pfiesteria*-like cells per milliliter. Levels of about one hundred to four hundred can cause sores, while fish usually die at concentrations of four hundred or more cells per milliliter. Something else must have been responsible for the fish kills—if it's not *Pfiesteria*, what is it?

It would be a long summer. Lawmakers, fearing horrible publicity over dying rivers, practically tripped over themselves on their way to the capital to pass new legislation. In late June, the Democratic-controlled state senate pushed through the sweeping Clean Water Responsibility Act by a forty-to-ten vote. It was considered among the most far-reaching environmental bills ever passed in Raleigh. Introduced by New Bern's Beverly Perdue, the bill authorized crackdowns on municipal sewers and other point sources of pollution. It also called for a two-year moratorium on new hog confinements and—to the surprise of

Rick and others—county control over siting them. The GOP-controlled House had already passed a one-year moratorium.

Meanwhile, the pork people fanned out into the mass media with talking-point criticisms of the Perdue bill. "The real danger of the moratorium is that it will spread to other states," Walter Cherry, executive director of the North Carolina Pork Council, told *The News & Observer*.[24] He warned that the industry might move overseas, abandoning "family farms" and workers who built hog barns. Still, he was pleased that lawmakers had not singled out hog manure, but tackled human waste, too.

Despite the hog-industry campaign, a statewide moratorium was put in place, though not until mid-1999.

North Carolina was getting the lion's share of media attention for *Pfiesteria piscicida*, but the dangerous dinoflagellate was turning up in other states as well—specifically the eastern shore of the Chesapeake Bay in Maryland. The area—especially Wicomico, Somerset, and Worcester counties—was the largest chicken-producing region in the country, home to tens of millions of birds, and headquarters to Perdue Farms, in the farming city of Salisbury. The three counties, home to about 180,000 people, slaughtered approximately ten million chickens a week. That meant a steady net poultry population of seventy million birds.[25]

In late 1996, Rick first learned that familiar lesions were appearing on fish catches from the Pocomoke River, a seventy-mile waterway that ran from the Delaware border southwest to the Chesapeake. Pocomoke passes through some of the most heavily concentrated poultry precincts in the world. By June 1997, thousands of fish in the river were dying. Similar reports were coming in from Maryland watermen near Annapolis, and even in the Potomac River south of Washington.

Scientists suspected *Pfiesteria*, but no one had confirmed its presence yet. Unlike officials' response in North Carolina, health officials in Maryland quickly warned against the consumption of ulcerated fish and urged handling them with gloves. They said it was safe to swim only in areas with no recent fish kills, and where fewer than 20 percent of the fish had sores—without explaining how one was supposed to count the diseased population.

In August, the Pocomoke had some thirty thousand dead fish, most of them with telltale sores. Similar but smaller kills were reported in the Kings Creek branch of the Manokin River. This time, state scientists identified the killer as the "cell from hell." Local environmentalists said that very high levels of phosphorus and nitrogen found in the rivers were to blame for the algae, and the most likely source of those nutrients were the thousands of huge broiler farms squeezed into the rivers' watersheds. But in September, another batch of lesion-speckled fish turned up dead. This time, it happened in the Chicamacomico River, just outside the chicken zone in Dorchester County. "It raises the question," one state agent said, "is it really the poultry?"

Environmentalists suggested that crop farms in the area were using chicken manure, just as farmers across the county line were doing, by scattering the dry chicken "litter" (wood chips, feathers, feces, and spilled food) liberally around their fields. Fertilizer runoff from crop farms near rivers and the bay had been a proven contributor to the growing eutrophication and algal blooms found in Chesapeake Bay.

8

It was January 1998. CARE's official paperwork to bring a federal lawsuit against Henry and Henrietta Bosma was filed in federal court in Spokane. CARE accused the farmer and his wife of violating the Clean Water Act. Charlie Tebbutt was not a member of the bar in Washington, so he took on a well-known Spokane cocounsel named Richard Eymann.

"Defendants have discharged pollutants to the waters of the United States without a permit," CARE's official complaint alleged, "and have violated and continue to violate their Washington State general dairy permit, the Clean Water Act and the Washington Clean Water Act, by discharging animal manure wastes into waters of the state from a concentrated animal feedlot operation."[1]

These illegal discharges were negatively impacting the quality of life for residents near the river who "recreate there by fishing, rafting, hiking, walking and boating; they observe and enjoy wildlife in the watershed; and they have an aesthetic and health interest in keeping the water free of animal manure."

As restitution for these violations, CARE would seek "a declaratory judgment, injunctive relief, the imposition of civil penalties, and the award of costs including attorney and expert witness fees."

Charlie laid out the "facts of the case."

In January 1996, the DOE had issued a general dairy permit to one of Henry Bosma's two dairies. Under department rules, there were to be no discharges of waste to "surface waters of the State," except during a "twenty-five-year, twenty-four-hour rainfall event."

The complaint alleged that Hank Bosma had violated his permit by repeatedly discharging liquid manure from a point source—the dairies—into drains and irrigation ditches connected by other waterways to the Yakima River. One of those ditches, called Joint Drain 26.6, was little more than a natural gulch with a small stream running through it in the winter. But the drain emptied into the Sunnyside irrigation canal during the summer and, in the winter, into the Granger Drain—a larger confluence of man-altered intermittent or "ephemeral" streams—that received rainwater and irrigation runoff within a 62-square-mile watershed called the Granger Drain Basin.

Specifically, CARE was alleging that Bosma deliberately allowed a variety of illegal discharges to escape from his two dairies, including wastewater seepage, wastewater discharged from drainpipes and leaking from hoses, runoff from overapplication on sprayfields and from spraying on frozen ground, lagoon waste from breaches and overflows, and manure that was deliberately dumped into ditches and canals. The discharges were found to contain fecal coliform and *E. coli* bacteria, phosphorus, nitrogen, ammonia, and suspended solids.

In its "Prayer for Relief," CARE requested that the court

- Declare that Bosma violated, and continued to violate, the CWA, state laws, and his federal permit.
- Ban him from running the dairies in a way that would cause further discharge of manure waste into waters of the United States.
- Issue civil penalties up to $27,500 per day for violations since January 1, 1997, and $25,000 per day before then.
- Allow CARE to sample discharges from the dairies, with Bosma covering the cost.
- Order Bosma to provide CARE with all documents and reports pertaining to any discharges for one year.
- Order Bosma to pay for environmental restoration or remediation "to ameliorate the water degradation caused by defendant's violations."
- Award CARE its costs, including reasonable attorney and expert witness fees, and award "other relief as this Court deems appropriate."

Dairy-industry reaction to the lawsuits was swift. The Washington State Dairy Federation's Debbie Becker told the *Daily Sun News* that CARE members refused their pleas for negotiation.[2] Letters to the editor were more belligerent. "I am outraged, but not at the dairy industry," one woman wrote. "Are we so simpleminded that we do not see money connections between system exploiters and organizations created instantly to make us believe in half truths?" Another woman urged readers not to consider CARE a Lower Valley group, adding: "We booed them out of the Grange Hall this fall."

But Mary Lynne Bos argued that CARE's environmental complaints were heeded only after the group threatened legal action, and that several dairies not named in the letters of intent had begun making significant improvements over the past two months.

"We are happy that they are taking some action, but it's unfortunate it took the threat of lawsuit to bring this about," Shari Conant told the newspaper. "Contrary to what the Dairy Federation has been saying, we want to work with the dairies to solve these problems, and come to a settlement which will prevent future pollution."[3]

The newspaper also commissioned two guest editorials about the lawsuits for that day's edition. The first was from then Yakima County Commissioner Bill Flower, under the headline DO YOU REALLY CARE, CARE? Flower claimed that area dairies had made great efforts to comply with state regulations over the past two years, spending hundreds of thousands of dollars. He accused CARE of creating an atmosphere of anxiety throughout the region's agricultural community.

"No farmer can survive when there is an overt risk of paying legal fees to out-of-state organizations," Flower wrote. "If you really care, CARE, come back to the table with a clear agenda and make a real difference in the community by helping our valley to be a better place to live. Litigation is not the answer. We all care!"

He went on, "This explains why large dairies with good records are threatened with proposed lawsuits, along with other dairies who have spent hundreds of thousands of dollars over the past two years addressing runoff issues from unusual heavy snow and rainfall. The interesting thing is that CARE actually has accomplished a great deal without litigation!" Flower continued, in an unexpected nod to the homegrown environmentalists. "CARE got the attention of the farming community—not just the dairy farmers!"

The reply editorial came from CARE president, Helen Reddout. "Our basic purpose is to get legally binding commitments from [dairies] to build and operate waste management facilities that will no longer pollute our water," she said, adding that citizens cannot file CWA suits "because they feel like it," but only if pollution "has occurred or continues to occur." She said Flower's essay had "several mistakes or misinformed ideas," which she would correct in a personal letter. Days later, he received it:

I have attended four workshops and heard how the problems with the feedlots have been solved. Yet I regularly drive through air heavily laden with particles. Sometimes the dust is so thick it looks like a low-lying fog. The smells that originate from these lots will turn your stomach.

Ammonialike gases burn your nose and eyes. Today, with the addition of 67 factory dairies, the problem has become overwhelming—there is no escape. The buildup of thousands of tons of fecal material has turned the land into a disposal system. The valley floor has become pocked with open sewage pits the size of several football fields.

At one time, we thought the manure sprayguns were as bad as it could become, but with the new misting systems, the problem has grown worse. Now the fermented urine and fecal materials are pumped, in mist form, into the air, where it floats unimpeded onto neighboring yards, homes, crops, children, pets or anything that unfortunately happens to be outside at the time. Yakima's "dairies" are milk factories, highly capitalized industrial facilities that corral several thousand animals on a few acres around a milking parlor, minimize their movement, feed them highly concentrated mixtures of feed and chemicals, and force milk production to levels that are 50 percent higher than state averages. The area's herd of seventy thousand dairy cows is creating a million gallons of liquid waste daily, and 150,000 tons of dry manure per year—roughly the equivalent of 2.5 million people, three Seattles.

You ask "does CARE really care?" I think they do. If we let this thing go, groundwater and air quality will deteriorate even more. CARE is not out to destroy the dairy industry in the valley. It is a valuable tax base for Yakima County. The problem we have here is negligent dairies. Factories and processing plants for fruits and vegetables are required to take care of their wastes; this is what dairies must also do. Maybe the only confusion we have is in the minds of the negligent dairies and the author of the editorial.

In early 1998, Charlie sent a letter to Bosma's attorneys, formally notifying them about the tape that Helen made during Hank's visit to the Reddout home. Bosma's lawyers were ready for hardball. They sent a curt letter back to Charlie, asking if he was aware that Helen had broken state laws by recording a conversation without permission. She could do jail time for such an offense, the lawyers said.

Charlie called Helen to break the news. "It seems that, in Washington state, well, you may have broken the law."

"What to do you mean, Charlie?"

"Well, because when you started taping Bosma, you didn't say into the tape, and in front of him, 'Hello, this is Helen Reddout, and I am taping Mr. Henry Bosma at my home in Outlook, Washington, on such and such a date . . .'"

"My *God*, Charlie, I had no idea! I thought that the sign I made was good

enough. I read that brochure and just assumed that was what you were supposed to do. I didn't intentionally break the law, Charlie."

"I know. You didn't do it *intentionally*. But . . ."

Helen felt dizzy. "I'm going to jail!" she cried. "I'm an old lady and I'm going to be in jail! We've got to do something about this. Can we destroy the
tape?"

But Helen knew that would be obstruction of justice. There was a similar
case on the news. After all, it was the summer of Monica Lewinsky. Linda
Tripp was facing criminal charges for illegally taping phone chatter with the
intern. Charlie tried to soothe his rattled client. "Helen," he said, "please don't
worry. We'll take care of you. We'll provide you with legal services and whatever else you need."

"Really, Charlie? You would do that?"

"Of course. And anyway, with the courts being so full and everything, it
would be hard to find a prosecutor who considered this a priority."

"Is that supposed to make me feel better, Charlie? Because it doesn't. What
if they *do* find a prosecutor like that?"

An awkward pause ensued as Helen contemplated life as a criminal defendant. Then Charlie broke her grim thoughts. "Besides, Helen, if we did lose the
case, I would come to visit you every Sunday in prison." And with that, he burst
out laughing.

"Damn it, Charlie!" she shouted. "That's not funny. That's not funny at all!"

Charlie assured her the chance of criminal charges was minimal. (In the
end, he turned out to be right; Linda Tripp would likewise escape prosecution.)
Helen remained nervous about the existence of the tape nonetheless. But Charlie insisted he would not turn it over to anyone—unless doing so was necessary
as part of the pretrial process.

One brisk morning in early 1998, Shari and Helen were on patrol, scouting
around for more violations. They came across a drainage pipe that was
emptying dairy sludge into an irrigation ditch. Helen climbed from the car and
began snapping photos.

Almost immediately, a surly-looking young man drove up in his pickup.
Helen recognized Hank Bosma's son Steve. Helen scrambled up the embank-
ment and into the passenger seat. Shari rolled down her window and smiled
coolly at the young man.[4]

"What the hell are you doing here?" he shouted. "I want you to get out of
here! You don't got no right to be here!" Shari started the ignition and began
to pull away.

"Let's turn right up here, because that takes us away from Hank's place,"

Helen said. They had driven on about a quarter mile when Helen heard screeching rubber behind them. Steve Bosma was approaching quickly, his truck growing in Shari's rearview mirror. "He's coming up on us fast," Helen said, turning around. The truck, now going about 70 miles per hour, was a few yards away. "Damn!" Shari shouted. "This maniac's going to ram us!"

Helen unfastened her seat belt and turned around to stare the young man in the face. Shari shouted at her: "What are you doing?" Helen didn't answer. Instead, she reached for her trusty Canon, dropped in a long lens, and began shooting the whole crazy chase on film. "If we're going to go out like Karen Silkwood, at least I'm going to have some good photos of it!" The young man saw the camera and dropped his pursuit.

Within one week, CARE filed two more lawsuits: one against the DeRuyter Brothers Dairy, in Outlook, and another against Herman teVelde's Sunnyveld Dairy, next to Mary Lynne.

Jake DeRuyter issued a terse response to the media. "We have had our attorney contact their attorneys to try to arrange a meeting, so we could have a face-to-face discussion, which we thought would occur next week," he told reporters. "They have consistently said they would rather talk than litigate. But filing a lawsuit doesn't seem like a way to promote discussions."[5]

The week of March 1, 1998, the *Tri-City Herald* ran a five-part series on the impact of the dairy industry in the Yakima Valley. It did not paint a flattering picture.[6]

Helen was encouraged by the articles. She hoped they might help deflate some of the heated rhetoric and threats that had come in the wake of the CARE lawsuits.

The articles reported that waste from at least two dairies—owned by Henry Bosma and Jake DeRuyter—had "repeatedly leaked" into irrigation and drainage ditches since the mid-1970s. From August 1995 to June 1997 alone, the DOE fined the two farms for "substantial water quality violations" totaling some $42,000. "These are the two that we've been working the hardest with," said the DOE's Max Linden. But Bosma said he had just installed a $125,000 waste system that included three new lagoons with more than forty-nine million gallons' capacity. "He's hoping all that work and money will keep the agency—and valley citizens groups filing Clean Water Act lawsuits—off his back," the paper said.

Jake DeRuyter refused to comment. But records from his dairy revealed at least fifteen illegal manure discharges since 1976. In January 1995, he was caught pumping waste into a ditch along Van Belle Road, even though his lagoon had available space. Water samples from a nearby drain revealed seven hundred thousand colonies of fecal coliform bacteria per one hundred millili-ters of water, or seven thousand times over the state limit. He was fined three thousand dollars.

Two years later, DeRuyter workers were caught on film pumping manure into another irrigation drain. This time, he was fined thirty thousand dollars after inspectors saw two empty lagoons on-site that could have taken the waste. DeRuyter paid the fine but didn't admit guilt. That same year, three more ma-nure discharges were verified at his facility. In two of the cases, a pivoting spray gun was stuck in one position, sending wastewater in giant streams off the property.

Meanwhile, Henry Bosma had several disturbing incidents in his own file, according to the article. Among them were the following:

March 1993: Two manure discharges ran into an irrigation drain from overap-plication of waste, for which he received a six-thousand-dollar penalty. Bosma said the worker who ran the spray guns left the site when his wife went into labor. The fine was cut in half on appeal.

April 1996: Bosma was hit with a nine-thousand-dollar fine for discharging manure water into an irrigation drain. The fine was deferred until he completed his waste-management plan. But the discharges continued. He was ordered to pay the fine up front and hit with an additional three-thousand-dollar penalty for "permit violations."

September 1997: A drain was found to be "pure green" from animal effluence. Coliform counts were more than 480 times the state limit. "It was clean water going through a dirty ditch," Bosma told the paper. "I am not the only one who uses that ditch."

January 1998: During a large storm that impacted several farms, the DOE confirmed two more cases of manure in drains near Bosma's dairy.

Bosma spoke out in defense of his "thick file," the paper wrote. "'A lot of this stuff isn't verified. And if it is, we address it immediately,'" he said, adding that he wished people who had complaints about his dairies would come to him before going to the DOE.

By May 1998, Charlie Tebbutt's process of examining all the relevant Bosma documents he received through discovery was well under way. His

office was stacked with boxes of papers documenting Bosma's rocky relationship with Mother Nature—and the authorities. Bosma seemed to have been in
trouble right from the start; some violations dated back twenty-five years. In
March 1976, soon after he opened Bosma Dairy, a DOE inspector named
Marc Horton paid a visit. Bosma was petulant and intransigent, Horton indicated in his report. "I told Mr. Bosma I would like to see the discharge from his
dairy *not* entering the drain that runs toward the Sunnyside Canal," he wrote.
"He told me that he plans on digging a lagoon for containment of his manure
by this spring."[7] The inspector returned in July to see if Bosma had, indeed,
built his lagoon by spring:

> Mr. Bosma informed me that a lagoon was not "high on his priority
> list" and he would get around to it when he "felt like it." His attitude
> was negative toward any governmental interference, and I feel that
> system improvements will not occur without application of CWA per-
> mits on this dairy.[8]

Months went by, and still Bosma rebuffed "government interference." DOE
agents were losing patience, but still preferred to get Bosma's cooperation
through persuasion, rather than force. In October, DOE supervisor Clar Pratt
sent a very polite letter to Bosma.

"I sent you a simple form which covered the application for NPDES [Na-
tional Pollutant Discharge Elimination System] permit," Pratt wrote in 1976.
"My purpose was to primarily afford you the opportunity to conveniently submit an NPDES application before the required date. Failure to [do so] would
have exposed you to potential action by the state, federal government and civil
suit by any concerned citizen under the federal law"—such as the suit that
CARE was about to bring.[9]

But Bosma never bothered to fill out the permit. "That leaves you, legally,
hanging way out there, and I did go to some length to see that that would not
happen," Pratt said. "Please get hold of me and let me know what the problem
is so we can work something out." He hinted that the state might engage in
"cost-sharing" for waste-control measures.

And still Bosma ignored them. In March 1978, inspectors once again
caught his dairy in the act of discharging liquid manure into a ditch that emptied into the Granger Drain. This time, he was ordered to cease and desist.[10]

A month later, the DOE *finally* issued a violation notice to B & M Dairy
for illegal discharges of liquid cow manure to waters of the state. The fine was
$250.[11] But two years went by, and Bosma never paid even this token fine. By

1980, however, the dairyman's obduracy had stirred the Washington State Office of the Attorney General in Olympia. Assistant Attorney General Jeffrey Goltz told Bosma it was pointless to "push this relatively small controversy to a court confrontation."[12]

That was followed by an angry missive from the DOE. "Your lack of response to our previous attempts to contact you by visit, letter, phone and finally delivery of a cease-and-desist order by the sheriff has resulted in our recommendation for an additional penalty." The DOE wanted far more than the original $250 fine—now it sought $250 per *day* for a period of twenty-one days, or $5,250 overall. Bosma had complained that a manure plan would cost him $15,000 to implement. "Perhaps the magnitude of our proposed fine, which we feel is not at all unreasonable, puts the implementation of a waste management plan into proper perspective," DOE agents wrote. "We would much rather have seen you spend that money on wastewater control facilities than to have to recommend a penalty."[13]

But still no reply. On June 10, 1980, the DOE filed suit against "Henry Bosma and his wife, if any." The summons gave the Bosmas twenty days to respond or face a default judgment and fines up to five thousand dollars per day.[14]

Bosma was starting to get the message. He revamped his lagoons by digging two small pits next to a larger basin. But the new system didn't work for long. Three years later, "a discharge of black manure solids-laden water" was running off of the Bosma property across the road and into a canal.[15]

The Sunnyside Valley Irrigation District, owner of Joint Drain 26.6, was fed up. On July 27, 1984, manager James Trull penned a "get off your ass" letter to the DOE, saying that waste from the lagoon was still running into the canal. "The impact has been enormous," he wrote. "We have complaints from water users that their weed screens have plugged in a matter of one or two hours, as opposed to the normal 12–24 hour intervals (and) irrigation systems plugging, causing overflow and erosion. These are not isolated complaints. The above situation is frustrating because it is typical of the experience the District has had with dairy waste problems for the last several years." And, he added, "We have a number of water users who would be most willing to testify in court, contact area legislators, or do whatever else is necessary to assist you with your enforcement responsibilities."[16]

Still, Bosma paid nothing.

In June 1986, the DOE ordered the obstinate dairyman to apply for an NPDES permit within thirty days, and file a new waste-management plan in ninety days, or face a ten-thousand-dollar-per-day fine.[17]

Bosma did not seem to give a damn. "From the sounds of the enclosed orders, you must have been promoted to some type of deity," he wrote to the DOE inspector. "Congratulations. As per your request, I return your permit forms herewith. Unfortunately I don't understand any of it, and therefore, can't act on them. I would be happy to discuss this at your convenience at more reasonable terms."[18]

Bosma's attorney said he had no intention of paying anything. Two years went by. On March 30, 1988, the DOE proposed another fine, for three thousand dollars, when an agent caught workers building a manure drain line from Bosma's cow barns to a culvert crossing under East Zillah Drive. He had also dug an unauthorized lagoon to the east of his calf pens.[19]

Bosma fired back with a defiant, menacing letter to the DOE about the agent they had sent to his property. "I get very tired of fighting off incompetent experts who are off on their ego trips," he began. "After this incident, I called you and told you that I did not ever want to see this man again, that he was totally incompetent and has a dangerously twisted mental attitude, and if he ever showed up again I would run him off with a pair of Dobermans."[20]

He continued: "I'm told that 'Bosma needs to be taught a lesson.' I find that rather presumptuous. I have not violated any state regulations, I will not pay any fines, I will not attend any hearings, I will not waste any more of my time trying to debate various interpretations of state regulations, and I will no longer dignify with a response anything coming from your agent. I've never written a letter like this, please don't take this lightly. Sincerely Yours, Hank Bosma."

The DOE agent who had so riled Bosma filed his own account of the incident, including Bosma's "unwillingness to take control of the dairy's wastewater" and his "indifferent attitude" that led to intentional discharges by hired help. "Mr. Bosma's responses have varied from rapid, poorly planned, unreviewed construction to indefinite delays and avoidance of communication. Mr. Bosma can best be described as uncooperative." The agent recommended a fine of three thousand dollars.[21]

Unbelievably to Charlie and Helen, Bosma just kept on polluting, right up until 1997. Reports filed against his dairies in 1993 *alone* included the following:

January 12: A caller complained that Bosma was spraying liquid waste on frozen ground, and manure was running into Joint Drain 26.6.[22]

March 26: A caller complained that Bosma was discharging dairy manure into an agricultural drain.[23]

March 31: DOE inspectors saw wastewater from Bosma Dairy running on Liberty Road, and an irrigation line was set so that runoff floated across a field and entered a culvert under Liberty Road and into a drain.[24]

October 1: Agents found manure in the main canal by Granger Drain caused by Bosma's dairy and sprayfield runoff. "During irrigation season, this is sent into the main canal, which it is doing right now. Farmers are mad. Please contact Hank Bosma!!" one wrote.[25]

October 7: Bosma called to complain. "He seemed extremely upset and agitated," an agent wrote. "He stated he would be extremely upset if that minor discharge resulted in action by [the DOE] and emphasized that with the use of 'God damn' numerous times."[26]

October 8: Bosma typed a letter to the DOE saying, "I do not believe that it is necessary for your department to issue a notice of violation in connection with our spill. All this does is create hard feelings and antagonism. This was accidental. We took immediate corrective action and the problem has been solved. I do not feel the situation calls for legal actions and bureaucratic interferences. It is taken care of, period."[27]

November 2: Bosma was issued a violation after his dairy was observed discharging manure water into Joint Drain 26.6 on September 30 and October 1.[28]

By late 1993, Bosma's intransigence had become legendary at the DOE. On December 21, an agent called to see if he was going to respond to his violations. "Mr. Bosma indicated he had not responded to the notice. It was apparent from his tone that he did not consider it to be a big deal. He stated that the problems were all corrected," the file notes. "I told Mr. Bosma that the department considered that situation a significant water problem, and based upon his response, may take further action. He indicated that he would try to respond to the violation by the end of the year."[29]

There was another intriguing handwritten note in the Bosma file, dated December 23, 1997—the time when CARE members were receiving those unwanted visits and creepy cut-and-paste letters in the mail. The note was from Hank Bosma to the DOE. It said: "Max—can we do this before the end of the year? I need some protection on this 1997 Notice of Violation—Say $1,000?"[30]

To Charlie, this was a blatant, perhaps illegal attempt to get the state to issue a fine—any fine for any CWA violation—and preempt a dreaded citizens' lawsuit in federal court. It didn't work, of course. But the note would make its way into the trial as evidence against Henry Bosma. Charlie was certain of it.

The year 1998 brought some tidings of encouragement for Helen, Charlie, and the CARE members. In January, Henry Bosma filed a motion to dismiss the case against him based on legal technicalities about proper notice.[31] The motion failed. Meanwhile, Charlie won a motion for limited consolidation of the suit against Bosma with three more civil actions—against the Koopmans, DeRuyter, and teVelde dairies. Each case would still be heard separately, but for purposes of discovery, many of the same witnesses could be deposed at one sitting.

May 1998 brought even more welcome news. The original judge assigned to the cases—Alan McDonald, a federal judge appointed by Ronald Reagan, with a conservative, probusiness record—was being replaced by a younger, relatively unknown judge, Edward F. Shea, who had recently been appointed by President Bill Clinton. The CARE lawsuits were to be Shea's first cases as a federal judge. After appearing before Judge Shea, Charlie felt that he was someone who would listen.

What lay ahead, Charlie said, was more than a year of trial preparation: There would be depositions from people on both sides, expert testimony would be developed, site inspections were needed, and more lab tests of water quality would have to be done.

For the Reddout family, the summer of 1998 settled into its usual rhythms of backyard barbecues and grueling cherry harvests. Helen thought about the lawsuits constantly and felt deep trepidation about the whole endeavor.

For one thing, there was the rather sticky legal matter of that tape that she had recorded. Helen wanted the tape played in an open courtroom—if only to humiliate Bosma and the dairymen he had trashed during his visit. Charlie provided the tape to the other side with restrictions: He would send a copy of the tape if they would commit in writing not to press charges against Helen. They agreed.

Eventually, Charlie received notice that Bosma's team wanted to submit the first seventeen minutes of the tape as evidence—of his responsible farming. He called up Helen, giddy with the news. "I can't believe this!" he said. "They actually want to *use* the tape. But they don't seem to realize, as long as they want to use any part of it, then the whole tape comes into evidence. Your entire conversation with Bosma will have its day in court!"

The Lower Valley was consumed with news of the Bosma lawsuit and other dairy affairs. Then, in February 1999, DeRuyter Brothers Dairy had a massive manure spill. The *Yakima Herald-Republic* estimated that seven hundred thousand gallons of liquefied manure had blown out of the lagoon, and some of that had emptied into the Yakima River.[32] The incident "comes at a time when the dairy industry is under fierce scrutiny for its environmental record," the paper said, noting that valley dairies were at that time producing nine hundred thousand tons of waste per year.

DOE inspector Ray Latham told the paper the cause for the spill was unknown, pending investigation. But Jake DeRuyter offered an explanation: A decades-old pipe had broken, allowing manure water to rush out.

On the hot seat, DeRuyter emphasized his green interests. "I'm very much concerned with the environment. I live here. I plan on living here a long time," the paper quoted him as saying. Disputing the seven-hundred-thousand-gallon figure, he added, "What happened here is truly an accident, but I do believe we need to clean up, all of us neighbors."

Later that spring, Koopmans Dairy decided to settle its case with CARE, rather than face them in Judge Shea's courtroom. Koopmans was a moderate-size operation of around one thousand head, compared with Bosma and De-Ruyter, who each had more than four thousand cows. Sid Koopmans did not admit to any wrongdoing, but agreed to pay out $7,500—including $500 to the U.S. Treasury, $2,500 to Heritage College (now known as Heritage University) to help fund a groundwater survey, and $4,500 to the Western Environmental Law Center to cover legal costs. CARE also won the right to inspect the Koopmans property.[33]

Lawyers for the other dairies said Koopmans's decision would not have an impact on their own trials.

Sid Koopmans sold his cows and closed his dairy, and went on to manage someone else's farm. "Financially, I couldn't make everything work," he told the local media. "It was a way of life, and it isn't there anymore. I can't pass it on to my kids." He declined to say how much influence the CARE lawsuit had had on his decision. "They filed the suit to accomplish what they wanted to accomplish," he said, "but they went about it the wrong way." Now he was looking for a job.[34]

Helen was not very sympathetic. "He's known the law for a long time," she told Don. "If he can't get with it and clean up his act, well, 'So long, my friend!'"

Meanwhile, Judge Shea had scheduled the *CARE v. Henry Bosma* trial to begin on June 1 in Richland, Washington. He also set a September 27 trial date for DeRuyter Brothers.

The work of CARE would finally be displayed in a court of law—and in the local media. Helen was nervous. Already her work had taken a social toll;

old friends would cross the street to avoid running into her downtown. "So many people have been so brainwashed by the agencies and commissioners," she told Mary Lynne. "Some actually believe these megadairies bring wonderful economic benefits."

"Either we will be successful and prove our point," Helen added, "or we'll be running around with sacks on our heads."

On June 1, 1999, *CARE v. Henry Bosma Dairy* began precisely at 8:45 A.M. in the Richland federal courthouse—a squat, bone-colored, rather Soviet-looking affair with small, irregularly placed windows.

Helen would make the trip from Outlook almost every day; sometimes Mary Lynne would drive in with her. Inside Judge Shea's courtroom, the CARE people sat in the back of the room with fellow opponents of the megadairy. Mr. and Mrs. Bosma and megadairy supporters sat up front. On either side of Mrs. Bosma sat the other dairy wives: Mrs. teVelde and Mrs. DeRuyter were both in floral print dresses with lacy white collars. They would occasionally pat Mrs. Bosma's hand in warm solidarity.

It made Helen nauseated. "Look at them, sitting up front, looking up at the judge with their pathetic little cocker spaniel faces, begging for clemency," she said later to Mary Lynne. "We would never pull that kind of crap. And I don't think the judge is buying any of it, either." Helen thought Bosma came across as cocky and unlikeable, a bigwig who was actually a petty tyrant.

There was no jury, at the request of both sides. Charlie had worried that too many potential jurors relied on the dairy industry for a living. Defense lawyers worried about the opposite problem—that the area harbored numerous CARE cheerleaders; the valley was dotted with handmade signs opposing the factory dairies. (One of Helen's favorites declared: SUNNYSIDE—COME SMELL OUR DAIRY AIR!)

Charlie launched the trial with a blistering opening statement: "Your Honor, the defendant has been on notice to cease and desist discharges from the Henry Bosma Dairy since 1978 and was specifically requested by the Department of Ecology in 1986 to get a permit, but the defendant returned the application to the DOE and refused to even submit an application for an NPDES permit."[35]

Ouch, my God, this is actually happening, Helen thought. I hope we win this.

"Essentially, the defendant thumbed his nose at the DOE all these years and he got away with it," Charlie said, promising to walk the judge through the litany of violations, fines, summonses, and angry letters involving Bosma, dating back to the legal statute of limitations: five years and sixty days from the date of CARE's original complaint.

Another important issue was the extent of injury to the plaintiffs. Charlie promised evidence of how Bosma facilities had impaired the quality of life of CARE's members. Charlie summed up his plan of attack by saying: "CARE will establish that Bosma has discharged pollutants to waters of the United States, drains and canals and eventually the Yakima River, on more than sixty occasions, including numerous violations of the water quality standards, as well as failures to report any discharges from the facilities on any occasion at any time."

Jerry Neal, attorney for the defense from the Spokane office of the Preston, Gates & Ellis law firm, rose to offer his opening statements. A stout man pushing sixty, with salt-and-pepper hair and a well-tailored suit befitting his position in a large firm, he wasted no time in arguing that CARE's case was without merit and illegitimate on its face—an argument that already had been lost at summary judgment on the basic legal issue. Neal said he would argue that the plaintiff suffered from "lack of standing" in the case. "In order for CARE to have standing, they must establish three elements," Neal said. "There must be an injury, there must be traceability, and there must be redressability; that is, that by this action their injury can be redressed."

CARE's complaint was not about the loss of recreational use in drains and canals, but rather about recreation on the Yakima River. And its pollution would not stop, regardless of the trial's outcome; therefore CARE lacked legal standing to proceed. "Whether Mr. and Mrs. Bosma had any future discharges would not make any difference to the plaintiff's action," Neal claimed. "They will not use the Yakima River regardless of what Mr. Bosma does."

Neal would also talk about the improvements Bosma had made at his properties, and said that no fines had been issued since then. True, the DOE had issued four violations in 1997, but all four had been corrected and "therefore that issue is moot."

Finally, Neal promised testimony showing that "there are a number of sources of these fecals in the drains and that those sources are unrelated to Mr. Bosma's dairy. Your Honor, we believe at the end of this case, the testimony will warrant a finding in the Bosmas' favor."

When it came time for witnesses, Charlie called Harold Porath, a former DOE inspector who was now an expert for Bosma, to the stand. He testified that runoff from a Bosma sprayfield was reaching Joint Drain 26.6, and from there, the Yakima River.

Porath later tried to suggest that some wild birds he saw near Joint Drain 26.6 might explain the elevated *E. coli* levels in the water. Charlie grilled him about how many waterfowl, exactly, he had observed on the day he made his inspection.

"Two, three," Porath said flatly.

"And they were flying where? Overhead?" Charlie inquired.

"Yes, sir."

"How high?"

"Fifty feet, a hundred feet."

It was silly to suggest that a few birds flying at one hundred feet could hit a three-foot-wide ditch with their droppings. "They must have had pretty good aim, huh?" Charlie joked with the witness. Earlier, on the same line of questioning with another witness, Charlie had asked, "Did you see any cows flying overhead?" He was quickly admonished by Judge Shea: "Mr. Tebbutt, I think you're having just a little too much fun right now." Charlie had smiled and said, "Yeah, I think so, too, Your Honor."

Porath's questioning was followed by a revealing exchange with Bob Barwin, the DOE's water-quality manager for central Washington. Charlie grilled Barwin about dairy-industry pressure against enforcing pollution permit requirements.

"Nobody really *prevented* us," he testified, "but the Dairy Federation would have seen [enforcement] as some sort of breach, and initiated some kind of action at the legislature to more directly address their concern, which ultimately did happen in 1993."

Charlie pounced: "You were negotiating with the industry over regulation of the industry?"

"Through an advisory committee, yes."

"Isn't it your job to *regulate* the industry?"

"Yes."

"It's not the industry's job to regulate the industry, is it?"

"No, but we—"

"That's why we're in this mess in the first place, isn't it?"

"Perhaps."

Over the next day or two, Charlie and Richard Eymann would interrogate many more witnesses from state government, and from their own list of experts, about Bosma property inspections over the past few years. The evidence was bruising to Bosma's case.

DOE inspector Ray Latham took to the stand. Charlie asked him if the overtopping of Bosma's lagoon had been caused by erosion of its earthen wall. Latham said yes.

"So let's see." Charlie moved toward the witness. "We have complaints about discharges in January from overapplication. We have complaints in February, and we have complaints in March, which you verified. And now we have reports of continuing problems at Mr. Bosma's facility in April of '97?"

"Yes," Latham replied.

On June 4, Charlie called Bosma himself to the stand. Charlie jumped right in.

"Mr. Bosma, were you ever requested by the Department of Ecology to get an NPDES permit in the 1980s?" Bosma said he did not recall. Charlie produced a letter, dated June 2, 1986, showing that Bosma had indeed been asked to get the permit. Charlie read it aloud.

"Mr. Bosma, having read that to you, does that refresh your recollection whether you've been required to get an NPDES permit in the 1980s?"

"No, it doesn't, Mr. Tebbutt," Bosma testified. "I don't recall this document at all. I don't recall seeing this document or any conversation about this document." Charlie pushed on. "Were you ever ordered to cease and desist discharges into the drains around your property by the Department of Ecology back in the 1970s?"

"I don't remember that, either, Mr. Tebbutt," Bosma said again, looking like he believed it.

Charlie moved in for the kill, this time producing a letter from DOE dated May 17, 1978. Again, he read aloud: "'It is ordered that B & M Dairy shall take appropriate action to cease and desist from further discharge of liquid cow manure into the Granger Drain and the Yakima River, public waters of this state,'" he read. "Mr. Bosma, does that document refresh your recollection whether you were ordered to cease and desist discharges to the Granger Drain in 1978?"

Bosma paused a moment before answering. "Well, this document is addressed to me. I don't recall this document," he said. "I may have received it. I don't know if I have or not. But I do know that in 1978 we devised—we made a—we had some kind of management system. We dug some lagoons and we addressed this issue."

"Mr. Bosma, are you familiar with the Clean Water Act?"

"I am familiar with the Clean Water Act. I am today much more so than I was a number of years ago."

"When did you become familiar with the Clean Water Act?"

"We were taking our cues from the Department of Ecology, basically. We did not necessarily look at the Clean Water Act as a body of legislation that we were totally familiar with."

The confession was a bombshell, and Charlie knew it. It was essential to pin Bosma down on when he had become familiar with the CWA. Charlie knew that, as Bosma was the recipient of a federal CWA permit, it was his responsibility to know what the law said. "I don't recall a specific moment in my life, Mr. Tebbutt," Bosma said. "It probably was a few years ago when the

Clean Water Act was being mentioned more in the literature that was available. But way back when—we were taking all of our cues from DOE."

Charlie lay in waiting, attempting to seem nonchalant. He knew he was about to ensnare his prey in a series of lies. Helen was impressed. Give them enough rope . . . she thought.

And so, the hippie Eugene lawyer with the bushy red beard (which he had trimmed back a bit for trial), picked up a weighty copy of the deposition he had taken from the burly, blue-eyed dairyman on November 4, 1998, and confronted his nemesis with the volume. Charlie handed the defendant, now looking rather glum, a copy of his own deposition. "I asked you the following question: Are you familiar with the Clean Water Act?" Charlie read aloud. "Answer: 'I didn't become—I didn't hear much about the Clean Water Act until about a year or so ago.' "

Bosma had been issued his CWA permit in 1996—and now he had contradicted himself, under oath, as to when he first learned about the law. Score one for CARE.

Charlie was about to set another trap. "Mr. Bosma, one of the Clean Water Act requirements is to have calibrated equipment for application of manure. You don't have any calibrated equipment, do you?"

"Maybe you should define for me, Mr. Tebbutt, what you mean."

"Well, you helped prepare that waste-management plan, didn't you, Mr. Bosma?"

"Yes, I did."

"What do you understand 'calibrated equipment' to mean?"

"These are manure spreader trucks and, to a certain extent, they're calibrated," Bosma said. "I'm not sure what you—the process you would go through—"

Charlie kept reading. " 'When you apply solid manure, do you have some way of determining the rate of application?' Answer: 'No. You know, not every truck is the same.' Question: 'So you don't have calibrated equipment?' Answer: 'No, we don't.' "

Strike two against the dairyman, Helen thought.

"Mr. Bosma, you apply lagoon wastes to your fields during the months of November, December, January, and February, don't you?" Charlie changed the subject.

"Well, we try not to do that, but there are certain conditions—some years there wasn't any frost on the ground. People plow it in at that time, but normally it's discouraged."

"You've never notified the DOE before you applied waste during the winter, have you?"

"I don't believe I have, Mr. Tebbutt. I didn't realize that I needed to be doing that."

"If you would take a look at the waste-management plan, Mr. Bosma, it states: 'Land application of solid or liquid manure during the winter months must be at agronomic rates. It is recommended whenever possible that these liquids be applied during a period of good weather. Notify the Department of Ecology prior to application.' Part of your waste-management plan, isn't it?"

"That's . . . it's in there, yes."

"And you signed off on that waste-management plan, didn't you?"

"Yes, sir. Yes, sir."

Strike three, Helen thought. Isn't this guy out yet?

Charlie proceeded to the illegal discharges that Bosma had been accused of. "Those discharges, you don't contest that they actually occurred, do you?" It was going to be very hard for Henry to answer yes without perjuring himself. But he tried.

"We went to a hearing on that, Mr. Tebbutt, and the hearing officer found that those were discharges and we were penalized and we did not appeal this. We didn't go to any further process. We paid our fines."

"So you had, in fact, a discharge. And during 1997 there were verified discharges as well?"

"That's what the, what the report indicated."

"Yet you still checked 'no' on your application, correct?"

There was no denying it. Bosma had clearly checked "no," right there on the document. "Well, I did. I'm not so sure what that sentence all necessarily has to imply. If this is just, 'Do I normally do this, just discharge in the river for different things?' Of course not."

Bosma looked as though he desperately wanted to get off that stand. Helen thought he looked as if he missed his cows, and he probably did. But Charlie was just getting warmed up. He went through each of the violations that Bosma had admitted to, beginning in 1993 and running up to 1997.

Charlie then returned to impeaching Bosma's character. He grilled the dairyman on his visits to Shari Conant and Helen Reddout. "Did you threaten Ms. Conant in any way during that conversation?" Bosma said he had not. "Did you threaten to investigate or bring civil action against Ms. Conant during that conversation?" Again, he said no.

"And did you ever threaten to investigate Mrs. Reddout during that conversation?"

"I don't believe so, Mr. Tebbutt, but you have it all on a tape."

"Did you threaten to bring civil action against CARE if it proceeded with a case against you?"

"I don't recall that, Mr. Tebbutt."

When Bosma's attorney rose for cross-examination, he tried out a rather flaccid "everyone does it" line of defense. "Do you know of anybody in the industry that has a calibrated manure dumping vehicle?" he asked. Bosma did not.

A few days later, when Helen's turn came at the stand, Charlie had her describe family picnic lunches down by the river. Those days were long gone now. "The last two times I've been there, about a year ago, there was foam on the river," she testified. The riverbank, she added, had the smell and texture of dried manure. The pollution had forced Helen to abandon her use of the waterway altogether.

Then it came time to play "the tape." Bosma's lawyer objected, even though it was the defense's exhibit. After some back and forth between parties, Judge Shea ruled: "On the one hand, the defendant is going to like it because of certain things that are in there. On the other hand, the plaintiff likes it for different reasons. But while it is tedious, it seems to me clear that both parties are going to benefit from having their discussion in here."

And so Helen's tape had its day in court. The clerk played the entire thing, right there in the courtroom. Helen had her eyes glued to the dairy wives. She noticed that Henrietta Bosma had got up and left the courtroom just prior to the tape being played. Mrs. Bosma knew what was coming. Her farmwife attendants, Mrs. teVelde and Mrs. DeRuyter, stayed on. They grew white as they listened to Hank Bosma trash their husbands in such frank language on Helen's surreptitious recording.

When it was finished, the court took a break for lunch. Helen noticed that the other farmwives did not return, and she wouldn't see them at the trial again until closing arguments.

Under withering cross-examination later that day, Helen was pressed about charges of runoff from Bosma Dairy since November 1997 that would affect the Yakima River. Had Helen actually seen anything like that? No, she had not, she admitted. And wasn't it true that, after November 1997, she had no evidence of any runoff to the Yakima River from any of Mr. Bosma's operations? She had no such evidence. And out of all those discharges, could Helen testify if any of them ever reached the Yakima River? The answer again was no.

It was one of the most winning moments for the defense. Neal was on a roll. He pressed on, trying to tear into Helen's credibility and her claims of "injury" from river pollution. And he attempted to slash holes through Helen's schoolmarm character. His grilling of Helen ended with three simple, pointed questions. Helen's curt answers didn't help:

"Did you announce to Mr. Bosma that you were going to tape his conversation?"

"No, I did not."

"You don't personally try to recreate in any of the irrigation ditches, do you?"

"No."

"Do you know how many lateral drains run to 26.6 before it reaches the Granger Drain?"

"No, I do not know that." Helen could not wait to get off the stand when it was over. She drove home, limp and drained.

"How did it go?" Don asked that night.

"I cannot understand how a person can sit on the witness stand and tell whoppers like I heard today," Helen said as she stared at her dinner.

"Maybe they live in a fool's paradise and they really believe what they say."

"Well, Charlie will make short issue of that. He is so sharp. I think he has every document for both sides memorized."

On June 16, both sides presented their closing arguments in front of Judge Shea.

Charlie began. When Congress passed the Clean Water Act, cases like Bosma's were probably "beyond their wildest imaginations," he said. They could not have anticipated that someone could get away with "over twenty years of flouting laws, manipulating government agencies, ignoring orders to cease and desist, flatly refusing to even apply for a permit, and calling the agencies some kind of deity simply because they were trying to do what Congress required more than a decade earlier." And yet, Charlie alleged, "none of this" deterred the defendant.

"At least sixty-four days of discrete discharge events have occurred," the plaintiffs had proved. They showed a "continuing pattern of misconduct that in many cases is not only negligent but willful." The violations were chronic and ongoing: "Failure to fill out manure application records, failure to notify the DOE before winter application of wastes, and never reporting a single one of the scores of discharges from his property.

"Mrs. Reddout, who owns land along the Yakima River, has had manure solids clog her irrigation systems. She has had to apply contaminated water to her lawn and garden. The odors from the manure discharges permeate the valley, increase fly populations, and increase risk of disease to humans. Mrs. Reddout no longer uses the Yakima River for recreation and is repulsed by its aesthetic appearance. She no longer gathers wild plants in the area out of fear of contamination. Ms. Conant, an avid water user, won't even allow her dogs to swim in the river out of fear for harming her pets.

"Now," Charlie continued, "defendants' answer might be that everyone else is doing it, too, so why pick on us? The reason is, because Mr. Bosma and his facilities constitute one of the biggest dairies in the state and one of the biggest polluters of all the dairies in the state. He's got a rap sheet five pages long."

Charlie then ripped through a list of other excuses Bosma and his legal team had offered for the repeated violations. There was, for instance, the "oh, the lagoons aren't contaminating 26.6" excuse, he said. "Well, that one doesn't fly because of the weakness of defendants' experts by failing to perform any rigorous scientific investigation."

There was also the "it's everybody else's fault" defense. "Mr. Bosma is on tape using derogatory barroom terms to describe his fellow dairymen, saying, 'It's their problem, their problem, but trust *me*, I'm a good guy,'" Charlie asserted. "Again he's trying to deflect the problems from him, and manipulate the situation so that CARE does not sue."

And then there was the "birds did it" defense—"as opposed to the six thousand cattle," Charlie said, sporting a mischievous grin. Recalling Harold Porath's testimony about two wild birds who might have dropped feces into the drain from one hundred feet aloft, he stated: "This defense is best summed up by a playground rhyme, Your Honor: 'Birdie, birdie, in the sky, drop a turdie in my eye. I'm no baby, I don't cry, I'm just glad that *cows* don't fly!'"

The courtroom fell so silent you could hear someone's watch ticking. The judge stared in bemusement, possibly thinking the same thing that Helen did: Did Charlie Tebbutt, Esq., just say what I *thought* he said? In federal *court*!?" After that, during the penalty phase, every time Bosma's attorneys raised the bird defense, Judge Shea told them not to mention it again because that argument just wasn't going to cut it.

"Then we come to Mr. Bosma himself," Charlie went on, "a man who said he never threatened to countersue Ms. Reddout or Ms. Conant or CARE and who said just the opposite on tape; a man who begged DOE not to put violations in his file and then who challenged DOE and hired lawyers to do so, to fight discharges which have now been conceded in litigation; a man who knowingly failed to inform his experts of information that could have proved to be detrimental to him."

The Clean Water Act was not a voluntary law, Charlie said. "And then we hear the argument, 'Hey, I've corrected that problem, now leave me alone.' It just shouldn't work that way. This is a man who's tried to portray himself as an 'aw, shucks, I'm just trying to make a living' kind of guy, but in reality is really a sophisticated manipulator and bully. Your Honor, what this man and his operations have done to the people and in the environment of this area is truly criminal, and we would ask you for relief in this case to specifically find Mr. Bosma has violated the law in a number of respects."

Helen wanted to shout and cheer, but instead sat on her hands. Besides, it was now the defense's time to close.

"I would ask the court to balance and weigh the rhetoric versus what has been admitted in this case," Neal began. "And I'm particularly referring to all these unsubstantiated attacks on Mr. Bosma and the attacks on Mr. and Mrs. Bosma's witnesses.

"There is no evidence that the Bosmas' activities at their dairies have caused the plaintiffs any injury to their use and enjoyment of the Yakima River," he said. "The plaintiffs have totally failed to meet their burden to trace any condition in the Yakima River to the Bosmas. And there has been no evidence after September 9, 1997, about any surface-water discharge from the Bosma property."

But what about the sixty-four alleged violations? "The vast majority are merely making the leap that all of those exceedences are the result of Mr. Bosma," he said. "There's no connection, there's no linking up to any of the testing."

Neal concluded, "This is not a case where the court needs to send a message. The Bosmas were well along making their improvements long before the plaintiffs were even organized. The plaintiffs in this case have the burden. They have failed to satisfy that burden, and Mr. and Mrs. Bosma ask the court to render a verdict in their favor."

Judge Shea promised to work on his ruling "in the weeks ahead," and hoped to have a decision within a "reasonable" amount of time. His court adjourned precisely at 5:00 P.M.

Helen was home on July 29 when Charlie Tebbutt called her with the verdict in the Bosma trial. She sat down, nervous as a hen, and braced for whatever decision had been reached. Charlie read Judge Shea's ruling very slowly to Helen.

" 'The Court finds that CARE has standing to sue the Defendants," he began reading. "CARE established (1) an injury in fact, (2) an injury that is traceable to Bosma, and (3) a redressible injury.' " [36]

Helen knew that this was going to be very good. "Oh my God," she said. "Did we win?"

Charlie kept reading.

CARE had proved "a continuing violation and a reasonable likelihood of recurrent violations," Shea said. Bosma was liable for illegal discharges of wastewater from his truck wash to Joint Drain 26.6, overapplication of wastewater to a field that ran off into the same drain, and "a long history of repeated violations and discharges." Of the sixty CWA violations alleged by CARE, Judge Shea found liability proven in fifteen of them.

On the downside for CARE, they failed to prove "continuing violations or reasonable likelihood of recurrent violations" related to Bosma's operating without a permit, and to "seepage and capacity of the storage ponds."

But CARE had won a lot. The decisions came on top of an earlier summary judgment from Shea, in which he made a landmark ruling that sprayfields and other areas of a CAFO are indeed subject to the Clean Water Act, and that drainage ditches on Bosma's property were in fact "waters of the United States" and thus subject to protection under the CWA. (Years later, *CARE v. Bosma* would be cited by Justice Antonin Scalia in another Clean Water Act case before the U.S. Supreme Court.)

For the next week, Helen's phone did not stop ringing. There were national and international media—everyone from the Associated Press to the London *Times* wanted comment. There were also national environmental groups calling, such as the Sierra Club and Natural Resources Defense Council. There were public-interest lawyers and citizens around the country dealing with CAFO issues of their own.

Locally, the news ricocheted around the valley like a sonic boom. "An Outlook group's long and sometimes lonely battle to force changes in the way the Yakima Valley dairy industry handles its waste paid off in court," the *Yakima Herald-Republic* proclaimed. "The decision is a blow to a fast growing industry that provides hundreds of local jobs while struggling to manage vast amounts of manure."[37]

But the *Tri-City Herald* was far less laudatory. It ran a news article warning that Shea's ruling could "severely limit irrigation canal operations by forcing districts to keep the water in their canals clean—not just the water that spills back into the river."[38] Meanwhile, the pro-agriculture *Capital Press* issued a decidedly unhappy editorial, speculating that "Charlie Tebbutt must have figured he'd arrived in heaven," after the verdict. It could not fathom why a court "regarded discharge into an irrigation drain as a Clean Water Act offense."[39]

Now Judge Shea had to determine damages in the case against Bosma. CARE would have to wait for the outcome until after the penalty phase of the trial, in December.

9

In its first year, FARM had fought hard and carved out a reputation for itself in western Illinois and beyond. Karen and the group may have failed to halt the Highlands project, but at the close of 1997 they were better positioned than ever to ramp up their campaign against CAFOs.

Karen had been invited to speak at a major conference in February 1998 in Ames, Iowa, sponsored by the Soil and Water Conservation Society. Though its title was decidedly unglamorous—"Managing Manure in Harmony with the Environment and Society"—the biggest names in livestock would be there, both pro- and anti-CAFO. Nothing, Karen vowed, would keep her away.

Except, that is, for her thyroid condition. After Christmas, Karen developed a tumor on her thyroid so large, it was blocking her windpipe. Doctors were unsure if it was cancer, so Karen was scheduled for surgery on New Year's Eve. When she woke up, Rocky and Nina were at her bedside.

"Wendell Murphy was here to see you," Rocky joked. "But he left."

Karen turned toward her husband; a stab of pain shot through her throat, which had been sliced open for surgery. "Screw Wendell Murphy," she whispered. And then, despite the fog of anesthesia, she said, "I got a paper to finish for my manure conference."

Fortunately, the biopsy results were benign. Karen spent the next week in bed, sipping tea with honey and regaining her strength, and completed her conference paper, which she called "A Patchwork of Rural Injustice." Jane, her librarian friend and FARM board member, guided Karen on how to properly reference all the data in her presentation. "Jane, you're like a mom to me," marveled Karen, whose own mom had passed away the year before.

As manure meetings go, this one would turn out to be remarkably worth-while. The conference was already making news before it began. The Peoria and Galesburg papers ran feature stories on Karen's impending manure mo-ment in Iowa, and sent reporters to cover the meeting. Rocky, Jane, and her husband, Joe, drove the four hours across the Mississippi and up to Ames. Karen felt exhilarated.

Support for FARM's positions came from a somewhat unexpected source at the conference. The National Catholic Rural Life Conference (NCRLC) had called for a moratorium on new CAFOs, citing their "negative health, environ-mental economic and social impacts." The Catholic group, formed in 1927, "ap-plies the teachings of Jesus Christ for the social and economic development of rural America," according to its Web site.[1] Brother David Andrews, a rising voice in the growing ecumenical movement against factory farming, was to speak on a panel with Karen.

"The NCRLC has for seventy-five years been a voice for participative de-mocracy, widespread ownership of land, the defense of nature, animal welfare, support for small and moderate-sized independent family farms, economic justice, rural and urban interdependence," the moratorium resolution said. "Such values are drawn from the message of the Gospel and the social teach-ings of our Church. Furthermore, we see such values best represented in the agricultural arena by what is called sustainable agriculture."[2]

Karen obtained copies of the NCRLC statement and handed them out ev-erywhere she went during the conference. If the Catholic Church is willing to be involved in such a contentious issue, Karen reckoned, then everyone should.

A moratorium on "farm factories" was just a first step, warned the resolu-tion, which went on to call for "a serious consideration of their replacement by sustainable agricultural systems that are environmentally safe, economically viable, and socially just."

NCRLC even had the gumption to dispute hog industry claims of deliver-ing economic benefits to rural communities. "Studies have shown that for ev-ery job created by a hog factory, three are lost," it noted. "Every year, hog factories put almost 31,000 farmers out of business, out of their homes, and out of their communities. In 1990, there were 670,350 family hog farms; in 1995, there were only 208,780. While concentration in pork production grows, inde-pendent family farmers are being forced out. The same can be said about dairy, beef, and poultry farming."

The meeting lived up to its own hype as an unprecedented gathering of groups and people from all sides of the animal-factory wars. Among them were representatives from community groups, agricultural schools, state gov-ernments, the federal EPA, the National Pork Producers Council, and the

American Farm Bureau Federation—a well-funded trade group for large and small farmers nationwide. With its myriad investment tentacles tightly wound with agribusiness interests, the Farm Bureau found itself under fire from anti-CAFO activists, who routinely referred to it as "the enemy."

Karen got to meet Brother David Andrews, as well as Kendall Thu, the pig-impact expert, and North Carolina's own Don Webb of ARSI. The three-day conference was held on the sprawling Iowa State University campus and drew more than 450 people from thirty-four states. It would have been impossible for Karen to take in all of the proceedings, but she did manage to hit some of the highlights. Among them were the following.[3]

NUTRIENT "IMPORTS"

Two researchers from the University of North Carolina, Wilmington—Lawrence Cahoon and Michael A. Mallin—presented data on the net importation of nutrients into the Cape Fear and Neuse river basins, in the form of animal feed. The lowlands of eastern North Carolina cannot grow enough feed to sustain the millions of pigs and chickens in the area, they said. In 1995, 87 percent of all grains and 94.5 percent of soybeans fed to animals living in the Cape Fear River Basin were "imported" from outside, mostly from the Midwest. In the Neuse River Basin, 60.6 percent of grains and 73.6 percent of soybeans were imported. That meant that trainloads of nitrogen and phosphorus were hauled into the region every day. Most of this nitrogen and phosphorus would eventually end up in the sprayfields. Farmers often grew hay or Bermuda grass to absorb the nutrients from the soil, but none of that was exported back out of the region.

For the Cape Fear River Basin, in 1995 nearly ninety thousand metric tons of nitrogen and some twenty-eight thousand metric tons of phosphorus in feed were imported from outside. The imported nutrients made up 90 percent of all field applications in the basin. "The magnitudes of nitrogen and phosphorus imports and loadings as manures to the Cape Fear and Neuse River basins pose a significant management challenge," the authors said. "Loadings of nitrogen have received much attention recently, particularly with reference to nitrogen stimulation of algal blooms in North Carolina coastal waters."

A DEADLY SMELL

Also on hand at the conference was Julie Jansen, the hydrogen sulfide–plagued mom from Minnesota, whose letter Karen had read aloud at the Elmwood meeting two years before. Karen learned a lot about that weekend about the gas, which is often called H₂S.

Hydrogen sulfide smells like rotten eggs, which actually do emit the gas. H_2S is why flatulence stinks. It is also one reason why YouTube has an entire "Fart Lighting" section. The more colorful names for H_2S include "sour gas," "sewer gas," and "stink damp." Many people mistake its smell for sulfur, which is actually odorless. In nature, H_2S can emerge from volcanoes, swamps, and natural gas deposits, in addition to flatulent mammals. Industrial sources include refineries, cement plants, and manure pits and lagoons. It is heavier than air, and builds up in low-lying areas, even basements. It tends to concentrate during cooler evening hours, when families are more likely to be home.

The gas is a "broad-spectrum poison" because it can affect many different systems, though the central nervous system (CNS) typically suffers most. H_2S interferes with the brain's signaling system to the lungs and impedes red blood cells from carrying oxygen. The populations most sensitive to it are fetuses, children, and heart and asthma patients. Toxicity at the eight hundred to one thousand parts per million level is well documented. Anyone exposed at that level will die almost instantaneously. But low-level or long-term exposures were considered to be less harmful. Most agencies held that, if H_2S was not present in fatal levels, then there were few, if any, lasting health effects. (This notion has since been disputed.)

HOG FARROWING IN SWEDEN

In 1971, Sweden banned the use of tethers for restraining sows because the practice created an "extremely high incidence of traumatic injuries," reported Marlene Halverson, an advisor to the Animal Welfare Institute. A second study showed a higher rate of disease among "dry sows" (sows that were pregnant or not lactating) in crates, versus those loosely housed in groups.

By 1985, "deep-bedded housing systems" with individual feeding stalls had become (and remain) the method of choice for housing dry sows in Sweden, because of their improved efficiency, aesthetics, and neighbor relations, and the health and well-being of the animals.

Pigs are highly sentient, intelligent, and social creatures, and sows have inherent rules of group identity and hierarchy. While these attributes are virtually ignored in CAFOs, Swedish farms take steps to ensure proper socialization and reduce stress on the herd. Females require about six and a half feet of space when meeting, to establish rank and avoid fights. Each sow needs at least twenty-seven square feet to avoid stress on lower-ranked sows. Karen was amazed. She knew that dry sows at the Highlands barely had room to turn around.

Meanwhile, the correct mixing of urine and feces with straw can nearly eliminate strong odors, especially compared to a pit-and-lagoon system. As fresh straw is added to wet spots, it helps keep bedding dry while sustaining aerobic decomposition. "The straw-to-manure-balance provides a high carbon/nitrogen ratio, which binds nitrogen. The beds do not give off ammonia or hydrogen sulfide," Halverson said. "Two major manure emission sources are thus controlled, and composting also destroys pathogens."

What about farrowing sows? In Sweden, farrowing houses offer each sow her own seven-by-ten-foot pen, big enough to include separate areas for bedding, feeding, and dunging, plus a "creep area" where piglets can sleep without getting squished by their mother. Again, Karen was impressed. These pens were palatial compared to the farrowing crates she saw at the Baird place, which had tiny cages only five feet long and two feet wide—or ten square feet.

The Swedish system had a clear manure advantage. Since waste was never liquefied, but rather composted aerobically, used bedding was ready to be spread as dry fertilizer. There was no need for lagoons and sprayfields, with their inherent environmental hazards.

Eventually, society would press the hog industry to reform modern production, Halverson predicted, adding that farmers "who have mastered the techniques for operating alternative swine production and manure systems are likely to be a giant step ahead."

THE INDUSTRIAL FOOD CHAIN

William D. Heffernan, Ph.D., a professor of rural sociology at the University of Missouri, said that virtually all concerns about factory farming could be traced back to the "increasingly industrialized model of global food production." He said activists could reform CAFOs all they want—ban lagoons, eliminate odors, and let pigs be pigs—but "worrisome changes within the food system" would persist.

"A simple technological solution to narrowly defined water and air quality concerns is not going to reduce much of the opposition to CAFOs," Heffernan warned. "My purpose is to raise some of the other societal concerns currently highlighted by CAFOs."

More and more farmers were being alienated from the critical decisions being made on their own farms, he said. They were being told, "This is how it will be done if you want to have a market." That meant almost total concentration of the U.S.—and global—system. "The food system resembles an hourglass with many producers and millions of consumers," Heffernan said, using an oft-repeated analogy. "Between the two are a few firms controlling the processing. These firms exert disproportionate control in the food system. Not surprisingly, they receive a disproportionate share of the economic benefits."

Processing is the all-important gate between producer and consumer. The fewer the number of processors, the narrower the gate. Whoever controls the gate, controls the system and the flow of goods through it. In most cases, the processing of each major food commodity produced in the Midwest is dominated by just a few big companies: Four firms control 45 percent or more of the processing for poultry, beef, and pork.

NAMES OF FOUR LARGEST FIRMS
AND PERCENTAGE OF MARKET SHARE THEY CONTROL[4]

Commodity	Percent of Market Controlled	Four Largest Firms
Broilers	45% of production	Tyson, ConAgra, Gold Kist Perdue
Beef	87% of slaughter	IBP, ConAgra, Cargill, Beef America
Pork	60% of slaughter	Smithfield, IBP, ConAgra, Cargill (Excel)
Turkey	35% of production	ConAgra, Rocco Turkeys, Hormel (Jennie-O), Carolina Turkeys

For farmers, this meant a rapidly shrinking number of markets to unload their commodities, undermining "the most basic condition of competition and leaving farmers with few or no alternative markets. A farmer must produce a product meeting the specifications of the processing firms (i.e., genetic material and production practices) or no market is available for their product."

There was, however, a growing backlash to this domination of the food chain. "Today we see the emergence of a growing interest in an alternative food system," Heffernan said. And for people interested in this alternative system, their concerns reached far beyond manure, to include "social justice, food safety, food quality, the sustainability of the food system, humane animal treatment and quality of life in rural communities," he said. "Why is the public being asked to contribute large sums of research funding to promote a system that has such a questionable future?" he asked about the booming animal factories.

When it was time for Karen's presentation, she grew jittery. Her knees rattled as she looked out at the auditorium of two hundred or so. In the front row sat Rocky and the Kucks, smiling and giving Karen thumbs-ups and buckets of confidence.

"CAFOs are taking over the rural landscape, extracting commodities and profits from the soil and leaving debt and devastation behind," she began tentatively. "In response to this invasion, grassroots citizens' groups have sprouted throughout America in an attempt to confront this crucial issue." The pollution and economic upheaval caused by CAFOs was degrading the quality of rural life, with little or no chance for citizen recourse, she said. In their wakes have come deep anger and frustration, and severe, even violent divisions within small communities. "Members of our organization have experienced verbal threats, trespassing, and vandalism of private property," she said. "And they've been subjected to litigation by the nation's largest pork producer in an arrogant attempt to silence them into submission."[5]

For the activists, quality family time had taken a backseat to fighting "the issue," she said. "Members of FARM have also exhibited the classic symptoms of a 'we versus them' mentality. This obsession to fight for our basic democratic rights has resulted in symptoms of physical and mental exhaustion in many of our group members."

The blight of "rural stress" was real. Iowa State University researchers had recently reviewed a dozen studies showing that corporate agriculture "produces social consequences that reduce quality of life for rural communities," Karen said. Consequences extended to the political alienation. "Members of FARM and their supporters now realize that the normal political channels for redress we thought we possessed are very limited," she said.

"In an attempt to discredit us, corporate sympathizers claim our concern is based on emotion, not science. This lack of respect for legitimate problems has led us to be highly skeptical that our concerns will be addressed through normal political processes."

One of the people who most impressed Karen during the Ames manure conference was Terry Spence, a grower of grass-fed cattle from Lincoln Township in north-central Missouri who is a real-life cowboy, and looks the part. His crow's-feet and wizened face reveal a tale of many years spent out on the range, in courtrooms, and in hearing rooms fighting the hog giant Premium Standard Farms (PSF).

As Midwestern neighbors, Terry had much in common with Karen Hudson; the two quickly became extremely close friends and allies. Terry had been fighting CAFOs long before most people had ever heard of the term, and he was indefatigable. His true grit inspired Karen.

Terry explained to Karen that his township's concerns over Premium Standard Farms's swine operation began even before the company moved into the Lincoln Township area, a beautifully pastoral and undulating stretch of land carved into low hills and woodland-filled ravines. In 1989, the company had been fined for its attempt to build a new hog CAFO near Ledges State Park, in next-door Iowa. PSF had begun digging a lagoon without any permits, or approval, from the Iowa Department of Natural Resources, which slapped the company with a stiff $700,000 penalty and banned it from any further construction.[6]

"The Iowa governor's office said that talks with company leaders showed they had an attitude of 'we're building regardless of approvals,'" Terry told Karen. "After hearing this, it didn't set well with me at all."

After the Iowa incident, Premium Standard Farms turned its focus to Missouri, "where they were met with open arms," Terry said. "People like Governor John Ashcroft and Senator John Danforth put the links together for them to relocate in three of Missouri's northern counties, including ours."

Terry and his wife, Linda, their children, and their neighbors, were alarmed by the welcome mat being offered to PSF. They knew that a Missouri corporate farming law passed in 1975 banned large corporations from owning land and operating industrialized farms within the state, but they also knew that laws were made to be rewritten. And they were right.

In 1993, during the final exhausting hours of the 1993 Missouri legislative session, a little-noticed amendment was piggybacked onto an economic development bill that would exempt Sullivan, Mercer, and Putnam counties from the corporate farming law for the raising of swine.

"We raised a ruckus about that amendment and how it got approved without public knowledge or participation by the very citizens who would be affected," Terry said sadly. "But the fix was in, and it was all hurriedly hushed up." The amendment also gave Premium Standard Farms access to millions of dollars in new financing for their planned "Missouri operations."

It didn't take long for the company to start moving into all three counties once all the deals were made; the locals soon learned that PSF was planning on raising more than two million hogs a year in this area.

"As soon as construction neared completion over in Mercer County, in 1994, they changed their focus to Lincoln Township in Putnam County," Terry told Karen. He sat on the Lincoln Township Board when this was happening. "They proposed a megacomplex consisting of ninety-six hog buildings and twelve lagoons with a total capacity of over 240 million gallons of feces and urine. It would house about 106,000 head and be built within a mile of nearly thirty family homes. We could not believe what we were hearing. It was worse than anyone had imagined."

Over the next several months, the Spences and others in the township met repeatedly with company officials, and the Missouri Department of Natural Resources (MoDNR), but got nowhere. So they decided to create a new zoning ordinance to defend their tiny hamlet. "We needed one to protect the health, safety, and welfare of the general public; to protect property values; and to secure the most economically sustainable use of the land." Missouri law grants townships the authority to place zoning ordinances to preserve and protect land use, as well as the welfare of their inhabitants.

On June 30, 1994, Lincoln Township had voted to approve a zoning ordinance that would not exclude hog feedlots or CAFOs, but simply require setbacks from family residences and a security bond for new lagoons, "to hold the company liable for cleanup if it went out of business, rather than leaving that burden on the township, or county," Terry said.

The township's victory was exceedingly short-lived. One day after the ordinance was passed and recorded, the MoDNR issued letters of approval for nine lagoons in Lincoln Township. The MoDNR had been properly notified that the new ordinance was imminent and would be in effect on June 30. "They approved the lagoons even though they knew the region would be under a zoning ordinance," Terry said.

Construction began four days later. Township officials protested and demanded that the company comply with the ordinance. Their request was met with a lawsuit. "Premium Standard Farms was suing our little township for $7.9 million for, get this, taking away their property rights!" Terry said. "They were trying to intimidate and harass the local citizens, but it didn't work. Those people in their suits, and corporate offices, vastly underestimated how much pride we have in our rural community, our way of life, and how determined we were to preserve and protect it." On October 6, 1994, Lincoln Township filed a countersuit, seeking enforcement of its ordinance and abatement of the facility on the grounds that it was a public nuisance.[7] The following April, Willie Nelson and Farm Aid traveled to Lincoln Township to take part in a rally protesting against the hog giant, and its lawsuit. Some three thousand people attended the event in deference of the "David and Goliath battle in North Missouri," as it was being billed in the press. Days before the rally, PSF dropped its demand for $7.9 million, but kept the lawsuit against the township's ordinance.

In the end, Lincoln Township lost.

On May 31, 1996, the Putnam County Circuit Court ruled that the state law giving zoning powers to townships was unconstitutional and voided Lincoln Township's new ordinance. The judge also ruled that townships could not require "closure bonds" on hog lagoons because they were part of agriculture, and agriculture was exempt in Missouri.

The township appealed to the Missouri Supreme Court, which ruled that agricultural buildings, structures, and water impoundments were, in fact, exempt from zoning.

"Since then, this endless battle has been a nightmare," Terry said. "We have attended relentless meetings and hearings at the Missouri legislature, Department of Natural Resources, Missouri Clean Water Commission, the Governor's Office and the Attorney General's Office. We said the state put the cart before the horse when they allowed Premium Standard Farms to begin operations in Missouri, with little understanding, or realization, of the magnitude of the problems that were to later develop."

The first of many manure spills began in 1995. Several miles of creeks and streambeds were contaminated, resulting in the slaughter of more than 180,000 fish in northern Missouri.[8]

"We complained like mad, but the state did nothing," Terry said. "As usual, the bureaucrats were reluctant to enforce any of their own compliance standards against the conduct of this company. So we did the only thing we could: We applied pure pressure by demoralizing the state in the press. And you know what? The bureaucrats finally figured out that these CAFOs weren't built to design plan. The engineer had put his seal of approval on the construction without ever inspecting the facilities! I may be a farmer and not a professional engineer, but anyone with common sense knows that you can't drain water, or effluent, uphill."

The next year, DNR finally made a move to penalize the company for its environmental mishaps and fish kills. PSF agreed to a fine of $241,084 in a settlement negotiated by the state.[9]

In 1997, Terry and his allies formed a group called Citizens Legal Environmental Action Network (CLEAN), with the intention of filing a federal lawsuit against the company for noncompliance with state and federal regulatory standards.

Shortly after, "and just by 'coincidence,' the official state files on the environmental compliance of Premium Standard Farms were sealed," Terry said with mock disbelief. "They were sent to the state AG's office nine days after our intent letter for the lawsuit was filed. The attorney general decided he would file notice against the company. PSF was told if they entered into a consent agreement within sixty days that addressed the violations with a permanent remedy, the state's federal lawsuit could be avoided," Terry added. "But as usual this was nothing but hot air and media attention, with no actions, remedies, or follow-up taking place."

But on January 19, 1999, the Attorney General's Office filed a state suit against Premium Standard Farms alleging violations of state environmental laws. Again just by coincidence, twelve days after the U.S. Department of Justice and the federal EPA joined the CLEAN lawsuit, the State of Missouri reached a settlement with Premium Standard Farms, in which the company would pay a million-dollar fine with $650,000 up front, plus $350,000 on condition of future compliance, and would adopt next-generation technologies for its operations.

On July 2, 1997, CLEAN filed its lawsuit against Premium Standard Farms and the federal EPA for ongoing violations of the federal Clean Water Act and Clean Air Act; the EPA was named as a defendant because of its failure to properly oversee Missouri's Department of Natural Resources and for failing to enforce federal environmental law. (Later, CLEAN dropped the EPA as a defendant, hoping it would be more beneficial as a partner in the litigation that was to follow.)[10]

Two years later, in July 22, 1999, the United States filed a motion to intervene on behalf of CLEAN's suit. "We welcomed the move, after so many years of wasted time and energy working with the Missouri government," Terry told Karen. "But it was a devastating mistake. We would regret it later." CLEAN, the EPA, and the U.S. Department of Justice (DOJ) hoped that Missouri would join with the suit, but the state declined, saying its 1999 consent decree would bring the changes in technology needed to force the company into compliance.

"With the EPA and the DOJ taking over the case, we at CLEAN soon realized that we were being shut out, with the main negotiating being done by the federal government and industry attorneys," Terry recalled. "We were in attendance at every meeting that took place, mostly in Washington, D.C., and a few times in Kansas City. And through that process, we knew it wasn't headed in the right direction, but we had no control or guidance on what was being discussed. Little did we know that the EPA had been told by White House officials to exit the case and never take on another of this type; two of the main EPA officials involved with our case resigned due to the injustice.

"For now, we remain in legal limbo, and drowned in air pollution," Terry said. "This fight has taken a big toll on all of us—me, my family, my friends, and our close allies—but we all stayed dedicated to our cause. We really do believe that justice will prevail at some point in time if we, as individuals, stay dedicated and committed to preserving the environment that must be sustained for future generations."

A lifelong farmer, Terry said he was never one to be involved in issues that didn't relate to farming or to his personal business. "But with the lawsuit and Willie Nelson's presence, I went from being a quiet person to one that was traveling and constantly on the phone. Suddenly I found myself organizing, strategizing, doing press interviews, and dealing with attorneys," he said.

Karen could utterly relate. "It's amazing how a person can react when something is about to jeopardize their family, home, livelihood, or community," she said.

Terry nodded. "Not everyone felt that way, though," he said sadly. "As time wore on, we saw that friends and associates we'd known for years, and even relatives, were now distancing themselves from us. Either they disagreed with the stand we took, or didn't want to be seen associating with someone that criticized the state's ugly stepchild, Premium Standard Farms. Local outlets we had done farm business with for many years suddenly seemed bothered by our presence. It was very ugly. My wife and I, and our children, began noticing that people in our church started ignoring us. Those who did speak had little to say. We had belonged to that congregation for thirty-two years before we decided to leave and find another church that appreciated our presence at their services, and didn't judge us for the fundamental things in life we believed in. And the minister at our old church never once attempted to visit or make contact, to see what was wrong, or to find out why we left."

Their small-town struggle had taken a hit on their financial security as well. Linda had been the deputy circuit clerk and recorder of Putnam County for sixteen years before her boss retired from the Circuit Clerk's Office in 1998. In prior years no one had made a bid for the Circuit Clerk's job until Terry's wife, with her many years of experience, placed her name on the ballot for election. Putnam County has always been a Republican stronghold and Linda ran on the GOP ticket. Nine other candidates, some of whom the Spences suspected were backed by Premium Standard Farms, ran against her in the primary.

"She survived the primary and only won the general election by a mere forty-two votes. Never before had the Republican ticket come close to losing in Putnam County," Terry explained. "This just goes to show how far a company town will bow to try and intimidate anyone that interferes with the company's business. The company wasn't after her position. They wanted to get to me in whatever way they could, to deflect my determination on pursuing them any further. It didn't work. Little did the company know that our thirty-eight years together were more binding, and carried more strength, than their stupid corporate mentality." Linda's four-year term expired in the fall of 2002, and she lost her bid for reelection just two years before reaching a full retirement.

"What has been left behind is animosity, mistrust, and division within our community, as well as environmental degradation," Terry went on. "It's been a no-win situation since they first located here. If there was true justice," Terry said sadly, "Premium Standard Farms would be held accountable for its misconduct."

But all was not lost, Terry added. "Even though we were mere private citizens," he told Karen, "we left a trail through the legal system that clearly shows how democracy in America is not of the people, by the people, and for the people, but rather of the corporations, by the corporations, and for the corporations. Maybe, when more people realize that, and fight against it, things will finally change."

Karen Hudson had learned enough about navigating the Internet that she was no longer dependent on Jane Kuck. FARM hired a local Web site designer who got the group's official site up and running. It was one of the first anti-CAFO Web sites run by a grassroots group.

Karen was unprepared for the onslaught of pleas for help that reached her via the new site. People all over the country were craving information on how to confront a CAFO in their own small-town backyards. Often, they were drawn to the reasonable and reassuring mission statement that appeared on FARM's homepage, which said the group was "organized to educate the public about the facts surrounding livestock factories, to promote responsible agriculture, and to work with decision makers in crafting laws and statutes that balance the needs of agriculture with those of the environment and society."

FARM quickly had become a national clearinghouse of information for desperate homeowners from Fresno to Florida. Karen's phone never stopped ringing. The frantic cries for help became known around her house as SOS calls as Karen realized that CAFOs were sprouting up in rural towns at a breathtaking pace. Neighbors were being taken by surprise—often not learning about a facility until it was under construction, when it was too late to do anything about it. Callers grilled Karen on peer-reviewed research that would support their claims when they petitioned their county commissions. They asked about state and federal laws, about stopping CAFOs in court, and about working the media angle. Mostly, they wanted to know what FARM had done that worked.

Karen found herself on the phone with people fighting against pig factories in Iowa, Missouri, and Ohio; megadairies in Idaho, Utah, Michigan, and Texas; and poultry operations from Maryland southwestward. Before long, Karen had created a standard "How to Fight a CAFO" packet culled from her eighteen months of activism. At least once a week she would drive to Peoria to visit Kinko's and run off several copies to mail out. It was time-consuming, and not cheap. But Karen would not turn her back on so many people needing her help.

In 1998, Dave Inskeep had decided to use recombinant bovine growth hormone (rBGH) on his Inwood Dairy cows. Karen knew little about the dairy industry, but she already had reservations about the controversial product.

That summer, Karen and Jane began reading up on the use of growth hormones, which are utilized to boost production in modern dairies. Debate over rBGH had a long, rancorous history.

Bovine growth hormone is the common term for bovine somatotropin (BST), which cows naturally produce in their pituitary glands. Some BST is used to make another hormone, insulin-like growth factor-1, or IGF-1. High levels of these hormones accelerate the burning of fat for energy, and prevent mammary cell death. In 1993, the FDA approved a synthetic form of BST developed by Monsanto called recombinant bovine growth hormone, or rBGH. The commercial product name is Posilac.

Posilac injections do not increase daily production: They prolong the life of milk-producing cells during the lactation period, about 300–305 days after the cow gives birth. Usually milk production peaks and then declines before the cow "dries up." Posilac prevents that drop, boosting total yields of 10–15 percent during lactation.

Consumer groups, family farm advocates, and some scientists said the drug was harmful to animals and dangerous or even carcinogenic for humans. And it was a threat to small dairies, who were already struggling with low prices owing to overproduction.

But Monsanto, the dairy industry, and the USDA said Posilac had been tested in cows for years, and that it was completely safe. They said that milk from treated cows had no sign of rBGH and was not "significantly" different from that of untreated cows. But Europe wasn't buying it. In 1993, the European Union slapped a moratorium on its sale (it issued a permanent ban in 2000). Canada was just about to follow suit, because of safety concerns for the animals, not humans.

In the United States, consumer groups were raising the alarm about elevated levels of BGH and IGF-1 in commercial milk, and their potential links to breast, colon, and prostate cancer in adults, as well as precocious puberty in girls. Many consumers also worried about the presence of antibiotics in milk from treated cows, which are more prone to infections, especially in their udders—a serious condition known as mastitis.

And despite dairy-industry assurances that milk is routinely tested for antibiotics, those tests only detect drugs in the penicillin (beta-lactam) family. Officials do spot checks of samples of nonpenicillin antibiotics just four times a year.[11] Consumer groups were also worried about "comingling" of milk collected from different dairies in the same stainless-steel tanker trucks.

Family farmers complained that Posilac was making an already bad milk market worse by giving megadairies a serious edge in production capacity, while also damaging the brand images of milk, butter, and cheese.

Animal-welfare groups said the drug was sapping healthy cows of their vitality and sending them to a premature and painful demise. A 1998 survey by Family Farm Defenders showed that megadairies that used rBGH had an annual cow mortality rate of 40 percent. Most only produced for about two and a half years before they were sent to the hamburger factory.[12] Typically, dairy cows produce for about ten to fifteen years.[13]

Treated cows were apparently not as healthy as untreated cows. In addition to mastitis, many developed hoof problems so severe they could not walk. And despite Monsanto's pronouncements that Posilac was safe for animals, the company's own packaging carried the following warning:

Posilac has been associated with increases in cystic ovaries and disorders of the uterus. Cows injected with Posilac are at an increased risk of clinical mastitis (visibly abnormal milk). The number of cows affected and the number of cases per cow may increase. In addition, the risk of subclinical mastitis (milk not visibly abnormal) is increased. Posilac has been associated with increases in somatic (nonreproductive) cell counts. Posilac is associated with increased frequency of use of medication in cows for mastitis and other health problems. Use of Posilac may result in an increase in disorders such as indigestion and diarrhea. Studies indicated increased numbers of enlarged hocks and lesions (i.e., lacerations).[14]

Monsanto was widely rebuked in corporate circles for its clumsy handling of the Posilac controversy, and it never seized the upper hand in the court of public opinion—no matter what its science said. The company and the dairy industry were looking at polls showing that 90 percent of American consumers wanted labeling for dairy products that were made from rBGH-treated cows, mostly so they could avoid buying them.[15] Knowing that it had a potential marketing meltdown on tap, Monsanto furiously lobbied FDA to prevent supermarket labeling.

Monsanto's muscle was put to the test in 1994, when Vermont passed legislation calling for mandatory labels on all rBGH-related products. A group led by Kraft/Philip Morris and the International Dairy Foods Association sued the state federal court and forced it to repeal the law. When some stores, co-ops, and dairies began advertising themselves as rBGH-free, Monsanto threatened to sue *them*. Most backed down.[16]

It was not hard to see why Monsanto was so jealously guarding its product. In 1998, the company boasted that nearly one-fourth of the nation's nine million dairy cows were in Posilac-treated herds. "Since its introduction in

1994, POSILAC has become the largest-selling dairy animal health product in the United States," its Web site said. "Sales continue on a strong growth curve with nearly a 30-percent increase in 1997 compared to 1996."[17]

But Monsanto had some annoying detractors. Chief among them were Dr. Michael Hansen of the Consumers Union, and Dr. Samuel Epstein, a University of Illinois at Chicago professor of environment and occupational medicine and one of the earliest and fiercest critics of Posilac. Epstein has earned three medical degrees, has authored several books, and has testified before Congress. He began to investigate Posilac before most people had even heard of it.

Epstein published an op-ed piece in the *Los Angeles Times* in which he alleged that cows were "hyperstimulated" by rBGH and suffered from increased stress and greater susceptibility to infection, infertility, loss of fat, heat intolerance, and "lactational failure."[18] He said that bovine growth hormones "pose grave consumer health risks that have not been investigated by the industry or FDA" because they were not natural. "The FDA now admits that they are up to 3% different in molecular structure from the normal hormone," Epstein wrote. "Increased rBGH levels in milk and blood have been found in injected cows. RBGH and its digested products could be absorbed from milk into blood, particularly in infants, and produce hormonal and allergic effects." Plus, elevated levels of cell-stimulating growth factors (IGF-1) might cause "premature growth and breast stimulation in infants, and possibly promote breast cancer in adults."

Epstein went so far as to urge states and the FDA to ban artificial hormones "until all safety questions can be resolved." He called on Congress to investigate the industry's "misleading and self-interested claims on rBGH" and warned consumers to recognize it as "industry's latest unsafe contribution to the brave new world of chemicalized food and mechanized farming."

Executives at Monsanto were apoplectic. Soon after his op-ed ran, Epstein claimed the *Los Angeles Times* was visited by senior Monsanto officials who were furious about his column and accused him of being scientifically unqualified. "They urged against acceptance of any further contributions from me," he said. "This protestation was firmly rejected."[19] The paper ran a rebuttal from the FDA, which wasted no time in belittling Dr. Epstein and his anti-rBGH ideas. Epstein had resorted to "a great deal of scientific exaggeration, designed more to frighten than enlighten," said Gerald Guest of the FDA's Center for Veterinary Medicine.[20]

Guest's argument was not exactly concise. He wrote: "The exaggerations (e.g., that increased bacterial infections in cows will require treatment with antibiotics that will pass to man and create antibiotic-resistant infections in the general population, that somehow the use of bovine somatotropin may create infections in man similar to AIDS, that cows are widely contaminated with carcinogens in their body fat) do a significant disservice to your readers who do not have firsthand knowledge of their lack of scientific merit."

According to Guest, all tests showed the product was safe. Anyone suggesting otherwise was promoting scientific illiteracy and fear-mongering. "The men and women at the FDA are not dumb," he said. "Food safety scientists at FDA are among the most knowledgeable and capable in the world today and we do care about the people we serve. Please be assured that we, at the FDA, will deal with this animal drug as with any other, in a fair, objective and scientific manner. We welcome constructive criticism from well-informed scientists."

The year 1997 had been a boom period for hog prices and the world of pork. But by the end of 1998, the market was crashing. The rapid CAFO-fueled boom in production had undermined prices. The smallest producers were the first to take the hit—within months, thousands of them were wiped out of business.

Overproduction flooded the market. Processors throughout the country began offering staggeringly low prices that had not been seen in decades. It was one of the bleakest gluts that anyone could remember. Packers were simply unable to slaughter and process all of the pigs being raised around them. Because of that, they began bidding down the price they would pay per pig.

Farmers were getting $29 for an entire pig at the slaughterhouse, less than a third of the $110 they were paid a year before. Consumers, however, were not benefitting. *The New York Times* noted that high-grade pork chops were fetching $3.99 a pound.[21] When hog farmers complained about the outrageous wholesale-to-retail differential, federal officials began to investigate whether the meatpacking plants were illegally taking advantage of producers and consumers. It would have been possible in a market where 75 percent of the packing was dominated by only six corporations—Smithfield, IBP, Swift, Excel, Farmland, and Hormel Foods.

Processors denied that they were doing anything illegal. Record supplies had kept wholesale prices low, but increasing demand had sustained supermarket prices, they contended. "There are hogs everywhere," Jens Knutson, of the American Meat Institute, told *The New York Times*. "These are market forces at work." But Clinton's agriculture secretary, Dan Glickman, wasn't buying it. He asked the Justice Department and the Federal Trade Commission to look into price fixing or other illicit activities.

Meanwhile, independent growers were being squeezed out of the business altogether. "Although prices typically decline in the winter months, the drop this year has some farmers wondering if they should leave the business," the

Peoria Journal Star reported. Just one year earlier, processors were paying farmers fifty to sixty dollars per hundred pounds of hog. In 1998, at the Peoria stockyards a grower was lucky to get fifteen dollars per hundredweight. It was a catastrophic price. The break-even cost for farmers—for all but the very biggest—was at least thirty dollars per hundredweight.

"The corporate approach to hog farming has left smaller producers in the industry worried," the *Journal Star* reported.[22] One Fulton County grower, Robert Marshall, ran his farm "the old-fashioned way." He and his father grew about thirty-six hundred hogs each year, from farrow to finish, plus about 480 acres of corn and soybeans. "Somebody like me that is trying to do it with a very labor-intensive approach, I'm afraid that our days are numbered and we may be out of it," he said.

Smaller, diversified farms could no longer keep up with million-dollar hog operations that hired thirty to forty people. "The time when a person could make a good living from a few hundred acres, some cows and sows, are leaving quickly. Obviously, there have been people who have gotten into the hog business, thinking they are going to be able to make it," Marshall said. "But they're driving the little guy out of business."

Neil Curry, another independent producer, ran a hog farm near Alpha in Henry County, the state's leading pork-producing county. The recent plunge in hog prices was about to ruin him, he said. "We hope it doesn't last terribly long," he said. "I'm taking about two hundred head to market each week and I'm only getting between seventeen and nineteen dollars per hundred pounds. To break even, I need to get about thirty-five dollars. I'm losing nine thousand to ten thousand dollars a week."

Part of the problem was exports. The Asian financial crisis had cut into projected growth in that vast market, and the economy of Russia—another big pig consumer—was teetering. While exports to Japan, Mexico, and Korea were holding steady, total growth had fallen far short of expectations. But mostly, as one market analyst put it, the real reason for the price collapse was because "there are just too many pigs."

Even with all those surplus hogs, the actual numbers of producers had declined. In 1987, there were nearly eighteen thousand farms that sold pigs—by 1992, that figure was just above fourteen thousand. But in those same five years, production rose from 9.9 million head to about 10.3 million in 1992. "The number of hog producers has actually decreased but the amount of hogs has increased," said the expert. "There has been a real structural change."

Hard times were easier to weather for the big hog producers, even as the little guys were winnowed out of the market. The biggest winners of all, naturally, were the largest vertical integrators, the "semen to cellophane" corporations who stood to make a profit no matter where on the production chain it was extracted.

News of the victory in *CARE v. Henry Bosma* sped through environmental circles. An alert arrived in Karen Hudson's in-box. She was delighted to read it, and somewhat awestruck that another group, very similar to FARM, had achieved such a triumph.

Karen made sure that FARM's Web site was updated with links to news about the precedent-setting legal victory. She was fascinated by the case, and by some of the expert reports that had been filed on behalf of CARE. She also wanted to know more about the group's leader, that cherry-farming schoolteacher from Yakima Valley, Helen Reddout.

The next day, Karen called Helen, eager to learn about CARE's legal strategy. She asked for copies of the reports used at the trial. "It's so good to know that someone like you is out there," Karen said to Helen. "We're fighting a dairy factory, too, here in Elmwood. But most people in Illinois are dealing with hogs. In fact, almost all the information online is about swine or poultry. My hog file is a giant box; my dairy file is a thin little folder."

Over several months, the two women bonded. Instead of swapping recipes as some middle-aged wives might do, they exchanged data on fly populations and *Cryptosporidium parvum* outbreaks. They traded hundreds of e-mails, faxes, and phone calls. They shared industry research, court rulings, university studies, and proenvironment opinion papers. They shared studies proving that pathogens in manure water used for irrigation can be absorbed by plants: It was possible that *Cryptosporidium parvum*, listeria, salmonella, and dangerous strains of *E. coli* could contaminate fresh greens and other vegetables from the *inside*. Even the most thoroughly washed spinach would still be harmful if eaten raw.

The correspondence and phone calls marked the beginning of a long and close friendship. Karen affectionately referred to Helen as "that nice dairy lady out west."

Dave Inskeep's Inwood Dairy was proving to be as troublesome as Karen Hudson had predicted. There had been a hose rupture and discharge into Walnut Creek, FARM discovered. That event followed previous mishaps: A lagoon pump had broken down, and there was creek pollution during construction.[23]

There was also the signature stench of the place. In the past, summer evenings in Elmwood had been redolent with the sweet scents of cornstalk and cut straw, prairie grass and wildflowers. Now it smelled like poison gas. On warm nights when the breeze shifted in the wrong direction, the stink would suddenly settle over Elmwood like a toxic veil. Karen could actually hear the frantic clatter of shutting windows. Women would run to clotheslines to rescue bedsheets; backyard barbecues and pool parties were promptly canceled.

Some Elmwood locals began keeping "manure logs." The details were the same: the eye-watering stench, the release of effluent through pivot irrigators into 40-mile-per-hour winds, the filthy mist carried aloft, the coating of passing cars when misted cow feces blew onto nearby roads. Karen's neighbors would keep candles alight around the clock to burn off the stench that permeated their homes.

"I think I will send Dave Inskeep my candle bills as a message of our suffering," one woman wrote in her diary.

Others kept perfume spray bottles throughout the house to mask odors the candles couldn't burn off. For many, a solid night's sleep had become a sweet and distant memory since the clouds usually descended between 2 and 6 A.M.

Another neighbor noticed that the odors had infiltrated her rugs and drapes. Steam cleaning, chemical treatments, and shampoos had no effect. She was compelled to rip out thousands of dollars of wall-to-wall carpeting.

The public grumbling did elicit an official response. From May through August, the Illinois Environmental Protection Agency (IEPA) sent inspectors to Inwood, where they found a number of violations. On August 19, 1999, IEPA officially notified Inwood that it was in violation of state regulations on odor and water contamination. "We are committed to stepping in when we find significant environmental violations," Illinois EPA director Thomas Skinner said. "This is such an instance."[24] His agency found that Inwood had allowed too much waste to be stored in its livestock lagoon, creating the chance for overflow during heavy rains; had diverted storm water from the lagoons to prevent manure overflows; had managed livestock waste in a way that permitted odor pollution; had failed to use adequate odor controls and technology; and had improperly discharged wastewater into waters of the state.

Dave Inskeep was given forty-five days to respond with "proposed corrective actions" for each violation. The IEPA recommended several such actions, though they were purely voluntary at this point, and Inskeep could request a meeting to discuss how best to correct the problems. To Karen, Inskeep had gotten off with a gentle slap on the wrist. There was no talk of fines—yet.

The suggestions for corrective actions included keeping a minimum of three-feet distance between the liquid surface and the rim of the lagoon (the freeboard) and installation of a freeboard marker and rain gauge. To prevent rainwater from filling up the lagoons, the IEPA also recommended the installation of gutters, downspouts, berms, curbs, and dikes to divert clean storm water away from the lagoons. Finally, the agency urged the dairy not to expand operations until successful odor-control techniques were in place.

As an official reprimand to a violator, Karen thought, the letter seemed to offer too much chummy wiggle room.

In the fall of 1999, Karen Hudson stared aghast at her kitchen table. It had become her impromptu office desk, and now there was no room for a bowl of cereal. But she knew that a messy kitchen table was the mark of a committed activist. Karen was beyond committed. She was obsessed. She lived, breathed, and dreamed of CAFOs. Nothing could supplant the subject in her mind. She relocated piles of papers, along with her computer, to more suitable quarters down in the basement.

Her CAFO obsession had grown so intense, she couldn't separate the animal-factory crusade from everyday life.

Karen's various radio appearances were getting noticed in faraway places. One of them was New York City—not a traditional hotbed of agricultural activism. It was, however, home to a new group forming to help rural communities confront CAFOs, called the Global Resource Action Center for the Environment (GRACE) Factory Farm Project.

One day, Karen took a call from a young woman in New York City named Diane Hatz, who worked out of GRACE's headquarters on Lexington Avenue. Diane had heard Karen on the radio, and was impressed with her knowledge, experience, and gritty determination. She explained how the GRACE Factory Farm Project had been created by the Colorado College economist Dr. William J. Weida to push for so-called sustainable alternatives to industrial animal production. Diane and Karen hit it off right away, and they spoke for two hours on the phone that day.

"Listen, Karen, we're putting together something called the GRACE Factory Farm Project Team," Diane said. "It's made up of independent family farmers across North America, plus people here in the New York office. The idea is to act as a consulting force that can rush in to help communities that are trying to stop CAFOs in their area. Our goal is to create a sustainable food production system that is healthful and humane, economically viable, and environmentally sound. I was wondering if that sort of thing might be of interest to you."

GRACE carried with it a certain sense of mystery; the group was funded by a wealthy individual in New York City who wished to remain anonymous.

Karen liked the idea: a factory farm SWAT team that could swoop into to rural communities and teach locals how to tackle CAFOs. Legal counsel, scientific research, public relations expertise, and so on—all for free. A few days later, Bill Weida called Karen and formally asked her to join the GRACE Factory Farm Project Team.

Along struggle had been under way between Knox County and the Highlands hog farm. State's Attorney Paul Mangieri had worked with Nina and Bill Baird to try to block building permits for the CAFO, and to assert local county control over where and how it was zoned. Now, in late 1999, that effort had sputtered to an end. After nearly three years of sparring, losing, and appealing, Mangieri was finally giving up his crusade for local control of CAFOs. On December 2, the Illinois Supreme Court ruled firmly in favor of the hog operation and against county authority in regulating factory farms.

The eleven-page opinion upheld lower court decisions that hog confinements of *any* size are purely "agricultural" in nature, and not industrial or commercial. Illinois state law permitted counties to zone and regulate industry and commerce, but not agriculture.

Mangieri had argued before the justices in September that the Highlands and operations like it were indisputably industrial, while the attorney for the Highlands told the court the opposite: He insisted that the facility was clearly "a core agricultural use." The Highlands' position won the day. "It is clear that hog facilities fall within the meaning of agriculture or animal husbandry," the court ruled. "In plain and unambiguous terms, the legislature has prohibited zoning regulation of agricultural uses, such as animal husbandry, other than to conform to building or setback lines."[25]

It was up to the Illinois General Assembly to decide whether it wanted to give counties the authority to regulate CAFOs. The justices seemed almost to be punting the issue back to lawmakers. "At what level of activity does a hog production facility cease to be 'agricultural' and become 'industrial'?" the majority wrote. "This is an exercise in line-drawing classically meant for the legislature." The prospects for such reform were dim. Key legislators had already let that be known.

Mangieri was finished. "This is the highest court in our state," he told reporters. "So based upon that, while we may respectfully disagree with the court's decision, we respectfully abide by it. And it would be my opinion that that would end this litigation."

Doug and Jim Baird were relieved to put the entire civil war behind them. "I just want to see it over with," Doug told reporters. "It's been a long three years." Shortly after that, the Highlands' countersuit—the one filed against Mangieri, Nina and Bill Baird, and others—was quietly dropped.

Doug and Jim Baird may have emerged victorious in the courts, but there was another legal challenge aimed at them. This time it came from the office of the Illinois attorney general, Jim Ryan. During 1999, the IEPA had logged some 230 complaints about odors emanating from the Highlands facility. Several inspections confirmed that it was producing "a strong swine odor" since starting operations in 1997.[26] Ryan's office decided to take action. The attorney general filed a two-count lawsuit on December 2 with the state's Pollution Control Board. It was filed not only against the Highlands, but also Murphy Family Farms and Bion Environmental Technologies, the firm that designed the Bairds' touted high-tech wastewater system.

According to the article, back in 1997, at the Highlands open house, Bion officials had guaranteed that their clients would not cause any environmental problems. But now, two years later, the attorney general's lawsuit alleged that the Highlands was "unreasonably interfering with its neighbors' use and enjoyment of their property." It also charged that the $2.5 million, 3,650-sow operation was violating state air-quality laws. It sought an injunction against any further violations, fines of up to fifty thousand dollars for each violation, and a ten-thousand-dollar-a-day fine for every day that the violations persisted.

The lawsuit said that most odor complaints were made by seven homeowners living within a quarter mile to one and a half miles of the CAFO. "We're not talking about a whole lot of people here," Assistant Attorney General Jane McBride said. "But they're impacted, and they're impacted severely."[27] The lawsuit alleged offensive odors were coming from "animal-confinement buildings and the waste-treatment system, which does not perform in a manner consistent with the claims of Bion Technologies." And though the facility met minimum setback requirements, there was still "inadequate separation" from one home located just a quarter mile to the east.

Jim and Doug Baird had been warned about this issue seven months before the Highlands opened. The IEPA told Jim Baird he should have minimum setbacks, and also urged the adoption of antiodor measures, but apparently those suggestions had been ignored.

Jim and Doug were working closely with Bion to improve the wastewater-treatment system. "They are dedicated to being good neighbors," the Highlands' attorney argued.[28]

Meanwhile, local papers reported that a separate lawsuit against the Highlands had been filed in Knox County Circuit Court, by the same couple who lived just a quarter mile away, Roy and Dianne Kell. Their four-count complaint alleged that odors had harmed their property and lifestyle and aggravated Diane Kell's asthma. The couple sought $150,000 in damages and asked that the Highlands be ordered to cease and desist from generating offensive odors.[29]

That suit was eventually resolved out of court. The specifics are unknown, however, as the Kells agreed to a gag order as part of their settlement.

According to the *Journal Star*, Bion Technologies worked out its own settlement with the AG's office wherein it would pay a fine of nine thousand dollars without admitting liability or violation of any law. Bion also withdrew from its contractual obligations at the Highlands, contending that Jim and Doug Baird were not properly operating its waste-management system.[30]

There was more news. As Ryan's office continued to litigate against the Highlands and Murphy Family Farms, it now had a new ally: Bion had agreed to cooperate in any future prosecution of its former client.

PART II
GOING NATIONAL

n the closing years of the twentieth century—and the waning days of the
Clinton administration—factory-farm activists soberly realized that they
were in this fight for the long haul. Fortunately, they were also coming to realize that they were not alone. The years to follow would usher in a new phase
of the American animal-factory wars, in which small, discrete groups of concerned citizens began joining forces and winning major battles, from Yakima
to Elmwood to New Bern and beyond.

The work was grueling, time-consuming, and expensive. The opposition
was well funded and well organized. But retreat was not an option.

Even as they braced for a new century of defending their communities, these
groups were beginning to come to terms with an unsettling realization: Nobody
was going to make factory farms disappear altogether. Reform them, yes. Promote smaller independent farms, of course. But the CAFOs could not be legis-
lated, litigated, or even shamed into obsolescence.

It was a situation filled with irony. Rick Dove, Helen Reddout, and Karen
Hudson all knew it. The more the activists chipped away at the factory-farm
system—by forcing reforms and reducing the risk to public health, the environment, and rural communities—the more they were helping to sustain the
entire corporate food system.

Were activists unwittingly reforming CAFOs into perpetuity?

Considering the prospect of no reforms at all, most figured they had no
choice but to keep fighting. This new phase of the animal wars would unify
many activists, whether their issues were pollution, food safety, rural preservation,

or animal welfare. Along the way, they would encounter new allies from the fields of law, politics, science, and health.

Their goal was to regulate factory farming for the benefit of all, and to work for the eventual elimination of the CAFO system altogether. Their battlefields had been drawn: The fight would continue in all three branches of government, in the court of public opinion, in the realm of scientific investigation, and in the vast and powerful global marketplace.

This fight over human laws would become highly visible and increasingly vitriolic. But another battle was also being waged, a struggle that received far less attention than the fight between people—even though it could ultimately determine the final fate of factory farming.

It was the battle against Mother Nature.

Rick Dove was becoming convinced that the fight over human laws would eventually submit to the unbendable laws of nature. "In the end, it doesn't really matter what we try to do to control odor, or water pollution, or animal exploitation," Rick began saying when he spoke in public. "Mother Nature is starting to take control. We're trying to change the environment that she provided for us, but I'm not sure she'll let us."

Rick, Helen, Karen, and other activists already recognized emerging evidence of nature's backlash against the growing of food in an unnatural way. *Pfiesteria* was a prime example.

Over the coming years, Mother Nature would reveal to humans the new and frightening consequences of violating her laws.

These would grow in frequency and severity: *E. coli* and salmonella in food, antibiotic resistance in medicine, avian flu, swine flu, mad cow disease, hormone imbalances, arsenic poisoning, cancer clusters, childhood asthma, MRSA, global warming in the skies, and dead zones in the waters would all be linked to industrial animal production by 2010.

Did Rick Dove have Pfiesteriosis? By the early spring of 1998, the question had become the subject of considerable speculation in the media. Rick, at fifty-eight years, had been feeling chronically unwell. His symptoms always appeared during the time of the autumn fish kills, and then would dissipate by the end of the year. He had suffered periodic headaches, breathing problems, sinus and lung infections, and loss of voice for almost a decade.

Rick was seeing the Duke University doctor who treated North Carolina scientists Burkholder and Glasgow, and he diagnosed the problem as related to exposure to *Pfiesteria* toxin. Two other treating physicians came to the same conclusion. They all urged him to stay off the water.

Rick did not want to get off the water, though he believed that *Pfiesteria* in the river was making him sick. He cautioned the Neuse River Foundation that this could be his last year as Riverkeeper. "The bane of polluters and bureaucrats alike may be serving his last year," *The News & Observer* reported.[1]

But Rick cautioned the paper, "It would be far too soon for the polluters to start dancing in the street yet. I'm nowhere near throwing in the towel."

That would prove to be unwelcome news to the mammoth hog corporation Smithfield Foods, which had recently bought out two large North Carolina swine producers, Carroll's Foods and Browns of Carolina.

By 1998, a loose coalition of Riverkeepers, Baykeepers, and Soundkeepers had melded into the Waterkeeper Alliance. The formal confederacy was headed by Robert F. Kennedy, Jr., out of his Pace Law School office in White Plains, New York. Rick, who had come to know Kennedy well over the years, became a board member of the Waterkeeper Alliance. Kennedy was seeking a viable target for a national campaign, and he focused on the CAFOs.

Smithfield Foods and its swine operations in North Carolina soon emerged as the favored targets. Kennedy knew that the Clean Water Act had a special provision allowing citizens to file suit against polluters in federal court. But those cases required plaintiffs to take on polluters one at a time. At that rate, it would take decades to bring suits against the hog facilities suspected of polluting North Carolina waterways. Instead, Kennedy, Rick, and others opted to file a suit in state court against all Smithfield CAFOs with a single across-the-board lawsuit.

The lawsuit, *Waterkeeper Alliance v. Smithfield Foods, Inc.*, was filed in Wake County Superior Court in Raleigh, with the help of attorneys from the capital. The suit alleged that Smithfield Foods and its contractors had caused injury to the state's rivers and damaged property owned by the people of North Carolina. The litigation sought damages and the costs of restoring the river.

Even before trial, there was behind-the-scenes drama. North Carolina's then attorney general, Mike Easley, was furious at Kennedy for filing a lawsuit that should have originated from his own office. He urged the Waterkeeper Alliance to withdraw the litigation threat, and to work with him to craft a State of North Carolina action against Smithfield. Kennedy told Easley to take a hike—the state had been given years to fight the pork industry, but had done nothing.

The judge in the case, however, agreed with Attorney General Easley. He upheld a Smithfield motion to dismiss the lawsuit, concluding that Waterkeeper did not have the "standing" under North Carolina's public trust law. Only the state's attorney general could bring such a suit on behalf of the people of the state. Easley had reason to be territorial: He was planning a run for governor. Within months, he formally took action against Smithfield.

Easley also issued a written campaign pledge vowing to close down every livestock lagoon in North Carolina within five years if elected. He was elected governor in 2000 and served two full terms—a total of eight years. By the end of his term, there were many more lagoons in North Carolina than there had been when he took office. Almost all are still there.

At year's end, Rick, still ailing, received a moving honor. *Time for Kids* magazine named him one of the "Heroes for the Planet" of 1998 for refusing to "turn his back on the long, lazy river that winds through the farmlands of eastern North Carolina to the sea."[2]

Rick Dove knew that, one day, raising thousands of animals in close quarters would come back to haunt humanity in a major way. He predicted that the laws of Mother Nature could be ignored for only so long before she meted out new and terrible punishments—not only for those who violated her strict unwritten rules, but for all humanity.

In mid-1999, Rick and the world learned that a novel and insidious threat had emerged from a sow-farrowing operation in Sampson County: A strain of swine flu had mixed with human influenza genes and, soon after that, with avian influenza components, to create a powerful new virus that swept across hog herds throughout North America.

In this case, humanity dodged a potentially deadly bullet when the epidemic failed to jump over to people. But experts warned that the new hybrid virus was still out there in circulation, and it was only a matter of time before it mutated to become infectious in humans.

The new bug was discovered in August 1998, at a twenty-four-hundred-head breeding facility near Fayetteville, where all the sows suddenly came down with a phlegmatic cough and those that were pregnant spontaneously aborted their litters. Nasal swabs from the pigs were sent to the state agriculture department's animal disease lab in Raleigh.[3]

State scientists at first did not think the outbreak was extraordinary. To them, it sounded like another case of "classic" swine flu, which had appeared many times before in North Carolina. That virus was known to cause fevers and miscarriages in sows.

But when scientists ran the regular tests for swine flu, they were stumped. They simply did not recognize the virus they were looking at. Even more alarming, some of the sows who got sick had been vaccinated against classic swine flu. That vaccine had clearly failed to stop this particular infection. "It started to look like we might have a novel, new strain of swine influenza on our hands," Dr. Gene Erickson, director of microbiological testing at the state lab, told the Raleigh *News & Observer*. "That is when I started to get a little worried."[4]

His lab isolated the novel influenza virus and discovered that it contained the inner structure of a swine virus, but was encased in a coating of human proteins. The new swine virus had picked up three human flu genes. By December, the new bug had acquired two bird flu gene segments as well, evolving into a previously unseen "triple reassortment" virus, a worrisome and unprecedented monster of human, hog, and bird flu.

Outbreaks were soon reported in Texas, Minnesota, and Iowa swine herds, and within months, pigs were sick nationwide. More than forty-three hundred samples were taken from swine in twenty-three states, and on average, 20.5 percent of them had the new triple-assortment flu virus. In Illinois and Iowa, 100 percent of the animals were infected, while Kansas and Oklahoma each reported rates of 90 percent. The long-distance transport of live animals—from farrowing to fattening to slaughtering—was blamed for the rapid dissemination of the virus.

Scientists were frantic to discover if this new strain could infect people. Health experts tested swine workers who had been in contact with the sick pigs. Only 10 percent of them showed antibodies to the new virus and none had fallen ill. It appeared that the virus was not a threat to people—for now, anyway.

Most flu outbreaks in people can be traced to waterfowl. But birds and people are very different genetically, and it is difficult for a purely avian virus to jump over to people. Pigs and people are much more similar, making pigs the perfect viral bridge for transferring bird flu to humans.

In fact, pigs are nature's "mixing bowls" for interspecies infections, and many swine flu viruses have long contained genetic components of human influenza. One theory behind the 1918 flu pandemic that killed twenty million people is that waterfowl cross-infected U.S. pigs with a new type of avian-swine supervirus that was quickly transmitted to farmworkers, possibly in Iowa, who went off to military training camps for World War I and then spread the pathogen worldwide.

Even though people had just dodged an infectious bullet, North Carolina's chief epidemiologist cautioned that the new virus could still jump back and forth between pigs and people. And Dr. Newton MacCormack, chief of communicable disease control at the state health department, added that, "We don't know how often these reassortments occur in nature—probably more than we want to realize. We're pretty lucky that most of these viruses reach a genetic dead end. The big problem is the rare occasion when one of these viruses gets into a human and begins to be passed from person to person."[5]

Indeed, the planet was way overdue for a global human pandemic, warned one of the top virologists in the world, Dr. Robert Webster, at St. Jude's Children's

Research Hospital in Memphis. He said that children, teenagers, and young adults born after the 1968 Asian flu pandemic would be especially vulnerable, because they would have zero immunity to a reconstituted Asian flu virus. He added that it was possible for the next pandemic to begin in North Carolina, which had more pigs than any state except Iowa.

Dr. Nancy Cox, a flu expert at the CDC, said the outbreak was a "wake-up call" for guardians of both human and animal health. "It showed a human flu strain has gotten into pigs and that strain may permanently establish itself in pigs," she said. "It can go both ways. You have veterinary consequences as well as human consequences of this interspecies transmission."[6]

The prestigious journal *Science* concurred. "After years of stability," it said, "the North American swine flu virus had jumped on an evolutionary fast track."[7]

Meanwhile, Dr. Erickson said his lab had introduced new types of diagnostic analyses that were advanced enough to identify emerging "reassortments" of new viruses that mixed human and animal components. "These influenza viruses can shuffle like a deck of cards, but we will at least have one more diagnostic tool in our hands when this happens again," he told *The News & Observer*. "That might give us some extra time when there is a true outbreak of a new virus." He added that "the best way to view this whole series of events would be as a valuable learning experience for all of us. We will be much better prepared should it happen again."[8]

Ten years later, in 2009, a new and deadly outbreak of swine flu would appear in people, beginning in Mexico and then spreading around the world— even before it was isolated and identified. Most of the victims were born after the 1968 Asian flu pandemic.

Six of the virus's eight genetic components would be indentified as direct descendants of the 1998 pig farm outbreak in Sampson County. But in 2009, the Mexican government clearly was not endowed with the same sophisticated testing equipment and regimes as those Dr. Erickson had in his lab in Raleigh. If such precautions had been in place, a global pandemic might have been averted.

Hurricanes Bertha and Fran had wreaked chaos on the hog belt, but they were nothing more than meteorological dress rehearsals compared to Floyd. The storm slammed into North Carolina in September 1999 and dropped up to nineteen inches of rain on ground that was still soaked by its predecessor, Hurricane Dennis, merely two weeks earlier. The deluge set off the worst river flooding in state history. The floods lasted for weeks, leaving some twenty-four thousand homes uninhabitable. Rick braced for the worst. The sight of dead pigs in Fran's floodwaters still played in his mind. The Neuse, Tar, New, and Cape Fear rivers all burst their banks and flooded CAFO-filled areas for miles around. Rick knew what must be going on out there, but for days on end he could barely leave the house; blankets of rain pelted the windows, and the river was invisible. There was nothing to do but wait.

Meanwhile, news reports were filled with tragic deaths and heroic rescues. There was coverage of oil slicks, sewage spills, and other disgusting pollutants swirling around homes and businesses, but no one was talking about the farm animals, CAFOs, or waste lagoons. Rick was practically scratching at the door to go out and investigate.

As soon as the rain stopped, he headed for a Neuse Air Force plane. Once aloft, Rick was shocked by the extent of the devastation: Everywhere he looked, CAFOs had been wiped out. Rick could not count the lagoons completely overrun by black floodwaters. In shallower areas, he could still make out the rims of the submerged cesspools. In every case, their contents had been flushed into the still-rising floodwaters, and Rick could see ribbons of Pepto-Bismol-colored waste streaming into the Neuse.

Everywhere pink, wet, dead pigs were floating aimlessly in a brown ocean of muck. "It's so quiet down there," he said to the pilot. "The countryside is covered in silent death."

A few pigs, still in shock, had found their way to the barn roofs or higher ground. Rick's heart went out to the survivors. These pigs had never been outside their barns, had never seen sunlight or the elements. Now they were floating around like fat beach balls.

On occasional dry patches, Rick saw farmers with bulldozers piling up dead hogs by the hundreds. More swine hung high in the trees as the waters receded. Thousands of lifeless, bloated pigs littered the landscape in a surreal tableau of stench and death. There were even reports of hog carcasses bobbing around out in the ocean, a rare treat for the sharks.

Millions never had a chance. Hundreds of swine and poultry barns were flooded up to the roof, trapping the hapless creatures like rats in a cage. Little if any attempt was made to rescue them—though some farmers did try. Ultimately, hog deaths alone were estimated at one hundred to four hundred thousand, though farmers claimed only about thirty thousand.

For several days after the flooding began, no one in the media was reporting on the CAFO damage. Rick was apoplectic about it. He got on the phone with local and national reporters to tell them what he'd seen from the air. Within eight hours, national media teams were arriving from New York and D.C. That night, people around the globe were confronted with the death and destruction inflicted upon the animals of eastern North Carolina, and the manure-filled floodwaters left in Floyd's wake.

The first report aired on ABC *World News Tonight* and featured Rick. His phone rang soon after; on the other end of the line was an old colleague with a dire warning.

"Some swine producers don't like what you're doing with the media, Rick," he said. "They wanted to keep the CAFO situation hush-hush. They didn't want anyone to know the lagoons flooded and the animals died. Now they're talking about killing you, and I honestly believe they mean it."

Before long, the threats started coming in directly, including one from an irate dentist, of all things, who was financially invested in the community and furious that Rick was tarnishing New Bern's good name. Friends counseled Rick to cool it. But he refused. He did talk to the sheriff, who suggested he consider getting a personal firearm; guns are legal to carry and conceal in the state. Rick got the permit and carried his Colt .45 pistol with him, especially while on the water.

State reaction to the floods was swift, but not very reassuring. Governor Hunt blustered that he would shut down every swine facility built in a floodplain. A week later, he backtracked, promising closure only for those facilities that had suffered 50 percent or more damage. A week after that, he announced that no CAFOs were damaged enough to warrant shuttering.

Most lagoons had survived and were still operational. But the rain had filled them to the brim, and their adjoining sprayfields were too soaked too absorb anything. Even so, desperate farmers asked for and were given permission to keep on spraying, despite the fact that most of that effluent would end up in state waterways.

Outraged, Rick and the Neuse River Foundation sued the state and won. When the state appealed, State Attorney General Mike Easley refused to defend the spraying policy. The state lost again, and farmers were hit with an order not to overapply the waste. They did it anyway, Rick complained. But such was the chaos in Floyd's wake—environmental law enforcement was simply not a top priority.

Meanwhile, dead pigs piled up by the thousands. Farmers around the hog belt were trying to incinerate them, but without much success. It was like trying to roast a hot dog with a match. Mostly, the pigs were disposed of by burying them in the waterlogged ground. This posed a substantial threat to local wells, but state officials didn't seem to care.

Burial could not get rid of the carcasses fast enough, though. Some farmers likely took a page from a North Carolina State University paper that had put forth a novel idea for disposing of dead pigs: Feed them to live pigs.[9]

According to this paper, the grinding and decomposition of hog carcasses was shown to be "one of the most promising technologies for disposing of dead animals." Anaerobic fermentation was achieved through several steps. The recipe was gruesome: Place several dead hogs in a grinder until reduced to one-inch pieces. In a large, noncorrosive container, mix chunks of flesh with plant matter and acid-forming bacteria. Let the bacteria acidify the flesh until the fermented tissue becomes a stable slurry. Yield: several gallons of added nutritional value for pig feed. "This product has a sweet-sour smell," the report helpfully noted.

Before long, another rash of fish kills began popping up in the Neuse, though not as bad as incidents in prior years. Floods depleted oxygen from the water, but levels returned to normal fairly quickly. There were no major *Pfiesteria* outbreaks that year. Floyd had wiped the basin clean—far more than Fran or Bertha had. Over the next few years, conditions on the river would return to levels that were healthier than they had been in a decade.

But there was something else, something very unsettling about Floyd that Rick could not shake from his consciousness. The hurricane had been a "hundred-year rain event"—dumping more water on the state than any storm in the past century—but it *caused* a "five-hundred-year flood." How was it possible that the heaviest rainfall in one hundred years had caused the worst flooding in five hundred years?

"It's because we messed around with nature," Rick told Joanne as 1999 finally drew to a merciful close. Much of the state had become heavily developed, and land that used to absorb rainfall was reconstructed to divert water into the rivers. "But Mother Nature didn't design these rivers to handle all that water at once, so she deluged the floodplains—and washed out all those CAFOs in her path." Rick didn't even think about storms becoming more severe because of global warming, though 1999 ended as the nation's second-hottest year on record.

It gave Rick the shivers to ponder the other ways that nature might exact revenge for the warehousing of so many thousands of creatures trapped within a single confinement. Floyd, floods, and *Pfiesteria* were perhaps just omens of more havoc to follow. And it enraged him to think that when Mother Nature acted, she would not discriminate between those who had endeavored to stop the CAFOs and those who got rich from them.

By the dawn of the new millennium, consolidation of the U.S. pork industry had achieved a powerful momentum. In January 2000, Murphy Family Farms—though racked with $200 million in debt—was acquired by the giant agricultural conglomerate Smithfield Foods, Inc. It would join Smithfield's other hog subsidiaries, including Brown's of Carolina, Inc., which would now be called Murphy-Brown, and Carroll's Foods, Inc. Together they would supply some twelve million hogs a year to the domestic and foreign markets.[10]

The New York Times was impressed with Smithfield's vertically integrated assault on the pork market. "By aggressively acquiring its larger rivals over the last two years and using precision genetics, huge hog farms and giant meat-packing plants to control every stage of production, Smithfield has ballooned into a $5 billion company that accounts for more than a fifth of the nation's pork," the paper gushed.[11]

In 1997, the company was the seventh-largest pork producer in the country. Now, three years later, it was number one. But there were potential pitfalls in going so big, so fast. Unwanted attention from federal authorities was chief among them. After the Murphy acquisition, Smithfield had become "absurdly big," the USDA alleged. It asked the Justice Department's antitrust division to look into the deal.

Smithfield officials said such criticism was unwarranted. Smithfield considered itself to be a pioneer in creating and selling a leaner, healthier, more consistent pork product. After all, it was just following the model of successful chicken companies.

"What we did in the pork industry is what Perdue and Tyson did in the poultry business," said Joseph W. Luter III, chairman and chief executive of Smithfield (quoted in the same article). "Vertical integration gives you high-quality, consistent products with consistent genetics. And the only way to do that is to control the process from the farm to the packing plant."

Smithfield was hardly a family farming affair. CEO Luter was a "tart-tongued sixty-year-old Virginian who runs the company from his Park Avenue apartment in New York City and his home in Aspen, Colorado," the *Times* also wrote. Luter was unfazed by the small but growing number of independent pig farmers who were growing fatter, more flavorful meat for fine restaurants and niche markets that demanded hogs free of antibiotics and additives.

To Luter, American livestock farming had irrevocably changed. "The bottom line is, the small farmers have been disappearing for one hundred years," he said. "If you want to protect the small farmer, you are going to do it on the back of the American consumer."

In early 2000, fresh off their Clean Water Act victory in federal court, members of CARE were beginning to enjoy their newfound clout in the Lower Valley. They had emerged victorious over Bosma and settled with Koopmans and Sunnyveld dairies. Their next battle would be with DeRuyter Brothers Dairy.

But their opponent caved. On February 1, a DeRuyter attorney filed papers in Richland agreeing to a half-million-dollar settlement with CARE. It was the largest deal ever offered by a dairy in the American Northwest. In lieu of paying fines to the feds, the DeRuyters would donate $200,000 to a nonprofit group called the Valley Institute for Research and Education (VIRE) for a landmark study of groundwater pollution in the area.[12]

The dairy also agreed to spend $250,000 in "engineering improvements," such as a new fully lined lagoon and new berms around the cow pens. DeRuyter would embark on a four-year soil-testing regime to detect overapplication of manure, and submit to water testing in drains that ran through its property. DeRuyter would also pay CARE's legal costs, estimated at about fifty-five thousand dollars. CARE also won the right to conduct its own inspections of the dairy several times a year over the next four years. In addition, DeRuyter pledged to hold annual training seminars for its workers on proper waste handling and disposal.

"We have been waiting a long time for this day," Helen told reporters. "We can now move beyond the legal hoops in this case and finally get down to the business of cleaning up the water in our valley."

The DeRuyters were in no mood to sing CARE's praises, nor were they particularly contrite. But the settlement made economic sense, their lawyer said, even though the allegations had been "grossly overstated." In the end, the dairymen felt they'd been singled out "among hundreds of dairies," partly because of their financial success.

Helen received DeRuyter's grousing with equanimity. It didn't really matter: Her side—CARE and its attorneys—had turned a corner into the brave new century. "After all these years of defending ourselves against the megadairies, we may finally bring about the changes we need to finally clean up this filthy valley," she said to Don that night. "Let them become an example for others to follow."

But Helen was no longer just thinking in terms of her little community. She realized that far beyond the sheltered walls of the Lower Valley, in places like Texas, California, Colorado, Illinois, and elsewhere, massive dairy farms were bringing many of the same headaches to people throughout the country.

Helen Reddout and Karen Hudson had conferred on the phone many times over the past year or so, without ever meeting. Likewise, neither woman had met their admired ally Rick Dove. In June 2000, their paths would finally converge at the Sierra Club meeting in Washington, D.C. The occasion was a conference on using rBGH in factory-farmed dairy cows. It was an anti-Posilac conference, as evidenced by its name: "The Threat Recombinant

Bovine Growth Hormone Poses to Small Dairy Farms, Public Health, Animal Welfare and the Environment."

The Sierra Club pulled no punches in promoting the event. A promotional flyer warned that small family farmers, milking fifty to three hundred cows each, faced bankruptcy from tumbling milk prices, which had fallen below 1978 levels. "This fall has been manipulated through the dumping of large quantities of cheese from factory dairy operations in California, Arizona and Idaho." The megadairies—some as massive as forty thousand head—imprisoned cows in "inhumane industrial settings," and continued to proliferate, despite the threat they posed to water and air quality, the flyer warned.[13]

Recombinant growth hormones were playing a key role in the industrialization of American dairies, the Sierra Club asserted. "RBGH produces a 15 percent increase in individual cow milk production during the first lactation. This onetime increase in production combined with the externalizing of the environmental and human health costs AND corporate and government subsidies for large industrial animal production give dairy animal factories a significant and unfair production cost advantage over small dairy operations," the group alleged. It added that rBGH significantly harmed animal welfare and threatened human health "through contamination of the food supply."

Karen Hudson walked into one presentation, being given by a woman she did not recognize, about the overwhelming amount of dairy cow manure that was literally backing up in Yakima Valley. (It was Helen, of course—Karen had seen her at two previous conferences but never put two and two together.)

Helen explained how so much of the cow muck had been scraped off dry lots—with no immediate place for it to go—that dairymen began piling it up into a gargantuan heap that locals soon started calling Manure Mountain. Still there, it had now reached the height of a seven-story building.

Karen was equally transfixed by Rick's presentation, especially when he played an underground video shot by volunteers from PETA (People for the Ethical Treatment of Animals). The video showed that factory farming involved not only efficiency but also cold-blooded cruelty. It showed workers inside a hog barn terrorizing and beating animals with steel rods. One man is seen sodomizing a screaming hog with a crowbar. In another segment, two workers cull out the runts (who won't make it to market size in time) and, grabbing them by their hind legs, slam their heads repeatedly into the cement floor until they are dead. The other pigs, completely aware of what is happening, squeal in horror. Scientists say pigs have the intelligence and awareness of three-year-old children.

In the slaughterhouse, the assembly-line nature of CAFOs was made more vivid. Live pigs were shoved onto sharp hooks and dangled from an elevated conveyor belt. Workers shot them in the head with a bolt bullet and then, after they died, sliced open their bellies in a rush of blood and entrails. The living pigs waiting on hooks witnessed all this.

In the video, one of the pigs survives the bullet. A worker slices the pig's throat and, in the process, knocks the poor animal off its hook. In agony, the whining, bleeding beast crawls around the floor, seeking the merciful deliverance of death.

Rick continued speaking over the screams of the pigs on the video. Both Karen and Helen were horrified. Tears welled in their eyes and Karen had to look away. From that moment on, Helen would never buy pork again; when she saw it in her market, she would hear those screams of agony in the industrial slaughterhouses and feel sick to her stomach.

The whole group—Helen, Karen, Rick, Bill Weida, and staff members from the GRACE Factory Farm Project—had dinner together that night. Joining them were two seasoned Midwest activists, cattleman Terry Spence of Missouri and former hog grower Chris Petersen of Iowa. Both were significant figures in the CAFO wars.

For Karen and Helen, it was the beginning of a long and very close friendship.

Chris Petersen is the archetypal Iowa hog, corn, and bean farmer. Friendly and plainspoken, with a pronounced Upper Plains twang and a cap constantly perched on his head, the fiftysomething Iowa native is also a powerhouse in local Democratic politics.

Chris owns an independent family farm just outside Clear Lake, Iowa, a rather affluent vacation community in the north-central part of Iowa. For more than thirty-five years, Chris has been involved in varying degrees of farming, politics, and rural social action.

In the 1980s, Chris worked in a local factory, Iowa Mold and Tooling, but also began to wade into the hog business, starting off with a few sows at first and then gradually expanding his herd in a home-based farrow-to-finish operation. The pigs spent some of their lives in bedded confinements, but were also allowed outside in warmer weather. In the bitterly cold winter months, sows were farrowed indoors and weaned piglets were kept in a "hot nursery." At forty pounds, the young animals were then let outside into open-air pens, with heavily bedded shelters for sleeping.

By 1990, hog farming was looking pretty sweet for the Petersens. Chris doubled his herd to 250 sows and sent some 3,000 market-weight hogs to slaughter each year. He quit his job to dedicate himself full-time to his lifelong dream of farming.

Back then, the market was wide open, and any producer could sell his or her pigs to any packing plant that offered the highest price. Chris would call around to various packers to see what price they were paying on any given day. He soon learned that during planting and harvesting seasons, most farmers were out in their fields and not willing to be bothered selling hogs. Packers would grow desperate during these times and call their lists of growers, asking if they had any pigs ready for slaughter. Chris knew they would pay a premium to keep their shifts humming at full capacity, and he tried timing his herds around these cycles, for maximum profit.

The system worked. As soon as production grew too high, prices would fall and farmers would immediately cut back their herds, and within months, prices would stabilize. There were very few wild swings in the amount that a processor would pay for a pig.

"But then corporate hogs started to control the market," Chris explained to Karen one weekend when she and Rocky drove up to Clear Lake for a visit. "Big hog companies like Iowa Select moved in." Others, like Smithfield Foods, were banned under state law from owning animals in Iowa because they also owned processing plants. This "packer ban" prevented processing companies from owning the animals they slaughtered, thus encouraging free and open access for all growers to the all-important "hourglass" gateway to the market.

But Chris believed that Smithfield and others conspired to drive small producers out of business. "The big companies came in and manipulated the markets to where prices would hit bottom more often, and stay there longer," he explained. "It became harder and harder for smaller farmers to ride out the price slumps, and they would go deeper into debt waiting for prices to come back up. But then the next drop would come."

Packers favored the new, larger producers because they could deliver, say, one thousand animals all at once, each exactly the same size, weight, fat content, and meat texture—or, as Chris derisively called them, cookie-cutter pigs. Processors like Smithfield and Hormel no longer had to scramble to keep their factories humming, and exploding competition drove prices ever downward, even as feed prices were going way up.

Things got so bad that Chris went back to work in town, and his wife, Kristi, took a job as well. As the prices fell lower, small producers were forced to aggregate their pigs and sell them through "hog packagers" because they could no longer sell small quantities of animals on their own. It got the job done, but everyone was losing a few dollars more per pig to the aggregator.

"By 1997, I'd seen the handwriting on the wall," Chris said sadly. "You could no longer sell your pigs when you wanted to, but only when the plant wanted to buy them. By then, packers were in long-term contracts with the CAFOs, and it might be a two-week wait or more before they were ready to take your pigs. But pigs are like parking meters: They keep eating and costing you money. And I had to get new pigs into their pens ASAP, so every day was costing me more. They killed the market."

Chris said CAFOs and packers "worked together to form a very accommodating situation for them both that kept the little guy on the outside, begging for scraps. The CAFOs were buying bulk feed and vet supplies. Theirs was a gravy train and they had full access into a vertically integrated market." The longer this went on, the more the smaller independent producers got squeezed out, he said.

Over the years, things got considerably worse: Lawmakers voted to overturn the state ban on processors owning the animals they slaughtered. This opened the door for Smithfield and others to run their own CAFOs in the nation's number-one hog-producing state.

Another blow came when rural activists failed to defeat a bill that would ban counties from exercising any local control over factory farms in Iowa. "That was the last straw," Chris said. "It cleared the way for the CAFO industry to finally come in and take over the state."

By the end of 1998, the packers—through market control or outright ownership of the animals—were able to manipulate prices down to an abysmal eight cents a pound, Chris recalled bitterly. "Iowa lost tens of thousands of producers right there." Prices had already fallen ridiculously low before they bottomed out. "It had been around forty cents, which was not great, but it could pay the rent," Chris said. It cost him about thirty-seven cents a pound to raise the pigs, so he made just enough to get by. But eight cents was a catastrophe. Chris lost more than seventy thousand dollars in herd value in a six-week period, and saw his net worth plummet by 75 percent. He could not even sell the buildings, equipment, and breeding herd for very much. What farmer was going to raise pigs for eight cents a pound?

Chris barely held on. He was forced to remortgage everything. And because he carried so much debt, he had no choice but to ride things out. The appalling eight-cents-a-pound price remained for several weeks, then rose to the low twenties for many more. He lost money until prices recovered to the forty-cent range. But even then, for the next few years, Chris was barely able to cover the interest on his debt. He and Kristi were still working in town to make ends meet. It wasn't the farmer's life he had envisioned.

Without competitive markets, Chris knew, independent producers like himself would be pushed out of their own businesses and driven into demeaning lives as low-wage employees of corporations on their own farmland.

"That's when I got into the animal-factory fight, big time," Chris told Karen. "Within a few weeks, there were six of us farmers who came together. One guy called me up, John Crabtree from the Center for Rural Affairs. Back in the sixties, his dad used to farm across the fence from my dad. And he said, 'Want to raise a little hell together?'" Soon, they were holding meetings with hundreds of farmers at a time, and the gang of six became known as the Freedom Fighters. Chris was a ringleader.

"We need to force state and federal officials to listen to the public and the farmers!" he would say at rallies in support of independent family farms. "Why the hell are they destroying markets and running independents out of business, and how are we going to make them stop it?"

In 2001, Chris and Kristi completely switched over to what he considered to be a more sustainable thirty-sow herd of Berkshires, a "heritage" breed of hogs, producing about seven hundred piglets a year. All were sold directly to consumers, or to niche pork companies and high-end restaurants that valued the fattier and more flavorful meat. Chris and Kristi also raised some grass-fed cattle for local consumers, grew vegetables for area restaurants, and produced hay to sell commercially.

Chris became more politically active. Colleagues had introduced him to Senator Paul Wellstone, the liberal Democrat from Minnesota who would die in a small plane crash during his 2002 reelection campaign. Chris's introduction to Senator Wellstone had led to meetings with Vice President Al Gore and his staff and, when Gore began campaigning for president in 1999, Chris suddenly found himself as a friend and advisor to the candidate and his campaign.

Chris was also very active in the Iowa Farmers Union, a chapter of the National Farmers Union and a more left-of-center, environmentally oriented group than the American Farm Bureau Federation. In 2000, he was elected vice president of the state group (and in 2004, would become its president). Chris was also featured extensively in a CBS *60 Minutes* broadcast that was highly critical of the Farm Bureau, from which Chris had publicly and conspicuously resigned, citing its many ties to corporate agriculture and CAFOs.

Chris had impressed other activists in Washington with the Iowa Farmers Union's list of demands. The very contentious issues they were pushing for included the following:

- A nationwide temporary moratorium on new industrial animal confinements "until the issues of human health risks are properly analyzed and dealt with."
- A requirement to protect CAFO workers with written warnings (in their own language) on the "health impacts of working in these facilities," and for employees to be at least eighteen years old, receive health insurance, and be covered for up to five years after termination for any health costs arising from working in the CAFO.

- A retroactive requirement for all CAFOs greater than five hundred animal units (1,250 hogs) to obtain an annual operating permit through county supervisors, after completion of an environmental impact study.
- A fifteen-parts-per-billion limit on CAFO emissions of ammonia and hydrogen sulfide; a minimum one-half-mile setback from animal buildings and lagoons to streams, lakes, drainage wells, and other waters; and a ban on all new confinements "within the watersheds of lakes or a source of drinking water for a town, city, or residence."
- A ban on confinements being built in flood-prone areas.
- A federal law to ban any packer from owning or contracting livestock, or from discounting the price paid on the basis of volume, and to enforce violations with penalties.
- A "contract grower bill of rights" that would require that contractors have recourse to litigation to redress grievances, instead of the current contractual stipulation of forced and binding arbitration of disputes.
- A ban on confidentiality clauses in contracts, and the right of growers to obtain all information about prices paid to other growers and about their ranking as producers.
- A requirement for manure to be applied as close to planting time as possible, and never when the ground is frozen or when soil temperatures are fifty degrees and falling. Disposal of waste through gun methods should be prohibited.

Chris knew that the laundry list was a long shot. But there were several key provisions that he and thousands of Iowa farmers were unwilling to compromise on, he told his friends. Those included price transparency, antitrust enforcement, a packer ban, and local control.

North Carolina's attorney general, Mike Easley, was still fuming at Robert Kennedy, Jr., and his Waterkeeper group for trying to sue Smithfield Foods on behalf of the people of his state. But since the judge had ruled that only the attorney general could take such an action, in July 2000, gubernatorial candidate Easley made his big move.

Rather than take Smithfield to court, however, Easley forced the hog behemoth and its major subsidiaries—Carroll's, Carolina Foods, and the recently acquired Murphy Family Farms—to enter into a binding settlement that would ultimately phase out lagoon-and-sprayfield operations statewide.

"The attorney general has concluded that the public interest will be served by the development and implementation of environmentally superior swine waste management technologies," the official agreement between the parties declared, stipulating Easley's "commitment to use the full power and authority of his office to diligently pursue expeditious implementation [of alternative technologies] under North Carolina law, regardless of ownership or operational control of the farms."[14]

It was a historic legal strategy, and it would prove a difficult order for the companies. They argued that lagoons were the best available technology for managing swine waste, but moving to alternative methods was far better than facing an ambitious and rising North Carolina politician in court.

Smithfield and its companies were vowing to help develop and then adopt "environmentally superior technologies" to replace all of their waste lagoons. Soon after, Premium Standard Farms—which had a considerably smaller presence in the state—also signed the agreement. Smithfield would cough up $15 million and Premium Standard Farms $2.1 million to test out various alternative technologies.

Under the settlement, a manure expert from North Carolina State, Mike Williams, would evaluate lagoon alternatives to see which met the criteria as an environmentally superior technology. The alternatives had to be technically and economically feasible, while also eliminating wastewater discharges, ammonia emissions, detectable odors beyond CAFO boundaries, nutrient and heavy-metal contamination of soil and groundwater, and the release of "disease-transmitting vectors" and other pathogens into the air.

The state issued a request for research proposals from experts around the nation. Eventually, Mike Williams would settle on eighteen of the most innovative proposals to test for environmental superiority. Many of the candidates incorporated a process to separate solid material from the liquid waste, dry it, and then use it in "value-added" products such as commercial fertilizer. Dried solids dramatically reduce both odor and ammonia emissions.

It would be years before Williams announced which technologies met the criteria.

On July 4, 2000, Rick Dove stepped down after seven years as the Neuse Riverkeeper. It was one of the hardest decisions he had ever made. But his declining health would no longer permit him to be out on the river at 7 A.M. each morning for a sixteen-hour day. Each night at quitting time, he was drained, short of breath, and racked with a migraine. Now in his sixties, he was unable to sleep well at nights. His short-term memory was withering away.

His tenure on the river drew accolades from leaders of the environmental movement. "He's been able to tell the story in human terms of how we hurt our rivers and ourselves," Molly Diggins, North Carolina director of the Sierra Club, told reporters. "And he's done it in a way that has captured the minds and hearts of people in the state and around the country. There is as much poetry as there is steel in Rick Dove."[15]

The Raleigh *News & Observer* hailed Rick as someone who "antagonized the swine industry, chambers of commerce and other groups." And, the paper said, "Politicians heard the message." Rick's innumerable hours on water, on land, and in the air had helped force the state to spend "millions on clean water projects and environmental research, impose a moratorium on new swine operations, tighten pollution controls and enforcement at sewage plants and adopt a cleanup plan for the Neuse River that is one of the nation's most comprehensive."

Rick was humbled by the recognition, but he also knew the work was not completed. He was far from retiring; he remained a board member of the Waterkeeper Alliance and soon accepted a paying position with the group to help bring CAFO abuses to a halt. Waterkeeper had not given up on bringing a suit against the worst factory-farm polluters in North Carolina. Rick was still on the job.

In late 2000, Kennedy and the group decided to target six North Carolina swine facilities owned by Smithfield subsidiary Murphy-Brown with a lawsuit under the federal Clean Water Act—in which Congress provided for ordinary citizens to litigate against alleged polluters if the government had failed to do so.

Kennedy planned to create, in his words, a team of "superstar lawyers" to take on big agriculture and the worst-offending CAFOs. The coalition included Jan Schlichtmann, whom John Travolta portrayed in the movie *A Civil Action*, and Steve Bozeman, one of the attorneys who sued the tobacco companies, as dramatized in the film *The Insider*. Rounding out the lineup were Charlie Speer and Richard Middleton, both of them charismatic trial lawyers who would later go on to win some high-profile, high-paying nuisance lawsuits against CAFOs on their own.

For the North Carolina action, Kennedy chose Nicolette Hahn, an attractive young litigator with medium-brown hair worn long, and a winning smile that concealed a fearless "I eat nails for breakfast" demeanor in court.

The plaintiffs eventually honed in on four Jones County hog farms as their targets, identified as Browns Nos. 5, 6, 9, and 22. Rick, who had monitored these facilities for some time, stepped up his surveillance with more flyovers, photos, and videos. Water testing turned up high levels of fecal coliform bacteria. While Browns No. 5 had been completely submerged underwater during Floyd, the CAFO was now back up and running, despite the fact that it was situated in a Neuse River floodplain. In its letter of intent to sue, Waterkeeper said the CAFOs were point sources of pollution and, as such, were required to have a National Pollution Discharge Elimination System permit under the rules of the Clean Water Act.

But no CAFO in the state had an NPDES permit, which was slightly ironic, since that rule had been pushed through by then U.S. Senator Robert Dole. (His North Carolinian wife, Elizabeth, would be elected a senator from the state in 2002.) Smithfield argued that it didn't need a permit, and the battle was set.

On December 6, 2000, the Waterkeeper Alliance put the lawsuits in motion by filing formal notice letters against the hog-farming operations. Rick and Nicolette arranged press conferences in Washington, D.C., and in Raleigh for the occasion. Robert Kennedy, Jr., and Jan Schlichtmann were slated to come to North Carolina. In Raleigh, Rick was thrilled to see the room packed with farmers, environmentalists, and lots of reporters. Kennedy set the place on fire with his speech, without the use of notes. He condemned the industrial farms for polluting, for being inhumane to animals, for wrecking rural economies, and for bankrupting independent farmers.

"Federal environmental prosecution against the meat industry has effectively ceased," he charged. "Congress has eviscerated the EPA's enforcement budget while the political clout of powerful pork producers has trumped state enforcement efforts. This collapse of environmental enforcement has allowed corporate hog farms to proliferate with huge pollution-based profits."[16]

In other words, CAFOs could only make money if they broke the laws protecting the environment.

New Year's 2001 dawned as a brave new day in America. George W. Bush had just been declared president by a five to four Supreme Court vote, and the country was flush with a "peace dividend." Contentment was hardly universal. In the anti-CAFO camp, many people were nervous about the future; the incoming Bush administration was already noted for its probusiness and antienvironmental stance. Many activists assumed that Bush would side with factory farms in most disputes and, though weary, they prepared for more battle.

But the anti-CAFO forces knew they could not simply maintain a strategy of antagonism and rejection toward factory farms. If industrial animal production was an unacceptable means of feeding the nation at an affordable cost—a controversial assertion, to be sure—then it was incumbent upon critics to offer up a feasible alternative.

The alternative they liked was a concept called sustainable agriculture. Hardly a new idea, it had been making inroads in the 1990s as a buzzword among environmentalists. The very word "sustainable," however, remains wide-open to subjective interpretation—one reason why the idea has so many detractors in industry, academia, and government.

But back in 1990, the USDA decided to give the term a government definition that was, typically, vagueness inside denseness wrapped in legalese:

Sustainable farming is an integrated system of plant and animal production practices having a site-specific application that will, over the long term, satisfy human food and fiber needs; enhance environmental quality and the natural resource base upon which the agricultural economy depends; make the most efficient use of nonrenewable resources and on-farm resources and integrate, where appropriate, natural biological cycles and controls; sustain the economic viability of farm operations; and enhance the quality of life for farmers and society as a whole.[1]

Consumers could be forgiven for having lingering questions, so the GRACE Factory Farm Project offered a more straightforward definition: "A way of raising food that is healthy for consumers and animals, does not harm the environment, is humane for workers, respects animals, provides a fair wage to the farmer, and supports and enhances rural communities." This would include the following:[2]

Conservation: "What is taken out of the environment is put back in," so that water, soil, and air are available to future generations. Farm waste stays with each farm's ecosystem and cannot build up or pollute—it is a "closed system."

Biodiversity: Sustainable farms raise various kinds of plants and animals, and rotate both around fields and pastures to improve soil, reduce disease, and avoid oversaturation of nutrients. Chemical pesticides are kept to a minimum.

Animal Welfare: Animals are treated humanely and with respect, and "permitted to carry out their natural behaviors," such as grazing, rooting, or pecking.

Economic Viability: Farmers are "paid a fair wage and are not dependent on subsidies from the government," which strengthens small-town viability.

Social Justice: There is fair treatment and living wages for farm workers, who are afforded safe and healthy workplaces and proper living conditions.

For many, "sustainable farming" was not just a trendy buzzword but a goal and mission. Entire conferences were being dedicated to it. In January 2001, the Waterkeeper Alliance's Rick Dove and Nicolette Hahn, along with Gary Grant—the activist from Tillery and head of the thirty-member North Carolina Hog Roundtable—organized the Summit for Sustainable Hog Farming at the new Riverfront Convention Center in downtown New Bern.

Billed as a "National Gathering of Environmentalists, Family Farmers, Humane Farming Advocates, Scientists, Public Officials, Attorneys, and Citizens," it was one of the biggest anti-CAFO conferences held in the short history of the movement. Some eight hundred people came from across the United States and Canada, packing the place to hear Robert Kennedy, Jr., and other stars of the fledgling national movement speak out against industrial animal production, and in favor of smaller-scale, more "sustainable" types of farms. Their message had grown increasingly popular over a brief time, as large-scale animal confinements were becoming a hotbed of discontent among consumers and opinion makers nationwide.

The all-day event offered talks by fishermen and farmers, lawyers and scientists, clerics and labor leaders, politicians and animal-welfare advocates. Rick was stunned by the turnout. Key people in the movement had registered: Karen Hudson and Kendall Thu from Illinois, Chris Petersen from Iowa, Terry Spence from Missouri, Bill Weida from Idaho, and Julie Jansen from Minnesota.

Speakers included Brother David Andrews of the National Catholic Rural Life Conference; attorneys Jan Schlichtmann and Charlie Speer; and sustainable-livestock farmer Bill Niman, cofounder of Niman Ranch, which furnished the pasture-raised Iowa pork that was served up by local caterers. Rick's ally, Professor Steve Wing of the University of North Carolina at Chapel Hill, spoke on the effect of hog odors on residents in Duplin County and elsewhere. The affable Don Webb, in his trademark bib overalls and booming drawl, gave a rousing address as well.

Karen split her time between staffing the FARM booth—displaying her IL-LINOIS, LAND OF STINKIN' posters, a favorite of the media, and handing out pamphlets and public-health fact sheets—and attending seminars. She was happy the meeting was not merely an anti-CAFO gathering; experts provided numerous road maps to sustainable farming.

A major tenet of sustainable animal farming, of course, is to raise livestock and poultry in the most natural way possible, and that means keeping antibiotics and other drugs to a minimum. It was a hot topic for the new century, and one of its leading champions had come to New Bern to speak. Karen was excited to meet him.

David Wallinga, M.D., is the director of the Food and Health program at the Institute for Agriculture and Trade Policy (IATP), a liberal think tank in Minneapolis that purports to "work locally and globally at the intersection of policy and practice to ensure fair and sustainable food, farm and trade systems."[3] The group's positions often put it at odds with the ambitions of agribusiness and other industrial interests.

Both Helen and Rick hit it off with the Minnesota doctor, whose extensive research included studying the impact of modern food production on human health, especially from the "inappropriate use of antibiotics and arsenic" in livestock and poultry. Months before, he and the IATP joined with the Cambridge, Massachusetts–based Union of Concerned Scientists (UCS) and others to form a group called Keep Antibiotics Working.

"We support limiting the overuse of antibiotics in human medicine," David said, "but our primary goal is ending their overuse and misuse in animal agriculture." Low-dose or "subtherapeutic" use of antibiotics to boost growth and prevent disease was leading to rapid development of multidrug-resistant bacteria in the environment, he said.

The Keep Antibiotics Working campaign had three main goals: phase out nontherapeutic use of any antibiotics that are or may become important to human medicine; restrict the treatment of sick animals with antibiotics that are essential for treating humans, especially fluoroquinolones—the last class of drugs that has not yet experienced bacterial resistance; and ensure public transparency in tracking antibiotic use and the development of antibiotic resistance.

"When animals are given antibiotics to artificially boost weight gain and compensate for their terrible growing conditions," David said during his talk at the summit, "they are given fairly low doses of the drugs in their feed, which kills only the most susceptible bacteria and leaves surviving bacteria to pass on their resistant genes." This "extensive and unnecessary" use drastically shortens the life span of any antibiotic, he explained.[4]

"Given the rapid evolution of bacteria, all antibiotics have a limited period of effectiveness. But the more often bacteria are exposed to an antibiotic, the more chances they have to develop resistance against it," David continued. "That's why it is so critical to extend the useful lifetime of any drug used against human disease for as long as possible," especially since very few new antibiotics are being or have been developed in the last quarter century.

"It is a practice which puts human health on the line," he told a hushed audience. "Antibiotic resistance has the potential to plunge us back into medicine's Dark Ages, when doctors couldn't treat infections caused by bacteria."

People can be infected with multidrug-resistant bacteria by eating undercooked contaminated meat, or foods and utensils that come in contact with meat juices. But farmers, their families, and meat-plant workers are exposed to antibiotics and antibiotic-resistant bacteria on a regular basis. "And of course," David added, "large quantities of antibiotics and antibiotic-resistant bacteria also enter the environment through the nearly two trillion pounds of animal wastes produced each year in this country. This poses an important, though little-studied, risk to the people and communities who inhabit those environments."

Karen also spent time in New Bern with Marlene Halverson—whose lecture on Swedish pig farming had captivated her at the 1998 Ames manure conference—and Marlene's sister Diane, from the Animal Welfare Institute (AWI).

AWI, founded in 1951, initially crusaded against the abuse of animals in experimentation. By 2001 much of its focus was on the conditions inside animal factories. The group compiled a set of animal-welfare standards that exceeded not only industry standards but also the bewildering patchwork of criteria created by the USDA's National Organic Program, the American Humane Association's Free Farmed program (now known as the American Humane Certified program), and Humane Farm Animal Care's Certified Humane Raised & Handled program.

For example, in order to earn the AWI "Animal Welfare Approved" label, a product had to come from an independent farm owned by a family that lived on the site and partook in its daily labor. Liquefied manure systems were prohibited, partly because gases in waste pits beneath the barns are unhealthy for animals.

The group prohibited the otherwise routine industry practice of "docking"— the removal of a pig's tail shortly after birth with scissors, cauterizing iron, or "burdizzo," a clamp that crushes the tail and causes it to drop off after two or three days. Docking was adopted when CAFO farmers began noticing much higher rates of tail biting among confined animals than among pasture-raised pigs. Scientists say the exact reason why such cannibalism increases inside a CAFO is a "mystery," though some have suggested that lack of sunlight, concrete slats for bedding, mechanical ventilation, and high-energy grain-based diets are possible factors. Farm animal advocates scoff at this speculation, and say the reason is clear: Crowding and incarceration can drive sentient beings to violence.

But until researchers learn how to control cannibalism, tail docking is highly recommended to prevent wounds and infections that lead to spinal abscesses and "carcass condemnation" (rejection as human food) at the slaughterhouse.

Not required by the animal-production industry, the USDA National Organic Program, or the Certified Humane and Free Farmed labels are these AWI standards:

Debeaking: AWI prohibits cutting off part of the beak of laying hens. Though this removal prevents fights, it also is excruciating for the birds and impedes their ability to eat and preen.

Farrowing Crates: Banned under the AWI program, they are allowed by the others—even the USDA National Organic Program gives certifying agents discretion to grant permission.

Nesting Material: It may not sound like much, but sows have a hormonally driven need to prepare for birth that, if prevented, causes undue stress in the animal.

Heritage Breeds: Standard-bred chickens and turkeys have fewer skeletal defects and other health problems than CAFO-bred birds, whose large breasts make it hard for them to walk.

Natural Daylight: Animals need light from the sun for optimal health. Aside from the AWI, only the USDA National Organic Program makes it mandatory.

Outdoor Access: All vertebrates need some form of exercise; allowing them ample time outside helps prevent abnormal behaviors and enhances vigor and immune health. Again, the organic label is the only other program to mandate outdoor access for all species.

Some food companies were beginning to adopt the AWI standards; first among them was Niman Ranch—which required its hog suppliers to follow AWI's humane husbandry standards. During a powerful speech, chairman Mike McConnell urged people to lobby their grocers, restaurants, and local markets to offer meat from "humane and sustainable family farms."

The issue of environmental racism was another hot topic in New Bern that day. Rick learned how African-American residents were mobilizing in places like Duplin County. There, a couple named Devon Hall and Dothula Baron-Hall had established the grassroots group Rural Empowerment Association for Community Help (REACH). Initially created to provide services to empower low-income families and people of color after Hurricane Floyd, REACH was also addressing the potential health effects of living in an area crowded with animal factories.

"They are everywhere in Duplin," Devon explained to Rick that afternoon during a conference break. "They are ruining people's lives and property."

A case in point was Elsie, an African-American woman whose grandfather had been a tobacco farmer on about sixty-one acres of land outside a small town in North Carolina.

"Several years ago, a white family just walked into the register of deeds office and rewrote the deed on our property," Elsie contended to Rick, who had a hard time believing that something like this could happen in late twentieth-century America. "They took forty-five acres—they said we'd never registered the deed on that parcel. There was nothing we could do," she said. "The land they took goes right up to eight feet away from our house."

Then the neighbors put in a hog CAFO.

"Ever since, it's a living hell," Elsie claimed. "They spray manure right onto our property, and they haul their sprayer behind a tractor, so they know exactly where it's going. And when we complained, they just sprayed some more—on our lawn, on our house, even the laundry on our clothesline. It's like rain comin' down, but it's raw sewage. You can't stand out there. You can't open your windows, you can't cook out, you can't have company over, and you got these flies everywhere. Meantime, everyone's got a headache, our eyes water, it's hard to breathe or swallow from the ammonia. You know, it actually makes you *itch*."

Devon explained that lots of people in the area were having similar problems. Many were worried that their shallow wells might have been contaminated with dangerously high nitrate levels. Rick sat in silence and disgust as he listened. "What did you do?" he asked Elsie.

"Well, I tried to go talk to the people, but I was afraid to even walk up to their door—they got a lot of guns and ammo on that farm," she said. Instead, Elsie approached the owner one day out on the road, on what she called neutral territory. She tried to reason with the man, but he barked at her amid a rash of racial obscenities. "This is *my* investment!" he shouted.

Days later, the farmer's son appeared at Elsie's home and burst into the living room, where her elderly mother was caring for Elsie's brother, who had severe Down syndrome. "He ran inside and grabbed my mama and started cursing and shaking her," Elsie said.

Elsie went to the local police department, but was told she would have to drive over to the town of Kenansville, to file a complaint with the Duplin County Sheriff's Office. They sent someone out to have a look, and Elsie pressed charges.

The case was dismissed.

It was a "he said, she said" situation, Elsie was informed, but she told Rick that she knew it was more than that. Her own sister had witnessed the attack on their ninety-eight-year-old mother, according to Elsie, but her sister was not allowed to testify in court. Elsie, her family, and her friends had seen this brand of Duplin County "justice" many times before.

Elsie spent the next nine months calling the health department, the water-quality division, county commissioners, the state attorney general, and her member of Congress. "Sometimes people actually did come out when we complained," she said, "but it was four or five hours later, after the spraying stopped. We showed 'em the dark ground that had been saturated, but they just went back to Raleigh and filed reports saying there was no problem at all."

Several weeks and many complaints later, the sheriff returned to the house, this time bearing handcuffs. "He'd come over to arrest me!" Elsie said. "I was out mowing the lawn, and he wanted to put me in handcuffs. My mother had passed away by then, and I said my Down syndrome brother was in the house—he could barely move his head at this point. They were going to take me away and leave him there alone. It was a disgrace."

"But what did they want to arrest you for?" Rick asked in disbelief.

"My neighbor said I was trespassing. He lied, and the police believed him," she contended. By this time, Elsie had gained some help from a lawyer in Durham, who jumped on the phone to defuse the situation: Elsie agreed to appear at an arraignment later that day, if the sheriff wouldn't haul her off in handcuffs, marooning her brother. She cleaned up from gardening and arranged for someone to look after her brother. Before leaving, she called her lawyer again. He advised her to seek a warrant against the neighbor for trespassing.

"And so I asked the magistrate, and she laughed in my face," Elsie said angrily. "She was the same person who signed my arrest warrant! And she said to me, 'We're just going to let this whole thing play out in court.'" Eventually, Elsie had to make the forty-five-mile round-trip drive many times to Kenansville, where, eventually, a judge ruled that this was a civil and not a criminal matter, and dismissed the case.

Rick was having a hard time fathoming that this kind of Jim Crow bullshit was taking place just two hours away from the sparkling new convention center in downtown New Bern, with its modern terrace overlooking the sleek sailboats crisscrossing the river. Devon assured him that such harsh injustice and harassment was not at all uncommon inside the hog belt.

"If you look at the makeup of Duplin, it's an agriculture county," he said. "And when you look at the power structure, and your county commissioners and the various county boards and so forth, those people are always connected with the industry somehow. So when the little people like us have a complaint, we're always shut down because of the power and intimidation of the pork industry. And most of their farmers are white."

Finally, the long day came to a close with a calming prayer as Sister Evelyn Mattern of the North Carolina Council of Churches read from the writings of Saint Basil the Great:

> O God, enlarge within us the sense of fellowship with all living things, even our brothers and sisters the animals, to whom you have given the earth as their home in common with us. We remember with shame that in the past we have exercised our high dominion with ruthless cruelty so that the voice of the earth, which should have gone up to you in song, has been a groan of pain. May we realize that they live, not for us alone, but for themselves and for you, and that they love the sweetness of life.

Most people who attended the New Bern summit came away with positive feelings about traditional and sustainable alternatives to industrialized hog production, but not everyone. During the day, Rick had noticed small groups of men in farmer's clothing milling about the convention hall or conferring with other men in expensive suits. Rick knew they were contract swine growers and the "hog barons" that ran companies like Murphy-Brown. Throughout Kennedy's talk, he noticed, they had remained seated—silent, with tape recorders on—as the rest of the room stood up to cheer.

Big food interests were pushing back hard against the campaigners, starting with the Center for Consumer Freedom (CCF), a nonprofit group "devoted to promoting personal responsibility and protecting consumer choices. We believe that the consumer is King. And Queen." [5] (SourceWatch, an online listing of industry groups from the Center for Media and Democracy, says CCF "claims its mission is to defend the rights of consumers to choose to eat, drink and smoke as they please," but is really just a "front group" for agribusiness, tobacco, restaurant, and alcoholic-beverage interests.) [6]

CCF wrote about the New Bern hog summit on its Web site, deriding the talks by "multi-millionaire lawyers," environmentalists who "warned of the evils of 'Big Pork,'" and "animal-rights activists who touted Sweden's 'humane' hog industry as the example to follow (in Sweden, by the way, pork typically costs the equivalent of eleven dollars per pound)."

The summit had been more sinister than a mere carnival for "environmental zealots to run amok," the group warned. "Kennedy and the Waterkeeper lawyers just might win a significant payoff from their anti-corporate jihad," it said. "A big enough jury verdict could force mainstream corporate producers from the marketplace entirely, drastically raising food prices and ultimately narrowing the choices open to American consumers." Kennedy and Waterkeeper had "declared war on America's pork industry," and many in the anti-agribusiness movement were backing "any initiative that will raise prices and make 'organic' and 'sustainable' meats more attractive to consumers."

Zealots in the anti-CAFO movement "claim to know 'what's best for you,'" the industry group said. "In reality, they're eroding our basic freedoms—the freedom to buy what we want, eat what we want, drink what we want, and raise our children as we see fit. When they push ordinary Americans around, we're here to push back."

February 2001 brought nasty weather to Elmwood: ice, snow, and rain. The weather turned the soil into a mucky, soupy mess—a condition that justifies why manure application is usually illegal in northern states during winter months. Frozen or oversaturated ground blocks the absorption of liquid and leads to runoff.

But that had not stopped Dave Inskeep and the Inwood Dairy. Local media reported that they had continued to spray liquid waste onto cropland just east of the operation. A thousand yards away from Inwood's lagoon lived farmer Bill Wagner. On February 13, Wagner noticed that rainwater washing onto his property from next door was running brown. And it reeked of cow poop.[7]

Wagner had been friends and neighbors with Inskeep for more than forty years, and had advised the Caterpillar executive against opening such a large operation. But Inskeep wouldn't listen to him, any more than he would to Karen Hudson or his other concerned neighbors. And now, shit-water from Dave's cows was streaming across his front lawn and into the lake behind his house.

He called the state EPA.

Inspectors came over that day. There was reason for their promptness; Inwood had been on their radar for quite some time. The place had built up a rap sheet of leaks, spills, and unyielding odor complaints from local residents. Now, given the miserable weather, the Illinois EPA had a potentially monstrous problem on its hands.

After visiting Wagner's property, the inspectors got back in their car and drove through the pounding rain to the dairy. They walked past the long white animal barns and attractive brick milking parlor, and over toward the above-ground lagoon. What they saw there was unnerving.

Farmhands were feverishly piling up sandbags along one edge of the eight-acre lagoon. Inskeep had allowed it to become too full. Instead of the required two feet of freeboard between surface and rim, this lagoon was an inch or two from catastrophe. And the rain just kept falling.

The inspectors slapped the dairy with an emergency injunction on the spot, ordering Inskeep to stop pumping waste from the cow barns and flushwater from the milking parlor into his lagoon, until they could help him devise some makeshift solution. And they forbade him to spray any of the wastewater onto the nearby soaking fields.

The next morning, the state officials returned, unannounced, to find the pumps still running, still sending thousands of gallons of water, urine, feces, and spilled milk into the ever-rising lagoon. Inwood's forty-million-gallon lagoon was perhaps hours from overflowing.

The officials were outraged. They said Inskeep had to lower his lagoon immediately—by a foot or more—before he even *thought* about turning the pumps back on. That meant removing several million gallons. Spraying was out of the question, so his only option was to haul the stuff out. Since one tanker truck could accommodate only six thousand gallons, this would be a very expensive process.

Inskeep refused. He said he had to keep operations going to avoid a total economic collapse. He would continue milking cows and hosing down his buildings on an intensive schedule. When agents asked how he planned to dispose of the effluent, he "threatened to pump the waste into the West Fork of Kickapoo Creek," IEPA documents revealed.

This time, the inspectors slapped Inskeep with a court order to stop pumping, and added a summons: Inskeep would have to appear two days later in Peoria County Court, where the matter would be taken up by the office of Attorney General Jim Ryan.

Inskeep must have panicked, because he made some very bad decisions that afternoon—decisions that haunt him to this day.

Inskeep had his men lay thick snakelike hoses out to a long, narrow, twisting ravine that had been left over from the old strip mining days. Workers pumped somewhere between one and two million gallons of muck from the lagoon. Its freeboard now showed six inches of room; not ideal, but better.

Unfortunately for Inskeep—and Elmwood—an earthen dam plugging up the end of the ravine couldn't withstand the strain of two million gallons of sludge combined with the torrential rain. A fissure in the dam began to grow, and suddenly widened into a small chasm. Foamy brown and yellow liquid gushed through the opening, eroding into a full-grown breach. The waste cascaded down in a stream of filth into a fishpond below. From there, it began draining into the west fork of Kickapoo Creek.

Dave Inskeep would have a lot of explaining to do at his hearing in Peoria. Karen Hudson had learned that the attorney general's office had prepared a sixteen-page criminal complaint against the dairy. Karen and FARM members needed to be there as witnesses, telling reporters they had been predicting such a disaster from the get-go. Unless CAFOs regulations were stronger, they had warned, these environmental tragedies would continue.

Karen ran down to her basement office, a room crammed with news clippings, government papers, academic studies, and stacks of CAFO photos. She picked up the phone and began gathering the troops.

Judge Richard Grawey's Peoria County Courtroom was unusually full that Friday, February 16, as the hearing against Inwood Dairy got under way. FARM members sat on one side; Inskeep, his lawyers, a few investment partners, and his family were on the other. Several reporters milled about the back.

Karen instantly admired the judge's demeanor—he seemed consistent and fair, if a little gruff around the edges. Nearby, Inskeep listened to the opening remarks. Dressed in a conservative business suit, he looked ravaged and pale, Karen thought.

Jane McBride, the assistant attorney general handling livestock cases, made the oral arguments. She was short and fiftysomething, with a no-nonsense sartorial sense. Her approach was equally no-nonsense. McBride reminded the court this was not Inwood's first pollution problem, noting that "IEPA officials [had] previously warned the owners about the handling of livestock waste in general, and management of the lagoon in particular." Despite these warnings, Inskeep had let his lagoon level creep dangerously close to the rim. "'The defendant has failed to properly manage the lagoon in order to prevent discharges or overflows,'" she read. "'For now, the violations are ongoing, and they may not be abated until the defendant is restrained and enjoined by order of this court.'"

The ravine, which still held at least a million gallons of foamy, discolored water, was still discharging liquid into the pond and creek, McBride said. Many fish had died. EPA officials were working to repair the berm and stem the release of more waste into the pond and creek. They were also documenting the entire mess for future prosecution.

"That ravine is now a loaded gun," McBride warned. Any more rain and the entire berm could blow, spewing tons of effluent into the creek and killing thousands more fish. And now, major thunderstorms were forecast.

Karen looked at the judge for a reaction. Grawey was growing increasingly agitated as he took in the scope of what Inskeep was calling a "controlled spill."

The state sought an "immediate injunction" against any further discharges of lagoon waste and an order to clean up all the affected land and water. It did not take long for Grawey to decide. As he prepared to announce his opinion, Karen and the FARM posse sat squirming in anticipation. They squeezed hands and gave silent winks to one another. Finally, almost five years after they first banded together, their concerns were being taken seriously by powerful people.

But Grawey's decision exceeded their expectations.

Inskeep was ordered to sell off nearly half of his herd, more than six hundred cows, within three months. He was to cease pumping waste into the lagoon until its freeboard measured at least two feet from the rim. He was told to build an earthen levee to channel storm water away from the lagoon, and to clean up manure in an area that drained into it. And he was compelled to "ensure that waste applied to farmland will not run off."

As for the disaster on his property, Inskeep was given until Saturday evening to extract and dispose of the two million gallons of waste currently residing in the ravine and the contaminated pond beneath it.

Inskeep, looking dazed, quietly agreed to each condition without argument.

Court was adjourned. A scrum of media waited outside the courthouse in the chilly drizzle, seeking comment. "This should not have happened. We think it violated the injunction order which prohibited discharging into waters of the state," said Tom Davis from the attorney general's office. Inwood could be slapped with a fine of fifty thousand dollars or more, just for the damage that had already occurred. If the whole ravine blew, it could run much, much higher. "We're keeping our options open on levels of sanctions," he said.

Karen was still reeling from the judge's decision. But she stressed to reporters the damage that had already been caused. "Dave Inskeep has turned the waters of my town into an open sewer system. People downstream need to be warned what is happening," she said, and then quickly added, "These events verify exactly what we at Families Against Rural Messes have warned about all along: Factory farms and their lagoons are dangerous to the environment; they're million-gallon bombs of manure just waiting to spill into public waters." Flashbulbs popped and reporters scribbled as she continued.

"The big problem is that the IEPA steps in only after so much damage has been done. What's it going to take to have stronger livestock laws that would prevent disasters like this?"

As she spoke, an unsmiling Inskeep, along with his attorneys and family, left the courthouse without comment.

Inwood has until eight tonight to clear the ravine of up to two million gallons of cattle waste," Karen read in the *Journal Star* the following Saturday.

He would not meet the deadline.

The cleanup was taking much longer than anticipated as bureaucrats dithered over waste-removal methods. Some wanted tankers to haul it away; others said the big trucks would tear up township roads. In the end, they decided to use hoses to cautiously pump waste from the ravine and onto surrounding fields—wet as they were.

The attorney general's office had no choice but to let the cleanup continue. "They did a lot of pumping, but with storm water and runoff, there's more wastewater now than a few days ago," said Tom Davis. He described the water as "brown, turbid and smelling like manure. It's not something we want discharged into creeks."

Jane McBride warned that it might take several more days before the crisis passed. "[Inskeep has] got a lot of water to move and bad conditions," she said. "This is the worst time of year to be dealing with this kind of thing."

By Monday, a second crisis emerged. Though sandbags were still holding waste within the lagoon, and no new effluent had been pumped in, the endless rain had brought the surface back to just inches from the rim. If it overflowed, the wastewater would flood Watkins Cemetery, a small family graveyard from the 1800s containing the plots of two Civil War soldiers and one from the Black Hawk War.

It's hard to measure the devastation caused by a major lagoon spill. Karen knew she had to get airborne to fully appreciate, and document, the mess on the ground. But she loathed flying, and had rarely been in a sputtering little prop plane. The very thought petrified her, but Rocky convinced her it would be okay.

A neighbor agreed to take her up in his own plane—anonymously, to avoid reprisal. Karen's FARM colleague Jack Leonard would go up with her, and Jane Kuck furnished a camera and telephoto lens. All they needed now was press coverage. Karen placed a few calls and, as expected, the media lined up to get a live aerial shot of the catastrophe.

Reporters from two stations and the *Journal Star* reserved separate flights in the four-seater plane. Karen closed her eyes tightly and murmured a small prayer as they took off from a grass runway on the first sortie. The flight was bumpy and noisy as the plane ascended and flew over the site, which reporters were now calling the Big Spill. They circled Inwood in small, dizzying arcs. Karen quickly discovered that peering through a telephoto lens at the swirling earth below can make you very disoriented—and airsick—very quickly. When they landed, she dashed from the plane and ran behind a small hangar, where she promptly threw up.

It was a tough day, but the aerial strategy paid off. Images taken by Karen and the news crews aired on stations throughout western Illinois, and the *Journal Star*'s front page was splashed with an eight-by-ten-inch color photo taken from a FARM flight. Later, Karen's photos would be used by the attorney general's office in prosecuting the case.

Karen stressed to reporters that a lack of local county control was to blame for the mess. "There's local control in Illinois for things like low-level nuclear waste and garbage. But when it comes to forty million gallons of raw urine and feces right near my house, I don't have a voice. I think I'd rather live next to a garbage dump. At least it's more regulated."

Given the Inwood calamity, lawmakers agreed it was time to rewrite Illinois's livestock laws. "If it were not for the vigilance of citizens and the Illinois EPA, this situation would not have been discovered," a *Journal Star* editorial declared. "It is time Illinois enact sensible legislation that allows input from local governments. Only when we work together will we be able to protect our environment from the mismanagement and corporate greed which too often is associated with factory farms."

But *Journal Star* columnist Mike Bailey portrayed both Inskeep and Elmwood residents alike as corporate victims. His was a plaintive meditation on strained small-town loyalties and bedrock Midwestern sensibilities.

"Elmwood is not an in-your-face place. Disappointment is more common than anger," Bailey wrote. But beneath its sad surface smoldered a "perceived intrusion of a corporate culture and callousness to a community where people look you in the eye and make business deals on a handshake."

Bailey defended citizen Inskeep. "At 59 and retired from Cat, he didn't intend to hurt anybody, and seems genuinely sorry about what has happened. He acknowledges 'mistakes,' but believes some media have unfairly maligned him," he wrote. "He's taking measures to ensure this will never happen again. He wants to be a good neighbor. He's also a businessman who concedes that, even at 1,200 head, his dairy is not profitable."

Another Inskeep ally was Gene Vaughan, the brother-in-law of Karen Hudson; Bailey identified Karen as Inwood Dairy's "most vocal critic." A deeply divided town does not "make for happy Easter gatherings," Bailey lamented. "A rural community's essence is in that code that says you don't do anything on your land that damages a neighbor's."

In February 2001, Helen Reddout received an exciting call from Charlie Tebbutt: Judge Shea had finally handed down a decision in the penalty phase of *CARE v. Bosma.*

Charlie read from the decision in a triumphant voice. CARE had proven that Bosma's farm posed a public health risk and also potentially harmed aquatic life and contributed to the degradation of Granger Drain and the Yakima River, Judge Shea ruled. CARE had also offered convincing evidence that Bosma was continuing to violate the Clean Water Act. Bosma's "lax attitude" made him one of the most difficult dairymen in the region, he said.[8]

The dairyman and his wife were slammed with a civil penalty of $171,500, payable to the U.S. Treasury by April 27. It was only about 40 percent the maximum that Shea could have levied, but he also ordered Bosma to reimburse CARE for attorney fees of $326,166, plus $36,561 in related costs and $65,576 in expert witness fees.

Total penalty for Bosma: $599,303. And that did not include his own legal fees.

"Which means," Charlie told Helen, who was now grinning like a mad-woman, "if you add his own legal fees, this whole mess cost him well over a million dollars. Maybe two."

Helen allowed herself to gloat. "And to think, that little weasel thought he could make it all go away by begging the DOE to fine him one thousand dollars," she said. "He never saw this coming."

It wasn't a total slam dunk for CARE. Shea commended Bosma for taking some "serious steps" as a result of the lawsuit, and rejected CARE's demand for ongoing surface and groundwater monitoring, and for unannounced lagoon inspections.

Even so, the penalties made headlines around the country and proved that CARE was a force to be reckoned with.

Helen was beside herself with satisfaction over winning this battle, even though she knew that much work remained in the fight to defend her valley. Despite a decade of citizens' efforts to clean up the watershed, there was just too much cow manure being spread around to achieve much progress. Recent tests showed that water draining into the river at Granger Drain possessed ten times the fecal coliform—from cow manure—allowed by law. It was one of the most bacteria-infested waterways in the state.[9]

Helen knew that CARE could sue the dairies until—well, until the cows came home—but the valley would stay polluted. One could not litigate CAFOs into oblivion. The bovine overpopulation would continue to excrete more waste than local fields could absorb.

More people were noticing the problem. "The fields may have had enough," declared an article in the *Yakima Herald-Republic*. Yakima County's big dairies were the worst offenders, with about eight cows per acre of available cropland—even higher when calves were included. The county average was five per acre, far exceeding agronomist recommendations of a maximum of two cows per acre.[10]

"By that standard, nearly two-thirds of Yakima County's dairies have too little land," the paper said. But available cropland was shrinking, because farms were getting bigger and bumping into one another. Remaining land was growing too costly for many dairies hit by stagnant milk prices.

Still, there was good news for the valley. Most dairies had cleaned up their acts somewhat since CARE had come out swinging. Moreover, water quality had actually improved over the decade. Fecal coliform levels had fallen by 90 percent, though they were, disquietingly, still ten times over the limit. Though Helen found it very hard to cheer *any* water that contained ten times more toxins than it should, it was gratifying to read that most dairies had improved since CARE began suing, even if the litigation had "bathed the valley in bad blood."

Charlie reminded CARE it was time to crow a little. "You should feel great," he said. "Thanks to CARE, there's been a drop in bacteria." The ten dairies CARE had threatened to file suit against housed thirty-seven thousand cows within the Granger Basin, he said. "And we won or settled cases involving more than twenty thousand of those cows."

Almost unbelievably, the troubles at Inwood Dairy LLC kept mounting. On March 2 its main lender, AgStar Financial Services, filed suit to physically repossess Inwood's 1,250 cows, in an attempt to recoup part of the $2.8 million owed by Inskeep and his partners. Judge Richard Grawey of the Peoria County Circuit Court was not in the mood for clemency, and set another hearing to assess the cleanup process and give AgStar a chance to argue for repossession of the Holsteins. "Get better people," he wrote to the dairy. "Do it or be closed down."[11]

Karen and fellow FARM members drove back over to Peoria for the court hearing. Two weeks had passed since the Inwood Dairy spill, yet constant rain had already caused lagoon wastewater to rise two inches closer to the rim. Just as troubling, the ravine was now estimated to hold three million gallons of wastewater (its ruptured berm had been repaired).

Meanwhile, Assistant Attorney General McBride testified that waste being sprayed onto saturated land was running off into local waters. The cleanup plan wasn't working. McBride suggested the entire operation might need to be shut down, perhaps permanently. Between the messed-up lagoon and the swollen ravine, there were ten million gallons that "need[ed] to be moved as quickly as possible," she said.[12]

Inwood Dairy lawyer Jeffrey Ryva protested that it would be unfair to shutter Inwood, and that it would strike a "death knell" for the entire Illinois dairy industry. He insisted that Inwood workers were doing their best and asked that the hearing be postponed a week.

His Honor was unmoved. He asked if his order to remove six hundred cows had been carried out.

"We haven't taken any steps on that, Your Honor," the lawyer replied. "If we get a plan in place, we would ask the court to modify the injunction."

"It's apparent to me," Grawey grumbled, "that you can't run the operation without being a threat to the environment."

The dour judge read a laundry list of violations at Inwood beginning in 1999. Then he made his ruling: The dairy was to reduce its herd immediately. It was to pump out all of the discharged wastewater from the ravine and pond.

It was to remove enough waste from its faltering lagoon to leave two feet of freeboard. It was to truck out all that liquid waste in tankers, at its own expense, and take it somewhere else for storage until the spring thaw, when the manure could be applied without runoff. The dairy was also ordered to stockpile an additional five hundred sandbags, just in case.

Karen was thrilled with the ruling, but there was one thing she didn't understand. What was to become of all that waste being trucked out of there? There was nowhere for it to *go*. (It was finally sent to nearby farms and injected into topsoil.)

Then it was time for AgStar to make its case for repossession of all 1,250 cattle. Inwood's loans were in default, the lawyers said. The cows—part of the loan's collateral—were worth $1.2 million. The judge put off a ruling in that case.

Meanwhile six "silent partners" had guaranteed the dairy's loans, and each owed various amounts. They included Caterpillar vice president Gerald Shaheen, surgeon James DeBord, M.D., and Albert Zeller, a restaurant owner. None were from Elmwood.

After the hearing, Karen went home to disseminate the good news to her comrades. Her list of like-minded activists was rapidly growing, and included people around the country.

"We have had fecal coliform counts high as eighty-one thousand units per one hundred milliliters in nearby tributaries downstream from the site," she wrote. "This is not a farm, it's a factory—exploiting workers, animals, and the environment while tarnishing the very reputation of agriculture. The investors do not live in our community—they are in other areas of the state and country hiding behind the skirts of agriculture—afraid to show their faces!!"

On March 9, nearly a month after the spill, Inwood was only halfway toward its court-ordered goal. Gregg Hardy, an environmental consultant from Michigan retained by the dairy, said four to five million gallons still needed to be removed. It would take another four days.

Tanker trucks ran on and off the property every few minutes as they ferried the muck off-site. The goal was to remove about a million gallons—about 170 truckloads—a day. Dave Inskeep himself had been spotted kneeling at the rim of the lagoon with an ice scraper to show reporters how much room there was—the lagoon now had about two feet of breathing room, just as Judge Grawey had ordered.

Gregg Hardy said that poor structural design, not poor management, had produced the disaster. Rainfall was draining into the wastewater sewers that emptied into the lagoon. Newly created ditches and berms would now channel rainwater away from it. Two smaller lagoons were also being installed, as a backup in case the main basin ever got too full. Once these flaws were remedied, lagoon failure would not recur, Hardy said.

Speaking to reporters, Inskeep expressed hardly any contrition over the spill. "All I can say is that we were always cognizant of the environment and never once was there anything done that was a deliberate attempt to do anything bad," he told the media. "You can hear all kinds of stories. If you call six people, you can probably get six stories. That's all I can say."[13]

Even Karen had to concede that the mess was getting better. "From what I have seen in the last couple of days, they have finally gotten their act together," she told the *Journal Star*. "But when the consultant leaves, the same people are going to be managing the place. What then? Are we going to be back at square one?"

Karen's apprehension was well founded. Just one day later, she received a tip from a FARM member that the truck-away-manure plan had opted to take shortcuts. Tankers were seen dumping the manure on the roadside in unapproved areas. The mess got under the cars of many local residents, requiring several trips to the car wash to vanquish the stench. The fire department was dispatched to hose down the highway.

"It is BUSINESS AS USUAL for this CAFO," she wrote angrily that day to her e-mail network. "We have been sold downstream and justice has not been served. They will continue to DUMP when heads are turned and desecrate our neighborhood. This dirty deal stinks worse than the manure flowing downstream!!"

Over at Inwood, workers had finished draining the pond. The ravine was about 75 percent clean. Tanker trucks were still arriving and departing every few minutes. Estimates of the round-the-clock removal bill were approaching $750,000.

Karen flashed back to the words of Inskeep's engineer back in 1997: "It's unlikely it would fail," he had said, "unless ten years down the road they let it fill up and water goes over the top."

In mid-March, Inwood Dairy reached an agreement with the attorney general's office that allowed the dairy to keep all 1,250 cows on-site. But the dairy was required to "drastically" change its waste management to keep its herd. At the courthouse, attorneys for both sides spent an hour banging out an accord before going in to see Judge Grawey. Under the terms of this accord, Inwood would overhaul its system and cut the total liquid waste. It would completely empty the pond and ravine and scrub them clean of all sludge and sediment.

About one hundred thousand gallons remained in the ravine, and that would have to be removed within days.[14]

One other reform was mandated: Workers could no longer clean the barns by hose. Instead, they were ordered to use more straw and other absorbent material to soak up urine and feces. This would then be stored in compost piles for use as solid fertilizer. The milking parlor and other areas would still be hosed with water at frequent intervals. (Consultant Gregg Hardy had said one hundred gallons of liquid per cow per day was entering the lagoon, when the industry standard was just thirty gallons.)

In return for these efforts, Inwood would no longer have to thin its herd. The new agreement would permit the dairy to remain open, but gave the state considerable oversight and the authority to intervene if problems arose.

Karen thought the deal fell short. "This is business as usual for factory farms," she told the *Journal Star*. "I want 600 more cows out of there." She was equally unimpressed with the backup lagoons, saying, "All we have now is more holes in the ground to put poop in."

Karen Hudson was now a five-year veteran of the animal-factory wars. She had seen and heard some fairly outlandish things in her tenure. But this new development in the Inwood saga, she thought, was insane. Dave Inskeep had still been scraping crap off the land when the Illinois Milk Producers Association, an affiliate of the Illinois Farm Bureau, came up with a novel idea.[15]

The milk people suggested that Illinois write a check for $248,000 in taxpayer funds to buy milk from Inwood Dairy for a scientific study, conducted by the Illinois Council on Food and Agriculture Research (C-FAR). But this wasn't just any milk they wanted. It was "waste milk"—too contaminated with antibiotics to be fit for marketing to people. The proposed study would earmark funds for renting sick cows being treated with antibiotics, along with healthy "control" cows, to study differences in their milk, and minimize any potential chemical hazards in treated milk. The data would be shared with all dairy operators.

It was a sweet deal for Inskeep, to be sure: Instead of dumping waste milk into the lagoon whenever a sick cow was being treated, he could simply rent her and her milk out to C-FAR.

FARM members went on the warpath. Karen worked the media phones. "Those poor cows at Inwood are injected with rBGH and it causes increased infections in their udders," she said, "as well as higher somatic cell counts, pus, in their milk. There's more antibiotic use among rBGH treated herds." She told reporters no public funds should go to "support this factory farm, which constantly violates the law to stay in business."[16]

Only after FARM member John Belz informed C-FAR about the specifics of Inwood's environmental and regulatory record did the project die.

In April, Dave Inskeep had big news: He was giving up milking. "The dairy is for sale," he said during another hearing before Judge Grawey. "Selling was a decision that the investors had to make," he added. "It remains to be seen what a buyer will pay."[17]

A month later, one of the investment partners at Inwood, Peoria restaurateur Albert Zeller, announced he would take over as sole owner. Karen had always regarded Albert as a nice, hardworking businessman who stepped too deep into it. Inskeep, meanwhile, would still sell feed to the dairy and spread its manure on cropland for other farmers. The rebranded facility and company would henceforth be called New Horizons Dairy LLC.

It was the end of Inwood Dairy, and Karen hoped the change of ownership would mean a real reduction in air and water pollution. Only time would tell, but things couldn't get much worse. An IEPA supervisor warned Judge Grawey that storm runoff could still mix with manure and drain off the property. Meanwhile, the lagoon had been pumped down but continued to be a problem. "It's a major source of odors that travel three to four miles," the supervisor said. There had been seventeen odor complaints in March alone.

But Zeller seemed to be making strides to improve things. He hired an experienced dairyman named Jeff Trapp to run the farm, an improvement over "a clueless Caterpillar employee," Karen quipped to Rocky. Zeller also invested more than $5 million, much of it his own, to finish cleaning up the Big Spill and to rebuild the dairy to more water-efficient and eco-friendly specs. Even the state offered help: It kicked in $300,000 for a new system to compost manure and burn excess methane to generate electricity.

Trapp was working overtime to clean up the dairy's reputation, as well as its operations. He paid weekly visits to all the homes in the immediate area, and even came bearing gifts on special occasions—such as baskets filled with cheese and sausages.

One of those neighbors was Bill Wagner, the farmer whose home was just thirty-three hundred feet from the lagoon and who had initially called the IEPA back in February. Wagner told Trapp that things were better, and credited Trapp's dairy experience with turning the situation around. "We do smell it now and then but it's not a septic sewer smell," he said. "It's a manure smell."

The new PR measures seemed to be working. Even the *Journal Star* conceded Trapp's management style was a winning one. "Now," the paper noted, "his neighbors wave to him with all five fingers instead of just one."[18]

On June 19, the last of CARE's four original lawsuits was settled. Lawyers for Herman teVelde and his Sunnyveld Dairy filed a consent decree in U.S. District Court, while still denying any liability for the "alleged" violations.[19]

TeVelde would allow CARE to make annual inspections of his dairy, and agreed to hand over $21,500 for a study of groundwater quality in the Sunnyside–Granger area. The funds would be used by Heritage College—a small private school on the Yakima Indian Reservation—to conduct tests on well water in homes of people living near megadairies.

And CARE extracted even more concessions—something that Mary Lynne, a next-door neighbor, felt was a reasonable comeuppance for the loss of her swimming pool. To begin with, teVelde agreed to put in a two-hundred-foot "cow-free barrier" between his dairy and the Bos property line. He also agreed to pay an additional $24,500 for soil testing on his cropland, put in two-hundred-foot setbacks from all waterways, install odor-abatement measures like a lagoon bubbler (or aerator), improve fly control, and write a new employee-training manual.

TeVelde also vowed to restrict manure applications between November and March. The rest of the year, he would spray only after a full week of above-freezing temperatures. He committed to clean up after every manure spill caused by his trucks, and promised to divert his truck-wash water into a lagoon. CARE members were thrilled with the terms.

September 2001 was an exceptionally busy time for Rick, Karen, and Helen. The Yakima cherry farmer had recently been asked to join the GRACE Factory Farm Project Team, at the urging of her new friend Karen from Illinois.

Down in North Carolina, Rick was working closely with Waterkeeper attorney Nicolette Hahn, who was preparing to make oral arguments in the Clean Water Act lawsuit against two of the Murphy-Brown hog facilities in Jones County. The one-day hearing was held on September 7 in the federal district court in Greenville. Rick watched with admiration as Nicolette took on seven well-clad Smithfield lawyers who were defending Murphy-Brown. To Rick, it didn't look as though Judge Malcolm Howard had much patience for the Smithfield attorneys. Then again, the judge was from Duplin County.

Smithfield lawyers had moved to dismiss the case, arguing that the Waterkeeper Alliance and the Neuse River Foundation did not have legal standing to sue. More important, they insisted that hog operations were not required to have national pollution permits—at the time, no CAFO in the state had an NPDES permit—and so Smithfield didn't need one, either. But the judge seemed to be siding with Hahn and the Waterkeeper Alliance, or so it seemed to Rick. The judge was due to make his ruling within two weeks.

Shortly after the Smithfield hearing, Rick and Nicolette were scheduled to depart for a Waterkeeper-sponsored "whistle-stop tour" through several Midwestern states, stopping at grange halls and county fairgrounds in farming towns from Champaign, Illinois, to Northfield, Minnesota—where Kennedy would join them.

The week of September 10 was also National Clean Water Week, to be marked by a conference in Washington, D.C., sponsored by the Natural Resources Defense Council. Helen and Karen were due to fly in on September 11 to join up with Bill Weida and GRACE Factory Farm members Chris Petersen of Iowa and Terry Spence of Missouri.

The night before her trip, Karen was a nervous wreck; she was still anxious about flying. That night, just hours before 9/11, she had a vivid dream filled with violence and the threat of death. In the dark vision, someone held a gun to her head as a malicious voice whispered, "We've got you now."

The next morning, as she was preparing to leave for the airport, Karen noticed a newscast on the TV from the corner of her eye. One of New York's Twin Towers had a plume of black smoke spewing from its flank. It was a surreal and awful sight. Karen called Rocky inside. "A plane flew into the Trade Center," she said.

"Well, I guess that could happen," Rocky replied, sensing how jittery his wife was. "But don't worry, hon, you're going to Washington, not New York. Let's get you to the airport." But as he spoke, a second 757 hit the south tower, live on TV.

Terry Spence was at the Kansas City airport when the attacks began, waiting for a now-canceled flight to Washington. Chris Petersen was already there—at a meeting on the fifth floor of EPA headquarters in D.C., right across the Potomac from where American Airlines flight 77 slammed into the Pentagon.

The War on Terror was engaged. Soon, the feds would list agriculture as a prime target for those who wished America harm. Agribusiness interests would start comparing groups like CARE, FARM, and Waterkeeper—incredibly—to terror outfits like Al Qaeda. Nonviolent farmwives would be likened to Osama bin Laden. It was going to be a hell of a decade.

The nation was still in shock and mourning in the weeks following the 9/11 attacks, but that did not stop Rick Dove and Nicolette Hahn from going ahead with their planned whistle-stop tour of the Midwest, explaining the tactics of defending local communities who opposed having an animal factory in their midst. To their amazement, hundreds turned out at every flag-studded stop on the trip, despite the deep sense of loss that permeated each event.

All sorrow aside, the tour began with some uplifting news for Rick and Nicolette. When they arrived in Champaign, Illinois, Rick picked up a voice-mail message on his cell phone. A Waterkeeper staffer had called to say they had just won a major decision in the case against the two Murphy-Brown hog operations.

It was a thirteen-page declaration of victory against Smithfield and its subsidiary. The court was "unpersuaded" by the giant company's argument that no discharge permits were required at its swine CAFOs. Judge Howard had ruled that the trial could proceed.

Rick was elated. He felt like buying a glass of bubbly for everyone in the airport. "They are dead in the water!" he whooped to his colleagues. "We already proved they violated the CWA by operating without a permit. Now we have to prove at trial that they were also illegally discharging crap into the water." Each violation could command up to twenty-five thousand dollars in fines per day.

Nicolette was equally thrilled. She had a feeling that Smithfield might want to settle now, given the legal blow it had just sustained. Her intuition was correct.

Soon after the decision, Smithfield and Murphy-Brown notified the court that they wanted to move ahead toward hashing out a deal with the triumphant environmentalists.

In the end, it would take four years for the warring parties to reach a final settlement.

By early 2002, the debate over Posilac growth hormone in modern American dairying was growing louder and more vitriolic. Monsanto tried to exercise damage control to protect its battered brand among skeptical Americans. But consumers weren't buying it. A solid majority told pollsters they wanted to know—at the store—which brands of milk, butter, cheese, and other items in the dairy aisle were from cows given rBGH.[1] Most consumers preferred to buy goods marked "rBGH Free." The furor over labeling laws was brewing, and could prove a nightmare for Monsanto.

Canada and Europe had banned the sale of rBGH milk, and much of the developed world regarded U.S. food rules with bewilderment. More than 30 percent of American herds being milked were injected with Posilac.[2] The Canadians and Europeans saw the United States again taking its own probusiness and isolated path: Just as with the Kyoto climate treaty, when it came to artificial growth hormones, the Bush administration would go its own way. But many scientists, foreign and domestic, viewed FDA policy as reckless and grossly unscientific.

Karen Hudson was captivated by this story. She found that Canadian scientists had studied data previously reviewed by the FDA and charged that American regulators ignored or "suppressed" evidence showing that milk from Posilac cows caused adverse health reactions in rats.

Dr. Shiv Chopra was one of five Canadian scientists writing that the FDA had "ignored the harder information." For example, in one rat study, the drug entered the bloodstream and produced lesions and dangerous antibodies. "I'm afraid to say that, despite all that is known about the adverse reactions that cows have to this drug, and the evidence of human health concerns, the U.S. Government took an expedient route to approval," Chopra said. Monsanto had "significantly profited as a result."[3] To Karen, it was a typical tale of corporate greed winning out over human health.

During this period, *The Indy*, the college newspaper at Illinois State University at Bloomington-Normal had been gently pushing Karen to write a factory farm piece. Now she had fresh ammunition. Karen minced no words with her title: "Lab Rats for Monsanto: The Uncontrolled rBGH Experiment on Americans."[4] It was a broadside against the now-common drug and its impact on people, places, and cows. "FDA documents show that cows injected with rBGH were 79% more likely to contract mastitis," she wrote.[5] "A University of Vermont test herd of rBGH-injected cows showed all of the problems identified by the FDA, plus an alarming number of dead and deformed calves born to treated cows."

More evidence had surfaced to suggest that insulin-like growth factor-1 (IGF-1), which Posilac increases in cows, was a risk factor for breast, colon, and childhood cancers, Karen wrote. One study showed substantial but indirect evidence of a relation between IGF-1 and breast cancer. IGF-1 enhanced growth of cancerous breast cells in mice, and the growth of normal breast cells in rhesus monkeys.[6] (Tamoxifen, a breast-cancer treatment, is known to reduce IGF-1 levels in blood).

Dr. Samuel Epstein, the researcher from the University of Illinois at Chicago and author of this study, put it bluntly: "With the active complicity of the FDA, the entire nation is currently being subjected to an experiment involving large-scale adulteration of an age-old dietary staple by a poorly characterized and unlabeled biotechnology product," he wrote. "It poses major potential health risks for the entire U.S. population."[7]

But American consumers were being kept in the dark, Karen warned. They weren't notified by current labeling if their milk came from Posilac cows or not. "The US public is being treated as Monsanto's lab rats," she wrote. "The only difference is that the results aren't being documented for science. We must demand testing, clear food labeling and mandate FDA removal of this drug from the marketplace. The uncontrolled experiment on US citizens must be stopped."

Meanwhile, she alleged, the FDA had curled up in the lap of corporate agribusiness.

North Carolina's search for a viable alternative to its lagoon-and-sprayfield system on hog CAFOs continued, as various candidates were ruled in or out based on the environmental and financial criteria agreed to in the Smithfield settlement with Attorney General Mike Easley. It was a tall order. The winning technology would not only have to eliminate odors, groundwater contamination, air emissions, and the like—it would have to do so for an established sum of money.

That amount had been set through a complicated calculus, which included the cost of building a new lagoon-replacement system and operating it over a period of ten years. In order to be deemed economically feasible, the winning technology could not cost more than eighty-nine dollars per thousand pounds of live animals (thousandweight) raised at a time—about nine cents a pound over and above the cost of a lagoon-and-sprayfield system.[8] Those nine cents would be passed on to consumers, which made producers fret that it could make North Carolina pork less competitive in the U.S. and world markets.

Rick, however, didn't think the cost limit was high *enough*. He and other clean water advocates were highly doubtful that any effective technology could be adopted for nine cents a pound. The industry could then say it tried, and legally walk away from the settlement. "This will give the big boys an out," he complained to colleagues, "and they know it."

Some hog contractors actually welcomed new alternatives to lagoons. They had initially built lagoons because the state assured them it was the most effective method for managing swine waste. But now they saw the downsides. They were tired of dealing with leaks and spills; they were canceling vacations to stay home and nervously monitor the earthen sewage basins. They were weary of neighbor complaints or bad press, and kept edgy eyes to the sky, waiting for the next big tropical storm that might send wastewater surging over their lagoons' rims.

As early as 1996, some of these contract growers began speaking among themselves about developing their own lagoon alternatives. One farmer was Chuck Stokes, a large, solid, and charismatic man with a quick mind and a professed impatience for fools. Chuck ran a number of giant hog operations out of his flagship farm, Little Creek Hog Farms, near the Greene County town of Ayden. He went on to form a group of about 250 contract growers called Frontline Farmers.

By mid-2000, Rick was in regular contact with Chuck and the Frontline Farmers, who had just agreed to sign on to the attorney general's settlement with Smithfield. They were committed to voluntarily adopting the alternative technology chosen by Mike Williams, the North Carolina expert entrusted with the task.

Chuck Stokes was a force to be reckoned with in the North Carolina hog industry, and his independent ways won him plenty of enemies on both sides of the conflict. But Chuck liked the middle ground—he was friendly with Wendell Murphy, of Murphy Family Farms, as well as Robert Kennedy, Jr. Rick had come to respect Chuck and the work he did, though he still kept an eagle eye on Chuck's hog operations via the Neuse Air Force surveillance program.

"Rick," Chuck said one day in a phone conversation, "I see you flying over my farms, and it gives me the jitters. If you see anything wrong going on at one of my farms from up in the air, please tell me before you go to the state; give me a chance to go fix it first. I want to do what's right. I got enough headaches as it is."

Rick agreed to the arrangement. The more he got to know Chuck, the more he realized the mega–hog producer was trying to do the right thing. "I gotta tell you, my life is complicated enough. And I have to pick and choose my battles," Chuck confided in Rick one day. "I've got people in the industry who don't like me, and I got some people in the environmental community that don't like me, either, because our group's blowing up their little scheme of throwing rocks and making us look like we're doing something wrong."

What irked Chuck most was that not all hog farmers were doing their part to avoid pollution. "And it ticks me off," he said. "I spend so much time and trouble and paperwork on all the things I do—most of my expenses, really— for applying and monitoring the waste. And then some guy somewhere just decides to let it go, and then that paints a bad picture for all of us." But instead of confronting the bad apples, or closing them down altogether, he said, the pork industry tried to keep quiet and insist there were no problems. "The mistake in our industry has been to shun people like you and run you out the door," he said to Rick, "and give you some pamphlet saying everything's hunky dory on a hog farm. And through the years that's created a frustration within the environmental community—and the media."

Chuck wanted to help develop and use an alternative technology to replace lagoons, but he still defended the basins as safe and effective. "I moved over 150,000 yards of clay to line various lagoons around my farm, eighteen inches thick, compressed with a roller to over ninety-five percent compaction, that I had to send off to a lab and get them to certify before I could put the first drop of water in it," he explained. "I've spent millions building these lagoons. They're not just holes punched in the ground that leak manure into the water tables. That's just ridiculous."

Even so, Chuck was personally involved in the hunt to make lagoons obsolete. He and a small group of investor/hog farmers were developing their own system for adoption by the state. One day, Chuck invited Rick and Nicolette Hahn to see the prototype he was developing.

Chuck introduced them to the inventor, an old farmer named Don Lloyd. Rick and Nicolette watched in wonderment as Chuck and Lloyd explained how it worked.

"We take all the wastewater washed from the barns and pump it into this underground holding tank, where heavy solids settle to the bottom," Chuck said. "Now, this is all the stuff that would normally go into the lagoon. So you see, we've already eliminated the need for a lagoon right from the get-go." Rick liked what he was hearing so far.

Once the solids had settled out, Chuck and Lloyd siphoned water off the top and ran it to a large above-ground tank. "Once there, we inject the water with something called TCM, or trichloromelamine; it's a sanitizer, attacks the bad organics and stuff," Chuck said. "Makes it like pure water. The United States uses it in Afghanistan for our troops."

After the microorganisms were killed, a polymer was then injected into the water—the tiny polymer beads bound with particulate matter that got through the separator and clumped them together, pulling them down to the bottom of the tank. "You can actually see the liquid getting clearer," Chuck marveled. When that process was finished, the water was removed from the top and the residual matter was ejected through a hopper at the bottom of the tank.

Some of the cleaned water was then recycled back to the barns—to hose down the floors and flush the manure pits back out into the underground separator tank, starting the whole closed-circuit process over again. The remaining liquid was mixed with fresh aquifer water, diluting its particulate content to the point of human drinkability.

To prove it, Don gulped down a glass of the former hogwash. The guests gasped. "Why, it tastes just *fine!*" he said, smiling and wiping his mouth. "But we don't usually drink it—we give it to the pigs to drink. It cuts down our groundwater use by about 40 percent."

That left the solids. Raw manure cannot be used on food crops because of the harmful pathogens it contains, limiting its commercial value as a fertilizer. Most of the germs can be killed through composting, though that takes time and money to accomplish, without adding enough market value to the manure to make the system economically feasible.

"Then we discovered an answer," Chuck said proudly. "It was worms—vermiculture, they call it." Lloyd devised a system that feeds waste solids to worms on a continual basis. Inside a barn with dirt floors, he had dug several rows of trenches—three feet wide and about twenty-two inches deep—the entire length of the floor. A mix of worms and organic matter were introduced into the trenches, and then specially designed machinery deposited an inch of solids into each trench every morning. By the end of the day, the worms had consumed the entire inch of food, turning it into clean, odorless, disease-free castings. The worms returned to the bottom of the trench, and another layer of solids was applied to begin the process again.

"I chose a type of worm that turns this stuff into some kind of superfood for plants," Don said. "Farmers and gardeners can't get enough of it; they pay top dollar for it." The worm barn could yield about three tons of the coveted "black gold" each day, he said, adding that the state department of transportation had told him they wanted to buy it for roadside plantings.

"And because of the value added on the manure from those little worms," Chuck concluded with a big grin, "it brings our net costs down to about fourteen dollars per thousandweight," or a penny and a half per pound. "But this is still in its early stages. We're just a little Chitty Chitty Bang Bang kinda outfit up here."

B y the middle of George W. Bush's first presidential term, it became apparent that scientists were being pressured to publish papers that were uncritical of concentrated livestock operations and their impact on the environment, rural communities, animal welfare, and human health. It gave a brand-new meaning to the term "political science."

"University and government scientists studying health threats associated with agricultural pollution say they are harassed by farmers and trade groups and silenced by superiors afraid to offend the powerful industry," said a lengthy investigative article in *The Des Moines Register* that ran in April 2002 under the headline AG SCIENTISTS FEEL THE HEAT.[9]

"Scientists say the pressure is stopping important work meant to protect the taxpayers, who foot most of the bill," the article said. "Even when the work gets done, they worry about efforts to manipulate or muffle the results." Many researchers blamed the increasingly cozy relationship between the USDA and the industry it was supposed to regulate, and according to some scientists, the coercion was increasing.

The USDA had stifled many proposed controversial studies by driving them through a lengthy approval process, critics alleged. The resulting delays would dry up grant money and the research would often get canceled. Some accused the USDA of collaborating outright with industry to squelch data that did not meet desired results or expectations.

"Such pressure tactics have been reported in the tobacco, pharmaceutical and oil industries," the *Register* reported. "But they are every bit as intense, if not more so, in the agricultural arena."

None of this surprised JoAnn Burkholder, Rick Dove's ally, who still maintained her lab in Raleigh. "I have seen some very sad practices in this country," she told the *Register*. "Industry has a stranglehold on environmental issues to the point that this muzzling goes on all the time." She was backed up by an Iowa State University economist, who reported more outside pressure in the last year or so than during his entire thirty-eight years at the school.

Not surprisingly, the USDA recoiled at charges of collusion. Sandy Miller Hays of the agency's Agricultural Research Service (ARS) said that though the feds did work with agricultural organizations on studies, the USDA would never let producers change or suppress data. "We put the findings out there, and we let the chips fall where they may," she said. "The work was consistently objective and independent."

The pork people also denied having any influence over government research.

National Pork Board spokeswoman Cindy Cunningham said her group would not shy away from controversial issues, such as subtherapeutic antibiotics. In fact, the NPB had just offered forty thousand dollars per project for scientists to study the spread of pathogens from CAFOs, and their potential health risks. The group also wanted to fund studies of alternatives to antibiotics in feed.

"Any criticism that the pork board is trying to stifle objective research or skew the USDA-reviewed study plans is just ludicrous," Cunningham said.

Few nonfarming Americans are familiar with the term "land-grant college." Yet these institutions wield tremendous influence over virtually every item we eat, how it was raised, and the technology that was applied to produce it in record amounts per acre.

They are called land-grant colleges because they were awarded property by Congress under the Morrill Act of 1862 and 1890, the first of which was signed into law by President Lincoln. Lawmakers decreed that each state should select one institution of higher learning to be given large tracts of federally controlled land in order to build places "to teach agriculture, military tactics, the mechanic arts, and home economics, not to the exclusion of classical studies, so that members of the working classes might obtain a practical college education."[10]

In 1887, Congress passed the Hatch Act, bankrolling a network of "agricultural experiment stations" to be administered by each state's land-grant college. These stations would disseminate new information and technology—especially on soil agronomics and plant growth—to local farmers.

Congress expanded the system in 1914 to include "cooperative extensions" to dispatch agents out into the countryside with results from all the latest agricultural research. Each land-grant college receives money from the federal government annually for research and cooperative-extension work, as long as the state government matches the funds.

Among the most prominent and influential land-grant schools are: Purdue University in Indiana, Iowa State University, Ohio State University, New York's Cornell University, the University of California at Davis, the University of Illinois at Urbana-Champaign, and Texas A&M (Agricultural and Mechanical) University.

Big Ag has traditionally found comfortable quarters at land-grant schools, where it has reliably been able to fund studies that, to critics at least, reach scientific conclusions that usually demonstrate the safety and efficacy of their products and technologies.

Many of those same critics contended that the George W. Bush administration began slashing funds for the land-grant programs, leaving a gaping hole in research that corporate agribusiness was only too happy—and able—to fill. That would help explain Monsanto Auditorium at the University of Missouri and Monsanto-funded graduate fellowships at Iowa State, or the Dow Chemical Professor of Biological and Agricultural Engineering at Texas A&M, or the famed agriculture school at UC Davis that is partly funded by DuPont and Calgene.

Faculty at these institutions often work hand-in-hand with big players like Cargill, ADM, Smithfield, and ConAgra, which fund research; sponsor academic chairs; and build labs, classrooms, experimental farms, and agricultural pavilions on university campuses from California to the Carolinas.

Kansas State even has its own spin-off company, Wildcat Genetics, which sells genetically engineered soybean seeds that can survive the weed killer Roundup, which is made by Monsanto, whose relationship with the school goes back more than a decade. The many threads of these chummy relations between agribusiness and university research seemed to run almost universally through the U.S. Department of Agriculture, many critics contended.

As it turned out, a major CAFO conference in Iowa in 2002 would become an object lesson on the tangled web of government and industry influence in which so many independent scientists were becoming increasingly ensnared.

In April 2002, Karen Hudson was scheduled to speak at the second Summit for Sustainable Hog Farming, in Clear Lake, Iowa—home of Chris Petersen, the GRACE Factory Farm Project member and former pig farmer she had met at the D.C. meeting on Posilac.

The event's keynote address, sponsored by the Waterkeeper Alliance and Robert Kennedy, Jr., was held at Clear Lake's Surf Ballroom. Brochures for the event promised that Kennedy would deliver a sermon on "the urgent need to revitalize a culture of humane, environmentally sound, independent family farming."

Karen was so excited about going, she couldn't sleep. Of the numerous factory farm activists booked to speak, many were now her friends, and she looked forward to catching up with them to exchange information and reports on victories.

Waterkeepers' senior attorney, Nicolette Hahn, who helped organize the conference, spoke to a *Journal Star* reporter before the event began. She praised Europe for aggressively regulating animal production. "The EU is way ahead of us in recognizing the problems of animal factories," said Hahn, who would go on to marry Bill Niman, owner of the Niman Ranch pasture-fed beef and pork company, in 2004. She accused most U.S. research of being funded by agribusiness, often in association with state universities, resulting in toothless research that offered a general dismissal of the dangers of CAFOs.[11]

Hundreds showed up in Clear Lake. One very big draw was Steve Ells, founder of Chipotle Mexican Grill. Chipotle, a growing food chain, had begun buying Niman pork exclusively. It was part of a mission that Ells, a rising star in the sustainable food movement, called Food With Integrity. As his Web site described it:

> In pursuing new sources of pork, we discovered naturally raised pigs from a select group of farmers. These animals are not confined in stressful factories. They live outdoors or in deeply bedded pens, so they are free to run, roam, root and socialize. They are not given antibiotics. Consequently the pork they produce has a natural, moist, delicious flavor. We think it tastes better and is better for you. By creating a market for meats raised in a healthier environment, we make it worthwhile for these farmers to raise even more.[12]

But not everyone was excited about the Clear Lake conference. Officials at the USDA's Agricultural Research Service banned their own scientists from attending.

One of them was Dr. James Zahn, who had a Ph.D. in microbial physiology from Iowa State and worked at the ARS's Swine Odor and Manure Management Research Unit of the National Swine Research and Information Center in Ames, Iowa. Zahn was deeply respected for his landmark studies in CAFO hazards, such as antimicrobial resistance. His vast knowledge base had earned several awards, including one from the American Society for Microbiology.

In 2001, Zahn had presented his findings at a conference in Indianapolis, where he broke ranks with his peers in George W. Bush's Agriculture Department by reporting that "aerial transfer of antibiotics and antibiotic-resistant bacteria from swine CAFOs may represent an important and previously overlooked mechanism for transfer of antibiotic resistance to humans and the environment."[13]

It was a fairly radical statement for a USDA employee, but he seemed to get away with it, at least for the time being. Zahn vowed to publish his data in the journal *Applied and Environmental Microbiology*. He had investigated the drug Tylosin, part of an important antibiotic class called macrolides, which are used to treat and prevent disease in humans and animals—and to promote growth in animals. (Tylosin itself is used exclusively in veterinary medicine.)

Some studies had looked at meat—and CAFO discharges into water-ways—as potential vectors of human exposure to resistant bacteria, but no one had ever looked at aerial transmissions. Zahn measured concentrations of Tylo-sin and Tylosin-resistant bacteria (TRB) in the air outside three finishing farms that had giant expulsion fans at the end of each barn. The drug was mixed with hog feed in subtherapeutic doses—to prevent, rather than treat, disease and to promote growth (scientists don't know why antibiotics promote growth).

Air exhaust from the fans revealed both Tylosin and Tylosin-resistant bugs. In fact, 80 percent of the bacteria captured were resistant, Zahn reported.[14] The shocking findings were widely circulated in public health circles, and quickly found their way to Kendall Thu, Karen Hudson's mentor at Northern Illinois University. In March 2001, Thu invited Zahn to present his data on a panel at the summit at Clear Lake. Zahn needed to check first with USDA brass for permission. It was promptly denied by Dr. Brian Kerr, research leader at the ARS.

"USDA employees are to cooperate fully with civic, education and con-sumer groups," Kerr wrote back to Zahn. "As a cautionary note, however, we are expected to factually discuss our research without speculative extrapolation to larger, sensitive controversies," he said. "Politically sensitive and controver-sial issues require discretion." Kerr added that he had visited the Waterkeeper Web site "to try to understand the mission of the April 5th meeting to which you are invited." He wrote that "the wording of the press release about the 'Hog Summit,'" indicated that "this is not the method by which we should get our information out to the public. Thus, I would like you to inform Dr. Thu that you will not be speaking."[15]

It was classic bureaucratese. But it didn't matter: Zahn told Thu he could not attend. "I don't agree with it," he told *The Des Moines Register*. "This is taxpayers' information, and I should be able to disclose my research."

It was not the first time he had been muzzled by his bosses. The censorship began in February of that year, when health officials from Adair County, in-vited Zahn to present his swine research data at a meeting. Zahn requested travel authorization, and Kerr approved it—until he saw a press release for the event that was faxed out by the (anti-CAFO) Iowa Citizens for Community Improvement.

The meeting would discuss the benefits of "local air quality rules for fac-tory farms with more than three hundred thousand pounds of livestock," the press release said. Featured speaker Dr. Zahn would discuss "the health risks to neighbors of mega-hog confinements." Zahn's permission was yanked just thirty minutes before he left for the meeting. He went anyway, but sat obedi-ently in the back without speaking.

Clear Lake was the fifth speaking invitation in three months blocked by Zahn's higher-ups. "It's frustrating," he told the *Register*. "My whole career I've never had to deal with censorship issues. I thought it was important to speak to the citizens that are paying my salary." Now his antibiotic research had been canceled altogether.

Sandy Miller Hays, of the ARS, explained that Zahn could not speak at the Adair County meeting because he lacked expertise on the health risks of CA-FOs. "He's simply an odor specialist," said Miller Hays. "It just made us very uncomfortable that it was being presented [as] he was going to talk about something he has no expertise in."

Zahn had a different take. But he could not share it until after leaving his job for a position at a pharmaceutical firm. "The USDA has a long-term relationship with pork producers," he told *The Des Moines Register*. Zahn charged that his lab work had been closely watched over by an "advisory panel" of hog farmers, selected by USDA officials. "In fact, national pork groups have at times had offices in the same government buildings as the USDA labs," the *Register* reported.

"The USDA ought to be ashamed of themselves," Kendall Thu told the paper. "Jim Zahn is one of the best researchers in the country, if not the world, on emissions from swine facilities. It is demeaning and absolutely ludicrous." Zahn's harassment, he added, was now a common tale. "It fits a pattern of industry intimidation, the muzzling of freedom of speech and erosion of academic freedom," Thu said.

On May 2, 2002, the good people of Peoria County awoke to news about justice being served in the mammoth Elmwood dairy spill, the largest intentional discharge ever in the history of Illinois. The dairy, now called New Horizons, reached an agreement with the attorney general's office in which it would pay a fifty-thousand-dollar fine for the largest spill in state history. Furthermore, the dairy would install new treatment facilities to reduce odor complaints, while also maintaining a minimum of two feet of freeboard in its waste lagoon.[16]

"Much has been accomplished to improve operations at Inwood," Attorney General Jim Ryan said in a written statement. "Today's order calls on management to continue rectifying what had become an intolerable as well as environmentally dangerous situation." Dairy manager Jeff Trapp told reporters that he and the dairy's investors were "just happy it's over. We worked hard with the attorney general to comply with all the issues and are ready to move forward."

The agreement required the dairy to minimize wastewater by scraping manure from the barns, rather than flushing them out with water (though water would still be used to clean the milking parlor, holding pen, and "east cow transfer lane"). The dairy was also banned from applying waste to land within nine hundred feet of where Illinois Route 78 crosses Taggart Road. It agreed as well to excavate wastewater and sludge from the seven-acre lagoon by September 30, and to turn in proposals for regular sludge removal and disposal in the future.

Violations of the consent order would carry fines of one hundred dollars per day.

But over in Williamsfield, Karen Hudson and Nina Baird knew it was just a matter of time before the Highlands pig CAFO had an environmental accident and, on June 18, 2002, it happened. After an excess of lagoon waste was applied to a nearby field, Highlands runoff resulted in a fish kill along a 1.5 mile stretch of a tributary of French Creek, the Illinois Environmental Protection Agency said.

Doug Baird told IEPA inspectors that he had misjudged the amount of manure water that the soil could absorb. The ground was already saturated from heavy rainfall when he applied the waste. "I goofed. It won't happen again," he told the *Journal Star*.[17]

The runoff killed sixty-six hundred minnows, darters, green sunfish, crayfish, and others. The Illinois Department of Natural Resources estimated the value of the fish at nine hundred dollars, but was expected to increase that figure because the value of the dead crayfish had not yet been calculated. (Minnows were valued at eight cents each, darters at thirty-five cents each, and green sunfish between twenty-five and forty-six cents each.) Any fines collected would be used in restocking fish in the creek.

For groups such as CARE, FARM, the Factory Farm Project, and the Waterkeeper Alliance, defending the environment, preserving rural communities, and protecting human health were their main motivating factors. But that didn't mean they had no regard for the animals themselves.

In some ways, it was a deliberate decision on their part to generally avoid the animal-rights issue (which most CAFO opponents prefer to call animal welfare, because the question over whether animals have actual legal "rights" is a highly contentious one). Groups such as People for the Ethical Treatment of Animals (PETA), and in particular the Humane Society of the United States (HSUS), are constantly subjected to industry attacks for promoting "radical, vegetarian, antiagricultural zealotry" to eliminate all poultry and livestock farms, regardless of size or type of operation.

On the other hand, most CAFO fighters cared deeply about animal welfare, even if it wasn't always at the top of their agenda. What happened in Florida in November 2002 warmed their hearts.

By a 55/45 percent margin, voters in Florida passed the Animal Cruelty Amendment: Limiting Cruel and Inhumane Confinement of Pigs During Pregnancy. It was the first-ever ballot initiative to take on gestation crates in hog factories. The state legislature had originally dodged the gestation issue, so a group called Floridians for Humane Farms, with support from the Humane Society, turned in more than 650,000 signatures to get the amendment on the November ballot.

Rick was extremely happy with the news. He had been following the measure very closely and rooting for the reform. "We needed some state, somewhere, to stand up and say, 'This imprisonment of helpless sows is so against the laws of nature, and so terrible that it's got to stop,'" he told Joanne on election night.

To activists like Rick, CAFOs were acceptable to the public only because very few members of the public had ever set foot inside one. In most cases, the animals were kept out of sight, behind closed doors in windowless buildings. Millions of people drove by farrowing houses every day of their lives, Rick thought, without any inkling of the thousands of pregnant or lactating sows crammed within cold steel bars behind those anonymous white walls.

"If only people could see for themselves what it looks like inside these factories," Rick said. "Very few of them could stomach it." But, he added, those same people who drive blithely past a hog factory might come upon an open pasture down the road, where the horses look undernourished, sickly, or neglected. "They will call the sheriff, and someone will go to jail, I guarantee it," Rick said.

"And they still grossly disregard the abuse and suffering of the pigs, which are just as much part of God's creatures. The horse has a life in nature that's respected by man—why does a pig rate less than that? Because the pig is meat—a food product, not a living thing. It's an idiotic double standard—you can't kick a dog, but you can lock a pig up in a small crate and take her piglets away before she can nurse them properly, as any mother is programmed to do. This is man's insane inhumanity at its worse. We are turning into something that's, well, that's not very nice."

When Rick went on his Midwestern whistle-stop tour with Nicolette Hahn, he was shaken to find that some local organizers did not want him talking about animal welfare in the battle against CAFOs. Rick didn't acquiesce. "No honest-to-God farmer would ever treat his animals this way," he told them, "so if you're doing that, by gosh you are not a farmer. These crates, they're an industrial practice, not a farming one."

Rick reserved particular ire for industry veterinarians—who he thought should know better—and the American Society for the Prevention of Cruelty to Animals (ASPCA). "I have never once heard of the ASPCA looking into animal-factory cruelty," he said to Karen one night on a phone conference. "If you have a pig on a film set, the ASPCA has an officer there to make sure it is treated well. Actor pigs get a guardian; food pigs get squat."

Karen was equally impressed with the Florida vote. "It's because they showed people what these crates actually look like," she said. "Once people are confronted with the facts, they side with the pigs." But, Karen knew, far too often the public is treated to old-fashioned farm images of haylofts, gamboling calves, and clucking chickens scratching around in the dirt. "They don't want people to see how the animals are really raised," she said. "But when you force people to see the real thing, then they will take ethical action every time. It must be industry's worst nightmare."

Karen had another reason to support animal welfare, and it had nothing to do with ethics. She had read studies showing that animal stress can actually increase "pathogen shedding"—so animal welfare also affects the amount of pathogens produced. "Animal welfare is a human public health issue," she said. "Most people just don't realize it."

Agribusiness supporters were apoplectic over the Florida vote. The Center for Consumer Freedom complained that the state had just "extended human rights to farm animals." But, it noted, few hog farmers used gestation crates anyway. The initiative was a solution in search of a problem, it said.

The much-anticipated well-water study, conducted by the nonprofit Valley Institute for Research and Education, was released to the public in the spring of 2003. Helen Reddout and her fellow CARE members now had a new weapon in their arsenal. The study reaffirmed the role of CAFOs in contaminating Lower Valley drinking water.

Funded with ninety-five thousand dollars from the Bosma and DeRuyter settlements, VIRE had conducted drinking-well tests, free of charge, for low-income families across a wide swath of the valley during 2001 and 2002. Its main goal was to inform residents of the fitness of their drinking water. But it would also gather baseline data on groundwater quality in the study area—between Rattlesnake Ridge in the north and Horse Heaven Hills to the south.

The area was one of the most heavily irrigated districts in the country, the study noted. It was also unusually dairy intensive: The southern portion of the valley was home to more than sixty milking operations with some one hundred thousand animal units. Tellingly, drinking water quality was found to be "significantly better" in the *northern* portion of the area. In fact, none of the wells tested there exceeded the EPA maximum for nitrates in drinking water of ten milligrams per liter. In the southern sector, 40 out of 195 wells (21 percent) were contaminated enough to cause "serious medical problems" for infants and pregnant women, it said. Ammonia and chloride were also "significantly higher" in these wells.[18]

The authors recommended that local residents and agricultural interests form a "groundwater management area" to conduct more extensive well monitoring, indentify the most contaminated sections to study, and "determine the effects of agricultural practices and other human activities on contaminants."

The study was not designed to determine the source of the contaminants, but to Helen and the other members of CARE, the source was obvious. "There is a direct correlation between the location of large confinement dairies and the pollution of private wells," Helen said in a statement. "If you take the zip codes of where the dairies are located, and where the tests were taken, there's a direct connection to the presence of nitrates."[19]

Mary Lynne Bos was much blunter. "You don't have to be a rocket scientist to know what is causing the well water pollution," she said in the statement. "Contaminated water was not a problem when cows were allowed to graze on pasture."

"This study shows the same thing as similar studies across the United States where animal factories operate," the CARE statement continued. "We need to return to sustainable farming practices before the danger to our water is beyond repair."

A year later, the second lawsuit-funded report—conducted by Heritage College—would confirm CARE's assertions. It found nitrate levels above ten milligrams per liter in three areas of the valley, and fecal coliform bacteria in a significant number of the wells with elevated nitrates. "The source of these bacteria can only be animal feces," the report said. "These results suggest that sources of contaminants are feedlots and/or dairy operations."[20]

In mid-2003, Karen Hudson realized that seven years had passed since she first heard rumors about Dave Inskeep's plan to bring a megafarm into sleepy little Elmwood. Since then, the dairy had changed hands and, gradually, with each investment in new technological advances, it had managed to cut back odor emissions while also limiting the risk of water contamination from leaks, spills, or overflowing lagoons.

In doing so, New Horizons Dairy had, in a sense, become emblematic of the larger debate over factory farming in America. In an age of innovative technology, factory farms were slowly—if not completely—cleaning up their acts. But they were still underregulated, in Karen's perspective, and some were still being monitored just once every few years. Even worse, the IEPA didn't even know where all the CAFOs were in Illinois.

But was it possible for a concentrated animal feeding operation to reform itself into total acceptability? Of course there were still hazards to tackle: particle contamination, dangerous pathogens, antibiotic-resistant bacteria, heavy metals. But to what extent should neighbors be asked to tolerate a measure of odor, some water pollution, and the occasional spill?

Even an eco-friendly CAFO is still a CAFO, critics charged. You would still have tons of manure to dispose of. You would still have economic disruption of rural communities. And you would still have thousands of animals living their lives in concentration-camp confinement.

For some people, there is no such thing as a "good" CAFO. But in Elmwood in 2003, others were beginning to believe that New Horizons Dairy was capable of coming pretty close. Emerging technology was to be thanked for this development. (Though Karen today points out that the megadairy "still stinks up the town, especially on warm summer nights when the band concerts are held in Central Park.")

New Horizons had installed a state-of-the-art, $1.8 million system to capture methane from composting manure in a massive anaerobic digester.[21] The biogas was then burned off in a pair of roaring Caterpillar generators to create power to run the operation, slashing the electric bill from $7,000 to $500 per month, according to dairy officials. It was the first dairy in Illinois to invest in such a complex system, though nearly half the funds ($550,000) had come from the Illinois Department of Commerce and Economic Opportunity and the Renewable Energy Resources Program, with utility ratepayer money.

The grant had seemed odd to Karen and other activists. After all, New Horizons had been forced to install this system as part of its settlement with the attorney general, under which it also wrote a check for fifty thousand dollars to the state. Maybe, Karen laughed to herself, it would have gotten $600,000 if not for the fine.

On the other hand, there were genuine public benefits in return for the public investment. Capturing methane cut the odor emissions. And because manure and urine in the cattle barns were regularly scraped into pipes that drained into a catch basin and digester, little water was needed, which relieved extra pressure on lagoon levels.

Meanwhile, heat that was captured off the generators helped the digesters to extract methane gas from the solids, while liquids were separated out into the lagoon. Solid waste left over from the process was relatively odor free and could be sold for commercial fertilizer. At the time, a semitrailer truckful could fetch $120.

The new arrangement seemed to be helping. "Now it smells like a dairy farm," said Phyllis Cook, a FARM member who lived nearby. "It doesn't smell like a sewer anymore."

Karen wasn't completely sold yet. "The smell seems to have improved, though somebody from Elmwood called recently and said they had to close the door of their business because it was so bad in town. I can still smell it some days. There are still emissions from methane digesters that must be monitored—it's a Band-Aid on top of a poop pile," she told the *Peoria Journal Star*. "At the Factory Farm Project, we say, 'Do not concentrate animals to the point where manure becomes a liability,' " she said. "It's subsidizing the wrong way to produce our food."

She criticized the $550,000 grant that New Horizons had received from ratepayer money, calling it "corporate welfare" in the newspaper. "They took money from the community to subsidize their unsustainable operation," she said. And then, the humble, once-apolitical Midwestern farmwife and schoolteacher told her hometown newspaper that New Horizons "could make amends for past pollution by providing free electricity to people who have suffered from the odors and other problems caused by the dairy."

On May 20, 2003, Helen and Don Reddout had finished dinner and switched on the TV. The CNN anchor, Bill Hemmer, wore a worried knit across his usually boyish brow. "Mad cow disease is striking a little closer to home," he announced grimly. Hemmer said that a cow in Alberta, Canada, had tested positive for the disease, which had swept the United Kingdom in the 1990s and killed more than a hundred people.

It was only the second time that a cow afflicted with the disease had been reported on this side of the Atlantic. The first, also in Canada, had been diagnosed back in 1993. Officials hoped they had thwarted further spread of the dreaded infection. But now, a full decade later, here it was again.

Mad cow disease was first identified in 1986 when farmers in Britain reported an unusual number of "downer" cows—animals that are very sick and unable to walk—among their herds. By 2003, it had spread to twenty-four countries, infected nearly two hundred thousand animals, and led to the killing of millions more as a precaution.

The formal veterinary name for the illness is bovine spongiform encephalopathy (BSE), which means, literally, "cattle spongy-brain disease"—because it causes nerve and brain tissue to waste into a spongelike mass of dead cells. BSE is transmitted by a little-understood infectious agent called a prion—an improperly folded protein that is almost impossible to kill except at extremely high temperatures. Prions are known to concentrate in the brain, spinal cord, and eyes of infected animals. But recent research in Europe has found noninfectious prions in the blood, muscle, and even milk of some animals,[22] including sheep—which can get a similar prion disease called scrapie.

BSE is transmitted to cattle when their feed contains prion-contaminated material from other cattle (or sheep). Infectious cattle parts are said to be the brain, spinal chord, and central nervous system tissue. In most countries, these are removed from the carcass before processing.

When people consume the infected tissues, they are at risk of developing the human form of the illness, called variant Creutzfeldt-Jakob disease (vCJD). It is always fatal. Symptoms of vCJD can take from two to eight years or longer to develop. Patients typically first display a rapidly deteriorating form of dementia, followed by a loss of memory, changes in personality, and hallucinations. Physical symptoms are ghastly and include speech impairment, spastic movements, ataxia (coordination and balance problems), and seizures. Some patients die within months or even weeks of the onset of symptoms. Others suffer for years before succumbing.

Mad cow disease is the most frightening of potential health threats staring up from our dinner plates. It easily trumps *E. coli*, salmonella, and cholesterol on the scale of health horrors. Cooking infected meat will not kill the prions, though officials insist that muscle cuts are safe to eat because prions are found only in the tissues of the animal's central nervous system.

In 2003, some consumers wondered whether beef might be the food that bites us back the hardest. Canadian officials had the Alberta cow destroyed and quarantined the herd. Inspectors did not "think" there was any contamination of beef in the human food chain. Even so, the United States issued an instantaneous ban on all beef imports from Canada. But the move may have been moot. Canadian officials announced later that day that the cow may have originated in the United States, though they weren't sure.

Helen was shocked to learn that the cow had been found to be sick back in January; why was this alarming news only being broadcast now?

A meat inspector said at the time that the animal was underweight, suffering from pneumonia, and unfit for human consumption. But no one had really suspected mad cow. The animal was slaughtered and its carcass was "rendered"—a process of drying tissue and separating out the liquid fats. The grease and tallow from this process is sold for soap, cooking, cosmetics, biodiesel, and other uses, and the dried tissue is ground into meat and bone meal (MBM). In the United States, MBM is widely used in animal feed, including inexpensive dog and cat food. Most countries have banned feeding MBM to cattle, however, for reasons that are explained below.

Some of the Canadian cow's tissues were reserved for testing, but its samples were low on the waiting list, and were only analyzed months later.

The confirming test had just come back positive. Health officials were quick to point out that the monitoring system was effective, even though the infected cow had presumably been rendered into bath soaps and floor wax. "While the impact this disease has on cattle is disturbing," Hemmer said on CNN, "U.S. health officials say the fact that the infected cow was found is a good sign, trying to reassure American consumers that there is no need to be worried now." [23]

CNN's chief health correspondent, Dr. Sanjay Gupta, sounded a cautionary note, but then said it was fine to plan a big steak dinner. "The toughest thing about this is the incubation period, two to eight years," Gupta said. "That's important because you've got to trace the steps back two years ago to find out where this particular disease came from. Was this cow eating a particularly contaminated feed two to eight years ago, and if so, how are you going to figure that out? You can see the investigative dilemma."

Gupta predicted that BSE would not make it across the border. "We haven't seen it in the United States ever. I don't think it's going to come as a result of this," he said. "I think Canada has staved off, will probably stave this off as they staved off SARS not too long ago. I don't think we're going to see it in this country."

Seven months later, Dr. Gupta would be proved wrong.

By 2003, the Factory Farm Project Team had settled into a fairly regular routine of helping residents around the country to confront incoming or already established CAFOs nearby. Helen, Karen, Chris, Terry, and a few other paid consultants began to refer to themselves, jokingly, as the SWAT Team. All incoming calls would be directed to Karen, who would take down the basic information of the new client's situation and then assign the case to the appropriate SWAT Team member. The resulting investigation was gratis. Dairy calls went to Helen, beef calls to Terry, and pig calls to Chris. Karen would also take on a number of hog and dairy cases herself.

They advertised themselves as working to "create a sustainable food production system that is healthful and humane, economically viable, and environmentally sound. When invited by regional or grassroots groups, our team helps rural communities, family ranchers and farmers around the country oppose the spread of new factory farms, and close down existing operations that adversely affect the health and well-being of communities." The team offered to provide assistance on many of the following fronts:

- Community organizing and support.
- Identifying "major players," concerned citizens, important elements of the opposition, and general preferences of the local government.

- Generating scholarly research on social and economic costs, externalities, employment impacts, and multiplier effects of factory-farm operations.
- Teaching communities how to access, understand, and use existing regulations concerning the development of factory-farm facilities.
- Participating in hearings and other speaking opportunities in order to educate the public and government officials about the realities of factory farms.[24]

In 2003, Diane Hatz of GRACE's Sustainable Table campaign began developing a DVD cartoon to get its story out. *The Meatrix* was released in November 2003 and, according to the group's Web site, "broke new ground in online grassroots advocacy, creating a unique vehicle by which to educate, entertain and motivate people to create change."[25] Within three months, well over four million people had watched the humorous film at least once, including residents of Europe, South America, Canada, Mexico, Australia, New Zealand, China, Korea, and Japan.

At just four minutes long, *The Meatrix* is an animated spoof of the ultrapopular *Matrix* movies that starred Keanu Reeves, but uses factory farms as the grim gulags from which the animal heroes decide they must liberate their brethren. It was based on "the many similarities between the film and today's corporate system of agriculture." In the film, a young pig named Leo, wondering if he is "the one," unites with Chickity, "the feathered family farm defender," and Moopheus, a cow in a trench coat longing for greener pastures. Afterward, viewers are invited to visit an "action page" for more information on animal factories, and for help in finding locally produced meat, poultry, dairy, and eggs that were raised on sustainable family farms.

GRACE did not shy away from calling it "the most successful online advocacy film ever." The flash animation short film went on to be translated into more than thirty languages, with well over fifteen million views worldwide. It won more than a dozen film and Web awards, including a coveted Webby Award.

Much of the media also loved *The Meatrix*. "We swear you'll never look at pigs the same," wrote the *Los Angeles Times*. "*The Meatrix* achieves something we didn't think possible—a pretty funny exposé on the evils of factory farming," a *Seattle Post-Intelligencer* review raved.

As part of the release, GRACE also launched the Sustainable Table project's online Eat Well Guide, in conjunction with Dr. David Wallinga and his team at the Minneapolis-based Institute for Agriculture and Trade Policy. The goal, the two groups said, was to teach consumers "how to shop smarter, eat healthier and enjoy an abundance of fresh, nutritious meat and produce grown by local family farmers."[26]

The Eat Well Guide offers an online list of producers, farmers' markets, grocery stores, restaurants, and mail-order outlets that carry sustainably raised meat, eggs, and dairy produced without antibiotics or growth promoters. Items can be searched by zip code, and by categories such as "certified organic," "free-range," "cage-free," "pastured," "no antibiotics added," and so on. The Web site also carries a list of questions to ask "your local farmer, butcher, store manager and/or waiter," plus information on community-supported agriculture—or CSA, where members buy part of a farmer's animal, fruit, or vegetable production in advance.

The guide was launched on November 3, 2003, just in time for Thanksgiving, and featured a special turkey section to help consumers find that "perfect" bird, one that was "raised sustainably or organically on a small farm in their area."

A month after BSE was reported in Alberta, and the United States banned beef imports from Canada, the American media was rife with stories about the fear of mad cows and Happy Meals. The year 2003 was shaping up to be year of the mad cow, Karen thought.

In June, *USA Today* ran an exposé on the trend of lax monitoring for beef products in cattle feed. Cattle by-products were finding their way into cattle feed in ways that most consumers would find unimaginable: The same cow-eats-cow cannibalism that had spread BSE in England.

USA Today reported that the FDA was testing just six hundred samples of domestic feed and six hundred imported samples each year for prohibited materials, such as meal made from ruminants (cud chewers such as cows, sheep, and goats). "Consumer groups say this is woefully inadequate," the paper said. Meanwhile, remnants of cattle were making their way into food for U.S. cattle in at least four ways:[27]

Chicken Feed: Birds cannot catch BSE from eating beef, so they are often fed a ration fortified with meat and bonemeal and other cattle by-products. This feed is typically delivered to caged factory-farm chickens along long conveyer belts. As the birds peck at the feed, some of it invariably spills into their bedding/litter. This litter is usually made of wood chips, feathers, bird droppings—and spilled feed. Chicken litter is then spread onto cropland as fertilizer in some states, including Arkansas and Maryland; in other places it is incinerated. In regions with large poultry and cattle operations in the same area, it is most cost-effective to feed it to cattle. This practice has been outlawed in Canada.

Restaurant Scraps: In 1997, a new law banned the practice of feeding most mammalian remains to cattle. There remained, however, one significant but largely under-the-radar loophole to that rule: the "restaurant-plate waste" exemption. This rule allowed restaurants and institutional food suppliers to sell food scraps and leftovers to animal renderers, which routinely turn them into feed for cattle and other animals.

Pet Food: "Retail pet food frequently contains ruminant meat and bonemeal, but unlike agricultural animal feed, there's no requirement that it be labeled 'Do not feed to cattle or other ruminants,'" *USA Today* reported. But dry cat and dog food past its expiration date sometimes finds its way into the rendering salvage market. From there, it routinely ends up being mixed into cattle feed. "The FDA is wondering whether all pet food should be labeled, just in case," the paper noted.

Dried Blood: Spray-dried cattle and pig blood meal is often mixed into animal feed to boost protein levels. Most commonly, blood serum is used as a milk replacement for dairy calves, which are yanked away from their mothers within twenty-four hours of birth so as not to "waste" marketable milk on the offspring.

John Stauber, coauthor of the book *Mad Cow USA*, said U.S. policy toward its human blood supply was laughable. While America cautiously banned anyone who lived in the United Kingdom in the 1980s from donating blood, it still fed cow blood to cows. "The question is whether it can be transmitted by oral feeding," he said. "But those experiments involve years, if not decades. We have to err on the side of caution."

Janice Swanson, a cattle specialist at Kansas State University, said the American public should share the blame for the problem, which is mostly due to their insistence on low-priced meat. "It's not just the fault of the producers," she said. "The pressure on them is to produce a product that's so cheap that they have to capture every efficiency. The average consumer doesn't care, and they're not going to pay one penny more."

Public and scientific pushback against overuse of antibiotics in farm animals was having an impact in the marketplace. In June, McDonald's rattled agribusiness by ordering its global suppliers to phase out growth-promoting antibiotics in cows, pigs, and chickens because the practice increased the risk of antibiotic-resistant bacterial infections in people.[28]

A year earlier, McDonald's—facing intense pressure from animal-welfare groups—ordered poultry suppliers to begin adopting minimum humane standards for raising chickens, setting a precedent that was soon followed elsewhere in fast food. None of them went out of business in doing so, and animal-welfare supporters called it a success.

The move by the world's largest restaurant chain followed a year of consultations with consumer and scientific groups, including the Union of Concerned Scientists and its affiliated organization, the Keep Antibiotics Working coalition. McDonald's was the first major fast-food chain to do so. (Under the McDonald's arrangement, sick farm animals could still be treated with therapeutic levels of antibiotics.)

"As a company committed to social responsibility, we take seriously our obligation to understand the emerging science of antibiotic resistance and to work with our suppliers to foster real, tangible changes in our own supply community and hopefully beyond," said Frank Muschetto, a McDonald's senior vice president.[29]

But the Coalition for Animal Health, an industry trade group, took McDonald's to task for its new policy, alleging that animal disease *increased* in Europe after subtherapeutic antibiotics use was drastically reduced.[30]

Offering an opposing voice was the Union of Concerned Scientists, which complained that the burger giant had not gone far *enough*; its new policy failed to address antibiotic use for disease prevention, as opposed to treatment or growth stimulation. According to the group, 70 percent of all antimicrobials sold in the United States were given to healthy pigs, cows, and chickens to promote growth and prevent disease, not to treat illness.[31]

For Rick, Karen, and Helen, the McDonald's announcement was welcome news. "What do you know?" Rick said to his wife, Joanne. "I guess we're really getting somewhere. Do you have any idea how many millions of pounds of bacon and ham McDonald's buys right here in North Carolina?" Rick was certain that public pressure had moved the chain to demand that its giant supplier, Smithfield, change the way it raised pork.

"It's good to win one, once in a while," Rick said, smiling.

Five years had passed since Rick Dove and other clean-water advocates had convinced North Carolina to finally address the dismal condition of the Neuse River Basin. New rules had been enacted to reduce nitrogen levels in the river by the end of 2003. It was now November 2003; had the plan worked?

No one was quite sure.

At a special meeting in New Bern to review the health of the Neuse River,

Ken Reckhow, director of the University of North Carolina's Water Resources Research Institute, confirmed there had been a downward trend in nitrogen concentrations since 1997.[32]

Rick went to the meeting to listen, but was not impressed by what he heard. Reckhow could not explain the reason for the decline. It could have been due to improved wastewater treatment, or major hurricanes flushing out the basin, or new buffers installed to capture runoff. Or a combination thereof.

But hog farms, and the one million acres of farmland in the river basin, were still the biggest threat to the Neuse estuary, scientists warned. Crop farmers in the seventeen-county river basin reported a 37 percent drop in nitrogen fertilizer use over the previous five years. That exceeded the plan's goal, but it may have been an unintentional side effect; there had been increased market demand for cotton, which requires far less nitrogen than corn.

Meanwhile, the thirty biggest municipal wastewater-treatment plants had reduced nitrogen discharge by nearly 50 percent. Rick understood the implication: Hog farmers had done little to reduce the amount of nutrients they discharged into the Neuse through their farms and sprayfields.

JoAnn Burkholder did more to deflate the good news. She and her colleagues at North Carolina State and University of North Carolina Wilmington were completing their own review of ten years of data collected from the Neuse Basin. The report was due out in late spring.

JoAnn explained to *The News & Observer* that though total nitrogen in the Neuse had declined since 1993, it was a statistical anomaly. The period 2000–2002 had been extremely dry, greatly reducing runoff. When the team analyzed data that excluded the drought years, they found that nitrogen levels had actually remained flat. "Folks might be tempted to say that we've made wonderful strides in the last decade," JoAnn said, "but that drought makes us look better than we are."[33]

Human population in the basin had increased 25 percent since 1993, but its swine population was up 277 percent, she added. "When you think of it that way, it's something of an accomplishment that total nitrogen concentrations stayed where they are. We're running to stand still."

Besides, nitrogen was not the only problem, JoAnn continued. Dissolved oxygen levels had fallen, creating a threat to fish and plants. But the most staggering information in their study, which was published in the prestigious journal *Limnology and Oceanography*, is that ammonia in the Neuse estuary had increased by 500 percent.[34] This form of nitrogen is preferred by many algae, and has been related to increases in some harmful algal bloom species in the Neuse and elsewhere.

Whatever progress had been made, Rick Dove deserved the credit. Marion

Smith, a consultant to the Neuse Basin Oversight Committee, praised the former Riverkeeper to *The News & Observer* for "focusing enough attention on the problems in the 1990s to build political momentum to clean up the river."

Rick was grateful, but pointed out that the job wasn't completed—fish were still dying in the Neuse. Heavy rains that summer had ended the drought, but now runoff into rivers and streams was bringing back the nightmares. In September alone, more than a million fish had died from "oxygen sags" caused by noxious algal blooms.

ate December 2003 was not a very merry affair in Yakima County and other parts of the country where cattle are raised for food and milk. Late on the afternoon of December 23, Helen Reddout was busy, not with Yuletide preparations—she and Don would spend this year at their daughter's place—but with the dust and clutter of a partially remodeled kitchen. Then the phone rang.

"Helen? There're rumors flying around the valley." Helen recognized the voice of a CARE member from Mabton. She was speaking nervously. "We've heard there's big trouble brewing around here."

"Trouble?" Helen asked. "What is it?"

"I'm not sure, there's just lots of rumors flying."

"Can you get anyone to give us more information?"

"No. But it sounds big."

"I'd really like to know what is going on. Keep in contact if you find anything solid," Helen replied, and then returned to the clutter. But the phone kept ringing, each time with vague reports of "something big" going on with a dairy in Mabton. Helen knew that nothing goes on in a small community without everyone catching wind of it, so something odd was definitely afoot.

The news broke that afternoon: Local media reported that a single Holstein dairy cow from the Sunny Dene Ranch in Mabton had tested positive for bovine spongiform encephalopathy, the first such case ever reported in the United States. The diseased cow was "likely" slaughtered for hamburger after it stopped milking, state officials said.

News reports said the cow was a "downer"—unable to walk when it arrived at the plant. Cattle in that condition usually had tissue samples taken when slaughtered. This cow's tissue had tentatively come back positive; now it was on a military jet to England for a definitive diagnosis.

Most disturbing to Helen was that nobody knew for sure if the contaminated beef had already been sold, cooked, and eaten. Perhaps, she speculated with growing panic, it had been ground into patties and frozen. Perhaps those patties were sitting in a warehouse awaiting shipment to a school lunch program.

Federal officials insisted that the nation's food supply was perfectly safe. They were quick to confirm that the infection of the cow was not terrorist related, which did not calm Helen's chief concern. They assured the public that the animal's brain and spinal tissue had been sent to a rendering plant. Those items did not enter the food supply.

Even so, the Moses Lake slaughterhouse—where the animal had been killed and ground into hamburger—announced a "voluntary recall" of some ten thousand pounds of beef. The feds said the move was taken "out of an abundance of caution." Later it was revealed that beef from the animal was sent to Midway Meats in Centralia, Washington, and then on to Willamette and Interstate Meat. (Eventually, thirty-eight thousand pounds would be recalled.)[1]

Because BSE takes several years to manifest symptoms, even healthy-looking cows could be sick. Therefore, additional cows were marked for destruction as a precautionary measure. "Very likely, the rest of the herd is toast even if they are not contaminated," Gordon Kelly, Yakima County's director of environmental health, told reporters. In Mabton, the dairy farmer who raised the cow said he had sent twenty animals to slaughter in the past two weeks. "I'm glad I sent them now," he mused. "I've got kind of a cushion—I got sixty-five cents a pound for one cow."

The day before Christmas, Helen's phone kept ringing. About to answer what must have been the fiftieth call, Helen rolled her eyes. But this time, it was a welcome, recognizable voice: Karen Hudson.

"Hey," Helen said, "I take it you've heard what's happened out here?"

"I have, and it's just awful," Karen said. "Has CARE put out a press release yet?"

"No, I can't get off the phone! People keep calling me, wanting to know if their families are safe. I haven't had time to deal with the media yet."

Karen said she'd take a crack at a statement, working with Diane Hatz and Alice Slater from the GRACE office in New York. Helen thanked her and hung up, only to have her phone ring once again with a call from another frantic valley dweller.

Back in Elmwood, Karen spent hours on the phone with Diane and Alice in Manhattan drafting the GRACE Factory Farm Project's response. As she banged away on the keyboard, Karen was overwhelmed by disgust, outrage, and adrenaline. By this point, she knew the USDA's Yuletide announcement was carefully planned; one of the key rules of the PR game was to release your worst news when the fewest people are paying attention.

Karen was so caught up, she had neglected her traditional Christmas Eve feast of manicotti, baked clams, and stuffed mushrooms. It sat uncooked on the kitchen counter. "There's no way I can let this one fly by," she apologized to her family, who were waiting patiently for dinner. "The authorities who are supposed to be protecting us—the consumers, our children—they're asleep at the wheel!" Rocky popped his head into Karen's basement office to remind her of holiday duties.

"Rocky, I promise, fifteen minutes more," Karen pleaded. Rocky knew it would be more than fifteen minutes. Fortunately, he had learned how to make this meal from his wife and set to work in the kitchen. The GRACE press release was completed on time, and so was the big Italian Christmas dinner. That evening, the activists' statement was delivered via e-mail to media around the globe.

"Evidence indicates that mad cow disease is the product of an increasingly industrialized food system," the statement said, "where parts of deceased animals are routinely fed to live animals to keep costs down."

"Mad cow disease is a red flag that exposes the deadly flaws employed by our broken food system," Karen's quote read. "The corporate industrial model of agriculture has brought us to the position we are in today. Grinding up dead farm animals to feed to live animals should be banned worldwide."

Testing animals for BSE was not enough. "The only viable answer to this problem is to change the way animals are raised," the GRACE Factory Farm Project asserted. "Consumers can help create this change by supporting family farmers who raise animals sustainably."

Back in D.C., Agriculture Secretary Ann Veneman rushed to the airwaves on Christmas Eve to reassure a nation sitting down nervously to holiday meals. "We remain confident in the safety of our food supply," she said.[2] "The risk to human health is extremely low, and my family and I plan to have beef for Christmas." She added that "muscle cuts of meat have almost no risk," though Helen, Karen, and Rick wanted to know the definition of "almost."

"I know of no science that's shown that you can transmit BSE from muscle cuts of meat," Veneman said. More than twenty thousand cows had been tested that year by U.S. officials—triple the number in 2002. But that hardly reassured the activists, who knew that the country slaughtered some thirty-five million cattle each year. Nor were they comforted by official declarations that BSE is found only in brain and nerve tissue, thus rendering milk and other dairy products safe.

"For them to be guaranteeing that the entire food supply is safe is a total lie to the American public," Karen said to Rocky that uneasy holiday night. "It's outrageous."

On this holiday of faith, Karen and Rocky had lost whatever belief they once held in the USDA. Karen knew that Secretary Veneman's chief of staff, Dale Moore, was the former chief lobbyist for the National Cattlemen's Beef Association, and her spokesperson, Alisa Harrison, was the group's former PR director. Soon afterward, Veneman appointed a special mad cow committee that included William Hueston, whom the beef industry had hired to testify against Oprah Winfrey in their famously failed 1997 lawsuit against her. The Texas cattlemen sued Winfrey for $12 million after vegetarian activist Howard Lyman said on her show that mad cow disease "could make AIDS look like the common cold," and Winfrey responded, "It has just stopped me *cold* from eating another burger!"

Much of the world seemed to agree with Oprah. Almost immediately after the mad cow announcement, U.S. beef exports to Asia were blocked. Foreign sales had reached more than $3.2 billion in 2002, but now numerous countries were enacting bans on American beef imports, especially Japan and South Korea, two of the leading foreign buyers of U.S. beef.

Beef purveyors scurried to tamp down consumer alarm at home. Gayland Pedhirney, president of Washington Beef, a Yakima Valley slaughterhouse that processed more than three hundred thousand head a year, called for "common sense and calm" to prevail. "Finding one animal that has the disease shouldn't be reason for huge panic," he told reporters. Pedhirney estimated his company had $1.8 million worth of beef en route to the Asian markets when exports were halted. Now it was offering "salvage" prices for the returning meat.[3]

Meanwhile, from its headquarters in Colorado, the National Cattlemen's Beef Association held a conference call with reporters, also aimed at reassuring jittery consumers. Chief Executive Terry Stokes spoke calmly about the industry's "triple firewall": testing downer cows; an import ban on cattle and bovine products from BSE countries; and a ban on bovine-derived material in cattle feed.[4] (He failed to mention that some cattle were still eating bovine material in the form of calf formula, plate scraps, and chicken litter.)

Stokes did make one comment that soothed the nerves of rattled beef-eaters: "One can derive a fair bit of comfort from statistics and epidemiology:

when there were sixty thousand to eighty thousand infected cows in the UK, approximately 150 people out of 60 million developed the disease," he said. "One cow is not likely to translate into any cases in the U.S."

But some officials did not brush off the bad news so casually. "This is certainly a big concern. We now have evidence of a disease that we didn't have before in the U.S.," Dr. W. Ron DeHaven, the USDA's chief veterinary officer, told *The New York Times*.[5]

The news galvanized other anti-CAFO forces. They wasted no time in calling for a ban on the practice of sending downer cows into the human food supply. Wayne Pacelle, vice president of the Humane Society of the United States, told the *Times* that downer animals that can't walk into the slaughterhouse are routinely pushed in by bulldozers or dragged by chains. By contrast, in Japan and most of Europe, inspectors culled cattle with ambulatory problems before they entered the abattoirs and remanded them to a rendering plant.

Meanwhile, despite government assurances, consumers were clamoring to know what the "safest" cuts of beef might be. Food-safety advocate and author Marion Nestle opined that boneless steaks and roasts were "probably" safest. The riskiest products were ground beef, hot dogs, cold cuts, taco filling, and pizza toppings—foods preferred especially by children. Many processed-meat products are harvested from the carcass using "advanced meat recovery" machines, whose rubber fingers strip bone and tissue of any remaining flesh. Banned in Europe and Japan, they are legal here, despite a 2002 USDA study showing that just 12 percent of the plants examined had recovery systems that were free of bovine nerve tissue.[6]

Helen, Karen, and Rick were nauseated by reading of the flesh-recovery machines, but also relieved they had given up commercial meat long ago. In fact, Helen was trying to buy only organic dairy products. But now she worried about that, too.

"I can go out to the dairy and see that the cow's been out on pasture, it's being treated great. But unless I can go back and examine whether it was nursed by its mother or on starter with blood meal, then I'm in twilight land, because I just don't know," she told Don one night while they ate dinner in the kitchen.

"But, Helen," Don said, "you don't know that there's mad cow in milk."

She regarded her husband for a moment as if he had mad cow disease himself. "Don, don't you remember when I was first nursing Terri and I ate onions? Remember how the onion flavor showed up in my milk? And what a problem that was? Do you really think when you're sick, all your germs stay in your spinal column?" Helen said. "There are studies from Europe showing that prions are found in every neuron, not just the brain and spinal cord. And besides, if you lived in Britain over a certain period, you are banned from giving blood, remember?"

Don knew Helen was on a tear. So he just nodded his head in agreement.

"Well, if BSE prions are found in blood, then they are found in *milk*, too."

On Christmas morning at the Hudson household, in between opening presents, Karen fielded phone calls from the media. They were calling from Seattle and California, Texas and New York. One reporter asked if her family was eating beef for Christmas dinner.

Karen responded that her family was fine; they would dine that night on grass-fed beef whose rearing and processing she could trace. Yet she was worried for the nation's food supply. She was also ashamed at the USDA's devious timing of the news. But if industry leaders and the administration hoped to bury this story, they had failed.

The media got the message. "National attention is now shifting to the larger debate of just how much surveillance or testing should be conducted," the *Houston Chronicle* reported. "Some, like Karen Hudson of the Global Resource Action Center for the Environment, say 100 percent of suspect cattle should be tested, instead of 2 percent as is currently the case."

Dan Murphy of the American Meat Institute, a trade group of packers and processors, dismissed Karen's demands. "It's comparable to looking for early-stage Alzheimer's disease by testing everybody in grade school and high school. It would be a waste of time and money," he said. "If the infected Holstein cow is the tip of the iceberg, as some people claim, more cases would have been found in thirteen years of looking."

But the *Seattle Post-Intelligencer* quoted Karen Hudson's "red flag" comment about the broken national food system and said that many experts agreed with her that testing was inadequate. "This was just an accident waiting to happen," said Lester Friedlander, a former veterinarian for the USDA and a federal whistle-blower who left his job in 1995. The testing of twenty thousand brain samples from a national herd of 120 million was "nothing," he said, adding that downer cows should never be eaten by people.[7]

Dr. Michael Greger, a mad cow coordinator to the Organic Consumers Association, said the practice of feeding blood-containing formula to dairy calves (to save the mother's milk for the market) was to blame. "By continuing to feed cow blood to cows, we're creating the cannibalism circuit that these prions love so much," he said.

Meanwhile, down in New Bern, North Carolina, Rick Dove took in the news with a deep sigh. He was grateful his family had dined on nonindustrial Christmas turkey and ham, but he was troubled by the bigger picture.

"Remember what I said after Floyd, about Mother Nature pushing back against humans breaking her rules?" he said to Joanne. "Well, here we go again. Cows don't eat meat. I never heard of a cow eating a cow until the dairy industry said it was okay.

"You know, after I die, I'm going to run into some of these factory farm barons face-to-face," said Rick, a devout Catholic. "But I hope to God we'll be heading in opposite directions."

The discovery of a BSE-infected dairy cow in Yakima County had turned the American cattle industry on its head. Now, in January 2004, the issue was about to fluster the poultry people as well. Late in the month, Tommy Thompson, secretary of the U.S. Department of Health and Human Services (HHS), shocked the layer and broiler industries by announcing a ban on feeding chicken litter to cattle.

The move would be implemented by the FDA to add another layer of protection to the "multiple existing firewalls" keeping dangerous prions off the American dinner plate.

Poultry litter is used bird bedding, made of wood chips and sometimes rice hulls, plus feathers, urine, feces and spilled feed—some of which contains beef by-products. In most large poultry states, land application of litter was still the most common method for disposal. But with rapid growth in the industry, using it as cattle feed was an attractive alternative for growers running out of land to spread their mountains of litter.

If the chicken industry was apprehensive about the ban, its leaders didn't let on. The National Chicken Council's Richard Lobb said it would barely impact poultry producers. Just 1 percent of chicken litter is fed to cattle, he said, so poultry growers would not encounter much trouble finding "an acceptable, environmental way to dispose of it."[8]

In addition to litter, Secretary Thompson also banned the use of blood and blood products in feed or starter formula for calves. The feeding of plate scraps to cattle was also prohibited—not because of infection fears, the FDA said, but because it interferes with tests for prohibited proteins in the animal feed.

Also prohibited was the use of any part of a "downer cow" in a product meant for use by people. This included cosmetics and dietary supplements as well as food. One thing that was not covered, which worried some scientists, was cattle feed made with meal from chicken and pigs that were themselves fed beef by-products.

For the most part, consumers had been blissfully unaware that cows were being fed chicken shit—with or without beef meal mixed in. Some people were tempted to ditch commercial beef forever on the spot. Their collective revulsion was summed up by natural-food author, professor, and animal-factory irritant Michael Pollan.

"It's hard to say whether an American hamburger was appreciably less safe to eat the day after a Holstein cow tested positive for bovine spongiform encephalopathy in Washington State last month than it was the day before, but it had sure gotten less appetizing," he wrote in *The New York Times Magazine* on January 11, 2004. "You can't help feeling that the convoluted new food chain that industrial agriculture has devised for the animals we eat (and thus for us) is, to be unscientific for a moment, disgusting."[9]

Before long, the FDA would cave in to beef industry pressure and reverse itself on even these sensible preventive measures.

As mad cow concerns continued to frighten Americans, meat producers, marketers, and lobbyists hit back fast and furiously with a carefully orchestrated damage control operation.

The Center for Consumer Freedom issued a petulant screed against the "Mad Cow Scaremongers," offering colorful rhetoric in calling activists the "masters of disaster."[10]

"Every reputable expert tells us that the American meat supply is still safe. And yet a cabal of animal-rights activists and radical opponents of modern farming are already hitting the airwaves for one purpose: to spread fear and needless alarm," the CCF Web site declared. "These people are activists, not knowledgeable scientists. Their goal is to promote animal rights and organic-only, 1800s-style agriculture. And their track record is full of doom-and-gloom predictions that never came true."

Heading CCF's list of mad cow doomsayers was the Center for Media and Democracy's John Stauber. CCF railed at him for telling CNN that the Yakima case was "the tip of an invisible iceberg." Sharing equal blame, the Web site said, were Michael Hansen of the Consumers Union and Ronnie Cummins, head of the Organic Consumers Association. Their offense was claiming "consumers and farmers would be better off if people paid twice as much for their meat and ate half as much." The group also mocked author Marion Nestle, "New York University's food scold extraordinaire," and *Fast Food Nation* author Eric Schlosser.

Also on the list: Karen Hudson, "a consultant for GRACE Factory Farm Project, which can't stand the idea of efficient, large-scale agriculture," CCF said. "Hudson insists—without providing any evidence—that 'mad cow disease is the product of an increasingly industrialized food system.'"

Karen knew that hostility from well-funded industry groups was something to celebrate. "I think it's a sign that we're making progress," she told Helen one day. "Industrial agriculture is on the defensive. They're scrambling."

Helen agreed. Then she dropped her own bombshell.

"I got an anonymous call today from someone who worked at the dairy slaughterhouse in Moses Lake, where that cow was processed," she said. "He told me it *wasn't* a downer cow—it was a standing cow. And the thing is, almost all the other cows that came in from that Mabton dairy were downers, and the workers didn't feel like walking this cow all the way down to the standing pen, so they just left her in the downer pen with the other sick cows. If this cow had been in the proper pen, she *never* would have been tested and no one would ever know about the contamination."

"My God," Karen said. "So other standing cows have gone into the food chain, untested, who could also have BSE. What did you tell this guy?"

"I said, 'You need to go to the media. Tell them it was a standing cow with BSE, but they only want to test the downers.' I gave him some reporters' names, so we'll see."

The press paid attention. Trudy Bialic, a guest columnist for the *Seattle Post-Intelligencer*, reported that the Mabton cow "didn't show symptoms, according to three witnesses, including the man who killed her. Dave Louthan remembered her because she was a rare, white cow and says she walked off the delivery truck; she had a birthing injury but wasn't sick."[11]

Helen thought Louthan must be the man who called her. "She was a walker, not a downer," he said. "My walking cow was tested by accident." Louthan said the plant had only recently started testing cows. "We had taken maybe one hundred tests and we found that one that fast," he said.

Inexplicably, Bialic reported, the USDA stopped testing cows at the slaughterhouse after the first case was found. It also stopped searching for fifty-two of the eighty-one cows from the Mabton herd sent to the hamburger factory. "The USDA says the paper trail turned cold and it couldn't trace those fifty-two cows, so it gave up," she wrote. "You may have eaten them."

The USDA announced it would now test 268,000 primarily downer cows each year, and also do a random sampling of healthy cows over thirty months old, an age when BSE usually becomes apparent. "But Europe and Japan have found the disease in younger cattle; one was twenty-three months, another twenty-one months," she wrote, adding that it would cost "pennies per pound" to test all U.S. beef.

Bialic demanded new policies, including better traceability, testing, and recalls. "We also need to create an independent Food Safety Agency, as Britain did after conflicts of interest surfaced in its regulatory system. We need rules to stop herbivores from being force-fed their own kind and other animals."

I
n April 2004, the U.S. government announced it had tracked down the feed that had created the first U.S. mad cow in Yakima County: It was found in Yakima County and had come from a Canadian mill.

Meanwhile, the proposed ban on feeding blood, chicken litter, and restaurant scraps to cattle was still pending. But within days of proposing the changes in January, the FDA was inundated with complaints, concerns, and "troubling feedback" from the agricultural sector, said Stephen Sundlof, director of the agency's Center for Veterinary Medicine.[12]

CAFO industry resistance had successfully stalled enactment of the new rules. Now major export markets were balking more loudly at buying U.S. cattle. Even lawmakers from beef states were growing increasingly impatient with the Bush administration. After all, if the nation could not produce its own protein without feeding feces and old meatloaf to farm animals, there was something seriously wrong with the system.

But the FDA's Sundlof refused to commit the agency to a deadline for enacting the bans.

One obstacle was chicken-industry opposition to the litter ban. Mixing chicken litter into cattle feed was "one of the primary methods of waste disposal for the chicken growers, especially in the Southeast," he said. What else would growers do with their mounds of litter—which would quickly grow into mountains—if it weren't disposed of quickly? "One benefit of doing this," he said, "was that it was an environmentally sound way of recycling the material."

Chicken waste is densely concentrated with nitrogen and phosphorus, so its field application uses are limited. However, "as disgusting as this may sound," Sundlof said, "poultry litter is really utilizable in cattle feed, because it contains high nitrogen content that cattle can convert back into protein." Cattle's ruminant stomachs convert urea, a chemical found in urine, into protein. Chicken litter has lots of urea, which lets cows and steers build plenty of lean, nutritious, ready-to-grill muscle.

A ban on feeding blood to cows was also "problematic," Sundlof said, adding that the FDA was considering a number of exemptions, beginning with fetal calf serum. "The question is, 'How risky would fetal calf serum be?'" he mused. "We think that it's not very risky because it's from cattle that are not even born yet, so they haven't reached the age when they could be infected."

And the ban on restaurant scraps? Its urgency also waned. "Plate waste doesn't seem to have many issues related to it," Sundlof said. The FDA planned to submit new rules about feed in the future. For now, much to the alarm of food-safety advocates, adding plate scraps to cattle feed was fine.

Were conditions in North Carolina's rivers getting better, worse, or staying the same? It was the subject of much debate in 2004, and everyone seemed to produce data to support their own particular positions, including the Frontline Farmers.

In June, Frontline Farmers released a report claiming that water quality in four North Carolina river basins had remained stable or even improved, according to thirty-two years of data.[13] Frontline had ponied up thirty thousand dollars to pay for the review, conducted by University of Kentucky investigator Dwayne Edwards, Ph.D.

"This is not a study done by the industry or environmentalists," Chuck Stokes said at a news conference to promote the research paper. He claimed that it had been peer reviewed, but the paper was not published in a scientific journal, which would require a thorough and anonymous review by a panel of scientific experts in the field.

Edwards had looked at official state data from 1970 to 2002 and focused on the Cape Fear, Neuse, Tar-Pamlico, and White Oak river basins. He looked at seven different measurements considered to be indicators of livestock pollution in water, including fecal coliform counts showing the presence of ammonia nitrogen. He found that 46 percent of all sampling stations showed "a trend toward improving water quality," while 23 percent showed stable water quality. Only 5 percent of the samples revealed deteriorating water quality, which may have been exacerbated by urban growth in those areas. The other 26 percent was "unaccounted" for, owing to inconsistent data, Chuck told the media.

Water pollution in the river basins seemed to be "generally independent of hog populations," he said, "and any detectable trends were usually in the decreasing direction, even downstream of counties with very high hog densities."

For the next several weeks, Chuck and other Frontline members conducted a media blitz on their report. They appeared in news stories across North Carolina, insisting that their industry had done nothing to impair state waterways.

The Frontline review was not received with universal enthusiasm. Negative reaction began with the North Carolina Department of Environment and Natural Resources, whose data Edwards had used in the paper. Department officials agreed about an overall drop in pollution in the rivers, but said the data used by Edwards did not track smaller creeks and streams, which often carry pollution from hog farming.

Rick was annoyed with Frontline and its report, especially when he discovered that a PR firm had commissioned Dr. Edwards, who consistently wrote papers that were generally favorable to livestock producers. And he was put off by Frontline's insistence that the paper had been peer reviewed. Several times, Rick e-mailed Chuck asking for information on who had reviewed the paper, and under what auspices.

Chuck admitted that Edwards had sent the paper to a single colleague, who approved it. Rick asked to see a copy of the review, but it never materialized.

Finally, Rick called Edwards himself.

"I asked if he'd ever been to the Neuse River or conducted any independent water sampling, and he said he hadn't," Rick recounted to Don Webb one night. "Instead, he relied on what the industry had given him." When Rick contacted the person who allegedly reviewed the work, the man explained that he couldn't release his review without Chuck's permission.

Furious, Rick denounced the Frontline paper in a statement issued to reporters. He began by saying that the environmental group American Rivers had designated the Neuse one of North America's most threatened rivers in 1995, 1996, and 1997, citing swine pollution as a leading problem. And he went on:[14]

The report of Dr. Edwards was generated by a public relations firm. This firm and Dr. Edwards were selected, hired and funded by the hog industry. Dr. Edwards works out of the University of Kentucky, where he specializes in projects that support industrial agriculture. While the university system of North Carolina contains many of the world's leading experts on water quality, most of whom have been directly involved in water monitoring programs here, none was selected by the hog industry to conduct their analysis. Instead, through their public relations firm, they hired a professor from the University of Kentucky (Ag school) who was a good friend of the industrial animal industry. They further intentionally limited the materials provided to him. It was a result preordained to favor the industry. As a result, it is grossly lacking in credibility.

The hog industry has stated that the data they sent to Dr. Edwards were found buried in state files and had not been previously analyzed. In fact, these data had been known and used by many scientists doing water quality analysis in North Carolina. In the late 1990s, Dr. Carl Wagner used these data and applied another method of analysis that is designed to determine if a known event, such as the development of the hog industry over a specific time period, was likely to have indicated a change in water quality. In comparing the periods 1988–1990 and 1991–1993, a significant 11% increase in nitrogen concentrations was noted.

Rick Dove was a lifelong Republican, and a fairly conservative one at that. But he hated George W. Bush like poison. "Our president is the very worst thing that Mother Nature ever produced," he told anyone who would listen.

"And he's the worst thing that could happen to this country." Bush was still tremendously popular in North Carolina, so Rick's attacks didn't always endear him to people. But he felt too strongly about Bush's environmental record—which he considered abysmal—to shut up about it.

"The GOP is supposed to be conservative," Rick complained, "meaning it *conserves* and protects things, like the environment." But Bush had been an ecological disaster. When Bush ran again, Rick did something he'd never done before: He sent a contribution to a political candidate of another party—in this case, Massachusetts senator John Kerry, the liberal Democrat running against Bush. He even joined a group called Republicans for Kerry.

In July 2004, the left-of-center political group MoveOn.org asked its members to film thirty-second spots in support of Kerry. Among some twenty thousand responses was an endorsement from Rick.

Two weeks later, Rick learned his story was one of forty-one that had been selected for filming. MoveOn.org had commissioned Oscar-winning documentary filmmaker Errol Morris (*The Fog of War*) to interview people who voted for Bush in 2000 but were now backing Kerry. Rick was flown to New York City and put in front of a camera to talk about why he was voting for Kerry. In fact, he had not voted for Bush in 2000, Rick explained to the producers. "You would have to be pretty 'out there' not to be able to see Bush for what he is—an antienvironmentalist," he noted.

Rick knew just what to say. "When am I going to hear my president say, 'I blew it, folks, the buck stops here, this is my mistake, and I'm going to learn from this and we're going to go on'? I've never heard it," he began. "It's not that I'm looking for an apology. I want an admission when things are wrong that, 'I'm responsible for that.'"[15]

MoveOn.org posted seventeen of the ads online, allowing members to vote on their five favorite spots. Of the hundred thousand votes tallied, votes for Rick sent him to second place. During the 2004 Republican National Convention in New York, and for weeks before the election, swing-state voters were treated to a TV ad titled *Fishing*, and featuring the retired marine speaking in front of a plain white field saying:

My son and I did fish and then the fish got sick and we got sick and the river went belly-up. We had to give it up. We found the source of pollution. And then we began to get regulations in place that would change it. And as soon as George Bush took office, within months, he just canceled all those regulations. Essentially, he just wiped them off the books. I've been registered as a Republican for a long, long time and I cannot see four more years of that kind of leadership.[16]

In early October 2004, Helen flew to Louisville, Kentucky, for a Sierra Club conference. It was her first as an official member of the GRACE Factory Farm Project. Her duty was to staff GRACE's Sustainable Table display.

Her display offered a wide array of information: a continuous loop of *The Meatrix*, photos comparing sustainably raised to animal-factory cows, and literature on finding non-CAFO foods close to home. Helen also arranged two table place settings. On the plate marked SUSTAINABLE were printed the names of various vitamins, minerals, and trace elements, along with phrases like "less total fat" and "lots of antioxidants." On the plate labeled FACTORY FARM was a different meal, including "bacterial endotoxins," "*Cryptosporidium parvum*," "heavy metals," and "salmonella."

Children approached the table to watch *The Meatrix* over and over, enthralled with the adventures of "Moopheus" and his animal friends. Helen was thrilled by the young people's response. Now *this*, she thought, gives me hope for the future.

Helen left Louisville in triumph, making a stopover to visit her parents in Granby, Missouri, for a few days, before heading home. Don was busy with the harvest and said it would be a good time for her to spend with her folks.

On her second day in Missouri, October 8, Helen called Don. It was 6 A.M. in Outlook and he was already heading out the door for the orchards. She told him how great things had gone in Louisville, and Don said how proud the whole family was of her.

Two hours later, Helen's son David called. He told her that Don had suffered a heart attack and was on the way to the hospital.

The words pummeled Helen like falling rocks. Don had endured a severe cardiac arrest and quadruple bypass ten years before. "Call me when you get there," she said.

When David called back, the attending physician was just walking up to him. But the doctor would not talk to Helen on the telephone. Hospital policy said he could only talk to relatives present in the room. David held the phone up so Helen could hear.

"An expert medical team worked to their full potential on the way over," the doctor said bluntly and coolly. "And when he arrived, Mr. Reddout was pronounced DOA."

Helen heard a deep, gut-wrenching groan on the line. It was her son.

"David?" she said in a panic. "David, did he just say Dad is *dead*?"

"Yes, Mom. He's dead." The news was delivered flatly, surreally. Don was sixty-seven.

For a moment, all Helen could do was rage against the doctor. How could that cold-hearted bastard break this news as though he was talking about a broken arm? But Helen was not one to let anger interfere with a critical task. She pulled it together. "Tell your brother and sisters I'll be home on the next plane," Helen said. "I love you."

When Helen got home, her kids told her the details. Don had been out in the orchards on that crisp fall morning, splitting wood for the coming season, one of his favorite activities. His trusted hand Esequiel found him lying on the ground and immediately gave him CPR and called 911 on Don's cell phone.

Completely distraught, Helen was able to find a glimmer of comfort in knowing that Don died doing what he loved. And he had died the way he wished. "He always said he didn't want to linger and suffer for months," she told Karen her first night home. "And he was out on that land he cherished on a brilliant day when the sky was blue like a giant sapphire."

Don had passed away just weeks before their fiftieth anniversary, and the Reddouts had planned a long Hawaiian sojourn. But Helen's wicked sense of humor clearly had not died along with her beloved husband.

"When I go and walk into that bright light, and your father is there waiting for me," she told her kids after the funeral, "I'm going to go over and kick his *butt* for not waiting until after our anniversary! He couldn't wait a few more weeks?"

But inside, Helen was demolished. She thought back to that warm summer morning when she first saw Don. How could time pass so quickly? And how on earth was Helen going to continue to lead a family, run a fruit business, and defend her valley against the dairies without her best friend and confidant? She thought again about the handsome young cherry picker she first saw through the chipped mirror, and broke down sobbing.

The year 2004 would end on a terrible note for Helen. After Don's funeral, she had to deal with the end-of-year financials, bills from the harvest, company taxes, and closing the estate. The stress was taking its toll. Helen was tired, and she felt sick a lot.

At the urging of her children, Helen took refuge in the work of the GRACE Factory Farm Project and the Sustainable Table. The kids convinced her to fly to a weeklong gathering of the team in New York. It would be nice to see Karen and the others, Helen agreed.

It was a terrific getaway, and everyone received Helen like a cherished family member, comforting her and listening to her stories about Don. But Helen was there on serious business, too. She and Karen wanted the GRACE Factory Farm Project Team to invest in two emission-monitoring machines,

UV Hound multigas air analyzers—the canine name applied because of their accuracy in sniffing chemicals such as hydrogen sulfide and ammonia from the air. They had seen a Hound at an Iowa meeting and had been awed by its precision.

It was a large metallic canister, hooked up to a laptop computer. It pulled air in through a valve, analyzed it, and printed out a color-coded, tamper-proof report on the gases detected in parts per million or billion. Helen had borrowed one of the thirty-thousand-dollar machines before her trip and took air measurements at one of the dairies in the valley. She showed the data printouts to everyone in the room.

"These come from a huge dairy, up in Moxee, Washington," she explained. "On several return visits, the Hound showed forty-eight hundred parts per billion ammonia. This was not just peaks, but the high for hours. Anything over fifteen parts per billion is considered dangerous. Now, to get a baseline of what it was like inside one house nearby, we set the Hound up in the living room, and it read twelve hundred parts per billion, but only when the furnace came on."

Hounds had been very useful in measuring hydrogen sulfide levels as well as ammonia outside of megadairies, Helen said. One study from the State of Iowa used six air monitors to measure hydrogen sulfide emissions outside several thousand hog, chicken, and dairy CAFOs. It found that a dairy called Milk Unlimited had some of the highest hydrogen sulfide readings of all.[17]

"The State of Iowa says that people should not be exposed to more than fifteen parts per billion of hydrogen sulfide," Helen said, "but a hound outside Milk Unlimited had levels well above that limit within one month of testing. One reading came back at seventy parts per billion. These things are nothing more than hydrogen sulfide factories, even more than the pigs.

"Please, I need this new machine so badly in the valley," Helen continued, "and people all over the country could really benefit from having access to one, too."

The GRACE project agreed to purchase five of the Hounds. Helen flew back to Yakima, a feeling of satisfaction momentarily offsetting her mourning.

In November 2004, the Minnesota Farm Bureau released a twenty-seven-page booklet titled *When an Activist Group Comes to Town*. The handy little guide was created to demonize people who opposed CAFOs, especially "anti-farming" groups such as the GRACE Factory Farm Project. The bureau urged its membership to "take square aim at those who oppose farm expansion, minimizing them as 'outsiders' dividing 'vulnerable' communities and farmers."[18]

It wasn't the first time that GRACE had been labeled as dangerous. Earlier in the year, Karen had been invited by the Bureau County Board in Illinois to speak at one of their meetings. As she began her talk, warning about a proposed forty-eight-hundred-hog facility, a dissenting voice arose from the audience. The local Farm Bureau president stood and called the farmwife/schoolteacher/mom a "radical activist" who was spreading "junk science."

And then there was Trent Loos, a cattle rancher and self-proclaimed "attack dog" from Nebraska. Loos had his own platforms: a newspaper column and a syndicated radio show. He was also founder of a group called Faces of Agriculture, which, according to its Web site, www.facesofag.com, was formed to "provide producers with empowering information so they can confidently champion their industry." Loos's taste for combativeness was matched by a sharp pen and acerbic tongue. He had taken to calling Karen a "smooth-talking radical" and accused her of spreading dangerous and damaging misinformation.

Soon afterward, Faces of Ag issued a press release in which Loos blasted "activists bent on the demise of livestock agriculture in the United States." He warned that rural residents were being "misled by a bunch of well-funded, smooth-talking radicals."[19] He was referring to people like Karen Hudson and her work for the GRACE Factory Farm Project.

"GRACE claims to support family farms against corporate operations but actually favors the abolishment of all animal agriculture," Loos said in a statement. "They will stop big operations first and then they will close down the others. No livestock producer is safe."

On January 3, 2005, Canadian officials announced that a second case of mad cow had been found in an Alberta herd. Agents tracking the 141 cattle in the herd said that infected animals may have been consumed by people. Nonetheless, Canadian health officials insisted the risk of BSE entering the food chain was "very low."[20]

A week later, on January 11, a third case was found, also in Alberta. Investigators said the animal was born after 1997, when Canada banned the feeding of cattle remains to cattle. This cow had been infected, they claimed, by leftover feed produced before the ban was enacted.[21]

Food-safety advocates were stunned the next day when the USDA declared that the border with Canada would *reopen* to beef imports on March 7. But the USDA said it would monitor the latest mad cow investigations in Canada "very closely." It would also dispatch a team of American experts to Alberta to help with the effort.[22]

GRACE and Sustainable Table jumped into the fray—capitalizing on mad cow mania to get their message across. "American consumers worry that open-ing markets to Canadian beef may risk contaminating the U.S. food supply," a GRACE Factory Farm Project statement said. "The best solution for families concerned about mad cow is to buy meat from traditional family farmers who raise cows on natural feed."[23]

Alice Slater, who was now president of GRACE, said the problem was not the border, but the beef. "Cows were never meant to eat other cows," she said. "For centuries, farmers raised cows safely on grass and natural feed. Now fac-tory farms cut corners by using chicken manure, blood, and the carcasses of other animals as filler in artificial feeds. No wonder we have to worry. You can only bend nature so far before it snaps back. When cattle are raised natu-rally on pasture, the conditions for spreading BSE are virtually eliminated," she claimed.

The farm activists blasted the USDA for *still* not banning blood and animal parts in cattle feed. Other safety rules were not enforced, raising the chance for BSE to slip through the regulatory cracks. "The USDA is in a dangerous guess-ing game that plays Russian roulette with our food. Natural rules are simple concepts," Karen said in a Factory Farm Project statement. "You can be sure that food is safe without guessing or putting your faith in a government bureau-cracy."

Terry Spence, the Missouri cattle grower, agreed. "I'm not comfortable with the so-called safeguards implemented by the USDA," he warned in the state-ment. "When the USDA can't even oversee the food inspection system without regular recalls, why would consumers think they are doing their jobs on mad cow?"

In its statement, the GRACE Project listed four reasons why buying "sus-tainable" beef is healthier:

1. Sustainable ranchers do not feed their cattle animal parts, relying instead on natural diets free of growth hormones and excess antibi-otics.
2. Sustainable farmers rarely slaughter sick or injured "downer" cows and do not normally use dairy cows for beef.
3. Most traditional, sustainable farmers use smaller, independent slaughter facilities that decrease the risk of cross-contamination with factory-farmed cattle.
4. Tracing an animal's history is easier and more reliable. Sustainably raised cows are normally tracked throughout their lives by the same farmer. They are not bought at auctions, but are born on the same premises where they graze until slaughter.

The reelection of George W. Bush hardly came as good news to anti-CAFO activists. Big Ag had overwhelmingly supported Bush and the GOP over John Kerry with all the largesse that campaign finance laws would allow. Activists feared what the next four years would bring. It took only one day for them to get a taste of things to come.

On January 21, 2005, the EPA announced an unprecedented program that granted amnesty to large CAFOs that violated the federal Clean Air Act. In return, the offenders would participate in a voluntary program of monitoring air emissions at some, but not all, of the participating farms.[24]

Under the proposed plan, participating CAFOs would be cleared of any air violations in the past as well as during the two years of the program. The EPA would collect data on air emissions. As part of the agreement, the EPA would delay new CAFO regulations until the data-collection period ended. Once final standards were established, all CAFOs would then apply for their own air-emission permits and install pollution-control measures as needed.

For environmentalists, the deal carried the stench of cronyism. If the agreement seemed like a free ride for Big Ag, there was ample reason for that. Factory-farm giant Tyson Foods, supported by a fleet of lobbyists, had pushed hard for the voluntary monitoring program. Not coincidentally, Tyson had contributed $100,000 to the second Bush inauguration celebration, more than almost any other entity in the country.[25]

Federal regulators hailed the deal as a breakthrough that would finally set national standards for air emissions from livestock facilities, environmentalist protests notwithstanding. It would provide one-stop shopping for officials to determine the extent of the problem, and establish a nationwide program to address it. They claimed that the alternative—hitting offenders with lawsuits one by one with Clean Air Act violations—was too costly and time-consuming.

Data gathered from the two-year program would provide a "representative sampling from which we can estimate the emissions from all kinds of farms around the country," EPA spokesperson Cynthia Bergman told reporters. "This way we can get far more CAFOs into compliance than by the traditional case-by-case approach."[26]

The pig people were also pleased. The National Pork Producers Council said monitoring would offer "sound scientific data" that farmers needed to cut emissions. But now it was time to celebrate. "This has been a long, exhaustive and costly endeavor that NPPC has led on behalf of America's pork producers," said one NPPC leader.[27]

Activists were galled that all farms that signed up for the program would get amnesty—even if they did not submit to air monitoring. In fact, some four thousand CAFO operators were expected to register for the program, mostly hog and poultry producers. But only thirty or so would actually have their air quality monitored.

Critics also denounced the low fees and penalties that the four thousand farms would have to pay. Participants would transfer $2,500 into a fund to cover monitoring costs on the thirty sites. Each CAFO would also have to pay a onetime penalty that would then "pardon" the facility for any "presumed" violations. The penalties, based on size, ranged from $200 to $100,000. Clean Air Act fines can reach $27,500 per day, per facility.

"It's chump change," scoffed Michele Merkel, a leading attorney for NRDC. Merkel, a former EPA staff attorney, had seen the writing on the wall when Bush became president in 2001. Predicting that the EPA would be rendered toothless by the Bush administration, she resigned her EPA post and headed for the private sector to continue the battle.

The crusade for "sustainable" food was initially a difficult one; Karen, Rick, and Helen realized that consumers saw only higher price tags and higher grocery bills. Clearly, "happy pork" and "certified humane" chicken at Whole Foods (or Whole Paycheck, as some call it), would cost more than Tyson chicken at Safeway. They doubted that the public would cheerfully be willing to spend more on food simply because it was not produced in an animal factory. But, to their surprise, a May 2005 poll of Midwestern consumers showed that they would.[28]

The survey, conducted by researchers at Ohio State University, showed that 92 percent of people in that state agreed or strongly agreed it was important for "farm animals to be well cared for," and 85 percent said that farm animal quality of life was important, even if the animal was being raised for their meat, milk, or eggs. Perhaps most stunning—and annoying to agribusiness—was the finding that 81 percent of respondents agreed that "the well-being of farm animals is just as important as the well-being of pets." Three-fourths agreed that "farm animals should be protected from feeling physical pain" (undoubtedly, the vast majority of farmers also agreed with that).

The survey tended to support the practice of what Sustainable Table and *The Meatrix* were preaching. More than half of those polled said they would spend more on meat, poultry, or dairy products if the products had labels proving they came from humanely treated animals. Some would pay up to 25 percent more, they said.

Karen read about the study in the news and smiled to herself. "At least people in Ohio won't think we're crazy," she said to Rocky. "They know we need to respect our food."

In June 2005, the U.S. government confirmed what had been suspected for months: It had identified the nation's second case of mad cow disease. And this one was not imported from Canada; it was homegrown. The beef cow from Alabama had been a "downer" and was sent to a rendering plant for animals unfit for food.[29]

The suspected cattle had been slaughtered seven months before, but the animal's records had been mislabeled. Tissues from that animal were mixed with others, causing a serious delay in pinpointing which herd the cow had come from. A lab in England had confirmed the new case after U.S. tests proved inconclusive.

Despite the Keystone Kops–like handling of such an important public health issue, federal officials insisted that government food inspectors were doing their jobs. "The fact that this animal was blocked from entering the food supply tells us that safeguards are working exactly as they should," USDA Secretary Mike Johanns told reporters.[30]

American consumers may have been reassured, but foreign governments were not. Since the first cow with mad cow disease was discovered in Yakima in 2003, more than fifty nations had banned U.S. beef.[31] Japan, the largest customer for American beef, did not lift its ban. One country had since lifted its prohibition: In 2003, Taiwan bought more than $76 million worth of beef from the United States. But within hours of the second case, it announced that it was reinstating its blockade. It was another blow for the owners of America's ninety-six million cow herd, the world's largest.

It had now been eighteen months since the first mad cow was discovered in Washington, but the United States had done nothing to prevent the feeding of cattle to cattle. The FDA had proposed its ban on mixing bovine blood, restaurant scraps, and chicken litter into feed, but in June 2005, all three practices were still thriving.

The FDA wasn't giving interviews on the subject, but issued a written statement saying only that it would implement new restrictions. However, there was no firm timeline for putting such new restrictions in place. Many Democrats weren't buying it. Representative Rosa DeLauro (D-CA) groused to reporters, "It's a lot of talk, a lot of press releases, and no action."

Karen Hudson had received so many "SOS calls" and frantic letters from neighbors facing the arrival of factory farms, she had lost count. In August, she received yet another e-mail. Angie Litterst lived near the town of Reynolds, not far from Quad Cities.

Before writing to Karen in exasperation, Angie had detailed her concerns about factory farming in a guest editorial of her hometown paper, the *Quad-City Times*:[32]

> In May, I discovered that Jim O'Leary, of O'Leary Farms, was planning to build a 2,400-head hog confinement within a half mile of my rural Rock Island County home. A dozen homes are within about a mile radius of this site, and the entire town of Reynolds is within two miles. In similar situations, surrounding property values have dropped 5 percent to 90 percent. It seems unethical for one person to create financial hardship for all those around them. The *Quad-City Times* reports a new manure spill from these types of facilities almost weekly.

Angie also shed light on a little-known fact of factory farming—much of it is actually subsidized by American taxpayers:

> I foolishly assumed the government would protect us from such threats. Instead, it offers incentives to factory farms. From 1995–2003, Mr. O'Leary received over $688,000 in government subsidies and his wife received over $672,000. Our tax dollars are being given to someone who is now turning around and destroying our homes, our rural environment and our community. This situation is wrong, and if things do not change, these confinements will continue to pollute our air and water. I beg Mr. O'Leary not to destroy our homes. Will he use this opportunity to abandon construction at this location and in doing so, become the local hero, or will he continue acting only for his own personal gain?

Angie would soon get her answer, as neighbors began reporting mysterious illnesses. Eventually, her own family would also be affected.

It had been four and a half years since Dave Inskeep had pumped dairy lagoon wastewater into a ravine. In September 2005, Inskeep was indicted on one count of knowingly discharging pollutants into the waters of the United States without a permit. He faced up to three years in prison and fines of fifty thousand dollars per day for his violations of the Clean Water Act.[33]

"These allegations suggest a blatant disregard for the laws that protect them," Acting Assistant Attorney General Kelly A. Johnson said in a Justice Department statement.

"The Justice Department takes violations of the laws that protect our waters very seriously and will prosecute such violations to the full extent." In the same statement, U.S. Attorney Jan Paul Miller declared that environmental laws "are not suggestions; they are mandates that will be enforced."

The Justice Department said that a summons would soon be issued for Inskeep to appear in federal court in Peoria.

Finally, Karen thought, justice was about to be done.

14

The topic of strange and deadly emerging diseases is common fodder for tropical medicine conferences, cocktail party chatter, and Syfy channel movies. People are captivated by tales of nature run amok: bacteria that eat flesh, birds that spread flu, cows that go mad. By the late twentieth century, a new threat was being added to the bizarre list. It was barely pronounceable but it was deadly: methicillin-resistant *Staphylococcus aureus*, better known as MRSA.

MRSA had emerged in the United Kingdom in the 1960s, and was first detected in North America in the early 1980s, mostly among IV drug users. It is a highly tenacious strain of a common staph bacteria that has developed resistance to a wide range of antibiotics, including methicillin, dicloxacillin, nafcillin, and oxacillin. MRSA is spread easily in hospitals and health care settings; patients with open wounds, catheters, and immune-deficiency problems are most susceptible to infection.

At the end of the 1990s, U.S. hospitals were treating 127,000 cases of MRSA a year. In 2005, that number had doubled to 278,000; more than 94,000 of those cases would be life-threatening and 18,650 would end in death—50 percent more than the number of AIDS-related deaths that year, which numbered about 12,500.[1]

A healthy person could be infected with MRSA without showing symptoms for months or even years. MRSA first appears in the form of small pimplelike bumps, sometimes with fever or skin rash. Over the next few days, the bumps become painful, pus-filled boils. About 75 percent of cases remain on the skin, and usually respond to treatment. But more virulent strains are more invasive, rapidly infecting organs and causing systemwide sepsis, toxic shock, "flesh-eating" pneumonia, and, ultimately, death.

These fast-spreading types of MRSA are called community-associated MRSA, or CA-MRSA. These strains, which first emerged in the late 1990s, seemed to occur in nonhospital settings. One study done in San Francisco in 2004–2005 showed that an alarming one in three hundred residents was infected with MRSA, and more than 85 percent of those cases occurred outside of any type of health care setting.[2]

Where was all that MRSA coming from? Many CAFO activists suspected the culprit was low-dose antibiotic use in CAFOs to prevent disease and promote growth. Scientists would soon confirm their suspicions. In December 2005, a Dutch study was published in *Emerging Infectious Diseases*, concerning twenty-six pig farmers in the southeast region of the Netherlands who found their rate of MRSA was more than *760 times* greater than among patients admitted to Dutch hospitals. In fact, the general Dutch population had one of the lowest rates of MRSA in Europe, yet Dutch farmers were disproportionately infected.[3]

"Here we demonstrate transmission of MRSA between an animal and human," the authors wrote. The farmers' unexpectedly high rate indicated that their profession greatly increased their risk for MRSA colonization. While the authors called for larger studies to confirm the observations, they could still state with confidence that "pig farming poses a significant risk factor for MRSA carriage in humans."

As 2005 came to a close, Rick Dove read all the new MRSA stories with an increasing sense of alarm. Here, he thought, was yet another example of payback when man messes around with the laws of nature. And nobody likes payback.

"Pigs were just not meant to be raised on drugs, it's that simple," Rick wrote in an e-mail to fellow activists Karen, Helen, Don Webb, and Chris Petersen. "It's not what Mother Nature intended, and it's coming back to haunt us." MRSA had already been reported in North Carolina, and Rick wondered how much of it was being carried around by the thousands of people who worked in the state's swine factories.

Rick also wondered if MRSA was breeding in the state's lagoons and sprayfields. But it didn't look as though North Carolina's waste systems would be replaced any time soon. After five years and $17 million in research, Mike Williams and his panel of experts were set to issue their final report on candidate technologies to replace the lagoon-and-sprayfield system, as stipulated in the agreement between the attorney general, Smithfield, Premium Standard Farms, and Frontline Farmers.[4]

The good news was that five systems had been deemed technically feasible and effective in protecting the environment. One method used metal tanks to treat liquid waste before discharging it; one mixed hog manure with organic matter like wood chips to make a marketable compost; two systems burned solids to produce energy while also yielding methane and hydrogen to sell to energy companies, and ash that could be sold as fertilizer; and the final method created biogases, which were also marketable. Don Lloyd's vermiculture system was not selected.

The bad news was that none of the five came in under the crucial nine-cents-a-pound limit.

Smithfield Foods was suddenly off the hook, as Rick had predicted. Having first dodged litigation from Attorney General (and now Governor) Easley, the company was now freed of the looming requirement to replace the lagoons at its North Carolina facilities. Smithfield was happy, and Rick was livid.

Costs aside, there was much to admire in the five systems that Mike Williams and his team had identified. The trick was to make them more affordable for contract producers. In early 2006, Frontline Farmers began talking with the North Carolina chapter of Environmental Defense, a mainstream national group, to explore ways to make the lagoon alternatives economically feasible. Now they were going public with their plan.

"Five years ago, a partnership between hog farmers and environmentalists may have seemed as unlikely as sprouts on a BBQ sandwich," Chuck Stokes and North Carolina Environmental Defense attorney Daniel Whittle said in a *News & Observer* guest editorial on January 15. "Today, members of our two groups are working toward a common goal: making hog production in North Carolina profitable and clean."[5]

The pig farmer and the environmentalist both agreed that the five alternatives offered a "logical starting point," and said they "symbolize the significant progress that has been made in the collective thinking about hog farms." In fact, the whole search had brought at least some parties in the warring sides together. "Over time many farmers began to realize that the environmentalists involved in the process are not out to put them out of business, and environmentalists began to see that some farmers are ready to move beyond lagoons to cleaner waste systems," they wrote.

But, they added, "We cannot be intimidated by the current estimated costs of new technologies." Pollution-control costs drop with economies of scale. Stokes and Whittle called for pork companies and state and federal agencies to provide financial incentives for lagoon conversions.

Back in 2001, lawyer Nicolette Hahn had argued successfully in federal court that all swine CAFOs were required to have Clean Water Act permits. Soon after, Smithfield lawyers said they would enter into settlement negotiations with the plaintiffs—Waterkeeper, the Neuse River Foundation, and the Lower Neuse Riverkeeper—to avoid going to trial.

It was now January 2006. (Nicolette had left Waterkeeper to raise cattle with her new husband, cattle rancher Bill Niman, in Bolinas, California.) The long dispute was coming to an end. Waterkeeper managed to extend the deal well beyond the facilities initially sued; the settlement would now affect every swine facility owned by Murphy-Brown in North Carolina—more than 275 in all.[6]

Among the details of the settlement was a commitment by Murphy-Brown to install a computerized weather alert system that would send "red flag" warnings to all 275 facilities, prohibiting them from spraying onto fields when a rainstorm was imminent. This provision would cut down significantly on pathogenic runoffs into area waterways, the Waterkeeper Alliance noted. Murphy-Brown would install automatic shut-off devices as well to halt spray guns whenever the wind speeds reached 15 miles per hour, to prevent aerosolized liquid manure from blowing into ditches and streams.

The company also agreed to a "comprehensive groundwater risk assessment" by an independent consultant who would evaluate every Murphy-Brown swine operation for signs of leaking lagoons or "sprayfield infiltration." Any significant risk to human health or the environment would be addressed by the company. Independent surface-water experts would likewise conduct a two-year program at select Murphy-Brown facilities to identify how sprayfield runoff reaches waterways.

In addition, Murphy-Brown would hire an independent consultant to review its current "structural measures" to prevent runoff waste from entering ditches, streams, and rivers, followed by a $1.2 million upgrade on pollution-control measures at its North Carolina CAFOs. These "best management practices" might include wetland creation, buffer zones, and/or filter strips, plus improved water control through dikes and detention areas.

Murphy-Brown also consented to get Clean Water Act permits for all of its hog CAFOs in the state, as well as those of its contractors—something that Smithfield lawyers had argued in court was unnecessary. If it did not comply with the terms of the settlement, Murphy-Brown was obliged to pay "significant monetary penalties." Penalty money would be earmarked for wetlands creation and preservation by North Carolina Coastal Land Trust. The court would keep jurisdiction over the process for at least seven years.

The deal was a breakthrough for activists against factory farms. Indeed, it was an unabashed victory for the plaintiffs, who got virtually everything they had asked for. In addition, it was an important move toward reducing the impact of lagoon-and-sprayfield systems. Rick allowed himself to savor the victory, but privately he received news of the deal with mixed emotions. It had not come close to accomplishing their ultimate goal, to eliminate lagoons and sprayfields altogether. That is why Rick had always wanted to go to trial, although he realized that a settlement was inevitable. He and his fellow activists viewed the Murphy-Brown settlement as a stopgap measure, a temporary step toward reducing lagoon and sprayfield pollution, until a new method was found.

Smithfield executives put on a happy public face and congratulated themselves for their robust defense of ecology. "We are very pleased with this settlement," said Dennis Treacy, Smithfield's vice president for environmental and corporate affairs, "which acknowledges Smithfield Foods' environmental stewardship efforts, and its position as a food-industry leader in helping preserve and protect the natural resources in the communities where we live and work."[7]

For years, America's giant poultry producers had been purposely using subtherapeutic levels of antibiotics in broiler operations. For biological reasons that remain unclear, low-dose antibiotics cause birds to grow faster, bringing them to market more quickly and thereby cutting costs on feed and labor. But in the mid-2000s, the biggest chicken companies discovered through extensive market research that consumers would not only prefer antibiotic-free chicken but would pay a premium for it.

By January 2006, four of the country's top ten producers were removing low-dose antibiotics from broiler chicken feed: Tyson Foods, Gold Kist, Perdue Farms, and Foster Farms.[8] Scientists and activists were impressed. "It is the first time that these companies have admitted to major quantitative reductions in antibiotic use. And it's not just one company but a tier of companies—the top tier of companies," said Margaret Mellon, director of the Union of Concerned Scientists, a member of the Keep Antibiotics Working coalition.

Tyson, the number-one chicken company in the United States, reduced antibiotic use the most—with a 93 percent drop between 1997 and 2004—from 853,000 to just 59,000 pounds. By 2004, less than 1 percent of the company's broilers were given antibiotics, company officials boasted. Perdue Farms had stopped using antibiotics for growth promotion a few years earlier after it "became obvious that it was a concern," said the company's chief veterinarian Bruce Stewart-Brown. Foster Farms reported that just 1 percent of its flocks were now receiving antibiotics.

But as huge as the four companies were, they still only accounted for 38 percent of the broiler chickens produced in the nation.

Even so, consumer groups, environmentalists, and infectious-disease specialists all applauded the move. Rick saw it as another victory in following the laws of nature. And it was manna for the chicken industry's vast PR, marketing, and advertising campaigns.

Arkansas-based Tyson Foods, founded in 1935, likes to maintain a folksy image on TV and in the supermarket—even though it is the largest processor and marketer of chicken, beef, and pork in the world and the second-largest food company on the Fortune 500. Ending the antibiotic practice was not only consumer-friendly, it kept Tyson in line with its own corporate values to "strive to be faith-friendly, provide a safe work environment, and serve as stewards of the animals, land, and environment entrusted to it."[9]

In January, Frontline Farmers and Environmental Defense had vowed to make alternatives to waste lagoons affordable for North Carolina farmers. In March 2006, the two groups announced they would develop a voluntary plan to encourage widespread implementation of the five new technologies available.

"It's time to turn research into reality and put the results—and the benefits—directly into the hands of farmers," said ED's Dan Whittle in a press statement. "There are a lot of motivated farmers who are stepping forward and want the new technologies as soon as possible. They should get them, and be rewarded for their pioneer spirit."[10]

Frontline's president, Lamont Futrell, said that North Carolina farmers truly cared about protecting the environment and public health. "Alternative technologies can help us do that and still protect the future for our families and the pork industry," he insisted.

The two groups estimated that $20 million would help fifty to one hundred swine producers in the state install the alternative technologies on their properties and kick-start the transition away from lagoons. Money could come from the hog industry and federal and state sources, as well as the North Carolina Clean Water Management Trust Fund, they said.

The innovations would not only benefit the environment, they would stimulate business. "Putting a sufficient number of new technologies on the ground will increase competition, prompt engineering improvements and spur the development of markets for new by-products that will increase farm revenues," continued Dan Whittle in the statement.

Rick and other environmentalists applauded the move; they viewed it as a step toward eliminating lagoons, and not perpetuating them forever. *The News & Observer*, in a March 13 editorial, also heralded the effort.[11]

"State legislators should make permanent the moratorium on new lagoons, set to expire in 2007, to encourage the use of the new options. And they should consider requiring power companies to generate a portion of their energy from sources like the biogases that the new technologies create," the paper declared. "Give hog farmers every chance to operate cleanly and affordably, so the state can preserve jobs and the industry that creates them."

On March 13, the USDA announced the country's third case of mad cow disease. It was discovered in a herd in Alabama. John Clifford, the US-DA's chief veterinarian, told reporters on a conference call that the cow in question lived its last year on a farm in Alabama, but investigators had not yet figured out where the animal was born and raised. The cow had been put down by a vet and buried on the farm, and "did not enter the human food or animal feed chains," Clifford said.[12]

The announcement came weeks after the Canadian Food Inspection Agency confirmed Canada's fourth case of BSE since its first case was confirmed in May 2003. The animal was still on the Alberta farm where it had been born. No part of it entered the food chain.[13]

Inexplicably, the federal government followed the news the next day with plans for reducing its BSE-testing program, which critics had already said was anemic and ineffective. Back in 2003, just fifty-five BSE routine tests were performed each day on U.S. herds. By 2006, that number had reached one thousand tests per day. But that was still a miniscule fraction of the ninety-five million head of U.S. cattle being raised at any given time.[14]

The testing program had detected the infected cow in Alabama. But the USDA was still planning to gut the program. USDA Secretary Mike Johanns insisted that testing was "not a food safety measure" but rather a "way to find out the prevalence of the disease." The increase in testing that was implemented two years earlier, Johanns said, was always meant to be temporary and was not meant to ensure food safety. Activists like Helen and Karen hardly found those words reassuring.

The new USDA plan would test 40,000 cattle each year, or about 110 animals daily (a 90 percent reduction). That figure alarmed safety advocates. "This would be a tenth of a percent of all animals," Jean Halloran of the Consumers Union protested. It was such a small sample size, she said, "it approaches a policy of 'Don't look, don't find.'"[15]

But industry groups bristled at the idea of wider testing. If consumers got their way, every bovine in the country would need to be tested at great expense, bemoaned Gary Weber, head of regulatory affairs for the National Cattlemen's Beef Association in Colorado. "It's not cost-effective; it's not necessary," he said. "The consumers we've done focus groups with are comfortable that this is a very rare disease and we've got safeguards in place."[16]

In March 2006, GRACE Factory Farm Project—which was in the process of transforming itself and its consultants into a new group, the Socially Responsible Agriculture Project (SRAP)—released a sequel to *The Meatrix* called *The Meatrix II: Revolting.* This time, they took on megadairies and the use of rBGH growth hormone.

Given that Helen and Karen were the SRAP experts on milking operations, they were assigned to help Diane Hatz gather a list of factoids and other information for the script. Helen and Karen spent weeks online pulling together studies, papers, and other findings on the effects of milk factories on health, the environment, the cows, and their milk. Among the things they found:

- In the mid-1800s, the average cow yielded just under two quarts of milk per day. In 1960, the yield was just over nine quarts. Today, due to "selective breeding, and genetic engineering," cows produce twenty-four quarts per day on average, and some can yield fifty quarts.[17]
- The U.S. dairy industry sometimes has difficulty replacing worn-out cows. Here, the average dairy cow is productive for about 1.75 lactations (each lactation lasts from 300 to 340 days) compared to 6 or 7 lactations in New Zealand. About 40 percent of U.S. heifers never even see a second lactation.[18]
- The Nebraska Center for Rural Affairs estimated that each new one-thousand-head dairy in Nebraska had the capacity to displace ten or more family-sized farms.[19]
- A preliminary study from seven dairy feedlots over six years indicated there was "significant contamination" from waste lagoons. High levels of nitrate, ammonia, chloride, nitrogen, and total dissolved solids were discovered in nearby monitoring wells, and these rose as dairy herds grew.[20] Even a lined dairy lagoon can leak a million gallons a year.[21]
- An Oregon State University study found that salmonella, *E. coli*, and other bacteria in feed samples from Oregon dairies had a high rate of antibiotic resistance. All of the samples of Enterobacteriaceae—a bacterial family that includes salmonella and *E. coli*—were resistant either to ampicillin, tetracycline, or streptomycin.[22]
- A 1988 Illinois survey found more than two hundred different animal drugs on dairy farms, 58 percent of them not approved for use on dairy cows. Meanwhile, routine FDA tests only detect four types of antibiotics, which are sold without prescription at farm-supply stores.[23]

- The Consumers Union says that cows injected with Posilac have higher rates of mastitis, cystic ovaries, reproductive problems, digestive disorders, bloat, diarrhea, enlarged hocks, and lesions causing lameness, increased body temperature, and reduction in hemoglobin.[24]
- The Government Accountability Office advised the FDA not to approve Posilac in 1993, saying the resulting risks of increased antibiotic residues in milk posed an "unacceptable risk" for human health.[25]
- According to author Dr. Samuel Epstein, IGF-1, a powerful tumor promoter, is up to ten times more prevalent and more than ten times more potent in milk from treated cows. He claims that it resists pasteurization and digestive enzymes and is absorbed by the human intestinal wall.[26]
- The connection between IGF-1 and cancer has been corroborated by two ongoing studies at Harvard: the Physicians' Health Study[27] and the Nurses' Health Study.[28]
- The average bovine produces 170 kilograms of nitrogen waste per year. Fifty percent of this nitrogen waste is in the form of urea in the urine.[29]
- Ammonia production from bovine waste is at least ten times greater than human waste, and cow waste products are responsible for 48 percent of ammonia emissions in the United States. Poultry causes 16 percent, soil 14 percent, households 5 percent, fertilizer 3 percent, and motor vehicles 30 percent.[30]

Spring of 2006 brought welcome news for animal-factory activists, proving just how far the CAFO issue had entered into the national consciousness. The Pew Charitable Trusts announced a $2.6 million grant to the Johns Hopkins Bloomberg School of Public Health that would establish an expert inquiry into the potential risks of modern livestock farming.

The National Commission on Industrial Farm Animal Production (later renamed the Pew Commission on Industrial Farm Animal Production) brought together medical professionals, veterinarians, religious leaders, ethicists, nutritionists, experts in state and federal policy, infectious-disease experts, public health leaders, and livestock producers to carry out a two-year study into the impacts of CAFOs on the environment, public health, animal welfare, and rural communities.

The commission was charged with developing consensus recommendations to solve the problems created by CAFOs in the areas of public health, the environment, animal welfare, and rural communities. Among the specific issues it would examine included "zoonotic diseases (animal-to-human), such as avian influenza, *E. coli* and salmonella; manure and waste disposal systems; chicken litter; air and water pollution; and the use of chicken feed supplemented with arsenic-based growth promoters."

John Carlin, the former Kansas governor, was appointed chairman of the group, which also included Dan Glickman, USDA secretary under Bill Clinton; Thomas Hayes, president of Cargill Meat Solutions Corporation; Bill Niman of Niman Ranch, Inc.; Fedele Bauccio, cofounder and CEO of Bon Appétit Management Company, a sustainable food–service outfit; Mary Wilson, M.D., associate professor in the Department of Population and International Health at Harvard School of Public Health and associate clinical professor of medicine at Harvard Medical School; James Merchant, M.D., Dr.P.H., dean of the University of Iowa College of Public Health; Frederick Kirschenmann, Ph.D., Distinguished Fellow at the Leopold Center for Sustainable Agriculture at Iowa State University; Alan M. Goldberg, Ph.D., professor at Johns Hopkins Bloomberg School of Public Health; Brother David Andrews of the National Catholic Rural Life Conference; Marion Nestle, author, nutritionist, and professor at New York University; and others.

The commission would hold two public hearings and eleven invitation-only meetings, culminating in a comprehensive report with recommendations for legislators, the agricultural industry, and the public.

Not every member was thrilled to be there. Some, like Thomas Hayes of Cargill, the pork giant, agreed to sit on the commission as a way of making sure that industry's voice was heard (he later quietly resigned). And Christopher Galen of the National Milk Producers Federation expressed concern that the study panel might vilify large-animal farmers. But he welcomed the chance to share farm research that he promised would "debunk . . . urban legends about food production."

Kay Johnson of the Animal Agriculture Alliance also expressed alarm. "Our concern is that there is a lot of potential for bias in the report based on the makeup of the commission," she told the media, "because we see that the commission has a dearth of experts in the field of animal agriculture."[31]

The AAA is a pro-industry organization that promotes the message that raising livestock boosts the national economy. The AAA also claims to support animal well-being, which its Web site says is "central to producing safe, high-quality, affordable food and other products essential to our daily lives":[32]

The positive message of feeding the world safely and inexpensively doesn't sell papers or network advertising. Therefore, animal agriculture has often found itself on the defensive and must become proactive in order to make a real impact. . . . The image of the family farm with its red barn, a few chickens in the yard, some pigs in the mud, and cows in the field isn't accurate anymore. Today, U.S. animal agriculture is a dynamic, specialized endeavor—the envy of the rest of the world. Modern American agriculture allows 2 percent of the people to feed 100 percent of the population. Well cared for, healthy livestock and poultry is the key to this efficiency, resulting in the highest quality and most affordable food in the history of the world.

The AAA also lists several "myths and facts" about modern animal agriculture. For example, it says it is a myth that "'factory farms' confine animals in crowded, unventilated cages and sheds." Instead, they are "generally kept in barns and similar housing . . . to protect the health and welfare of the animal. Housing protects animals from predators, disease, and bad weather or extreme climate. Housing also makes breeding and birth less stressful, protects young animals, and makes it easier for farmers to care for both healthy and sick animals. Modern housing is well-ventilated, warm, well-lit, clean, and scientifically-designed to meet an animal's specific needs—including temperature, light, water and food."

Johnson also worried that the panel was based at Johns Hopkins. "[Johns Hopkins's] Center for a Livable Future sponsors some programs that are extremely anti-modern-animal-agriculture," she noted, but then softened her assertion a bit: "I think it's important for us as an industry to continue to monitor; to be engaged with the commission, providing information and input; to continue to be very open with them about our concerns and to ensure the final outcome is fair and balanced."

At one point, Johnson prepared a PowerPoint presentation to warn industry leaders about the commission and its appointees, and posted it on the AAA Web site. Among the "Industry Concerns About the Commission & Potential Threat," the slides said, were the "potential for predetermined, biased conclusions based on funding source and makeup of the commission; negative findings and recommendations may receive considerable media attention; next step could be recommendations for intolerable legislation and regulation; and potential loss of business opportunity and profitability."

But Johnson still held that her group would "continue to be cooperative with the commission as long as there is a sincere effort to work on the issues." But AAA would also maintain a watchdog role and reply "aggressively to mischaracterizations and inaccuracies of the issues being addressed and challenge and correct misinformation."

If the AAA was playing watchdog, the Center for Consumer Freedom was a pit bull, calling the Pew effort a "stealth campaign against meat production and consumption stacked with opponents of animal agriculture and advocates of strict vegetarianism, which threatens to attack farmers and demonize the meat on America's dinner tables."[33]

"This Pew-funded panel is a Trojan horse for organized activists who want to radically change the way meat is produced or eliminate it entirely," said David Martosko, director of research for CCF. "If you wanted to assemble a kangaroo court to rubber-stamp the opinion that modern meat production is the root of all evil, you could hardly do better than this group. The only thing missing is PETA. As it is, the current panel of activists can't possibly be taken seriously."

David Inskeep, age sixty-four, pleaded guilty in federal court in March 2006 to a misdemeanor violation of the U.S. Clean Water Act.[34] Inskeep had originally been charged with a felony offense that carried a three-year prison term. But in order to take a plea deal, he admitted to committing one count of negligently discharging pollutants into waters of the United States without a permit, a misdemeanor. Sentencing was scheduled for July 13, 2006. He faced up to a year in jail and fines of up to $100,000.

"Mr. Inskeep had many opportunities to lawfully dispose of the waste, but chose instead to disregard them and violate the Clean Water Act by discharging millions of gallons of waste generated by the dairy operation into nearby tributaries," a U.S. assistant attorney general announced. "The defendant's actions introduced pollutants into the environment and he now faces the consequences of his actions."

In July, Inskeep would be sentenced to thirty days' imprisonment, a year of supervised release, and a three-thousand-dollar fine. That was later reduced further to thirty days at a halfway house. Until the end, Inskeep insisted that he had done the right thing back in 2001. He believed his actions had saved Elmwood from a much larger spill caused by the complete failure of his lagoon. "The right thing was to prevent the dam from blowing," he said in court.

Is animal waste a pollutant? Federal statute is surprisingly vague on the subject, and a rancorous fight has broken out over whether the government should classify animal waste as a hazardous substance.

The real question is how to interpret the federal Superfund law, technically called the Comprehensive Environmental Response, Compensation, and Liability Act, or CERCLA. It was created in 1980 after the scandal of Love Canal and other toxic debacles. CERCLA gives the government sweeping powers to force polluters to stop, or clean up, discharges of hazardous materials that could endanger the environment or public health.

People and groups can legally bring CERCLA lawsuits against polluters, but the statute had never been tested when it came to manure—until 2001, when the city of Tulsa sued poultry companies for polluting the Lake Eucha watershed district. A federal court ruled that phosphate in chicken litter was a "hazardous substance" under the Superfund law. The ruling was later vacated, but it started a precedent, one that left many in the agricultural sector extremely nervous and agitated.

Then their worst fears materialized. In 2004, the city of Waco, Texas, filed lawsuits against fourteen dairies upstream from the Lake Waco watershed, which supplies the city's drinking water. The city alleged that phosphorus in cow manure was a hazardous substance. A federal district judge declined to dismiss the case. The next year, Oklahoma's attorney general filed suit against large chicken producers in Arkansas, claiming under CERCLA that damage had occurred to the Illinois River watershed from their improper poultry litter use.

"The amount of phosphorus dumped every year into this area from our friends across the border in Arkansas equals the waste of 10.7 million people, more than the population of Oklahoma, Kansas, and Arkansas *combined*," Attorney General Drew Edmondson told reporters when filing the suit. He said that more than 70 percent of one of the state's most beautiful recreational jewels, Lake Tenkiller, was oxygen-dead, and Lake Francis, "once a recreational Mecca along the Arkansas border, is a mere marsh today," he said. "Unless we stop this, our future is rancid."[35]

The Oklahoma lawsuit was the last straw for Big Ag, whose lobbyists mobilized on Capitol Hill in 2005 and lobbied for a House bill to amend CERCLA "to provide that manure is not considered a hazardous substance or pollutant or contaminant."[36] The Senate bill, introduced the following summer, would carry thirty-five sponsors, thirty-one of them Republican. Industry wanted the law passed badly. In early 2005, it formed the Farmers for Clean Air and Water Coalition, whose mission was to lobby for a permanent manure exemption in CERCLA.

The coalition claims to represent farmers and ranchers across the country, though its roster reads more like a who's who of major trade organizations, including the American Farm Bureau Federation, American Meat Institute, Dairy Farmers of America, Farm Credit Council, Fertilizer Institute, National Cattlemen's Beef Association, National Chicken Council, National Council of Farmer Cooperatives, National Milk Producers Federation, National Pork Producers Council, and the National Turkey Federation. It is not clear how many small, family-run farms are members.

The coalition's mission was to fight against what it termed "frivolous multimillion-dollar lawsuits" against farms, and to battle against efforts to declare them Superfund toxic-waste sites simply because they generated animal manure.

The group would soon throw its $600,000 war chest behind the effort, lobbying on Capitol Hill to warn legislators: "If normal animal manure is found to be a hazardous substance under CERCLA, then virtually every farm operation in the United States could be potentially exposed to liabilities and penalties."[37] The resulting legal explosion, they further warned, would push factory farms overseas and devastate the U.S. market.

To Rick, Helen, and Karen, the coalition's mission to classify factory-farm poop as safe for health and the environment was both laughable and dangerous. The CERCLA battle would soon become another front in the war to defend rural communities.

On June 28, 2006, the Pew Commission on Industrial Farm Animal Production held its first invitation-only meeting in Des Moines. Among those testifying was a University of Iowa group presenting research into avian flu and the threat it posed to people via swine.

These researchers warned that an emerging avian flu viral strain could find its way into a swine CAFO. There, it could rapidly mutate and be passed to workers and others beyond the farms. New strains of avian flu could combine with swine flu viruses, resulting in a strain of swine flu that would be deadly to people. Viruses pass easily between pigs and people, so a new avian component could make swine flu more virulent, the scientists said.

Hog CAFOs are supposed to be completely closed environments, in order to protect the pigs from outside diseases. Visitors are usually required to shower and don special protective clothing (for the animals' health) before going inside a confinement. But these are not hermetically sealed environments, scientists told the panel; pathogens can enter and exit a CAFO in a number of ways other than via swine workers.

Flies are a proven vector of CAFO diseases.[38] Another source is lagoon wastewater from swine CAFOs that is recycled back into the animal housing to wash out the barns. The nonstop recycling of pig viruses in CAFO herds and flocks gives a virus ample opportunity to mutate or recombine to create much more efficient modes of transmission, including from human to human.

In addition, wildfowl routinely land in CAFO lagoons, where they can easily shed influenza viruses into the water. This can also happen at facilities that use water from ponds or rivers.

The forensics of rapidly mutating pathogens makes investigations challenging, the scientists testified. Populations exposed to CAFO pathogens are difficult to define because bugs such as a novel avian influenza virus may be highly transmissible well beyond a farm community setting. Those who worked in CAFOs might serve as a "bridging population" between the animals and other people in their communities.

Providing a different perspective that day was Iowa's sustainable hog farmer, Chris Petersen, who testified on his ecological practices. Recounting the event afterward via e-mail, he wrote: "First, I quickly realized that I was the only one there as an actual producer involved in any type of sustainable agriculture! In the room were the 'sharks and alligators' of the world who claim to represent farmers while 'feeding the world,' like Farm Bureau, commodity groups, and industry entities. These fellas trip over themselves and pride themselves in telling the biggest lies again, again, and again."[39]

Industry was "farming the farmer for extreme economic gain while externalizing every cost when and where possible," Chris had testified, but on "real family farms," those costs were internalized. "Externalization on behalf of nonfarm entities is outright cheating," he said, "and it comes from those who claim to participate in a 'fair' system while their political and government clan supports it!"

Chris had offered a mini–history lesson in sustainable agriculture, telling the panel that "local farmers who own the land and livestock are far better stewards, so why are we moving away from localized family farm agriculture, which has documented proof of success in feeding this country since 1776? Sustainable family farms can raise a far safer, superior product more efficiently in a level playing field, a fact that the politicians ignore."

The commissioners seemed to take notice of his straight-talk presentation, Chris concluded. He had returned to Des Moines in triumph to alert his fellow activists. "Everything else I said was built around these highlights, and over my concern about new animal diseases arising from these filthy, crowded conditions," he wrote. "In my calendar this goes down as a day for a home run for our side."

Barbara Sha (pronounced *shay*) Cox, a diminutive grandmother and former nurse with an eastern Indiana farmer's twang, packs a lot of wallop into her five-foot-three frame. Her no-nonsense approach to fighting CAFO pollution had earned her both fear and grudging respect among Indiana state officials. Karen Hudson loved Barbara from day one.

Indiana was relatively new to the CAFO game, Barbara explained one afternoon to Karen, who had driven over from Illinois to Barbara's home in Wayne County, on the straight, flat border with Ohio. Barbara had grown up in neighboring Randolph County, whose largest town, Winchester, is home to fewer than five thousand souls; and Lynn, whose most infamous son was Jim Jones, of the People's Temple and cyanide-laced Kool-Aid.

Barbara's father had owned dairies, and she was intimately familiar with cows. "I learned that you treat the animals right, and you will prosper," she told Karen. "We had the most pampered cows in the county! About eighty to one hundred of them."

Barbara met her future husband, Dan Cox, in high school before going to nursing school at Ball State University, while Dan launched a career in banking. Their son Todd was born in 1961 and daughter Lisa arrived two years later. Sadly, by age ten, Lisa would become almost completely blind from a rare eye disease.

Lisa was often home from school for treatment, and Barbara drove over to the school to fetch books to bring home to read to Lisa. One day, however, without warning, the school announced a change in its policy: Parents could no longer bring schoolbooks home for ill children.

It flabbergasted and infuriated the conservative, bedrock Republican.

"I went on the warpath," she told Karen. "I met with her teachers, I took the matter to the school board, and I complained until we got change." Soon after that, the school not only allowed books to go home, they purchased large-print editions and books on tape for visually impaired students. Barbara forced the school to provide those materials for free.

Her small victories set the stage for much larger battles in the decades to come. "I was not an activist, but I got involved," she said. "And I won."

After Barbara's father passed away, she decided to keep up the family farm, if only to generate income to care for her ailing mother with Alzheimer's. She sold the dairy equipment, rented out most of the 240 acres to corn and bean sharecroppers, and spent much of her time maintaining the property, painting its buildings, clearing its ditches, and cutting its grass and wood.

One day in 2003, she was working on the land when a neighboring farmer came by with a polite smile, a pen, and a petition.

"They want to put a dairy in around here, and this petition is to try and stop that," the farmer said.

Barbara was dumbfounded. She loved dairy cows. Why on earth would anyone want to stop a dairy?

"But then I read the petition," she explained to Karen. "This was no dairy they were talking about. It was unlike anything I had ever heard of before. It was huge. And it was industrial."

Barbara signed the petition. She also got together with the farmer and a group of neighbors to take their concerns to the county commissioners, who were unmoved by their pleas.

"You just don't want this in your neighborhood," one of the commissioners had told Barbara—rather haughtily, she thought. "If this weren't in your backyard, you wouldn't care about it."

"That's not true!" Barbara had protested. "I wouldn't want twelve hundred cows in one place *anywhere* in this county."

Eventually, the dairy was approved, but for the other side of the county. And, true to her word, Barbara still fought against it. Before long she was joining forces with residents in neighboring counties who were fighting similar battles against other incoming dairy CAFOs.

By late 2005, Indiana had emerged as a new front in the animal-factory wars, and Barbara Sha Cox became a leading opponent of industrialized animal agriculture in the flat, green Hoosier State.

"We saw the handwriting was on the wall," she said. "We knew what happened in North Carolina and we sure didn't want that to happen in our state. We didn't want our watersheds destroyed. But then Mitch came in here and welcomed Big Ag's factory farms with open arms and without regulations"

"Mitch," in this case, was Mitchell Daniels, Jr.—the newly elected Republican governor of Indiana, former Bush White House budget director, and, before that, senior executive at Eli Lilly and Company—who had vowed to double pork production in the state over the next twenty years.

One headline in the trade journal *National Hog Farmer* blared: HOOSIER STATE EMBRACES HOG GROWTH. Barbara read the piece with trepidation. "Government officials in Indiana have said they want more pigs produced and fed out in the state," the article began, "and several large hog production companies have accepted the challenge. After decades of decline, Indiana's farming economy is on the verge of an upswing, fueled by seven initiatives designed to boost employment and revenue."

The initiatives had come from Governor Daniels and his staff, and included an ethanol-production plan beginning with a dozen new plants that were expected to burn up 35 percent of the state's corn crop—and put pressure on hog-feed prices. One solution was to feed the spent corn by-product back to livestock.

To help small towns "embrace livestock production and to facilitate siting," the Daniels administration began something called the Economic Development Initiative, which sought to encourage environmentally responsible growth in the industry, according to state agriculture director Andy Miller. "We want them to know that we are committed and stand ready to help them, and most importantly, to let them know that we have very high standards as to the kind of producers we want," he told *National Hog Farmer*. "We want good-quality producers who are going to be good to their communities and environment."

This cooperative spirit to work with producers "has been a key reason why large swine production companies are expanding into Indiana," the paper said. Barbara had to grimace as she read it. She did not feel any better after reading on:

IDEM [Indiana Department of Environmental Management] Commissioner Thomas Easterly stresses the charge of his agency is to protect human health and the environment, and not to promote any business interests. But he makes it clear where he stands on hog growth. "Some people from other states, including North Carolina, are proposing hog projects in Indiana. We think that is a good thing." And IDEM is backing up that support with an expedited permitting process, adds Dennis Lasiter, technical environmental specialist. The pace of approvals has almost doubled. Last year, 25 permits were issued for confined animal feeding operations (CAFOs), plus a number of modifications approved for existing operations. In the first quarter of 2006, IDEM has approved 19 CAFO permits, 11 of which were for new farms, says Lasiter. All were approved for hog farms.

Barbara had read enough. She was more interested in what IDEM did *not* say rather than what it said. IDEM did not mention that Indiana had no air regulations for CAFOs, for example. "So neighbors beware," she began warning people at town hall meetings, "if the hydrogen sulfide, ammonia, and dust come into your yard and home, there's no one to call for help."

Nor did IDEM officials mention that most CAFOs in Indiana were inspected just once every five years. CAFO owners are self-reporting, Barbara would explain to people, "so if they are less than honest, who would know?"

IDEM had failed to acknowledge that its "plan for mortality" was insufficient, and that she had sent it pictures of hog heads and cow skins that were carried by wild animals and found in the yards of people who lived a half mile from the facility.

A few days later, as Barbara was driving home from the farm, passing through the mist of a sprayfield, her car was splattered bumper to bumper with liquid hog manure. "They don't have any respect for anyone!" she said to Dan when she got home. "They leave their crap on the roadways, they spray it on the cars, and it smells horrible. My car is going to stink for weeks. At least the car washes around here will do well."

One of the first people she allied herself with was State Senator Allen Paul, a Republican from Randolph County. In 2004, Paul introduced one of the very first CAFO-related bills in Indiana, known as the "good character clause." If passed, it would require the state to study the past history of all new CAFO-permit applicants, and deny permits on the grounds of past performance. Such a provision was in place for operators of landfills, but not CAFOs.

The bill met with stiff resistance in committee and failed to become law. (Over the following years, Barbara would work hard with Democratic state senator Tim Lanane and his GOP counterpart, Allen Paul, plus state representatives Phil Pflum [D], Tom Saunders [R], and David Cheatham [D] on a variety of CAFO regulation bills, not all of which succeeded. During these years, citizens from all over the state made their way to Indianapolis on their own money to testify regarding their desire to protect their water, air, property value, and quality of life.)

Randolph County seemed to be the epicenter of the new development— More than forty CAFOs had set up shop there in the past few years, Barbara learned. It didn't take long for complaints to be filed about overapplication of manure on cropland. The next summer, Barbara noticed that some plots of land could barely support the growth of corn—on these patches, the plants looked yellow and stunted, as if burned by acid or, in this case, too much nitrogen.

But it was the health complaints that really started piling up. People such as Eric and Lisa Stickdorn—organic farmers outside of Cambridge City—even coined a term for how the gases and stench made them feel: "manure flu," which they described as throbbing pain in joints and muscles, a debilitating headache, and a low-grade fever that sucked the energy right out of one's body. They also complained of "olfactory fatigue," the temporary or permanent loss of sensitivity to the offending odor. Eric Stickdorn told Barbara he could no longer smell the manure—he only knew it was a problem because it still made his mouth burn like fire.

Judy and Allen Hutchison, who lived in a small farmhouse surrounded by dairy and hog CAFOs, also complained of "burning mouth syndrome." Respiratory illness also befell Brenda Jones, a Henry County resident who came down with chronic obstructive pulmonary disease, or COPD, something often associated with cigarette smoking. She was hospitalized and put on a respirator not long after the farm across the road from her house began spraying hog waste on the crops.

Around this time, Barbara also began communicating regularly with Karen Hudson in Illinois. The two quickly became friends. "We are desperate here in Indiana," she told Karen one morning on a call. "My phone is ringing constantly with complaints on the animal-factory operators. People call IDEM,

324 | ANIMAL FACTORY

but they are all too often told that IDEM does not regulate that. I also hear from a lot of people who want to sell their homes, but can never find buyers. Who wants a home where you can't have a picnic outside in the yard?"

Karen offered to guide Barbara through the treacherous shoals of grass-roots activism. Barbara gratefully accepted.

The Factory Farm Project was bringing the animal-factory fight to Indiana, where skirmishes were breaking out all over. In July 2006, Barbara Sha Cox's fledgling statewide grassroots group sponsored a public meeting where Karen, Helen, Bill Weida, Terry Spence, and others were invited to speak at the Anderson Center for the Arts in Anderson. It was organized by Cox and other CAFO opponents around the state. More than a hundred people showed up to listen to dire warnings about their own futures.

"The only reason the CAFO industry is coming to Indiana is that they can pollute easier here than they can anyplace else," Bill Weida told the anxious crowd. "If you have any delusions that it's for any other reason—maybe they like shopping in downtown Indianapolis or something—then you need to talk to me at greater length. Because there is no evidence that they move here for any reason other than pollution shopping."

Weida reminded everyone that Indiana governor Mitch Daniels—the former Bush White House budget director—had vowed during his 2004 campaign to double pork production in the state by 2025. Daniels had moved quickly to develop Indiana's reputation as a place with soft environmental regulations. "Industry is thrilled. Permits are getting through in forty days," Weida said.

The Indiana Department of Environmental Management, meanwhile, was "doing nothing more than an entry-level clerk would do in reviewing these permits," Weida continued. Daniels had his eye only on doubling production, "so it doesn't matter to him that the hogs are raised in East Central Indiana and slaughtered four or five counties away in Delphi and Logansport," he said. "What do slaughterhouses in Delphi and Logansport do for the region here? Not a dang thing."

The remarks by Weida and others brought a swift retort from state officials and the Indiana Farm Bureau. IDEM and the Indiana State Department of Agriculture issued a joint response, accusing GRACE Factory Farm Project members of being antifarming zealots and outside agitators.

"These statements are being made from a group whose agenda is to stop livestock agriculture," the joint statement declared. "They want to scare you into thinking farming is bad. We believe that most of the residents of East Central Indiana want to learn facts from various sources to make up their own minds.

We also believe in local control and trust the citizens of Indiana, through their elected local officials, to be able to decide what is best for their community."

Agriculture was among the most heavily regulated industries in the nation, the statement said. Livestock operations were the only businesses in America with a zero-discharge policy. And the scrutiny was relentless, it claimed. For each CAFO application, IDEM workers pored over soil information and manure-management plans; new building plans; nearby homes and water sources; specific floodway locations; and restrictions due to nearby karst formations, wetlands, and old mines. And even after approval, agents "routinely conduct site visits to ensure construction is done according to the permit."

The Indiana Farm Bureau launched a personal attack on GRACE Factory Farm Project members, challenging their authority on agricultural matters. "We find it disturbing that the opponents to livestock agriculture are forced to rely on so-called experts from Idaho, New York, Missouri and Illinois," IFB's Mike Baise said. "We suspect that GRACE is nothing more than a front group for activists who want to drive out all agriculture from Indiana."

In his ad hominem attack, Baise had overlooked some telling details about these so-called outsiders: They, too, were farmers. Karen Hudson farmed corn and beans, Helen Reddout owned fruit orchards, Chris Petersen bred hogs, and Terry Spence raised cattle.

This wouldn't be the last time the Factory Farm Project would be pilloried for its forays into Indiana.

By 2006, the animal-factory wars were raging, having spread from rural communities to state courthouses and now all the way to Capitol Hill. The tactics were fiery, and the rhetoric simplistic, as each side agitated to smear its opponents. Anti-CAFO forces portrayed industrial livestock leaders as part of an immense network of greed, without regard for health and the environment. Agribusiness was ramping up its counterattack that naysayers were anti-farming, overemotional, irrational, and a threat to economic development, affordable food, and national security.

In April, the Animal Agriculture Alliance warned members that the GRACE Factory Farm Project was organizing people in Indiana. "We have learned that professional activists from New York–based GRACE offered to lend citizens in Indiana and Ohio one of the organization's five 'UV Hounds,' " it said. "The extremist group lends the monitors exclusively to activists who plan to sue agricultural enterprises [they] consider to be 'factory farms.' " They detailed the group's multipoint strategy, which included pleas for locals to vote for farming reformation, document infractions, file suits where merited, and buy organic. AAA called GRACE's actions "off-base" and "off-beat."[40]

Karen phoned Helen and read aloud the alert. She didn't know whether to laugh or cry. "Can you believe this?" she said. "We're the 'extremists,' but they are the ones who think it's 'off-base' to do things like, um, *vote*? Are these folks nuts?"

"They must be," Helen said. "And they're after our hides, Karen."

The AAA warning systematically dismissed the activists' entire case, including claims of animal cruelty, overuse of antibiotics, and the dangers of antibiotic-resistant CAFO bacteria passing to the public at large.

The true danger, according to the AAA, was the anti-CAFO activists themselves. "The AAA urges its members in Indiana and Ohio to prepare themselves for this coming threat, along with forwarding this alert to your friends, neighbors, suppliers and customers."

Helen, Karen, and Rick were used to being called antifarming, alarmist, unscientific, and even communists. But in mid-2006 their opponents ramped up the rhetoric, linking the factory-farming activists to Al Qaeda–style *terrorists*.

"Documents recovered from al-Qaeda training camps indicate that the USA's food supply is a high-priority target," the AAA charged in a news release. "Domestically, terrorist-activists within our own borders have declared war on modern food and agriculture.[41]

"Incited by GRACE activists' inflammatory rhetoric," the release continued, "some extreme elements of the anti-agriculture movement may take matters into their own hands."

The implication was that anti-CAFO activists shared an agenda with Al Qaeda. For a nation still wounded by 9/11, the allegation was powerful.

To react to the alleged threat, AAA created a farmers' training course called "Managing Activist/Terrorist Threats to the Food, Agricultural and Animal Industries: A Common Sense Approach." The seminar was slated for October in Columbus, Ohio, and was cosponsored by the Ohio Livestock Coalition and the Law Enforcement Academic Research Network (LEARN).

"The increasing number of incidents of violence at farms, processing plants, research centers, and other business locations emphasizes the need for better managing threats to our food and animal industries," the announcement said. LEARN operated an antiterrorism training team whose mission was to "prepare those in both public and private sectors to protect critical infrastructures from internal and external threats."

The FBI had estimated that "eco- and animal-rights extremists" had inflicted more than $200 million in damages to livestock facilities in recent years," the AAA said. The bureau was currently working more than 150 open cases in the area of "agriterrorism."

A flyer promoting the session pressed the alleged activist-terrorist connection, claiming that the GRACE Factory Farm Project had conducted "anti-agriculture activist training sessions" recently in Indiana.

The antiterror pushback aimed at GRACE and others did not stop there. Even scientists were jumping into the fray. Dr. Bob Norton, professor of veterinary microbiology and biosecurity in the Department of Poultry Science at Auburn University, warned the public about how the country was "now a target from adversaries, both foreign and domestic, who would like to destroy the American way of life and devastate our people."

Professor Norton exhorted everyone responsible "for securing food and agriculture facilities from internal and external threats, along with protecting their workforce and the public" to take an AAA training session to "help them effectively execute this task."

Joining the debate, the Department of Homeland Security awarded $2 million to the University of Tennessee to find ways to fight agriterrorism.[42]

In May 2006, Karen received an SOS e-mail from Angie Litterst, the farmwife from Reynolds, near Quad Cities, who had been worried about a new hog CAFO nearby. Now the CAFO was up and running, bringing torment to her family. It depressed the hell out of Karen to read: "My way of life has been attacked, and I've done nothing to bring this on. Who exactly is being terrorized here?"[43]

Three days later, Angie took her daughter to the University of Iowa hospital, which diagnosed the young girl with a lung tumor.

In November, the Pew Commission headed out West and arranged to take testimony during two days of invitation-only meetings in San Francisco. Commission staff reached out to Helen and to Bill Weida for their perspectives, and both agreed to fly to California to give a presentation. Western dairy operations were sure to be a big part of the talks.

Helen could not have been happier. Until now, dairy issues had been getting short shrift in the overall national CAFO debate. The dairy industry was the last to be integrated, and most Americans still assumed their milk, butter, and cheese came from Farmer Bill's favorite cow Bessie, who was peacefully munching clover in a pasture somewhere up in Wisconsin. Dairy farms—as opposed to, say, pig sties—held a special bucolic place in the American imagination. Few people wanted to think of their friendly local dairy as a massive, polluting factory that could be hazardous to human health and the environment. But to Helen, that is exactly what many dairies had become.

Helen found it mystifying that megadairies were getting such a relatively free pass from the press and public. It seemed that for every ten news stories about pigs and chickens, there was only one about milk cows. And yet, she thought, when one considered the average family's grocery-store cart, there were far more dairy-based sources of food than beef, chicken, or pork combined. "Bacon is in bacon," she said, "but milk is in everything."

In 2004, Americans consumed 582 pounds of milk equivalents per person, compared to 63 pounds of beef, 59 pounds of chicken, and 51 pounds of pork. Americans consumed ten times more dairy than pork, yet pigs got far more media attention than cows. Helen prayed that the Pew Commission could help change that calculus.

Moreover, Americans were consuming more of the stuff—cream, sour cream, ice cream, cottage cheese, yogurt, and flavored milk. Demand for dairy products was continuing to grow from new sources: School lunch programs were now offering single-serve plastic milk containers to offset sugary soda consumption; fast-food chains were putting flavored milk on their kids' menus, leading to "skyrocketing milk consumption by children," as one journal put it;[44] and adults were gulping down energy drinks that contained whey proteins and other "milk protein fractions."

When the time came to speak, Helen gave her presentation calmly and methodically. She began her slide show by showing bucolic images of the Yakima Valley, with its views of snow-covered Mount Adams, the tree-lined banks of the Yakima River, and small, grass-fed dairies with cows lolling around on green pastures. "This was our valley," she said wistfully.[45]

"Then, out-of-state dairies invaded us, mainly from the Chino Valley in California, and this is what we got." The slides of pasture cows switched to images of pathetic-looking animals resting on piles of crap, or wading through foot-deep pools of brown liquid. "That's not mud," Helen said to audible gasps.

Successive slides offered images of polluted wetlands, overflowing ditches, and giant spray guns spewing thick braids of a coffee-colored water right up to the property lines of other people's homes. "And here you can clearly see them spraying liquid manure onto snow; it's an intentional violation of law. So is the dumping of dead animals, used hypodermic needles, and medicine bottles into streams. This is a constant problem, not a once-only type of occurrence. There is not one bad apple in the barrel; there are only one or two good apples in the barrel," she said softly. "And nothing has been done to correct any of these problems. There is no enforcement, and these giant factory dairy operators get a blank check to destroy our environment."

Helen was not merely tugging at heartstrings; she had data to support her claims. A recent EPA study measured *E. coli* levels found in the Granger Drain: 31 percent of all bacteria DNA was linked to cows, which were believed to be the largest single source, Helen stated. "They found concentrations that were seven times greater than state standards allowed, and manure application to fields were the prime source."

She also presented Hound readings that CARE members had taken outside one dairy near the town of Moxie, Washington. Some results cataloged concentrations over 7,000 parts per billion, Helen told the commissioners. Those figures were cause for alarm—a new University of Iowa study warned that concentrations over 150 parts per billion could cause damage to human health.

Helen also discussed the two well-water studies funded by CARE's Clean Water Act lawsuits against the dairies. "Many people's wells were filled with fecal matter, *E. coli*, and nitrates and other contaminants. Some said their drinking water was turning brown. Others were told by doctors not to drink, bathe in, or even come in contact with water from their wells," she added. "So residents began to suck up the costs of the irresponsibility of these dairy operations, and we have to buy reverse osmosis machines or we have to bring in bottled water in order to have clean drinking water in our own homes. Those who cannot afford to use such things take a real risk with their health."

Then there was Manure Mountain, "the mother of all manure piles," Helen said as the room again filled with gasps when she projected an image of the big brown mound. "Millions of tons of raw manure and sludge are being stored on top of a high water table area, without a containment floor or walls to control seepage or runoff. This area is populated by many low-income or minority families whose only source of drinking water comes from these shallow wells."

On the slide, one could easily see eroded ravines in the "mountain," where rain had washed fecal matter away into the soil below. "It is over half a mile long and three football fields wide," she said.

The mountain was a depressing and glaring symbol of economic discrimination in the valley as well. "Most people who live near this monstrosity are poor; they can't afford to hire a lawyer to fight damage to their property and houses," she said. "The very agencies that are being paid to protect us are not doing their job. And they have submitted to the political power of corporate agriculture. And the economic chokehold that dairy operations have on the valley makes it impossible to get into the legal system so we can retain the rights that are ours." Helen completed her tour of industry injustice with a final slide depicting an American flag. The commission panelists understood the implication.

"We simply believe as rural residents we have the right to clean air and safe drinking water; we have the right to have sustainable farms around us that will keep the soil productive," Helen said. "And we have the right to democratically led community development, to our property values, and to a healthy wildlife habitat. And we have the right to keep a quality of life and health that is safe and enduring. As you conduct your investigation I would ask you to try real hard to separate the dairy myths that you see on a regular basis from the reality that you have seen here today."

When it was over, commission members were so moved, they invited Helen and Bill to have dinner with them. Later, Helen would realize that her hard-hitting testimony had shaped the content and tenor of the commission's final report.

On Election Day, November 7, 2006, voters in Arizona approved a ballot initiative to outlaw inhumane practices at livestock operations in their state. Proposition 204, the Humane Treatment of Farm Animals Act, passed with 61.5 percent of the vote, carrying all but four counties.[46] As in Florida, where a similar law was passed, this measure would phase out the use of gestation crates for sows by 2012. But Arizona went a step further, banning the use of veal crates, or "hutches," which completely confine the movement of calves.

The Humane Society of the United States claimed victory against the CAFO operators, who had been backed by a well-funded industry campaign. "Arizona voters stood up to factory farming lobby groups and affirmed that farm animals should have basic protections such as being able to turn around and extend their limbs," HSUS president Wayne Pacelle said in a statement. "The overwhelming passage of Proposition 204 will not only help thousands of animals in Arizona, but will also send a message to factory farming operations across the country that they must end the most abusive practices."[47]

The Animal Agricultural Alliance called the outcome "disappointing" and accused HSUS of "a multimillion dollar campaign of misdirection."[48] The benefits of veal and sow crates, the AAA argued, had been proved through "scientific examination at leading universities and pragmatic experience from both farmers and veterinarians." But the voters were duped by animal-rights activists, and soon they would pay the price, the statement said, predicting "significant long-term deterrent to Arizona's agriculture industry," which was now adding an impressive $9 billion a year to the gross state product, more than half of it from animal agriculture.

The problem was not poor animal conditions, but poor marketing, AAA's Kay Johnson said. "Tuesday's vote indicates that America's farmers and ranchers need to continuously communicate their commitment on critical issues, including animal welfare and their dedication to providing the safest, highest quality food supply in history," she said. "The vote also shows that America's farmers and ranchers need to remind consumers that 98% of America's farms are family farms. The understanding generated by expanding communications initiatives will impede the success of anti-agriculture initiatives like Prop 204 in other states."

Johnson added that death threats had been sent to members of the anti-204 Campaign for Arizona Farmers and Ranchers, and "the threat of violence to coerce an action, by definition, is terrorism."

Karen was dismayed to read about the threats. She in no way wished to be associated with violence or radicals. But there was nothing radical, she thought, about 62 percent of the people in this conservative state voting to protect and enhance the welfare of food animals and, by extension, consumer health.

She also agreed with the Humane Society's campaign for better conditions among U.S. livestock and poultry. The society had identified the "six most egregious standard agribusiness practices"[49] and was working to end them all. Karen, Helen, Rick, and many others supported the effort:

Battery Cages: Nearly 95 percent of all U.S. laying hens live in small "battery cages"—wire enclosures offering "less space per hen than a single sheet of paper," stacked several tiers high in long rows inside huge, windowless buildings. The birds cannot engage in natural behaviors including "nesting, perching, walking, dust bathing, foraging, or even spreading their wings."

Rapid Bird Growth: More than 90 percent of land animals consumed by Americans are chickens—about nine billion are eaten per year. Selective breeding and antibiotic use was yielding birds whose bodies "struggle to function and are on the verge of structural collapse." The University of Arkansas reported that if people grew at the same rate as industrial chickens, "we'd weigh 349 pounds by our second birthday." As a result, 90 percent of broilers have leg problems and structural deformities, and more than a quarter "suffer from chronic pain as a result of bone disease."

Forced Feeding for Foie Gras: "Two to three times daily for several weeks, birds raised for foie gras are force-fed enormous quantities of food through a long pipe thrust down their throats into their stomachs. The birds' livers can swell to ten times the normal size, causing pain, discomfort and immobility."

Gestation Crates and Veal Crates: Sows are pregnant for four months, and 60–70 percent of them in the United States are kept in cramped crates during gestation. Veal calves are also kept in hutches, and are "generally chained by the neck" to keep them from turning around. "The frustration of natural behaviors takes an enormous mental and physical toll on the animals." Two months after Arizona passed the ban on crates, Smithfield Foods announced it would begin transitioning to "group housing" for its gestating sows, calling it a business decision based on consumer demand.

Electric Stunning: At the plant, live birds are hung upside down by their legs in shackles, HSUS alleged. Their heads are dipped into electrified water to stun them before their throats are slit. "From beginning to end, the entire process is filled with pain and suffering," HSUS said, adding that federal rules do not require anesthesia for the animals, "many of whom already suffer leg disorders or broken bones. And electric stunning has been found to be ineffective in consistently inducing unconsciousness."

Long-Distance Transport: Billions of animals are subjected to long truck journeys every year, in vehicles that are often overcrowded, without food, water, or rest, HSUS said. "The conditions are so stressful that in-transit death is considered common."

After Election Day in Arizona, Karen walked with a lighter clip to her step. Even though the Factory Farm Project and Sustainable Table were focused on environmental health and rural sustainability, she was ashamed of the way humans treated animals inside industrial confinements. And she knew that voter measures like those in Florida and Arizona were elevating public consciousness about what happens to our food before it is neatly wrapped and brightly packaged at the supermarket.

She was also excited that Illinois had just elected a promising young politician from Chicago to represent her state in the U.S. Senate. Karen had watched him on TV during the Democratic Convention in 2004 and, like many, was engrossed by his keynote address. Some people were even joking about how he would one day become the first African American president.

Karen had always disliked electoral politics and partisan bickering. And like most CAFO activists, her disdain for George W. Bush grew deeper each day. But this new guy, Obama, Karen really liked. Her intuition told her that Barack Obama was a decent man who would fight for the little people—even if that meant taking on moneyed interests like Big Ag.

Karen's intuition was prescient. Within two years, President Obama would promise to implement many of the reforms and regulations that the GRACE Project, FARM, CARE, Waterkeeper, and so many others had been seeking for fifteen years. Chris Petersen, who lived in the critical caucus state of Iowa, would gain privileged access to candidate Obama and wield impressive influence over the development of his rural agenda.

Much of Obama's farm agenda would be equally informed by the Pew Commission. Having just taken testimony from Chris, Helen, Terry Spence, and others, they would soon hear from Rick Dove and Don Webb in North Carolina. Ultimately, commission officials would warn the Obama people that CAFOs could potentially breed new and dangerous diseases that would threaten human health and disrupt economic activity.

No one had any idea that that scenario would come true within Obama's first hundred days.

15

Back in 2004, some of the leading environmental health experts in the world had come together in Iowa City to examine the risks posed by large-scale concentrated animal production and to suggest ways to mitigate its impact on air, water, human health, and rural communities.

In November 2006, the "minimonographs" that were prepared by thirty-seven national and international CAFO experts who had gathered in Iowa City were published in the online edition of *Environmental Health Perspectives*. It wasn't good news for the industry.

The series, "Environmental Health Impacts of Concentrated Animal Feeding Operations: Anticipating Hazards—Searching for Solutions,"[1] made one thing exceedingly clear—most independent scientists agreed that CAFOs cause pollution and hurt communities. The challenge was to find ways to mitigate those harmful effects.

"Traditional crop–livestock farms were balanced," the scientists concurred, "in that livestock manure supplied nutrients to grow the crops to feed those livestock." But in industrialized settings, nutrients from feed are drawn in from a wide area to a single concentrated landmass, "resulting in soil accumulation and runoff of phosphorus, nitrogen, and other pollutants," and pollution of the air and water.

A serious lack of oversight was the main culprit, the scientists said: "There was general agreement among all workgroups that the industrialization of livestock production over the past three decades has not been accompanied by commensurate modernization of regulations to protect the health of the public, or natural public-trust resources."

The major findings were well known to anti-CAFO activists. But this time, esteemed scientists were making the claims, and they would not be as easily ignored. Among the most important issues and recommendations included in the monographs were the following.

WATER QUALITY

This panel, chaired by Dr. JoAnn Burkholder, found "substantial documentation of major, ongoing impacts on aquatic resources from CAFOs." U.S. farms produced 133 million tons of dry-weight manure each year, thirteen times more than the human population produced.

Meanwhile, lagoons were designed to let nitrogen evaporate into the air in the form of ammonia, the paper said. That volatilization, plus ammonia from sprayfields, was reentering local waters in levels far above the minimum that causes noxious algal blooms.

Nitrates in well water above the standard of ten milligrams per liter had been implicated in cases of blue-baby syndrome, diarrhea, and even respiratory disease. At the same time, there was an increased risk of hypothyroidism from long-term exposure to levels between eleven to sixty-one milligrams per liter; exposures below the ten-milligram-per-liter safety limit had been associated with insulin-dependent diabetes in some studies (though other studies said it happened at levels greater than fifteen milligrams per liter).

Reproductive health risks were also associated with nitrates in drinking water, even below the ten-milligram-per-liter level. These included central nervous system malformations in children, and even neural tube defects, which has been linked to some cases of autism. Equally frightening were anecdotal reports of spontaneous abortions among women who drank nitrate-tainted water (at levels of nineteen to twenty-six milligrams per liter) from private wells.

AIRBORNE EXPOSURES

CAFOs emit ammonia, hydrogen sulfide, and carbon dioxide, among other gases. Odor emissions, in particular, were associated with quality-of-life issues, though the question of air quality and public health was "open and controversial." Most likely, stress caused by odors, rather than the foul smells themselves, was making people feel ill. Another potential hazard was the presence of endotoxins, found in certain bacterial cell walls, which have powerful proinflammatory properties.

Extremely common to CAFOs, they can cause a wide range of respiratory infections and illnesses, including asthma.

INFECTIOUS DISEASE AND
ANTIBIOTIC RESISTANCE

"As a general principle, the concentration of humans or animals in proximity enhances potential transmission of microorganisms among members of the group," wrote this panel, which included Dr. David Wallinga of the IATP. "It also creates greater potential for infecting surrounding life forms, even those of different species. The conditions created also may be a breeding ground for new, more infectious, or more resistant microorganisms."

In fact, escalating resistance "has raised concern that we are entering the 'post antibiotic era,' meaning we may be entering a period where there would be no effective antibiotics available for treating many life-threatening infections in humans," this panel wrote. "Deaths due to infection will once again become a very real threat."

Antibiotic overuse in medicine was contributing to resistance, but agricultural use of the drugs was thought to be much more of a problem. The Union of Concerned Scientists estimated that 24.6 million pounds of antimicrobials are used each year as growth promoters and for other nonessential purposes in U.S. beef cattle, hogs, and poultry each year, compared to about 3 million pounds in humans, an 87 to 13 percent ratio. One study did suggest lower rates, however, finding that less than 40 percent of U.S. antibiotics use is in animals. The UCS criticized that report for using "flawed reasoning."

Resistant genes can easily pass from one type of bacteria to another. "Ultimately, these genes may pass into pathogens, and diseases that were formerly treatable will be capable of causing severe illness or death," the paper said.

Resistant bacteria were also showing up in food. In 2001, a team of researchers bought two hundred samples of hamburger meat in the Washington, D.C., area and found that 20 percent contained salmonella. Of the contaminated samples, 84 percent of the organisms were resistant to at least one antibiotic tested, and 53 percent were resistant to three or more.

"Several recent studies clearly demonstrate the transmission of multidrug-resistant pathogens from swine to humans," the report said. One French paper looked at forty-four samples of nasal *Staphylococcus aureus* taken from healthy pig farmers, and twenty-one controls. Five of the isolates in the farmers were methicillin resistant (MRSA), and others were resistant to penicillin, lincomycin, erythromycin, pristinamycin, kanamycin, and pefloxacin. "The authors concluded that transmission of these resistant organisms from swine to pig farmers may be frequent," the panel said. One U.S. study found airborne enterococci, staph, and strep bacteria with resistant genes to the drugs erythromycin, clindamycin, virginiamycin, and tetracycline. A shocking 98 percent of them showed resistance to two or more of the antibiotics and 30 percent were resistant to all four drugs.

Animal production was far more reliant on antibiotics in the United States than in Europe. Scandinavian growers, for instance, used less than three grams of antimicrobial agents for every pig killed; U.S. producers used forty-seven grams. The use of routine antibiotics as growth promoters was not always more profitable, either. U.S. farmers raised bigger chickens, but at greater cost; antibiotics are not cheap. In the end, it was a wash: "The decrease in production, in terms of decreased feed efficiency, is small and offset by savings in the cost of antimicrobials," the panel said. As for pigs, it cost 1 percent more to raise them without antibiotic growth promoters, the World Health Organization (WHO) said, adding that this should be weighed against the "likely human health benefits to society of antimicrobial growth promoter termination." WHO said there was no reason not to get rid of the antibiotics for growth promotion.

INFLUENZA VIRUS

CAFOs are breeding grounds for a number of diseases that can infect people. One study found that hog workers were 35.3 times more likely to be infected with swine flu virus than controls, while veterinarians were 17.8 times and meat processors 6.5 times more likely. "The transmission of influenza is a continuing concern," the panel said. "Whether it comes to humans from avian species or swine, or from avian species via swine, or perhaps from humans to swine, strains of high transmissibility and pathogenicity are likely to evolve and create another pandemic." And because CAFOs cram lots of animals into close proximity, "they facilitate rapid transmission and mixing of viruses," the paper said.

Of particular concern was the increasingly common—and alarming—practice of siting swine facilities right next to poultry confinements, something that "could further promote the evolution of the next pandemic." Transmission of avian flu from birds to swine could provide the biological bridge a virus needed to finally become highly infectious in people.

CAFOs are so concentrated that once an organism gets in, it is very hard to get rid of it, the paper said. And because pathogens get amplified in CAFOs, that makes them more difficult to eliminate at the processing plant.

Among the paper's public health recommendations were: a phasing out of nontherapeutic antimicrobials in farm animals; national surveillance to detect "ecological reservoirs of resistance," fingerprinting of antibiotic-resistant bacteria; minimum separation distances for swine and poultry CAFOs; and the replacement of lagoons with solid tanks and municipal-style waste treatment to reduce water pollution.

COMMUNITY AND SOCIOECONOMIC HEALTH

"Economic concentration of agricultural operations tends to remove a higher percentage of money from rural communities than when the industry is dominated by smaller farm operations, which tend to circulate money within the community," wrote the members of this workgroup, who included Steve Wing of the University of North Carolina and Kendall Thu of Central Illinois University.

One 1988 analysis showed that industrialized agriculture was associated with economic and community decline, while other Midwestern studies found a drop in tax receipts and local retail sales in areas with large operations. One of these studies showed how a drop in local purchases was specifically linked to growing livestock facilities and not crop production.

"These findings consistently show that the social and economic well-being of local rural communities benefit from increasing the number of farmers, not simply increasing the volume of commodity produced," the authors wrote.

Quality of life also suffered. CAFOs were found to be "significantly disruptive of rural living," the panel said. "Highly cherished values of freedom and independence associated with life oriented toward the outdoors gives way to feelings of violation and infringement. Homes are no longer an extension of or a means for enjoying the outdoors, [but] a barrier against the outdoors that must be escaped."

Social and legal redress had also been restricted. For example, thirteen states had passed laws limiting disparaging speech about agriculture, and all fifty states had some type of "right to farm" rules that "protect farming operations"—including CAFOs—"from zoning laws or lawsuits that would overly restrict the ability of farmers to do business."

Big Ag hated the Iowa papers, and went to war with the authors and the journal *Environmental Health Perspectives*, a publication of the NIH.

"The process of developing these reports was flawed," Liz Wagstrom of the National Pork Board wrote in a letter published in *Environmental Health Perspectives*. She accused the authors of lumping all animal-production risks together with those of CAFOs. "For example, Burkholder et al. gave the impression that pathogens in manure would not exist in manure from animals raised in facilities that do not meet the definition of a CAFO," she said.[2]

Wagstrom also complained that the authors had evaluated risks based on the mere presence of potential pathogens or toxins, when a "true assessment" would also evaluate exposure and volume.

"Additionally, Burkholder et al. did not in any way differentiate between the normal operation of a CAFO and potential impacts on water quality versus the results of a single catastrophic event, such as failure of a lagoon wall," she said. "Repeated reference to a single catastrophic event involving a single lagoon does not aid scientists or the public in understanding how CAFOs are operated on a daily basis."

Burkholder had been pilloried for more than a decade by scientists who falsely discredited her research, and claimed that their own work proved that *Pfiesteria* cannot make toxin. Research on *Pfiesteria* toxin by scientists from the National Oceanic and Atmospheric Administration (NOAA) in Charleston that was peer reviewed and published in 2001—and that supported Burkholder's findings—was ignored or ridiculed by her detractors. Burkholder was also accused of not sharing her toxic cultures with other scientists, which was untrue, and she was slammed in the worldwide press, including *The New York Times*. Her work, discoveries, and early conflicts were the subject of a gripping 1997 book, *And the Waters Turned to Blood*, by Rodney Barker. Finally, in early 2007, Dr. Peter Moeller, a chemist at NOAA-Charleston, and his research team identified a group of *Pfiesteria* toxins, new to science, that kill fish and cause cell death in mammals. Their findings were published in *Environmental Science and Technology*.[3] The Raleigh *News & Observer*, traditionally a supporter of Burkholder's detractors, ran an editorial admitting that she had been "on solid ground" all along in her research on *Pfiesteria* as a cause of massive fish kills in North Carolina and the Chesapeake Bay. And though Hurricane Floyd and other big storms seemed to have flushed the cell from hell from local waterways, Burkholder had nonetheless "blazed an important scientific trail," the paper acknowledged.[4]

After downplaying Burkholder's conclusions about the effects of CAFOs on water quality, Wagstrom continued with her rebuttal. The Iowa monographs had made no mention of the "relative rarity" of lagoon failures, she contended, making them seem to be commonplace. She also took issue with the claim that pathogens are "amplified" in CAFO animals, and thus harder to eliminate in meat processing. The assessment was inaccurate, Wagstrom said, offering the example that *Trichinella spiralis*, once a prominent pork-associated pathogen, had mostly disappeared since pigs were moved indoors.

Contamination with salmonella and other bacteria was "consistently lowest in the large packing plants," which were most likely to process CAFO animals, she added. "This clearly invalidates the argument that these pathogens are more difficult to eliminate in the packing process."

Finally, the authors "were unaware or intentionally overlooked the fact" that the National Pork Board had recently launched the "Take Care. Use Antibiotics Responsibly" program, which covered more than fifty million pigs a year, Wagstrom said. "We do the public, producers, and the research community a disservice when the discussion is driven by misinformation and subjective opinion."

Conference chair Dr. Peter Thorne responded to the charges by pointing out that "recognized scientists with peer-reviewed publications on the subjects of the workgroups," as well as three state regulators, were asked to take part in the monographs, which also received multiple levels of peer review prior to publication.[5]

Thorne said the conference focused on CAFOs because they were the site of 85 percent of all U.S. and western European pork and poultry production. In the United States, more than half of all pigs were raised at just 110 facilities, each housing fifty thousand hogs or more.

Wagstrom also alleged there had been no assessment of the risk of exposure to pathogens and toxins, but Thorne found that "particularly perplexing" since all the articles had "addressed exposure assessment issues," and two of them dealt almost exclusively with exposures. And, he added, "Wagstrom's suggestion that we should ignore lagoon breaches or manure pipe ruptures with regard to water quality and focus on daily operations is misguided because these events occur with regularity and lead to significant surface water contamination, fish kills, and loss of recreational use of surface waters."

While the agricultural industry took exception to the Iowa monographs, mainstream media regarded them as a sober indictment of the entire system.

"Growing so large that they are now called factory farms, livestock feedlots are poorly regulated, pose health and ecological dangers and are responsible for deteriorating quality of life in America's and Europe's farm regions, according to a series of scientific studies published this week," the *Los Angeles Times* reported.[6]

"Feedlots are contaminating water supplies with pathogens and chemicals, and polluting the air with foul-smelling compounds that can cause respiratory problems," it said, "but the health of their neighbors goes largely unmonitored."

But Farm Bureau spokesperson Don Parrish disputed that harsh assessment, saying the livestock industry was subjected to more than a decade of intense scrutiny and, as a result, "has gone to great lengths and very high expense to try to improve their environmental record, across the board," he told the *Los Angeles Times*. "We've definitely improved our game over the past 10 years. Most growers are being very sensitive to their neighbors and doing the best job they can."

By mid-2007, Karen was fielding several CAFO complaints every week— many from central and western Illinois.

In April, she received an e-mail from a woman named Diane Ward, a resident of Rushville in Schuyler County, about eighty miles south of Elmwood. A large contractor operation for Cargill had moved into the area, and the smells were already unbearable. The Wards' neighbors, a young couple with three children, had bought the quaint little farmhouse next door, with its tidy fields and vineyard, and had begun a quiet life of organic farming. Now they were desperate to sell the place.

"On April 23rd the house was shown to the maintenance supervisor at Cargill as a potential buyer," Karen read. "Although he and his wife liked the house and said they personally would not be bothered by the hog confinement, they had to keep in mind resale value, because Cargill was going to be moving him eventually, and he would then have to sell it. He also said that Cargill does its own property value studies and that houses within a five-mile radius of a hog confinement lose 50 percent of their value."[7]

Karen was also contacted by a couple in the southwestern Illinois town of Mendon, independent grain and hog farmers Dan Trent and Kim Ward. In 2006, their neighbor decided to put in a three-thousand-head hog-finishing operation on his property, directly in front of their farmhouse, right across the narrow country road. They had tried to stop him, but failed. Now their lives were overwhelmed by having so many pigs so close.

Kim told Karen how guests would arrive at their home, and practically keel over from the assault of hydrogen sulfide wafting over from just thirty feet away, where the hogs were kept. At night, when dark fell, no one was working over at the CAFO, and the pigs were on their own.

That's when Kim and her family would hear the sound.

It was like something you might hear in a haunted mansion at Halloween, Kim told Karen. It was so eerie, so disorienting, and so awful, it took visitors a moment to realize that the ungodly racket was coming from the pigs. Anyone could tell just from the sound that they were overcrowded and stressed in there, fighting and biting, she said.

"My God," she told Karen, "it sounds like a hundred small children all being tortured at once in there."

Eventually, Dan and Kim gave up, and moved off the property to another home they owned about two miles away. Two years later, the foul odor of hogs from a new CAFO near the other home came wafting through their windows, which they could no longer open.

In February, the Pew Commission held a public hearing in Durham, and the North Carolina anti-CAFO movement mobilized to have their voices heard. Rick was scheduled to speak, as well as Gary Grant, Don Webb, Devon Hall, Dothula Baron-Hall, and others.

The hearing was held at the old brick Durham Armory in downtown, and the room was packed. People came from all sides of the debate—environmentalists, citizen activists, academics, hog producers, industry reps—some from as far away as Texas and Wisconsin.

Plenty of hog farmers turned out to get their side of the story on the record, and they often conveyed poignant tales of how contract farming with the big corporations saved their business and kept them and their families down on the farm.

Isaac Singletary, for example, was owner of Reedy Branch Farm, which had belonged to his family since before the Civil War. After years of traditional pig farming, he switched over to contract production for Murphy-Brown in 1994. It was one of the best decisions he ever made.

"I feel like that's the reason I still own my farm," Singletary said. "My business relations with Murphy-Brown have been good. As a hog farmer, I accept the responsibility and care for my animals. And I'm not paid to be here today. I came because I felt that someone on ground zero needed to talk to you." He ended by stating that he lived within five hundred feet of one of his two hog confinements. "I know what the ramifications of living by a confined pig operation is," he testified. "So my neighbors and I get along just fine. We don't have some problems, never have."[8]

Richard Eason, CEO of Cape Fear Farm Credit, which had given loans to twenty-seven hundred North Carolina farms, confirmed that vertical integration was a godsend for many small farmers, beginning in the mid-1980s. "I saw that it was a great opportunity for our customers and hundreds of family farmers that embraced this technology; they embraced this way of production and saved their family farms," he said.

In the process, they had increased net income, employed seasonal labor year-round, and eliminated the use of commercial fertilizers on their row crops. "The return on investments for these farmers is somewhere between 15 and 22 percent," Eason claimed. "Family farms survived because of this. And the sons and daughters of these family farms were able to come back and realize the dream of making a living."

The majority of contract growers lived on their farms, Eason said, without providing documentation. "They care about the water, because they drink it. They care about the way these operations smell, because they live right next to them, and they try to be good neighbors." Eason also argued against the conventional wisdom that CAFOs reduce property values. "I have over six certified appraisers on my staff, and we can formally show you that land values started to rise with the advent of this industry," he said.

Dr. Liz Wagstrom, chief veterinarian for the National Pork Board, also spoke in defense of swine growers. Mostly, she discussed antibiotic use and the "other white meat" group's two-year-old Use Antibiotics Responsibly program, which promoted "the responsible use of antibiotics" to "minimize the risk of developing antibiotic resistance to thereby protect public health." Wagstrom claimed that small producers were using the same amount of antibiotics per pig as large producers.

Rick Dove's head jerked to attention at Wagstrom's allegation. He made a mental note to fact-check her claim later on.

"Right now over fifty percent of pigs in the U.S. market are coming from producers who've signed an endorsement form that says: 'I will protect animal health, animal welfare, and public health, medical welfare and human health responsibly,'" she added.

Now that the praises of CAFOs had been sung, the opposition testified. What to one party was a godsend, to another was hell on earth. Duplin County's Dothula Baron-Hall told the commission what it is like to live on a backcountry road surrounded by five giant hog farms. "There is a constant stench and respiratory problems that I experience on almost a daily basis and my sinuses and allergies have become just really, really severe," she said.

One woman recounted her tale of how her family's land had been partly appropriated by a neighbor and turned into a hog factory, and of the harassment campaign that she alleged had followed. "They've done everything they can to make me not speak out about the injustices that we're enduring," she said. "A lawyer sent me an intimidating letter, telling me that, should I continue to call [the Division of] Water Quality, I could be arrested or made to pay the hog farmer for the monies that he loses. But this man is making a living off my family's property."

Rick's presentation really impressed the panel members, commissioners said later. He told them the days of the lagoon-and-sprayfield system were numbered. "It's failed. It never will work," he said. "So what do we do? In North Carolina, it's over. I'm telling you, for this industry in North Carolina, the use of lagoons and sprayfields is over in 2007. The legislature in North Carolina this year is considering a permanent ban, which I believe will pass."

What was needed now was "a date certain at which there will be no lagoons or sprayfields on the ground in North Carolina," Rick said, "and benchmarks along the way to be established for the phaseout, with some help for the contract growers." That would require more expensive technology, which presented industry with a stark choice: "You either spend the money to protect these communities and protect their waters, or get back to the family farmers, because the family farmers in America can raise these animals without any problem and feed the market. Nobody has ever stood in line in America to buy a pork chop."

Big old Don Webb, however, brought down the house, as usual. "How many of you would want your mothers to live within twenty-five hundred feet of a factory hog farm owned by the rich guy that lives on Park Avenue?" he asked the commission, adding that, "I was the first one in North Carolina to stand up to them, and you know what, I'm proud of that."

Don also warned the panel not to be taken in by industry claims that people would go hungry if not for cheap protein produced in CAFOs. "If you think those hog people are that worried about feeding somebody? They're worried about buying new homes," he bellowed. "The Constitution of the United States says these poor people that have to smell that stench—have the right of domestic tranquility, and they don't have it!"

Helen was angered by the lack of attention being paid to megadairies in these debates (with the exception of the Pew Commission), and Karen shared her frustration. After all, one of the CAFOs that had first dragged Karen into this protracted war was Inwood, a dairy.

One late night in mid-2007, Karen was still scouring the Internet for documents to support one client's campaign against a megadairy when she came across an intriguing Web site—Inside Dairy Production (http://www.inside-dairyproduction.com)—run by a California group called East Bay Animal Advocates. The group's main message was simple—most of the milk cows in California are not of the happy TV variety, wisecracking on the grassy hills of Sonoma County.

"Each year the California Milk Advisory Board spends $37 million to promote the Happy Cows Campaign. CMAB's marketing promotion depicts computer-animated cows praising life on picturesque dairies in California," the Web site says, adding that these cuddly images are nothing like outdoor feedlots that make up modern dairying in the Golden State.[9]

The reality of the situation, the Web site continues, would not make a good TV commercial. "The pastureless dry lot system increases the incidence of infection, disease and injury among the cow population," the site claims, adding that California cows are often infected with "Laminitis, Johne's Disease, Milk

Fever, Bovine Immunodeficiency Virus and Bovine Leukemia Virus." A University of California, Davis, study showed that air quality in the state's central San Joaquin Valley was among the worst in the nation, and that dairy cow belching was a leading factor in pollution. Ozone levels there had surpassed that of Los Angeles.

In San Joaquin and Stanislaus counties, dairies were the single largest source of water pollution, according to Bill Jennings of Deltakeeper, a San Joaquin Valley environmental protection group. "Our volunteers frequently encounter massive discharges of dairy waste that literally cauterize waterways and kill fish," he wrote on the Web site.

California's "happy" cows were also reportedly threatening human health. A recent study from the South Coast Air Quality Management District warned that California dairies "pose a serious threat to humans living in surrounding rural communities," the Inside Dairy Production Web site said, adding that flies, dust, and odors wafting off the facilities were sickening people living in the valley. Another study showed a significant association between "living close to a dairy and a higher reported rate of diarrhea and asthma in children."[10]

Meanwhile, it cites a USDA Economic Research Service report that "dairy workers exposed to toxic-gas-releasing manure may experience nausea, diarrhea, sore throats, stress and alterations in mood."[11]

Karen quickly telephoned Yakima Valley. "Helen," she said, "I've got some new ammo for our dairy campaign."

In April 2007, Rick got a call from Bill Gerlach and Scott Edwards of the Waterkeeper headquarters in New York, with a special mission for Rick—one they knew he would not refuse.

They planned to investigate the poultry industry's impact on the eastern shore of Maryland and the effect of nutrient runoff on the polluted Chesapeake Bay. Significant funding from a Waterkeeper donor had made the study possible. Bill and Scott asked Rick if he would head up the effort, as he had done in North Carolina.

Rick immediately agreed. He loved the idea. First of all, he had grown up on the Chesapeake, and the meandering bay waters had always held a special attraction for him. "You know, nobody's ever thought about taking our hog strategies and tactics and applying them to poultry," he said. "But this will have to be a different approach. Swine waste is liquefied—you can track it through ditches, drains, and culverts right back to a lagoon or sprayfields. But broiler poultry litter is composted and spread dry on the land—it makes it harder to document a violation."

Rick planned to travel to the peninsula, known locally as the Delmarva (after Delaware, Maryland, and Virginia, which share the landmass), go up in an airplane to have a look around and see if he could spot any Clean Water Act violations. "If I do," he assured them, "we can sue those damn producers, just like we did in North Carolina."

To help Rick out, people at Waterkeeper introduced him to a young coastal wildlife biologist, wildlife manager, and boat operator named Jordan West, who was born and raised on Virginia's Chincoteague Island, a picturesque fishing village and vacation haven on the eastern flank of the narrow tip of the Delmarva Peninsula.

Rick also enlisted the help of another eastern shore local, Carole Morison, who ran a large poultry CAFO with her husband near the town of Pocomoke City, in Worcester County, Maryland. The Morisons had been raising broiler chickens for years for the Perdue company, whose world headquarters is in nearby Salisbury.

Carole is a gregarious blond woman with a quick wit and easy smile. Rick first got to know her back in the mid-1990s, when *Pfiesteria* outbreaks began to show up in the Pocomoke River and other eastern shore tributaries of the Chesapeake. Rick had also watched Carole on public television, speaking out quite harshly against the poultry industry—the first food animal sector to go vertical, way back in the 1950s. Today, the Delmarva is a leading broiler production center in the United States, raising 567 million birds a year.[12]

Rick had never seen a contract grower rail so decisively against big agribusiness, and he was impressed. In 2007, after twenty years in the business, Carole and her husband, Frank, were trying to get out of the business. They said they were tired of the top-down dictates coming directly from Perdue.

Carole was born and raised at the beach in nearby Delaware. She met Frank through a mutual friend and married him in 1985. Frank's parents were chicken and grain farmers on a ninety-three-acre parcel of gently rolling fields and woodlands called Bird's Eye View Farm, about a half mile from the Pocomoke River in Worcester County, Maryland. In 1987, Frank, Jr., was born.

The young couple received fourteen acres to raise crops and build a couple of chicken houses. At the time, seven poultry integrators dominated Delmarva; today only four remain: Tyson Foods, Allen Family Foods, Mountaire Farms, and Maryland's own Perdue Farms. Frank's parents had been contracting with Perdue for years. The newlyweds chose to follow family tradition.

People who raise chickens for big integrators have little choice in the birds they will grow. Generally speaking, there are two types of chickens bred in the United States: layers and broilers. Most layers produce eggs for human consumption, but some facilities produce eggs for hatching meat chickens (broilers).

Layer houses are run quite differently from broiler houses. In the former, the goal is to get hens to deliver eggs as quickly as possible, and in the latter, it is to fatten them for market as quickly as possible. Layer CAFOs are typically where one sees the "battery cages" stacked in long rows that fill massive buildings. Food is carried in along one conveyor belt and eggs are carried out along another.

Delmarva used to have many laying operations that provided broiler chicks to the hundreds of producers in the area (layers that produce eggs for food are more common in states such as Ohio and Indiana). But in the early 1990s, Perdue shuttered these operations and transferred them down to North Carolina. From there, eggs are shipped back up to Delmarva for incubating and hatching. Fear that an avian influenza outbreak could wipe out both broilers and breeders in the same area is what prompted the move.

These days, broilers are the name of the game for Delmarva farmers. Broilers are raised in giant cageless barns. There are three main types of broilers (plus a few specialty breeds):

Chickens: The most common broiler on display at the supermarket is labeled simply as "chicken"—either whole or in parts. "Chicken" is usually a certain hybrid breed of bird, male or female, that is raised until it is seven weeks old. At that age, the males are just starting to show the features of a full-grown rooster—including the iconic comb and wattle, but not the legendary sex drive. Chickens don't start reproducing until about twenty-two weeks of age.

Cornish Game Hens: Another type of chicken, Cornish game hen, has nothing to do with Cornwall and nothing to do with game. Cornish game hens are simply young females from breeds different from broiler chickens, slaughtered at a tender four weeks of age.

Roasters: While the females of this breed are sold as Cornish game hens, the males are separated out early and sent to be raised as "roasters," those very large whole birds found in the market. Roasters are roosters that are slaughtered at eight or nine weeks, and they are always bigger than broiler chickens.

In addition to these three types of broilers, some birds are slaughtered at about six weeks, to be sold as smaller "fryers," or other specialty sizes for institutional food or catering companies. And finally, some stores will occasionally put out something that's marketed as a "whole hen," or "large hen." This is an egg-producing bird past her prime, known in the industry as a spent hen. These birds usually start producing fewer eggs at about one year of age, when they are slaughtered for food—even though "backyard chickens" can continue producing eggs for years.

"The big companies have genetically modified and engineered their laying hens to do a specific thing, which is to put out as many eggs as quickly as possible," Carole explained to Rick. But after a year of that kind of biological pressure, their egg production becomes more sporadic and they are not worth the feed to sustain them. These birds, kept confined to cages, grow quite large and fat. Because their meat is tougher than that of broilers, they typically end up in prepared foods such as soups, frozen dinners, and pot pies. When surplus whole hens are sold in the supermarket, it is usually at a lower price because their meat is meant for stewing, not slicing.

Perdue gave Frank Morison a contract to raise roasters, and the couple built two chicken houses—entirely according to Perdue specs—with a $210,000 loan from the bank. "The company owns everything except the buildings," Carole complained, "and they let you pretend like you're a little family farmer."

When the couple first started out, she said, they were able to make ends meet. But over time, rising costs for feed, propane, and electricity quickly gobbled up their modest profits. Despite rising costs, she said, they were not paid more for the chickens.

After the Morisons had raised just two flocks of roasters, Perdue announced it was moving all roaster operations to the northern part of the peninsula, close to a Delaware slaughterhouse. According to Carole, the Morisons were given a choice between raising regular broilers and getting out of the business. They switched.

Not only did they have to invest in new upgrades to raise broilers, their net gains had just been reduced, too—and for more work. "We built our houses to spec for roasters, and Perdue knew as we were building it they would switch us over to broilers, so why didn't they just tell us?" Carole asked.

Genetically designed to have bigger, meatier breasts, the broilers were given a proprietary feed provided by Perdue. Carole suspected that the feed contained low-dose antibiotics and significant amounts of arsenic, though the company refused to disclose the ingredients. Arsenic in chicken feed promotes growth because it inhibits the intestinal presence of *Coccidioides immitis*, a dangerous fungus. One common though unproven belief is that the heavy metal makes birds eat and drink more to flush the poison from their systems. Other industry observers say that arsenic in feed lends supermarket chicken skin its trademark consistently opaque appearance that shoppers expect.

Under the terms of their Perdue contract, the Morisons were expected to cull out broilers that were not going to make it to market size on time. Some chickens have leg problems or skeletal issues that will prevent proper growth and must be destroyed. Others are the runts of the flock, which Carole called "bumblebee chickens" because they still retain some yellow chick down. They must be chased and killed on a routine basis, but are notoriously fast and hard to catch. Once in hand, the birds are dispatched with a quick thumb pressure to the skull, which neatly dislocates it from the spine.

"When we first found out we would have to destroy up to three percent of each flock, we were appalled," Carole told Rick. "A normal farmer doesn't raise animals only to have to constantly kill them because there is something slightly wrong with them."

"So, what happens to those birds?" Rick asked. "Do you get to eat them?"

Carole let out a cynical laugh. "My God, no, Rick!" she said. "Those birds belong to Perdue. If we eat so much as one of them, they could charge us with theft and cancel our contract immediately. Those birds get composted."

"That's a waste of food, and a waste of life," Rick replied. "What kind of farming is it when you can't even eat the food you raise on your own farm?"

"It isn't farming," Carole said. "If we want chicken for dinner, we have to go down to the supermarket and buy a Perdue like everyone else." At the time, she claimed that they were earning about twenty cents for every live chicken delivered to Purdue. A five-pound broiler might cost seven dollars or more. "So we have to raise somewhere around thirty-five Perdue chickens in order to buy one of them back," Carole said.

The Morisons believed they were buying back their own grain, too, at a big markup. "The only place we can take our corn and beans around here is to feed mills owned by the poultry companies," Carole complained. "The first thing they do is test it for moisture, and then deduct a certain price per bushel for that moisture. Then they grind it all up and sell it to the chicken contractors, but with the same moisture weight in it. So they have deducted that weight from the grain farmer, but included it in the price to the poultry farmer," she said. "They are turning water into money. And we are selling feed at one price, and buying it back at a higher price."

Meanwhile, getting paid for each chicken delivered to the slaughterhouse was a complicated calculus. "The grower is paid on the whole chicken—on total pounds of meat moved off the farm. Now, the market price for whole chicken might be sixty-nine cents a pound, and that is what they pay. What they don't pay us for is the extra revenue they receive from cutting the bird up into parts," she said. "In the market, chicken breast can cost $4.99 or more, but the company is acquiring that breast at sixty-nine cents a pound."

And yet, she said, the contractor doesn't get the whole sixty-nine cents, either.

"They start deducting the cost of the chicks, the cost of the feed, the medication, and the propane they sell you in winter for heat," Carole said. "Then they take all the contractors in your 'processing week' and average out how everyone has done. You may have done very well, and raised most of your birds to market weight, but others around you may not have matched that. But it all gets averaged into one pool of money, which is then divided among the growers. By the time you are finished, you are only making about four cents a pound, or twenty cents a bird."

"In the end, you are losing money," Carole continued. "People are forced to go off the farm and get a job. You are stuck in debt, but if you quit, you lose your farm, you lose your home. It's not like losing a regular small business—so you just keep taking it." Both Carole and Frank ended up getting jobs just to make ends meet. When they considered selling the farm, no one wanted to buy it.

All people had to do was look at the books. For raising fifty thousand birds at 4.13 cents per pound, they were lucky to net four thousand to six thousand dollars a year.

Meanwhile, every step of production was controlled by Perdue. "In the winter, we need steady heat to maintain temperatures at the exact degree specified, or they will cut our contract," Carole told Rick. "And they come out once a week, unannounced, to check the temperature of the litter, and see how the chickens are growing, and to make sure you are doing everything you're supposed to be doing, exactly according to their instructions."

Even the exact level of the feed pans was dictated by the company. As birds got bigger, contractors were required to raise the level of the pans each week with a motorized pulley system. "They don't want chickens having to bend down to reach the food," Carole explained. "That would be wasting energy. And they make sure there's plenty of feed in the pans at all times—those birds eat constantly." The same is done with drinking-water lines, only these were kept slightly above beak level. "It forces birds to raise their heads upward to peck at the little pin that makes water go down their throat," she said. "The company really wants water in that bird—makes it grow faster. And arsenic makes it drink more. They also put salt in the feed. These are some *very* thirsty chickens."

The brutal heat and humidity of eastern shore summers also took its toll on the birds. Normally, the way chickens cool off, aside from panting, is to stand up, lift their wings, and let all that heat under them escape. "But now, they are bred and fed in such a way that, after about five weeks, they are just too darn big to walk or even get up. So they just sit there," Carole told Rick. "They will die of heat if you don't do something. So during the summer, someone has to go into each confinement building every hour to 'walk the chickens'—

physically force them to get up and flap their wings around, otherwise they'd just sit there and die." (The National Chicken Council notes that most modern broiler houses have been or are being converted to a "tunnel-type" system in which outside air is blown into one end of the building and out the other.)

As the birds got bigger, the heat really became hard for them to handle. "You constantly have to pull out all the dead birds, up to one hundred or two hundred per day, per building," Carole said. "Many of them die of heart attacks or kidney failure, because they are growing so fast their internal organs cannot keep up with their muscles and skeletons." Industrial chickens are "on the verge of structural collapse" because they grow so fast, she said. One study found that 90 percent of all meat chickens have leg problems and structural deformities, and more than a quarter live with the chronic pain of bone disease.[13]

And then there was all that chicken shit.

About once every three years, the barns were cleaned out completely to their concrete floor, and new litter was set down for bedding for the birds. It was usually made with wood chips or shavings, though rice hulls worked pretty well; peanut shells proved not to be absorbent enough. After a few weeks, the birds would leave a smashed layer of manure, urine, feathers, and spilled feed that Carole referred to as the "cake." When each flock was removed, the cake was taken out to the manure shed until a local farmer came and hauled it to his fields. "Our land doesn't need any more phosphorus for another eight years," Carole explained.

The wretched environment did more than merely affect the birds, she said; it was also hell on the people who worked in the barns. Carole regularly saw farmers, including her husband, covered in a diaper rash caused by the heat and dust and sweat of working in those chicken houses. On some days, she said, the dust from dander, feathers, litter, and manure was so thick, you could not see from one end of the barn to the other.

Life was even more grueling for the teams of "catchers" that Perdue sent over five times a year, to collect the 27,200 birds in each barn. Seven men would arrive in a tractor-trailer, with stacks of plastic crates divided into "drawers," plus rolls of netting, temporary fencing, and a forklift. The forklift would carry in empty stacks of crates and haul out the full stacks. In the process, it would crack open the manure "cake" and release hundreds of pounds of ammonia, endotoxins, noxious gases, and dust into the barn.

As Carole told Rick, the crew would then section off the barn with fencing and netting and, section by section, scoop up the birds by the legs, clutching four in one hand and three in the other—leaving one finger free to open the cage "drawers." (CAFO efficiency knows no bounds.) The entire process was done in near darkness, because the chickens were more docile that way. But once nabbed, they would fight and scream and claw and peck—Perdue does not debeak its broilers. The ghastly process would routinely leave men cut and scratched, and hundreds of birds bruised and broken.

The workers wore no gloves and no masks, though most donned safety goggles to keep dust out of their eyes. They were dressed in jeans and T-shirts, leaving arms, necks, and faces fully exposed to the gray feces that flew from the terror-stricken birds. In hot weather, the men (women were never sent to catch) wore panty hose under their jeans and on their arms, to prevent the awful chafing that came from spending hours inside a choking-hot chicken house.

Up to the late 1990s, catcher crews were made up largely of African Americans who were paid near-minimum wage to perform the work. When workers attempted to unionize, Carole said, Perdue fired many of them.[14] By 2000, they began to be replaced, mostly by Latino workers from Mexico and Guatemala.

In 1995, Carole was so moved by the plight of the catchers that she volunteered for a group called the Delmarva Poultry Justice Alliance. Two years later, she became the group's executive director, an odd and precarious position for a Perdue contractor. For the next two years, Carole and the group brought together catchers, plant workers, large integrators, contract growers, union organizers, and community and environmental activists to hash out some new solutions for the workers.

Conditions in the processing plants were also horrible, Carole told Rick. Hours were long, conditions poor, and pay low. There were no bathroom breaks, and many women were forced to urinate where they stood, she said. Those who complained were fired.

Catchers were paid low wages. Around 1990, Carole said, Perdue declared that catcher crews were suddenly nothing but contractors, without rights or benefits. By 1997, the dispute landed in federal court, which sided with the workers,[15] who began filing lawsuits against all four Delmarva chicken companies to recover back pay and overtime wages. The cases were all settled, though the statute of limitations meant the companies would only reimburse workers for the past three years.

Meanwhile, catchers also won the right to perform their bodily functions as needed. In the past, there were no restroom facilities for them at the chicken factories, so they had to relieve themselves out in the fields—even in freezing weather. Now, at least, they carried a port-a-potty on their truck, along with their cages and nets.

"Sometimes," Carole explained to Rick as she gave him a tour of her farm, "even little things can make life a bit better, especially when you work in the darkest corners of hell."

In April, Rick drove up to the Delmarva Peninsula to begin the new Waterkeeper campaign for the Chesapeake Bay. Before leaving home, he took several simulated "test flights" on Google Earth over the big chicken-producing counties of Somerset, Worcester, and Wicomico in Maryland, searching for every factory farm he could find.

On the chicken farms, Rick could see giant mounds of dry manure piled up. These are typically kept protected from rain runoff by large open sheds, but Rick could see several that were outside and perilously close to waterways. Carole had explained that, during growing season, some farmers dump litter piles out by their fields, rather than moving it twice—from the barns to the shed and from the shed to the field. In many cases, Rick could see dark liquid leaching from the piles into ditches or canals. He identified seven of the most suspect sites, downloaded their coordinates into his mobile GPS system, and printed out the Google Earth image of each facility.

It was now time to take to the air. In a chartered Cessna, Rick used his GPS to guide the pilot to each site. Along the way, he kept an eye out for other suspect factory farms whose conditions had changed since the Google Earth photo was taken.

When he spotted a suspicious farm, Rick had the pilot circle overhead several times. He checked the property against the Google image. Then he grabbed his seventeen-million-pixel camera with its powerful seventy-millimeter lens and clicked away. He captured hundreds, sometimes thousands, of digital shots of outdoor manure piles, some the size of a three-story house, some with black, oily slicks at the bottom running off into ditches and creeks. Next, Rick turned to his video camera and did the same thing with its eight-hundred-millimeter lens. There was plenty of evidence that he could work with.

Back on the ground, Rick met with his new team—biologist Jordan West and chicken farmer Carole Morison—to plan out the next steps. Rick ran all the GPS coordinates through a program called Street Atlas USA, which printed out maps of each suspect CAFO, including roads, bridges, rivers, creeks, and tidal ditches.

Rick and Jordan spent the next few days driving around Delmarva and trying to take as many water samples as they could. Often, the suspected point of discharge—a pipe draining into a creek, say—would be well inside the private property of the chicken CAFO. But all navigable waters are considered waters of the United States, and that can include "blue line" waterways that look like ditches and are just big enough to allow for the passage of a small kayak.

The entire chicken-growing area in Maryland is very close to sea level, and laced with a complex system of ditches that flush in water from the bay during high tide, and flush back out at low tide. Once, Rick and Jordan got in kayaks to paddle up a tiny waterway and see what was going on. What they found shocked them. At high tide, water from the ditches would wash up into drainage pipes that led directly to the area of the chicken houses and manure piles. He could even see small fish swimming in and out of the pipes. When the tide went out, twice a day, it would wash whatever chicken waste was in the pipes into the ditch and back out to a river or the bay itself. Carole had explained to them that leachate gets washed into the bay year-round, whether it rains or not.

The men took water samples upstream and downstream from each CAFO. The samples were sent off to a lab while Rick returned home and waited for the results.

The lab tests confirmed the smoking gun. They showed the presence of animal waste in ditches that run to streams that feed the bay.

Rick and Jordan settled on nearly twenty sites that might be responsible for the greatest number of violations, and ended up taking repeated water samples outside six broiler CAFOs in the area. In many, they found extremely elevated levels of arsenic, *E. coli*, fecal coliform bacteria, total nitrogen, and phosphorus running into streams that run into the bay. Fecal coliform counts above two hundred colonies per one hundred milliliters of water are considered dangerous. Some samples they took had readings of forty thousand colonies or more per one hundred milliliters.

Normally, Rick would have filed a Clean Water Act sixty-day letter of intent to sue. But Maryland blocked the public from obtaining a critical tool in winning that effort: each facility's manure management plan. If the farm violated its plan by having a discharge, then it broke the law. In Maryland, however, manure plans were jealously guarded secrets. Rick wanted that information in order to make the sixty-day letter as airtight as possible.

Waterkeeper sued the state to relinquish the documents, but knew this would postpone any action under the CWA until that preliminary matter was settled. And besides, once the poultry producers knew they were being targeted, Rick believed, they would begin cleaning up their acts before any lawsuit could be filed.

Instead, Waterkeeper decided to take the water-quality data directly to the EPA, with a request that the EPA issue violations. But it didn't turn out that way. Rick was appalled to discover that EPA agents went directly to Maryland officials and the farmers. No enforcement action was taken.

For the time being, the legal pursuit of these farms was over.

It was a mixed blessing for Rick. Certainly, he took satisfaction in knowing that some pollution would be stopped from entering the bay. But the furtive move to correct the problem—away from the glare of TV cameras and court-room artists—would provide absolutely no deterrent to others in the watershed who might be violating the Clean Water Act. Without even a slap on the wrist for violators, Rick thought, the environmental message was unambiguous: If you are caught polluting, all that will happen is you will be privately and politely asked to stop.

Exasperated by the EPA, Rick and Waterkeeper shared their data with producers of the PBS investigative series *Frontline*, which was busy doing research for a special on water pollution titled *Poisoned Waters*. But that special would not air until April 2009, when it would go on to win the praises of a new EPA administrator working under an entirely new president.

First there were salmonella and *E. coli* emerging from America's CAFOs. Then it was mad cow disease and MRSA. In mid-2007, Americans had another new and unsettling concern while shopping in Safeway for bacon, pork chops, and chicken.

It was melamine—a common chemical used in plastics. But now it had a new and infamous reputation: It had begun turning up in U.S. brands of dog and cat food, sickening and killing countless pets and triggering a massive recall that came too late for thousands of heartbroken animal owners.

Melamine is rich in nitrogen. Machines that test animal food for protein levels often rely on nitrogen as a surrogate for actual protein. That makes the chemical a tempting but toxic filler for unscrupulous manufacturers in China and elsewhere.[16]

In May 2007, melamine was found in American-made livestock and industrial fish feed, manufactured by two companies in Ohio and Colorado. The FDA called it the first detection of melamine in U.S.-made animal feed. Even so, livestock food containing the deadly toxin was not recalled because melamine levels were low, according to the FDA, and posed "little risk" to animals or humans.

The melamine was discovered in a feed-pellet binder made by Tembec BTLSR of Ohio. Tembec stopped using the chemical in April, not chiefly because of the recall, but because world melamine prices were rising.

The livestock and poultry industries had little response to the melamine issue. But the fish-farming sector was distressed to learn of the problem. "Nobody in the United States would think of using fish feed that contained melamine," said Ron Hardy, director of the Aquaculture Research Institute at the University of Idaho.[17] The FDA said that the melamine concentrations in the fish and livestock pellets were relatively low, whereas the tainted dog and cat food had contained up to 20 percent melamine.

But there was an even bigger problem. Although domestic sources of melamine had been eliminated from U.S. livestock feed, Chinese melamine was still being fed to cows and pigs in this country. Giving surplus pet food to livestock was nothing new. But now more than one hundred brands and some sixty million packages of tainted food had been recalled. It had to go somewhere, and much of it wound up in North American animal factories.

Pigs raised on melamine-tainted pet food had now been traced to at least four rendering plants in California and to farms in North Carolina and Missouri. Swine from the American Hog Farm in Ceres, California, were quarantined after federal scientists discovered melamine in their urine samples. And pigs sold by American Hog Farm before the quarantine were now testing positive as well, though many of the animals could not be located. They had most likely already been slaughtered and rendered for human consumption.

Officials were desperately trying to track down a mass of American Hog Farm pigs that had been trucked to a slaughterhouse in Half Moon Bay, California, but they could not account for many of them. The FDA adopted a stoic posture. Even if the pigs went unfound, was their tainted meat really hazardous? Either way, FDA officials told consumers who bought American Hog Farm products to toss them out, "as a precautionary measure."[18]

A few days later, a swine herd in North Carolina tested positive for melamine. They had been fed dog food. That farm was quarantined as well. Its operators insisted that no pigs raised on the contaminated feed had been sold for slaughter. Soon after that, pigs at a Missouri farm also tested positive for melamine. They, too, had been fed the tainted pet food. It was enough to finally prompt the FDA to begin testing pork and poultry meat. Even so, the agency tried to reassure nauseated consumers that the risk of getting sick from eating melamine-tainted meat or dairy products was "minimal."

Helen had long worried about antibiotic use in megadairies, and the impact this might have on drug-resistant microorganisms spreading into the environment and our food supply. It had never occurred to her, though, that the antibiotics themselves might end up on her vegetarian dinner plate.

But a new USDA-funded study told her otherwise. In July 2007, researchers at the University of Minnesota looked at food crops grown in soil spread with antibiotic-containing manure, and published their findings in the *Journal of Environmental Quality*.[19] They examined uptake of drugs in corn, lettuce, and potato fertilized with liquid hog waste that contained sulfamethazine, a common antibiotic used on farms. The drug was absorbed by the crops in leaves and green tissue of the plants. As antibiotic concentrations in the manure increased, so did the levels in the food. The drug was also found in potato tubers, as root crops were the most vulnerable to contamination.

Helen thought she was going to be sick.

The notion of food crops absorbing pharmaceutical products raised serious questions about the human food supply. But one of the Minnesota researchers, Satish Gupta, tried to ease public fears by stating: "The adverse impacts of consuming plants that contain small quantities of antibiotics are largely unknown." This did little to reassure Helen.

The problem might be particularly acute for people with allergies to certain medications, including young children, the study noted. There was also the nagging concern about vegetable lovers developing antibiotic resistance merely from munching on salads.

"Around 90 percent of these drugs that are administered to animals end up being excreted either as urine or manure," said research team member Holly Dolliver. She added that antibiotics found in plants could be most worrisome to the organic farming industry, whose main source of nutrients is farm-animal manure. The USDA said that organic farms must manage manure "in a way that does not contribute to contamination of crops by residues of prohibited substances," such as antibiotics. The heat from composting will destroy some drug compounds, but not all of them.

"We need a better understanding of what takes place when chemicals are applied to sources of food and must be more vigilant about regulating what we use to grow food and what we put in our bodies," Gupta said. "We are a chemical society."

Consumer concern about antibiotics in food was starting to have an impact on the animal-factory industry. Back in January 2006, Tyson Foods announced it had reduced antibiotic use in its broiler chickens by 93 percent. Now, in June 2007, the company said it would no longer use antibiotics to raise chicken that was sold fresh in stores. They would back the new policy with a $70 million consumer ad campaign.[20]

Fresh chicken was soon shipped out to stores emblazoned with new labels proclaiming it to be 100% ALL NATURAL, RAISED WITHOUT ANTIBIOTICS. It was a big day for the big company. Tyson CEO Richard L. Bond told reporters, "We're providing mainstream consumers with products they want."[21]

The pharmaceutical-free birds would cost "slightly more," said Senior Vice President Dave Hogberg. But the price would be "below the cost consumers say they're willing to pay." Tyson's competitors were adding another $1.50 to $2 per pound for boneless, skinless chicken breast without antibiotics, he said.

The price hike for Tyson consumers would be kept under $1 per pound. The company hoped the new drug-free chickens would boost sales, despite the cost increase. But Wall Street was skeptical. "We question whether the average consumer will pay a hefty premium . . . that leads to a meaningful jump in profit margins," one market analyst said at the time.

Tyson would still use antibiotics on a small number of flocks destined for the fresh chicken market, but only to treat disease when there was an outbreak, and not as a prophylaxis against disease. Obviously, these birds would not qualify for the new label. Meanwhile, Tyson's frozen chicken parts would be drug free by the end of the summer, though its chicken nuggets and other processed foods would not be included in the drug-free policy.

The new Tyson ad campaign was called "Thank You," in which families smilingly thanked their loving mom for making dinner with healthy, all-natural chicken from Tyson.

Scientists were as delighted as the central-casting families. "With industry juggernaut Tyson proving that poultry can be grown without using antibiotics as a crutch," noted Margaret Mellon of the Union of Concerned Scientists, "we're hopeful that other poultry producers, as well as swine and beef producers, will follow suit."[22]

But it wasn't enough to simply hope that companies would "do the right thing," Mellon warned. She demanded that Congress approve the Preservation of Antibiotics for Medical Treatment Act, which would prevent all meat and poultry producers from using antibiotics important to human medicine as routine animal feed additives. "Until that happens, Americans remain vulnerable to drug-resistant bacteria that are often more virulent and much more costly to treat," she said.

Each year, grisly news reports surface about people working around manure pits who are instantly overcome by the fumes. Victims often topple into the thick brown muck, where, if they haven't stopped breathing already, they drown.

This happened again on a muggy July 2007 evening in Virginia's lovely Shenandoah Valley, on a Mennonite dairy farm in the shady hamlet of Briery Branch, in Rockingham County. There, the Showalter family milked 103 cows and kept active in the conservative Mennonite community that thrives in that part of the valley. Though they shunned many modern amenities, members did avail themselves of vehicles, telephones, and modern-day farm-safety procedures.

Late in the day on July 2, Scott Showalter, a thirty-four-year-old father of four, was conducting a weekly routine: pumping liquefied manure from a small pit into a larger holding pond. As he worked, a drainpipe in the pit became clogged. It had happened before, and Showalter knew what to do. He shimmied down through a four-foot opening into the concrete enclosure, essentially an underground tank, and attempted to clear the clogged pipe himself. But, unbeknownst to him, a cloud of odorless methane gas had engulfed the pit. Showalter passed out within seconds and fell face-first into eighteen inches of mire.

The dairy's farmhand, twenty-four-year-old Amous Stoltzfus, witnessed the accident. Thinking that Showalter must be having a heart attack, Stoltzfus waded in to rescue his boss. He, too, was felled by the fumes and dropped into the sludge. Another worker ran yelling toward the house, to alert Showalter's wife, Phyllis. She quickly scrambled down to the scene, along with her four daughters.

At the sight of her motionless husband, Phyllis screamed and climbed into the pit. She suddenly went limp. Her frantic daughter Shayla, eleven, went in after her, followed by Christina, nine. Workers had to restrain the other two screaming and sobbing daughters, ages six and two, from following suit. Five bodies now lay suspended in the muck.

The Showalter deaths rattled the quiet village to its core. The next day, grim headlines notified the rest of the country. But what happened that July evening remains a mystery. Dairy farmers are usually extremely careful about ventilating manure pits, where methane is prone to gather. But a cousin of Scott Showalter, Bruce Good, said that liquid runoff from some nearby cattle feed might have made its way into the pit, somehow exacerbating methane production. "It rained, and some of it ran down into this holding pit, it fermented and made a toxic gas," he told reporters.[23]

"Whether they suffocated from the fumes or drowned in eighteen inches of liquefied cow manure may never be known," the Associated Press reported in a story picked up all over the country. Since the deaths were clearly accidental, no autopsies were planned.

Helen read the story in her local paper, and a knot formed in the pit of her stomach. She knew that dairy lagoons were notorious methane generators. And even though this tragedy occurred on a small family farm, it illustrated the dangers of allowing animal gases to accumulate and hurt people.

Helen had read several accounts of similar deaths occurring on megadairies in Texas and California. Most recently, a young farmhand from Mexico had passed out in an electric cart while driving by a lagoon in the San Joaquin Valley. The vehicle went right into the waste, killing him instantly.

16

The ten-year-old ban on constructing new hog-waste lagoons in North Carolina was about to expire, and in the spring and summer of 2007, activists, environmentalists, industry barons, state lawmakers, and the office of Governor Mike Easley were engulfed in a protracted and complicated drama over what should come next.

Most swine lagoons are designed to last about twenty years or so before they start breaking down. That meant that hundreds of lagoons across North Carolina would need to be replaced over the next few years. But environmentalists did not want them replaced by other lagoons. For years, activists Rick Dove, Don Webb, Gary Grant, Devon Hall, Dothula Baron-Hall, and others had not only supported a ban on new lagoons, but had lobbied for the elimination of lagoon-and-sprayfield systems altogether. They wanted a new law on the books requiring CAFOs to install alternative technologies, and establishing a date certain when all lagoons would be outlawed.

Industry balked at any discussion of a permanent ban. They rightly pointed out that Smithfield, Premium Standard Farms, and Frontline Farmers had agreed to adopt new technologies—if they could be installed at an "economically feasible" rate. But that effort had failed (as Rick and others had predicted it would), and the big companies felt neither an obligation nor a compunction to pursue the matter further. Meanwhile, Frontline Farmers and North Carolina Environmental Defense were still seeking funds for their own voluntary pilot program for developing "feasible" lagoon alternatives.

In April, the state senate unanimously voted in favor of a permanent ban on all new hog lagoons and sprayfields as of September 1.[1] The bill also approved a pilot grant program to provide up to $500,000 for each producer who installed "environmentally friendly" waste alternatives. It would not affect current lagoons at the state's twenty-three hundred hog CAFOs. Environmentalists applauded the measure and vowed to push for its passage in the House.

The hog industry and its staunch supporters in Raleigh seemed to have read the tea leaves of public sentiment: They could not keep building new lagoons ad infinitum. "A great transition has taken place in this state," conceded State Senator Charlie Albertson, a Duplin County Democrat who was a friend of Duplin County hog baron Wendell Murphy and a longtime swine industry supporter.[2] In fact, Albertson was also the bill's sponsor. His reasoning was that by providing incentives and assistance for farms to convert to new technologies, he was helping to ensure the longevity of hog production in North Carolina, where the industry had become a pillar of the economy.

Deborah Johnson, CEO of the North Carolina Pork Council, said it was high time to recognize that most people did not want open cesspools anywhere near them, which had become apparent to producers, "just by looking at the economic and political climate," she said. Johnson said her council would work with lawmakers to develop state support for certain technologies, especially the conversion of methane from manure into electricity. Smithfield planned to sell the surplus power to the Progress Energy company.[3]

Amid all the plans, however, there was no talk of banning all lagoons, no mention of any "date certain" envisioned in vain by CAFO opponents. Their conspicuous absence planted a seed of dissent among environmentalists that sprouted into an internecine battle that lingers to this day. It would set mainstream environmentalists against grassroots groups in a bitter dispute over progress and compromise.

The House did not take up the Senate measure until late June. By then, activists statewide were ready for some good old-fashioned political theater. Hundreds of people, belonging to two dozen groups, camped out on the capital's Halifax Mall just behind the legislative building. There, they staged a fifty-one-hour rally and vigil (one hour for every day left in the legislative session), demanding that the House pass the Albertson bill, and that lagoons be banned outright by a certain date. Rick, Don, and Gary Grant helped lead the charge.

Protestors planned to arrange piles of fake pig poop for dramatic effect, but state police blocked them. And when the police saw some demonstrators filling baby pools with hog waste, they threatened to call in the hazmat team and fine the demonstrators for endangering public health if so much as one drop of the stuff spilled to the ground.

The irony of that threat was lost on no one.

"Hey hey, ho ho! Hog cesspools have *got* to go!" the crowd chanted. Reporters milled about, and many sought out Rick and Don for comment. "I've been fighting for this for 18 years and they are still stinking up our homes and getting away with it," Don told *The News & Observer*. And Rick scoffed at the idea of banning real swine waste from the event. "It's too *offensive*—can you imagine that?" he said. "Folks all over eastern North Carolina have feces and urine sprayed on their houses, their cars, their clothes and that's okay. But here at the State Capital where these legislators work and play, it's a health hazard. What nonsense!"[4]

Then came news that Rick and the others were hoping not to hear. The bill had been yanked from the Agriculture Committee and stalled at the request of Governor Easley, who was trying to push through an industry-backed companion bill to allow Smithfield and others to cover their lagoons, capture the methane, and use it to sell electricity to the public utilities, with heavy subsidies that would be passed on to consumers.

Encouraging methane collection would only serve to perpetuate lagoons forever, Rick and the others charged. "All they've got to do is throw a tarp over the lagoon and capture the methane gas, and they're home free," he told *The News & Observer*.

What Rick did not realize was that at that very moment, members of the North Carolina Environmental Defense and the Sierra Club were huddled in a closed-door meeting with the governor's staff and key House lawmakers, hammering out a compromise measure. Riverkeeper, Waterkeeper, REACH, Concerned Citizens of Tillery, and other groups had been left out of the negotiations. When they learned about it, they were furious. They didn't even know the meeting was taking place. On Monday, the revised House bill was passed 108 to 0.[5]

Like the Senate version, this bill would impose a permanent ban on all new lagoon construction for incoming or expanding hog CAFOs. But this time, industry had managed to insert two measures into the new bill that infuriated the protestors out on the plaza.

First was the Tucker Amendment, a measure largely drafted by Duplin County Democrat—and hog producer—State Representative Russell Tucker. It would create a pilot program to capture methane from lagoons at fifty farms, and then sell electricity at a subsidized price that would be absorbed by energy customers. Moreover, farms that adopted this measure would not be held to the same environmental standards as new or expanding farms coming online with alternative technologies—as required under the new law.

To Rick, this not only transferred the burden onto households, it would perpetuate the operation of lagoons and sprayfields well into the century and do nothing to encourage their elimination. "The more you support methane capture from existing lagoons, the less incentive you give these hog factories to convert to alternative technologies," Rick said.

But another new provision in the bill left activists downright apoplectic: CAFOs would be able to replace any lagoon that was in "imminent danger" of collapse.

"Well, they just gutted the whole damn thing," Rick grumbled to his colleagues when they got the news. With this new provision, he said, hog lagoons would never be phased out. "Now, the swine barons just have to wait until a lagoon gets old and looks like it might blow and become a threat to public health," Rick said. "And then, instead of replacing it with some new, nonpolluting technology, they can just build another lagoon that will stay there another twenty-plus years.

"While we were sleeping out here in the plaza, Environmental Defense was sitting around the table with the governor negotiating away everything we sought for more than fifteen years," he added. "We've been had, I'm afraid. It's a real bad deal. We would've been better off with no deal at all. The citizens of North Carolina would never have stood for this."

In fact, Rick was certain that Governor Easley would never have agreed to such a blatant backdoor loophole if he didn't have the cover of major environmental groups like the Sierra Club and Environmental Defense. "He never would have tried to pull this off if we were in the room," he told Don Webb.

Environmental Defense was unapologetic. The group issued a statement lauding "the first state in the nation to ban the construction or expansion of new lagoons and sprayfields on swine farms," and the new "voluntary cost-share program to help swine farmers convert existing lagoons to cleaner systems."[6]

"They sure make it sound nice," Rick said to Joanne when he read ED's spin on what, to many, amounted to a sellout. But even Environmental Defense had to concede that the new bill "does include two industry-sponsored provisions that will require close monitoring. The concern with both of these provisions is that they may lead swine farmers to continue using lagoons in lieu of converting them to cleaner systems."

"They *may* lead swine farmers to continue with their lagoons?" Rick laughed bitterly. "Why do they think the industry fought tooth and nail for that provision? They have no intention of ever giving up those lagoons. They're cash holes."

ED vowed to monitor implementation of the new regulations. "Environmental Defense will work to ensure that these two provisions are narrowly applied and that they do not hinder the overall effort to place cleaner systems on all hog farms across the state," Rick read on with incredulity. "More work will be required to meet the ultimate goal of converting all existing hog farms to clean treatment systems. Environmental Defense is committed to making that goal a reality."

Sure, Rick thought; maybe in 2050 when we're all dead.

Karen Hudson had been closely tracking pollutants for years now. She knew that waste, fertilizers, human sewage, and other effluent discharged into state waters must eventually end up somewhere downstream. Much of the particulate matter will settle out along creek and river bottoms, of course. Many pathogens will die off, and much of the nitrogen, ammonia, and other gases will aerosolize into the atmosphere. Even some of the heavy metals like mercury will be consumed by microorganisms and recycled through the food chain. The rest of it, though—including nutrients like phosphorus—can end up traveling all the way to the sea.

Karen was curious to know the ultimate fate of the millions of gallons of dairy waste that Dave Inskeep had pumped into Kickapoo Creek outside Elmwood, Illinois, back in February 2001. Some of those contaminants were surely washed down into the Illinois River, where they merged with pollutants from other upstream sources, including sewage plants, farms, factories, and fertilized front lawns. From there, the whole watery jumble would have flowed in a southwesterly direction across Illinois, until it united with the Mississippi just north of St. Louis. Karen traced the path with her finger on a road map.

Once the dairy waste from Elmwood was flowing in the mighty river, Karen could see how it would merge with other runoff and discharge from farms as far away as Montana and Pennsylvania. Nutrients and pollutants that spill into distant rivers and streams find their way into the Mississippi via a network of 250 tributaries. The 2,300-mile river drains nearly 1.25 million square miles of landmass—or 40 percent of the continental United States, making it the third-largest catchment basin in the world.

Eventually, waterborne contaminants flow slowly downstream past New Orleans, through the Louisiana Delta, and into the Gulf of Mexico, where the river spits out its nutrient-saturated waters into an eerie and dreadful site known as a dead zone. One of the world's largest algal blooms, it turns a sickeningly large swath of the Gulf each year into a suffocating cauldron of dirty water that destroys fish and other marine life.

In the summer, when sun-warmed seawater mixes with excessive nutrients carried downriver by the Mississippi, an enormous patch of the Gulf succumbs to oxygen depletion, called hypoxia. Nearly all the available oxygen in the water is used up by an unnatural overabundance of algae and microscopic organisms flourishing in the nutrient-rich soup.

The dead zone usually lurks many miles out at sea, away from the Gulf Coast. But in 2007, the hypoxic body of water had swollen to such immense proportions that its edge was now creeping dangerously close to shore. New satellite photos, released in September, confirmed the grim news: the zone had broadened to a 7,900-square-mile mass, roughly the size of New Jersey. It was the third-largest Gulf dead zone in history, and it was almost completely devoid of oxygen.[7]

That same month, fishermen and crabbers along the Gulf Coast began complaining to wildlife officials about some of the worst hypoxia conditions they had ever seen. Crab pots were being pulled up with dead and dying crabs. Fish harvests were down to record lows. And many of the Delta's famous shrimper boats had been idled: There was no reason to dispatch the fleet into a shrimpless sea. Anglers who did venture out into the turbid Gulf witnessed an apocalyptic vision of animal suffering and death. Bottom-feeders like crabs and eels were spotted swimming along the surface, gasping for air.

Their usual deepwater habitat had been entirely deprived of oxygen by the ubiquitous algae that was gorging itself on the detritus of human activity—including (one may speculate) nutrients discharged from a megadairy in Elmwood, Illinois, some seven hundred miles due north of the dead zone.

After the CAFO meeting that Barbara Sha Cox had arranged in Anderson, Indiana, for Karen, Helen, Terry, Bill Weida, and other GRACE Factory Farm Project folks, she found herself increasingly in demand among rural Hoosiers trying to stop incoming CAFOs in their far-flung counties. Phone calls and e-mails were coming in from all over the state from anxious people in wary communities. Barbara and other fledgling activists had formed an ad hoc citizens' group called Indiana CAFO Watch, which, by 2007, had become a force to be reckoned with among bureaucrats and lawmakers in Indianapolis, as well as the state's powerful animal agriculture groups and the Indiana Farm Bureau.

One night, Barbara had been invited to speak at a community meeting in LaPorte County, in northern Indiana, not far from LaGrange County, where a 1993 CDC report identified three women who reported a total of six spontaneous abortions between 1991 and 1993. All three lived near one another, and drew their drinking water from nitrate-contaminated wells. A fourth woman, from another part of LaGrange County, suffered two spontaneous abortions after moving to a new home with nitrate-contaminated well water. The area is known to have many livestock farms and CAFOs.

Before the meeting, Barbara braced herself with her usual tonic elixir, Coca-Cola (she downs them like springwater) outside the auditorium. There were several hog growers inside, she knew, and a decent number of CAFO supporters as well. These things sometimes got tense.

A nicely dressed young man with a friendly smile and disarming demeanor approached Barbara and introduced himself. "Hi, there," he said. "You know, we see you everywhere, at a lot of meetings and hearings around the state. We should get together and talk."

Barbara was not sure what to make of this. "Who are you?" she asked, with an outward smile but internal caution.

"I'm Mike Platt," he said, "Executive director of Indiana Pork."

Barbara did not do a spit take with her Coke, but she wanted to. And yet, this was not what the average CAFO activist thought of when she thought of "Big Bad Pork." Here was a nice guy in decent (but not too expensive) clothes, courteous and respectful. It was impossible to not like Mike. Barbara agreed the two should have lunch together soon, and went inside to give her talk.

The hog men were unhappy with the presentation, and they made their displeasure known through icy glares and under-their-breath oaths during Barbara's talk. When it was over, some of them followed Barbara around inside the building, yelling after her. Spooked and sincerely worried about her security, she ducked into the ladies' room to wait it out. Peering out the door, she spotted a group of people heading for the front exit and hurried to join the safety of their ranks.

Dan was supposed to be waiting for her outside with the car, but he was not there yet. Barbara nearly panicked. Out of nowhere, Mike Platt appeared and stood guard by her side, waiting with her until her ride showed up.

It was the beginning of a long and unexpected friendship.

In most other states, it is virtually unheard of for CAFO foes and CAFO fans to speak with one another, much less air grievances and propose solutions over a nice lunch of country ham, potato salad, and a Coke. But Barbara Sha Cox and Mike Platt were growing weary of the fighting and crossfire coming from both sides of the animal-factory wars.

Barbara and Mike both had to explain to a lot of people why they were lunching with the "enemy."

"The rest of the industry does not seem to want to work together with us, but Mike does," Barbara told Karen. "And I deeply respect him for that. When we go to lunch, we find common ground, which is very valuable for everyone."

Mike Platt was serious about improving the image and reputation of Indiana pork producers, and part of his job was to take journalists on tours of hog CAFO's that might be described as "industry models." It irked people like Barbara to think that reporters would never be invited to visit the facilities that gathered the most complaints by surrounding neighbors. But she understood that business was business, and all businesses want to present their best faces.

As those faces go, people like Mike Beard surely fit the "model" bill. Mike runs a large "wean-to-finish" operation called Meadowlane Farms out of Frankfort, Indiana, that raises thirty-three thousand hogs a year for TDM Farms. He uses his manure to fertilize sixteen hundred acres of corn and soybean crops. Mike's dedication to the environment and to keeping his neighbors satisfied is self-evident.

In fact, in 2007 Mike and his CAFO won two top honors: the Indiana Governor's Award for Environmental Excellence and a National Pork Board 2007 Pork Industry Environmental Stewards Award, presented by the Pork Checkoff, a trade group that is funded by pork producers who contribute forty cents on each hundred-dollar-value of hogs sold.

Meadowlane was one of four awardees selected for its exemplary "manure management systems; water and soil conservation practices; odor-control strategies; farm aesthetics and neighbor relations; wildlife habitat promotion; innovative ideas used to protect the environment; and an essay on the meaning of environmental stewardship," according to the Pork Board's Web site.

Instead of large open lagoons, Beard's CAFO uses deep pits to store manure under the barns, which are pumped out each fall for "field application using technology that is not only environmentally friendly, but also technologically advanced," according to the Pork Board. Trucks haul the waste out to fields, where hoses are connected to a special $150,000 high-tech tractor to inject the effluent into "no-till land," four to six inches under the soil surface.

"To get the best possible payoff from the application equipment, Beard, his son David, and son-in-law Chris run a thirty-million-gallon-per-year manure application business," the board said. "Their goal is to share their expertise and environmental philosophy with other pork producers and farmers in the area."

A brief video was also produced about the award, and Mike Beard shows it proudly to his visitors. According to Beard, manure is vastly preferable to chemical fertilizer, which he tried but didn't like. "My fertilizer bill went from near zero to something significantly more than that," he said on the video. "The manure-fertilized fields are greener, taller, don't seem to show near the firing that's due to the drought."

The video goes on to describe exactly what a state-of-the-art manure plan looks like:

Meadowlane Farms's most recent comprehensive nutrient management plan provides the details that tell Mike how to sample the fields he will apply swine-derived fertilizer on, how to handle the manure-derived nutrients, and how to maintain the records of these applications. Effluent is fed to a tractor-mounted injector through a flexible hose and supply pump, capable of delivering up to one thousand gallons per minute. The injector uses a power distributor to help assure even distribution over the width of the tool bar. Injectors place the manure approximately four inches below ground, with little disturbance to the soil surface. Odor is reduced and nitrogen volatization is minimized. Satellite technology helps guide application and record site-specific information. A flow meter provides gallons per minute rates to mapping software so precise maps and application reports can be produced. In the barn, detailed feed-management practices such as adjusting diets to the nutritional requirements of the pigs have helped Mike balance nutrient levels in the manure. Feed additives are also used to help control odor.

A tour inside one of the barns revealed comfortable-looking conditions, with dozens of young piglets—cute and pink—napping in big cozy piles or chasing one another about their indoor pens with squeals of delight. The young animals seemed clean, warm, dry, and happy.

Mike Beard insisted that this was just business as usual for his farm, and not done in order to win any of the awards. "Plus, we were complying with the requirements of Indiana Department of Environmental Management," he said. "We asked them to monitor our site, and if they thought there were any problems, we'd be happy to correct them. And if you check with the State, they'll tell you that we're quite good neighbors. We have added a buffer area all the way around our woods, to protect waterways and provide habitat for wildlife." Mike Baird does not apply manure onto wet soil, nor even when rain is expected, he added. "We don't apply right after it rains, and once the ground is frozen, that's it—we're done." Whatever he can't apply on his own land, he sells to other neighbors.

"A lot of people don't recognize that manure is a profit center for most hog farms," he said. "It's not just a waste product that they need to get rid of. And so just dumping it willy-nilly doesn't economically make much sense." Nitrogen fertilizer cost him six hundred dollars a ton, he said. Four years previously it was two hundred dollars. Phosphate and potash prices doubled in the same period.

Selling surplus manure, rather than trying to dump it onto the land, makes good economic sense, Mike said. "A barn can cost up to three-quarters of a million dollars to build," he explained. "You want to make sure you can operate that barn, and IDEM doesn't shut you down. You recognize the investment that you have. Using the manure to the fullest of your advantage is a way to offset that investment. It actually has value."

But even the best-run farms can have unforeseeable accidents.

In the summer of 2008, residents of Randolph County saw one of the strangest sights anyone could remember seeing in a long, long time. Rising high out of the cornfields nearly twenty feet into the air were six massive brown bubbles, growing by the day. It was the synthetic liner of a dairy lagoon: Gases had built up underneath the liner, bulging the material high up into the air. People were genuinely afraid that the whole thing was going to blow.

Allen Hutchison was one of them—the "bubble trouble" lagoon was very near his house. Instead of shutting down the dairy, IDEM actually approved a proposed expansion of the facility. Meanwhile, the whole time that the gas-filled old liner remained in place, IDEM never checked any of the neighbors' wells, nor did they require the dairy operator to increase his own groundwater testing. Hutchison and his neighbors not only grew increasingly worried about giant methane bubbles exploding into apocalyptic balls of fire, they also lost sleep over the potential contamination of their wells.

Another time, Allen Hutchison discovered that the USDA had come out to the dairy and put out poison bait for the thousands of starlings that often swirl around megadairies and create a nuisance and health hazard for cows and people.

No one had told the Hutchisons of the plan. They found out about it one night after waking up to the screams of dozens of dying birds—all over their property. The next day, Allen counted eighty-seven stiff and lifeless starlings, which he put into plastic bags for disposal. It took all morning, and no one from the dairy or the USDA offered to help. Allen has also found cowhides in his yard that he must pick up and dispose of because of the health risk of dead animal parts in the yard.

In the fall of 2007, the debate over animal waste and the CERCLA Superfund law was simmering once again. Only this time, the Democrats were in control of Congress, and they were far more divided on the issue than Republicans had been. The manure bills lived on, however, shepherded through the House by Agriculture Committee chair Collin Petersen (D-MN). A Senate version had also been introduced over the summer by Agriculture Committee member Blanche Lincoln (D-AR).

On the other hand, powerful members on the Hill, including California Democratic Senator Barbara Boxer, chair of the Committee on Environment and Public Works, appeared adamantly opposed to the exemption of manure from CERCLA. Boxer announced she would hold hearings on the matter in early September. Rick Dove was invited to testify.

It was an obscure piece of legislation on a topic that few Americans spent much time pondering. Even so, the manure exemption bill was "ruffling feathers on Capitol Hill," Politco.com reported.[8] Poultry giants like Tyson Foods were going "beak to beak with green groups such as the Sierra Club, a batch of state attorneys general, and local government organizations such as the National League of Cities," it added.

On the day of the hearings, September 6, 2007, Senator Boxer opened with a blistering proclamation against any bill that dared to claim that animal waste is not hazardous to the environment. She said all industries were held accountable for their bad acts—even accidental ones. There was no reason why agriculture should get a pass.

"Where there has been damage caused by these facilities, and there have been numerous instances of air and water pollution and contamination of wells and other water supplies," Boxer said, "the parties responsible can be held accountable and pay to clean up their messes."[9]

To drive home the potential harm of CAFO waste, Boxer mentioned the Virginia dairy tragedy that took five lives at the Showalter family dairy.

But the senator from California did not rely on drama alone to make her point; she reviewed the scientific evidence that had powered the cause of animal-factory opponents worldwide, she said.

"This waste can increase phosphorus levels in water, causing algae blooms that can foul drinking water supplies, increase treatment costs, and cause massive fish kills," Boxer reported with a stern look. "CAFOs can create significant air pollution, including foul odors, ammonia, volatile organic compounds, and hydrogen sulfide. CAFOs' air pollution can exceed the amounts emitted by industrial facilities. I believe this hearing will contribute to the public's clear understanding of the threats to environmental health associated with these facilities."

Environmentalists in the room clapped and cheered. Those representing the Ag interests looked dyspeptic. But the industrialists were not without their allies. Nearly a third of the Senate, and more than a third of all House members, had cosponsored the legislation. One of them was Senator James Inhofe, the committee's ranking Republican member. Inhofe, who is proudly proagribusiness, had the duty of welcoming his own state attorney general, Democrat Drew Edmondson, to the hearing. It was an awkward moment; Edmondson was suing Tyson and other poultry producers across the border in Arkansas for allegedly allowing chicken waste to contaminate large sections of Oklahoma's pristine watershed in the Ozark foothills.

After observing procedural etiquette, Inhofe ripped into the very idea of "criminalizing" animal poop. "The prospect of declaring animal manure a hazardous waste and thus regulating under CERCLA deeply concerns me," he said. "If animal manure is found to be a hazardous waste, then virtually every farm operation in the country could be exposed to liabilities and penalties under this act. Furthermore, how then do we categorize the producers of such hazardous waste? Are chickens and cows producers of hazardous waste and subject to CERCLA regulation as well? I do not believe this is what Congress intended."

But congressional intent went right to the heart of the argument, opponents contended. Congress never meant for the everyday, controlled use of manure on farms to be included under the Superfund rules. Those rules pertained to large spills and discharges only. The agronomic application of manure to enhance soil nutrients was already exempted under the law. This new bill, opponents charged, would extend that exemption to any discharge of agricultural waste—no matter how expansive, expensive, or even intentional it was.

Perhaps no one drove home that point more than Inhofe's fellow Oklahoman—and current political adversary—State Attorney General Drew Edmondson.

Farmers were not liable under CERCLA for the simple act of spreading manure on their crops at agronomic rates, Edmondson said. He read a passage from the law's Senate Report, calling it "powerful evidence of congressional intent." The "normal field application" of fertilizer was not a pollutant, but the term does not include the dumping, spilling, or emitting of waste anywhere but on fields, and then only at agronomic rates. Farmers were already exempted—unless they caused a significant spill that caused damage and incurred cleanup costs. Congress never intended to exempt *all* releases of hazardous substances from manure. Senator Lincoln's bill would be "a hundred-and-eighty-degree change in this carefully considered environmental law," Edmonson testified.

Meanwhile, Oklahoma was severely damaged by industrial chicken pollution from Arkansas, he said. Excess nitrogen, phosphorus, heavy metals, and pathogens were contaminating parts of eastern Oklahoma's Illinois River watershed—a million scenic acres of hilly land near the Arkansas border, dotted with woodlands and lakes, and beribboned with waterways.

"Pollution from industrial-scale animal feeding operations is a serious and growing problem," Edmondson said gravely. "States like Oklahoma need legal tools to help stop and clean up animal-waste contamination, which is destroying significant and irreplaceable public resources. Fortunately, CERCLA is there to provide one tool to help." But that tool could be snatched from the hands of environmentalists by a "coordinated effort" to weaken CERCLA. Proponents claimed it was designed to help family farms; to simply "clarify" that agriculture is exempt. But that was a lie, he said. It was nothing more than a transparent grab at the legalization of the dumping of hazardous material. "No other industry in the country has that kind of protection," he said.

The American Farm Bureau Federation did not agree. It brought an attractive young woman to tell its side of the story. Her name was Chris Chinn, chair of Farm Bureau's Young Farmers and Ranchers Committee. With her soft smile, rosy cheeks, and honey-colored hair, she put a fresh face on an old friend of Big Ag.

Chinn opened with a livestock apologia: a spirited defense of the industry she clearly loved and admired. She dismissed out of hand the terms "factory farm," and even "industrial livestock production," as attempts to "demonize" an honorable tradition.

"In fact, many of these livestock farms continue to be family owned and operated," Chinn testified. "Contrary to antilivestock rhetoric, this nation's livestock industry is proficient at producing safe and abundant food while protecting our natural resources. The industry is highly regulated and farmers often surpass requirements when fulfilling their roles as caretakers of the environment and good citizens of their communities."

Many farms were close to going under, and more "needless regulation" that did nothing for the environment or food safety would drive them out of business altogether, she said—though no one was calling for any new regulations at all.

"Additional regulation means dollars out of the pockets of farmers and ranchers, pure and simple," Chinn said. Animal farmers were already regulated under the CWA and their own nutrient plans, she said in a common refrain heard that day. It was a duplication of efforts to regulate manure, or, as she put it, the "overkill of CERCLA."

According to Chinn, if the nation were to classify manure as a hazardous substance, the threat of liability could forever change the face of American farming. Fear of manure lawsuits would drive farmers toward using more chemical fertilizers, which cost three times as much and would increase food prices. New monitoring technologies would hurt small and medium producers, but the largest operators "would be better able to absorb the compliance and cleanup costs." Chinn also pulled out the ever-reliable argument of CAFO supporters everywhere: If you regulate them too much, they will pull out and move to other countries, leaving the United States vulnerably dependent on foreign food imports.

Even the "green" movement would be derailed, Chinn claimed. The threat of manure lawsuits might herald the end of organic farming, and halt the widespread development of earth-friendly biofuels, making it "unclear how farmers who use organic methods would be allowed to continue applying manure to their crops." And, she added, "Using manure to generate energy—through methane digesters, for instance—could result in entrepreneurs and scientists being held liable for cleanup costs under CERCLA, which would preclude the use of manure as a potential energy source."

Chinn's tone grew serious, even ominous, in her closing remarks. And she cleverly used her opponents' own "sustainability" arguments to support passing the manure exemption amendment. "Livestock production in the United States must survive and profit," she warned. "If animal agriculture loses its economic sustainability due to overregulation, American consumers would be left to depend on foreign food imports, likely grown with less regard for food safety."

Rick was the last person to testify that day. Out of uniform, in a dark suit with his polished shoes and short graying hair, he was practically unrecognizable. Rick carefully recounted the long story of his fifteen-year fight to save the Neuse. He walked the committee through a saga of floods and hurricanes, lawsuits and legislation, as well as pollution, illnesses, and even animosity and occasional violence from opponents credible.

Barbara Boxer listened intently as the retired marine JAG recounted the many promises the pork industry had made to the people of North Carolina, especially those in the hog belt. "They claimed that as swine CAFOs were built, everyone would prosper; that new, good, high-paying jobs would be created; and that local crop farmers would benefit as they produced crops needed for animal feed," he said.

Regarding the matter of manure as a pollutant, Rick explained that when neighbors of swine CAFOs fell sick from the stench and the runoff, factory-farm owners denied any responsibility.

"Now, I am going to tell you why CAFO pollution must be brought under control," Rick said softly, to great effect. Several senators leaned forward in their tall leather swivel chairs to better listen. "By illegally polluting, industrial hog producers gained a critical advantage over their competitors—the traditional family farmer—in the marketplace," Rick said. "These are not businessmen making an 'honest buck.' Instead, they are lawbreakers who make money by polluting our air and water and violating the laws with which other Americans must comply."

Rick went on to rip apart industrialized animal agriculture. The corporate suits in the room must have been squirming in their seats, he thought:

> Environmental lawbreaking is an integral component of factory pork production, and factory hog producers are chronic violators of state and federal law. For example, North Carolina records show thousands of violations of environmental laws by Smithfield's facilities. State officials readily admit that at critical times they do not have the resources to enforce the law. As a result, enforcement is virtually nonexistent except for what private citizens are able to do pursuant to the provisions of the federal Clean Water Act. Meanwhile, the rare penalties and small dollar amounts occasionally dispensed by state enforcers never provide sufficient incentive for the industrial pork barons to stop their lawbreaking.

The scale of such pollution "can be truly shocking," Rick continued. At Threemile Canyon Farms, in Boardman, Oregon, 52,300 dairy cows were emitting 15,500 pounds of ammonia each day—or 5,675,000 pounds a year. "That's 75,000 pounds more than the nation's number-one manufacturing source of ammonia air pollution, CF Industries of Donaldson, Louisiana," he said. There was also the Buckeye Egg Farm (now Ohio Fresh Eggs) in Croton, Ohio, which released 1.6 million pounds of ammonia in 2003, or roughly 4,400 pounds per day—forty-four times over the "reporting threshold" established by the EPA.

If Congress were to amend the Superfund law with a special exemption for livestock waste, it would deny Americans a "critical legal tool for protecting their invaluable water supplies from pollution by large-scale agricultural operations that fail to properly manage their waste," Rick concluded. "Such an amendment would declare that water users, not polluters, must bear the burdens of pollution, a radical shift from the 'polluter pays' principle enshrined in CERCLA and in our common sense of right and wrong."

When Boxer closed the hearing that afternoon, she vowed to fight all efforts—including those from her own party—to exempt factory farms from CERCLA. "I wanted to have this hearing today to draw the lines of this battle," Boxer said. "My first priority is to protect the health of the people."

Many newspapers around the country agreed with Boxer, running editorials against granting a special Superfund exemption for animal manure.

LOOKING OUT FOR FARMER GOLIATH, blared an editorial headline in the Cleve-
land *Plain Dealer*. "Some members of Congress want to build a legal moat
around polluting megafarms to protect them from big, bad cities that want to
punish them," the paper said. "More reasonable lawmakers should block this
measure."[10]

The point of the Superfund law was to fight pollution, "whether from
smokestacks, swine, or any other source," the *Plain Dealer* contended. "Congress should not rush to protect factory farms from the consequences of their
actions. Cities seeking just compensation for environmental damages don't
need a moat blocking their way."

The following week, *The New York Times* published its own anti-CAFO
waste editorial, this one focusing on the risks of antibiotic-resistant bacteria
emerging from factory farms. "A recent study by the University of Illinois makes
the risk even more apparent," it said.[11] Scientists had examined groundwater
near two hog CAFOs and isolated a number of transferable bacterial genes that
confer antibiotic resistance, and in particular to tetracycline—a common human
antibiotic.

"There is the very real chance that in such a rich bacterial soup these genes
might move from organism to organism, carrying the ability to resist tetracycline with them. And because the resistant genes were found in groundwater,
they are already at large in the environment," the *Times* editors wrote, before
proposing two "interdependent" solutions. The first was sure to face industry
resistance: Ban the "herdwide" use of antibiotics. The other was to "tighten the
regulations and the monitoring of manure containment systems. The trouble,
of course, is that there is no such thing as perfect containment."

The editorial concluded, "The justification for this kind of farming has always been efficiency, and yet, as so often happens in agriculture, the argument
breaks down once you look at all the side effects. The trouble with factory
farms is that they are raising more than pigs. They are raising drug-resistant
bugs as well."

On November 1, the Waterkeeper Alliance sponsored a first-of-its-kind
Poultry Summit on the Delmarva Peninsula, at the Wicomico Civic Center in Salisbury. The summit brought together activists, environmentalists, industry reps, and contract chicken growers from Maryland, Delaware, and
Virginia to "discuss the impact that the poultry industry is having on nutrient
loads in the watershed and efforts to reduce the amount of chicken waste that
flows from poultry farms on the eastern shore into the bay," according to a
Waterkeeper bulletin.

The environmentalist group said that a large chunk of the Chesapeake Bay and its tidal waters suffered from nutrient pollution, which came "primarily from industrial farms throughout the region, [turning] much of the bay into an anoxic dead zone each summer, choking aquatic life, closing beaches and causing illness in people, livestock, and pets." Much of the pollution was chicken waste.

Meanwhile, the state's chicken industry and the government had flatly refused to release any specific information on how the CAFOs operated. The Maryland Department of Agriculture, which supervises the disposal of chicken litter, declared that chicken-manure management plans, which detail how farms dispose of their waste, were classified as secret. Data on the size, ownership, and even location of CAFOs were off-limits to the public, Waterkeeper charged.

The gathering would feature a keynote address by Robert F. Kennedy, Jr., and remarks by Maryland's attorney general, Douglas Gansler. Another speaker on the program was Bill Satterfield, spokesperson for Delmarva Poultry Industry, Inc., who must have known he would be received with something short of ebullience by most of the people attending.

"We're constantly being assured that the poultry industry is acting responsibly with respect to the mountains of chicken waste it generates each year," Waterkeeper's president, Steve Fleischli, said in a statement promoting the event. "But when an industry operates under the cover of state-sponsored darkness, there's no accountability. It's time to shine a light on these harmful practices and force the industry to act responsibly." He said the main goals of the summit were to encourage Maryland to issue NPDES pollution-control permits to chicken factories, step up water pollution enforcement, and make nutrient-management plans open for public scrutiny.

Rick came back up to Delmarva for the summit, where he spent a good deal of time with Jordan West and Carole Morison, as well as his old friend Bobby Kennedy, who brought most of the summit to its feet with another barnstorming speech.

According to a recent *Baltimore Sun* article, the poultry industry on Maryland's eastern shore was generating some billion pounds of manure a year, much more than available cropland could utilize.

Maryland had been slower than others to require Clean Water Act permits for the poultry industry, but was finally "considering" such permits, in addition to regular inspections and new fines ranging up to $32,500 per day for discharging manure into streams.

Even the mention of such measures had infuriated many chicken farmers, who complained that chicken houses don't pollute like factories, and that it was unjust to overburden family farms with too many regulations.

The farmers had their champion in Bill Satterfield, who presented a lengthy slide show defending chicken growers from their vocal and well-organized opponents.[12]

Slide number one pretty much summed up the presentation to follow: "It's Not Necessarily Us!" it declared.

Satterfield stated that high levels of nitrogen load and phosphorus in the Chesapeake Bay were not from chicken farming, since chicken-producing counties in Delmarva made up just 7.7 percent of the entire watershed area.

"The Susquehanna, the Potomac, and the James rivers contributed 95 percent of the annual nitrogen load and about 87 percent of the phosphorus from the nine major rivers draining to Chesapeake Bay," he asserted. Meanwhile, on Maryland's eastern shore, the largest river is the Choptank, but that contributed less than 1 percent of the total nitrogen and phosphorus load delivered annually from the nontidal part of the Chesapeake Bay basin.

Satterfield had other data to support the contention that chicken farming was not the biggest problem. Farming uses just 5 percent of the land in the Chesapeake watershed, and contributes only 7.75 percent of the total nitrogen, he said. Development was the real culprit. "Increasing human populations and the associated land-use changes continue to be the primary factors causing water quality and habitat degradation," Satterfield noted. But the state was unduly leaning on farmers to reduce loads even further, "in part because these measures are so cost-effective," he said.

In the meantime, Delmarva Poultry Industry had taken steps to reduce discharges. For one, "feed conversion" had improved 7.6 percent since 1998, meaning more grain was used by the birds and less was being excreted. And a feed additive called phytase was now being used that let birds better utilize phosphorus already in their feed. Because chickens lack enzymes to absorb phosphorus from corn, more was typically added to feed, making chicken litter unusually high in the nutrient. Phytase helped to eliminate the need for this. "Phosphorus levels in excreta have been reduced by approximately thirty percent in recent years," Satterfield said.

"Poultry and agriculture have been very aggressive on environmental issues" during the same period, he concluded. "If others in the 64,000-square-mile Chesapeake Bay watershed had been as proactive on environmental issues in recent years, things would not remain as challenging as they are and we would not need to be here today!"

Satterfield was treated politely, if not warmly, by the audience. And he was followed by Carole Morison, who was in no mood to extol the benefits of contract farming for big chicken companies. Over the summer, Perdue officials had come out to the farm for a little visit, and to inform Frank and Carole that they needed to make some very major "upgrades" to their chicken houses, yet again, if they wanted to continue their contract.

Perdue gave them one year to totally enclose the confinements with solid walls instead of heavy canvas curtains.

They would then have to install an expensive "tunnel ventilation" system that uses huge fans to draw in fresh air from one end of the long barn and spew out ammonia-filled air at the other. That system would require additional well water for use as a misting coolant, more electricity to pump the water, and a new automatic generator to keep the whole thing going if the power went out.

Carole said that the entire upgrade would cost more than $150,000, and it was entirely their responsibility to get the financing—or they would lose their contract by June 2008.

Frank and Carole were appalled by the idea of raising chickens in a totally enclosed building, and there was no way in hell they were going another $150,000 into debt for Perdue. They were already losing money as it was, even with two full-time jobs off the farm. And this was on top of their existing mortgage and debt on the chicken houses. With a net return of $5,000 or $6,000 a year, Carole told Frank, "it would take us two forevers to pay it all off."

This would be the Morisons' last year as chicken farmers.

It wasn't like the poultry industry was going to miss Carole Morison. She had been enough of a troublemaker as it was. Someone in particular was extremely unhappy with her activism.

After Carole was booked to speak at the Poultry Summit, two mysterious fires occurred right next to her property. In September, one of two large abandoned chicken houses on the adjacent land—not fifty feet away from the Morisons' own confinements—was set ablaze and destroyed. It had been a hot, drought-ridden summer, and there was nothing but tinder-dry weeds between the massive inferno and the Morisons' barns (which happened to be empty of birds at the time).

A month later, a second abandoned house went up in flames. Neither building had electricity, and there was no insurance policy on either structure. The fire department determined that both blazes were caused by arson.

The fires did nothing to stop Carole. "In 2006, the poultry industry on the Delmarva Peninsula produced almost 568 million chickens on less than 1,960 contract farms," she began her talk at the summit. "In fact, Sussex County, Delaware, is ranked number one in chicken production out of all of the counties in the United States."

The growth of the industry—and the chickens—had seemed nothing short of miraculous, at least at first blush. Back in 1928, when Herbert Hoover vowed to "put a chicken in every pot," it took American farmers 112 days to raise a 2½ pound bird, one that ate nearly 5 pounds of feed for every pound of meat it gained, Carole said.

But today's industrial farmers required just forty-eight days to raise a 5½ pound superchicken whose "feed conversion ratio" is so efficient it needs to eat only 1.95 pounds of food to gain 1 pound of meat. And even though Americans today consume more than 90 pounds of chicken annually,[13] "there are not enough pots to put those chickens in," she said.

"One could say that the billion-dollar poultry industry is a highly successful model to be admired," she added. "Or is it?"

The 568 million chickens that lived in Delmarva in 2006 left behind an unimaginable 2.27 billion pounds of manure. Where did it all go? The seven chicken-producing counties in Delmarva could count on just 638,356 acres of harvested cropland to absorb all those nutrients. Assuming the manure was distributed equally, that would leave over 3,500 pounds of manure to be spread on each acre.

"After decades of using poultry manure as fertilizer, the land has become saturated with phosphorus and nitrogen, resulting in nutrient overload," Carole said. "The continued practice, coupled with the fact that most drainage ditches on the peninsula are tidal, means runoff from fields ends up in tributaries, streams, rivers, and the bay."

Along with the "excessive nutrients spread on the land," Carole said, "we are adding a little arsenic for flavor. Arsenic does not break down in the environment. The most important question right now is, Where is all of that arsenic? Some research has been conducted, but much more is needed to determine if farmers have unknowingly turned their land into a toxic waste dump."

Carole then challenged something else that Satterfield had said. The chicken spokesperson had boasted that, since 2000, his industry had paid truckers to haul some 252,000 tons of manure out of the Chesapeake watershed. That sounds impressive at first, but maybe not so much when you begin to do the math, she said. Divided over seven years, it came out to 36,000 tons a year, or 72 million pounds, still a respectable amount to be sure, but just a tiny 0.3 percent of the 2.27 billion pounds produced in total.

"Have consumers really benefited from modern-day industrialized chicken production?" Carole asked in conclusion. "At the grocery store, maybe. But they are footing the bill through tax dollars used to clean up industrial waste, the increasing loss of clean and safe recreational waters, antibiotic-resistant bacteria, questionable safe drinking water and added withdrawal from an already low water supply, rising energy costs due to increased demand, and increased fossil fuel use contributing to global warming, acid rain, and water pollution.

"So the question then becomes, Just how cheap *is* that chicken?"

When the summit was over, Rick got to spend some more time with Carole Morison and Jordan West, along with Robert Kennedy, Jr. Among the most compelling topics that day, they agreed, were the possible connections between arsenic in feed, broiler litter, and cancer.

The most common brand of arsenic additive for chicken feed is roxarsone, manufactured by the company Alpharma Animal Health under the brand name 3-Nitro. By the early 1970s, contract poultry farmers noticed that large flocks of broiler chickens had serious problems with intestinal parasites, which stunted the growth of the chickens. Roxarsone became very popular among producers for its antiparasitic properties; even hog growers use it now.

The arsenic in roxarsone is organic—meaning there are carbon atoms in the molecule—making it much less toxic than the inorganic form of the metal. But even roxarsone will cause paralysis in chickens if they do not drink enough water while on the drug.[14]

Arsenic, especially the inorganic form, is very toxic to people. It can affect virtually all organs and tissues in the body and is considered a Group 1 carcinogen. The most common forms of cancer associated with exposure are skin, lung, liver, prostate, and bladder—but it can also cause leukemia and lymphoma, as well as cancers of the breast, colon, stomach, and throat. It can also cause neurological, immunological, cardiovascular, and endocrine effects; miscarriages; partial paralysis; diabetes; and hyperpigmentation and hyperkeratinization of the skin.[15]

As science has learned more about the dangers of arsenic, government officials have responded accordingly. In November 2001, the EPA said it would lower the maximum safe exposure level in drinking water from fifty parts per billion to ten parts per billion. Months later, when the Bush administration took office, it tried to overturn the new EPA rule, but eventually abandoned that effort.[16]

The poultry industry says that arsenic levels in chicken meat are negligible, though the USDA only tests the livers (and not the meat) of about twelve hundred birds a year (the European Union banned arsenic in chicken feed in 1999).[17] The FDA also sets withdrawal periods to allow the built-up arsenic in meat and organs to flush out of the system before slaughter, though critics say that significant residues remain in the slaughtered birds.

But in 2004, USDA researchers published a new paper showing that arsenic levels in chickens were considerably higher than previously acknowledged.[18]

That was followed by a 2007 study by David Wallinga, M.D., at the Institute for Agriculture and Trade Policy, whose team tested 155 samples of fresh chicken and chicken-based fast food and found some rather disturbing results.[19]

Most samples had relatively low levels, and 45 percent of them—including organic and Tyson brands of chicken (which says its growers ended roxarsone use in 2004)—had no detectable arsenic at all, proving that the poison does not always occur naturally in poultry. But some samples were considerably high in arsenic. Gold'n Plump boneless breast had 20.2 parts per billion and Perdue/Roundy's had 21.1. Some fast-food chicken was even more contaminated. Among the highest was Jack in the Box's chicken club sandwich (29.5 parts per billion), Popeye's chicken breast (32.4), and Church's chicken thigh 46.5. On average, the National Institutes of Health reported an "alarmingly high" level of arsenic in broiler flesh—at five to nine times over the EPA limit for inorganic arsenic in drinking water. One researcher suggested that a bucket of fried chicken has fifty times the allowable arsenic found in a glass of water.

The poultry industry insists that roxarsone is safe for birds, people, and the environment, because the arsenic is the more benign organic form. But recent studies have shown that some of the arsenic is converted to the inorganic form by bacteria inside chicken guts—and much of the rest is converted after it exits the bird, by bacteria found in chicken litter. In fact, the EPA found that 65 percent of the arsenic in chicken meat was already converted to the inorganic form.[20]

The U.S. Geological Survey notes that "direct evidence indicates that roxarsone degrades quickly into primarily inorganic arsenic species."[21] One study found that certain bacteria in chicken litter will quickly convert organic arsenic into one of two highly toxic inorganic forms within ten days: arsenite (or arsenic III) and arsenate (or arsenic V).[22] Not only does organic arsenic convert to inorganic in litter, but it also becomes volatized into airborne arsine gas. One study showed that the metal does not build up in soil because microorganisms found in litter convert it to gases.

Upwards of 350,000 tons of arsenic are applied to land every year in the United States—and not just on farms.[23] Chicken firms have partnered with Scotts fertilizer to put poultry litter into pellets for home garden use.

The National Chicken Council says that claims about the drug's dangers are faulty, stating that "there is no reason to believe that there are any human health hazards from this type of use."[24] The council's Web site says that arsenic naturally occurs in the Earth's crust and in rock, soil, water, and air, and is absorbed by plants and ingested by animals. And while inorganic arsenic "can be toxic," it says, the organic form used in chicken feed "doesn't present such problems."

In fact, high levels of inorganic arsenic can be found naturally in seafood, as well as meat, poultry, cereal products, fruits, and vegetables. The allowable level of arsenic in poultry meat is 0.5 parts per million in uncooked muscle and 2.0 parts per million in liver. "In contrast, shrimp has about 40 parts per million on average and an FDA limit of 50 parts per million, or one hundred times that allowed in chicken meat." Arsenicals are used to "prevent colonization of the chickens by organisms called *Coccidia*, whose presence can cause lethargy, lack of growth, illness, or death in untreated flocks."

Meanwhile, "Traces of organic arsenic that are sometimes found in broiler meat are not necessarily related to use of animal health products and could be related to naturally occurring arsenic in food and water ingested by the animals," the council claims. "FDA says the presence of arsenic at these trace levels is not harmful to human health."

Besides, it says, arsenic is helping to feed a hungry world: "Poultry producers using these products to produce healthy birds are contributing to a healthful food supply for consumers in America and around the world."

But if that is the case, critics contend, then why does the label on 3-Nitro state that arsenic is a poison and should not be inhaled?

Back on the Delmarva Peninsula, researchers were just as concerned about arsenic in drinking water as arsenic in the air. Dr. Ellen Silbergeld, of Johns Hopkins Bloomberg School of Public Health, reported in March 2007 that her team found higher levels of arsenic in tap water in areas where chicken manure is spread than in other areas of the peninsula.[25]

Carole wondered if this might help explain the exceedingly high rates of cancer being reported in the big chicken-producing counties of Delmarva. Sussex County, on the southern end of Delaware, seemed to be hardest hit: Its rates were among the highest in the nation (though the neighboring counties in Maryland had alarmingly high rates, too).

Carole found one study from the Delaware Division of Public Health showing especially elevated cancer rates near the town of Dagsboro.[26] The study showed that in the six zip codes around the Indian River power plant, cancer rates rose to 554 per 100,000 people, compared to the state average of 500 cases, a 10 percent increase. Twenty percent of all Sussex County cases were lung cancer, compared to 15 percent of patients statewide.

The cause of these clusters was "inconclusive," the state said, though some people suspected the power plant. "We now know there is a higher rate of lung cancer in the Indian River area," Delaware's lieutenant governor, John Carney, said in a statement. "It's critical that we get the best advice on how to determine the causes of this cancer cluster."[27] He said he was seeking advice from the National Cancer Institute. Meanwhile, a group named Citizens for Clean Power had contacted Carney about potential links between the power plant and unusually high rates of infant mortality, cancer, asthma, and childhood learning disabilities in the area.

Not everyone thought that the power plant was implicated. State Representative Gerald Hocker, a Republican from Ocean View, reviewed the study and concluded, "There is no way I can see how they can blame it on one particular thing. We need a deeper study because there is no way to pinpoint this. I know people who live within a mile of the plant and they are eighty years old and their minds are as sharp as a tack. But then I also know people who live miles away from the plant who have dementia and more health problems."

A quick look at the area on Google Earth reveals many huge chicken CAFOs—some with eight massive barns each housing up to forty thousand birds—just a few hundred yards from the center of Dagsboro, which is surrounded by poultry operations and cropland.

A few miles away across the Maryland border, things were just as bad:[28]

Type of Cancer	Statewide Rate	Local Rate	Rank in State	Comments
All Types Combined, Females	417.7	Worcester County 482.3	1	15.5% above state average Next highest county: 463.8
Melanoma, Both Genders	17.2	Wicomico Co. 42.8	1	148.9% above state average Way above all other counties
Melanoma, Females	13.2	Eastern Shore Counties 25.2	1	90.9% above state average Half of all cases were in Wicomico and Worcester counties
Melanoma, Males	22.8	Eastern Shore Counties 31.6	1	38.6% above state average Out of 63 cases, 20 were in Wicomico County and 11 in Worcester County
Cervical Cancer	7.9	Eastern Shore Counties 12.6	1	59.5% above state average
Lung Cancer, Females	56.2	Worcester County 76.9 Eastern Shore Counties 63.4	1	47.3% above state average
Non-Hodgkin Lymphoma, Females	15.8	Eastern Shore Counties 17.1	1	8.2% above state average
Malignant Breast Cancer	133.0	Wicomico Co. 148.5 Worcester Co. 148.2	2 2 (tied)	39.5% above average 39.4% above average
Leukemia, Both Sexes	10.8	Eastern Shore Counties 11.6	2	7.4% above average—Worcester and Wicomico counties have highest rates in eastern shore

Soon after the Delmarva Poultry Summit, Carole was asked to join Helen, Karen, Chris, Terry, and the others on the newly formed Socially Responsible Agriculture Project team. She didn't hesitate to say yes.

That night after the Poultry Summit, Robert F. Kennedy, Jr., had engrossed Rick, Carole, and Jordan with horror stories about the health and environmental troubles plaguing northwest Arkansas, home to Tyson Foods and one of the largest poultry-producing places in the country: Washington County.

Kennedy visited the area in 2004 and spoke with attorneys representing families of cancer patients who were planning lawsuits against Alpharma and several large chicken conglomerates that ordered contractors to use feed containing roxarsone in their CAFOs.

In a speech at the University of Arkansas, in Fayetteville, on the hazards of pollution from the chicken industry, Kennedy blasted Tyson and others for "forcing contractors to dump arsenic-laced waste" onto fields within the Arkansas River watershed.[29]

"When somebody dumps arsenic into a drinking water supply and a child drinks it, that's child abuse," Kennedy contended. "What Tyson is doing is cheating."

A Tyson spokesperson, Ed Nicholson, told the local paper that Kennedy was "entitled to his opinion," but complained that "he doesn't live here, we do. So do the chicken farmers." Kennedy possessed "some very elitist, idealistic ideas as to how food should be grown."

Nowhere was the debate over arsenic, litter, and cancer more heated and emotional than in the small Washington County town of Prairie Grove. It is one of those idyllic all-American hamlets that evoke images of fresh-baked pies, harvest festivals, and Fourth of July parades down Main Street. Its twenty-eight hundred residents live peacefully nestled in the shadows of the eastern foothills of the Ozarks.

But Prairie Grove was sick. Dozens of cancer cases and other serious disorders had been reported among its residents, including many who were under the age of twenty-one. Attorneys for the victims and their families claimed that cancer rates in Prairie Grove were fifty times higher than the national average.[30] State officials disputed that. Sometimes, visitors were led on an oncological tour of the town, strolling down streets whose homes have been rocked by cancer: an infant with a brain tumor lived in that house; a teenager with leukemia died next door; a woman across the street was being treated for breast cancer, and so on.

Up until 2004, all schoolchildren in Prairie Grove went to the same K–12 school, which was located directly in front of one of the chicken CAFOs. That land was regularly spread with dried poultry litter, which was distributed by being blown into the air from behind a truck. Like the school, the town is surrounded by fields on which arsenic-containing litter was spread—at a rate that plaintiff lawyers alleged was at least five tons per acre, per year, through the 1990s.

Court records show that since 1990, when litter began to be spread on the fields in large quantities, an extraordinarily high number of young people in Prairie Grove had been diagnosed with some type of cancer, plaintiff lawyers alleged. Several died.[31]

In 1990, a ten-year-old child developed an unspecified form of cancer. The next year, a fifteen-year-old grew a brain tumor.

In 1993, a fifteen-year-old girl was diagnosed with lymphoma, and, two years later, another teenager was diagnosed with the same malignancy. Also in 1995, a one-year-old infant developed liver cancer.

In 1995, a fifteen-year-old boy was diagnosed with leukemia; despite intense treatment and a short stint in remission, he died two years later.

In 1998, an eighteen-year-old girl was diagnosed with leukemia. And though she lived in nearby Lincoln, she spent a great deal of time at the ball fields of Prairie Grove School, where her mother was a cheerleading-squad coach. The girl also spent a lot of time at a babysitter's home at 601 N. Mock Street, near fields that were spread with litter.

A few months later, in 1999, Michael "Blu" Green, who lived across the street at 604 N. Mock Street (a leafy road that would become racked with cancer cases) also developed leukemia—a very rare myelogenous form of the blood disease. That same year, his schoolmate, thirteen-year-old Austin Johnson, got brain cancer. Austin was followed by a two-year-old who also lived near a field where litter was spread—he acquired a brain cancer called a medulloblastoma. Another unidentified Prairie Grove student was diagnosed with myeloma.

The cancer just kept rolling through town: 2000 brought lymphoma to a seven-year-old child; an unspecified cancer to a two-year-old; and another case of leukemia on Mock Street, this time afflicting a twenty-year-old, who did not survive.

The year 2001 ushered in a bizarre onset of testicular cancers. Three boys at Prairie Grove School all contracted the same exceedingly rare form of the disease, which is almost never found in young males. It only affects about one man in two million, lawyers for Blu Green contended, and the odds of three boys at the same school getting the same cancer at the same time—simply due to chance—were zero.

All three boys were fourteen years old, including one whose home's air filter was found to have 130 parts per million of arsenic, though the soil out-side the home was only 1.1 parts per million.

In 2002, a seventeen-year-old girl was diagnosed with leukemia and, though she lived in Fayetteville, she had spent all weekends, school breaks, and holidays at the home of her sister in Prairie Grove, at 301 S. Mock Street. The same year, a few months after that family moved away to Kentucky, one of the girls was diagnosed with a brain tumor at the age of eleven. That same year, a nine-year-old died of an unspecified cancer.

In 2003, a twenty-three-year-old died of leukemia. She had lived in Lin-coln, but was on the pom-pom squad and played softball in high school, which often brought her to Prairie Grove School. Two years later, a twenty-one-year-old boy was told that he had a medulloblastoma in his brain. He had attended Prairie Grove schools from 1997 through 2002.

In 2005, a twenty-four-year-old who had attended Prairie Grove schools was diagnosed with lymphoma.

In 2007, after living in Prairie Grove and then moving to Texas, a six-year-old was diagnosed with a brain tumor (glioblastoma), and died eight months later.

Not long after that, a three-year-old who was born in Prairie Grove in 2005 but moved with her family to Texas in 2006, was diagnosed with leuke-mia. While in Arkansas, her father worked in a poultry feed mill and came home covered in roxarsone-laced dust every day.

And those were just the young people (in whom one would normally ex-pect to find far fewer cancer cases). Many older adults over the age of twenty-one had also come down with a disturbing constellation of cancers and other disorders. All told, nearly one hundred plaintiffs in and around Prairie Grove were preparing lawsuits against the effects of roxarsone.

In 2004, the law firm of Lundy & Davis held a news conference on its own pending civil action against Alpharma and several large chicken producers, including Tyson Foods. Plaintiff attorneys had ordered tests on air filters in thirty-one Prairie Grove households and found arsenic in thirty of them. An independent lab confirmed that the arsenic contained the molecular "finger-print" of roxarsone.[32]

"We have found extremely alarming levels of toxic contamination and disease incidence in Prairie Grove, all of which can be directly linked back to the poultry industry's negligent management and disposal of chicken litter," claimed Hunter Lundy, one of the principals in the law firm, in a press release. "Decades of relentless growth in the quest for ever-increasing profits have re-sulted in more than an 80 percent increase in the number of chicken houses in Washington County over the last decade," he said.[33]

For years, litter was sold to crop farmers, who spread it liberally on their fields within a three-to-five-mile radius of Prairie Grove, Lundy asserted. "As the once-backyard chicken shacks have grown into factory farms, the sheer volume of waste, and the toxic chemicals it contains, has become overwhelming and hazardous," he added. "People in the poultry industry know this is true."

The press release went on to allege that staff at Children's Hospital in Little Rock confirmed there was an unusually high number of cancer cases in northwest Arkansas, especially among children. So many cases were coming in from the region that the hospital had established a new pediatric oncology program, the release claimed.

Nearly 150 health surveys had been completed and analyzed by experts, Baker added, and had revealed a host of illnesses—autoimmune diseases, skin disorders, and cancers among them, according to the lawyers' statement. At least forty-three residents of Prairie Grove had some type of cancer, including three in just one neighborhood who had liver cancer. "This is an extreme anomaly, considering that the national rate of liver cancer is just one in ten thousand," he said.[34]

The first case to go to trial would be that of Prairie Grove residents Michael and Beth Green and their son, Michael "Blu" Green, whose leukemia was now in remission. Their lead attorney would be an earnest and courtly young lawyer from Fayetteville who had recently joined Lundy & Davis, Jason Hatfield.

The Greens were suing for product liability, failure to warn, and negligence, and seeking damages of about $900,000 for medical care and other costs of Blu's lengthy and intensive treatment. They also sought $4.5 to $9 million for his pain and suffering. The suit was filed against Alpharma and its distributor, Alpharma Animal Health, and Tyson Foods, Peterson Farms, George's Farms, George's Processing, Simmons Foods, and Simmons Poultry Farms. But in a preliminary ruling, Washington County circuit court judge Kim Smith dismissed the cases against the chicken companies.[35]

Smith said that Arkansas law does not recognize "market share liability." In other words, even if Tyson had earned, say, half of all revenues from chickens in the area, there was no way to know how much, if any, of its litter was responsible for illness in Prairie Grove. Smith said toxic tort litigation must be lodged against a specific defendant; it cannot be a broad assault against an industry.

In another preliminary ruling, Smith decreed that the Greens had provided no evidence to support any allegation that the defendants intentionally sickened their son, and prohibited them from asking for punitive damages. Smith also barred Blu's parents from suing for their own emotional distress, citing state law against third-party distress suits.

In yet another blow to the Greens, Judge Smith made a pretrial ruling limiting testimony from one of the star plaintiff witnesses, Dr. Rod O'Connor, a retired professor of chemistry at Texas A&M. He barred O'Connor from presenting his calculations of the arsenic levels he had detected in the air filters of the thirty homes, saying that O'Connor's methods were "unreliable" and not generally accepted by science. Smith also dealt a huge setback to the plaintiffs when he barred testimony about the suspicious number of other cancer cases in Prairie Grove—though he did say he would allow discussions about three other town residents who had leukemia.

The trial got under way in September 2006, and the defendants came out swinging. In opening remarks, attorneys for Alpharma said that exposure to arsenic was not generally recognized by science as being a cause of Blu's form of leukemia. They also said the Greens could not show they were exposed to arsenic in levels known to cause disease.

During the trial, Blu testified about this illness, which had since gone into remission. He had grown up in Prairie Grove and spent as much time as possible playing outdoors, even as dusty chicken litter was spread on the fields around his home and school. "You just immediately notice the smell," he said.[36]

As a freshman, Blu started seeing inexplicable bruises on his body. Blood tests revealed a very high white blood cell count, and doctors diagnosed him with leukemia.

"I was afraid I was going to die," Blu testified at trial. "I was nervous about all the doctors and chemotherapy and losing my hair." Told he needed a bone-marrow transplant, he was put on oral chemotherapy to bring his blood count back toward normal, to prevent a stroke. He also got on a wait-list for a marrow donor, and then returned to school, "trying to scoop up the last little bit of time before I had the transplant," he said.

In March 2000, Blu and his mother traveled to Seattle's Fred Hutchinson Cancer Research Center for the operation—which was preceded by three days of radiation, twice a day for a half hour each. "That was about the worst right there," Blu said. "I got really sick and threw up all the time." He stayed in the hospital for a month after the transplant, dealing with serious graft problems as his body tried to reject the donated marrow.

On the flight back to Arkansas, Blu became seriously ill and was taken to the hospital in Fayetteville. His father barely recognized the boy, who had withered away to one hundred pounds and "looked just awful," he testified. By August, Blu was heading back to Seattle with pneumonia and several fungal infections, including *Aspergillus*. The *Aspergillus* fungus had been detected in poultry litter and house dust in Blu's home, and was now growing in his lungs.

The youth grew despondent and depressed, he testified, constantly warding off the fear of death. "I knew it was a real possibility," he said with deep sadness. His schoolmate from Prairie Grove, John Blakemore, and the little girl that went to the babysitter's house on Mock Street, Holly Green (no relation), had both contracted leukemia, and gone into remission. But both of them got sick again and passed away. Holly had been in the same hospital in Seattle while Blu was being treated there.

"Me and Holly were next door to each other," he testified to a somber courtroom. "I held her brother when they unplugged her."

Blu went back to Arkansas on Thanksgiving Day 2000, and rejoined his junior class in high school after the holiday. Since then, his health had slowly recovered.

Plaintiff attorneys alleged that roxarsone passed through chickens and converted to inorganic arsenic in the litter, which was then scattered onto Prairie Grove–area fields. From there the poison was carried by the wind into nearby homes, businesses, and the school, where investigators found arsenic dust traced to roxarsone. Alpharma was liable for selling a dangerous, defective product and failing to alert the public, they charged.

When the defense's turn came, lawyers contended that the Greens had filed suit prematurely, before state testing could be completed on soil, water, and air samples in the area, and before epidemiological studies could be done of cancer rates in Washington County. Those studies, now completed, had turned up nothing unusual in the area, the lawyers said. Cancer rates were no higher there than anywhere else in northwest Arkansas or the state, save for an elevated level of testicular cancer.

Alpharma attorneys attacked the Greens' credibility, questioning why they never moved from the house, and why they never complained about chicken litter either before or after Blu's diagnosis.[37] They presented experts who testified that breathing arsenic can cause cancer, but lung cancer, not the rare leukemia that afflicted Blu. One witness, Dr. Steven Lamm, said no environmental toxins were known to cause leukemia at all. And, he added, if roxarsone was causing cancer, there should be more cases in the rural outskirts of Prairie Grove—where most chicken houses and crop farms were located—and not in the town itself. But there were fewer cases in the areas outside of town.

Alpharma attorney Rob Adams then summed up the defense's position in what would become the most oft-quoted line from the trial: "Fear and blame without evidence," he told the jury, "have no place in the courtroom."

It took the jury just twenty-one minutes to reach a decision.

"The evidence, in my opinion, was overwhelming." said Floyd Belt, one of ten out of twelve jurors who voted for Alpharma.[38] He told reporters after the trial that roxarsone had been studied extensively for years and had been in use for five decades, without a single cancer-related lawsuit being filed, until now.

Blu's mother, Beth Green, walked out of the courthouse looking "like she had been punched in the stomach," the *North-West Arkansas Morning News* reported. Neither the Greens nor their attorneys would comment to reporters. Blu Green was now a senior at the University of Arkansas with hopes of becoming a basketball coach, like his dad. But despite his recovery, he would permanently be at risk for cancer and graft-illness disease. Radiation treatment had left him with cataracts and skin problems, and he was sterile—though he had banked sperm before the procedure.

Jason Hatfield, lead attorney for the plaintiffs, filed an appeal, citing Judge Smith's dismissal of the chicken companies, and his limiting of data presented by Dr. O'Connor. Judge Smith agreed to stay the other lawsuits until the appeal issues were settled in the Green case. In 2008, the Arkansas Supreme Court agreed with the plaintiffs that Tyson and other chicken companies could indeed be sued in this case and "that the poultry producers' chicken litter probably caused Green's injury."[39] The new trial was set for May 2009, back in the courtroom of Judge Kim Smith.

The day after the Delmarva Poultry Summit, Rick Dove helped organize a water-monitoring posse to obtain samples from local chicken CAFOs. Rick, Jordan, Waterkeeper's Bill Gerlach, and outreach coordinator Jillian Gladstone drove over to a stream near Crisfield, Maryland, that they had dubbed "Chicken Poop Creek."

They piled into kayaks and began paddling upstream toward a broiler facility suspected of discharging litter waste into the water. Once there, they planned to take several water samples to be tested for fecal samples, *E. coli*, ammonia, total nitrogen, phosphorus, and arsenic from the CAFO discharge.

Along the way, the floating party came across a metal culvert crossing under a road. They would have to carefully make their way through it to continue their journey upstream.

Then calamity struck. Bill cut his hand going through the culvert (within three days, it would end up as a nasty infection requiring intensive antibiotic treatment and take a long time to heal). Meanwhile, Rick was traveling in a canoe with Jillian, and they were unsure whether they could fit through the culvert. It might be better to get out and carry the canoe across the road, Rick suggested.

But as they attempted to beach the craft, Jillian stepped out and the canoe started to wobble. Looking back on it now, Rick realizes that he might have been able to save himself from going in. But he had that expensive video camera in his hand, and he tried to flip it over his head and onto the bank. The action only accelerated Rick's plunge into the fetid water. As things turned out, he would have been far better off losing the damn camera. Creek water shot up his nose and he could taste its acridity in his mouth.

The water was ugly. It hadn't smelled until Rick flipped into it. He was suddenly overwhelmed with the stench of hydrogen sulfide. Rick climbed out of the creek to shake himself dry. He was unhappy, but not too overly concerned—this had happened before. He told Jordon to keep going until he made it to the drainage pipe. When Jordan got there, the pipe was not discharging anything—the entire morning had been wasted.

Rick and Bill drove to a nearby gas station and mini-mart to buy disinfectant for Bill's gash. Discouraged and fatigued, Rick drove back to New Bern without changing. He got home late that night, exhausted and still wet from his spill into "Chicken Poop Creek." Joanne admonished him for driving all the way from Maryland in filthy, dank clothes, but Rick had little choice—he'd already checked out of his motel.

Rick told Joanne what had happened, though he wasn't concerned about himself, but about Bill Gerlach, who had cut his hand on the metal culvert. For the next week or so, Rick went about his business with no sign of trouble. Then he began to notice a little discomfort in his lower abdomen. He didn't give it much thought. "Aches and pains are something I've gotten used to in my 'old age,'" he joked to himself (though he didn't tell Joanne about it). By this point, the creek incident had faded from his mind.

Around Thanksgiving, the condition got much worse. Rick went to see his doctor, a urologist, who diagnosed an infection, although nothing showed up on blood and urine tests. The doctor prescribed the antibiotic Cipro, which Rick took for a week. It did no good.

Frustrated and in growing pain, Rick returned to the doctor. Throughout December, his antibiotic prescriptions were changed a number of times, all without results. Two days before New Year's, his urine darkened significantly and the pain was nearly unbearable. Once again Rick went back to the doctor, who ran a urine culture test.

On New Year's Eve, Rick and Joanne were in bed celebrating with their usual "party"—which meant watching the worldwide events on TV and ending the evening at midnight with a kiss. But around eleven, their phone rang. It was Rick's doctor.

"Rick, the culture tested positive for an extremely serious *E. coli* infection," he said. "You need to go to the hospital ER immediately for an IV. I've already called in the prescription. It is a very potent antibiotic."

At midnight, instead of kissing Joanne in bed, Rick was holding her hand in the emergency room, an IV infusion flowing into one arm. "It's a hell of a way to bring in the New Year, sweetheart," he said to her.

Rick was convinced that his ignominious tumble into that fetid creek was how he contracted multidrug-resistant *E. coli*. There were no other possibilities that he could think of. He had ingested some creek water that day in Maryland, then sat in his pathogen-soaked clothes for six hours on the drive home. A dumb move, he realized later.

Rick knew that *E. coli* incubation can take up to two weeks or longer, depending on where the bacteria are colonized, and how well the body fights back. "The doc said there was no way to be certain of the source," he told Joanne, "but the dip in Chicken Poop Creek was very likely it. No one else in our family got sick—so I doubt I caught it from food or something else around the house."

For weeks, Rick took antibiotics in infusions, injections, and fistfuls of pills. His doctor was alarmed. They had tried every class of antimicrobial known to fight *E. coli*, except one. The doctor didn't say so at the time, but Rick knew this was his last chance.

The irony was lost on no one. Colonel Richard Dove, U.S. Marine Corps (Retired), had dedicated almost two decades of his life to trying to keep animal waste from getting into the waterways. It was bad for the environment and dangerous—even deadly—for people. But instead of Rick vanquishing manure, it looked like the manure might vanquish Rick.

"What a way to go," he joked, sharing some gallows humor with family and friends. "Death by chicken litter."

Rick didn't fully recover until March 2009. That's when his doctor told him, gravely, that if the last-ditch antibiotic had failed, the *E. coli* might well have done him in.

Nobody had said anything to Rick while he was sick, but now he was taking an artillery of flack and a great deal of ribbing: When you row around in poop water, friends laughed, the idea is to stay *inside* the boat. Others could not resist remarks about being up you-know-what creek without a paddle.

Rick got the message, and made a vow to be more careful when working around animal waste. For the most part he stuck with it. But he refused to curtail his exposure.

"So long as I can get my boots on each morning," he told Joanne, "I'll keep fighting."

By the summer of 2007, the race for president was well under way, especially in Iowa, site of the upcoming first-ever primary-season voting—the famed Iowa caucuses—set for the unheard-of early date of January 4, 2008.

For most animal-factory opponents, the real action was on the Democratic side. Democratic candidates were crisscrossing the state with messages about saving the family farm, establishing local control, and reining in federal subsidy payouts to the biggest corporate operations. The Republicans tended to stick to their usual themes of taxes, immigration, and the war in Iraq.

Among Democrats, hogs were a hot-button issue. It had long been this way. Harry Truman once joked that no one should become president "who does not understand hogs, or hasn't been around a manure pile." Old-timers like Chris Petersen knew that every four years, rural issues get a thorough hearing leading up to the Iowa caucuses—before they are jettisoned for the rest of the campaign cycle. Now was the time to leverage Iowa's strategic electoral position to extract some solid promises from the politicians.

Chris began speaking to the major Democratic candidates in late 2006, including John Edwards, Hillary Clinton, Senator Chris Dodd of Connecticut, Governor Bill Richardson of New Mexico, Senator Joe Biden of Delaware, and the fresh-faced young junior senator from next-door Illinois, Barack Obama, who threw his hat into the ring in January 2007.

Chris had met with some of the Obama people at a Des Moines restaurant in December 2006. He diligently went over what he had told the Pew Commission. "You guys need to look at what that commission is doing, look at the testimony they are taking," he said. "You want your candidate to win Iowa? You tell him to listen to the people who are described in that report—go find out how their lives were wrecked by these damn factories. If you're going to let folks farm that way you really need to pay more attention to the consequences," he added. "Me, I want to see all CAFOs go away in time. But I know that this is America, and anyone can farm the way they want."

In January, Chris joined a small group of Democrats to meet with Obama himself, and some of his staff, to talk about local Iowa issues. Obama had announced his candidacy just days before on the icy steps of the Springfield statehouse (Karen watched the home-state event with great pride and joy, albeit from the warmth of her living room). But in Iowa, conventional wisdom held that Hillary Clinton would win this first, critical round of voting. Few people showed up to meet the long-shot senator from Illinois, and it gave Chris a golden opportunity to listen, learn—and *lecture*.

Chris was impressed with the young newcomer, who clearly spoke like someone from an agricultural state, even if he was a Chicagoan. Obama talked about his votes in the Illinois State Senate on CAFOs, including bills to impose stricter limits on illegal water discharges and emissions of nitrogen, phosphorus, hydrogen sulfide, and ammonia.

Then Chris chimed in. "Mr. Obama," he began, "we are anti-CAFO, but we are also much more than that. We are profamily farmers; we want to help them compete against the industrial producers here in Iowa. We want to give them a fair and equal chance to succeed." Obama listened intently, and Chris continued. "Now, I think you need to tackle this problem from the top down, and by that I mean you need new antitrust and competition laws. And you need to establish complete transparency in the marketplace."

It may seem counterintuitive, Chris said, but processors in Iowa were paying two or three dollars more per pig on deliveries of, say, one thousand head, than they would when buying pigs from a smaller producer who had just one hundred head to slaughter. That's because it was cheaper and easier for the integrator to acquire one thousand hogs from a single big source than one hundred hogs from ten smaller sources. The thousand hogs were more likely to have uniform size, shape, and leanness of meat. But the tactic was also an effective tool for quashing competition from smaller growers, Chris told Obama, adding that all growers should be paid an equitable price, and those prices should be made transparent for all to see.

"No one knows what the other guy is getting; these are secret contractual arrangements," Chris complained. "The company can keep farmers divided and stupid—the packers control eighty to ninety percent of all hogs slaughtered, through direct ownership or contracting, so you don't have to wonder why the markets are being destroyed—the farmers are getting farmed and the integrators are making a killing."

Chris also pleaded for help in reinstating a "packer ban," which had been challenged in Iowa and overturned by Smithfield and other integrators a few years back. He said the whole country should ban processing companies from owning the animals they slaughter. "This is real Teddy Roosevelt stuff we need," Chris told Obama. "You know, 'split 'em up and make 'em compete.' If you tackle this from the top down, many of the problems—environmental, rural, jobs, pollution, food safety—will go away, and the others will be far easier to address. We've been going about this ass-backwards, Senator."

He warned the candidate about the risks of a deadly influenza strain coming out of a large swine or poultry confinement. He explained how pigs, in particular, are very efficient mixing vessels of interspecies infection. And he worried that many hog CAFOs in Iowa were located right next to poultry CAFOs.

Antibiotic-resistant bacterial infections were another "ticking time bomb" waiting to happen, Chris said.

"CAFOs are unsustainable in every way possible, sir," Chris finished his spiel. "They are users of everything. They are the dinosaurs of the twenty-first century. They may not go away altogether, but they've already been proven to be a real bad way to raise livestock."

Obama seemed to hang on to every word uttered by the pig farmer from Clear Lake.

During much of 2007, Chris and other family-farm advocates would spend a good deal of time with the Obama people, and with the senator himself, who conducted fifty rural town hall meetings over the summer and fall. Chris would stop Obama—or Clinton, or Edwards, Dodd, Biden, or whomever he could grab for a few moments running down hallways or waiting backstage among the hay bales at county fairgrounds. Local control was always a crowd-pleasing topic at these stops—and it was something the candidates seemed to *get*.

Chris never missed a chance to talk as well about America's food, and the families who produce it. "Any issue dealing with food, whether it's safety, quality, or family farming—is an important issue," he told John Edwards one day. "Everybody eats, and everybody's worried about their health, or they should be. But when it comes to issues that win or lose elections, our food should be right up there with national defense and jobs."

As much as Chris admired Barack Obama, he was still leaning toward Edwards, despite his relatively spotty record in the Senate on rural issues. But Chris had worked closely with Edwards when he ran in 2004 and ended up on the ticket with John Kerry. This time around, Edwards and his family had spent virtually the entire year camped out in Iowa, with offices in even the most remote and sparsely populated counties. Much of his 2008 campaign showcased Edwards's trademark railing against "corporate interests." In Iowa, that largely meant denouncing large hog and chicken confinements. As such, the man from North Carolina, the *other* "other white meat" state, amassed a large and loyal following among family farmers and eco-preservationists.

Edwards was helped by bumper stickers around the state that said HOGS FOR EDWARDS, and by his appearance at an Iowa State Fairgrounds parade, where he walked with live pigs on a trailer and a sign that read SEND US BACK TO THE FAMILY FARM! Other posters said BE KIND TO SWINE. Mostly, though, he thrilled activists by calling for a national moratorium on all new or expanding CAFOs; he had already pledged his support for a national packer ban, and for breaking up vertically integrated pork companies.

Hillary Clinton, though the presumed front-runner, had her fair share of detractors in Iowa as well. Chris did not dislike her, but he wasn't sold on her, either. Her voting record on Big Ag issues was not bad. But Chris could not help but think back to Bill Clinton's presidency, when family farms and Big Ag issues were hardly addressed at all. Clinton's farm policy was little different from that of the President Bushes who came before and after. Hillary Clinton's reputation was not enhanced by her own close ties to Arkansas-based Tyson Foods, whose financial largesse helped elect Bill Clinton governor and president. Hillary had her own Tyson baggage, in the form of a $100,000 overnight profit she once made trading on cattle futures. The entire deal had been brokered by a leading Tyson attorney.

Nor did Clinton help herself among family farmers or environmentalists when she showed up at the Iowa State Fair, walked over to the Iowa Pork Producer Association's tent, threw on an apron, and started char-grilling chops for hungry reporters, mugging for their cameras. It thrilled big pork—and alienated rural activists.

Chris Petersen, as president of the Iowa Farmers Union and a leading Democratic organizer in the state, helped snag candidates for the October 27 National Summit on Agriculture and Rural Life in Ames, cosponsored by the League of Rural Voters and the Main Street Project. All the major Democratic candidates made their pitches—mostly in support of independent family farmers and more regulations on the CAFO contracting system. Edwards and Obama spoke in person; Clinton appeared live via webcam.

None of the GOP candidates showed up, though Iowa's senior senator, Charles Grassley, a courtly and conservative Republican, did attend. He thrilled the crowd by speaking out against vertical integrators and in favor of stronger antitrust and fair competition laws.

Backstage at the Ames event, Chris spoke with the candidates before they went on, and was impressed by how aptly they—especially Edwards and Obama—had absorbed and digested the problems facing rural farms. As far as Chris was concerned, they pretty much had it right. Obama seemed to agree with maybe 80 percent of what the activists wanted, and Edwards was closer to a perfect 100 percent.

Chris had been through the routine many times before. The candidates would come out, one by one, give their spiel and be picked over by the crowd, and then be shoved out the door rather unceremoniously. "It's like herding cows through the auditorium one at a time," he joked with Senator Obama as he waited his turn backstage. "We're going to send you out on that stage, and those five hundred people out there are going to look you over like livestock. Welcome to the 2007 Iowa Cattle Call, Senator!" Obama laughed.

He also wowed the crowd, and so did Edwards. And it wasn't just their personal charisma and passion—something that seemed absent in Clinton, especially over the webcam. Obama called for a 250,000-dollar limit on farm subsidies, and he vowed to reform the USDA to make it focus on the problems faced by independent farmers and ranchers. "When I'm president, I'll have a department of agriculture, not simply a department of agribusiness," he said to roaring approval. "Large corporate hog polluters should be required to pay for their own pollution—and not be bailed out at the taxpayer's expense!"[1]

The crowd ate it up; Obama flashed his famous grin. And then he hit a homer, as far as the Democrats in the room were concerned. If elected, Obama promised, he would convene a major national summit on all rural issues within one hundred days of taking office.

Edwards devoted much of his speech to blaming corporate farming for a variety of ills, including degradation of the rural environment. "And by the way, a lot of the money does not end up in the local economy," he said. Edwards reminded the crowd that he was the only candidate to back a nationwide CAFO moratorium. "You look at what's happened to hog farms here in the state of Iowa—we have fifty-thousand-plus less hog farms here than we had not very long ago—and it's all because these big corporate farming operations are doing it in CAFOs!"[2]

In the end, Obama and Edwards won the day. They both called for local control, stricter pollution regulations for CAFOs, a packer ban, a cap on farm subsidies, new antitrust and transparency laws, and the return of production decisions to the farmers who own the land. Edwards supported a moratorium, and Obama called for a rural summit. Otherwise, they were pretty close on the issues, and both were preferred over Clinton by the majority of the people Chris spoke with that day. For him, it would be a very tough decision to make between Edwards and Obama.

By late 2007, MRSA had become a household word to fear—and for good reason. Schoolkids were suddenly dying of the illness, from Brooklyn to the West Coast. Education officials were scrambling to disinfect desks, tables, bookshelves, computer keyboards, and bathrooms. It seemed that no place was immune from MRSA, not even Elmwood. On November 1, local papers reported that a student from the Elmwood Community School District had been diagnosed with MRSA. It appeared to be a fairly mild case. Just some bumpy skin, nothing invasive. Officials said that the student, a girl, would not miss class, as long as she kept her weepy red skin sores properly bandaged. But it was still front-page news in Peoria County.

Meanwhile, new science kept emerging to implicate the swine industry as a growing source of at least some of the infections among humans. An alarming new study was published in the November issue of *Veterinary Microbiology* showing that pig farms were likely a major force driving what could only be called an MRSA "epidemic."[3] The study found that one in five pig farmers in the United States and Canada in 2007 harbored methicillin-resistant *Staphylococcus aureus*. A second study, out of the Netherlands, revealed that 81 percent of Dutch pig farms had pigs with MRSA, and 39 percent of the animals at slaughter carried the bug. All of the infections were resistant to tetracycline and many were resistant to other antibiotics.[4]

"This groundbreaking research is a giant red flag that should be waved in front of the noses of our regulators and all elected officials not only in North America, but the entire world," Karen wrote in a bulletin to CAFO activists. "Until recently, it has been thought that virulent drug-resistant staph infections occurred mainly in hospital settings, but a *Journal of the American Medical Association* study recently stated it has found that even healthy humans are developing antibiotic-resistant bacterial infections."[5] According to media reports cited by the CDC, more people currently die of MRSA than AIDS in the United States."[6]

It was quite likely that Americans were being infected by the pork they handled and ate, and by some of the workers who raised that pork. But there was also a third potential route of transmission, a far more direct and frightening one: airborne emissions from the CAFO itself. One could stop buying commercial pork, and one could take precautions from being infected by others with MRSA, but one could not avoid breathing the air.

Karen mentioned a new study from Ohio that found high numbers of aerosolized staph bacteria downwind and inside homes near swine confinements. Follow-up research demonstrated that some of the bacteria had genes that were resistant to a number of antibiotics. The authors wrote that CAFOs should be built "with consideration of the location of human habitation."[7]

But that was not about to happen in Illinois, Karen warned. "Until state and federal regulators finally step up to the plate, helpless neighbors of factory farms will continue to be guinea pigs as they are exposed to unregulated emissions on a daily basis," she said. "Today I received a 'routine call' from yet another neighbor of a factory farm. This particular Illinois family has the misfortune of being completely surrounded by seven hog confinements. They are now forced to confine their child inside their home when they are assaulted by the dusts, odors, and gases created by their new industrial neighbors. In Illinois, industrial-sized factory farms can be constructed just about anywhere, even as close as a quarter to a half mile from a private home.

"Governor George Ryan signed 'new' legislation several years ago that barely strengthened Illinois livestock rules and still banned local control in our communities. After signing industry-watered-down legislation, he smugly posed with his Big Ag cronies for a celebratory photo op under the golden arches of a Springfield, Illinois, fast-food establishment. George Ryan never failed to demonstrate his unflagging support for livestock production in Illinois. Hundreds of new CAFOs and years later, we are still faced with the same reckless factory-farm problems in Illinois. Our own IEPA only has an inventory for about 30 percent of all the animal feeding operations in the state. The industry has padded political pockets and run free and unregulated for too many years."

It had only been six months since Tyson launched its big, splashy marketing campaign to hawk its "all-natural" chicken grown without antibiotics. The happy, grateful families were thanking their moms on TV commercials nationwide, and real-life consumers were forking over a few dollars more for the privilege of choosing Tyson.

But the campaign was about to tumble to an ignominious and, for the government, rather embarrassing halt. In early November, the USDA notified the company that official approval of the RAISED WITHOUT ANTIBIOTICS label had been a "mistake."[8] The label would have to go. The reason was because, although Tyson stopped using antibiotics in feed, they hadn't stopped using all antimicrobials. At issue was a class of drugs called ionophores—a U.S.-approved feed additive that is safe for use in poultry or livestock to protect against an intestinal disorder known as coccidiosis.

The USDA was forced to admit that its agents had "mistakenly overlooked" the fact that Tyson was using ionophores in its chicken feed when the new no-antibiotics label was approved. The Food Safety and Inspection Service of the USDA insisted that it had a longstanding policy of classifying ionophores as antibiotics.

Tyson was given forty-five days to stop feeding ionophores to its birds, or else cease and desist from using the current label. The company had already submitted a modified labeling scheme, one claiming that "no ingredients have been used that could create antibiotic resistance in humans." Despite this concession, Tyson executives still cried foul, insisting that ionophores were not antibiotics, that the FDA did not consider them antibiotics, and that Tyson had been victimized by bureaucratic bungling at the Department of Agriculture.

They also remained somewhat defiant. "We stand by the truthfulness of our product labels and remain fully committed to our program," the company said in a statement.[9] "Ionophores are not used in human medicine and do not contribute to the development of antibiotic resistance to important human drugs. They remain in the intestinal tract of the animal and do not carry over into the meat consumed by humans."

In December 2007, Chris Petersen knew he had to back a presidential candidate for the Iowa caucuses, and he had to do it soon. But he was torn. Obama offered inspiration and a promise of a better future. Edwards, despite his Senate voting record, offered a permanent moratorium on CAFOs.

By now, front-runner Clinton was out of the running, at least for Chris. Though she had spoken eloquently and at length about promoting local food systems and supporting family farms, she never really caught on among the anti-CAFO faithful. The last straw for many came in December, when Clinton named a recent former head of the National Pork Producers Council, Joy Philippi, as cochair of Rural Americans for Hillary. Chris and his comrades were appalled. They called Clinton and her people to bemoan the selection, flabbergasted that she would make such a pro-CAFO misstep so close to the Iowa caucuses, when every single voter counted, especially in rural precincts.

Indeed, one could argue that Hillary Clinton might be president today if she had taken a more aggressive stance against CAFOs before the Iowa caucuses. Had she won Iowa and gone on to victory in New Hampshire, her nomination would have been virtually unstoppable.

"She was never popular in rural districts to begin with," Chris told Karen. "And her rural campaign sucked anyway. But those Democrats tend to be pro–family farm, anti-CAFO, clean-water types, and they went to Obama or Edwards in droves after her screwup—and we helped make it happen!"

The appointment of Philippi cost Clinton votes she badly needed in rural precincts to make the vote close statewide, Chris said. Meanwhile, voters started drifting away from Edwards in the final week, possibly out of candidate fatigue. Chris rightly predicted that Obama would make significant inroads among anti-CAFO voters who were deserting Edwards—and now Clinton—in large numbers.

Hillary's move had a ripple effect that unsettled voters well beyond Iowa. Down in North Carolina, Rick practically had to scrape his jaw off the ground after reading the news. "What an idiot!" he cried out to Joanne across the breakfast table. "You can bet that decision will hurt her—a lot!" Until this point, Rick had been an avid Hillary backer, especially given Robert F. Kennedy, Jr.'s endorsement of her candidacy and environmental credentials. "And then out of nowhere, she picks a CAFO person for such a key position?" Rick said. "Well, she just lost me. And I'm going to urge everyone I know to go look for another candidate."

Two days after appointing Philippi, and perhaps in response to the backlash against her, Hillary Clinton finally came out in favor of local control over CAFOs. Just a week or so before Iowans would be the first Americans to have a say in the 2008 election, the senator from New York told *The Des Moines Register* that, yes, animal factories could be a threat to human health and the environment. "This is an issue I care deeply about," she said, describing her feelings as "long-standing" without explaining why her support for local control was so late in coming.[10]

Eight days before the Iowa caucuses, Chris Petersen endorsed John Edwards. But Obama defied the odds—and the pundits—and nabbed the first golden prize of the 2008 election.

Obama's victory speech stirred many that night around Iowa and the nation: Hopeful voters believed that he might usher in fundamental change in the way America conducted its business and politics. For them, his words bore great beauty and power. Chris watched the event live; Helen, Rick, Karen, Carole, Terry Spence, Barbara Sha Cox, and so many others also watched, some near tears, as Obama declared victory that night.

"Years from now, you'll look back and you'll say that this was the moment, this was the place where America remembered what it means to hope," the candidate said. "For many months, we've been teased, even derided for talking about hope. But we always knew that hope is not blind optimism. It's not ignoring the enormity of the tasks ahead or the roadblocks that stand in our path.

"It's not sitting on the sidelines or shirking from a fight. Hope is that thing inside us that insists, despite all the evidence to the contrary, that something better awaits us if we have the courage to reach for it and to work for it and to fight for it," Obama continued. And then he added what was music to the ears of animal-factory fighters: "You said the time has come to tell the lobbyists who think their money and their influence speak louder than our voices that they don't own this government—we do. And we are here to take it back!"[11]

Weeks later, Republican Helen Reddout attended the Washington State Democratic Caucus and stood up to speak out for Barack Obama—who won the vote two to one.

Soon after that, while campaigning in the North Carolina primary—which he would overwhelmingly win—Obama was asked by a voter if he had heard about the Pew Commission, and its report on animal factories, parts of which were now being released to the public. Rick, another Republican with an Obama sticker on his truck who drove around the North Carolina hog belt awash in McCain–Palin lawn signs, was watching the event live and was thrilled to hear the senator's reply: Obama had heard of the report. His staff had been briefed on it. Because of it, Rick concluded with pride, Obama was now more predisposed toward new and aggressive CAFO regulations.

Another voter asked about a bill in Congress to ban the "nontherapeutic" use of seven specific classes of antibiotics—including penicillins and tetracyclines—used in human medicine. Obama said he backed the bill. (The legislation also defined "nontherapeutic use" as adding drugs "in the absence of clinical signs of disease, for growth promotion, feed efficiency, weight gain, routine disease prevention, or other routine purpose.")[12]

Obama's support for the measure was hardly radical. It had the solid backing of the American Medical Association, the American Academy of Pediatrics, the American Public Health Association, the National Association of County and City Health Officials, and the National Campaign for Sustainable Agriculture, among 350 other groups.[13]

Industry National Campaign for Sustainable Agriculture opposed the bill, and said that, if enacted, it would drastically raise the price of protein for all American families. But the National Academy of Sciences disputed that claim. The esteemed body issued an estimate showing that such a ban would result in a five-to-ten-dollar increase in food costs, per person, each year.[14]

The price of protein in the United States is a very contentious issue. Large-scale industrial growers insist that CAFOs are the safest, most efficient, and most cost-effective way to raise large numbers of animals, and then sell their eggs, milk, and body parts at a price that virtually every American can afford.

But critics counter that a grocery-store price tag does not reflect the actual cost of producing a pound of protein. While corporations bank the profits, CAFO opponents say, contract farmers foot the bill for waste disposal. Should anything go wrong, taxpayers are left to clean up a big mess. If large integrators were forced to pay for the management of their own animals' waste—and for cleaning up after big spills—then food prices would rise. Everyone who pays income tax is forking over money to keep CAFOs in business, in the form of farm subsidies, which has only helped to perpetuate the animal-factory industry, many analysts contend.

In April 2008, the Union of Concerned Scientists joined the rising chorus of opponents to corporate farm subsidies with a damning report called "CAFOs Uncovered: The Untold Costs of Confined Animal Feeding Operations."[15] It methodically detailed U.S. policies that it claimed allowed CAFOs to dominate meat and dairy production in this country. Subsidies to grow animal feed, for example, saved CAFOs some $35 billion in operating costs between 1997 and 2005. (Cattle operations that raise animals exclusively on pastureland do not benefit from the subsidy.)

Some animal factories were even receiving millions of dollars in public money to install antipollution measures, through the federal Environmental Quality Incentives Program (EQIP), which was established by the 2002 Farm Bill. The report estimated that some $100 million in annual-pollution-prevention payments were made to CAFOs in recent years.

"Misguided federal farm policies have encouraged the growth of massive confined animal feeding operations by shifting billions of dollars in environmental, health, and economic costs to taxpayers and communities," the UCS said in a statement. "As a result, CAFOs now produce most of the nation's beef, pork, chicken, dairy, and eggs, even though there are more sophisticated and efficient farms in operation."

CAFOs did not evolve naturally through agricultural progress, nor did they come from "rational planning or market forces," said Doug Gurian-Sherman, a senior scientist in UCS's Food and Environment Program and author of the report. "Ill-advised policies created them, and it will take new policies to replace them with more sustainable, environmentally friendly production methods."

Margaret Mellon, director of the Food and Environment Program, said if CAFOs had to pay for their "ripple effects of harm," they would no longer dominate the industry. But it didn't have to be this way. "We can institute new policies that support animal-production methods that benefit society rather than harm it," Mellon asserted.

The UCS's report explained how alternative means of production can offer meat and dairy for about the same price as CAFO products. "Many farmers are succeeding when they work with nature instead of against it," Gurian-Sherman

404 | ANIMAL FACTORY

said. "These savvy producers are proving that hog hoop barns, smart pasture operations, and other alternative methods can compete with the massive CAFOs. And that's despite the fact that the cards are stacked against them."

Helen Reddout was disgusted to read about CAFOs profiting at the expense of taxpayers and individual farmers. And she knew that many of the megadairies in the Yakima Valley enjoyed federal subsidies of all kinds. She was starting to research the matter when she came across the Farm Subsidy Database Web site, run by the Washington, D.C.–based Environmental Working Group (EWG). According to EWG, the feds wrote checks for some $13.4 billion to American farmers in 2006; over the previous twelve years, that figure had totaled more than $177 billion.[16]

The wealth was hardly spread evenly, either. Half of all payments went to just twenty-two congressional districts (out of 435) in nine states.

"Taxpayers will continue to send billions more, even as the farm economy posts record prices for many crops, and record incomes for most farmers," the EWG said on its Web site. And a new House bill, if passed, would provide farm couples with new maximum direct payments of $120,000 per year, or $600,000 for five years. "To put this crop subsidy largesse in perspective, at [current] median home prices, $600,000 would buy eight or more homes in places like Youngstown, Ohio," the group said. "Some farmers would receive taxpayer dollars equivalent to five or more median-priced houses—one per year—in twenty-six metropolitan areas."

Enraged by this information, Helen immediately went to the EWG database, which is searchable by zip code, type of farm, or the name of the farmer. She learned that 80 percent of all farmers and ranchers in Washington State collect no government subsidy payments at all. Among those who did get checks, just 10 percent of them were paid 64 percent of all Washington State subsidies, which totaled $1.70 billion over twelve years. Among the top 10 percent, payments averaged $43,831 a year between 1995 and 2006, while the bottom 80 percent of recipients got just $1,586.[17]

Helen typed in the name "Henry Bosma" and found that he had received payments totaling $198,273 between 1995 and 2006. His brother John brought in $46,872.

At the end of April 2008—after two and a half years of study, fifty-four hours of testimony, and 139 pages of final text—the Pew Commission report on animal factories was finally released to the public. It was no exaggeration to label it a slam dunk for the anti-CAFO forces, and they celebrated its release exuberantly.

"Putting Meat on the Table: Industrial Farm Animal Production in America" was probably industry's worst dream materialized. It was extensive, thoughtful, and devastating. The paper had one stark, bottom-line message: CAFOs pose "unacceptable risks to public health, the environment, and the welfare of the animals," a press release from the Pew Commission said. [18]

"Commissioners have determined that the negative effects of the industrial farm animal production system are too great and the scientific evidence is too strong to ignore," the statement continued. "Significant changes must be implemented and must start now. And while some areas of animal agriculture have recognized these threats and have taken action, it is clear that the industry has a long way to go."

Rick, Helen, Karen, and all of their allies knew before they even read the thing that "Putting Meat on the Table" was going to put meat on their arguments. They eagerly devoured the entire report. The chairman—dairyman and former Democratic governor of Kansas John Carlin—said the panel's goal was to "sound the alarms" about badly needed changes in industrial farm animal production (whose acronym, IFAP, the commission chose to use over CAFO). "I believe that the IFAP system was first developed simply to help increase farmer productivity and that the negative effects were never intended," Carlin said. "Regardless, the consequences are real and serious and must be addressed." Industrial animal farms had blessed the world with "tremendous increases in short-term farm efficiency and affordable food," Carlin said, but the boom had not come without "serious unintended consequences and questions about its long-term sustainability."

Meanwhile, most Americans were blissfully unaware of their food's origins—and many did not know that factory farms now produced most of the animal protein they consumed:

> This transformation, and the associated social, economic, environmental, and public health problems engendered by it, have gone virtually unnoticed by many American citizens. These include contributing to the increase in the pool of antibiotic-resistant bacteria because of the overuse of antibiotics; air quality problems; the contamination of rivers, streams, and coastal waters with concentrated animal waste; animal welfare problems, mainly as a result of the extremely close quarters in which the animals are housed; and significant shifts in the social structure and economy of many farming regions throughout the country.

The panel also singled out a few of the people who testified before them, writing up little sidebar accounts of ordinary citizens dealing with animal-factory pollution. One of them was Helen Reddout, who had so impressed the commissioners during her presentation in San Francisco.

"The state of Washington has some of the toughest environmental protection laws in the country, but you wouldn't know it if you live in Yakima Valley, says longtime resident and family farmer, Helen Reddout," they wrote. "Reddout is credited by many as one of the first environmentalists to bring national attention to the issue of industrialized animal agriculture and its effects on the environment and public health. Reddout remembers the first time she was directly affected by a concentrated animal feeding operation. It was 2:00 in the morning when she was awakened by what she describes as a 'hideous smell oozing from the window.' "

The bulk of the report was divided into four sections: public health, the environment, animal welfare, and rural economies.

The health section covered all the issues of antibiotic resistance and other health threats to CAFO workers, neighbors, "and even those living far from the facilities through air and water pollution, and via the spread of respiratory illnesses, asthma, and diseases transmitted by animals. The emissions from confinement facilities, however, may affect communities proximate to those facilities as well as populations far away from these operations," it said. "Meanwhile, the physical stress caused by close confinement can raise the risk of infection and disease in industrial animal populations."

One of the most prophetic sections of the report dealt with the emergence of new and potentially lethal viruses from CAFOs, especially new strains of avian and swine flu. Taking what it learned at the Des Moines meeting, the commissioners noted that avian influenza viral components can easily mix with swine flu virus to create new bugs—and this can happen on both traditional hog farms and inside CAFOs, according to scientists.

The transmission of avian or swine influenza viruses to humans, the report said, "seems a rather infrequent event today." But the commission also issued this grave and perhaps prescient warning:

> The continual cycling of viruses and other animal pathogens in large herds or flocks increases opportunities for the generation of novel viruses through mutation or recombinant events that could result in more efficient human-to-human transmission. In addition, . . . agricultural workers serve as a bridging population between their communities and the animals in large confinement facilities. Such novel viruses not only put the workers and animals at risk of infection but also may increase the risk of disease transmission to the communities where the workers live.

"Reassortant" influenza viruses with human components have ravaged the modern swine industry. Such novel viruses not only put the workers and animals at risk of infections but also potentially increase zoonotic disease transmission risk to the communities where the workers live. For instance, 64 percent (forty out of sixty-three) of people exposed to humans infected with H7N7 avian influenza virus had serological evidence of H7N7 infection following the 2003 Netherlands avian influenza outbreak in poultry. The spouses of swine workers who had no direct contact with pigs had increased odds of antibodies against swine influenza virus. Recent modeling work has shown that among communities with a large number of CAFO workers, there is great potential for workers to accelerate pandemic influenza virus transmission.

The commission was concerned that new strains of avian flu combining with swine flu could make the swine flu more deadly. And because viruses pass so easily between pigs and people, the new avian component could make swine flu more virulent.

The environmental section dealt with health problems associated with all the usual suspects, including airborne emissions such as "toxic gases, odorous substances, particulates, and bioaerosols containing a variety of microorganisms and human pathogens." Meanwhile greenhouse gases—mostly methane, carbon dioxide, and nitrous oxide—were spewing forth from animal guts. The panel cited a 2006 UN report showing that global emissions from all livestock operations account for 18 percent of all anthropogenic greenhouse gas emissions on the planet, even more than cars, trucks, and planes.

Another overlooked environmental impact of industrial animal production is its high consumption of fossil fuels. It takes three units of fossil-fuel energy to produce one unit of food energy on average among all agricultural products. But for industrial meat, the ratio can grow as high as thirty-six to one.

The report discussed runoff into surface and groundwater, and how industrial animal waste can carry antibiotics, hormones, pesticides, and heavy metals into water supplies.

As for animal welfare, there was still considerable debate over "what constitutes a decent life for animals and what kind of life we owe the animals in our care," the panel said. But physical health is measured through the absence of diseases or danger, and these qualities "may be enhanced through confinement" because indoor animals are not as likely to be exposed to certain diseases or injuries. But, the panel stated, "It is clear that good animal welfare can no longer be assumed based only on productivity or the absence of disease."

The most basic concern was the "ability of the animal to express natural behaviors: rooting and social behavior for hogs, walking or lying on natural materials, and enough floor space to move around with some freedom at the minimum."

Reducing stress was good for the animals and good for the people who would eat them. "Scientists have long recognized that food safety is linked to the health of the animals that produce the meat, dairy, and egg products that we eat," the report said. "In fact, scientists have found modern intensive confinement production systems can be stressful for food animals, and that stress can increase pathogen shedding in animals."

Rural communities had "fared poorly" under the CAFO system, the report said. Industrialization had been marked by increasing farm size and gross farm sales, but also "lower family income, higher poverty rates, lower retail sales, lower housing quality, and lower wages for farmworkers." And even though the panel rejected the notion of "turning back the clock to the 1950s," it did say that corrective steps could be taken "to address the problems that industrialization of agriculture has brought."

As the food industry changed over to corporate contracting, economic power switched from farmers to integrators. "Farmers relinquished their once autonomous, animal husbandry decision-making authority in exchange for contracts that provide assured payment, but require substantial capital investment," the report said. "Once the commitment is made to such capital investment, many farmers have no choice but to continue to produce until the loan is paid off. Such contracts make it nearly impossible for there to be open and competitive markets for most hog and poultry producers."

And despite industry assurances that CAFOs were great at economic efficiency, the panelists worried that those benefits were not trickling down to local residents. In fact, they concluded that corporate ownership "draws investment and wealth from the communities in which [CAFOs] are located."

Finally, in one of the accompanying technical reports, there was an economic analysis of swine CAFOs in terms of benefits (i.e., affordable protein for consumers) and costs, which become "externalized" and borne by the surrounding community and society at large.

According to critics, the CAFO model appears to be efficient, but that is only because important costs "are not reflected in either the cost of the production system or its products, but are instead paid for by the public in other ways." Such "externalities" might include declining property values, the public health costs of pollution, the cost of fighting resistant infections, and the cost of cleanup of spills and other environmental disasters.

All of these costs are picked up by the public, "though they are not included in the cost of producing or buying the meat, poultry, eggs, and milk that modern industrial animal agriculture provides," the paper said.

What the researchers found may have surprised some people, who assumed that economies of scale meant that larger pig operations can produce each animal unit at a lower price. But it was externalization, not efficiency, that made industrial pork so cheap. "This analysis suggests that it is not the scale of production that has allowed industrial-style production to lower the cost of pork for the consumer," they wrote. "Rather, it has been the ability of IFAP operations to externalize a significant portion of their costs that has made them appear to be more cost efficient than smaller-scale, more traditional production systems or even newer systems like hoop production. This report calls into question the economic sustainability of the IFAP system of food animal production that exists today and, by extension, raises questions about other forms of IFAP."

The commission issued a number of recommendations—all of which were heartily cheered by activists, and roundly booed by the animal-factory industry. Chief among them were the following:

Phase Out Nontherapeutic Antimicrobials: The National Academy of Sciences had estimated that antibiotic-resistant bacteria had raised health care costs by at least $5 billion annually, or thirteen dollars per person. It also estimated that the banning of all antimicrobials in feed additives would cost each American consumer less than ten dollars per year from increased production costs.

Improve Disease Monitoring and Tracking: The panel endorsed a voluntary animal tracking system, the National Animal Identification System (NAIS), proposed by the USDA. It would be able to help identify exposures by tracking them back forty-eight hours—a time frame that can be critical for containing an infection. "The tracking system should follow food animals from birth to consumption," it said, "including movement, illness, breeding, feeding practices implemented, slaughter condition and location, and point of sale."

Improve Regulations: These are needed for zoning and siting of new CAFOs, with special attention given to topography, climate, and population density. New laws are also needed to mandate "sustainable waste handling and treatment systems that can utilize the beneficial components, but render the less desirable components benign." The panel said that CAFOs must be regulated as strictly as any other industrial operations, and that a "new system of laws and regulations for dealing with farm waste [must] replace the inflexible, patchwork, and broken systems that exist today."

Phase Out Intensive Confinement: "Conditions in many facilities are particularly harsh and stressful, and in many cases may cause undue suffering throughout much of an animal's entire life," the panel wrote. "Unbeknownst to most

Americans, no federal regulations protect animals while on the farm." The commission called for the phaseout, within a decade, of all systems "that restrict natural movement and normal behaviors, including swine gestation crates, restrictive swine farrowing crates, cages used to house multiple egg-laying chickens, and the tethering or individual housing of calves for the production of white veal." It also recommended a ban on force-feeding of fowl for foie gras, tail docking of dairy cattle, and forced molting of laying hens by feed removal.

Increase Competition in the Livestock Market: Every year, fewer Americans are employed in agriculture. "What was once a richly textured way of life supported by countless small-town businesses and a corresponding network of health, education, and social services that were once prevalent throughout many rural areas, has been dramatically altered," the authors said. "Quite literally, rural life in many parts of the nation has withered, leaving once thriving farm communities with an increasingly ghostlike appearance." The commission demanded "vigorous market competition" to improve the standing of consumers and the overall economy. It also called for "vigorous enforcement" of antitrust laws to restore that competition.

Improve Animal Welfare: Federal standards should be adopted to ensure that CAFOs have adequate housing that provides comfort to animals, especially in their lying areas; does not subject them to extreme temperatures; and offers each animal enough space to move around freely. And, in a move that was sure to spark particular industry ire, the commission called for allowing animals to exhibit "appropriate behavior" even while confined. "Animals should be allowed to perform normal nonharmful social behaviors and to express species-specific natural behaviors as much as reasonably possible," they said. "Negative emotions such as fear, distress, extreme frustration, or boredom should be avoided."

It was not made clear how one prevents boredom in farm animals.

Other demands were more clear-cut, including the elimination of practices and conditions such as: "cattle kept on concrete, left in excessive amounts of feces, and/or not provided shade and/or misting in hot climates . . . hogs that spend their entire lifetime on concrete who are prone to higher rates of leg injury . . . hand-catching methods for fowl that result in the animals' broken limbs, bruising, and stress . . . [poor] air quality in IFAP buildings: gas buildup can cause respiratory harm to animal health and to IFAP workers . . . ammonia burns on the feet and hocks of fowl due to contact with litter . . . [and] some weaning practices for piglets, beef cattle, and veal calves: the shortening of the weaning period or abrupt weaning to move the animal to market faster can stress the animals and make them more vulnerable to disease."

Finally, they called for a Food Safety Administration that would merge the food inspection and safety role of the USDA, FDA, EPA, and others into a single agency to improve food safety.

Karen sat down to read the Pew report page by page—yellow highlighter pen in hand. My God, she kept thinking as she read, this is everything that we have been demanding for years. For her, the paper would become an official handbook for policy making and grassroots organizing.

She called Helen when she finished. "It's a godsend—a home run!" she said, her grin coming through over the long-distance call. "I honestly expected a much more mediocre report, but this was very good. God bless you, John Carlin, for not letting someone tie your hands behind your back."

Helen agreed. They had been waiting for years for just this sort of concise tool to slam over the heads of lawmakers. "It is very comprehensive," she said. "And you know me—any time industry opposes something, I know it's good."

As with other reports that were critical of CAFOs, industry reps fought back fast and hard. A coalition led by the Animal Agriculture Alliance blasted the commission, its report, and the process by which the document had been created. "Despite a pledge to an open and public process, the last half of the commission's work was done behind closed doors," the industry statement complained. "This undermines the credibility of its recommendations and begs the question: 'Were these predetermined conclusions in search of supporting data?'"[19]

Industry leaders attacked the process, the makeup of the commission, and even its host, Johns Hopkins University—home to the Center for a Livable Future, which "made no secret of their opposition to contemporary animal agriculture." And, the Animal Agriculture Alliance added, "The commission is ignoring the scientific research it funded in favor of the opinions of commission members who believe they should be able to determine the future of animal agriculture in the United States."

Animal-industry reps had met with commission members early in the process, and had been informed that the Pew Commission had "already determined that problems exist in modern animal agriculture, and the commission's purpose was to find solutions and have them implemented through public policy." The Animal Agriculture Alliance had offered a list of seven candidates for appointment to the panel, but were told that none would be named, "nor would anyone else who could represent the interests of animal agriculture."

The statement was signed by the American Farm Bureau Federation, Animal

Agriculture Alliance, Animal Health Institute, National Chicken Council, National Milk Producers Federation, National Pork Board, National Pork Producers Council, National Turkey Federation, U.S. Poultry & Egg Association, and others.

Philip Lobo, of the Animal Agricultural Alliance, went on to eviscerate the Pew report in an essay, "What Smells in Washington, D.C.?" published in *Progressive Dairyman*.[20] "The report is essentially a rehashing of activist complaints about modern livestock and poultry production, some of which are decades old. Worse yet, they don't take into consideration advances agriculture has made," Lobo said. He predicted that the report's recommendations would be exploited by activists, "including the vegan-driven Humane Society of the United States," to demand new regulations on "everyone that is involved in providing our nation with meat, milk, and eggs."

Lobo argued that the responsible use of antimicrobials, whether to treat disease or for "subtherapeutic conditions," was indispensable to improve animal and human welfare. "If a problem existed, those most likely to be affected are those who work on farms and their families," he pointed out. "The commission's proposals gloss over this reality." He also ridiculed the panel for calling for an end to tail docking of dairy cows. He said the procedure was done to protect milk workers from being infected with leptospirosis and to keep cow udders cleaner, which reduced mastitis and improved milk hygiene. He cited studies showing that tail docking caused no more distress in animals than restraints or blood draws. "Again, if the commission had more agricultural representatives and fewer antiprogress activists, perhaps they would have recognized this reality as well," he said.

Perhaps the biggest worry for industry was that the commission was going to deliver its report to every senator and representative on Capitol Hill, as well as all fifty governors and state attorneys general. "It is important that all of agriculture point out the fallacies of the commission's unrealistic recommendations," Lobo implored dairymen. "The commission clearly fell short of its promise and everyone in agriculture must engage on both the state and federal levels to blunt the impact of its egregiously erroneous document."

And so the battle was engaged, just in time for the upcoming presidential election. On balance, industry did not seem to be winning the argument. In fact, it was starting to not look very good at all. As *The Des Moines Register* reported, Pew commissioners had complained about "livestock interests" trying to disrupt the study by threatening to pull funding from universities and scientists who contributed to the report. "We found significant influence by the industry at every turn," said Robert Martin, the commission's executive director, "in academic research, agriculture policy development, governmental regulation, and enforcement."

But farm groups countered that the Pew team was biased from the get-go, and complained that no major farm groups were included. "There's not a lot of respect for the process," said Michael Wegner, a National Pork Board spokesperson. "You knew when you looked at the people who were appointed how it would come out. It wasn't one of those broad-based, 'Let's start with a blank slate' kind of things."[21]

A Pew spokesperson declined to comment on the allegations. But Chairman John Carlin said that many livestock groups had attended commission meetings and submitted testimony—against any new recommendations. "Basically, they were all saying there is no problem here," Carlin complained to the *Register*. "We said, 'We are here to help, and we can't help you if you won't even admit there are problems.' There are problems."[22]

Most major newspapers agreed, including *The New York Times* in a scathing editorial titled "The Worst Way of Farming."[23]

"The so-called efficiency of industrial animal production is an illusion, made possible by cheap grain, cheap water, and prisonlike confinement systems," the paper of record claimed. "In short, animal husbandry has been turned into animal abuse. Manure—traditionally a source of fertilizer—has been turned into toxic waste that fouls the air and adjacent water bodies. Crowding creates health problems, resulting in the chronic overuse of antibiotics. And, because the modest profits in confinement operations require the lowest possible labor costs, including automated feeding, watering, and manure-handling systems, these operations have helped empty and impoverish rural America."

And the recommendations put forth by the panel, the *Times* said, were "useful guideposts for the next Congress and a new administration." No one could have imagined how heartily those recommendations would be endorsed by the next president.

Chris Petersen knew that, by the time the general election arrived in November, the CAFO question would not only take a backseat to war and the economy, it wouldn't even be riding in the campaign car.

Even so, nearly all animal-factory activists were going to vote for Obama–Biden over the GOP ticket of Senator John McCain and Alaska's governor, Sarah Palin, whose probusiness platform attracted lots of agribusiness dollars. Big Ag corporations spent $64 million in the 2008 election cycle, with sixty-four cents on each dollar going to Republicans. In the presidential race, CAFO interests donated $5.6 million to McCain and $3.7 million to Obama.[24]

John McCain could not really compete with Obama for the anti-CAFO vote, though he did hint at ending government support for ethanol, and vowed to slash farm subsidies.

The McCain campaign document on agriculture, "Prosperity for Rural America," contained many plums for the big food companies, including redoubled efforts to boost food exports. McCain vowed to "reduce barriers to trade, level the global playing field, and vigorously defend the rights of American agriculture."[25]

But many activists were turned off by McCain's vow to rein in the "unnecessary intervention of government regulations that severely alter or limit the ability of the family farm to produce efficiently." As Tom Philpott, food editor at the popular online environmental news and commentary site Grist.com, put it, "Despite the heartening reference to the 'family farm,' that statement is probably a coded promise to maintain comically lax oversight of confined-animal feedlot operations and their titanic output of toxic waste." And, he added, McCain came across as "utterly oblivious to the concept of sustainable agriculture; he never mentions it once in his rural document, nor in any other statement of his I can find. He seems intent on letting 'the market' work its magic on the food."[26]

Election night in the United States brought two victories for animal-factory opponents. Barack Obama was elected with 53 percent of the vote and won such big CAFO states as North Carolina, Washington, Iowa, Ohio, Michigan, Minnesota, and, most surprising of all, deep-red Indiana.

And just as Illinois had launched Obama into the history books, the people of California made a little history of their own, in the form of Proposition 2. With 63 percent in favor and 37 percent against, voters approved a measure mandating that veal calves, egg-laying hens, and pregnant sows "be confined only in ways that allow these animals to lie down, stand up, fully extend their limbs, and turn around freely." The practices would be phased out by 2015 with exceptions for transportation, rodeos, fairs, 4-H programs, lawful slaughter, research, and veterinary medicine. Penalties include fines up to one thousand dollars and/or 180 days incarceration.

Most affected by Prop 2 was the twenty-million-hen laying industry in California. Though they would not be required to eliminate battery cages altogether, producers would have to invest large sums of money to upgrade their houses, including making cages big enough to allow the birds to move around. Many egg CAFOs were expected to convert to "cage-free" housing, which, much like broiler houses, confines thousands of hens into huge "floor system" buildings, often with raised platforms to fit even more hens in.

The egg industry spent millions trying to defeat the measure. It predicted massive drops in supplies and price spikes up to 20 percent if Prop 2 passed (at the going rate of $1.80 per dozen in California, that would mean the retail price would rise by thirty-six cents).

Many argued that chickens were better off in cages, where they were less prone to predators, including other chickens. Others hinted that egg companies would simply pick up and move to other states or to Mexico, along with their jobs and other economic benefits. And they cited a UC Davis study predicting that Prop 2 would likely push the entire $300 million industry out of California or out of business altogether.[27]

The Animal Agricultural Alliance called the vote a "crushing defeat for animals, farmers, and consumers" that would shut down farms. "We are despondent that California voters didn't hear animal welfare experts' messages warning of higher rates of death in noncage systems, increased rates of smothering, increased incidences of aggression and much more," said the alliance's Kay Johnson Smith. "It is disappointing to learn that, in the tumult caused by all the various initiatives, consumers didn't hear that message."[28]

Two of the state's largest and most liberal newspapers, the *Los Angeles Times* and *San Francisco Chronicle*, had backed industry and opposed the proposition, along with the American Veterinary Medical Association, United Egg Producers, California Restaurant Association, and the California Hispanic Chamber of Commerce, among others.

Balancing that out was heavy support from A-list Hollywood types and financial backing by the Humane Society of the United States. The measure also drew support from the Pew Commission, which had called for the phasing out of veal and sow crates and battery cages for laying hens. Its endorsement gave HSUS and other Prop 2 supporters some more academically backed ammo to go after the CAFOs.

In fact, the Pew report's influence would stretch well beyond Golden State voters and into the highest levels of power in America in late 2008—all the way to the Presidential Transition Team. The Pew Commission's executive director, Robert Martin, made sure the report was personally delivered to top people on the president-elect's senior staff, including those overseeing the USDA, EPA, and Department of Health and Human Services, as well as to the incoming vice president, Joe Biden, and the first lady, Michelle Obama (who had long expressed interest in sustainably grown food).

Copies were also delivered to USDA Secretary Designate Tom Vilsack, the former governor of Iowa (and 2008 presidential candidate) and longtime friend and political ally of Chris Petersen. Chris worked his own extensive relationships within the incoming administration to ensure that the Pew report was widely distributed and read by the very people who would soon be running the United States and its food production policy.

Public revulsion at the way in which modern farm animals are housed, fed, and treated was proving to be one of the most contentious—and emotional—controversies facing the entire CAFO production system. It's not hard to understand why. When considering animal-welfare issues inside animal factories, it all comes down to real estate. The crowded quarters; the competition for a small amount of breathing room; and the attendant stress, conflict, and aggression are also found in overpopulated cities.

Our society, the argument goes, would never permit dogs, horses, or even zoo animals to be confined to overcrowded pens and cages their entire lives, with little if any opportunity to roam outside, breathe fresh air, or merely stretch their legs.

Even so, ballot initiatives to phase out the most restrictive apparatuses—battery cages, veal hutches, and sow gestation crates—rattled and infuriated large-scale animal producers, who felt under siege from voters and politicians who were forcing them to make upward adjustments in their square-foot-per-animal spreadsheets.

The industry was now bogged down in an acrid and expensive fight over animal welfare reform that put it squarely, bizarrely at odds with a majority of its own customers: those voters who passed or would pass measures to require a bare minimum of freedom of movement for American food animals.

According to at least one agribusiness reporter, farmers nationwide were furious over Proposition 2 because it banned "confinement of certain farm animals in manners that don't allow them to turn around freely, lie down, stand up and fully extend their limbs."[29] The villains in this war, the reporter said, included the Humane Society of the United States, and one of the most beloved personalities on American television: Ellen DeGeneres, who was selling old clothes on eBay to donate funds to the HSUS and encouraging her famous guests to do likewise.

Some animal-factory proponents tried to distance themselves from the "fully extended limbs" rhetoric, but still warned against the encroaching problem of voter-mandated animal-welfare regulations. At the American Farm Bureau Federation, the official position on animal care was that "generally, we support the right of producers to raise livestock in accordance with commonly accepted agricultural practices," said Kelly Ludlum, a Farm Bureau livestock representative. "The American Veterinary Medical Association has standards for each of those confinement practices that, if followed properly, will not harm animal welfare, and in fact can actually enhance animal welfare," she continued, adding that gestation stalls were "probably a fairly good example."[30]

Yes, one could still find gestation stalls "that are not in accordance with sort of industry guidelines, but I think that's going to be rare," Ludlum said. "I mean, gestation stalls, when installed, are typically done by people who know what they're doing and have the best interests of both producer and the animals in mind. And so if installed properly and managed properly, gestation stalls can be very effective in maintaining animal welfare of sows during their pregnancy."

But what if the question was merely whether the sow could stand up, turn around, or extend her limbs within the confines of her gestation "stall" (a term that the industry favors over the word "crate") and not whether such stalls should be eliminated altogether?

"That's how things work, if voters vote at the ballot box," Ludlum said, adding that farmers "sort of feel caught in between a public that says that they want free-range or organic or what we would consider to be niche-market attributes to their food product, and yet also want to pay the lowest amount possible." And even though Prop 2 was approved by 63 percent of the voters, "cage-free egg purchases in California continue to be well under 10 percent."

Farmers, she added, are willing to do "whatever they can, again, so long as the welfare of the animal is not compromised; they'll produce whatever consumers want them to produce, so long as consumers are willing to pay for the cost of that production. And I think the angst for farmers is that now they're being told we still want you to produce eggs at the exact same price that you were producing them in 2007, but oh, by the way, we're going to increase your production costs 300 percent. And it doesn't take a calculus degree to figure out that that's just not going to be sustainable for many producers."

Another argument against measures like Prop 2 was that some animals simply don't *need* the extra space mandated by nonfarming voters. "The question is, Why would I need to give a bird, you know, five feet?" Ludlum asked, throwing out that number as an example. "When all they're ever going to use is one foot. There's a cost to giving an animal five feet of space as opposed to less, and why pay that cost if it doesn't benefit the animal or the consumer or the quality of the food? Why do that if there's not the benefit?"

Ludlum said that we as humans are "sometimes guilty of applying our own thoughts and rationale to everything around us," including farm animals. "And so, because *we* would want to be able to stand up and turn around and fully extend our limbs, doesn't necessarily mean that a chicken, that is a prey animal, would want to do that."

Meanwhile, at Indiana's Purdue University, animal scientists were busy studying animal welfare, freedom of movement, and alternative housing designs, though most researchers at that land-grant school, not surprisingly, remained staunchly pro-CAFO.

For example, Ed Pajor, associate professor of animal behaviors (mostly swine) at Purdue, was looking into questions such as "Does it make a difference if animals have room or don't have room? How do the animals *feel* about this particular option, or that option?" he said.[31]

And Alan Sutton, a Purdue professor of waste management, nutrition, and swine intestinal microbiology, contended that CAFOs can actually enhance well-being by keeping animals apart from each other. "When you mix animals, they have to reestablish a pecking order and they're not always so friendly with each other," Sutton said. "And they could hurt each other, even kill each other."

There was also the issue of equitable feed distribution "because there are some individuals, a sow, that will just want to gobble it all up and they'll get fat, which may be counterproductive," he explained. "There's going to be some animals who won't get enough. So you need to make sure that each animal is given a fair share of feed and water." In other words, to *deny* an animal fair access to food and water, and to expose that animal to the risk of injury or death caused by another animal, is in itself a form of cruelty.

Other arguments that Purdue scientists offered in defense of confinement were that gestation and farrowing crates for sows increase litter size by reducing fetal and infant death; and that the health of confined animals is improved because the monitoring and delivery of care and medicine to individual members of the herd is greatly enhanced.

One scientist even suggested that young American pigs eat food that is better for them nutritionally than the food consumed by most American kids.

When president-elect Barack Obama selected former Iowa governor Tom Vilsack—a major ethanol supporter with ties to Monsanto who had joined Clinton's campaign after ending his own brief run at the White House—to head the USDA, it sent ripples of consternation and even protest through some corners of the sustainable-agriculture movement.

The Organic Consumers Association blasted the choice even before it was announced in a November 12 online communiqué titled "Six Reasons Why Obama Appointing Monsanto's Buddy, Former Iowa Governor Vilsack, for USDA Head Would be a Terrible Idea." Among them, it alleged, were Vilsack's support for genetically engineered crops, especially "pharmaceutical corn," his backing of efforts by the Trans Ova company to clone dairy cows, and his creation of the 2005 "seed preemption bill," which would prevent local governments from regulating the use of genetically engineered seeds.[32]

In addition to condemning his "being a shill for agribusiness biotech giants like Monsanto," which often flew Vilsack on a company jet, the OCA criticized his support of corn- and soy-based biofuels, "which use as much or more fossil energy to produce them as they generate, while driving up world food prices and literally starving the poor." The group neglected to mention that Obama was also a strong supporter of ethanol and other biofuels.

But other groups welcomed the choice. Ken Cook, president of the Environmental Working Group, said he was "encouraged" by it because Vilsack wanted to reform farm subsidies, supported local food programs, and had a solid conservation record.[33] National Farm Union's president, Tom Buis, called Vilsack a "great choice," saying Vilsack understood the problems of rural America and was willing to take them on.[34]

Helen and Karen didn't quite know what to make of the mixed signals, so they contacted their colleague from Iowa, Chris Petersen. They felt much better after the call.

Chris knew Vilsack and his wife, Christy, going back through years of politics in Iowa, long before he was first elected governor in 1998. "I supported him for this position through my various channels with the Obama people," he told them. "Tom and I worked together on a bunch of bills in the legislature. And when Farmers Union pushed for some truly progressive livestock bills, he stood behind us. He helped us refigure our packer ban bill to get it passed—before Smithfield got it overturned, of course."

In January 2009, the Waterkeeper Alliance sponsored yet another big conference, the Pure Farms, Pure Waters National CAFO Summit, once again in New Bern, North Carolina. Hundreds showed up on the cold, rainy weekend for Robert F. Kennedy, Jr.'s keynote address, and to hear dozens of other speakers from around the country talk about the progress they had made and the hard work that lay ahead, even under the more favorable climate of an Obama regime.

Rick Dove was the summit's unofficial host and for him, walking around the Riverfront Convention Center was like taking a pleasant stroll through the past twenty years of his life. He was delighted to welcome all of the people from Socially Responsible Agriculture (formerly GRACE Factory Farm Project), including Karen and Rocky Hudson, Chris Petersen, Terry Spence, Carole Morison, and Bill Weida. Helen, alas, was stuck at home in Outlook, Washington, recovering from surgery. There were old North Carolina friends, too, including Don Webb, Gary Grant, Devon Hall/Baron-Hall and Dothula, and Professor Steve Wing of University of North Carolina at Chapel Hill.

There were also some new anti-CAFO leaders making their way onto the national stage. In North Carolina, four Riverkeepers, including Larry Baldwin (Lower Neuse), Heather Jacobs Deck (Pamlico-Tar), Tess Sanders (White Oak-New), and Doug Springer (Cape Fear) were emerging. Rick was happy, and relieved, to introduce them. "Here are the future leaders in the North Carolina CAFO fight for generations to come," he said. "My bones are aging. These Riverkeepers are tough and full of life. I'm very proud of them."

The mood was both hopeful and apprehensive. After eight years of the almost-anything-goes, probusiness government of George W. Bush, many of those gathered in New Bern were guardedly optimistic that the Obama team would live up to its now somewhat overused "change" mantra and truly usher in a new era of agriculture: more sustainable, healthier for people, and easier on all God's creatures.

But another current ran through the conference, too. It subtly haunted many attendees, and most people knew that, despite Obama's election, nobody could let their guard down now.

There were just too many emerging threats out there for anyone to feel too complacent. Nobody knew when or where the next zoonotic disease might emerge, but everyone was certain it would happen sooner rather than later.

On the other hand, as Rick would say, they had been quite adept at changing the laws of man—in the courtroom, in the voting booth, in statehouses, on county commissions, in laboratories, and in health journals. The scrappy band of soothsayers ringing their once-dismissed alarm bells about industrialized animal production were being taken seriously by the media, by much of the public, and by the incoming president of the United States.

Obama's "Plan to Support Rural Communities" read like a manifesto from CARE, or FARM, or Waterkeeper, or any of the hundreds of grassroots groups around the country trying to defend their vision of what a traditional, sustainable agrarian way of life should be. The main problem that needed fixing today, Obama said, was that family farmers were being squeezed out by big industry. "Consolidation has made it harder for midsize family farmers to get fair prices for their products and compete on the open market," the plan began. "Rural communities are often left behind." To counter that, Obama vowed to enact these changes. (The following is a direct quote from BarackObama.com.)

Provide a Strong Safety Net for Family Farmers: Obama and Biden will fight for farm programs that provide family farmers with stability and predictability. They will implement a $250,000 payment limitation so that we help family farmers; not large corporate agribusiness. They will close the loopholes that allow mega farms to get around the limits by subdividing their operations into multiple paper corporations.

Prevent Anticompetitive Behavior Against Family Farms: Obama is a strong supporter of a packer ban. When meatpackers own livestock they can manipulate prices and discriminate against independent farmers. Obama and Biden will strengthen anti-monopoly laws and strengthen producer protections to ensure independent farmers have fair access to markets, control over their production decisions, and transparency in prices.

Regulate CAFOs: Obama's Environmental Protection Agency will strictly regulate pollution from large CAFOs, with fines for those that violate tough standards. Obama also supports meaningful local control.

Establish Country of Origin Labeling: Obama supports immediate implementation of the Country of Origin Labeling law so that American producers can distinguish their products from imported ones.

Encourage Organic and Local Agriculture: Obama and Biden will help organic farmers afford to certify their crops and reform crop insurance to not penalize organic farmers. They also will promote regional food systems.

Encourage Young People to Become Farmers: Obama and Biden will establish a new program to identify and train the next generation of farmers. They will also provide tax incentives to make it easier for new farmers to afford their first farm.

Partner with Landowners to Conserve Private Lands: Obama and Biden will increase incentives for farmers and private landowners to conduct sustainable agriculture and protect wetlands, grasslands, and forests. [35]

It was such a slam dunk for the activists that it made them nervous. "They're going to get their asses kicked," Chris said. "Barack has cojones, leaving this on his Web site."

Mostly, people at the summit wanted to know what Chris thought of Tom Vilsack. Was he a corporate apologist, as many had charged, or was he serious about cracking down on CAFOs?

"I just spoke with him recently, and we agreed on a lot of things," Chris said. "Now, not all his answers to everything were perfect, but it looked to me like he will be very interested in sustainable and organic farming. He wants to take a more big-picture view of things, like showing an interest in limiting the subsidies going to big players." And, he added, a friend had spotted Vilsack in a D.C. grocery store buying organic dairy products, "so his heart's in the right place, and that makes me feel good."

Vilsack and Obama understood what Chris and his friends had been fighting for all these years, he said. But no one was getting a free pass. "I said I was going to criticize the hell out of them anytime I don't like what they're doing." He grinned. "But I'll do so while offering them an alternative solution, and that's going to be smaller-scale, localized production, with decisions left to the people who're actually doin' the producing."

But what about Vilsack's connections to Posilac-maker Monsanto and other Big Ag companies, Karen asked. "We discussed all that," Chris said. "There's no love there for Monsanto, or Smithfield, for that matter," Chris said. "So I said to him, 'If that's the case, then why not just label the damn rBGH on the package, and let consumers pick which milk they want?'" He said he wouldn't have a problem with that. Labeling is the American way, he told me, especially with something you're gonna put in your stomach."

That night at dinner, Chris got up to address the six hundred people in the hall. He began with a friendly salvo to the new president. "Don't ever, *ever* let Barack Obama or Tom Vilsack say to your face, 'I don't know what you're talking about when you start speaking about CAFOs and family farms.' They know right from wrong! They went through a grueling little schooling we call the Iowa caucuses. Now, whether they do the right thing or not is their choice. But in the best interest of this country and our environment and our future, believe me, I hope Mr. Obama remembers what we told him."

Nothing less than the health of all Americans was on the line, Chris said. "Take avian flu, and swine flu, for example," he said soberly. "How many warnings have we had? And each time we expressed concern that swine flu could crawl out of one of these pig factories, industry said that was impossible. Well, that line's not going to work anymore.

"We're winning this thing," he continued. "I don't know when we'll reach a final victory, but we are winning. And soon, they won't have a leg to stand on with their dinosaur vision of how to feed the world. They know it and it scares the hell out of them."

E arly 2009 was a very bad time for swine. Media reports had already surfaced about MRSA showing up in raw pork meat at U.S. supermarkets. An investigative news team at Seattle's KOMO-TV purchased ninety-seven packages of pork chops and ground pork at stores in Oregon, California, and Idaho and tested them at a USDA-certified lab in Seattle.[1]

Three came back positive for MRSA.

And yet, the USDA has long resisted testing for the superbug in pork, even though U.S. hogs are known carriers, and a particularly virulent strain was found in pigs during a recent University of Iowa study, KOMO reported. The station confronted the USDA with the findings, but officials said the agency still had no plans to test American pork, even though Canada and Europe routinely test for MRSA in grocery stores.

The National Pork Board, meanwhile, began its own testing in retail markets in early 2009. Internet articles claimed that preliminary results were similar to KOMO's findings. About 3 percent of the samples, or one in thirty-three, tested positive for MRSA.[2] So a family that bought and cooked raw pork twice a week, say, was bringing MRSA into their home, on average, three times a year.

But the Pork Board said that the type of MRSA most commonly found in U.S. pigs was not dangerous to people. It did not even appear to make pigs sick, according to the Pork Board's Web site, Pork.org, "and there are no data to support that the humans carrying this pathogen are at a higher risk of developing infection than the rest of the U.S. population."

But MRSA is scary, and surely the pork industry knows that most Americans do not want to bring it home from the market. Matters were not helped in March by an alarming *New York Times* column by Nicholas Kristof titled "Our Pigs, Our Food, Our Health."[3] Filing from Camden, Indiana, Kristof described the tragic demise of a small-town family doctor, Tom Anderson, who began seeing patients with odd rashes more than a year earlier. "They began as innocuous bumps—'pimples from hell,' he called them—and quickly became lesions as big as saucers, fiery red and agonizing to touch," Kristof wrote.

Dr. Anderson was puzzled at first why there would be so many MRSA cases in a small town like Camden. Then he thought about all the large hog CAFOs just outside town. He was very worried—the level of MRSA he was seeing was "phenomenal." Anderson had offered to show Kristof around the area and go on the record with his fears that MRSA was coming from the hogs. "That was a bold move," Kristof wrote, "for any insinuation that the hog industry harms public health was sure to outrage many neighbors."

But before Kristof could finalize plans for his trip to Indiana, Dr. Anderson had very suddenly died, at age fifty-four. The cause of death was unknown, though blood tests indicated that he may have suffered a heart attack or aneurysm. But Anderson had also been sickened three times with MRSA, which Dutch researchers had linked to heart inflammation in humans.

"The larger question is whether we as a nation have moved to a model of agriculture that produces cheap bacon but risks the health of all of us," wrote Kristof, who grew up on a farm and even raised pigs for a while. "And the evidence, while far from conclusive, is growing that the answer is yes."

Kristof described the Dutch studies of swine workers infected with MRSA, and mentioned another small study showing that 45 percent of swine farmers sampled in Iowa carried MRSA, and so did 49 percent of the pigs tested.

As for the estimated fifty MRSA cases in Camden, population five hundred, Kristof thought they most likely came from the "routine use—make that the insane overuse—of antibiotics in livestock feed. This is a system that may help breed virulent 'superbugs' that pose a public health threat to us all."

The news only got worse for supporters of Big Pork. A month later, business wires were reporting that Smithfield Foods, Inc., the nation's largest pork producer, was struggling with rising costs and falling demand—and was said to be ripe for a sale. The reports said that COFCO, the biggest farm trading and processing company in China, was offering to buy Smithfield at a discounted rate. Reuters reported that Smithfield was suffering from a big slump in sales, and burning through cash each quarter.[4] "The industry is hurting due to commodity prices that reached record highs last year coupled with weak demand and a supply glut that is depressing prices," it said. Smithfield was also moving operations further into packaged meats, a more profitable end of the business.

In fact, Smithfield had already announced layoffs of eighteen hundred employees and said it would shutter six processing plants, including in its hometown Virginia headquarters, in order to focus more on packaged pork products.[5]

The swine industry may have thought that high grain prices, falling pork demand, and now MRSA were major headaches, but within days, in April 2009, a new and potentially catastrophic virus would be leaping from the world's headlines.

Soon after that, industry leaders would be frantically pressuring the U.S. government and the World Health Organization to call the new disease "novel H1N1 influenza." But everyone on earth knew it simply as "swine flu."

In late April, health officials from Mexico, the United States, and the WHO announced that a new form of influenza virus was spreading in Mexico, with a few cases also reported in Southern California and Texas. The previously unidentified pathogen carried one avian flu genetic component and one human flu genetic component, but two genetic components from swine influenza. Mexico's health minister, José Ángel Córdova, announced that the virus had "mutated from pigs, and then at some point was transmitted to humans," which may be why the media labeled the disease "swine flu."[6]

Thousands had already gotten sick in Mexico, and more than one hundred people had already reportedly died from the virus by the time news reached the United States. By the end of April, unsettling images of people running around Mexico City in surgical masks were plastered across the airwaves and newspapers of North America.

Almost immediately, CAFO opponents began saying that industrial swine operations in Mexico were to blame. Over the past decade, U.S. hog conglomerates like Smithfield began opening massive CAFOs south of the border, including dozens around Mexico City in the states of Mexico and Puebla. Smithfield Foods also operated a sixty-thousand-sow breeding operation outside La Gloria, a small village in the eastern state of Veracruz. Some early online reports traced the flu outbreak to that particular town.

Cheaper labor costs and a desire to enter the Latin American market drew more CAFOs to Mexico all the time, wiping out smaller, traditional farms, which by early 2009 accounted for only a very small portion of swine production in Mexico. And though it was far too soon to know if this new virus had mutated and incubated at a Mexican hog CAFO, the industrialized facilities unquestionably belonged on the list of suspects. For years, leading scientists around the world had worried that swine factories were breeding grounds for new pathogens that could more easily infect humans and then spread out rapidly in the general population—threatening to become a global pandemic.

Almost overnight, people around the world jumped online to look up the Pew Commission report, which had predicted that a global influenza epidemic could potentially emerge from a hog CAFO operation. Bob Martin, the former executive director, fielded a lot of media calls over the next few weeks. "We met with a team of researchers from the University of Iowa who are studying avian flu, and their real concern was the very scenario that may have happened in Mexico—that avian flu may get into a swine CAFO and rapidly mutate and then get passed to workers, and then on to other people very quickly," Martin told the *Huffington Post*.[7]

Martin said that researchers such as Gregory Gray, M.D., a University of Iowa professor of international epidemiology and expert in zoonotic infections, warned that CAFO workers could serve as a "bridging population" to rural communities sharing viruses with the pigs, and vice versa. Other scientists suggested that CAFO workers could theoretically spread disease quickly to great distances. An outbreak of infectious avian flu on the eastern shore of Maryland, for example, could reach the Rocky Mountains within thirty-six hours.

The Iowa team was also worried that CAFO production could lead to another 1918-style global pandemic. It was possible that waterfowl cross-infected U.S. pigs with a new type of avian-swine supervirus that was quickly transmitted to farmworkers, possibly in Iowa, who went off to military training camps for World War I, and then spread the pathogen worldwide.

In the United States, the National Pork Board had already urged producers to take steps to reduce avian-to-swine influenza transmission. "It is in the best interest of both human public health and animal health that transmission of influenza viruses from pigs to people, from people to pigs, from birds to pigs, and from pigs to birds be minimized," it said. "The global reservoir of influenza viruses in waterfowl, the examples of infection of pigs with waterfowl-origin influenza viruses, the risks for reassortment of avian viruses with swine and/or human influenza viruses in pigs, and the risk for transmission of influenza viruses from pigs to domestic turkeys all indicate that contact between pigs and both wild and domestic fowl should be minimized."

Dr. Liz Wagstrom, the board's chief veterinarian, said she did not know if Mexican producers followed the same precautions, though she did note that none of the Mexican herds under U.S. contract had reported any unusual health problems. She admitted that some U.S. farms use surface water in animal barns, but her group was moving to avoid the practice industrywide. She added that the new virus had not been detected in any U.S. pigs, and there was no importation of live swine from Mexico.

But Dr. Ellen Silbergeld, professor of environmental health sciences at

Johns Hopkins Bloomberg School of Public Health, and a leading researcher of pathogen evolution in CAFOs, said the genetic swimming pool that is found in modern swine—or poultry—production was probably where the killer bug evolved. "CAFOs are not biosecure," she said. "They have high rates of ventilation and an enormous number of animals that would die of heat stress unless the building was ventilated. We and others have measured bacteria and viruses in the environment around poultry and swine houses. They are carried by flies, too. These places are not biosecure going in—or going out. These mixing bowls of intensive operations of chickens and pigs are contributing to speeding up viral evolution." Dr. Silbergeld added, "I think CAFOs are contributing."[8]

What about traditional outdoor farms? Aren't those animals even more susceptible to wild-type viruses than animals kept indoors, as industry claims? "Well, let's say that animals in confinement are ten times less likely to be infected by wild animals," she said, "But there are one hundred times as many of them. You do the math."

A few days later, the Mexican government confirmed a case of swine flu in a five-year-old boy in La Gloria, Veracruz.

Hog-industry officials in Mexico and the United States said their operations were not to blame for any human illness. "We deny completely that the influenza virus affecting Mexico originated in pigs, because it has been scientifically demonstrated that this is not possible," said Mario Humberto Quintanilla González, president of Organización Nacional de Porcicultura y Porcicultores (the National Organization of Pig Production and Producers). "It must remain clear that the flu problem is caused neither by the proximity to swine operations nor by the consumption of pork meat or pork products."

Meanwhile, one of Mexico's largest producers, Granjas Carroll, which is co-owned by U.S. hog giant Smithfield Foods, which runs the CAFO near La Gloria, issued its own statement saying there was no sign of swine flu at any of its operations. It reported no signs of disease in any of its 907 workers—nor in its sixty thousand breeding sows or five hundred thousand feeder pigs, all of which were vaccinated against swine flu.[9]

But according to an April 5 article in *La Jornada* newspaper, more than four hundred residents in La Gloria had already been treated for respiratory infections, and more than 60 percent of the town's three thousand residents had reported getting sick. "Clouds of flies emanate from the lagoons where Granjas Carroll discharges the fecal waste from its hog barns—as well as air pollution that has already caused an epidemic of respiratory infections in the town," the paper reported. State officials disputed the claim, and said the illnesses were caused by cold weather and dust in the air.

The problems began in early March, when many villagers became sick with colds and flus that quickly turned into lung infections. Health officials imposed a "sanitary cordon" around the area and began a mass program of vaccination and home fumigation. "According to state agents of the Mexican Social Security Institute, the vectors of this outbreak are the clouds of flies that come out of the hog barns, and the waste lagoons into which the Mexican-U.S. company spews tons of excrement," *La Jornada* reported. "Even so, state and federal authorities paid no attention to the residents, until today."

The Veracruz state government demanded that Smithfield turn over all documents and environmental certifications on its three massive waste lagoons, but the company had only supplied information on one of them, news reports said. On Friday, the chairman of the state legislature's Committee on the Environment, Marco Antonio Núñez López, called on Veracruz's secretary of health to impose a sanitary cordon around all hog and poultry CAFOs in the area—as well as bus terminals and airports—to prevent the spread of influenza among the population. He said the factory farms should be considered "hot spots" of potential infection for the cities of Veracruz, Boca del Río, Coatzacoalcos, Córdoba, Orizaba, Xalapa, and Perote.

As the influenza virus continued to spread around the world—seemingly losing virulence as it traveled—scientists confirmed that six of its eight genetic components were direct descendents of the swine flu virus that had first appeared in North Carolina a decade ago at that twenty-four-hundred-head breeding facility in Sampson County. Fortunately, back in 1998, the virus did not become a threat to people—humanity had dodged one big epidemiological showdown. Even so, scientists had tried to warn the world that this would happen again, only next time it would bring far more calamitous results.

In May, it was erroneously reported that a Canadian pig farmer who had been in Mexico infected his own herd with the virus. Those pigs were quarantined and no other Canadian or U.S. pigs were reported with the strain, which U.S. and WHO officials were now taking great pains to call H1N1 influenza. For the most part, the media still called it swine flu, much to the despair of the USDA and the pork industry, which was losing millions of dollars a month due to export bans imposed by huge markets like Russia, China, and other East Asian countries (Japan, which requires irradiation of all imported pork meat, did not impose a ban).

The National Pork Council and the USDA took to the airwaves to remind consumers at home and abroad that properly cooked pork was perfectly safe to eat, and Secretary Vilsack—and President Obama—conspicuously began calling the outbreak H1N1 influenza, and not swine flu.

Within a few weeks, however, swine flu had been brushed aside from the headlines almost entirely. The number of new cases in Mexico dropped dramatically, and the official death toll was revised downward. Images of Mexicans in face masks no longer dominated the evening news and the world turned its short-term attention to other matters.

But the outbreak had still killed dozens, sickened thousands, and cost the world uncounted billions of dollars in lost productivity, travel, and other economic activities. Moreover, health officials warned that the virus, far from being eradicated, was still circulating and spreading throughout the world, and could return in an even more virulent form later in the year. They noted that the 1918 flu epidemic began with a relatively mild form of the disease in the spring, followed by a more serious return in the summer, and then, in the fall, the virus came back again in its supervirulent form that killed millions worldwide.

In May, the Obama administration was still deciding whether to order production of a new swine flu vaccine for fall delivery, haunted by the memory of the 1976 swine flu, in which President Gerald Ford hastily ordered millions of doses of vaccine that ended up causing a debilitating nerve disorder called Guillain-Barré syndrome in at least five hundred Americans (though some scientists believe the number of injured was actually in the thousands). A swine flu epidemic never materialized that year.[10]

For the flu outbreak in 2009, researchers at Iowa State University suggested they might have a better answer: They were developing a new type of genetically engineered corn that inserts flu vaccines into the DNA of the maize. One day, they said, both pigs and people could get a flu shot simply by eating corn, corn feed, or corn-based products like cornflakes, corn chips, or tortillas.[11]

When Karen Hudson first met Chris Petersen, he had warned her that she was stirring up a hornet's nest of controversy, and that Big Ag and the people who depend on it for their living would fight back hard. They would threaten her, ridicule her, call her nasty names. And the rhetoric heaped upon her on the anonymous Internet would be most stinging of all. Over the years, Karen had learned how rough it could get.

In May 2009, a reporter from the *Illinois Times* wrote an extensive profile on Karen and her history of opposing animal factories.[12] It was an exceedingly favorable article, and it incurred the wrath of Karen's enemies from around the Midwest. Under the headline BIGGER ISN'T ALWAYS BETTER—KAREN HUDSON HAS BECOME A RELUCTANT EXPERT ON THE CONSEQUENCES OF CONCENTRATED ANIMAL FEEDING OPERATIONS, was a picture of Karen with singer and rural activist Willie Nelson marching at Farm Aid 2007 and carrying a large banner reading FARMS, NOT FACTORIES!

The reporter, Dusty Rhodes, explained that Karen and her paid associates at the Socially Responsible Agriculture Project (SRAP, formerly GRACE Factory

Farm Project) were shifting their efforts these days more toward rebuilding rural infrastructure to provide the services needed to get their milk, meat, and eggs to market. Those services—independent feed mills, auction barns, and processing plants—had gone the way of the horse and buggy over time as big integrators moved in to hasten their planned obsolescence.

Rhodes reported that SRAP was in the process of "converting two fifty-three-foot refrigerated trailers into mobile slaughtering facilities to accommodate farmers with a few head of marketable meat, instead of a truckload." And though the SWAT Team members did collect a salary for their work, Karen said, "We are a group of people that would be doing this job even if we didn't get paid to do it. If I won the lottery tomorrow, it wouldn't change anything."

The reactions were swift. Comments praising Karen and ripping her to shreds came pouring in to the online comments section of the *Illinois Times* Web site. For example, someone identified only as "friend of the farm" wrote:

What a ridiculous overexposure of the overzealous queen of controversy! Karen Hudson is a blight on the landscape of agriculture—I really don't know how her husband, as a farmer, can stomach her crap. She and so many others are obviously blind to the elements of progress in animal agriculture—as we strive to keep up with the demands of feeding a growing global population, it's a no-brainer that we can't accomplish that by reverting back to the days when pigs, cows, and chickens roamed (and pooped) outdoors. Modern production facilities and animal husbandry practices allow producers to maintain better herd health (with less medications), oversee animal conditions, prevent fighting among animals, and produce meat and eggs in the most cost-effective and efficient means possible. As someone who's spent their entire life involved in agriculture, I'm embarrassed and saddened by the antics of people like Karen Hudson. And now she's getting PAID for it—UGGHHH!

Later, the same commenter got personal, if not a little creepy and stalkerlike:

Karen Hudson is a Chicago suburbs transplant to Elmwood, had never stepped foot on a farm (to my knowledge) before she married Rocky, worked at CILCO in Peoria (a cousin of mine knew her there) and then proceeded on her path of doing her best to destroy livestock farming. It sounds personal doesn't it? You bet it is. I got to know several of the farmers (including the Durkees) that Karen ravaged over the years. Not corporations, not faceless robots that live thousands of miles away, but farming families that were trying to grow and be successful in their industry. That picture of her and Willie up top of this story makes me want to vomit. And it sickens me even more when a farmer buddies up to her because of her anticorporation rhetoric. The sly leading the blind—and I'll have none of it.

Another writer piled on:

> Where are the stories about the communities that Karen has torn apart? I have personally witnessed Karen prance into a community, rile up neighbors, friends, and relatives of farmers who have proposed a new livestock operation, fill them full of misinformation and unfounded claims, demonizing agriculture to the point that people believed that wells would run dry, streams were doomed to be contaminated, hydrogen sulfide fumes would asphyxiate. Then after the lawsuits were filed and lifelong neighbors no longer would speak to one another, Karen would just move on to the next proposed operation and do it all over again. I fought against Karen and her ilk practically from the time she started, and the only air I ever saw poisoned was from Karen herself. Shame on *Illinois Times* for printing such a "manure-filled" puff piece written by a biased journalist.

But Karen had her supporters—they were just as ardent and vocal as her bitter foes:

> To all of us in Illinois currently fighting hellholes called CAFOs, Karen Hudson is an environmentalist godsend. Karen Hudson shows what can be done by anyone with creativity and a conscience. Factory farms are disconnected from the community, the people, and thus lack accountability. The push for cheap food has sad environmental, social, and ethical consequences that need to be reversed.

And yet another ally wrote this:

> I thank God for Karen Hudson. She understands the devastating effect of CAFOs on the humans who live near them, and the animals who live IN them. I do not know of one good thing that comes from CAFOs. To the people trashing Karen Hudson herein, know this: she is in very good company. Millions and millions of Americans nationwide agree with her! In fact, the most populated state in the United States—one that produces huge amounts of meat, eggs, and dairy—weighed in on

this very issue during the last election, with Proposition 2 passing in record numbers. Wake up and "smell" the message. CAFO farming is on the way out and sustainable farming is coming in!

On May 4, 2009, a new roxarsone trial got under way in the Fayetteville, Arkansas, courtroom of Circuit Judge Kim Smith. It was a continuation of the lawsuit against Tyson Foods and other chicken producers, filed by Beth and Michael Green and their son Blu, who contracted a rare form of leukemia in Prairie Grove. Judge Smith had dismissed those cases but, on appeal, they were remanded to his court.

During the new trial, the plaintiffs' star witness, retired environmental chemist Dr. Rod O'Connor, discussed his studies of air-conditioner filters and arsenic dust that he traced to roxarsone. And Dr. Devraj Sharma, an authority in "materials transfer," testified that Prairie Grove residents were exposed to "high levels of arsenic" during the times that broiler litter was spread near homes and schools, which he said was done "regularly."

Jason Hatfield, the Greens' lead attorney, urged jurors to consider the effects of airborne arsenic exposure "over and over and over again" in schoolchildren. "We know these kids were breathing it," he said in closing.

Hatfield also pointed out that since the lawsuit had been filed, Tyson had quit using roxarsone, chicken litter stopped being spread across the street from the Prairie Grove schools, and more than half the chicken litter was being transported out of the county. As a result, there were no more cases of childhood leukemia in Prairie Grove, he contended.

But Woody Bassett, representing defendant George's Farms, argued that the lawsuit never should have been filed, "because we have not done anything wrong." He accused the plaintiffs' witnesses of being paid to say anything necessary in order to "create a case out of nothing." They had offered no reliable science for the jury to consider, as opposed to the "first-class scientists" and experts brought in by the defense. The most salient point to remember, he instructed jurors, was that Blu's rare type of leukemia was not caused by arsenic. "That is the evidence you can rely on," he concluded.

In the previous trial, jurors had taken just twenty-one minutes to decide, ten to two, for the defendants. This time, on May 14, 2009, they took two hours to deliberate, and voted for the defendants once again, this time nine to three.

The Green family was crushed. "This was a case that had Blu's name attached to it, but it wasn't just about him," Beth Green told reporters after the verdict. "This was a case about seventeen children in a seven-year period in

Prairie Grove that were diagnosed with cancer," she said. "Our fear because of this verdict is that it opens the door for companies like Tyson to use this product again, or other companies to continue using the product."[13]

elen Reddout was getting tired of hearing about the pigs.

Swine flu mania had swept the world and, for a few weeks, it seemed to be the only thing people were talking about. To Helen, the pig obsession was irksome. But she knew there *was* something dirty, fecal, and pathogenic about swine that left many people with a visceral reaction to the animals, especially in terms of spreading disease. Dairy cows, on the other hand, were always portrayed as wholesome and clean, sweet as alpine meadow grass, and imbued with the innocence, purity, and natural goodness of milk.

Dairy cows. They have very good PR, Helen thought.

Helen felt like the nonstop focus on pigs—and, to a lesser extent, chickens—was masking the actual threat to health and the environment posed by megadairies. Life in the Yakima Valley had changed little since that first confrontational meeting at the Outlook Grange. The big dairies were still operating, the air quality was still often unbearable, asthma rates were rising, and even a school in Toppenish had its well water contaminated with nitrates, forcing the district to buy bottled water for students to drink.

In May, Helen got some sorely needed backup from the *Journal of Environmental Health*, which published a study on fungi and bacteria generated by dairy CAFOs and the threat they posed for spreading multidrug-resistant staph infections in people.[14] It was bad news for megadairies, but a welcome tonic to Helen, and a shot in the arm for her efforts.

The authors began by explaining that the risk of exposure to antibiotic-resistant pathogens is far greater from agricultural animals and products than from medicine-based pathways. Many scientists had studied fungal and bacterial concentrations in ambient air around swine and poultry CAFOs, but little such work had been done at the big dairies.

Helen could vouch for that—the dearth of dairy studies made her job that much harder.

"To our knowledge, this is the first study to evaluate bioaerosols of a cattle CAFO in an arid climate over multiple seasons," wrote the authors, who took multiple air samples outside a large New Mexico operation between the months of April and December. The dairy, which kept cows outside on large lots in an arid climate, resembled the huge operations in Washington, California, Idaho, Texas, and elsewhere.

The authors found that "a significant concentration of culturable fungal organisms and bacteria" were present in the ambient air. Even more disturbing, more than half of the *Staphylococcus aureus* bacteria found were resistant to one or more antibiotics.

In other words, Helen thought, you might get MRSA from handling raw pork, but you could also get drug-resistant staph just by living—or even walking—downwind from one of Washington's large dairies.

And there was more bad news, from a public-health point of view. More than half of the bacteria and 85 percent of the fungi at the dairy studied were attached to very fine particulate matter—coarser particles settle out of the air more quickly and finer matter stays suspended in the air for longer. Finer particles are more likely to reach the lungs, where infection can occur, because they are not filtered out in the upper airways of the respiratory system.

Bad as the air was outside this particular dairy, it was apparently much worse outside the average swine CAFO: Studies found that bacterial concentrations were twenty times higher, and fungal levels were ten times higher. But Helen was skeptical of this finding, and she had good reason to be. For one, the New Mexico dairy samples were always taken midmorning, when cows are not particularly active. Helen knew from experience that late in the afternoon, the cows—and especially their calves—would kick dust and dried feces up into the air. In Helen's opinion, that alone could increase particulate matter twentyfold. There was no reason to doubt that microbial concentrations would rise, too.

Helen also wondered about ambient air found at dairies that keep cattle confined to barns all of the time, like those in the wetter, colder states of the upper Midwest. She suspected that air quality around those sites would be poorer, because pathogens can thrive indoors. The authors concurred with this assessment. "The outdoor environment is more likely to suppress microorganisms by desiccation and UV light exposure," they wrote, "particularly in the arid southwestern U.S." And, they added, wind provides extra natural ventilation that was "likely to disperse these microorganisms."

Helen knew immediately that this was an important study with critical implications for the health of animals, dairy workers, and the general public.

"It is well known that livestock industry workers are exposed to a massive number of antibiotic-resistant airborne pathogens compared to healthcare workers and hospitalized patients," the paper said. "These workers are more likely to be colonized with these antibiotic-resistant organisms and to pass them to their families."

The authors then called for more research to determine the impact of repeated exposures to antibiotic-resistant bacteria of dairy workers and people who live near dairy operations.

Helen, of course, wanted to shout the news from the rooftop, channeling Howard Beale of *Network* once again. She knew that dairies using rBGH were more likely to rely on heavy antibiotic employment; and she knew that most of the big dairies in her area relied on rBGH. She worried her home and her community were being threatened by antibiotic-resistant pathogens drifting out of the huge open lots that spread out around her beloved valley.

On a warm afternoon in late May 2009, when the air was thick with humidity and the scent of honeysuckle, Rick and Joanne Dove were out in the backyard, enjoying their view of the Neuse River, when Rick's cell phone rang.

It was Don Webb.

Don and Rick were now old friends. They spoke on a regular basis about hogs and politics, feces and urine. The two had spoken often during the election season, the inauguration, and now the swine flu outbreak that was seriously threatening the U.S. hog industry, not to mention human health. Don had reluctantly voted for Obama, and only then after heavy prodding from Rick. Now he was waiting for action from the White House.

In fact, Don was feeling a bit of buyer's remorse, and he called Rick to chat about it. "I mean, where in the hell is that farm summit that Mr. Obama promised?" Don wanted to know. "And all those new CAFO regulations and fines? And what about that packer ban, Rick? Any idea when the Obama folks are gonna get a move-on with *that* one?"

Rick reminded his friend that Obama had been in office only four months, hardly enough to tackle the big farm issues, especially with two wars, an economic crisis, and now swine flu to deal with. On the other hand, it was clearly Obama's obligation and moral responsibility to keep his word and enact his promised reforms, Rick said.

Obama would have to make some good-faith efforts soon, or begin to lose support among a solid block of voters.

"I'm scared he's not going to keep promises," Rick admitted softly. "I'm afraid he won't make industry get off the dime and fix all these problems; won't tell them flat-out that 'Yes, you will make less money, but somebody has got to pay to stop all this pollution.'"

Don appreciated his friend's candor. "You hit it right on the head, Rick," he said. "They have the knowledge and the ability to put in new technology that would help, but they know it's cheaper to just keep on polluting. Now, if Obama would come down hard on them and force them to clean up, that would really be something, There's no way in hell you're going to get 'em to *volunteer* to do it, because the fox is guarding the henhouse."

Rick thought back through all the years that Don, Helen, Karen, Chris, Carole, Terry, Barbara, and so many others had put into this fight. He flashed back on the small victories and the crushing disappointments. Now he was thinking about the warnings.

"Don, do you remember when you spoke about swine flu way back when the state had that Blue Ribbon Commission? And you looked each one of them in the eye and warned them? I'll never forget it. You said, 'One day, in all this filth and stress we subject these pigs to, we are going to have another swine flu,' and they laughed at you. And now the swine flu is here and nature is once again trying to slap us in the face to wake us up."

"We predicted so *many* things," Don agreed. "We predicted the cesspools would break and the odor would stink and people would get sick. But our government went along with it anyway. Our government never listens to us, but they'll listen to a paid scientist who can make up anything, just to make Smithfield or some other hog producer happy."

Don recalled the time several years ago, at a demonstration in Raleigh, when he stood on the street outside the general assembly, staring up at the rows of dour official faces looking out the windows at him and the band of protestors. The activists had tried to enter the building carrying bottles of liquid hog waste, but were told it was too dangerous to allow inside. Don bellowed up at the lawmakers and their aides, shouting that they would never do anything serious about swine diseases until they had to "get out the body bags."

Years later, when Don sat on Mike Williams's committee that evaluated the alternative technologies to replace lagoons, he had brought up the same unpleasant subject. "I asked them, 'What are you going to do when swine flu comes around and starts killing people?'" Don told Rick. "'Are you going to help them? Don't you know it's coming?' And they didn't do nothin' but look at me like I was *crackers* in the head! And now these people turn their head for a dollar bill, but don't give one damn if a little child gets sick."

There was a long pause for a moment. Rick was beginning to feel depressed.

"You know something?" he finally said. "I get the feeling the battle is lost. And now the only way things will change is if something so bad, like killer flu, comes along to make the government do something. But why in the hell do we have to wait? Nature's been telling them the same thing that we have, all along. She's been warning them about the nitrogen and phosphorus in her waters, and how those nutrients were creating algal blooms and *Pfiesteria* and killing fish. She warned them with people getting sick from pollution, she warned them with dead zones and mad cow and MRSA and *E. coli*, even asthma in little kids. And now, swine flu.

"But the politicians didn't listen to nature any more than they did to us," Rick went on. "So now it's going to be something so bad that the government will have no choice but to fix it, in order to save mankind."

"This story isn't over yet," Don said. "And, you're right; nature will have the final word." And with that, the two friends said good-bye.

Rick hung up and put his arm around Joanne, who was staring out over the river. The late afternoon sun cast a warm arc of yellow-orange across the rippling waters of the Neuse Estuary. Off in the distance, a wild osprey wailed through the heavy air. The river looked the same, but Rick knew it was nothing like it used to be. There were so few fish anymore. Very few fishermen could make a living just from the water.

A week before, Rick had been in the river working on his boat, in water shoes, but with a small cut on his foot. That cut became so severely infected it required two antibiotics and four trips to the hospital to bring it under control. To Rick, it was just one more warning sign from nature.

And that made Rick think about swine flu again. Federal officials had just announced that one hundred thousand Americans in forty-eight states had contracted the new virus. More than two hundred had been hospitalized. H1N1 had just killed a vice principal in New York City, which was closing schools throughout the boroughs. Worldwide, the new flu was now in forty countries, with at least eighty deaths. Meanwhile, the virus was disproportionately claiming victims that were young. It was highly unusual to have so many people under twenty end up in the hospital with such severe cases of flu, many of them in the ICU.

Rick had watched the incoming CDC director, Dr. Thomas Frieden, tell reporters that ERs were seeing inordinately high numbers of patients showing up with fever and flu—most of them between five and seventeen years of age. Another CDC official, Dr. Anne Schuchat, told reporters that this was a serious problem that merited a serious response, and urged them to "dispel the idea that we're out of the woods."[15]

Meanwhile, Smithfield Foods was hardly out of the woods, either. In late May, the husband of one of the first people in the United States to have H1N1 filed a court petition against Smithfield on behalf of his wife, who died on May 4. The petition sought to investigate Smithfield's La Gloria operation for scientific evidence that the virus had emerged from what it termed the "horrifically unsanitary" conditions there.

Even big, powerful Smithfield, Rick thought, might have to pay a price for forcing pigs into what he thought amounted to animal concentration camps.

And that afternoon, May 22, 2009, scientists at the CDC had unveiled a detailed analysis of the novel virus's DNA and determined that, indeed, "the new swine flu may have been circulating undetected in pigs for years," according to the Associated Press.[16] It really was "swine flu" after all, no matter what Smithfield and the USDA wanted to call it.

Rick turned and looked deep into Joanne's eyes. His face had a painfully haunted look that almost frightened her.

"Right now, only God knows how bad this will get if this swine flu turns really deadly as it did once before," he said. "I am so afraid, Joanne. Not for us, but for Holly's family, and especially our grandchildren. Our lives would be over if we lost another child."

Human nature is a strange thing, Rick thought. We have an uncanny knack for ignoring warnings even as we are urged not to break the rules. Everyone knows that nature did not intend for humans to inhale tobacco smoke, yet millions of people do. But nature is generous with her admonitions. First comes the shortness of breath, then some wheezing, and then a deep phlegmatic cough. But these warnings are so often rationalized and brushed aside as mere annoyances, distractions from the overall pleasures of cigarette smoking.

In so many cases, the final alarm bell rings too late.

Maybe this swine flu outbreak would turn out to be nature's final alarm—"the big one," as Rick called it. Or maybe it was just one more generous wake-up call, one more slap in the face to remind us that rules are rules. Nature did not design farm animals to be crammed into buildings and confined indoors by the thousands. We broke her laws, Rick thought, and she will exact her price from all of us.

"You know something, Joanne? I have no idea where this story ends," Rick said with a deep sigh. "And that's what scares me the most."

EPILOGUE:
THE PRICE OF PROTEIN

Today, most Americans get their meat, milk, and eggs from highly productive, anonymous animal factories located hundreds or thousands of miles away from their home. Although the disconnect between people and their food has never been greater, the retail price of that food has never been cheaper.

Will it always be this way? No one can predict the future—especially when it comes to such a complex, emotional, and volatile issue as how our food is produced and processed. No one can know exactly what the typical American animal farm will look like in ten or twenty years: whether we will have all CA-FOs, all the time; a complete return to small, diversified, localized food production; or some type of patchwork hybrid.

Many people would like to see CAFOs fade away entirely, as have the eight-track tape player, ditto machine, and other clunky, outdated technologies we used to consider indispensable. But many people would also like to see world peace and a cure for cancer.

My one prediction is that animal-factory operators—under pressure from consumers, voters, environmentalists, community activists, regulators, politicians, scientists, journalists, animal-welfare advocates, and even celebrities—will continue to reform their operations by applying new technologies to help make their CAFOs more acceptable to their neighbors and the public in general.

In trying to determine where this complex story was heading, I attempted to interview people with a wide range of opinions about the current—and future—state of animal agriculture and what, if anything, should be done to change and improve the industry. While I had the generous cooperation of many people from the academic, scientific, agricultural, environmental, and rural activist communities, my efforts to include the voices of leaders from agribusiness and, especially, Barack Obama's federal government were less successful.

Requests to interview officials at Cargill, Smithfield, the National Milk Producers Federation, and the National Cattlemen's Beef Association were not fruitful. The National Pork Board referred me to the Animal Agricultural Alliance, which, after initial communications that were pleasant and respectful, suddenly and inexplicably stopped returning phone calls and e-mail inquiries.

Likewise, none of the dairy operators in the Yakima Valley or their attorneys responded to requests for interviews, and Doug Baird of the Highlands hog operation in Williamsfield, Illinois, politely declined an interview after careful consideration. (His father, Jim Baird, the former Knox County commissioner, passed away in July 2009.)

However, Mike Platt of Indiana Pork, and representatives from the National Chicken Council and the American Farm Bureau Federation, readily made themselves available to answer questions and provide their perspective on a wide variety of issues, for which I am indeed grateful.

As for the Obama administration, repeated attempts over a three-month period to speak with officials at the White House, the USDA (including Secretary Tom Vilsack), and the EPA (including Administrator Lisa Jackson) went nowhere, which was disappointing to me as a journalist (I also write about agriculture for *The Huffington Post*), and as a citizen who was looking forward to the president's promised new era of transparency and accountability.

Supporters of the animal-factory food system with whom I did speak argued that animals that are confined and restricted within CAFOs are much better off than their pasture- and grass-fed kin—protected as they are from predators, the elements, and one another. More important, they say, CAFOs are the one and only way to provide affordable protein to hundreds of millions of people who demand that their meat and dairy be not only cheap but also unwaveringly uniform every time they reach for a cellophane-covered package in their grocer's refrigerated aisle.

American food *is* cheap. People in the United States now spend about half the percentage of their incomes on food as they did in 1966.[1] But "cheap" at the checkout does not mean "cheap" for society as a whole. For every dollar per pound you spend on CAFO butter and chops, critics contend, there's an unspoken and almost incalculable social surcharge added to cover the additional costs of pollution and disease, plus federal subsidies, buyouts, and Farm Bill giveaways.

"You have to take into account the externalized costs," writes Ralph Loglisci, former communications director of the Pew Commission on Industrial

Farm Animal Production and current project director for the Johns Hopkins Healthy Monday Project, at the school's Center for a Livable Future blog. "Right now, Big Ag is very happy to let the public pick up the tab."[2]

Among the "externalized costs" that don't get figured into your grocery store bar code, he said, are "increased environmental health risks from the introduction of antibiotic resistant bacteria like MRSA or novel viruses like the current H1N1 swine flu, particulate matter known to exacerbate asthma, the emissions of countless toxic gasses from enclosed barns, and environmental pollution from excess nutrients (animal feces and urine) contributing to the dead zones in the Gulf of Mexico and choking the Chesapeake Bay."

And, Loglisci added, "Don't forget about the contamination concerns of nitrates and other pollutants in well water from all that liquid animal waste sprayed onto or pumped into the ground that is not agronomically absorbed."

So what's a concerned consumer to do? Some people are choosing (and can afford) to buy only "sustainably" and humanely raised milk and meat, vowing never to eat protein that was turned out in a factory-style environment. Others have reduced or abandoned eating meat—and sometimes eggs and dairy—altogether, and now somewhat smugly feel that all American families struggling to make ends meet should simply do the same.

I live in Brooklyn, New York, in a multiethnic neighborhood that spans the socioeconomic scale, from working class to comfortably affluent. The shoppers in my local supermarket are mothers mostly, and I can see the look on many of their faces as they do the math in their heads: How much protein can they actually afford to feed their families this week?

Then I see other people who sweep through the store, happily filling their baskets with organic this, grass-fed that, and free-range everything else. It looks great, but it is very expensive. At those times, I often think of the words of Helen Reddout, who fears we are heading into a "two-tiered food system" in this country, where the well-off get the hand-crafted, localized, "niche market" cream of the crop, while those below them nourish themselves on mass-produced, chemically and pharmaceutically enhanced, cheaply priced foodstuffs.

But these days, people in New York and elsewhere of all strata are growing much more aware of their food: where it comes from, how it was raised, what impact it had on the environment. Our farmers' markets are brimming with fresh meat and produce, our "locavore" restaurants pack in crowds with Hudson Valley pork and Long Island duck, and the idea of "urban agriculture" is fueling a miniboom Renaissance of rooftop crops, backyard coops, and community-run vegetable gardens.

But for now, at least, eating *only* animal protein that was raised in a non–factory farm setting is a prohibitively expensive proposition for many, if not most, of my neighbors. The dilemma—moral, economic, gastronomic—can be acute. A quick visit to my local supermarket, which reflects the high price of living in New York, tells the story:

EGGS
Commercial brand, 1 dozen large: $2.49
Specialty brand, organic "cage-free," 1 dozen large: $4.99

MILK
Commercial brand, ½ gallon: $1.59
Organic brand, ½ gallon: $3.89

BUTTER
Commercial brand, 1 pound: $4.99
Grass-fed brand, 1 pound: $7.98

CHEESE
Commercial brand, cheddar, 1 pound: $6.49
Organic brand, cheddar, 1 pound: $9.99

BACON
Commercial brand, 1 pound: $4.99
Pasture-fed brand, 1 pound: $7.45

PORK CHOPS
Store brand, center cut loin, 1 pound: $1.99
"Certified Humane," center cut loin, 1 pound: $3.99

CHICKEN
Commercial brand, whole chicken, 3 pounds: $5.47
"Certified Humane" brand, whole chicken, 3 pounds: $8.97

BEEF
Store brand shell steak, 1 pound: $8.99
Grass-fed shell steak, 1 pound: $14.99

TOTAL FOR "CAFO PROTEIN": $37.00
TOTAL FOR "NON-CAFO PROTEIN": $62.25

The "non-CAFO" bill was 68 percent higher.

"CAUGHT IN THE SYSTEM"

The American drive for cheap food drives everything in the modern American food chain, and even the biggest producers can get sucked into the discount-protein vortex.

Fred Kirschenmann, Distinguished Fellow for the Leopold Center for Sustainable Agriculture at Iowa State University, is also president of Stone Barns Center for Food and Agriculture in Pocantico Hills, New York, a certified organic farmer, a member of the Pew Commission on Industrial Farm Animal Production, and a leading figure in the modern national "food debate." He believes that many of the players in the corporate food chain are, in a way, unwitting victims in a structure that has lost all sense of control or boundaries in its unyielding drive to minimize "input" costs and maximize cookie-cutter "output": food products that can be sliced, diced, wrapped, and shipped in a manner that consumers find appealing, convenient, and, most of all, affordable.

"In a lot of ways, everyone is caught in the system; and the system is what we have to change if we want to change these production practices," Kirschenmann told me.[3] He had spoken with many CEOs at large food-processing and marketing companies and found this: "They understand the problems, but they are caught inside a system where they are obligated by law and by a responsibility to maximize returns to shareholders."

And even if these captains of animal industry wanted to change the way they do business, Kirschenmann said, "they would still have to take some of the company's profit and invest it on new infrastructure for the future. The problem is that shareholders always demand the maximum return on their dollar as quickly as possible. So we have created an industrial food system based on maximum production and short-term return, and everyone is caught up in it."

Kirschenmann was once seated at a dinner next to a meat marketer from Cargill, who complained that his company simply could not turn a profit when selling pork to Wal-Mart. "And it wasn't just Wal-Mart, but a whole concentration of retail food outlets. He said that when they need a new product, they go out to eight or nine suppliers and ask for proposals as to how and at what price they can deliver. So they have to give the buyer the best deal they can. Then the buyer will select three of those companies and tell them, 'Okay, you're in the running. Now give us the *real* price.' But their margins get so tight, they have no option but to keep reducing their costs, and that can only happen by giving contracts to bigger farmers, because it's cheaper to buy ten thousand hogs from one producer than one thousand hogs from ten producers."

Virtually everyone—including shoppers who scramble for the best buys at big-box stores with little regard for their own food's provenance, or "protein footprint" —bears some of the blame. "To some extent," Kirschenmann said, "we have all participated in the creation of this food system."

With all that in mind, then, how cheap *is* our meat? As Helen Reddout pointed out, "If you look at the actual cost of protein in the supermarket, and then factor in the corporate welfare system, and the cost of damaging the environment, creating antibiotic resistance, and sickening people who live nearby, and then if you consider the inferior product we are getting as a result, then in that sense, we have the most expensive food in the world."

Remove just two "crutches" from the system, Helen said, and CAFOs will collapse "like matchsticks." The big animal companies, she contended, cannot run without the "corporate welfare system under the Farm Bill," or without widespread antibiotic dependence.

AN ANTIBIOTIC BAN: COULD IT LEVEL THE PLAYING FIELD?

In August 2009, the American Veterinary Medical Association (AVMA) came out with a damning condemnation of the Pew Commission report on industrial animal production.[4] Although it took the AVMA fifteen months to articulate its protest, the passage of time did nothing to temper its abrasive rhetoric.

"The report contains significant flaws and major deviations from both science and reality," the AVMA said. "These missteps lead to dangerous and underinformed recommendations about the nature of our food system—and shocking recommendations for interventions that are scarcely commensurate with risk." The Pew report, which the vets' association called "biased," was little more than "a prolonged narrative designed to romanticize the small, independent farmer, while vilifying larger operations, based simply upon their size."

One of the group's biggest complaints was the Pew Commission's call for a ban on nontherapeutic antibiotic use. The AVMA opposes "seemingly simple but non-risk-based broad bans on certain labeled uses of antimicrobials, such as disease prevention, growth promotion, and feed efficiency," the statement said. "Not all antimicrobials or their uses are equal in their probability of developing resistance or creating a risk to human health."

The AVMA, like the Big Ag industry itself, pointed to data from countries that banned the use of antibiotics for growth promotion several years ago, and claimed that animal deaths and disease went up in Denmark after it enacted such a ban, "requiring more therapeutic antibiotic use to treat the resultant diseases."

People who worked on the Pew report quickly fired back. "It appears that leadership of the veterinary professional organization is attempting to misuse science to obfuscate and delay critically needed changes in the food animal production system rather than tackling very real public health and environmental threats head on," former commission staff member Ralph Loglisci wrote on the blog of the Center for a Livable Future at Johns Hopkins. "Following a grueling 2½-year discovery process, and despite several overt attempts by industry to discredit it, the commission concluded that the scientific evidence was too strong and the public health risk too great to ignore."

The AVMA had waited a long time to release its critique, but it still "contains very little scientific citation to back up its rebuttal," Loglisci wrote. "It's not a coincidence that this response coincides with the recent revelation that the Obama administration supports the idea of banning the use of key antibiotics as growth promoters in food animals."

The AVMA, he charged, "depends heavily on its relationships with the animal agriculture, pharmaceutical, and other industries." And the group's broadside against the Pew report "smacks of being more like an industry-choreographed campaign than a conscientious review of a hugely important document."

Loglisci cited a letter from one AVMA member, Dr. Raymond Tarpley, who was "dismayed that my professional organization has chosen to pursue a reckless policy that favors the misuse of critical antibiotic compounds for reasons other than medical necessity. Contrary to statements by the AVMA, the ban on antibiotics in Denmark has been shown to have positive benefits for human and animal welfare, while not harming the industry. Their interpretation of the Danish data reflects the bias of the AVMA in the spin of data favorable to industry."

Loglisci mentioned the two researchers from the National Food Institute at the Technical University of Denmark, Drs. Frank Møller Aarestrup and Henrik Wegener, who gave written testimony to a congressional committee hearing on banning nontherapeutic antimicrobials, in order to "set the record straight."

"As you may be aware, representatives of organizations funded by U.S. agribusiness have criticized and misrepresented the facts on the Danish ban of antibiotics since its inception," the two Danish scientists wrote.

In fact, the Danish ban had reduced antibiotic use by more than half, even though total pork production increased by 43 percent, Loglisci wrote. "AVMA's stance on public health prevention appears to be out of sync with the rest of the world," he added.

Loglisci was hardly alone in that assessment. "To my knowledge, [AVMA] remains the only major medical or public health organization not recommending changes in agriculture practices to help ensure sustainability where the use of antimicrobials is concerned," wrote Michael Blackwell, D.V.M., M.P.H., vice chairman of the Pew Commission and former dean of the College of Veterinary Medicine at the University of Tennessee, Knoxville. "As a public-health veterinarian I find this disconcerting and embarrassing."

But would a ban result in actual savings to society as a whole? It's not easy to say.

"How do you measure the cost savings or return on investment in cases where an antibiotics ban prevented people from getting sick and going to the doctor or the hospital?" Loglisci asked. "We know a great deal about the costs of drug-resistant infections in the United States in terms of health care costs, increased morbidity, and increased risk of death. Over longer periods of time we can measure whether doctor visits or reported illnesses are decreasing among certain populations or regions touched by industrial animal agriculture."

Loglisci was not surprised that Danish researchers found that farmers in that country initially saw increases in animal disease when the antibiotic ban went into effect. "However," he added, "after farmers improved ventilation systems and gave the animals more space, within a relatively short period of time they found production actually increased while at the same time they greatly reduced the need for antibiotics."

Dr. Ellen Silbergeld, the Johns Hopkins expert and lead author of the Pew Commission's antimicrobial-resistance technical report, said that removing antimicrobials from animal feed will unquestionably save money through reduced human medical costs, just as it did in Europe after the ban there. "There is clear evidence that this ban was associated with reduced prevalence of drug-resistant pathogens in people in hospitals in the EU," she wrote.

So why was Big Ag engaging in such "industry obfuscation and attempts to misuse science to muddy the issues?" as Loglisci put it. "The longer Big Ag can hold off on paying for upgrades and changes to the system, the longer it can continue to make money at the public's expense," he said.

OBAMA AND THE PROMISED "RURAL AGENDA"

For many animal-factory foes, President Barack Obama has not yet followed through on his promises of systemic reform, though that could always change. To be fair, with two wars, a health care imbroglio, a precarious economy, and a swine flu program to manage, the president has an extraordinary spoonful of troubles heaped upon his plate, and most CAFO activists remain patient and optimistic that their issues will not get buried and forgotten along with campaign slogans like the "audacity of hope" and the "fierce urgency of now."

And even though no one in Barack Obama's administration would return calls regarding agriculture policy (of all things), the White House did e-mail me this prepackaged statement:

> During the campaign the president outlined a vision for rural America that focused on rejuvenating local economies and protecting family farmers. That agenda has not changed. The administration's priorities are reflected in the president's budget, the allocation of critical Recovery Act funding, and a new culture of leadership at the USDA based on developing sustainable rural economies.[5]

"They put up a public shield, but all options are on the table. They understand all these connections between soil and food and health," Fred Kirschenmann explained. "They have to keep things held close, or else vested interests would clobber them. But if you think about it, why would the Obama administration put so much effort and energy into a public face around food with Michelle [and] her organic garden on the White House lawn? That statement is not lost on industry. One chemical company wrote a letter and thanked her for bringing more prestige to agriculture, but then added, 'Why do an organic garden, with all the progress we've made in chemicals?' They get the message, and they are concerned."

In June 2009, Dr. Bill Weida and members of the Socially Responsible Agriculture Project received notice via Chris Petersen that the USDA wanted to hear their ideas about how to enhance sustainable agriculture in the nation. The activists, needless to say, leaped at the chance.

"We hope these suggestions start a new dialogue between the USDA and the sustainable farming community," Weida and the group wrote back, attaching a paper listing several areas where "limited resources could reestablish the kind of agricultural system that fed this nation successfully for so long."[6]

But time was wasting. "Every core assumption on which corporate agriculture and confined operations are based, from cheap energy and cheap capital to cheap feed, has now been proved wrong," the SRAP group wrote to Vilsack. "The financials of these operations demonstrate that we face a stark choice of either increasing subsidies to keep failed enterprises afloat or reestablishing the proven alternative of conventional farms producing healthy, local food that consumers now demand."

Local food production and the rural economic stimulus it would bring could be assisted by targeted USDA funds, the activists said, helping to level the playing field in the marketplace.

"But small sustainable agriculture has been largely ignored in [Obama's] agriculture budget," they complained. Despite growing demand for sustainable food, USDA programs were still "structured to promote and subsidize the failed model of large, corporate farms and vertically integrated processing and distribution." Meanwhile, "local processing and marketing options that are critical to the survival of sustainable farms have largely been lost. As a result, subsidized food grown, on average, fifteen hundred miles from the average consumer replaced local food for most families."

Then the group, which included Karen, Helen, Chris, and Terry, put forth some "options for funding a local, sustainable agriculture program":

- Reduce or eliminate unnecessary inspection costs for small producers that favor large production and processing facilities that "created the hazards in the first place."
- Put greater focus on farmers beginning or transitioning to socially responsible meat production.
- Provide USDA funding for CAFOs to convert to sustainable models.
- Fund purchases of local, sustainable food for school lunches, colleges/universities, military bases, prisons, etc., to help local farmers and provide healthy foods.
- Help generate market access to food stores, farmers' markets, government institutions, local food banks, etc.
- Provide start-up assistance for small, multispecies processing facilities within thirty to forty-five minutes of one another and link them to mobile processing units.
- Prohibit nutrient generation from exceeding requirements of the land.
- Prohibit farms receiving federal money under these programs from using liquid manure systems.
- Limit animal ownership by meat packers to no more than fourteen days before slaughter and require that a daily percentage of meat-packer purchases come from an open-bid market.
- Publicize and educate the general public on the merits of supporting "local, safe and healthful food systems," and on what it means to local economies and the environment.

To everyone's astonishment, Vilsack dispatched a prompt and encouraging letter back. While he did not address all of what they had recommended, it was obvious that he was not only listening but thinking along some of the same lines.

"I hope the outcome of current USDA activities will reassure you that we are in sync with many of your views," he wrote to Weida and the group.[7] He listed three main points:

1. You can expect action from GIPSA (the Grain Inspection, Packers and Stockyards Administration) in the near future responding to USDA's responsibility to promote rules that level the playing field for livestock producers and to better define where unnecessary preferences are being granted to larger producers.

2. We will be announcing a program in August or September that we are calling "Know Your Farmer, Know Your Food" that would promote linking local production more closely to local consumption. We intend to use some of the program funding in Rural Development for the development of an enhanced supply chain infrastructure so we can ramp up sales to larger consumers (schools, hospitals) in a community.

3. Through the Recovery and Reinvestment Act, and the Energy Title of the Farm Bill, USDA is preparing to make the largest investment in rural development in my lifetime.

We look forward to keeping you informed as these efforts and many others are undertaken at USDA.

The words were something that most animal-factory activists had never heard before from a top government official. "Level the playing field?" Get rid of "unnecessary" preferences? Link "local production" to "local consumption?" "Ramp up" local food sales to schools and hospitals? It wasn't everything, but it was a hell of a lot more than anything uttered by the federal government in the past twenty years.

The correspondence wasn't the only promising news of the summer for animal-factory opponents. On August 5, Tom Vilsack and U.S. Attorney General Eric Holder announced that their two agencies would hold joint public workshops "to explore competition issues affecting the agriculture industry in the 21st century and the appropriate role for antitrust and regulatory enforcement in that industry," a USDA–DOJ statement said.[8]

The first workshops will be held in early 2010. Among the issues on the table are vertical integration and "concerns about the application of the antitrust laws to the agricultural industry." Other issues that might get on the agenda include "the impact of agriculture concentration on food costs, packer ownership of livestock before slaughter, market transparency, and increasing retailer concentration."

The announcement took many in the activist community by surprise, but made them smile nonetheless.

A WORD ON SWINE FLU

Should the multibillion cost of swine flu be factored into the purchase of every pork chop sold? And if so, what would that come out to, per pound? There is still no proof that the current strain of the H1N1 influenza virus circulating the globe sprang from a hog operation, big or small. But we do know that six of the eight genetic components in this bug came from a hog factory in North Carolina.

I personally believe there is still evidence to implicate the Granjas Carroll facility near the town of La Gloria, in Mexico's eastern state of Veracruz, as the possible ground zero of the current outbreak. On June 5, Reuters news agency reported that "genetic analysis shows new H1N1 came from pigs."[9]

World health officials had "underestimated" the possibility that pig farms were the new viral strain's source," Reuters said, instead opting to "focus on the threat of bird flu." But Gerardo Nava, of the National Autonomous University of Mexico, claimed that the current virus "most likely evolved from recent swine viruses," he wrote in the online journal *Eurosurveillance.* "These findings indicate that domestic pigs in North America may have a central role in the generation and maintenance of this virus."

Ironically, large pork-producing companies like Smithfield—which co-owns Granjas Carroll—routinely threaten to pull up their entire U.S. production operations and move them to more "receptive" places like Eastern Europe, Brazil, and Mexico.

"I think if this doesn't get resolved, it could eventually come to that," Purdue University's Alan Sutton said of the big pig firms. "The big companies would just say, 'You know what? This is too much headache for us; we're going to grow down in Mexico."[10] Sutton made his comments in November 2007, almost eighteen months before anyone had ever heard of novel H1N1 "swine flu."

What he said next was astonishing, given what we now know.

Sutton told me that Mexico and countries in South America do not have the same environmental regulations as those found in the United States. He had visited a massive hog facility in Mexico where, he said, "they are washing those farms down, with all the manure and feces, into a ditch, and that ditch goes into the river."

That was exactly what the people of La Gloria were telling Mexican health officials, members of the media, and just about anyone else who would listen.

Sutton continued with dark humor: "And I'm supposed to eat *lunch* in that place? Yeah right. Let's all have a glass of water, too!" he said of his trip to the Mexican hog CAFO. "And I thought, What is going on here? This wouldn't happen in the United States. And then I found out they had no rules or regulations whatsoever."

THE FUTURE

"The CAFO industry has lost the public relations game, no matter how hard they play and how hard they cheat. The tipping point has arrived," Karen Hudson told me. "Consumers have had enough meat and food scares, and now they are demanding to know about the biography of their pork chop. Change is coming that CAFO supporters and investors just cannot ignore."

Helen Reddout went so far as to predict that ten years from now, "We will have a lot more farms transition back to sustainable operations. And if the government can resist a bailout on large corporate farms, you will see a lot of them folding. They are having serious economic problems now, and if we don't come in and bail them out with more subsidies, then the free market will finish them off. Give us a chance and we can do it."

Like many animal-factory activists, Helen firmly believes that consumer education is key to defending rural communities from further encroachment by CAFOs. "Can you imagine if they had photos at the supermarket showing the living conditions of factory-farmed animals, and put those right next to photos of animals raised in humane and sustainable operations?" she asked. "People would gag and turn and run in the other direction. We need to make people in the city aware of how their food is being produced."

Helen fantasizes about one day having an advertising campaign that would show, instead of the dairy ads about happy cows, "the real California cow crammed into her miserable, filthy, crowded pen in the Central Valley. You would never buy that milk again. What they are showing now is nothing but propaganda."

But Rick Dove's vision is bleaker. He thinks the real price of protein will come back to bite us. And when that happens, "Unfortunately, we will *all* be made to pay the price," he predicted. "How much better it would have been for mankind if this problem was solved *before* nature was forced to step in. I feel sorry for all the innocent souls who will be consumed in the fury of this storm, but I don't feel a bit sorry for the greedy swine barons.

"They shall reap what they have sowed," the old marine said. "Let's pray that I am wrong. But prayer may be all we have left. We sure can't count on most of our elected officials."

NOTES

INTRODUCTION

1. USDA Agricultural Research Service, "National Program 206: Manure and Byproduct Utilization Action Plan," 2005, http://www.ars.usda.gov/research/projects/projects.htm?ACCN_NO=409616&showpars=true&fy=2008.
2. USDA National Statistics Service, "Farms, Land in Farms, and Livestock Operations," 2006, http://usda.mannlib.cornell.edu/MannUsda/viewDocumentInfo.do?documentID=1259.
3. USDA Agricultural Research Service, "FY-2005 Annual Report: Manure and Byproduct Utilization," 2006, http://www.ars.usda.gov/research/programs/programs.htm?np_code=206&docid=13337.
4. Charles P. Gerba and James E. Smith, Jr., "Sources of Pathogenic Microorganisms and Their Fate During Land Application of Wastes," *Journal of Environmental Quality* 34, no. 1 (2004): 42–48, http://jeq.scijournals.org/cgi/reprint/34/1/42.pdf.
5. U.S. Environmental Protection Agency, "Detecting and Mitigating the Environmental Impact of Fecal Pathogens Originating from Confined Animal Feeding Operations: Review," EPA/600/R-06/021, September 2005, http://www.epa.gov/nrmrl/pubs/600r06021/600r06021.htm.
6. J. Warrick and T. Shields, "Md. Counties Awash in Pollution-Causing Nutrients," *Washington Post*, October 3, 1997.
7. B. T. Nolan, B. C. Ruddy, K. J. Hitt, and D. R. Helsel, "A National Look at Nitrate Contamination of Ground Water," *Water Conditioning and Purification* 39, no. 12 (1998): 76–79, http://www.water.usgs.gov/nawqa/nutrients/pubs/wcp_v39_no12/.
8. U.S. Centers for Disease Control and Prevention, National Center for Environmental Health, "A Survey of the Quality of Water Drawn from Domestic Wells in Nine Midwest States," September 1998, http://www.cdc.gov/healthywater/statistics/environmental.
9. Confined Livestock Air Quality Committee of the USDA Agricultural Air Quality Task Force, Air Quality Research and Technology Transfer, "Risk Assessment Evaluation for Concentrated Animal Feeding Operations," July 12, 2000, 7, http://www.epa.gov/nrmrl/pubs/600r04042/600r04042.pdf.
10. H. Steinfeld et al, *Livestock's Long Shadow—Environmental Issues and Options* (Rome:

Food and Agriculture Organization of the United Nations, 2006), http://www.fao.org/do crep/010/a0701e/a0701e00.HTM.

11. Pew Commission on Industrial Animal Production, "Putting Meat on the Table: Industrial Farm Animal Production in America," a Project of the Pew Charitable Trusts and Johns Hopkins Bloomberg School of Public Health, 2008, http://www.ncifap.org.

PROLOGUE

1. EPA Pacific Southwest, "Animal Feeding Operations in Region 9," *Notes from Underground*, Fall 2001, 3, http://epa.gov/region09/water/notes/nfu1101.pdf.

CHAPTER 1

1. JoAnn M. Burkholder et al, "Letters to Nature," *Nature* 358 (July 1992): 407–410, http://www.nature.com/nature/journal/v358/n6385/abs/358407a0.html.
2. Pat Stith and Joby Warrick, "Murphy's Law," *News & Observer*, February 22, 1995.
3. Jim Barnett, "Raising a Stink," *News & Observer*, July 18, 1993.
4. S. S. Schiffman, E. A. Sattely-Miller, M. S. Suggs, and B. G. Graham, "Mood Changes Experienced by Persons Living Near Commercial Swine Operations," in *Pigs, Profits, and Rural Communities*, ed. K. Thu and E. P. Durrenberger (Albany, NY: State University of New York Press, 1998).
5. USDA, "CAFO Fact Sheets," 2003, http://www.nrcs.usda.gov/technical/afo/.
6. USDA and Natural Resources Conservation Service, *National Range and Pasture Handbook*, http://www.glti.nrcs.usda.gov/technical/publications/nrph.html (updated February 28, 2008).
7. Pew Commission on Industrial Farm Animal Production, "Putting Meat on the Table: Industrial Farm Animal Production in America," a Project of the Pew Charitable Trusts and Johns Hopkins Bloomberg School of Public Health, 2008, http://www.ncifap.org.
8. Ibid.
9. Julie Powers, "The Riverkeeper," *News & Observer*, August 22, 1993.

CHAPTER 2

1. This account of the visit to John Bosma comes from an interview with Helen Reddout in August 2007. John Howard is deceased, though his widow confirmed hearing the same account from him. Attorneys for John Bosma did not reply to requests to interview their client.
2. Rich Roesler, "Valley Economy Milking Benefits from a Burgeoning Dairy Industry," *Yakima Herald-Republic*, February 29, 1992.
3. Ibid.
4. Rob Taylor, "As Dairy Farms Grow Larger, So Do Some Complaints About Them," *Seattle Post-Intelligencer*, November 20, 1996, http://www.seattlepi.com/archives/1996/9611200019.asp.
5. Rob Taylor, "Dairies Spread Danger, State Is Failing to Regulate Pollution by Milk Producers," *Seattle Post-Intelligencer*, November 20, 1996, http://www.seattlepi.com/archives/1996/9611200001.asp.
6. Tom Paulson, "Cattle Harbor Deadly *E. Coli* but What Else Does?" *Seattle Post-Intelligencer*, November 25, 1996, http://www.seattlepi.com/archives/1996/9611200017.asp.
7. Cookson Beecher, "Washington Dairy Industry Under Scope," *Capital Press*, January 31, 1997.

8. Editorial, "Wash. Needs Guidance on State Dairy Waste Program," *Capital Press*, April 4, 1997.
9. "Agency Cracks Down on Water-Polluting Dairy Farms—EPA Has Issued 5 Fines for $10,000 to $20,000." *Seattle Post-Intelligencer*, May 23, 1997.

CHAPTER 3

1. Elaine Hopkins, "Livestock Facility Is Proposed: Operation Near Elmwood Would Center on Dairy or Swine," *Peoria Journal Star*, August 23, 1996.
2. Elaine Hopkins, "Hog Plant's Neighbors Sense Unwelcome Scents," *Peoria Journal Star*, August 28, 1996.
3. Terry Bibo, "'Smell of Money' Spells Bad News for Local Hog Farms," *Peoria Journal Star*, September 8, 1996.
4. Kelley J. Donham and Kendall M. Thu, "Understanding the Impacts of Large-Scale Swine Production," Iowa's Center for Agricultural Safety and Health, 1996, http://www.public-health.uiowa.edu/icash/publications/Swine/SwineProPDF.pdf.
5. Elaine Hopkins, "Strip Mine Site Unsuitable for Hog Plant, Firm Say: But Company Still Looking for Site Nearby," *Peoria Journal Star*, September 10, 1996.
6. Ibid.
7. Tim Meidroth, "County Board Decries Big Hog Projects," *Peoria Journal Star*, September 11, 1996.
8. Editorial, "Raising a Stink Over Hogs: It's Time to Declare a Moratorium on Huge Pig Farms in Illinois," *Peoria Journal Star,* September 11, 1996.
9. Julie Jansen, "Impacts of Odor and the Unknown Truth: A Comparison of Air Quality," DP-PEA, http://www.p2pays.org/ref/21/20013.htm.
10. Maureen Squires, "Knox Board Backs Hog Curbs, Chairman Is Eyeing Deal for 3,600-sow Confinement Facility," *Peoria Journal Star*, September 19, 1996.
11. Nina Baird, interview with the author, July 18, 2007.

CHAPTER 4

1. U.S. EPA, "Risk Management Evaluation for Concentrated Animal Feeding Operations," EPA/600/R-04/042, May 2004, http://www.epa.gov/nrmrl/pubs/600r04042/600r04042.pdf.
2. Douglas Phelps, "Another Nitrogen Leak from Hog Lagoons: Through the Air (Ammonia Volatilization)," Neuse River Foundation Research Committee, 1997.
3. State of North Carolina, "Status Report on Emissions and Deposition of Atmospheric Nitrogen Compounds from Animal Production in NC," DENR-DAQ report, June 7, 1999, http://daq.state.nc.us/monitor/projects/nstatusreport.pdf.
4. Pat Stith, Joby Warrick, and Melanie Sill, "Boss Hog" series, *News & Observer*. The series consisted of: "Boss Hog: The Power of Pork," February 19, 1995; "New Studies Show That Lagoons Are Leaking," February 19, 1995; "Corporate Takover," February 21, 1995; "Murphy's Law," February 22, 1995; "Hog-Tied on Ethics." February 23, 1995; "Money Talks," February 24, 1995; "Putting the Hush on Hogs," February 24, 1995; "Pork Barrels," February 26, 1995; and "When Hogs Come First," February 28, 1995. Permanently archived online at the Pulitzer Committee Web site, http://www.pulitzer.org.
5. Michael Mallin, "Impacts of Industrial Animal Production on Rivers and Estuaries," *American Scientist*, January–February 2000, http://www.americanscientist.org/issues/feature/impacts-of-industrial-animal-production-on-rivers-and-estuaries.
6. Joby Warrick, "Hog-Waste Spill Fouls Land, River in Onslow," *News & Observer*, June 23, 1995.

7. Stuart Leavenworth and Joby Warrick, "Jacksonville Joints Aren't Jumping After Spill," *News & Observer*, July 2, 1995.
8. Stuart Leavenworth, "Hunt Enlarges Waste Lagoon Inspection Corps," *News & Observer*, July 6, 1995.
9. Ibid.
10. Associated Press, "Inspectors Find Waste Lagoons Rife with Problems," August 26, 1995.
11. Joby Warrick and J. Andrew Curlliss, "Managers Get Blame for Spill," *News & Observer*, July 25, 1995
12. Joby Warrick and Jerry Allegood, "Spill Evidence Found at Edgecombe Farm of Top Pork Official," *News & Obsever*, August 5, 1995.
13. Ibid.
14. Warrick and Curlliss, "Managers Get Blame for Spill."
15. Joby Warrick, "Hog Spills Change Lawmakers' Views," *News & Observer*, August 6, 1995.
16. All dialogue from the New Bern meeting on the Neuse River taken verbatim from videotape of the event, provided by Rick Dove.
17. Nicole Brodeur, "Like a Scene from 'Jaws,'" *News & Observer*, October 8, 1995.
18. Rick Dove, interview with the author, April 22, 2009.
19. Stuart Leavenworth, "Health Warning Issued for Part of Neuse," *News & Observer*, October 7, 1995.
20. Betty Mitchell Gray, "Fishing Ban Lifted on Neuse River: Samples Taken by the State Show That the Concentration of a Toxic Algae Has Dropped," *Virginian-Pilot*, October 28, 1995.

CHAPTER 5

1. *Environmental News Network*, "Yakima Citizens Plan to Sue Local Dairies," November 3, 1997.
2. Scott Hunt, "Dairies Face Lawsuit Under Clean Water Act," *Daily Sun News*, November 4, 1997.
3. Ibid.
4. "Deposition Upon Oral Examination of Shari Conant," *Community Association for Restoration of the Environment v. Henry Bosma Dairy*, 65 F. Supp.2d 1129 (E.D. Wa. 1999), 2001 WL 1704240 (E.D. Wa. 2001), aff'd 305 F.3d 943 (9th Cir. 2002).
5. All quoted dialogue from the November 16, 1997, meeting at the Outlook Grange Hall comes from the following newspaper articles—Jennifer Hieger, "Dairy Farmers Listen to C.A.R.E. Concerns, Voice Disapproval," *Yakima Herald-Republic*, November 21, 1999; Jennifer Hieger, "Ten Valley Dairies May Face Lawsuits," *Yakima Herald-Republic*, November 4, 1997; Rob Taylor, "Activists May Sue 10 Dairies for Water Pollution," *Seattle Post-Intelligencer*, November 24, 1997; Rob Taylor, "10 Yakima Valley Dairies Notified of Pollution Suit," *Seattle Post-Intelligencer*, November 4, 1997; Terry Delman, "Pollution Keys Dairy Dispute," *Capital Press*, December 9, 1997—as well as a joint interview between Helen Reddout and Mary Lynne Bos and the author, September 3, 2007.
6. Charlie Tebbutt, WELC, interview with the author, Eugene, Oregon, February 11, 2008. This statement was confirmed by Mr. Barwin himself during testimony at trial in *CARE v. Bosma*.
7. Jennifer Hieger, "Dairies Seek Environmental Scrutiny," *Seattle Times*, December 7, 1997, http://community.seattletimes.nwsource.com/archive/?date=19971207&slug=2576634.
8. Ibid.
9. Shari Conant, "Notes to File: *CARE v. Bosma Dairies*." Exhibit #1, December 20, 1997.
10. Anonymous, letters mailed to Shari Conant and Mary Lynne Bos, December 1997. Photocopies provided by Charlie Tebbutt, WELC.

11. All dialogue from conversation between Henry Bosma and Helen Reddout taken verbatim from transcript of audio recording made by Mrs. Reddout at her home in early January 1998, as presented at trial during *CARE v. Bosma.*
12. Anonymous, letter mailed to Helen Reddout, January 1998. Photocopy provided by Charlie Tebbutt, WELC.

CHAPTER 6

1. Elaine Hopkins, "Hog-Farm Foes Plan Rally: Inskeep Confirms Purchase of Property Near Elmwood," *Peoria Journal Star*, October 29, 1996.
2. Nina Baird, interview with the author, Peoria, Illinois, July 18, 2007.
3. Lisa Cloat, "Dispute Over Mega-hog Farm Tears Family," *Peoria Journal Star*, September 28, 1997.
4. Elaine Hopkins, "Inskeep Outlines Plan for Elmwood Dairy Operation," *Peoria Journal Star*, February 18, 1997.
5. Cloat, "Dispute Over Mega-hog Farm Tears Family."
6. Nancy Millman, "Going Hog Wild Down on the Farm—As Large-Scale Operations Move in, Communities Debate the Economic, Environmental and Health Questions of Having Big Swine Producers Nearby," *Chicago Tribune*, July 6, 1997.
7. Ibid.
8. Elaine Hopkins, "Large Dairy Operation Gets Waste Lagoon Registered," *Peoria Journal Star*, August 4, 1997.
9. Lynne Padovan, Michael Plumer, press release from the cochairs of the joint Livestock Advisory Committee, Illinois State Legislature, September 24, 1997.
10. Cloat, "Dispute Over Mega-hog Farm Tears Family."
11. Stephen Elliot, "Bairds Hope to Dispel Rumors at Open House," *Register-Mail*, December 7, 1997.
12. John Pulliam, "Tour Fails to Deter Protests," *Register-Mail*, December 7, 1997.
13. Jill Dollan, "Hundreds Visit Bairds' Huge Hog Operation," *Register-Mail*, December 14, 1997.
14. Ibid.
15. Mike Kroll, "The Loyal Opposition: Karen Hudson and the Mega Opponents." *Zehpyr*, December 18, 1997.
16. "Baird Hails Redesign of Manure System," *Register-Mail*, December 14, 1997.
17. Ibid.

CHAPTER 7

1. Stuart Leavenworth, "Dead Bass, Bream and Crappie in Contentnea Creek," *News & Observer*, October 9, 1995.
2. Joby Warrick, "Contaminated Wells Linked to Robeson Hog Operation," *News & Observer*, October 14, 1995.
3. Ibid.
4. Joby Warrick, "Inspections Find Little Change at Hog Farms," *News & Observer*, December 1, 1995.
5. Joby Warrick, "Courts Take Action Against 3 Livestock Operations," *News & Observer*, December 20, 1995.
6. North Carolina Department of Environment and Natural Resources, "Neuse River Nutrient-Sensitive Waters (NSW) Management Strategy," 1997, http://h2o.enr.state.nc.us/su/Neuse_NSW_Management_Strategy.htm.

7. Blue Ribbon Commission on Agricultural Waste, *Report to the 1995 General Assembly of North Carolina* (Raleigh, May 16, 1996).

8. Joby Warrick, "State Hog Waste Panel Gets Tough," *News & Observer*, February 8, 1996.

9. Associated Press, "Pork Producer Group: Hog Farmers Have Gotten Bum Rap," *Sun Journal*, March 8, 1996.

10. Joby Warrick, "Lagoon Spills Waste into Neuse," *News & Observer*, July 16, 1996.

11. Erick Gill, "Spills Puts Farmer Out of Work," *Sun Journal*, July 16, 1996.

12. Editorial, "Spills Still a Threat," *Raleigh News & Observer*, July 17, 1996.

13. "Bertha Blamed for Recent Fish Kills," *News & Observer*, July 21, 1996.

14. Stuart Leavenworth, "Million Gallons of Hog Waste Spill in Jones County," *Raleigh News & Observer*, August 13, 1996.

15. Ibid.

16. Stuart Leavenworth and Todd Richissin, "Waste Lagoons That Withstood Fran Overflowing Now Due to Rain," *News & Observer*, September 12, 1996.

17. Ibid.

18. James Eli Shiffer and Steven Eisenstadt, "Lenoir County Awaits Worst," *News & Observer*, September 16, 1996.

19. Tinker Ready and Stuart Leavenworth, "Massive Fish Kill Hits Neuse," *News & Observer*, September 20, 1996.

20. Concerned Citizens of Tillery, "Tillery, North Carolina," http://www.cct78.org/about-cct .html.

21. Steve Wing, Gary Grant, Merle Green, and Chris Stewart, "Community-based Collaboration for Environmental Justice: South-east Halifax Environmental Reawakening," *Environment and Urbanization* 8, no. 2 (1996): 129, http://eau.sagepub.com/cgi/content/abstract/8/2/129.

22. Associated Press, "Environmentalists Want US to Look at NC Hog Biz," December 16, 1996.

23. Scott Batchelor, "Protesters Take Up Arms," *Washington Daily News*, March 19, 1997.

24. *Raleigh News & Observer*, "Senate Acts to Clean Waterways, Limit Hogs," June 19, 1997.

25. Delmarva Poultry Industry, Inc., "How the Broiler Chicken Industry Works," http://www .dpichicken.org/index.cfm?content=news&subcontent=details&id=205.

CHAPTER 8

1. Complaint, *Community Association for Restoration of the Environment v. Henry Bosma Dairy*, 65 F. Supp.2d 1129 (E.D. Wa. 1999), 2001 WL 1704240 (E.D. Wa. 2001), aff'd 305 F.3d 943 (9th Cir. 2002).

2. Olaf Elze and Scott Hunt, "Suits Start Against Local Dairy Farms," *Daily Sun News*, January 14, 1998.

3. Ibid.

4. As recalled by Helen Reddout in an interview with the author, Outlook, Washington, September 3, 2007.

5. Jennifer Hieger, "More Dairy Lawsuits Filed," *Yakima Herald-Republic*, February 21, 1998.

6. The series, "Yakima River Carries Troubled Water," by Mike Lee, ran in *Tri-City Herald* from March 1 to 3, 1998, and included the following articles: "Once-Clear 'Tapteal' Has Cloudy Future," March 1, 1998; "Pollution Widespread and Far Reaching," March 1, 1998; "Many Pollutants Added As Yakima River Runs East," March 2, 1998; "Climate, Space Put Valley at Top of Industry," March 3, 1998; "State Doing Little to Ensure Dairy Animals Aren't Polluting River," March 3, 1998; "State Legislators Wrestle to Regulate Dairy Waste," March 3, 1998; and "Legacy of Dairy Industry's Waste Problems Stretches Back Two Decades," March 3, 1998.

7. Marc Horton, "Subject: B & M Dairy," Memorandum to file, State of Washington, Department of Ecology, March 29, 1976.

8. Ibid.

9. Clar Pratt, letter to B & M Dairy, October 19, 1976. From archive.

10. Bruce A. Cameron, assistant director, Department of Ecology State of Washington, letter to B & M Dairy, May 17, 1978. From archive.

11. Jeffrey D. Goltz, letter to B & M Dairy re: docket no. DE 78-254, May 7, 1980. Papers from the Office of the Attorney General Slade Gorton, Temple of Justice, Olympia, Washington.

12. Ibid.

13. Jim Milton, District Supervisor, letter to B & M Dairy, May 12, 1980. From the Washington Department of Ecology, Olympia, Washington.

14. Superior Court of the State of Washington in and for Yakima County, "*State of Washington Department of Ecology vs. Henry Bosma and his wife, if any,*" Civil No. Summons, June 6, 1980. From the Washington Department of Ecology, Olympia, Washington.

15. Alan Newman, "Subject: Complaint Investigation July 20, 1984," memorandum of the State of Washington Department of Ecology, July 23, 1984. From the Washington Department of Ecology, Olympia, Washington.

16. James W. Trull, Secretary/Manager, Sunnyside Valley Irrigation District, letter to Russ Taylor, regional manager, Washington State Department of Ecology, Sunnyside Valley Irrigation District, Sunnyside, Washington, July 27, 1984.

17. Russell K. Taylor, P.E., regional manager, Department of Ecology, State of Washington, letter to Mr. Henry Bosma, "In the Matter of the Compliance by Henry Bosma Dairy, ORDER No. DE 86-539," June 2, 1986. From Department of Ecology, State of Washington, Yakima, Washington.

18. Henry Bosma, letter to Jim Milton, July 18, 1986. From Department of Ecology, State of Washington, Yakima, Washington. Obtained through discovery process by the Western Environmental Law Center in *CARE v. Henry Bosma*.

19. Kim H. Sherwood, letter to Corinna D. Ripfel-Harn, "In the Matter of the Penalty Against Henry Bosma dba B & M Dairy. NOTICE OF PENALTY No. 87-C381," March 30, 1988. From Department of Ecology, State of Washington, Yakima, Washington.

20. Hank Bosma, letter to Jim Milton, "Re: Hearing Scheduled Per Enclosed," May 30, 1988. From Department of Ecology, State of Washington, Yakima, Washington.

21. Kim H. Sherwood, letter to Russ Taylor, "B & M Dairy, Subject: May 2, 1988 Manure Discharge from B & M Dairy dba Hank Bosma," June 10, 1988. From Department of Ecology, State of Washington, Yakima, Washington.

22. Harold Porath, initial report/follow-up, "Environmental Report Tracking System," March 26, 1993. From Department of Ecology, State of Washington, Yakima, Washington.

23. Ibid.

24. Harold Porath, memorandum to files, April 2, 1993. From Department of Ecology, State of Washington, Yakima, Washington.

25. Vicki Wright, Central Regional Office environmental incident form, October 1, 1993.

26. Harold Porath, "Telephone Record RE: Mr. Henry Bosma," October 7, 1993. From Department of Ecology, State of Washington, Yakima, Washington.

27. Henry Bosma, letter to Harold Porath, October 8, 1993. From Department of Ecology, State of Washington, Yakima, Washington.

28. Robert F. Barwin, "In the Matter of the Compliance by Henry Bosma Dairy—Notice of Violation," November 2, 1993.

29. Harold Porath, "Telephone Record, RE: Hank Bosma Dairy."

30. Henry Bosma, handwritten note to Max Linden, 1997. Plaintiff's exhibit 95, *CARE v. Bosma Dairies*, 1999.

31. "Declaration of Henry Bosma in Support of Motion for Summary Judgment," *CARE v.*

Henry Bosma Dairy, United States District Court, Eastern District of Washington State at Spokane, January 15, 1999.

32. Staff and Wire Reports, "Manure Spill at the DeRuyter Dairy Draws State Probe," *Yakima Herald-Republic*, February 1, 1999.

33. Jennifer Hieger, "Settlement Closes Sunnyside Dairy," *Yakima Herald-Republic*, May 27, 1999.

34. Ibid.

35. All trial questions and testimony in *CARE v. Bosma Dairies* were quoted from the official trial transcript provided by the U.S. District Court Eastern District of Washington, Redmond, Washington.

36. "Findings of Facts and Conclusions of Law," *CARE v. Henry Bosma Dairy*, United States District Court, Eastern District of Washington at Richland, July 29, 1999.

37. Jennifer Hieger, "Judge Rules Against Dairy Owner," *Yakima Herald-Republic*, July 30, 1999.

38. Mike Lee, "Valley Dairy Faces Fines of $350,000," *Tri-City Herald*, July 30, 1999.

39. Editorial, "Wash. Dairy Waste Decision Needs to Be Appealed to a Higher Court," *Capitol Press*, August 20, 1999.

CHAPTER 9

1. National Catholic Rural Life Conference, "NCRLC Mission," http://www.ncrlc.com.

2. NCRLC Board of Directors, "A Moratorium on Large-scale Livestock and Poultry Confinement Facilities," 1998, http://www.ncrlc.com/on_factory_farms01.html.

3. Extended abstracts of papers and posters presented at the Manure Management Conference, February 10–12, 1998, Ames, Iowa. Online at http://www.p2pays.org/ref/21/20524.htm.

4. William D. Heffernan, "Societal Concerns Raised by CAFOs," http://www.p2pays.org/ref/21/20524/ManureMgmt/85.html.

5. Karen Hudson, "Rural Residents' Perspectives on Industrial Livestock Production: A Patchwork of Rural Injustice," North Carolina Division of Pollution Prevention and Environmental Assistance, http://www.p2pays.org/ref/21/20524/ManureMgmt/83.html.

6. Felecia Babb, "DNR Levies Fine, Halts Construction," *Boone (Iowa) News-Republican*, January 24, 1989.

7. Traci Carl, "70 Families Sue Corporate Hog Farm," Associated Press, October 7, 1994.

8. "America's Animal Factories—How States Fail to Prevent Pollution from Livestock Waste," Chapter 14, Missouri Natural Resources Defense Council and Clean Water Network, Washington, D.C., December 1999, http://www.nrdc.org/water/pollution/factor/stmiu.asp.

9. Terry Ganey, "Hog Producer to Pay $250,000 to Missouri for Spills," *St. Louis Post-Dispatch*, January 20, 1996.

10. Citizens Legal Environmental Action Network, Inc., Plaintiff; United States of America, Intervenor/Plaintiff; V. Premium Standard Farms, Inc., Defendant: case no. 98-6099-cv-w-6, United States District Court, Western District of Missouri, St. Joseph Division, http://www.epa.gov/compliance/resources/decrees/civil/mm/psfcd.pdf.

11. J. E. Rushing and D. P. Wesen, "Preventing Antibiotic Residues In Milk," North Carolina State University/A&T State University Cooperative Extension, 1995, http://www.ces.ncsu.edu/depts/foodsci/ext/pubs/antibioticresidues.html.

12. Pierre Harding, "Straight Talk," *The Milkweed*, no. 264 (2001).

13. Ibid.

14. The Monsanto Company, Animal Sciences Division, product label, available at http://www.the milkweed.com.

15. Ronnie Cummins, "Market Pressure: Busting BGH and Biotech," *Motion Magazine*, http://www.inmotionmagazine.com/ra02/geff13.html.

16. Ken Roseboro, "Monsanto, FDA Cracking Down on Hormone-free Milk Claims," *Non-GMO Source*, September 2003, http://www.purefood.org/rbgh/oakhurst101003.cfm.

17. Monsanto no longer owns Posilac, which it sold to Eli Lilly and Company in 2008. The Monsanto Web site has since removed the pages on Posilac.

18. Samuel S. Epstein, "Growth Hormones Would Endanger Milk," op-ed, *Los Angeles Times*, July 27, 1989, http://www.preventcancer.com/press/editorials/july27_89.htm.

19. Samuel S. Epstein, *What's In Your Milk?* (Victoria, BC, Canada: Trafford Publishing, 2006).

20. U.S. Food and Drug Administration, "Response by the FDA," *Los Angeles Times*, August 1, 1989.

21. Jean Anne Casey and Colleen Hobbs, "Lean Times on the Hog Farm," *New York Times*, January 29, 1999.

22. *Peoria Journal Star*, "No Profit in Pigs as Market Is Flooded: Some Area Farmers Can't Even Recover from Cost of Raising," December 13, 1998.

23. Adriana Colindres, "Dairy Farm Cited By State EPA—Peoria County Operation Faces Fines for Alleged Odor and Pollution Violations," *Peoria Journal Star*, August 31, 1999.

24. Ibid.

25. "Court Sides with Megahog Farms: Illinois Supreme Court Says Counties Can't Regulate Large-Scale Livestock Operations," *Peoria Journal Star*, December 3, 1999.

26. Adriana Colindres, "Settlement Reached In Lawsuit Alleging Hog Farm Odor," *Springfield (IL) State Journal-Register*, November 21, 2000.

27. Ibid.

28. Ibid.

29. Adriana Colindres, "State Sues Hog Farm Because of Odors," *Springfield (IL) State Journal-Register*, December 22, 1999.

30. Colindres, "Settlement Reached In Lawsuit Alleging Hog Farm Odor."

CHAPTER 10

1. Staff and Wire Reports, "Sickness May Force 'River Keeper' to Quit," *News & Observer*, April 24, 1998.

2. Sarah J. M. Tuff, "Fighting for the Fish," *Time for Kids*, October 26, 1998, http://www.time.com/time/reports/environment/heroes/tfk/0,2967,tfk_dove,00.html.

3. "Disease Detectives Untangle Mystery of Mutant Flu Virus," *News & Observer*, May 31, 1999.

4. Ibid.

5. Ibid.

6. Ibid.

7. Bernice Wuethrich, "Chasing the Fickle Swine Flu," *Science* 299, no. 5612 (March 2003): 1502–1505, cited in Brandon Keim, "Swine Flu Ancestor Born on U.S. Factory Farms," *Wired*, May 1, 2009, http://www.wired.com/wiredscience/2009/05/swineflufarm.

8. "Disease Detectives Untangle Mystery of Mutant Flu Virus."

9. NC Swine Odor Task Force, "Options for Managing Odor: A Report from the North Carolina Agricultural Research Service," North Carolina State University, March 1, 1995, http://www.ces.ncsu.edu/whpaper/SwineOdor.html.

10. Steve Marberry, "Smithfield Foods Completes Buyout of Murphy Farms," *Feedstuffs*, February 7, 2000.

11. David Barboza, "Goliath of the Hog World; Fast Rise of Smithfield Foods Makes Regulators Wary," *New York Times*, April 7, 2000, http://www.nytimes.com/2000/04/07/business/goliath-of-the-hog-world-fast-rise-of-smithfield-foods-makes-regulators-wary.html?pagewanted=3.

12. Mike Lee, "DeRuyter Dairy Agree to Settle Pollution Suit," *Tri-City Herald*, February 2, 2000.

13. Sierra Club, "RBGH and the Destruction of Small Dairy Farms," conference announcement, June 17, 2000.

14. "Agreement between the Attorney General of North Carolina; Smithfield Foods, Inc.; Brown's of Carolina, Inc.; Carroll's Foods, Inc.; Murphy Farms, Inc.; Carroll's Foods of Virginia, Inc.; and Quarter M Farms, Inc.," July 25, 2000, http://www.cals.ncsu.edu/waste_mgt/smithfield_projects/agreement.pdf.

15. James Eli Shiffer, "Neuse Advocate Quits to Recruit Other 'Keepers,' " *News & Observer*, June 8, 2000.

16. Nicolette Hahn Niman, *Righteous Pork Chop: Finding a Life and Good Food Beyond Factory Farms* (New York: William Morrow, 2009), 69.

CHAPTER 11

1. Mary V. Gold, "Sustainable Agriculture: Information Access Tools," USDA's Alternative Farming Systems Information Center, March 2007, http://www.nal.usda.gov/afsic/pubs/agnic/susag.shtml.

2. Sustainable Table, "Introduction to Sustainability: What is Sustainable Agriculture?" http://www.sustainabletable.org/intro/whatis.

3. Institute for Agriculture and Trade Policy, "Support Our Work," http://www.iatp.org.

4. David Wallinga, remarks at the Summit for Sustainable Hog Farming, Riverfront Convention Center, New Bern, NC, January 2001.

5. Center for Consumer Freedom, "What is the Center for Consumer Freedom?" http://www.consumerfreedom.com.

6. SourceWatch, "Industry-Funded Organizations," http://www.sourcewatch.com.

7. The descriptions of the lagoon spill at Inwood in February 2001 and its legal aftermath have been taken from the following articles printed in the *Peoria Journal Star*: Elaine Hopkins, "Attorney General Files Suit Over Lagoon—Environmental Officials Have Cited Dairy for Pollution," *Peoria Journal Star*, February 17, 2001; Elaine Hopkins, "Dairy Farm Ordered to Clean Up—Inwood Dairy Must Cut Herd Size, Clear Ravine of 2 Million Gallons of Waste," *Peoria Journal Star*, February 22, 2001; editorial, "State Should Send Corporate Farmers a Tough Message," *Peoria Journal Star*, February 23, 2001; Mike Bailey, "Dairy Farm Divides Elmwood, Families," *Peoria Journal Star*, April 8, 2001.

8. CARE, "Henry Bosma Dairy Fined $171,500 by Federal Court for Manure Discharges to Yakima River," press release, February 28, 2001.

9. Mike Lee, "State Acts on Dairies' Yakima River Pollution," *Tri-City Herald*, February 22, 2001.

10. Bill Heisel and Jennifer Hieger, "Not Enough Land—Local Dairies May Have Too Little Ground to Handle Their Waste," *Yakima Herald-Republic*, August 29, 1999.

11. Elaine Hopkins, "Inwood Dairy Knee Deep in Debt, Too," *Peoria Journal Star*, March 3, 2001.

12. Ibid.

13. Andy Kravetz, "Dairy Mess Almost Cleaned," *Peoria Journal Star*, March 9, 2001.

14. "State, Inwood Dairy Hash Out Agreement—Elmwood-Area Farm Won't Have to Cut Back on Its Herd, but Must Deal with Waste," *Peoria Journal Star*, March 14, 2001.

15. Steve Tarter, "Embattled Elmwood, Ill., Dairy Denied $250,000 Research Grant," *Peoria Journal Star*, March 20, 2001.

16. Steve Tarter, "Illinois Environmentalists Upset over Secrecy Policy for Agricultural Research," *Peoria Journal Star*, August 28, 2001.

17. Elaine Hopkins, "Dairy Mired in Cleanup Is Up for Sale," *Peoria Journal Star*, April 11, 2001.

18. "From 'Sewer' to Dairy Farm—Digester System Cuts Odor Near Elmwood," *Peoria Journal Star*, April 27, 2003.
19. Consent Decree, *CARE v. Sunnyveld Dairy*, United States District Court for the Eastern District of Washington at Spokane, June 19, 2001.

CHAPTER 12

1. OMB Watch, "Public Wants More Info on Food Labels," November 18, 2008, http://www.ombwatch.org/node/3839.
2. Terri Coles, "Posilac 'Mooves' Over," Reuters, September 4, 2007, http://future.aae.wisc.edu/collection/news_items/starbucks_rbst_free.pdf.
3. Francesca Lyman, "'Your Environment' on Claims That Gene-Modified Dairy Products Pose Health Risks," Special to MSNBC, March 29, 2007, available at http://www.organicconsumers.org/rbgh/msnbconrbgh.cfm.
4. Karen Hudson, "Lab Rats for Monsanto—The Uncontrolled rBGH Experiment on America," *The Indy* 1, no. 7 (January 2002).
5. Mark Kastel, "Down on the Farm: The Real BGH Story—Animal Health Problems, Financial Troubles," *Rural Vermont*, 1995, http://www.mindfully.org/GE/Down-On-The-Farm-BGH1995.htm.
6. Jo K. Perry, "Review: The Oncogenic Potential of Growth Hormone." *Growth Hormone & IGF Research* 16, no. 5–6 (October–December 2006): 277–289, http://www.sciencedirect.com/science/journal/10966374.
7. Samuel S. Epstein, "Unlabeled Milk from Cows Treated with Biosynthetic Growth Hormones: A Case of Regulatory Abdication," *International Journal of Health Services* 26, no. 1 (1996): 173–185; abstract online at http://www.ncbi.nlm.nih.gov/pubmed/8932606.
8. "Agreement between the Attorney General of North Carolina; Smithfield Foods, Inc.; Brown's of Carolina, Inc.; Carroll's Foods, Inc.; Murphy Farms, Inc.; Carroll's Foods of Virginia, Inc.; and Quarter M Farms, Inc." July 25, 2000, http://www.cals.ncsu.edu/waste_mgt/smithfield_projects/agreement.pdf.
9. Perry Beeman, "Ag Scientists Feel the Heat," *Des Moines Register*, December 1, 2002.
10. United States Congress, the Morrill Act of 1862.
11. Steve Tarter, "Activist Opposed to Mega-hog Farms Attends Conference," *Peoria Journal Star*, March 26, 2002.
12. Steve Ells, "Food with Integrity," Chipotle, http://www.chipotle.com.
13. J. A. Zahn, published abstract, National Swine Research and Information Center, Ames, Iowa, presented July 2001.
14. J. A. Zahn and Boyd E. Anhalt, "Evidence for Transfer of Tylosin and Tylosin-Resistant Bacteria in Air from Swine Production Facilities Using Sub-therapeutic Concentrations of Tylan in Feed," *Journal of Animal Science* 79 (supplement 1): 189 (abstract no. 783), http://www.asas.org/jas/jointabs/iaafsc83.pdf.
15. House Committee on Government Reform—Minority Staff Special Investigations Division, "Politics and Science in the Bush Administration," August 2003, http://oversight.house.gov/features/politics_and_science/pdfs/pdf_politics_and_science_rep.pdf.
16. Sarah Okeson, "Dairy Fined $50,000 for Waste Overflow," *Peoria Journal Star*, May 2, 2002.
17. Tom Nelson, "Mega-hog Farm Reports a Fish Kill," *Galesburg Register-Mail*, June 25, 2002.
18. CARE, "Link Found Between Nitrates, Well Water, and Factory Farms," news release, January 28, 2003, http://www.mail-archive.com/bdnow@envirolink.org/msg06697.html.
19. Ibid.
20. "Sunnyside Groundwater Study: Final Report," Heritage College, Toppenish, Washington, August 13, 2003, http://www.sec.nv.gov/cafo/tab_u_%20pt1.pdf.

21. "From 'Sewer' to Dairy Farm—Digester System Cuts Odor Near Elmwood," *Peoria Journal Star*, April 27, 2003.

22. Reuters, "Study Finds Illness May Promote Spread of Mad Cow Prion," January 20, 2005, http://www.rense.com/general62/amad.htm.

23. CNN, "Canadian Officials Move Quickly to Quash Mad Cow Disease," May 20, 2003, transcript at edition.cnn.com/TRANSCRIPTS/0305/20/se.12.html.

24. "GRACE Factory Farm Project," EnviroLink, http://www.envirolink.org/resource.html?item id/290413151796&catid/5.

25. Sustainable Table, "About the Meatrix," http://www.themeatrix.com.

26. Sustainable Table, "Factory Farm Fighting Cow Attends the All Things Organic Conference and Trade Show," press release, April 25, 2005, http://www.sustainabletable.org.

27. Elizabeth Weise, "Consumers May Have a Beef with Cattle Feed," *USA Today*, June 9, 2003, http://www.usatoday.com/news/health/2003-06-09-beef-cover_x.htm.

28. Environmental News Service, "McDonald's Tells Suppliers to Cut Antibiotics in Meat," June 19, 2003, http://www.ens-newswire.com/ens/jun2003/2003-06-19-09.asp.

29. *Pork* magazine, "McDonald's Sets Antibiotic Use Policy," June 19, 2003, http://www.pork mag.com/news_editorial.asp?pgID=675&ed_id=2026.

30. *Pork* magazine, "Science, Not Marketing Says Animal Health Group," June 17, 2003, http://www.porkmag.com/news_editorial.asp?pgID=675&ed_id=2027.

31. Union of Concerned Scientists, "70 Percent of All Antibiotics Given to Healthy Livestock," press release, January 8, 2001, http://www.sierraclub.org/factoryfarms/factsheets/antibiotics.asp.

32. *U.S. Water News Online*, "Neuse River Cleaner 5 Years After Nitrogen Reduction Began," December, 2003, http://www.uswaternews.com/archives/arcquality/3neuriv12.html.

33. Wade Rawlins, "Neuse Cleaner Than in 1998," *Raleigh News & Observer*, November 25, 2003.

34. JoAnn M. Burkholder et al, "Comprehensive Trend Analysis of Nutrients and Related Variables in a Large Eutrophic Estuary: A Decadal Study of Anthropogenic and Climatic Influences," *Limnology and Oceanography* 51, no. 1, part 2 (2006): 463–487.

CHAPTER 13

1. Phuong Cat Le, Chris McGann, and Claudia Rowe, "Mad Cow Case Feared at Yakima-Area Farm," *Seattle Post-Intelligencer*, December 24, 2003, http://www.seattlepi.com/local/153856_madcow24.html?dpfrom=thead.

2. "Excerpts From the Agriculture Secretary's News Conference," *New York Times*, December 24, 2003, http://www.nytimes.com/2003/12/24/us/excerpts-from-the-agriculture-secretary-s-news-conference.html.

3. Phuong Cat Le et al, "Mad Cow Case Feared at Yakima-Area Farm," *Seattle Post-Intelligencer*.

4. Matthew L. Wald and Eric Lichtblau, "U.S. Is Examining a Mad Cow Case, First in Country," *New York Times*, December 24, 2003, http://www.nytimes.com/2003/12/24/us/us-is-examining-a-mad-cow-case-first-in-country.html.

5. Ibid.

6. USDA, Food Safety and Inspection Service, "USDA Begins Sampling Program for Advanced Meat Recovery Systems," news release, March 3, 2002, http://www.fsis.usda.gov/oa/news/2003/amrsampling.htm.

7. Vanessa Ho, "Former USDA Vet—Testing 20,000 Cows Is 'Nothing,'" *Seattle Post-Intelligencer*, December 28, 2003, http://www.rense.com/general46/nothing.html.

8. FDA, "Expanded 'Mad Cow' Safeguards Announced to Strengthen Existing Firewalls Against BSE Transmission," press release, January 26, 2004, http://www.hhs.gov/news/press/2004pres/20040126.html.

9. Michael Pollan, "Cattle Futures?" *New York Times Magazine*, January 11, 2004, http://www .michaelpollan.com/article.php?id=9.

10. Center for Consumer Freedom, "Mad Cow Scaremongers," December 20, 2004, http://www .consumerfreedom.com/article_detail.cfm/article/138.

11. Trudy Bialic, "Tighten Rules to Safeguard Beef," *Seattle Post-Intelligencer*, April 30, 2004, http://www.seattlepi.com/opinion/171282_beef30.html.

12. Chris McGann, "Hot Debate Over Chicken Dung—FDA Wrestles with Whether to Ban It and Other Waste from Cattle Feed," *Seattle Post-Intelligencer*, April 22, 2004, http://www .madcowboy.com/01_FactsMC.000.html.

13. Frontline Farmers, "Water Quality: Study Shows Trend Toward Improvement," press release, June 8, 2004.

14. Rick Dove, "The Swine Industry's Attempt to Portray the Neuse River as Unaffected by Swine Pollution Is Not Credible," North Carolina Riverkeepers and Waterkeeper Alliance, November 2004, http://www.riverlaw.us/realhogfacts.html.

15. Philip Gourevitch, "Swing Time—Former Bush Voters Advertise Their Disaffection," *New Yorker*, August 23, 2004, http://www.errolmorris.com/content/profile/gourevitch_swing .html.

16. Richard Dove, *Fishing* (MoveOn.org advertisement for John Kerry for President, August 2004), video and scripts are online at http://www.errolmorris.com/content/election04/elec tion04_mo_dove.html.

17. Associated Press, "Toxic Gas at Some Confinements at High Levels," April 30, 2003.

18. Minnesota Farm Bureau, *When an Activist Group Comes to Town: Protecting Your Community from Unwanted Division* (Eagan, MN: Minnesota Farm Bureau, 2004). Copies may be ordered at http://www.fbmn.org or by e-mailing info@fbmn.org.

19. Faces of Agriculture, "Illinois Food Production Under Attack—Activists Bent on the Demise of Livestock Agriculture in the United States Have Taken Their Attack to Lee County, IL," press release, January 29, 2004, http://www.facesofag.com/illinois_food_production.shtml.

20. Canadian Broadcasting Company/CBC News Online, "In Depth: Mad Cow—Timeline of BSE in Canada and the U.S.," October 23, 2006, http://www.cbc.ca/news/background/mad cow/timeline.html.

21. Ibid.

22. Senate Committee on Agriculture, Nutrition, and Forestry, *Examining the Effects of Bovine Spongiform Encephalopathy (BSE) on U.S. Imports and Exports of Cattle and Beef: Hearing Before the Senate Committee on Agriculture, Nutrition, and Forestry*, 109th Congress, February 3, 2005, http://www.access.gpo.gov/congress/senate/pdf/109hrg/98459.pdf.

23. GRACE Factory Farm Project, "Best Solution Is to Eat Beef from Traditional Family Farmers," press release, New York City, January 13, 2005, http://www.enn.com/press_releases/ 314/print.

24. EPA, "Animal Feeding Operations Consent Agreement," *Federal Register* 70, no. 19 (January 2005): 4958–4960.

25. Donor lookup search function, http://www.opensecrets.org.

26. "A Big To-Doo-Doo—EPA Offers Air-Pollution Immunity to Factory Farms," *Grist Magazine*, January 24, 2005, http://www.grist.org/article/factory_farms.

27. Environmental News Service, "EPA Deal Allows Factory Farms to Avoid Air Laws," January 25, 2005, http://www.ens-newswire.com/ens/jan2005/2005-01-25-11.asp. (The person quoted was Dave Roper, chairman of the National Pork Producers Council's Environment Committee, and an Idaho pork producer.)

28. Andrew Rauch and Jeff S. Sharp, "Ohioans' Attitudes about Animal Welfare—A Topical Report from the 2004 Ohio Survey of Food, Agricultural and Environmental Issues," Social Responsibility Initiative, Department of Human and Community Resource Development, Ohio State University, January 2005, ohiosurvey.osu.edu/pdf/2004_Animal_report.pdf.

29. *CBS News*, "Mad Cow Timeline," http://www.cbsnews.com/elements/2003/12/29/in_depth_health/timeline590569.shtml.
30. Associated Press, "Tests Confirm New Mad Cow Case in U.S." June 25, 2005, http://www.foxnews.com/story/0,2933,160648,00.html.
31. Ibid.
32. Angie Litterst, "New Hog Facility Will Be Detrimental to Community," letter to the editor, *Quad-City Times*, August 29, 2005.
33. U.S. Department of Justice and Environment and Natural Resources Division, "Illinois Man Indicted for Criminal Violation of the Clean Water Act," press release, September 21, 2005, http://justice.gov/opa/pr/2005/September/05_enrd_495.html.

CHAPTER 14

1. E. Klein, D. L. Smith, and R. Laxminarayan, "Hospitalizations and Deaths Caused by Methicillin-Resistant *Staphylococcus Aureus*, United States, 1999–2005," *Emerging Infectious Disease* 13, no. 12 (2007): 1840–1846, http://www.rwjf.org/pr/product.jsp?id=23751.
2. C. Liu et al, "A Population-Based Study of the Incidence and Molecular Epidemiology of Methicillin-Resistant *Staphylococcus Aureus* Disease in San Francisco, 2004–2005," *Clinical Infectious Diseases* 46, no. 11 (June 2008): 1637–1646, http://www.ncbi.nlm.nih.gov/pubmed/18433335.
3. Andreas Voss, et al, "Methicillin-Resistant *Staphylococcus Aureus* in Pig Farming," *Emerging Infectious Diseases* (December 2005), http://www.cdc.gov/ncidod/EID/vol11no12/05-0428.htm.
4. Editorial, "Beyond Lagoons," *Raleigh News & Observer*, December 30, 2005.
5. Chuck Stokes and Daniel Whittle, "Getting It Together on N.C.'s Hog Waste," guest column, *Raleigh News & Observer*, January 15, 2006.
6. Waterkeeper Alliance, "Waterkeeper Alliance and Smithfield Foods Reach Agreement on Environmental Pact," press release, January 20, 2006, http://www.waterkeeper.org.
7. Ibid.
8. Marian Burros, "Poultry Industry Quietly Cuts Back on Antibiotic Use," *New York Times*, February 11, 2002, http://www.nytimes.com/2002/02/10/national/10CHIC.html.
9. Tyson Foods, "Our Core Values," http://www.tyson.com/Corporate/AboutTyson/Company-Information/CoreValues.aspx.
10. Environmental Defense Fund, "Environmental Defense, Frontline Farmers to Develop Plan for Cleaner Hog Farming," press release, March 9, 2006, http://www.edf.org/pressrelease.cfm?contentID=5109.
11. Editorial, "Pits Stopped," *Raleigh News & Observer*, March 13, 2006.
12. MSNBC.com, "Alabama Cow Tests Positive for Mad Cow Disease—Investigators Tracing Source; Meat Did Not Enter Food Chain, USDA Says," March 14, 2006, http://www.msnbc.msn.com/id/11809760/ns/health-mad_cow_in_the_us/.
13. Canadian Food Inspection Agency, *Report of the Investigation of the Fourth Case of Bovine Spongiform Encephalopathy (BSE) in Alberta, Canada*, March 3, 2006, http://www.inspection.gc.ca/english/anima/heasan/disemala/bseesb/ab2006/4investe.shtml.
14. Sarah A. Lister and Geoffrey S. Becker, "Bovine Spongiform Encephalopathy (BSE, or "Mad Cow Disease"): Current and Proposed Safeguards," report to Congress, updated May 18, 2007, available at http://www.nationalaglawcenter.org/assets/crs/RL32199.pdf.
15. Associated Press, "U.S. Plans to Reduce Mad Cow Testing," March 15, 2006.
16. Ibid.
17. Robert Cohen, *Milk, The Deadly Poison* (Englewood Cliffs, NJ: Argus, 2001), 15, 16.
18. Peter Harding, "Straight Talk," *The Milkweed*, no. 264, July 2001.

19. Nebraska Center For Rural Affairs, "Big Milk From Big Dairies," Nebraska Rural Action supplement, *Newsletter*, July 2000.
20. Steven D. Arnold and Edward Meister, "Dairy Feedlot Contributions to Groundwater Contamination," *Environmental Health* 62 (September 1999).
21. William J. Weida, "A Citizens Guide to the Regional Economic and Environmental Effects of Large Concentrated Dairy Operations," GRACE Factory Farm Project, November, 19, 2000, http://www.sraproject.org/wp-content/uploads/2007/12/acitizensguide.pdf.
22. Riam S. Kidd, Annette M. Rossignol, and Michael J. Gamroth, "Salmonella and Other Enterobacteriaceae in Dairy-Cow Feed Ingredients: Antimicrobial Resistance in Western Oregon," *Journal of Environmental Health* 64 (2002).
23. Michael K. Hansen, "Testimony before the Agriculture Committee of the Canadian Parliament on Potential Animal and Human Health Effects of rBGH Use by Michael K. Hansen, Ph.D.," March 9, 1994, available from Consumer Policy Institute, Consumers Union, Yonkers, NY.
24. Monsanto, "Posilac (sterile sometribove zinc suspension)," product label, available at http://www.sare.org/sanet-mg/archives/html-home/3-html/0312.html.
25. U. S. General Accounting Office, *ANTIBIOTIC RESISTANCE—Federal Agencies Need to Better Focus Efforts to Address Risk to Humans from Antibiotic Use in Animals*, report to Congressional Requesters (GAO-04-490), April 2004, http://www.gao.gov/new.items/d04490.pdf.
26. Cancer Prevention Coalition, "Monsanto's Hormonal Milk Poses Serious Risks of Breast Cancer, Besides Other Cancers Warns Professor of Environmental Medicine at the University of Illinois School of Public Health," press release, June 21, 2002, http://www.kitchendoctor.com/reprints/monsanto.html.
27. Julie Buring and J. Michael Gaziano, "Key Findings of the Physicians' Health Study," Harvard University, November 2002, http://phs.bwh.harvard.edu/phs20.htm. The study found that "IGF-1 is a mitogen for prostate epithelial cells," and that "men in the highest quartile of IGF-1 levels had a 4-fold increased risk of prostate cancer compared with men in the lowest quartile." *Science* 279 (1998): 563–566.
28. E. Giovannucci et al, "A Prospective Study of Plasma Insulin-like Growth Factor-1 and Binding Protein-3 and Risk of Colorectal Neoplasia in Women," *Cancer Epidemiology Biomarkers and Prevention* 9, no. 4.(April 2000): 345–349. This study concluded that "high levels of circulating IGF-1 and particularly low levels of IGFBP-3 are associated independently with an elevated risk of large or tubulovillous/villous colorectal adenoma and cancer."
29. Frank Mitloehner, Dept. of Animal Science, UC Davis, "SUMMARY—Utah State University Air Quality Symposium, September 21–22, 2005," http://www.airquality.utah.gov.
30. Ibid.
31. Allison Rezendes, "Commission Studies Effects of Animal Feeding Operations Potential Impact on Public Health, Animal Health, and Environment Evaluated," *Journal of the American Veterinary Medical Association* (December 2006), http://www.avma.org/onlnews/javma/dec06/061201l.asp.
32. Animal Agricultural Alliance, "Statement About Food, Inc.," press release, June 11, 2009, http://www.animalagalliance.org.
33. Center for Consumer Freedom, "Pew 'Farm Animal' Commission Tainted by Vegetarian Bias," press release, September 12, 2006, consumerfreedom.com/pressrelease_detail.cfm?release=173.
34. U.S. Department of Justice, Environment and Natural Resources Division, "Former Manager of Inwood Dairy Pleads Guilty to Violation of the Clean Water Act," press release, March 24, 2006, http://www.usdoj.gov/opa/pr/2006/March/06_enrd_170.html.
35. Tim Talley, "Oklahoma Attorney General Stresses Water Quality At Conference," Associated Press, November 14, 2006, http://www.nwaonline.net/articles/2006/11/20/news/111506ok water.txt.

36. Amendment to the Comprehensive Environmental Response Compensation and Liability Act of 1980 ("Superfund"), HR 4341, 109th Congress, 1st Session (introduced November 16, 2005), http://thomas.loc.gov/cgi-bin/bdquery/z?d109:HR04341:@@@T.

37. Texas Cattle Feeders Association, "Attempts to Regulate Livestock Manure Under Superfund (CERCLA/EPCRA)," newsletter, http://www.tcfa.org/Newsletter/superfund.html.

38. American Society for Microbiology, "Flies Implicated as vector for Cryptosporidium," press release, November 2, 2000, http://www.scienceblog.com/community/older/2000/A/200000712.html.

39. Chris Petersen, Iowa Farmers Union President, e-mail to colleagues and activists, Clear Lake, Iowa, June 28, 2006.

40. Animal Agriculture Alliance, "Alliance Announces First Midwest Anti-Terrorism Training Course: Protect Yourself from Agro-Terrorism," press release, August 10, 2006, http://www.animalagalliance.org/current/home.cfm?Section=2006_0810_Midwest&Category=Press_Releases.

41. Ibid.

42. Center for Agriculture and Food Security and Preparedness (CAFSP), "University of Tennessee College of Veterinary Medicine Mounts a National Response to Threats of Terrorism to Agriculture and the Food Supply," press release, October 16, 2006, http://www.vet.utk.edu/cafsp/about.php.

43. Angie Litterst, e-mail to Karen Hudson, May 13, 2006.

44. Michael Hutjens, "U.S. Dairy Consumption," Illini DairyNet, June 8, 2005, http://www.livestocktrail.uiuc.edu/dairynet/paperDisplay.cfm?ContentID=7447.

45. Helen Reddout, "Presentation to the Pew Commission on Industrial Farm Animal Production," San Francisco, California, May 6, 2008. Slides and audio presentation are available online at http://www.ncifap.org/videos/index.html.

46. Marlys Miller, "Arizona Voters Pass Proposition 204," *Pork* magazine, November 8, 2006, http://www.porkmag.com/directories.asp?pgID=720&ed_id=4478.

47. Humane Society of the United States, "Election '06: Animals Win in Arizona and Michigan," press release, November 7, 2006, http://www.hsus.org/legislation_laws/ballot_initiatives/election_06_animals_win_.html.

48. Animal Agricultural Alliance, "Proven Farming Practices Banned—America's Farmers and Ranchers Must Communicate Commitments on Critical Issues," press release, November 9, 2006, http://www.animalagalliance.org/current/home.cfm?Category=Press_Releases&Section=2006_1109_Farming.

49. Factory Farm Campaign, "The Dirty Six: The Worst Practices in Agribusiness," Humane Society of the United States, http://www.hsus.org/farm/resources/pubs/the_dirty_six.html.

CHAPTER 15

1. Peter S. Thorne et al, "Environmental Health Impacts of Concentrated Animal Feeding Operations: Anticipating Hazards—Searching for Solutions," *Environmental Health Perspectives* 115, no. 2 (February 2007), http://www.ehponline.org/docs/2006/8831/abstract.html.

2. Liz Wagstrom, "Environmental Health Impacts of CAFOs," correspondence, *Environmental Health Perspectives* 115, no. 7 (July 2007): A342–A343, http://www.pubmedcentral.nih.gov/articlerender.fcgi?artid=1913592.

3. Peter D. R. Moeller, "Metal Complexes and Free Radical Toxins Produced by *Pfiesteria piscicida*," *Environmental Science and Technology* 41, no. 4 (2007): 1166–1172.

4. Editorial, "Water Bug Wisdom," *News & Observer*, January 17, 2007.

5. Peter S. Thorne, "CAFOs: Thorne Responds," correspondence, *Environmental Health Per-*

spectives 115, no. 7 (July 2007): A343–A344, http://www.pubmedcentral.nih.gov/articleren der.fcgi?artid=1913572.

6. Marla Cone, "Foul State of Affairs Found in Feedlots," *Los Angeles Times*, November 17, 2006, http://articles.latimes.com/2006/nov/17/nation/na-livestock17.

7. Diane Ward, e-mail to Karen Hudson, April 23, 2007.

8. Pew Commission on Industrial Farm Animal Production, audio file from hearings, Durham, NC, April 9–11, 2007, http://www.media.jhsph.edu:554/oc/nc_public_meeting.rm.

9. R. M. Arrietta, "California Dairy Workers Face Danger and Abuse," *Dollars and Sense*, September–October 2004, http://www.insidedairyproduction.com/wst_page2.html.

10. Stephen Arnold, "Dairy Herds and Rural Communities in Southern New Mexico," *Environmental Health*, July–August 1999, 15–16.

11. Rebecca Clarren, "Got Guilt? Dairy Workers Grub for Minimum Wage in Sickening Manure Pits So American Consumers Can Have Cheap Milk and Cheese." *Salon*, August 27, 2004, http://www.salon.com/news/feature/2004/08/27/dairy_farms/print.html.

12. Tom Pelton, "An Environmental Game of Chicken," *Baltimore Sun*, October 14, 2007, http://www.severnriver.org/press/anenvironmentalgame.htm.

13. S. C. Kestin, T. G. Knowles, A. E. Tinch, and N. G. Gregory, "Prevalence of Leg Weakness in Broiler Chickens and Its Relationship with Genotype," *Veterinary Record* 131 (1992): 190–194.

14. Derrick Z. Jackson, "On the Chicken Line, People Are Treated Like Animals," *Boston Globe*, December 1, 1991.

15. *EHS Today*, "Perdue Farms Settles, Tyson Foods Fights Donning and Doffing Disputes," May 10, 2002, http://ehstoday.com/news/ehs_imp_35456.

16. Karen Roebuck, "Chinese Criticized in Pet Food Probe," *Pittsburgh Tribune-Review*, April 11, 2007, http://www.pittsburghlive.com/x/pittsburghtrib/news/rss/s_502101.html.

17. Elizabeth Weise and Julie Schmit, "2 U.S. Firms Recall Feed Ingredients," *USA Today*, May 31, 2007.

18. U.S. FDA, *Melamine Pet Food Recall—Frequently Asked Questions*, updated August 1, 2007, http://www.fda.gov/AnimalVeterinary/SafetyHealth/RecallsWithdrawals/ucm129932.htm.

19. Environmental News Service, "Livestock Antibiotics Can End Up in Human Foods," July 12, 2007, http://www.ens-newswire.com/ens/jul2007/2007-07-12-01.asp.

20. Tyson Foods, "All Tyson Brand Fresh Chicken to Be 'Raised Without Antibiotics'; Products Available to Mainstream Consumers at an Affordable Price," press release, http://www.tyson.com/Corporate/PressRoom/ViewArticle.aspx?id=2744.

21. Associated Press, "Tyson Fresh Chicken No-Antibiotics Campaign," June 20, 2007.

22. Margaret Mellon, "Largest Poultry Producer to Sell Chickens Raised Without Antibiotics," statement from the Union of Concerned Scientists, June 19, 2007, http://www.ucsusa.org/news/press_release/largest-poultry-producer-to-0041.html.

23. Dionne Walker, "Methane Gas Kills 5 on Virginia Farm," *Journal of Emergency Medical Services*, July 3, 2007, http://www.jems.com/news_and_articles/news/Methane_gas_kills_5_on_Virginia_farm.html%3Bjsessionid=130E4D5DDA5D25915E5DC9E93D4CAA71.

CHAPTER 16

1. Wade Rawlins, "Law Let Hog Industry Keep Growing in N.C.," *News & Observer*, March 23, 2007.

2. Wade Rawlins, "Senate Enacts Ban on New Hog-Waste Lagoons," *News & Observer*, April 19, 2007.

3. John Murawski, "North Carolina Power Program Will Convert Manure, Garbage into Energy," *Raleigh News & Observer*, July 12, 2005, http://www.wapa.gov/es/greennews/2005/jul1805 .htm.

4. Kristen Collins, "Activists Protest to End Pig-Waste Pits," *Raleigh News & Observer*, June 21, 2007, http://www.newsobserver.com/print/thursday/city_state/story/611664.html.

5. *American Agriculturalist*, "Legislation Bans Hog Waste Lagoons in North Carolina," July 27, 2007, americanagriculturist.com/story.aspx?s=12877&c=12.

6. Environmental Defense Fund, North Carolina Regional Office, "2007 NC Swine Farm Environmental Performance Standards Act," section analysis, Environmental Defense Fund, August 2007, http://www.edf.org/documents/6979_NC_Swine_Performance_Act.pdf.

7. Mike Hasten, "Study: Farm Runoff Feeds Dead Zone—Oxygen-Starved Gulf Area Now Closer to Shore," *Shreveport Times*, September 15, 2007, http://www.ewg.org/node/22580.

8. Erika Lovley, "Feathers Fly Over Pollution Legislation," *Politico.com*, October 2, 2007, http://dyn.politico.com/printstory.cfm?uuid=62B2EB54-3048-5C12-006779FF3A711497.

9. Senate Committee on Environment and Public Works, *An Examination of the Potential Human Health, Water Quality, and Other Impacts of the Confined Animal Feeding Operation Industry*, statement of Chairwoman Barbara Boxer (remarks as prepared for delivery), 110th Cong., September 6, 2007. Transcript and webcast of entire hearing is online at http://www .epw.senate.gov.

10. Editorial, "Looking Out for Farmer Goliath," *Plain Dealer*, May 4, 2006.

11. Editorial, "Antibiotic Runoff," *New York Times*, September 18, 2007, http://www.nytimes .com.

12. Bill Satterfield, "DPI Executive Director Remarks at Waterkeepers Alliance Poultry Summit," Delmarva Poultry, Inc., November 1, 2007, http://www.dpichicken.com/index.cfm?content= news&subcontent=details&id=303.

13. USDA Economic Research Service, "U.S. Per-Capita Chicken Consumption (2007)," Foodreference.com, http://www.foodreference.com/html/f-chick-consp.html.

14. U.S. Food and Drug Administration, "3-NITRO (roxarsone) granule (Alpharma Inc. Animal Health)," product label, http://dailymed.nlm.nih.gov/dailymed/drugInfo.cfm?id=10318.

15. Arsenic Health Effects Research Program Web site, "Research," University of California, Berkeley, School of Public Health, http://asrg.berkeley.edu.

16. Robert Perks et al, "Rewriting the Rules: The Bush Administration's Assault on the Environment," Natural Resources Defense Council, April 2002, http://www.nrdc.org/legislation/roll backs/rollbacks.pdf

17. Douglas Gansler, "A Deadly Ingredient in a Chicken Dinner," *Washington Post*, June 26, 2009, http://www.washingtonpost.com/wp-dyn/content/article/2009/06/25/AR200906250 3381.html.

18. Tamar Lasky, Wenyu Sun, Abdel Kadry, and Michael K. Hoffman, "Mean Total Arsenic Concentrations in Chicken 1989–2000 and Estimated Exposures for Consumers of Chicken," *Environmental Health Perspectives* 112, no. 1 (January 2004), http://www.ehponline.org/ docs/2003/6407/abstract.html.

19. David M. Wallinga, "Playing Chicken—Avoiding Arsenic in Your Meat," Institute for Agriculture and Trade Policy, Food and Health Program, April 2006, http://www.iatp.org/iatp/ publications.cfm?accountID=421&refID=80529.

20. Ibid.

21. J. R. Garbarino et al, "Environmental Fate of Roxarsone in Poultry Litter. I. Degradation of Roxarsone During Composting," *Environmental Science and Technology* 37, no. 8 (2003): 1509–1514, pubs.acs.org/doi/full/10.1021/es026219q.

22. Wallinga, "Playing Chicken—Avoiding Arsenic in Your Meat."

23. J. R. Garbarino et al, "Degradation of Roxarsone in Poultry Litter," U.S. Geological Survey, http://wwwbrr.cr.usgs.gov/Arsenic/FinalAbsPDF/garbarino.pdf.

24. Tim Lundeen, "Arsenic Paper Refuted," *Feedstuffs*, May 22, 2006, http://www.agobservatory.com/headlines.cfm?refID=87920.

25. E. K. Silbergeld and K. Nachman, "The Environmental and Public Health Risks Associated with Arsenical Use in Animal Feeds," *Annals of the New York Academy of Sciences* 1140 (October 2008): 346–357, http://www.ncbi.nlm.nih.gov/pubmed/18991934?dopt=Abstract.

26. Delaware Health and Social Services, Division of Public Health, "Cancer Cluster Investigation—Indian River Area," July 17, 2007, http://www.dhss.delaware.gov/dhss/dph/dpc/files/irrpt071707.txt.

27. Rachel Swick, "Sussex Residents Face High Cancer Risk," *Cape Gazette*, August 13, 2007, http://www.capegazette.com/storiescurrent/200708/cancerstudy081007.html.

28. Maryland Cancer Registry, Center for Cancer Surveillance and Control, Family Health Department, Maryland Department of Health and Mental Hygiene, "Cancer in Maryland 2000 Incident and Mortality Annual Report," Maryland Family Health Administration, fha.maryland.gov/pdf/cancer/2000report.pdf.

29. Chris Branam, "Kennedy Son Take on Tyson, Its Record," *Arkansas Democrat-Gazette*, April 9, 2004.

30. This and other information about the roxarsone litigation is from an interview with Jason Hatfield, plaintiff attorney in many Prairie Grove arsenic lawsuits, Fayetteville, AR, September, 2007; and from Lundy & Davis Law Firm, "Something 'Fowl' in the Air; Research Finds Toxic Contamination From Poultry Industry Linked to Disease and Death," press release, January 2003, http://www.infectioncontroltoday.com/hotnews/31h1015400.html.

31. Jason Hatfield, memorandum on cancer cases among minors in Prairie Grove, Arkansas, to Lundy & Davis Law Firm (no date).

32. Trish Hollenbeck, "Expert Posits Theory from Air Filters, Litter Samples," *Northwest Arkansas Times*, August 27, 2007, onibasu.com/archives/am/184588.html.

33. Lundy & Davis, "Something Fowl in the Air—Poultry Industry Contamination," press release, PR Newswire, January 2003, http://www.animalsvoice.com/edits/editorial/news/invest/fowl_air.html.

34. Ibid.

35. World Poultry, "Jury Selection for Poultry Arsenic Case," September 5, 2006, http://www.worldpoultry.net/news/jury-selection-for-poultry-arsenic-case-id478.html.

36. Ron Wood, "Plaintiffs Rest In Arsenic Cancer Case," *North-West Arkansas Morning News*, September 19, 2006, http://www.animalagalliance.org.

37. Ibid.

38. Trish Hollenbeck, "Alphapharma Acquitted," *North-West Arkansas Morning News*, September 26, 2006, http://www.animalagalliance.org/newsletter/main.cfm?EditionMonth=9&EditionYear=2006&DatabaseName=Alpharma&Email=contributor&Password=alliance1501.

39. "Appeal from Washington County Circuit Court," no. CIV 03-2150-2, Hon. Kim Smith, Judge, *Green v. Alphapharma et al. Supreme Court of Arkansas*, May 8, 2008, courts.arkansas.gov/opinions/2008a/20080508/07-382.pdf.

CHAPTER 17

1. Peter Shinn, "Presidential Candidate John Edwards Calls for a Moratorium on Factory Farm CAFOs; Front-running Democrats Woo Rural Voters," *Brownfield*, October 29, 2007, available at http://www.organicconsumers.org/articles/article_8040.cfm.

2. Ibid.

3. T. Khanna, R. Friendship, C. Dewey, and J. S. Weese, "Methicillin-resistant *Staphylococcus Aureus* Colonization in Pigs and Pig Farmers," *Veterinary Microbiology* 128, no. 3–4 (April 2008): 298–303, abstract online at http://www.ncbi.nlm.nih.gov/pubmed/18023542.

4. A. J. DeNeeling, "High Prevalence of Methicillin Resistant *Staphylococcus Aureus* in Pigs," *Veterinary Microbiology* 122, no. 3–4 (June 2007): 366–372, abstract online at http://www.ncbi.nlm.nih.gov/pubmed/17367960.

5. Bridget M. Kuehn, "Antibiotic-Resistant 'Superbugs' May Be Transmitted from Animals to Humans," *JAMA*, 298, no. 18 (2007): 2125–2126.

6. CDC Features, "Fighting Emerging Infectious Diseases," Centers for Disease Control and Prevention, Atlanta, Georgia, http://www.cdc.gov/Features/EmergingInfections.

7. P. V. Scarpino and H. Quinn, "Bioaerosol Distribution Patterns Adjacent to Two Swine Growing Finishing Housed Confinement Units in the American Midwest" (abstract from a paper presented at the 14th Annual Scientific Symposium of the Ohio River Basin Consortium for Research and Education, Oct. 14–16, 1998).

8. Terrence O'Keefe, "Natural Debate Rages On—Poultry Companies Can't Seem to Agree, and the USDA Has Yet to Rule," *Watt Poultry USA*, March 1, 2008, http://www.wattpoultry.com/PoultryUSA/Article.aspx?id=22004.

9. Reuters, "USDA Reverses Itself on Tyson Antibiotic Label," November 19, 2007, http://www.reuters.com/article/governmentFilingsNews/idUSN1952833420071120.

10. Dave Murphy, "The Great Pig Debate: How CAFOs Stalk the Future President," *Animal Welfare Institute Quarterly* (Winter 2008), http://www.awionline.org/ht/d/ContentDetails/i/2047/pid/2494.

11. Barack Obama, "Remarks of Senator Obama after Iowa Victory" (speech, Des Moines, Iowa, January 3, 2008), http://www.reobama.com/SpeechesJan0308.htm.

12. Environmental Defense Fund, "The Preservation of Antibiotics for Medical Treatment Act of 2005, Summary," http://www.edf.org/documents/4366_PAMTAsummary.pdf.

13. Ibid.

14. Committee on Drug Use in Food Animals; Panel on Animal Health, Food Safety, and Public Health; Board on Agriculture; National Research Council; Food and Nutrition Board; and Institute of Medicine, *The Use of Drugs in Food Animals—Benefits and Risks* (Washington, D.C.: National Academy Press, 1999), httpbooks.nap.edu/openbook.php?record_id=5137&page=R1.

15. Doug Gurian-Sherman, "CAFOs Uncovered: The Untold Costs of Confined Animal Feeding Operations" (Cambridge, MA: UCS Publications, 2008). Also available online at http://www.ucsusa.org/assets/documents/food_and_agriculture/cafos-uncovered.pdf.

16. Environmental Working Group, "In Recession, Modest Help for Most Americans, but Big Bucks for Big Farms," press release, April 14, 2008, farm.ewg.org/farm/newsrelease.php.

17. All farm subsidy info is available at the Environmental Working Group's searchable database at farm.ewg.org/farm/.

18. Pew Commission on Industrial Farm Animal Production, "Putting Meat on the Table: Industrial Farm Animal Production in America," a Project of the Pew Charitable Trusts and Johns Hopkins Bloomberg School of Public Health, 2008, http://www.ncifap.org.

19. Animal Agriculture Alliance, "Pew Commission Report on Farm Animal Production—Animal Agriculture Deserves Balanced Discussion," press release, http://www.animalagalliance.org/current/home.cfm?Category=Pew_Commission&Section=Statement6.

20. Philip Lobo, "What Smells in Washington, D.C.?: Recent Emissions from a Biased Commission," *Progressive Dairyman*, June 17, 2008, http://www.progressivedairy.com/pd/features/2008/0908/0908_lobo.html.

21. Perry Beeman, "Report: Livestock Industry Needs Overhaul," *Des Moines Register*, April 29, 2008, http://www.desmoinesregister.com/apps/pbcs.dll/article?AID=/20080429/NEWS/80429006/1001.

22. Ibid.

23. Editorial, "The Worst Way of Farming," *New York Times*, May 31, 2008, http://www.nytimes.com/2008/05/31/opinion/31sat4.html?_r=2&scp=5&sq=Pew&st=cse&oref=slogin.

24. "Politicians and Elections," http://www.opensecrets.org.
25. Tom Philpott, "Weighing Obama's and McCain's Stances on Food and Farm Policy—McCain: Food Maverick?" *Grist Magazine*, October 3, 2008, http://www.grist.org/article/politics-and-the-dinner-table.
26. Ibid.
27. Pooja Kumar, "Study Considers Economic Impacts of Prop 2 on Egg Industry," *California Aggie* (student newspaper of UC Davis), October 29, 2008, http://www.unitedegg.com/pdf/articles/CAaggie.pdf.
28. Animal Agriculture Alliance, "Crushing Defeat for Animals, Farmers and Consumers—Will Destroy Californian's Ability to Buy Locally Produced Eggs," press release, November 5, 2008, http://www.animalagalliance.org/current/home.cfm?Section=2008_1105_Crushing&Category=Press_Releases.
29. This quote was taken from an article that appeared on the Web site of Indiana AgriNews, but has since been pulled from the site.
30. Officials of the American Farm Bureau Federation, in a telephone interview with the author, July 9, 2009.
31. Animal science researchers at Purdue University, in an interview with the author, November 15, 2007.
32. Organic Consumers Association, "Six Reasons Why Obama Appointing Monsanto's Buddy, Former Iowa Governor Vilsack, for USDA Head Would Be a Terrible Idea," press release, November 12, 2008, http://www.organicconsumers.org/articles/article_15573.cfm.
33. Philip Rucker and Dan Morgan, "Obama to Pick Tom Vilsack to Lead USDA," *Washington Post*, December 17, 2008, http://www.washingtonpost.com/wp-dyn/content/article/2008/12/16/AR2008121602672.html.
34. Ibid.
35. Organizing for America, "Plan to Support Rural Communities," BarackObama.com, http://www.barackobama.com/issues/rural/index_campaign.php.

CHAPTER 18

1. KOMO-TV News (Seattle, WA), "Tests Find Drug-Resistant Bacteria in Store-Bought Pork," October 30, 2008, video online at http://www.search.komonews.com/default.aspx?ct=r&q=mrsa+97+packages+pork.
2. KVAL-TV News (Eugene, OR), "Drug-Resistant Bacteria Found in Pork," October 31, 2008, video online at http://www.kval.com/news/33646514.html.
3. Nicholas D. Kristof, "Our Pigs, Our Food, Our Health," *New York Times*, March 11, 2009, http://www.nytimes.com/2009/03/12/opinion/12kristof.html.
4. *Meat International*, "Smithfield could be ripe for sale," April 27, 2009, http://www.meatinternational.com/news/processing/smithfield-could-be-ripe-for-sale-id1310.html.
5. WRAL (Raleigh, NC), "Smithfield Foods to Cut 1,800 Jobs, Close Six Plants, Including One in Elon," February 27, 2009, http://www.wral.com/business/story/4551419.
6. David Kirby, "Mexican Lawmaker: Factory Farms Are 'Breeding Grounds' of Swine Flu Pandemic," *Huffington Post*, April 27, 2009, http://www.huffingtonpost.com/david-kirby/mexican-lawmaker-factory_b_191579.html.
7. David Kirby, "Swine Flu Outbreak—Nature Biting Back at Industrial Animal Production?" *Huffington Post*, April 26, 2009, http://www.huffingtonpost.com/david-kirby/swine-flu-outbreak----nat_b_191408.html.
8. Ibid.
9. Kirby, "Mexican Lawmaker."
10. Andrew Pollack, "Fear of a Swine Flu Epidemic in 1976 Offers Some Lessons, and Concerns,

Today," *New York Times*, May 8, 2009, http://www.nytimes.com/2009/05/09/health/09vaccine.html.

11. Iowa State University Press Service, "Pigs, People May Soon Eat Their Way to Flu Resistance, Say ISU Researchers," press release, April 30, 2009, http://www.public.iastate.edu/~nscentral/news/2009/apr/harriscorn.shtml.

12. Dusty Rhodes, "Bigger Isn't Always Better—Karen Hudson Has Become a Reluctant Expert on the Consequences of Concentrated Animal Feeding Operations," *Illinois Times*, April 16, 2009, http://www.illinoistimes.com/gyrobase/Content?oid=oid%3A9907.

13. *The Poultry Site*, "Companies Cleared Over 'Litter' Lawsuit," May 18, 2009, http://www.thepoultrysite.com/poultrynews/17759/companies-cleared-over-litter-lawsuit.

14. Carla S. Alvarado, M.P.H., et al, "Seasonal Changes in Airborne Fungi and Bacteria at a Dairy Cattle Concentrated Animal Feeding Operation in the Southwest United States," *Journal of Environmental Health* 71, no. 9 (May 2009), abstract online at http://www.neha.org/JEH/2009_abstracts.htm.

15. U.S. Centers for Disease Control and Prevention, "CDC Telebriefing on Investigation of Human Cases of H1N1 Flu," press briefing transcript, May 18, 2009, http://www.cdc.gov/media/transcripts/2009/t090518.htm.

16. Associated Press, "U.S. Moving Closer to Swine Flu Vaccine," MSNBC.com, May 22, 2009, http://www.msnbc.msn.com/id/30886851.

EPILOGUE: THE PRICE OF PROTEIN

1. Bryan Walsh, "Getting Real About the High Price of Cheap Food," *Time* magazine, August 21, 2009, http://www.time.com/time/health/article/0,8599,1917458-2,00.html.

2. Ralph Loglisci, "Public Health & Industrial Farm Animal Production: Setting the Record Straight," Center for a Livable Future, August 27, 2009, http://www.livablefutureblog.com/2009/08/public-health-industrial-farm-animal-production-setting-the-record-straight.

3. Fred Kirschenmann, telephone interview with the author, July 2009.

4. American Medical Veterinary Association, "The American Veterinary Medical Association Response to the Report of the Pew Commission on Industrial Farm Animal Production," http://www.avma.org/advocacy/PEWresponse/PEW_report_response.pdf.

5. Reid H. Cherlin, "Statement from the White House," White House Press Office, e-mail sent to the author, June 17, 2009.

6. Members of the Socially Responsible Agriculture Project, letter to USDA Secretary Tom Vilsack; signed by William J. Weida (president), Chris Petersen (Iowa), Helen Reddout (Washington), Kendra Kimbirauskas (Oregon), Carole Morison (Maryland), Genell Pridgen (North Carolina), Steve Campbell (Idaho), Karen Hudson (Illinois), Kathy Martin (Oklahoma), Terry Spence (Missouri), Megan Fehrman (Oregon), Laura Krebsbach (Nebraska), and Lisa Bechthold (Alberta, Canada), June 23, 2009.

7. USDA Secretary Tom Vilsack, letter to William J. Weida, president of the SRA Project, July 21, 2009.

8. USDA Office of Communications and DOJ Office of Public Affairs, "USDA and Justice Department to Hold Public Workshops to Explore Competition Issues in the Agriculture Industry," release no. 0368.09, August 5, 2009, http://www.usda.gov/wps/portal/!ut/p/_s.7_0_A/7_0_1OB?contentidonly=true&contentid=2009/08/0368.xml.

9. Maggie Fox, "Pigs An Underestimated Source of Flu," Reuters, June 5, 2009.

10. Alan Sutton, interview with the author, November 16, 2007.

INDEX